Scale 1:250,000
or 3.95 miles to 1 inch
(2.5km to 1cm)

**39th edition June 2016**

© AA Media Limited 2016

Revised version of the atlas formerly known as *Complete Atlas of Britain.*
Original edition printed 1979.

**Cartography:**
All cartography in this atlas edited, designed and produced by the
Mapping Services Department of AA Publishing (A05395).

This atlas contains Ordnance Survey data © Crown copyright and
database right 2016 and Royal Mail data © Royal Mail copyright and
database right 2016.

 This atlas is based upon Crown Copyright and is
reproduced with the permission of Land & Property
Services under delegated authority from the
Controller of Her Majesty's Stationery Office,
© Crown copyright and database right 2016. PMLPA No. 100497

 © Ordnance Survey Ireland/Government of Ireland.
Copyright Permit No. MP000616

**Publisher's Notes:**
Published by AA Publishing (a trading name of AA Media Limited,
whose registered office is Fanum House, Basing View, Basingstoke,
Hampshire RG21 4EA, UK. Registered number 06112600).

ISBN: 978 0 7495 7780 3

A CIP catalogue record for this book is available from The British Library.

**Disclaimer:**
The contents of this atlas are believed to be correct at the time of
the latest revision, it will not contain any subsequent amended, new
or temporary information including diversions and traffic control and
enforcement systems. The publishers cannot be held responsible or liable
for any loss or damage occasioned to any person acting or refraining
from action as a result of any use or reliance on material in this atlas, nor
for any errors, omissions or changes in such material. This does not affect
your statutory rights.

The publishers would welcome information to correct any errors or
omissions and to keep this atlas up to date. Please write to the Atlas
Editor, AA Publishing, The Automobile Association, Fanum House,
Basing View, Basingstoke, Hampshire RG21 4EA, UK.
E-mail: *roadatlasfeedback@theaa.com*

**Acknowledgements:**
AA Publishing would like to thank the following for their assistance in
producing this atlas:

**RoadPilot** mobile Information on fixed speed camera locations
provided by and © 2016 RoadPilot Ltd.
Crematoria data provided by the Cremation Society of Great Britain.
Cadw, English Heritage, Forestry Commission, Historic Scotland,
Johnsons, National Trust and National Trust for Scotland, RSPB, The
Wildlife Trust, Scottish Natural Heritage, Natural England, The Countryside
Council for Wales (road maps).

Transport for London (Central London Map),
Nexus (Newcastle district map).

**Printer:**
Printed in Romania by G. Canale & C. S.A

# Atlas contents

| Map pages | inside front cover |
|---|---|
| **Route planner** | **II–VII** |
| **Road map symbols** | **1** |
| **Road maps** | **2–115** |
| Britain 1:250,000 scale<br>Some islands are shown at slightly smaller scales. | 2–111 |
| Ireland 1:1,000,000 scale | 112–115 |
| **Motorways** | **116–121** |
| Restricted junctions | 116–119 |
| M25 London Orbital | 120 |
| M6 Toll motorway | 121 |
| **Street map symbols** | **122** |
| **Town plans** | **123–135** |
| **District maps** | **136–147** |
| Birmingham | 136–137 |
| Glasgow | 138–139 |
| Manchester | 140–141 |
| Tyne & Wear | 142–143 |
| London | 144–147 |
| **Central London** | **148–163** |
| Central London street map | 148–157 |
| Central London index | 158–163 |
| **Index to place names** | **164–200** |
| County, administrative area map | 164 |

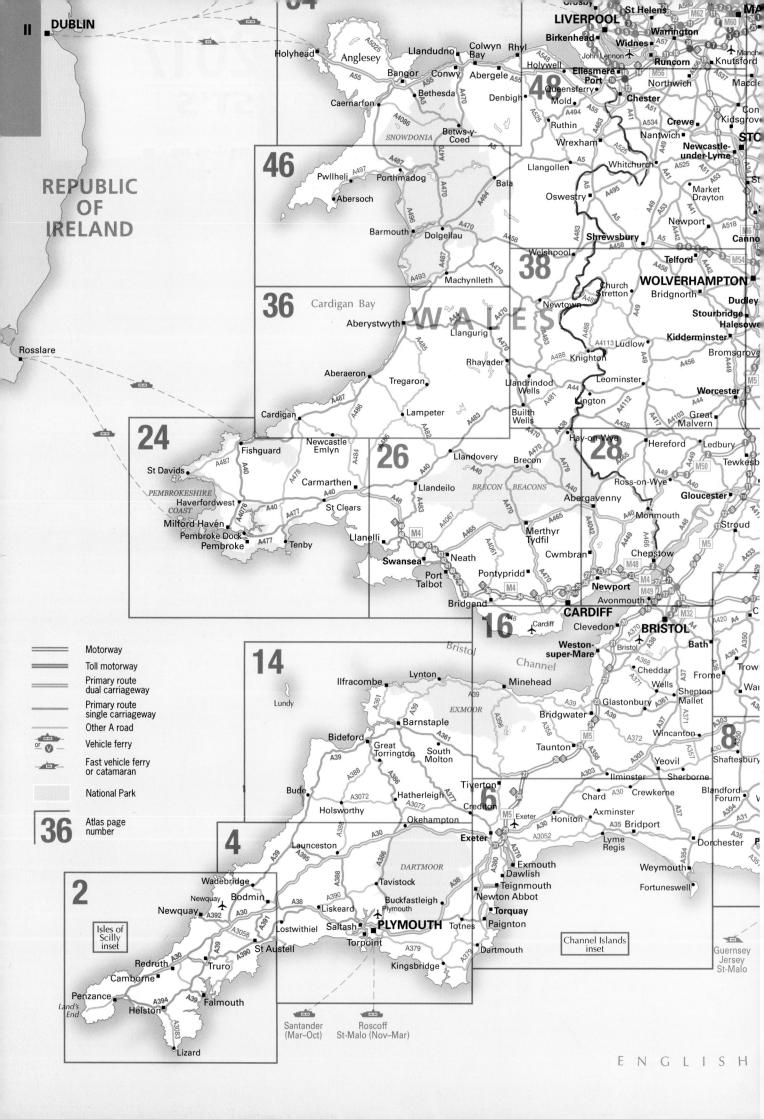

# Route planner

0    10    20    30 miles
0   10   20   30   40 kilometres

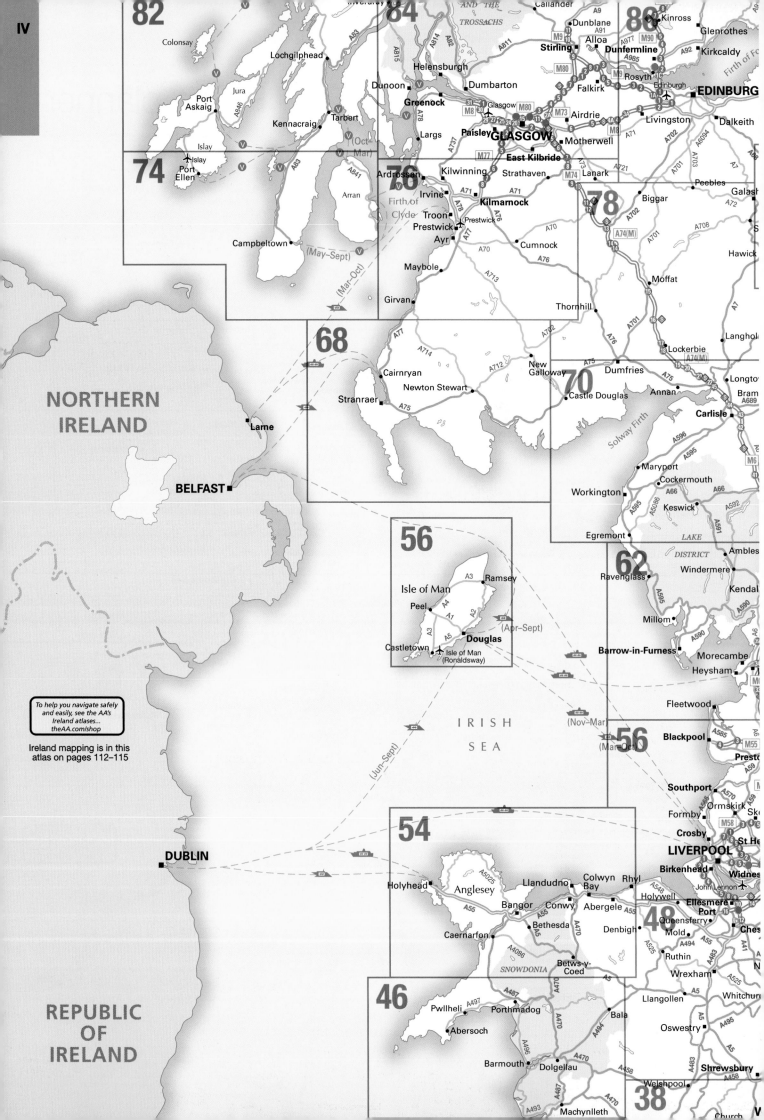

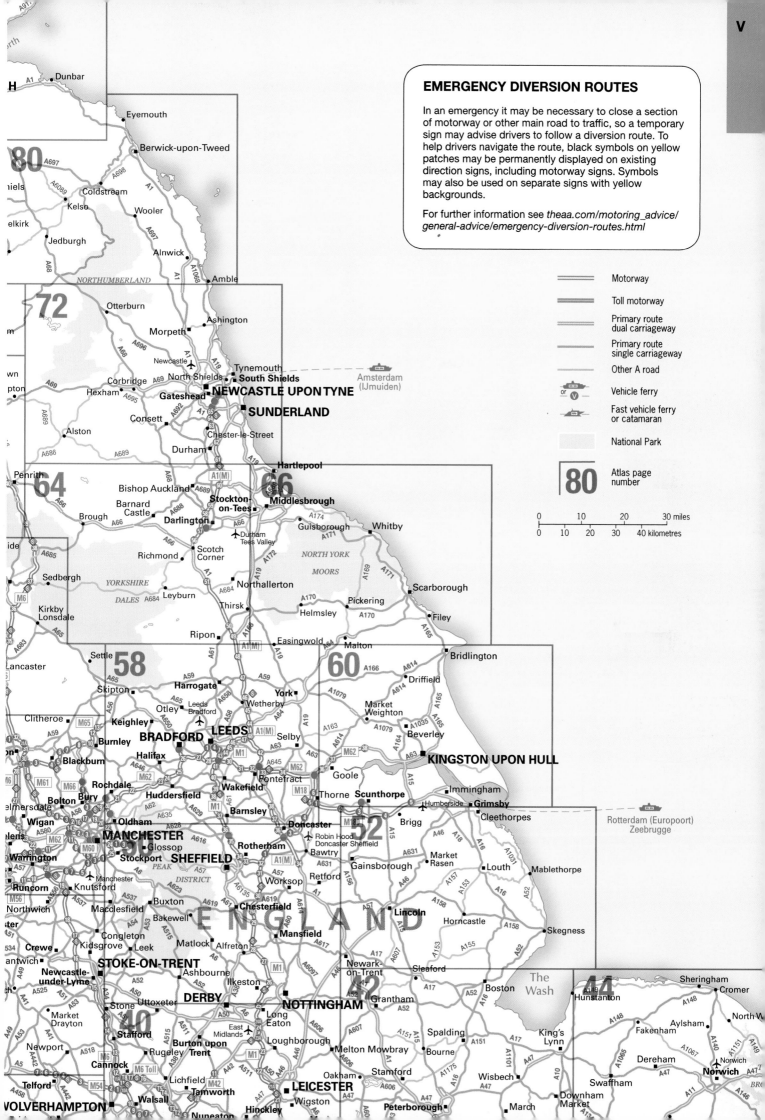

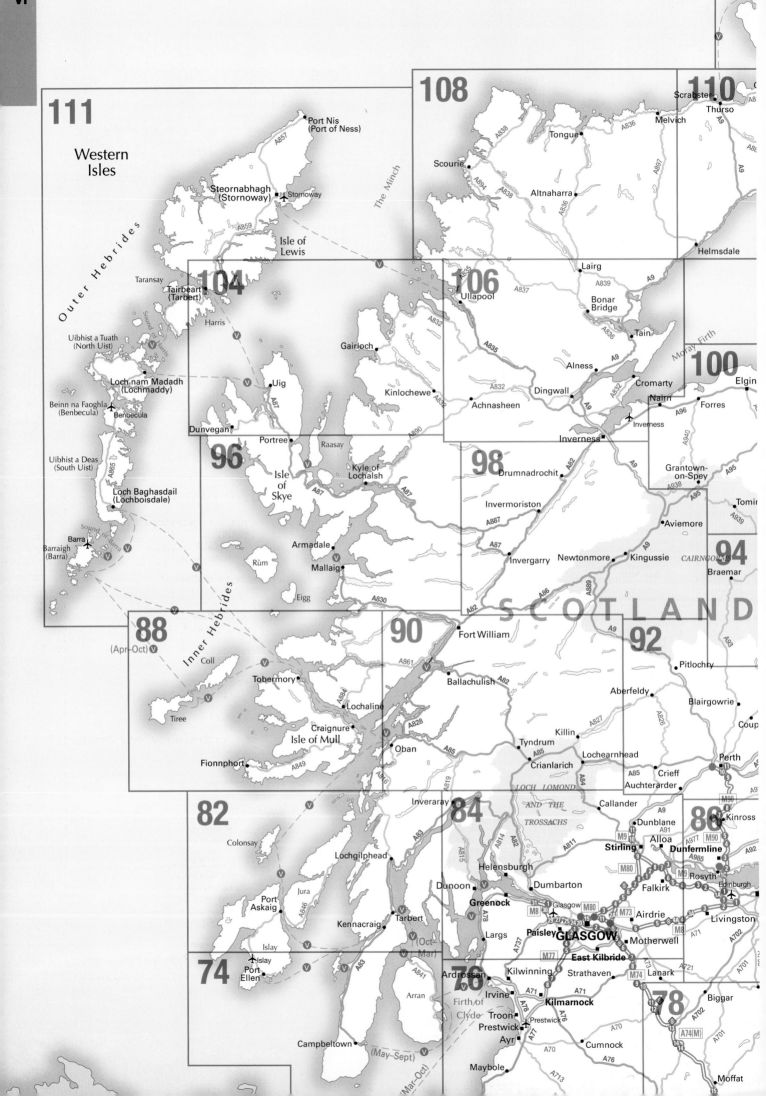

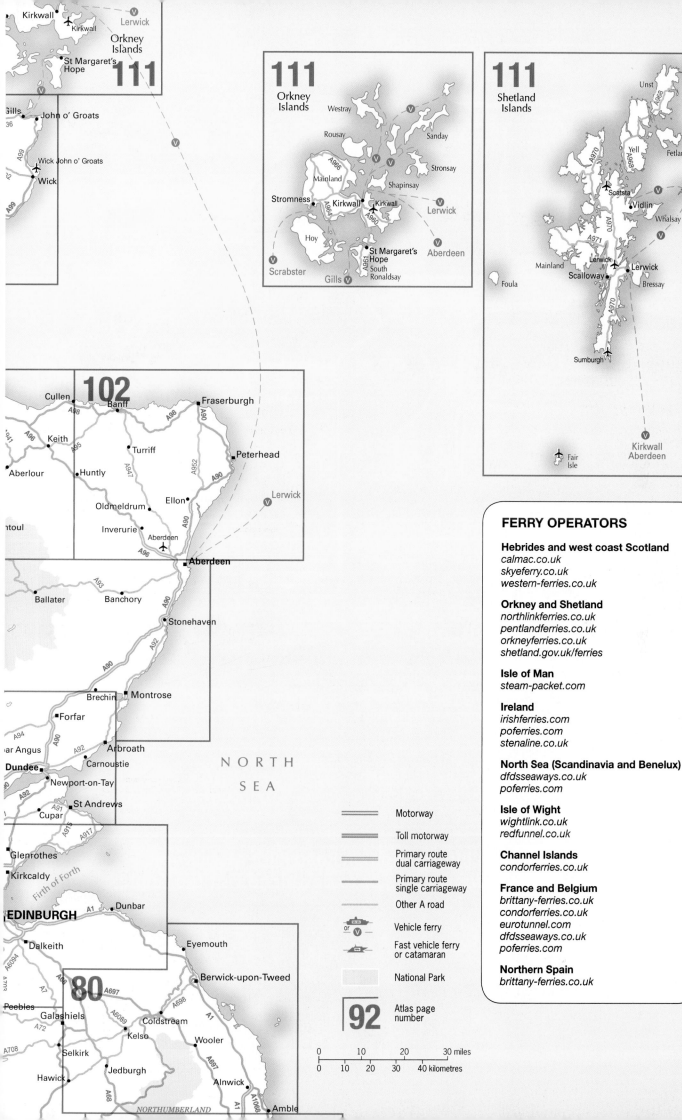

Kirkwall
Kirkwall
Lerwick
Orkney
Islands
111
St Margaret's
Hope
V
Gills
John o' Groats
A99
A36
Wick John o' Groats
V
A99
A882
Wick

**111**
Orkney
Islands

Westray
V
Rousay
Sanday
Stronsay
Mainland
Shapinsay
A966
V
Stromness
V
A965
Kirkwall
Kirkwall
Lerwick
A964
A960
Hoy
V
Aberdeen
St Margaret's
Hope
A961
South
Ronaldsay
V
Scrabster
Gills
V

**111**
Shetland
Islands

Unst
A968
Yell
Fetlar
A970
A968
A970
Scatsta
Vidlin
A971
Whalsay
A970
Foula
Mainland
Lerwick
Lerwick
Scalloway
V
Bressay
A970
Sumburgh
V
Kirkwall
Aberdeen
Fair
Isle

**102**
Cullen
A98
Banff
Fraserburgh
A98
A90
Keith
A96
A95
Turriff
A952
Peterhead
Aberlour
A941
Huntly
A947
A90
Oldmeldrum
Ellon
A90
Lerwick
V
ntoul
Inverurie
Aberdeen
A96
Aberdeen

Ballater
A93
Banchory
A90
Stonehaven
A92

Brechin
Montrose
A94
Forfar
A90
A92
Arbroath
ar Angus
Carnoustie
**Dundee**
Newport-on-Tay
A92
St Andrews
A91
Cupar
A915
A917
Glenrothes
Kirkcaldy
Firth of Forth
**EDINBURGH**
A1
Dunbar
Dalkeith
A6094
Eyemouth
A7
Peebles
A68
Berwick-upon-Tweed
**80**
A697
A1
Galashiels
A72
A6089
Coldstream
A698
A1
A708
Selkirk
Kelso
Wooler
A697
Hawick
Jedburgh
Alnwick
A68
A1068
NORTHUMBERLAND
A1
Amble

NORTH
SEA

Motorway

Toll motorway

Primary route
dual carriageway

Primary route
single carriageway

Other A road

**or** V Vehicle ferry

Fast vehicle ferry
or catamaran

National Park

**92** Atlas page
number

0      10      20      30 miles
0    10    20    30    40 kilometres

## FERRY OPERATORS

**Hebrides and west coast Scotland**
*calmac.co.uk*
*skyeferry.co.uk*
*western-ferries.co.uk*

**Orkney and Shetland**
*northlinkferries.co.uk*
*pentlandferries.co.uk*
*orkneyferries.co.uk*
*shetland.gov.uk/ferries*

**Isle of Man**
*steam-packet.com*

**Ireland**
*irishferries.com*
*poferries.com*
*stenaline.co.uk*

**North Sea (Scandinavia and Benelux)**
*dfdsseaways.co.uk*
*poferries.com*

**Isle of Wight**
*wightlink.co.uk*
*redfunnel.co.uk*

**Channel Islands**
*condorferries.co.uk*

**France and Belgium**
*brittany-ferries.co.uk*
*condorferries.co.uk*
*eurotunnel.com*
*dfdsseaways.co.uk*
*poferries.com*

**Northern Spain**
*brittany-ferries.co.uk*

# Road map symbols

## Motoring information

| | | | | | | | |
|---|---|---|---|---|---|---|---|
| M4 | Motorway with number | BATH | Primary route destination | | Distance in miles between symbols | 50 | Safety camera site (fixed location) with speed limit in mph |
| Toll T4 | Toll motorway with toll station | A1123 | Other A road single/dual carriageway | or V | Vehicle ferry | 60 | Section of road with two or more fixed safety cameras, with speed limit in mph |
| 11 | Motorway junction with and without number | B2070 | B road single/dual carriageway | | Fast vehicle ferry or catamaran | 50 50 | Average speed (SPECS™) camera system with speed limit in mph |
| 3 | Restricted motorway junctions | | Minor road more than 4 metres wide, less than 4 metres wide | | Railway line, in tunnel | V | Fixed safety camera site with variable speed limit |
| S Fleet | Motorway service area | | Roundabout | X | Railway station and level crossing | P·R | Park and Ride (at least 6 days per week) |
| | Motorway and junction under construction | | Interchange/junction | | Tourist railway | | City, town, village or other built-up area |
| A3 | Primary route single/dual carriageway | | Narrow primary/other A/B road with passing places (Scotland) | + H | Airport, heliport | 628 637 Lecht Summit | Height in metres, mountain pass |
| 1 | Primary route junction with and without number | | Road under construction/ approved | F | International freight terminal | | Sandy beach |
| 3 | Restricted primary route junctions | | Road tunnel | H | 24-hour Accident & Emergency hospital | | National boundary |
| S | Primary route service area | Toll | Road toll, steep gradient (arrows point downhill) | C | Crematorium | | County, administrative boundary |

## Touring information
To avoid disappointment, check opening times before visiting.

| | | | | | | | |
|---|---|---|---|---|---|---|---|
| | Scenic route | | Aqueduct or viaduct | | Forest drive | | Horse racing, show jumping |
| i | Tourist Information Centre | | Garden, arboretum | | National trail | | Air show venue, motor-racing circuit |
| i | Tourist Information Centre (seasonal) | | Vineyard | | Viewpoint | | Ski slope (natural, artificial) |
| i | Visitor or heritage centre | | Country park | | Hill-fort | | National Trust property (England & Wales, Scotland) |
| | Picnic site | | Agricultural showground | | Roman antiquity | | English Heritage site |
| | Caravan site (AA inspected) | | Theme park | | Prehistoric monument | | Historic Scotland site |
| | Camping site (AA inspected) | | Farm or animal centre | 1066 | Battle site with year | | Cadw (Welsh heritage) site |
| | Caravan & camping site (AA inspected) | | Zoological or wildlife collection | | Steam railway centre | ★ | Other place of interest |
| | Abbey, cathedral or priory | | Bird collection | | Cave | | Boxed symbols indicate attractions within urban areas |
| | Ruined abbey, cathedral or priory | | Aquarium | | Windmill, monument | | World Heritage Site (UNESCO) |
| | Castle | RSPB | RSPB site | | Golf course (AA listed) | | National Park and National Scenic Area (Scotland) |
| | Historic house or building | | National Nature Reserve (England, Scotland, Wales) | | County cricket ground | | Forest Park |
| | Museum or art gallery | | Local nature reserve | | Rugby Union national stadium | | Heritage coast |
| | Industrial interest | | Wildlife Trust reserve | | International athletics stadium | | Major shopping centre |

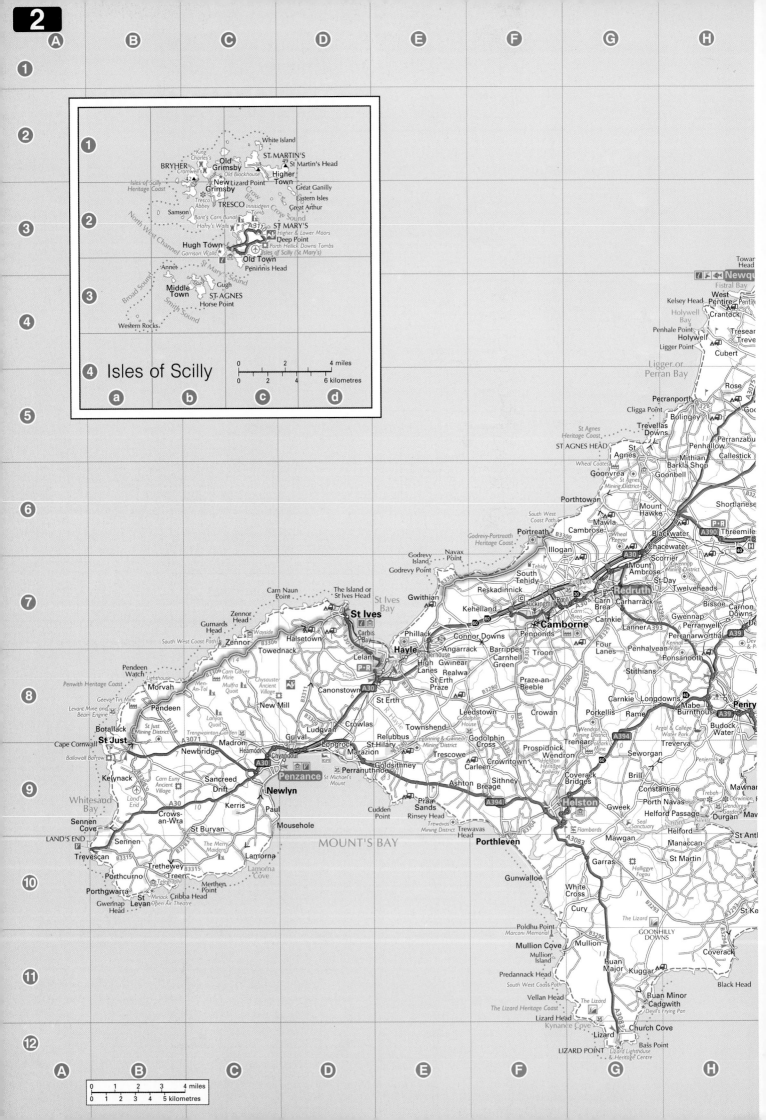

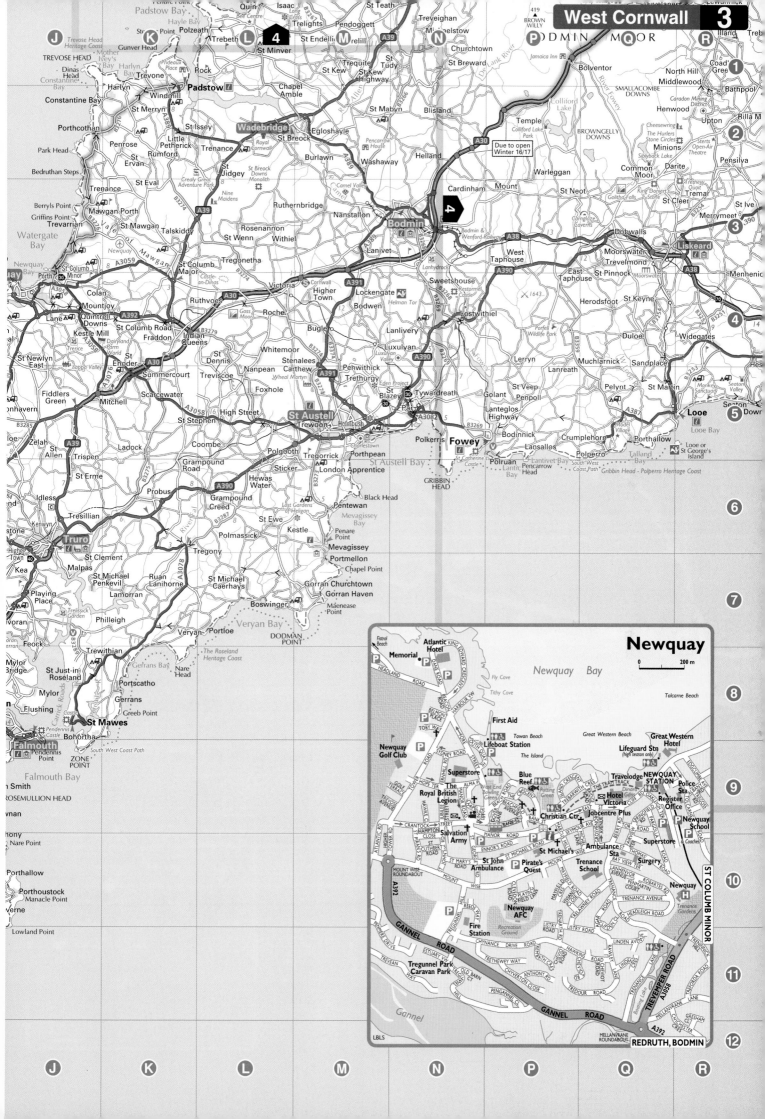

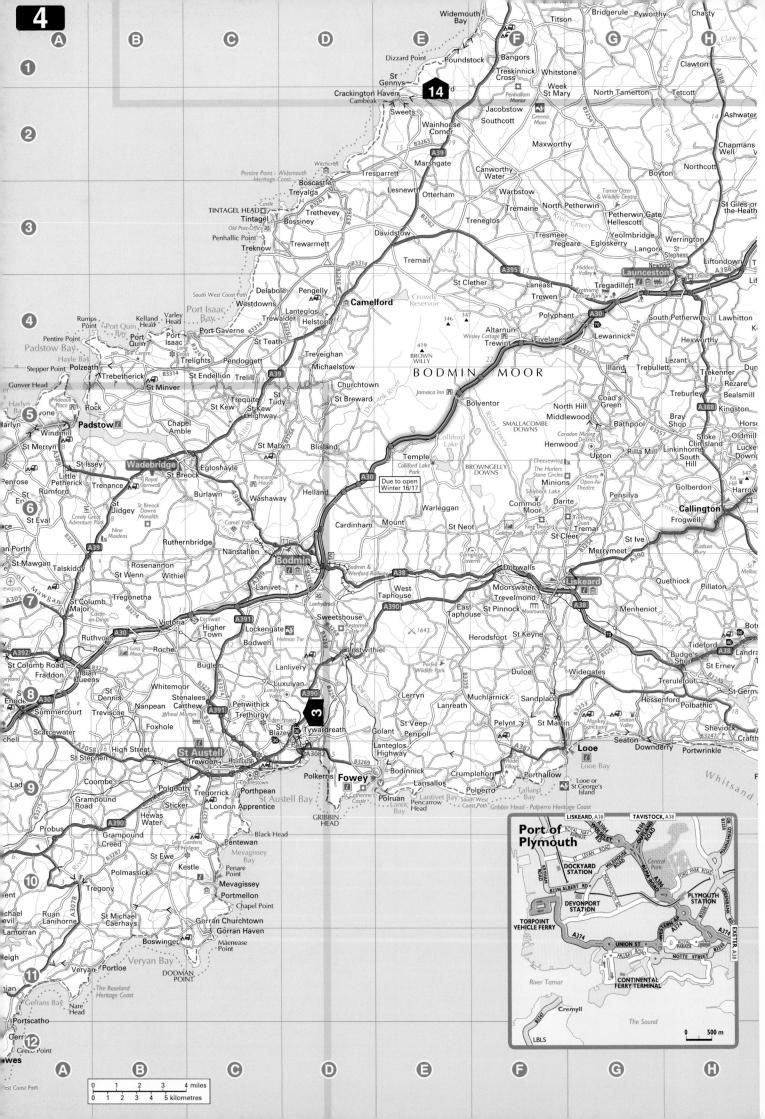

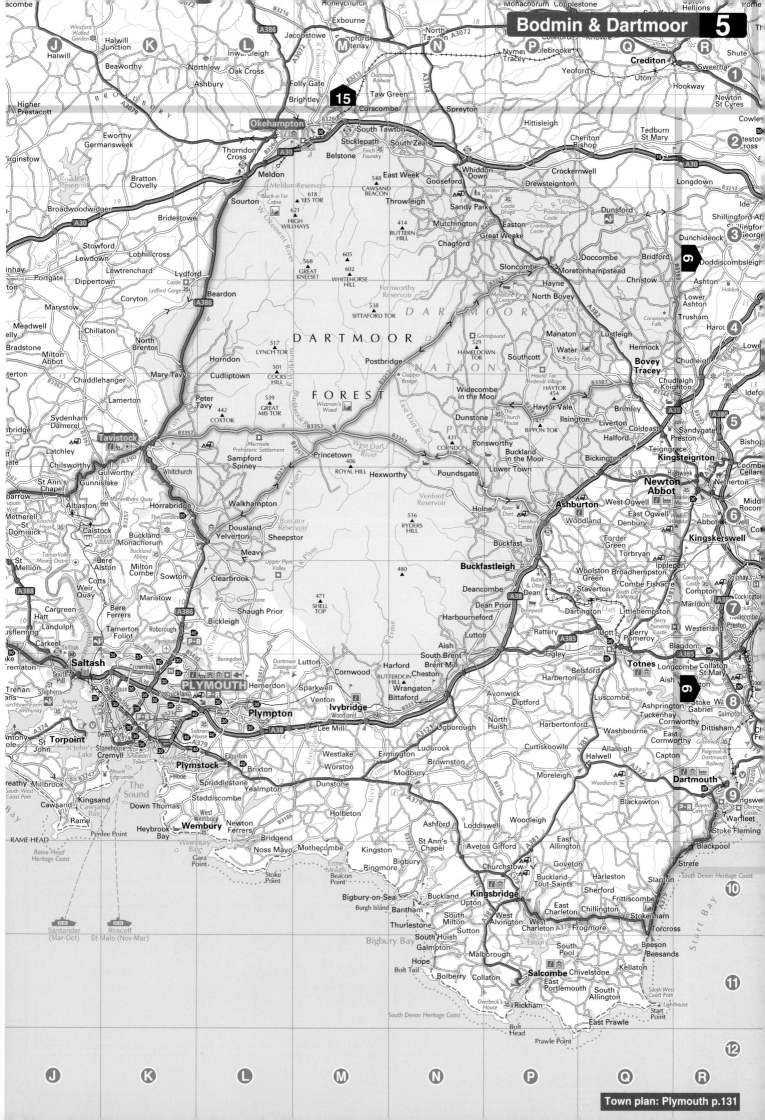

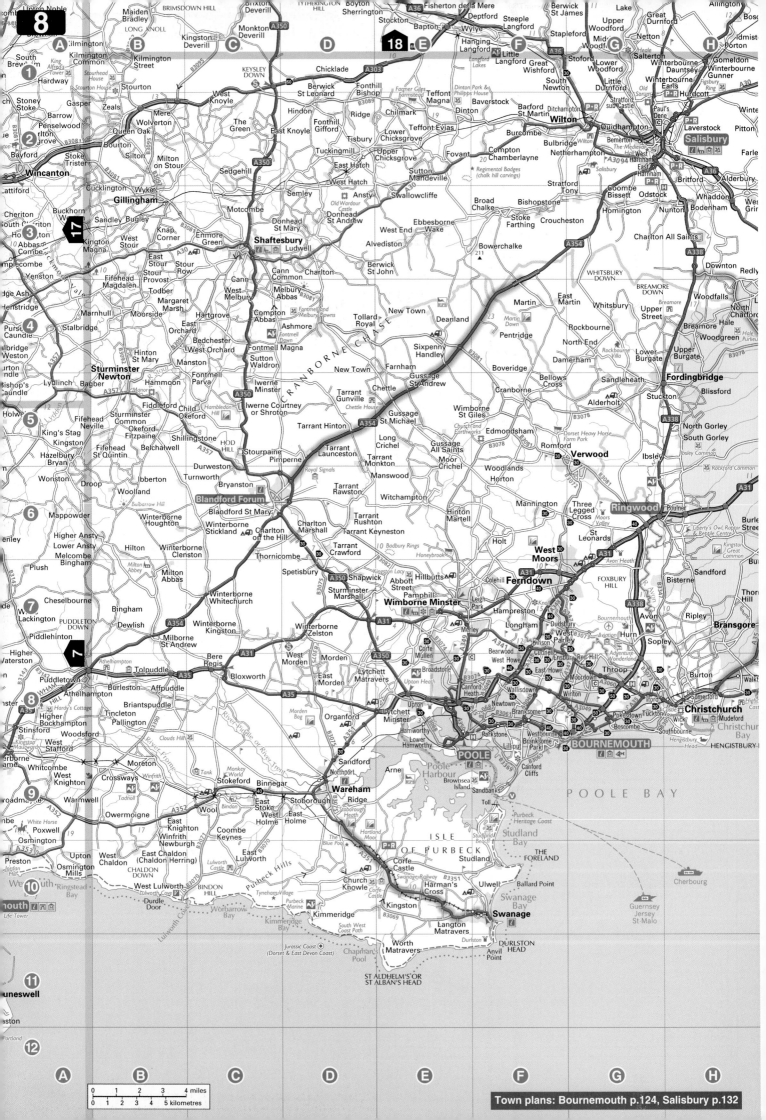

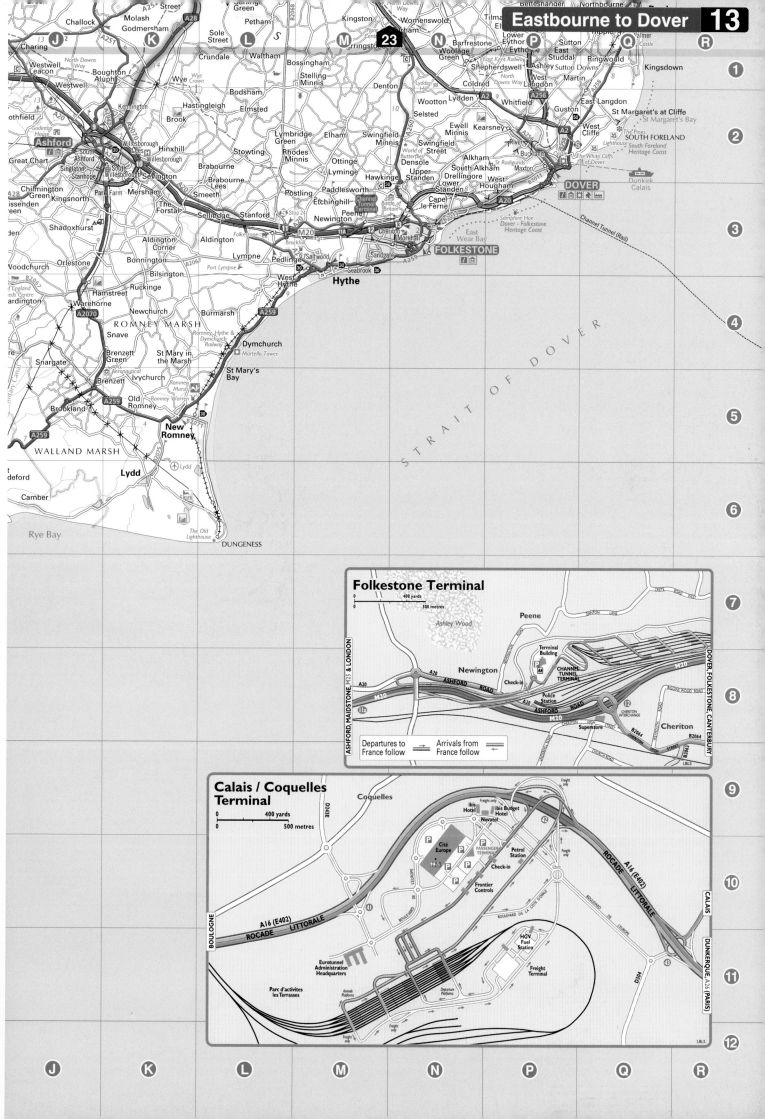

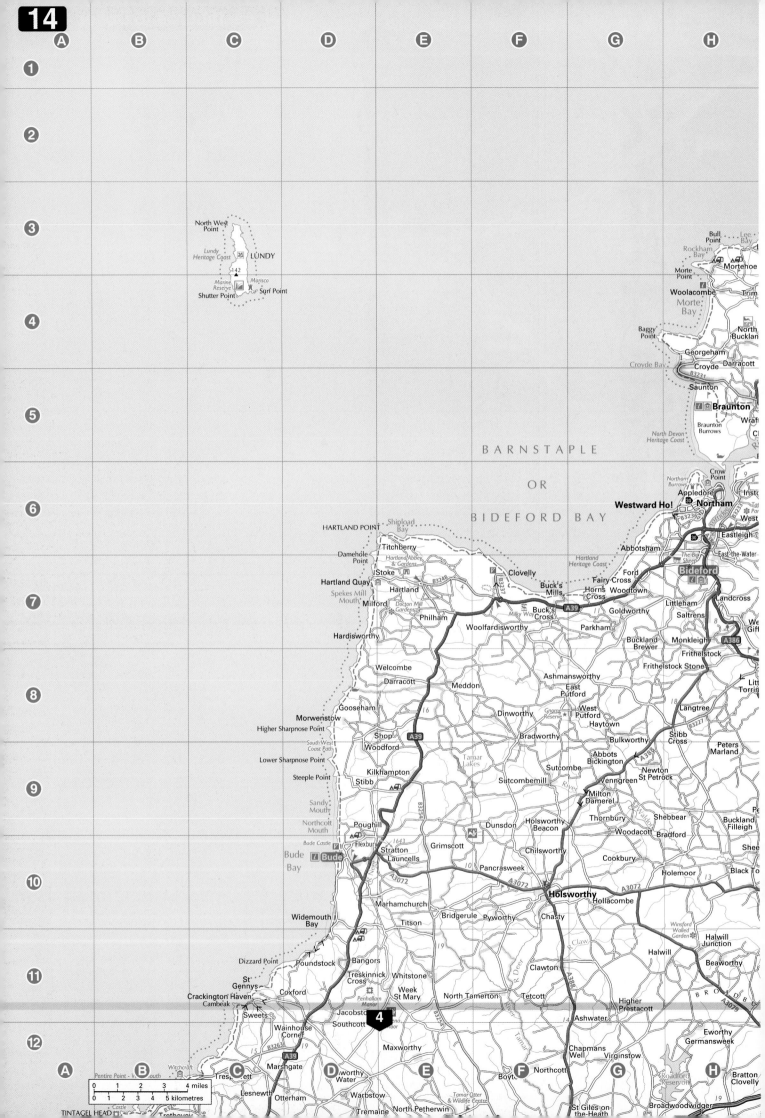

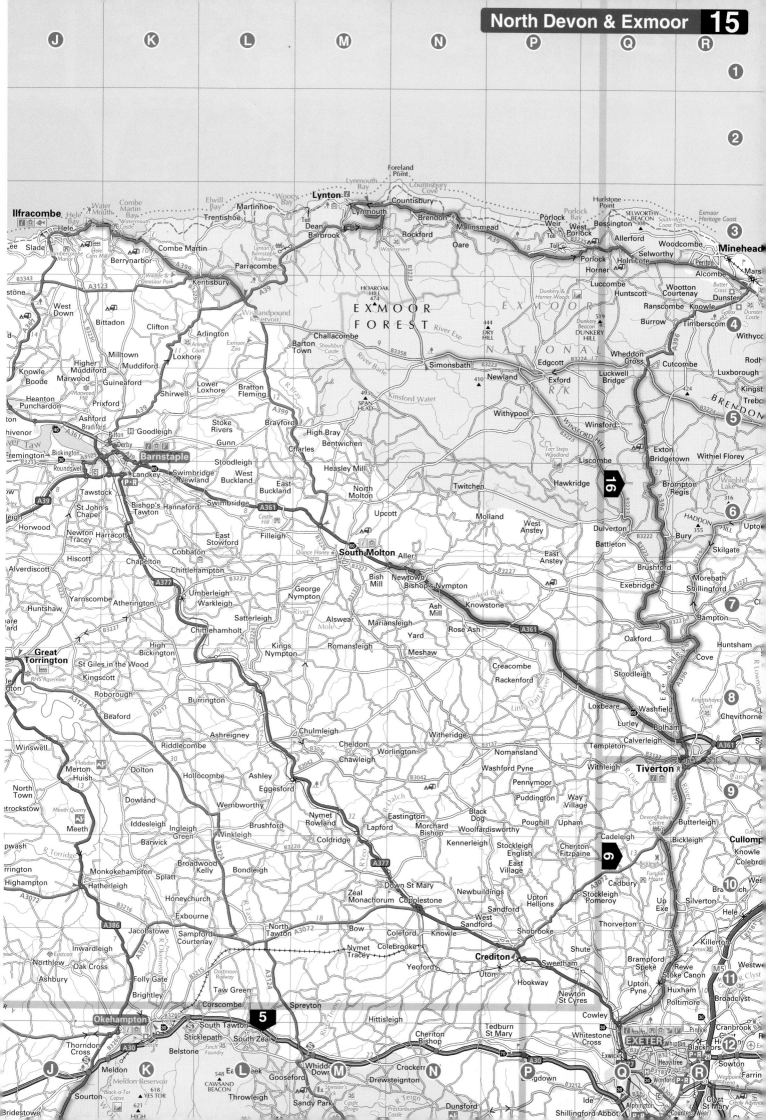

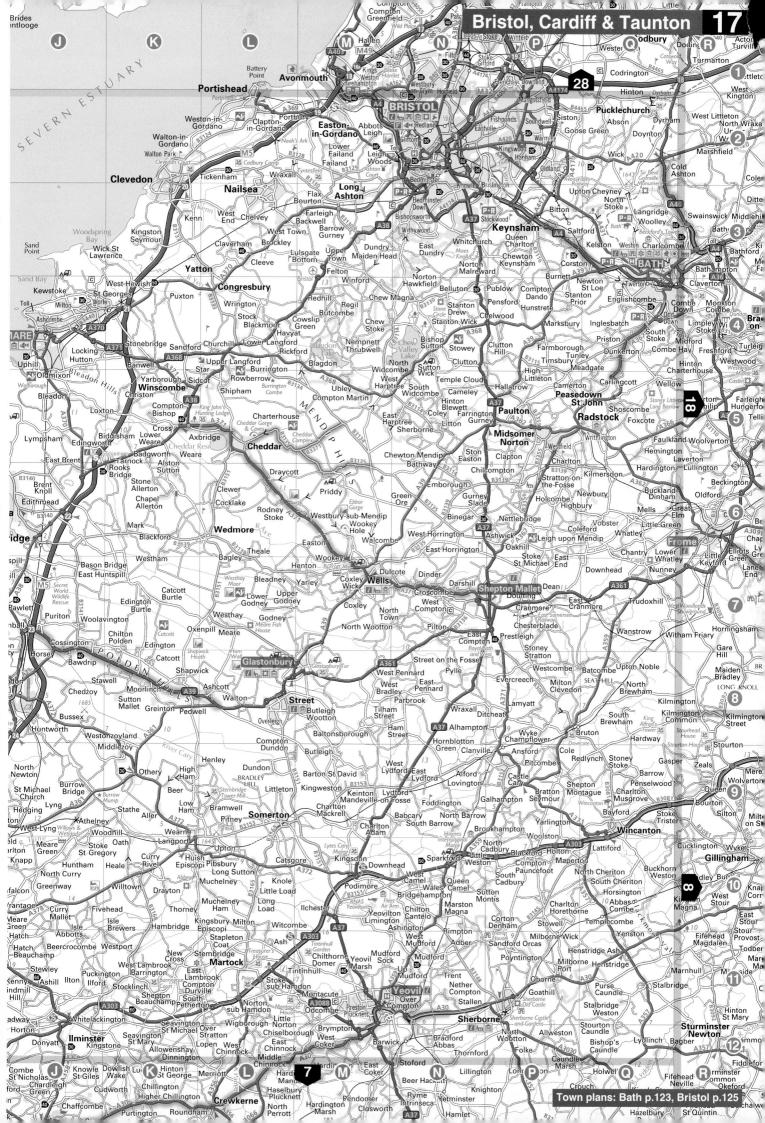

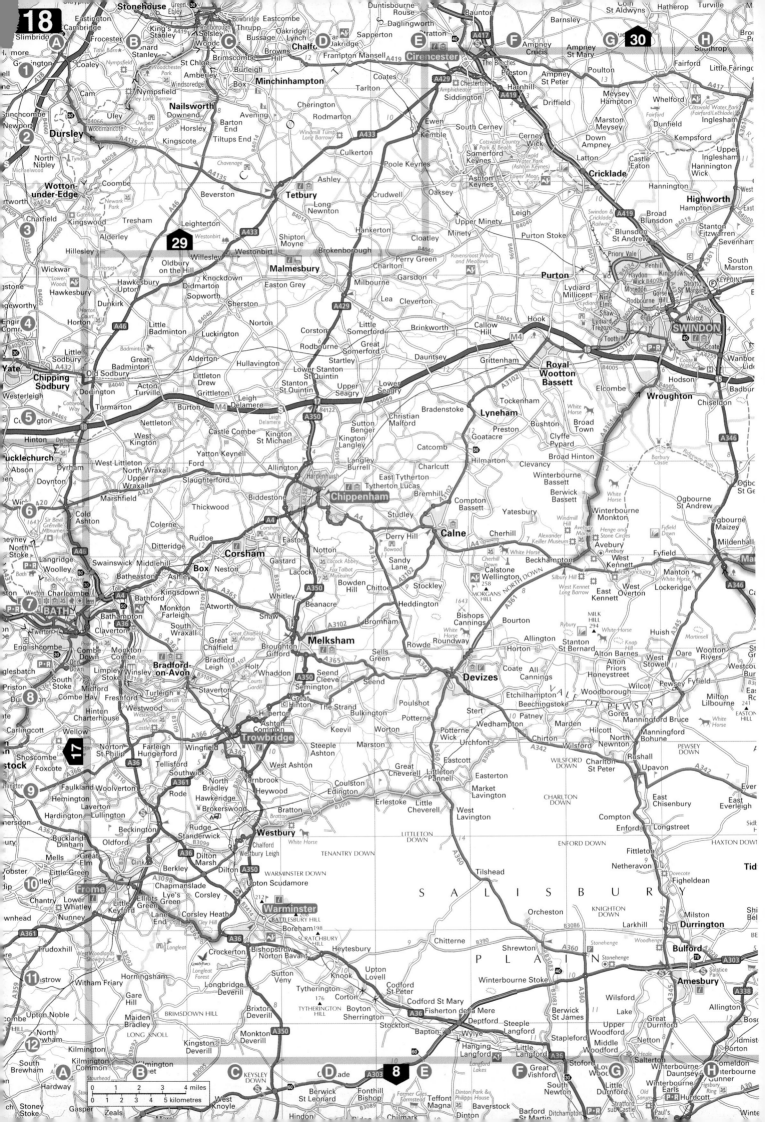

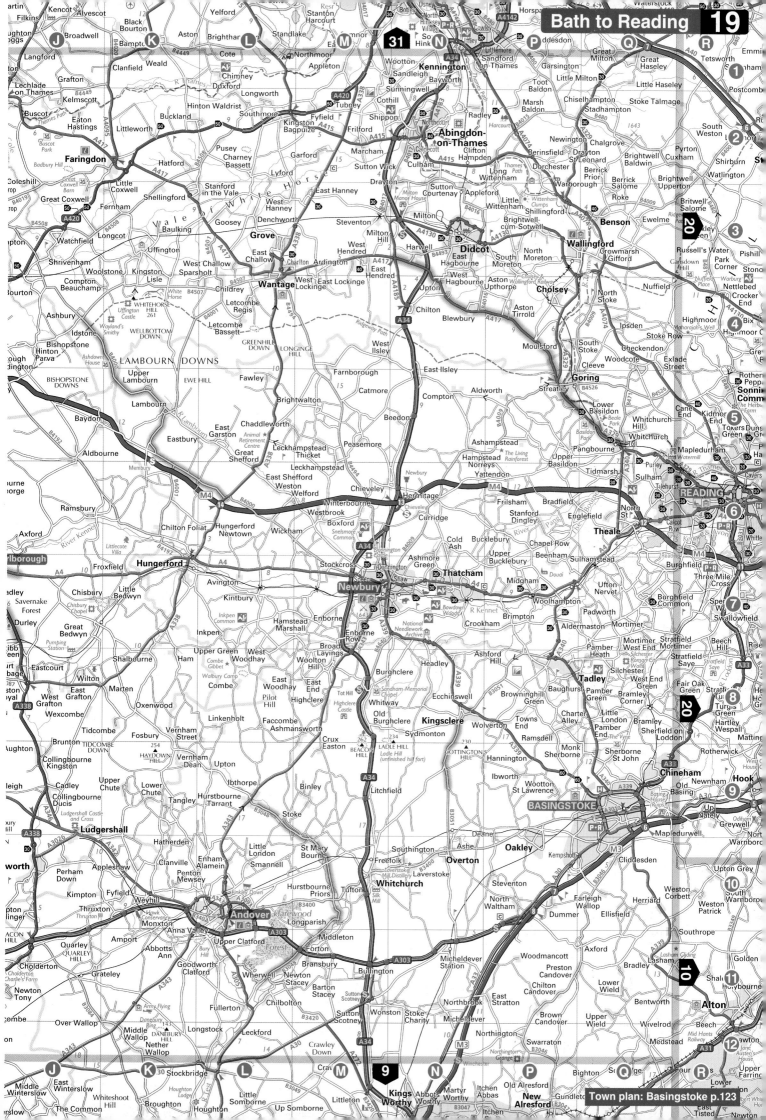

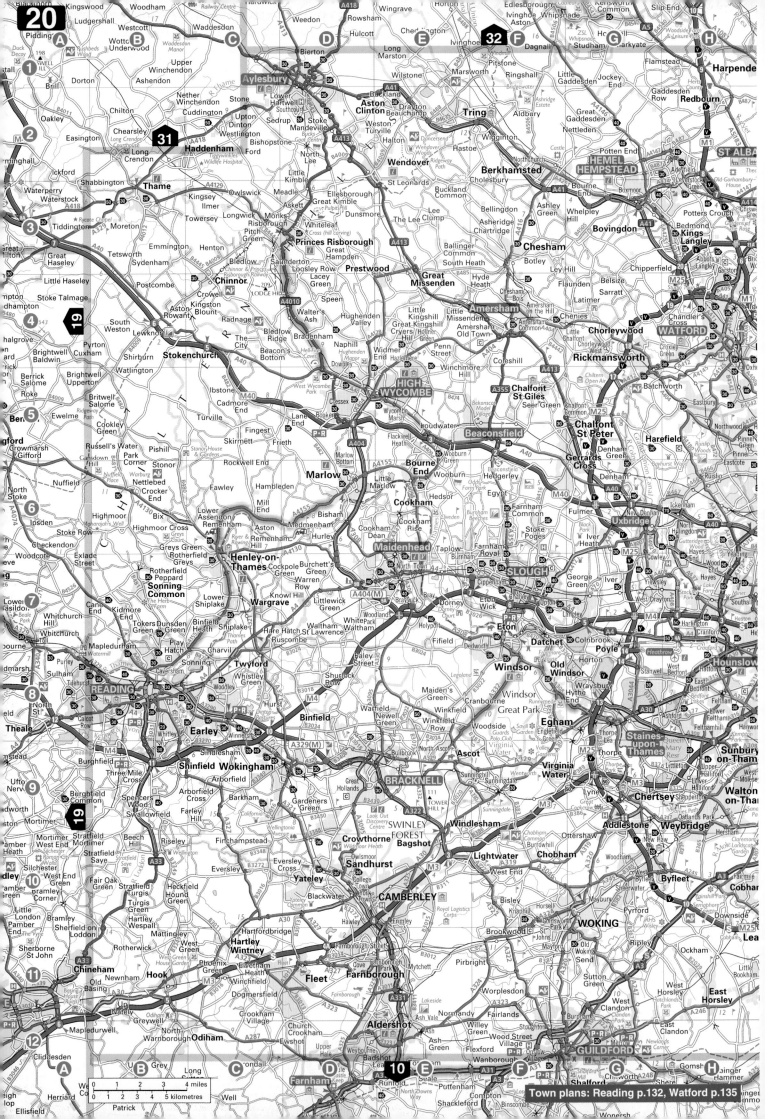

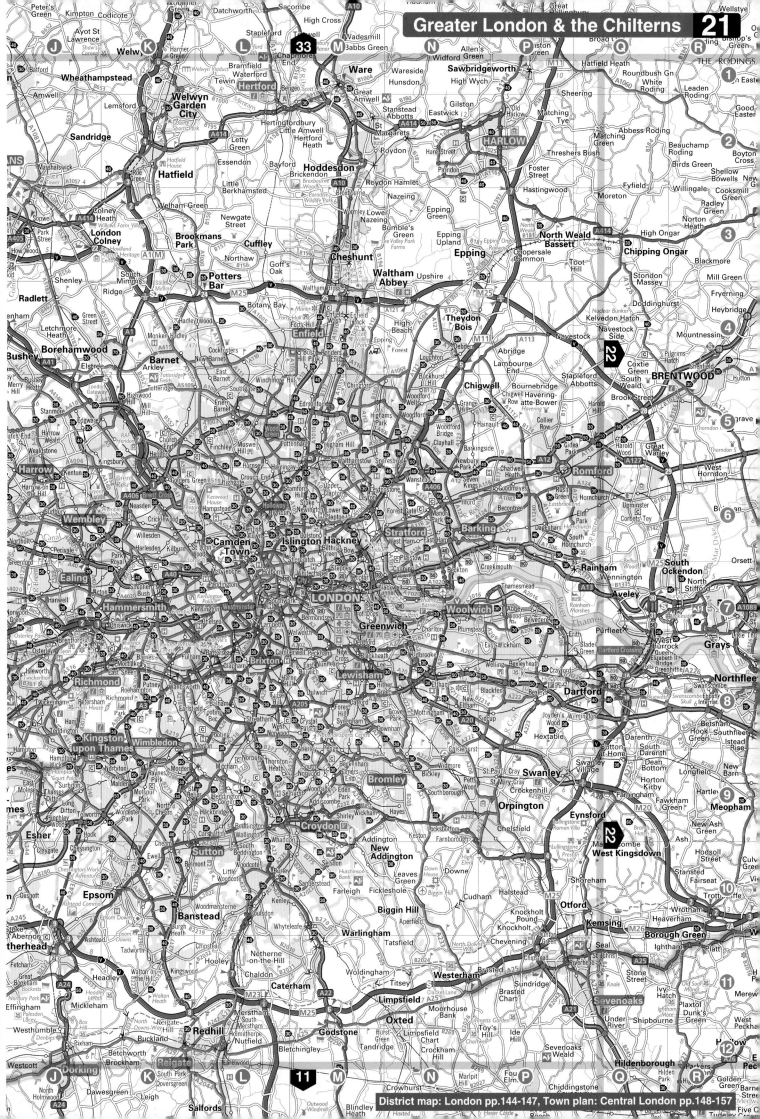

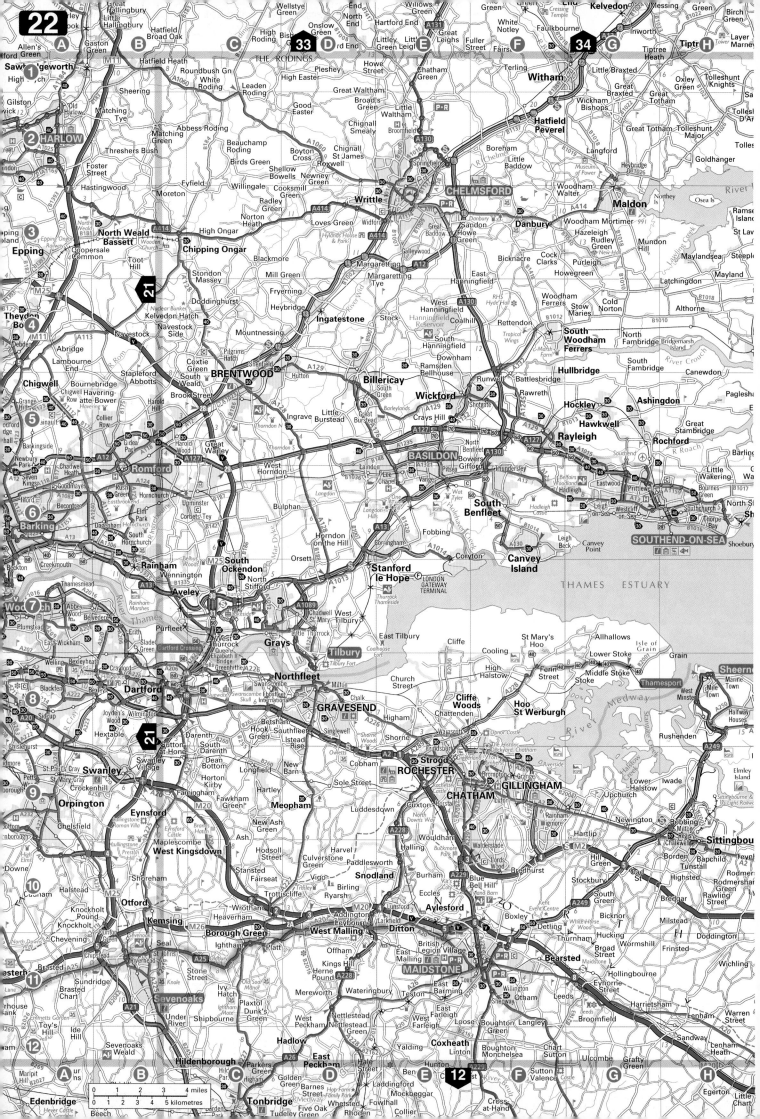

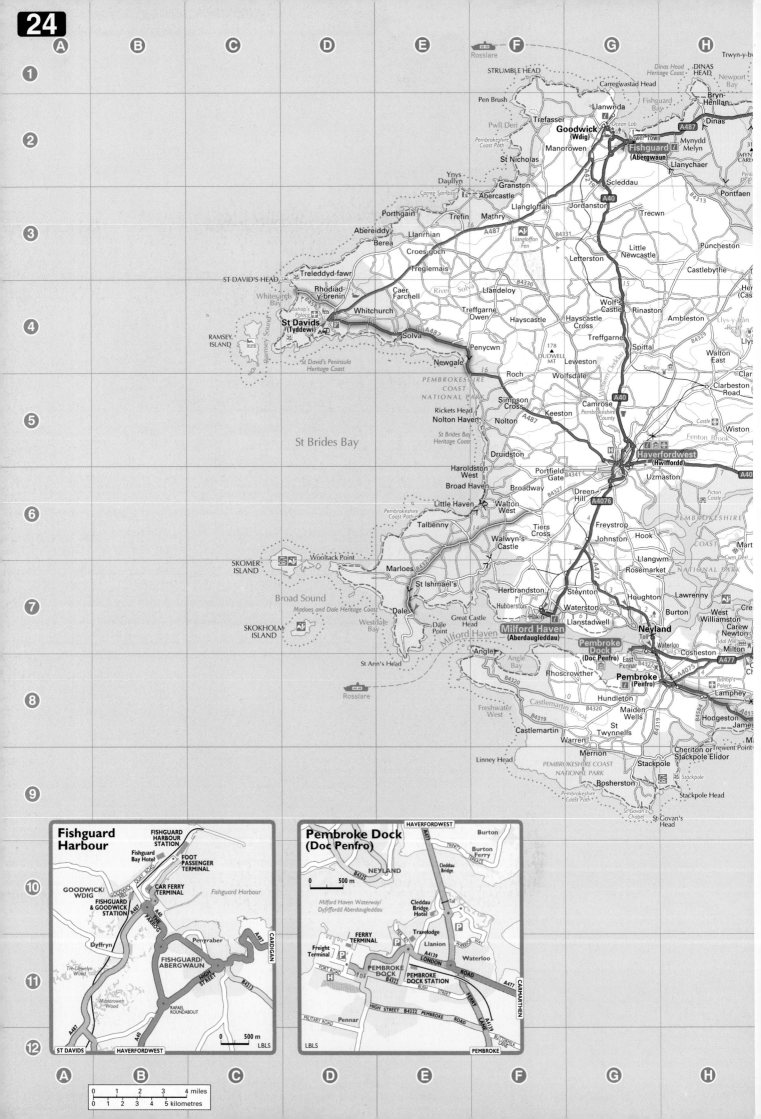

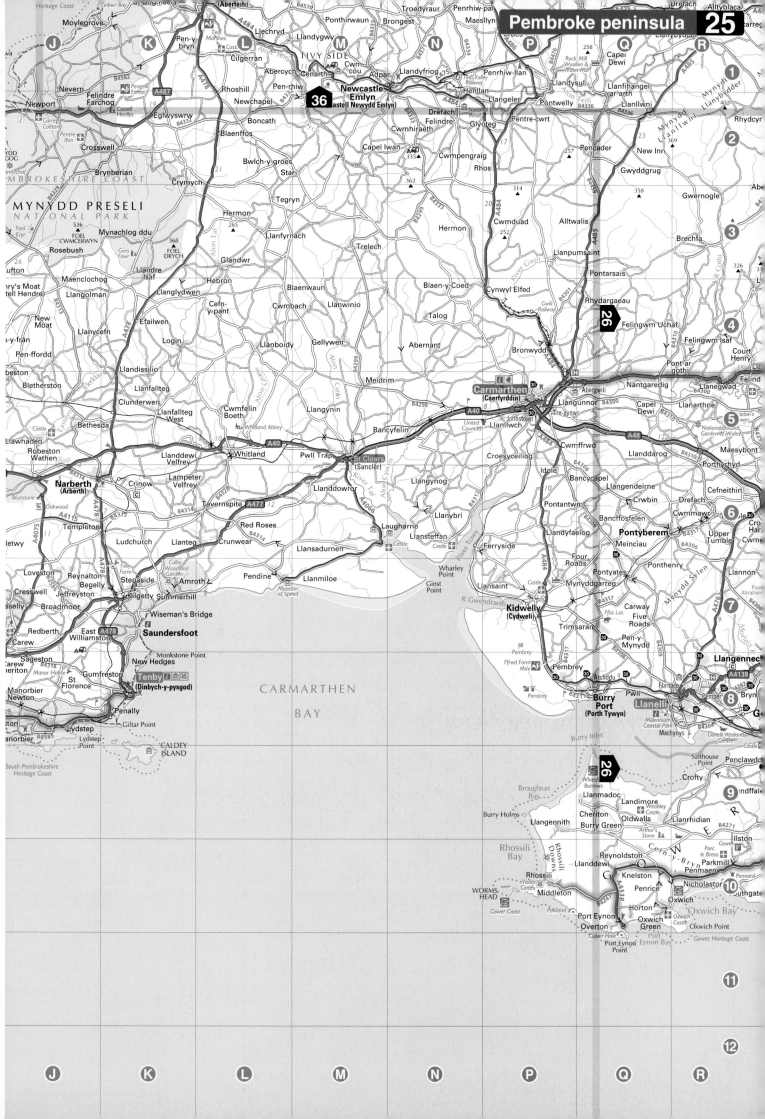

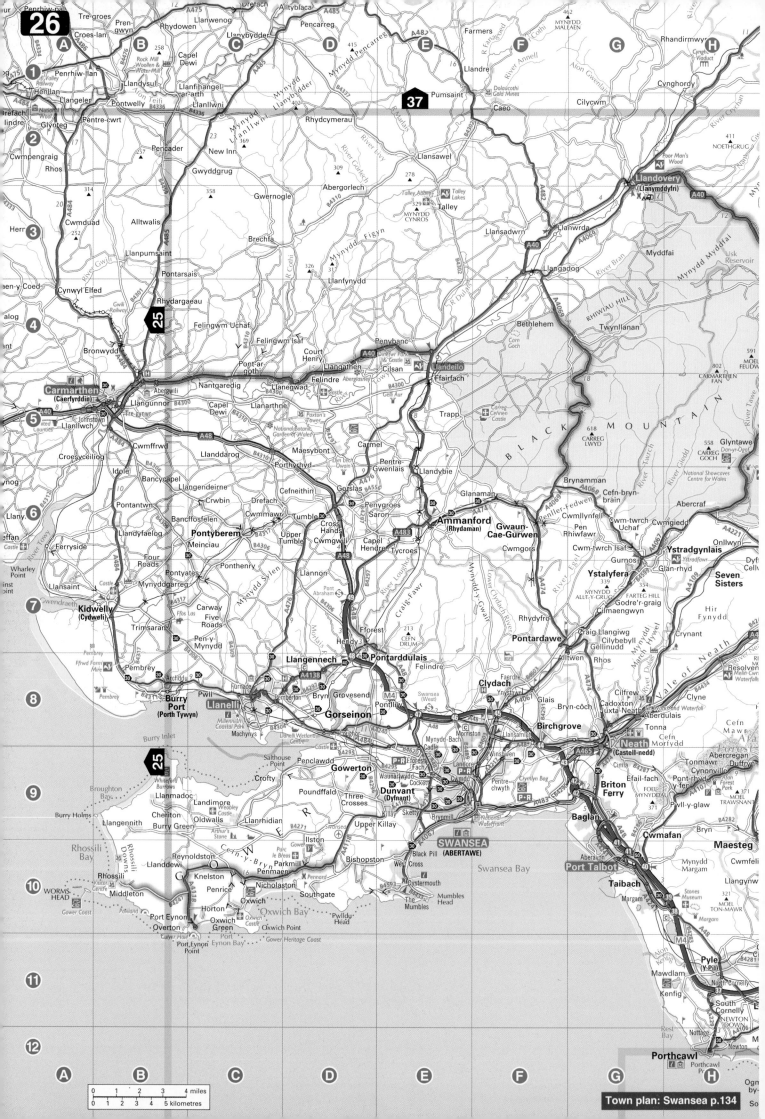

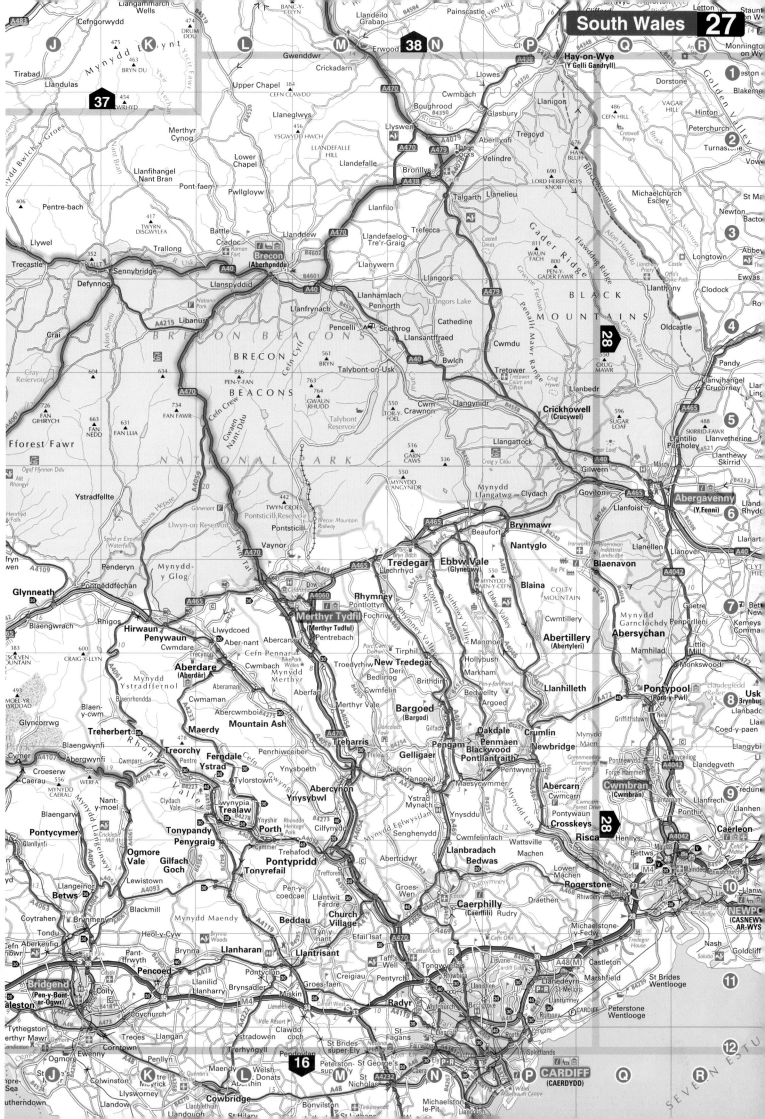

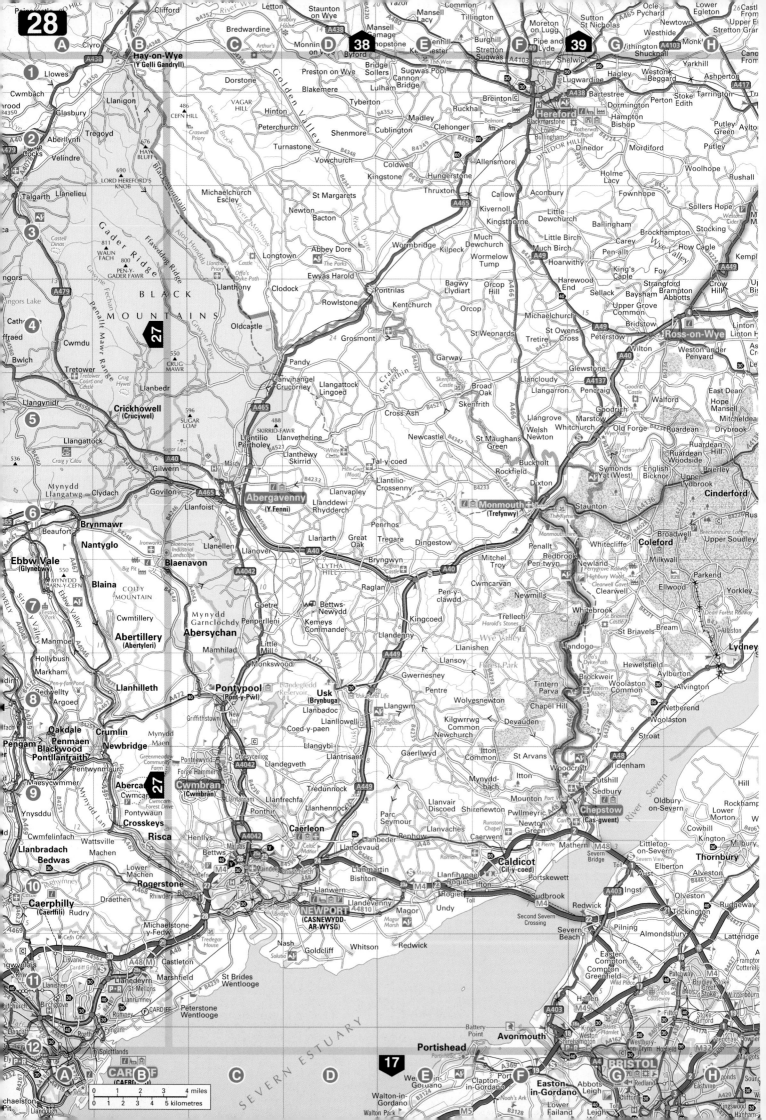

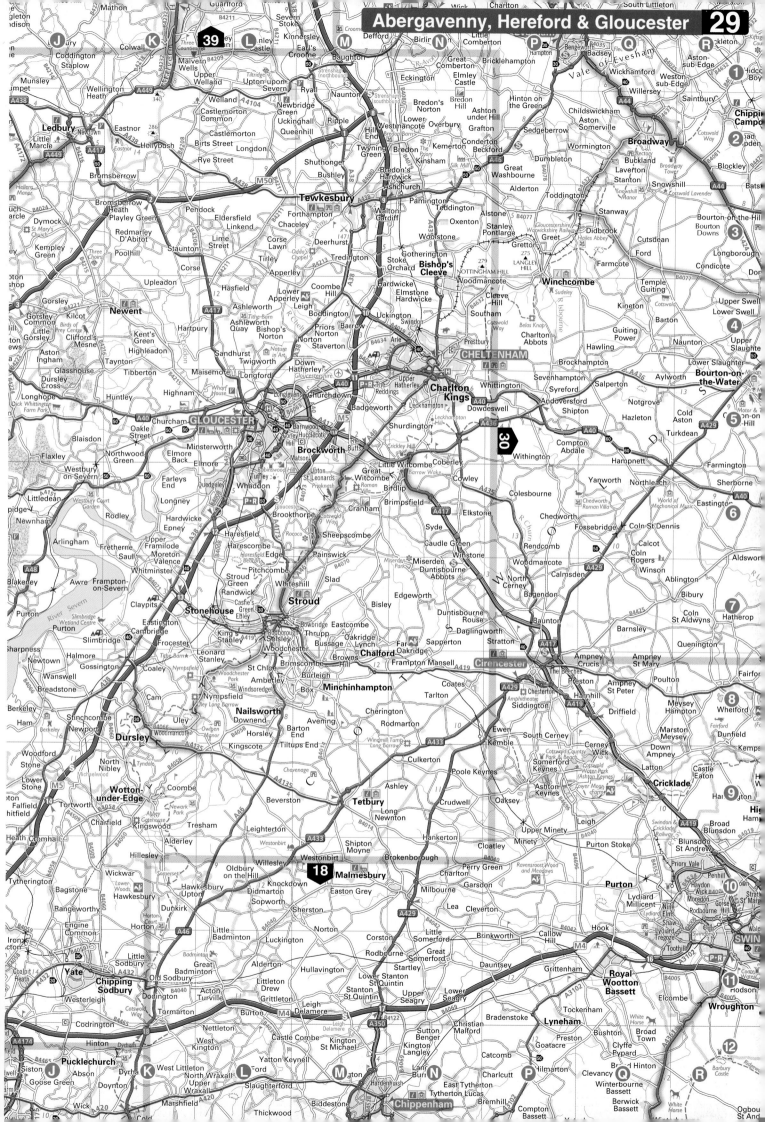

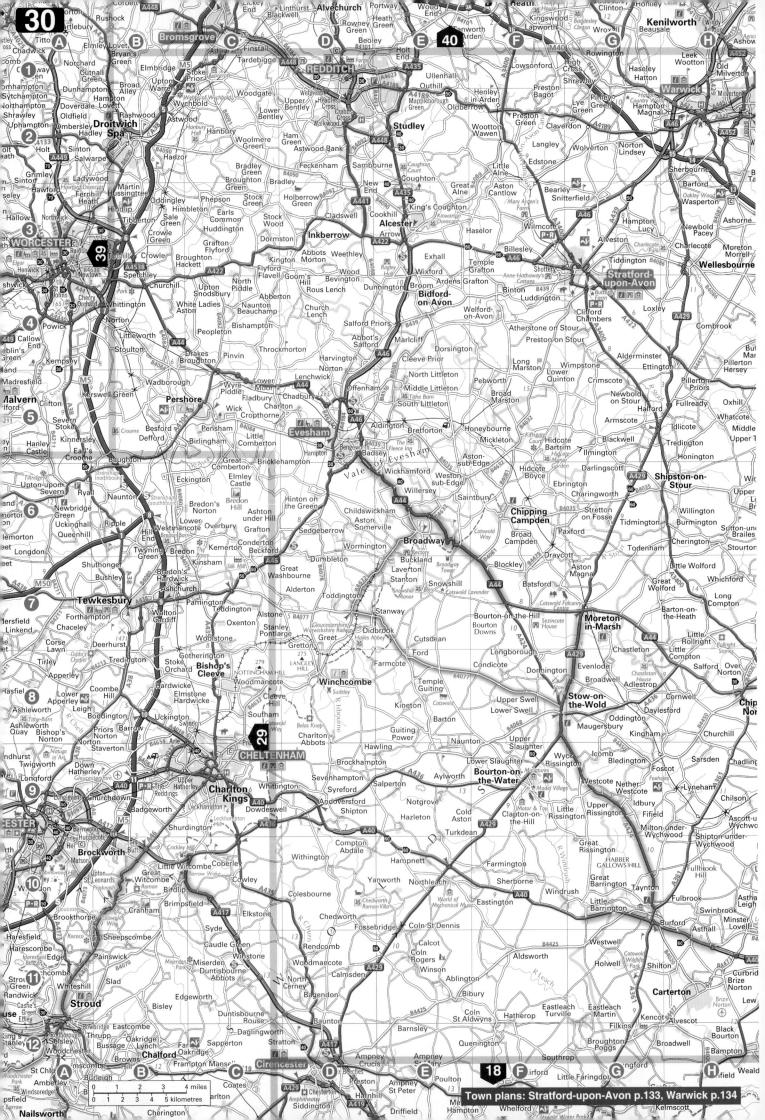

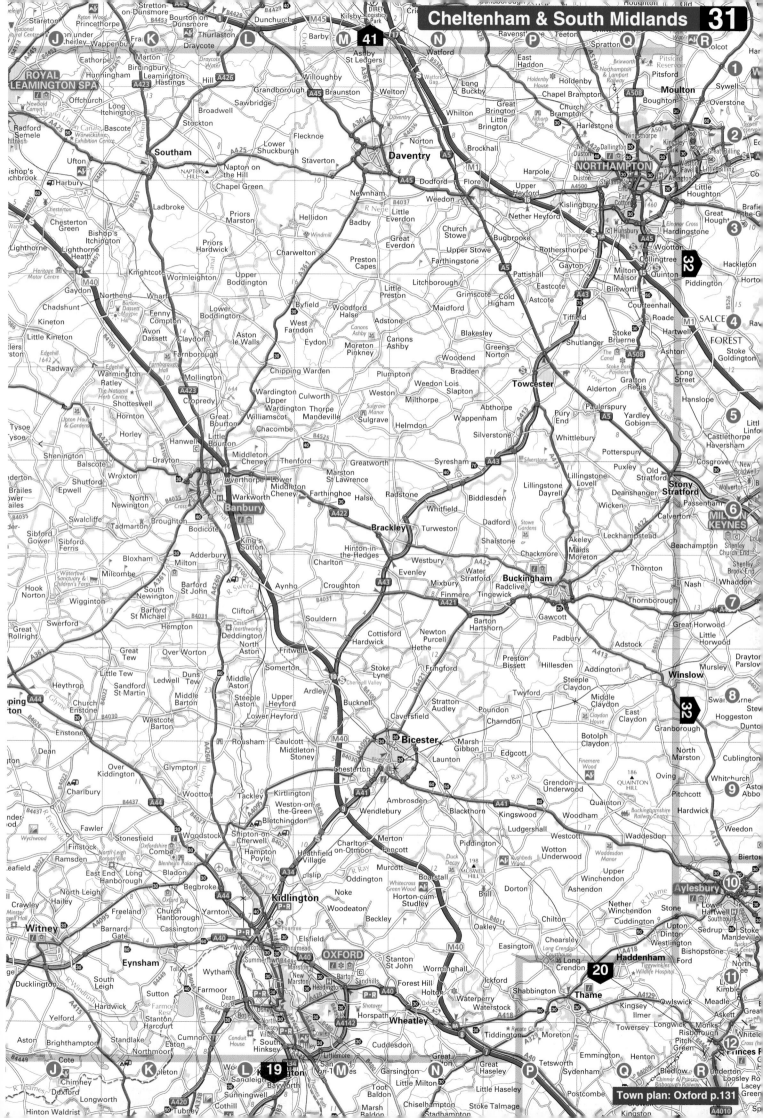

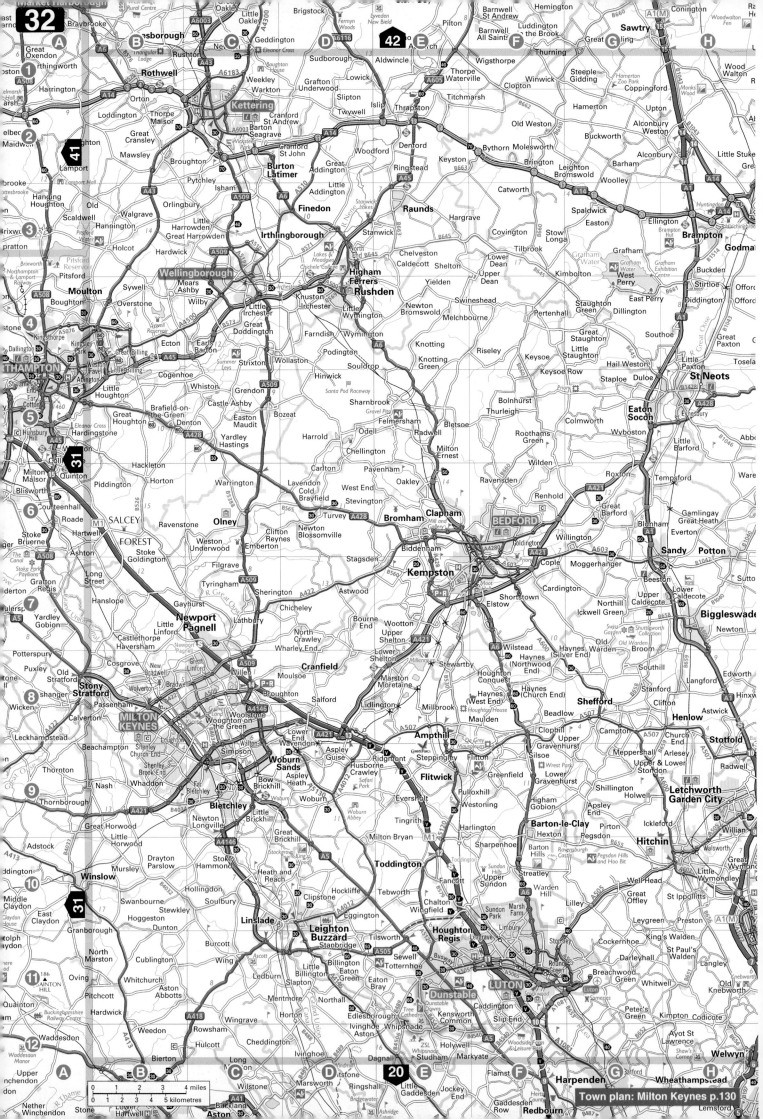

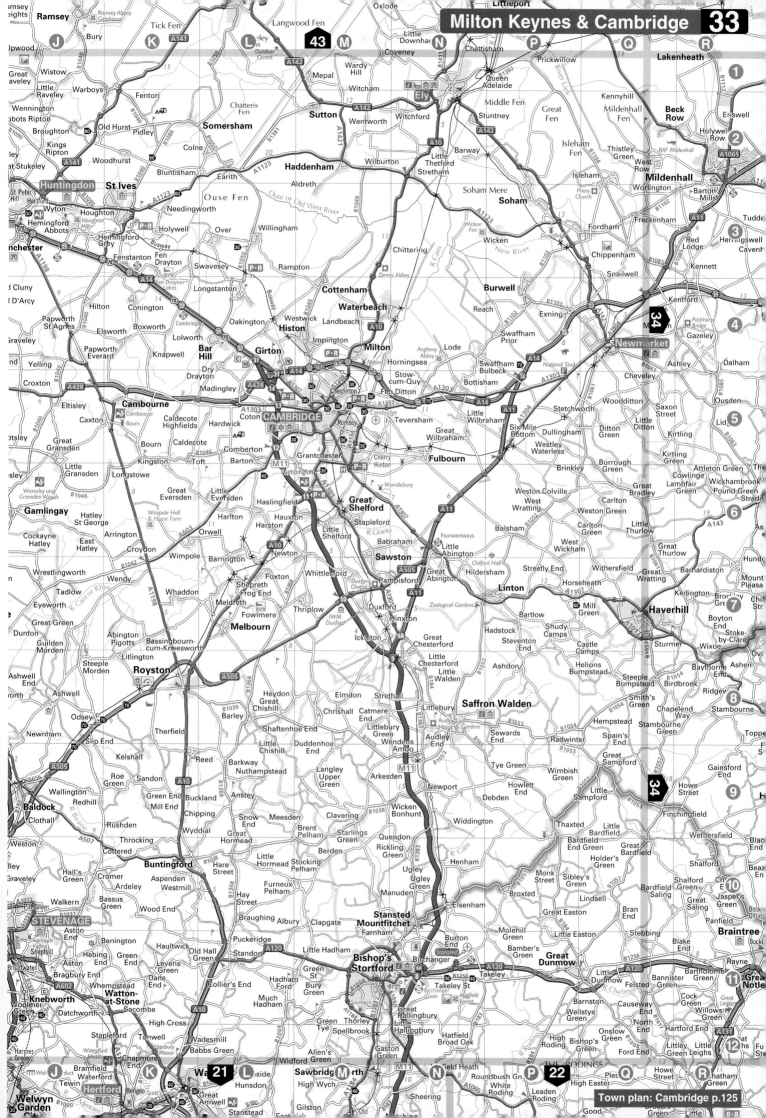

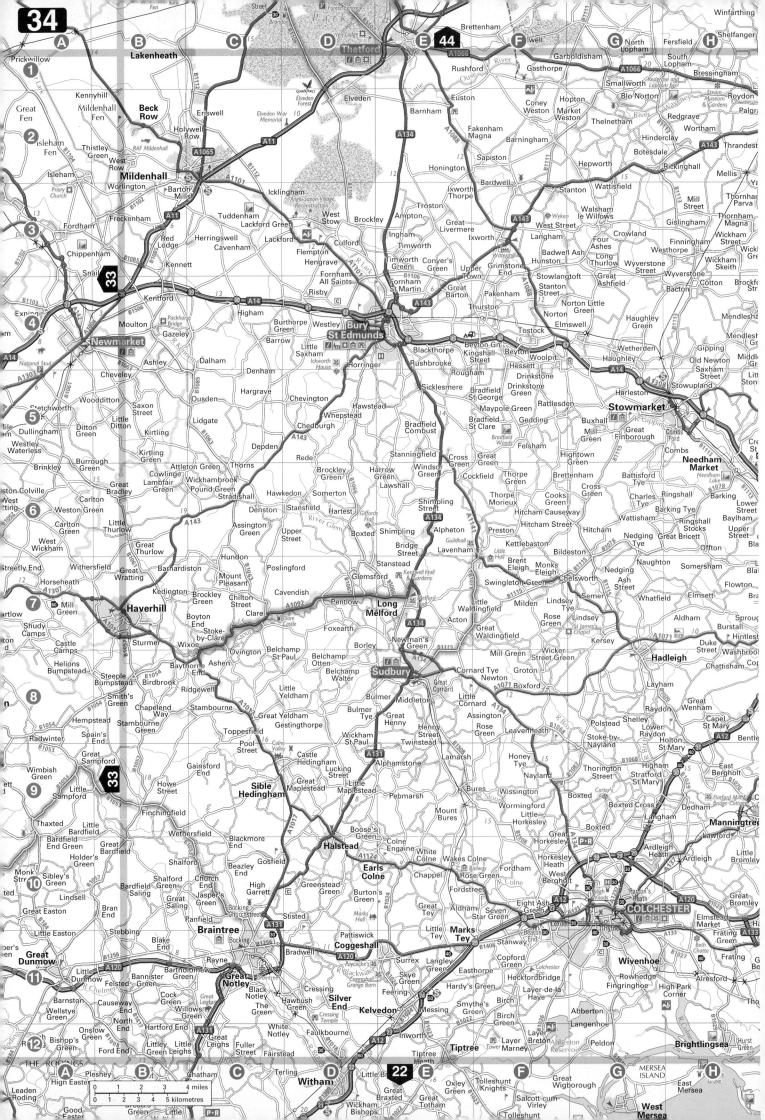

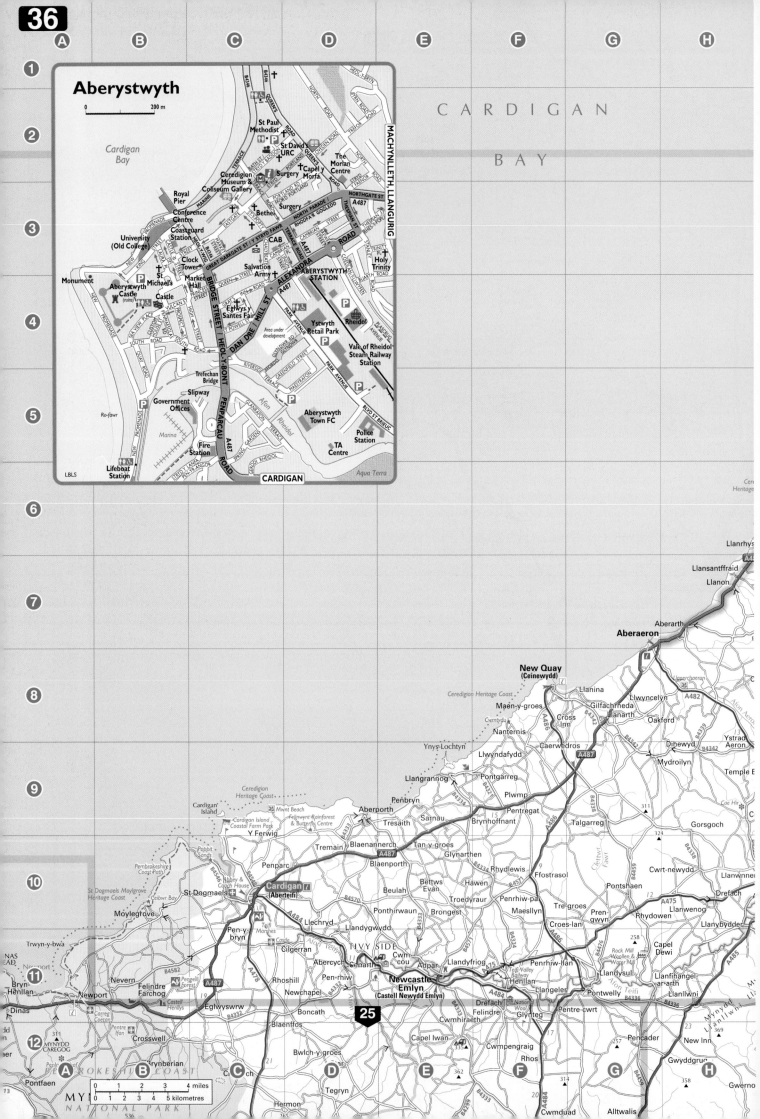

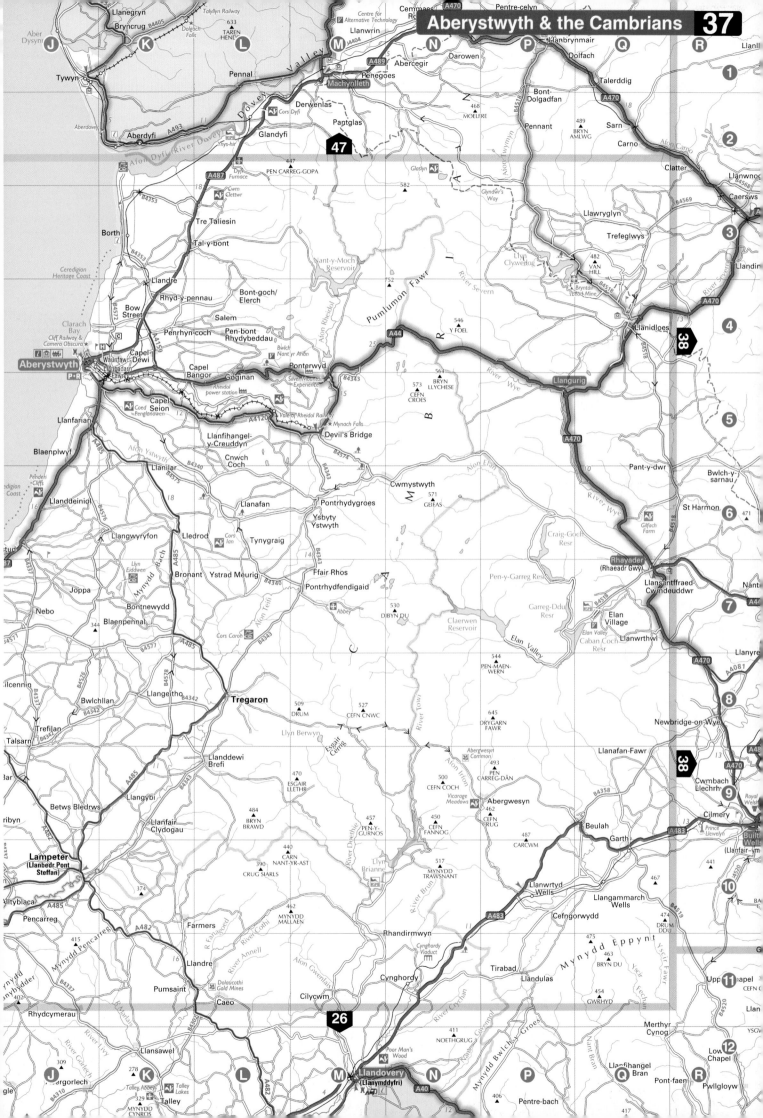

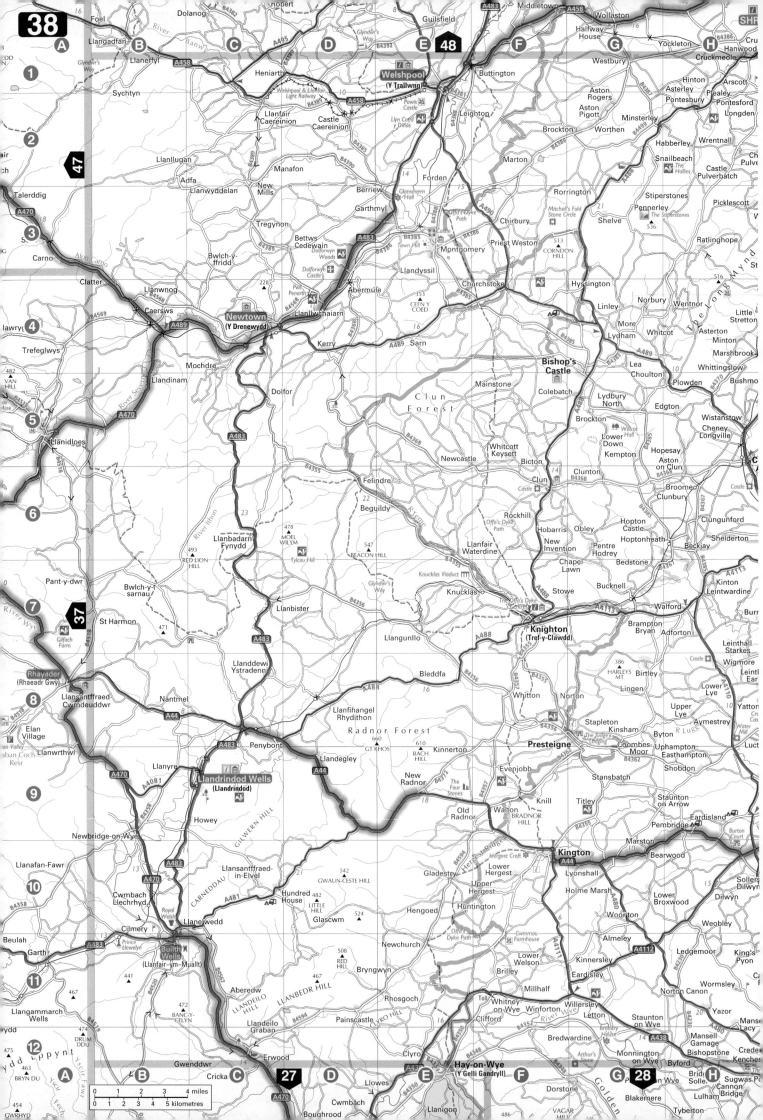

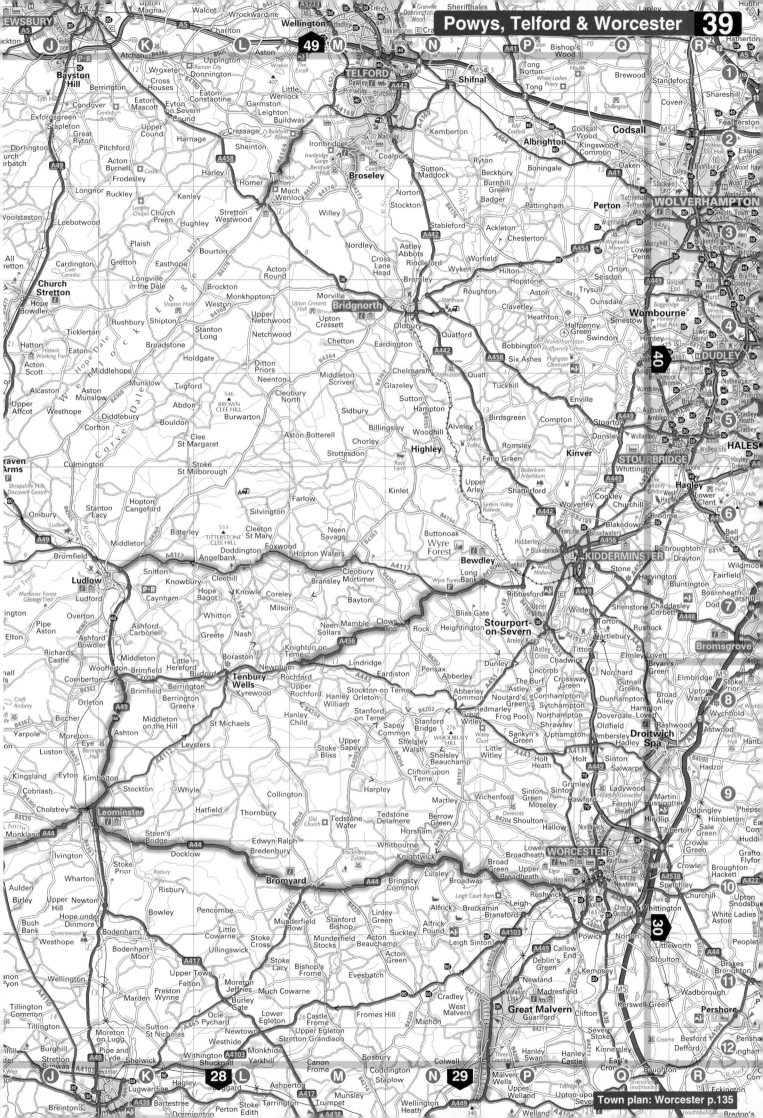

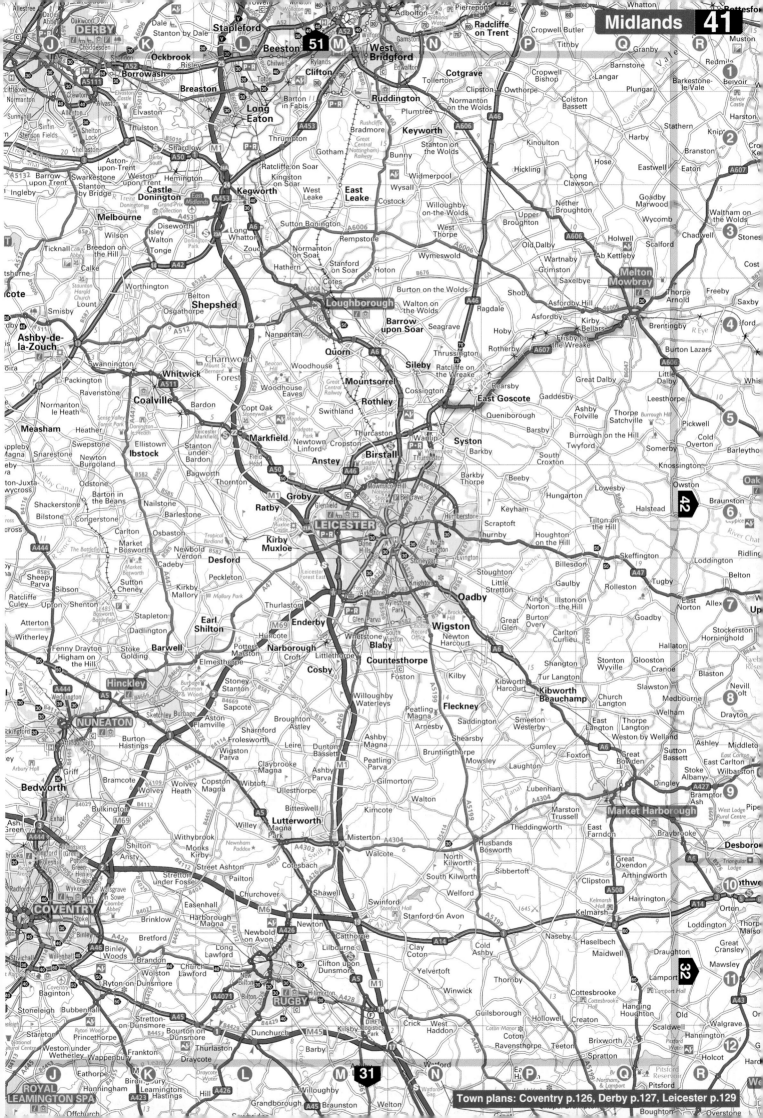

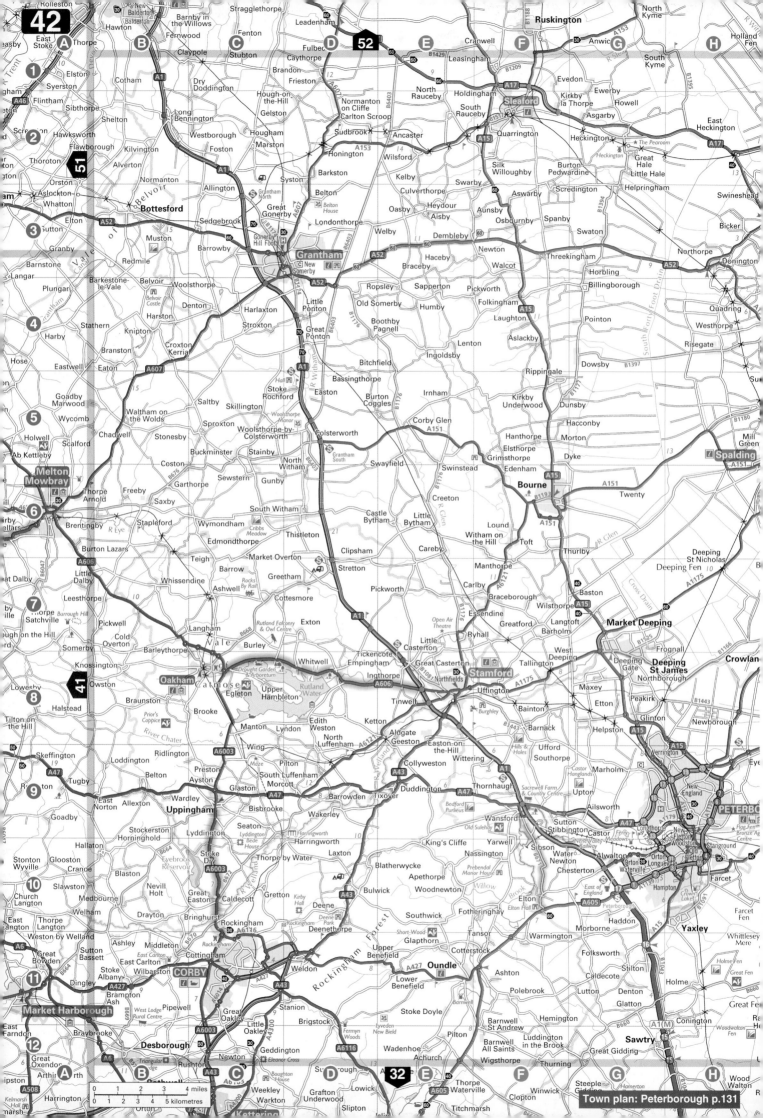

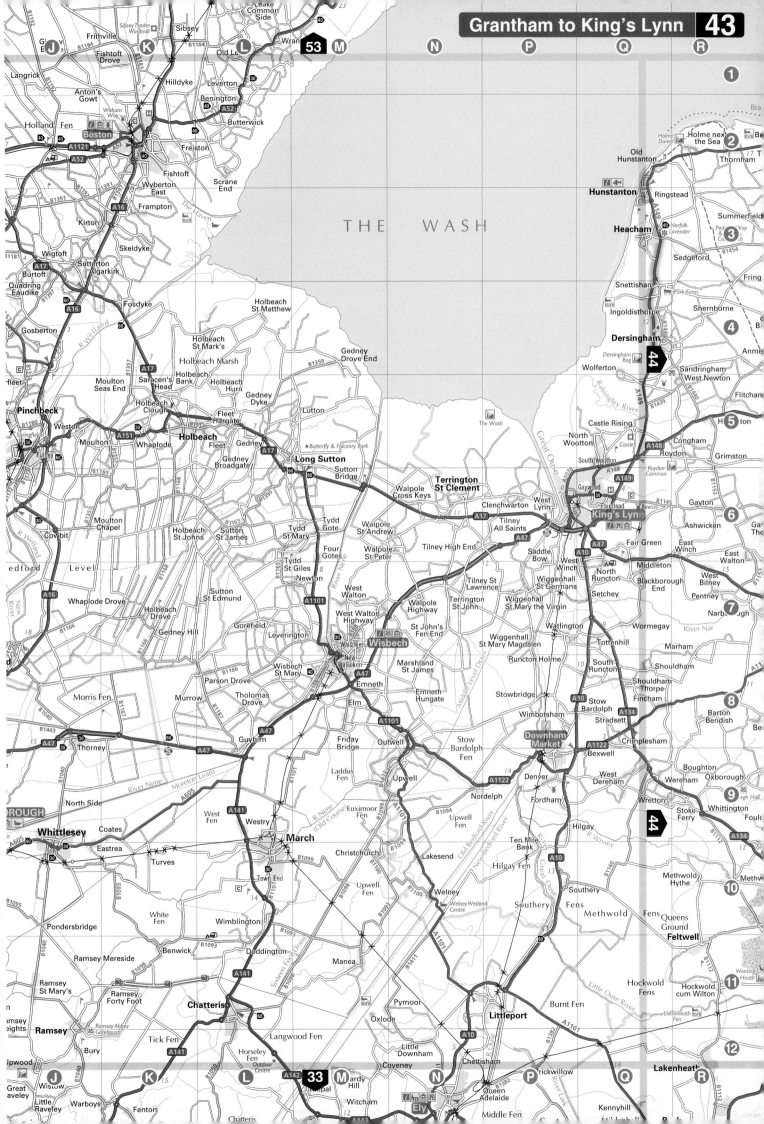

THE WASH

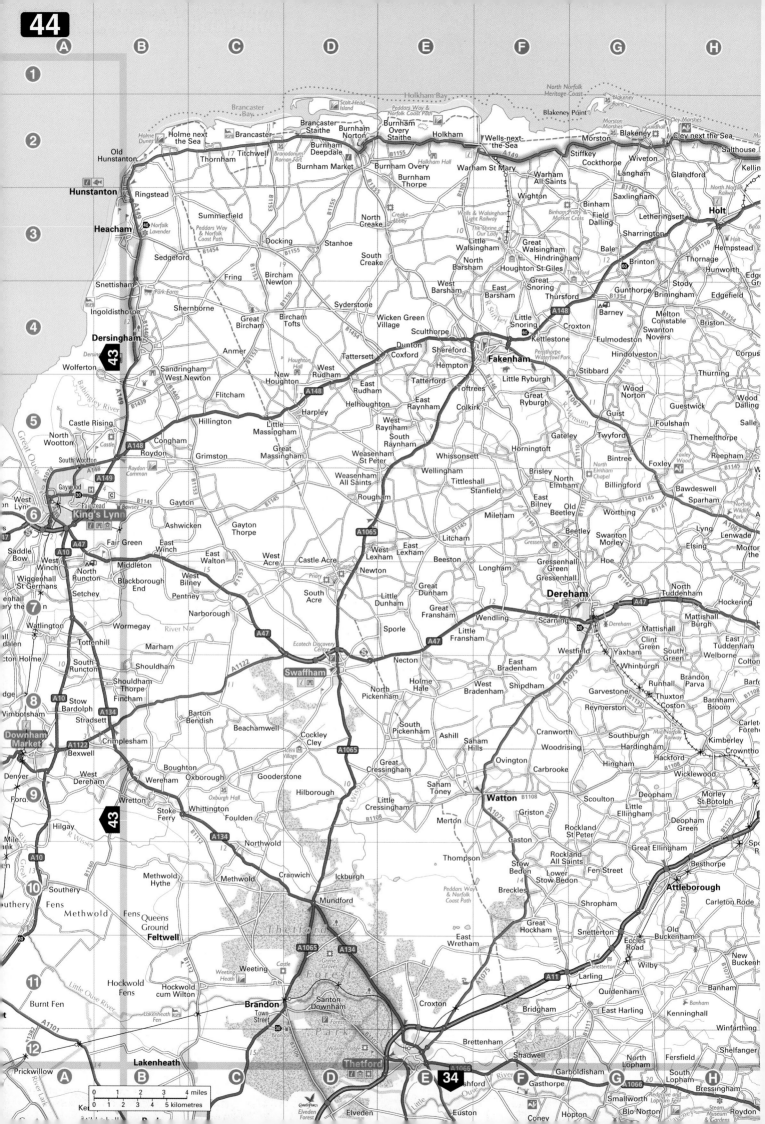

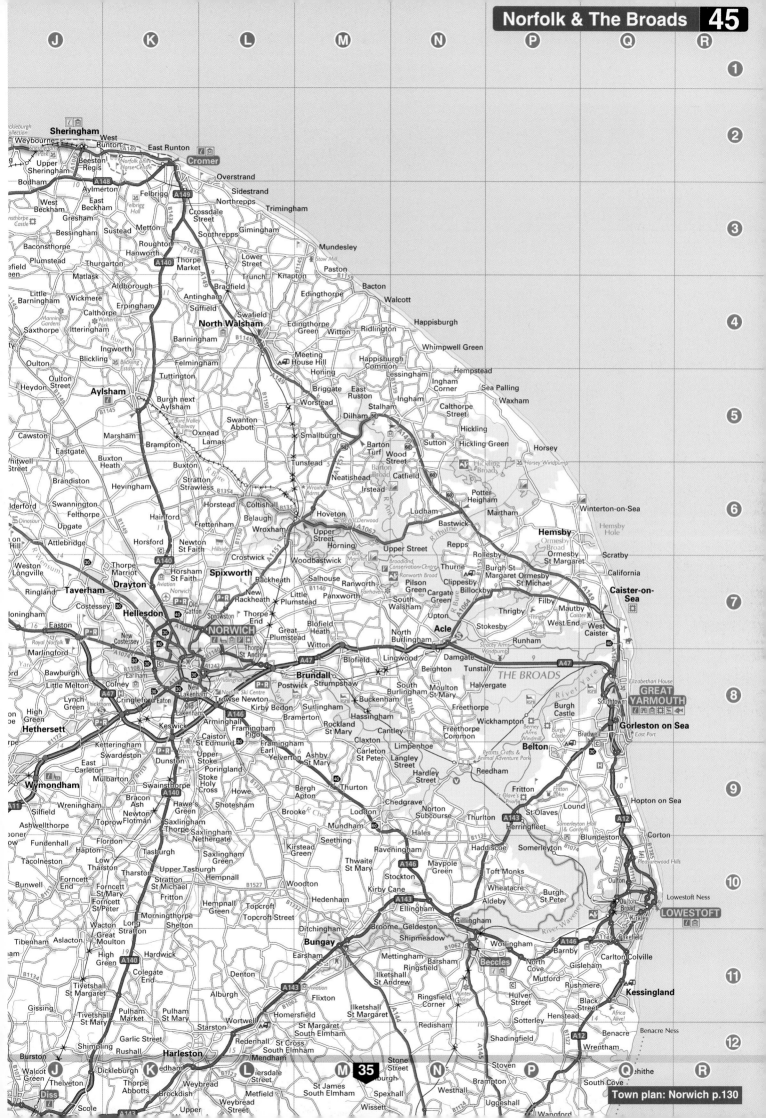

CAERNARFON

BAY

**54**

A  B  C  D  E  F  G  H

1

2

Clynnog-fawr

Caeau Tan
y Bwlch

522

Y GYRN-DDU

Trefor

Tre'r Ceiri
564
YR EIFL
20

Llanaelhaearn

3

Lleyn Heritage
Coast

Trwyn y
Grolech

Llithfaen

St Cybi's
Well

Llangybi

Carreg Ddu

Porth
Nefyn

Pistyll

Morfa
Nefyn

**Nefyn**

Edern

Bodfuan

Y Ffor

Llanystumdwy

Chwilog

Pentrefelin

Criccieth
Castle

4

Porth Ysgaden

Tudweiliog

Dinas

Corn
Fadrun
371

Llannor

Llanor

A497

B4415

Rhyd-y-clafdy

Efailnewydd

Abererch

Penarth Fawr
Medieval House

Pen-ychain

Tremadog
Bay

Porth
Colman

Bryn-
mawr

Llaniestyn

Pen-y-graig

Meyllteyrn

Llangwnnadl

Sarn

Botwnnog

Penrhos

**Pwllheli**

5

Porthoer

Bryncroes

Rhoshirwaun

B4413

B4413

Llanbedrog

Trwyn Llanbedrog

Plas yn
Rhiw

Llangian

St Tudwal's
Road

6

Porthor

Aberdaron
Bay

Porth
Ysgo

Y Rhiw

Llanfaelrhys

Porth Neigwl
or
Hell's Mouth

Llanengan

Bwlchtocyn

Marchros

**Abersoch**

St Tudwal's
Island East

St Tudwal's
Island West

Porth
Geiriad

Bardsey Sound

Lleyn Heritage
Coast

St Mary's

Ynys Enlli

**BARDSEY ISLAND**

7

8

9

10

CARDIGAN

BAY

11

12

A  B  C  D  E  F  G  H

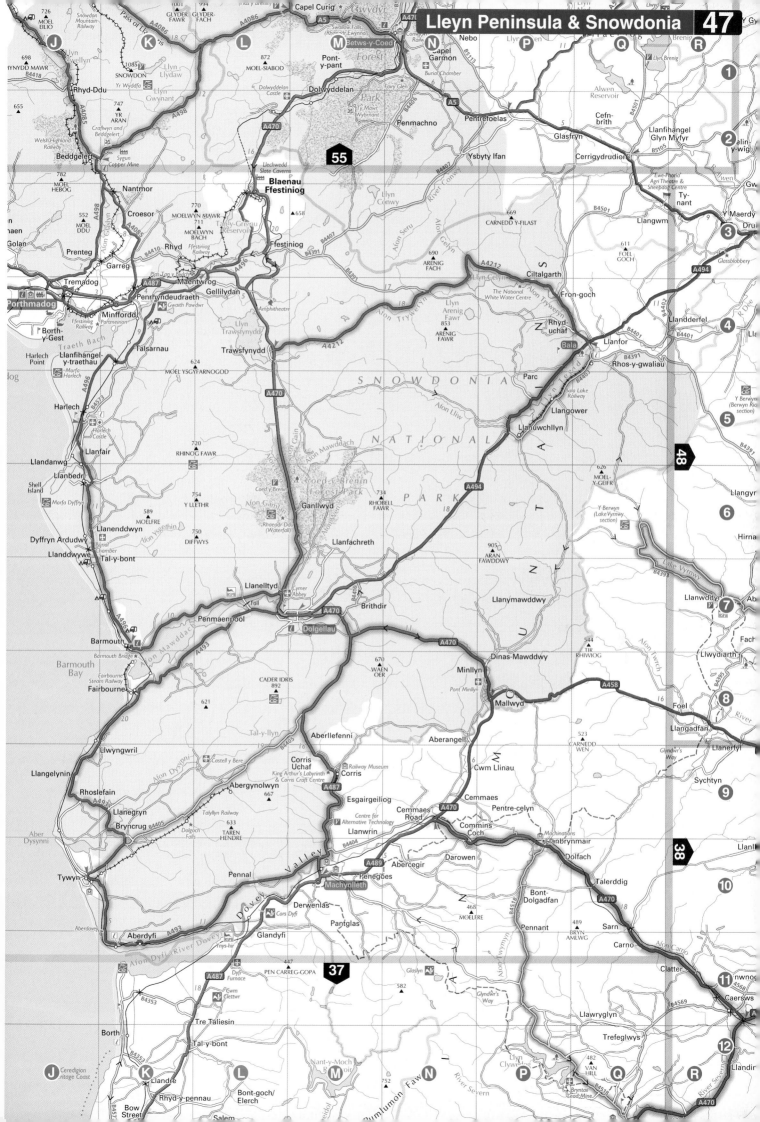

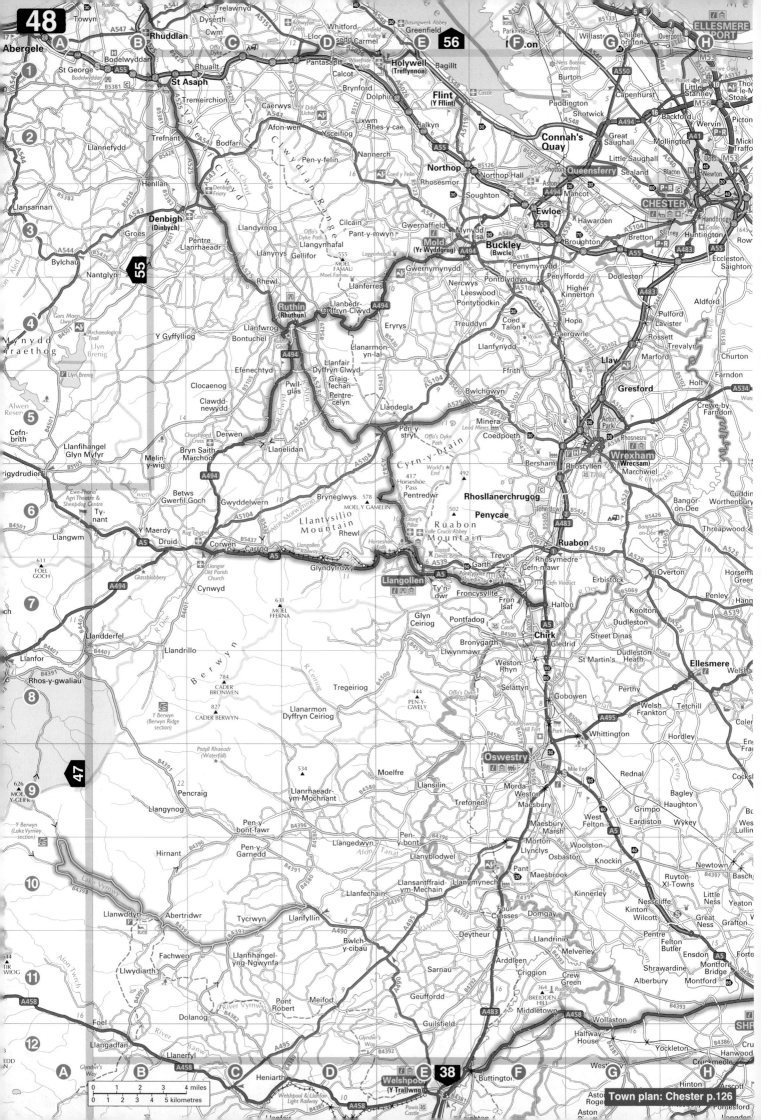

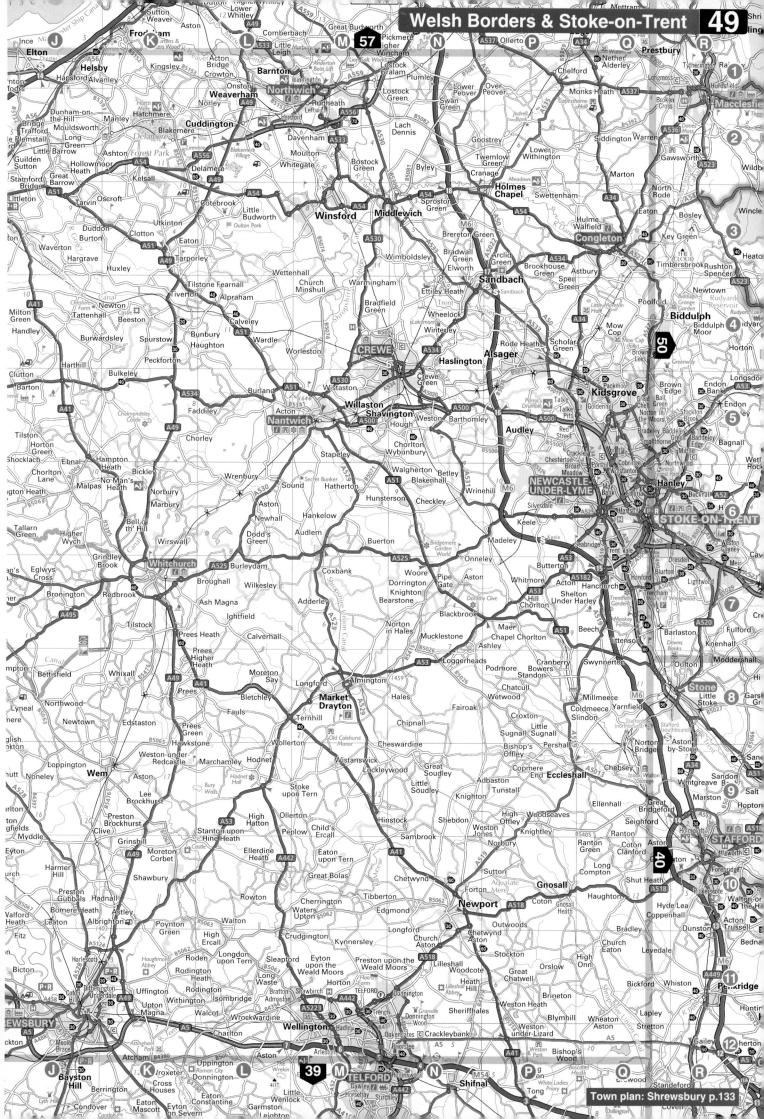

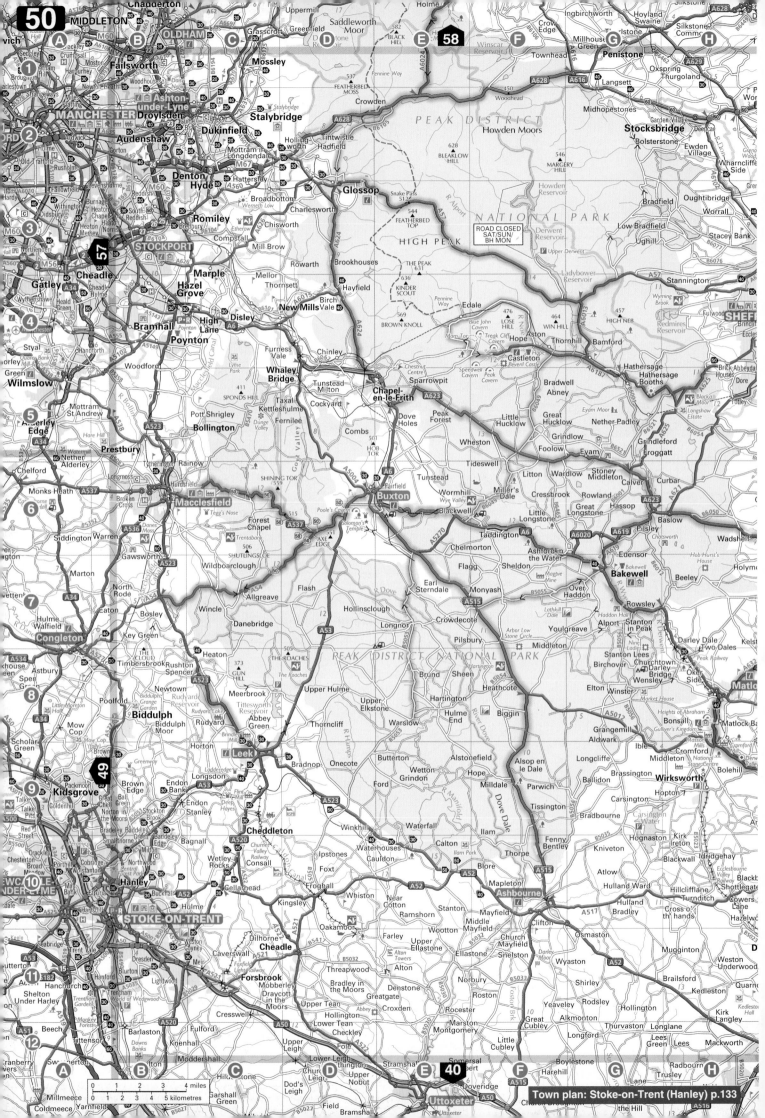

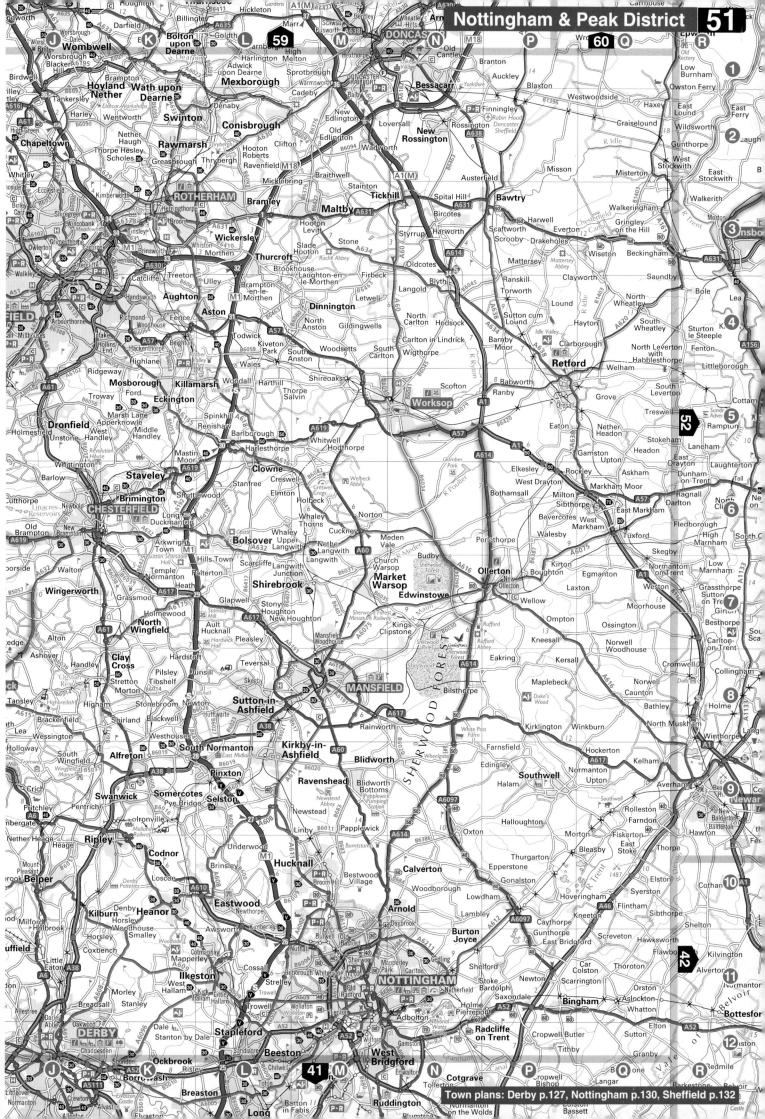

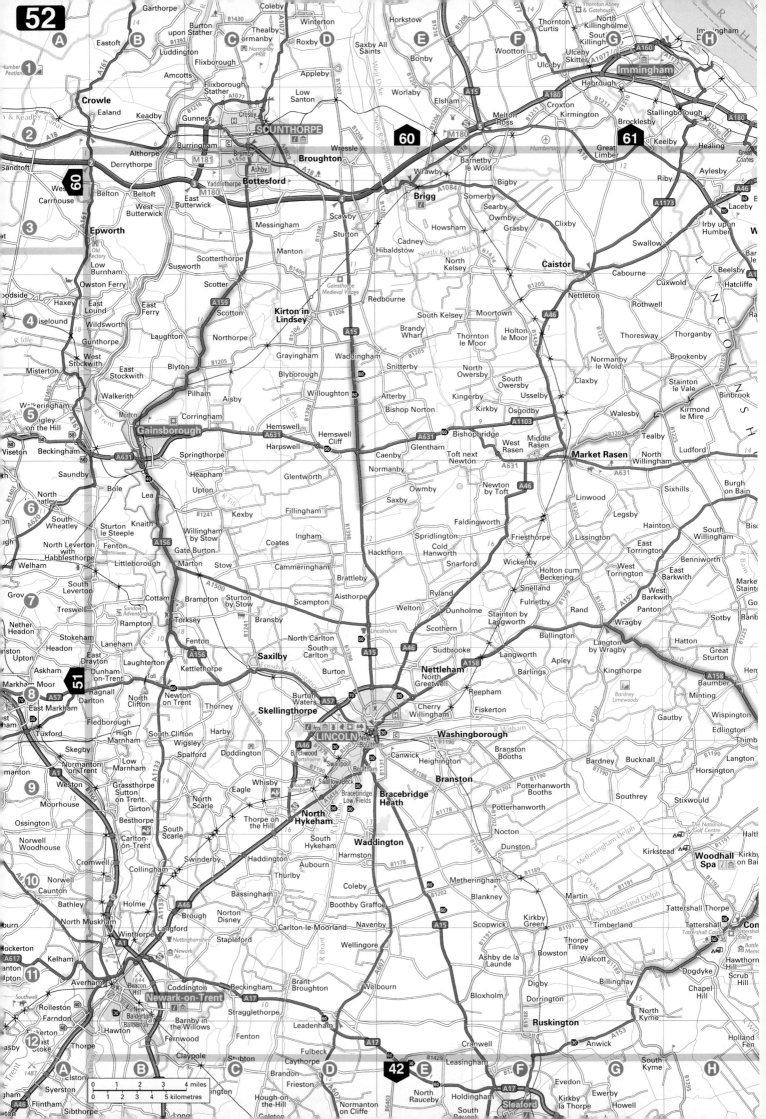

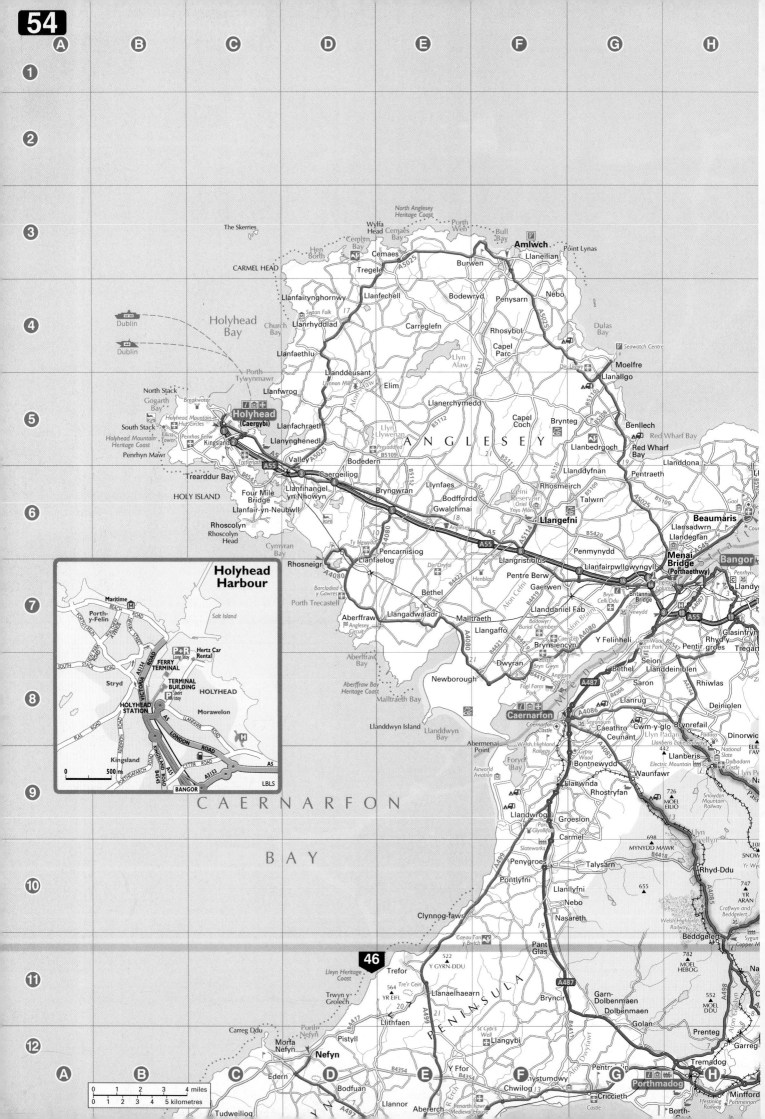

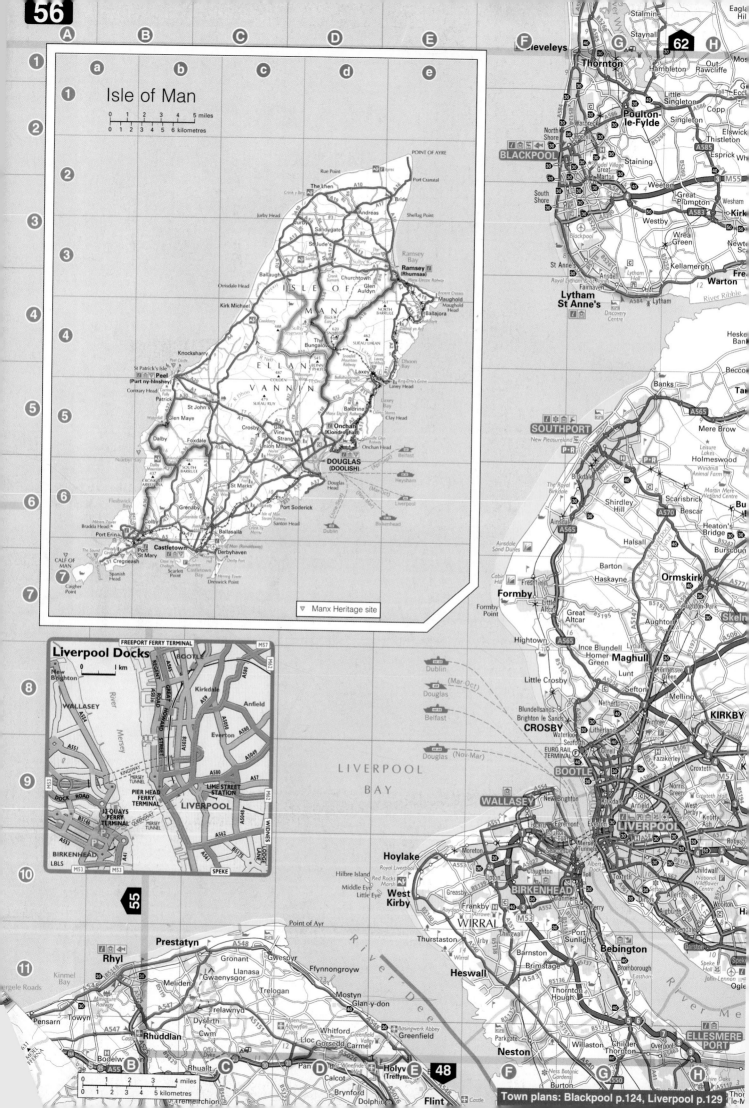

## Isle of Man

0 1 2 3 4 5 miles
0 1 2 3 4 5 6 kilometres

A  B  C  D  E  F  G  H
a  b  c  d  e

POINT OF AYRE

Rue Point
The Lhen
Cronk y Bing
Jurby Head
Jurby
Orrisdale Head
Ballaugh
Kirk Michael
Knocksharry
Peel
(Purt ny-hinshey)
St Patrick's Isle
Peel Castle
Contrary Head
Patrick
Glen Maye
Dalby
Foxdale
Niarbyl Bay
SOUTH
BARRULE
CRONK NY
ARREY LAA
Fleshwick Bay
Bradda Head
Port Erin
Miller's Tower
Calf of Man
Caigher Point
Spanish Head
Cregneash
Port St Mary
Colby
Grenaby
Ballasalla
Castletown
Derbyhaven
Scarlett Point
Castletown Bay
Dreswick Point

Port Cranstal
Bride
Shellag Point
Andreas
Sandygate
St Jude's
Sulby
Ramsey
(Rhumsaa)
Ramsey Bay
Churchtown
Glen Auldyn
Maughold
Maughold Head
Ballajora
NORTH BARRULE
Snaefell
The Bungalow
SLIEAU LHEAN
Dhoon Bay
Laxey
Laxey Head
Laxey Bay
Clay Head
ISLE OF MAN
ELLAN VANNIN
SLIEAU RUY
Crosby
Glen Vine
Strang
Union Mills
Onchan
(Kiondroghad)
Onchan Head
DOUGLAS
(DOOLISH)
Douglas Head
Port Soderick
Santon Head
Belfast
Heysham
Liverpool
Birkenhead
Dublin
St John's
St Marks
Baldrine

▽ Manx Heritage site

Cleveleys
Thornton
Staynall
Stalmine
Hambleton
Out Rawcliffe
Poulton-le-Fylde
Singleton
Little Singleton
Elswick
Thistleton
BLACKPOOL
North Shore
Warbreck
Hoohil
Staining
Great Marton
Model Village
Weeton
Great Plumpton
Wesham
Kirk
South Shore
Westby
Blackpool
Wrea Green
Kellamergh
Warton
St Anne's
Ansdell
Lytham Hall
Fairhaven
Lytham St Anne's
Royal Lytham
Discovery Centre
River Ribble
Hesketh Bank

SOUTHPORT
New Pleasureland
Birkdale
The Royal Birkdale
Ainsdale
Ainsdale Sand Dunes
Freshfield
Formby
Formby Point
Little Altcar
Hightown
Great Altcar
Ince Blundell
Homer Green
Maghull
Lunt
Sefton
Melling
Kirkby
Mere Brow
Holmeswood
Windmill Animal Farm
Martin Mere Wetland Centre
Scarisbrick
Shirdley Hill
Halsall
Barton
Haskayne
Ormskirk
Aughton Park
Aughton
Skelmersdale
Bescar
Burscough
Banks
Lydiate

Dublin (Mar-Oct)
Douglas
Belfast
Douglas (Nov-Mar)

LIVERPOOL BAY

EURO RAIL TERMINAL
Little Crosby
Blundellsands
Brighton le Sands
CROSBY
Waterloo
Seaforth
Litherland
Netherton
Aintree
BOOTLE
Fazakerley
Croxteth
Norris Green
West Derby
Knotty Ash
Childwall
Wallasey
New Brighton
Seacombe
Egremont
Liscard
Poulton
Wallasey
Mersey Tunnels
LIVERPOOL
Toxteth
Dingle
Aigburth
Allerton
Woolton
Garston
Speke
John Lennon Airport

## Liverpool Docks

FREEPORT FERRY TERMINAL
BOOTLE
New Brighton
WALLASEY
River Mersey
Kirkdale
Anfield
Everton
REGENT ROAD
GREAT HOWARD STREET
A5036
A565
A59
A5049
KINGSWAY MERSEY TUNNEL
PIER HEAD FERRY TERMINAL
12 QUAYS FERRY TERMINAL
DOCK ROAD
LIME STREET STATION
LIVERPOOL
QUEENSWAY MERSEY TUNNEL
BIRKENHEAD LBLS
SPEKE
WIDNES
LODGE LANE
0   1 km

Hoylake
Royal Liverpool
Hilbre Island
Red Rocks Marsh
Middle Eye
Little Eye
West Kirby
Greasby
Moreton
Upton
Claughton
BIRKENHEAD
Tranmere
Rock Ferry
Frankby
Roydon
Arrowe
WIRRAL
Thurstaston
Irby
Thingwall
Wirral
Barnston
Brimstage
Port Sunlight
Bebington
Bromborough
Eastham
Heswall
Thornton Hough
Willaston
Childer Thornton
Neston
Parkgate
Ness Botanic Gardens
Burton
ELLESMERE PORT
Overpool
Whitby

Prestatyn
Rhyl
Kinmel Bay
Abergele Roads
Pensarn
Towyn
Bodelwyddan
Rhuddlan
Gronant
Meliden
Gwaenysgor
Llanasa
Gwespyr
Ffynnongroyw
Trelawnyd
Dyserth
Cwm
Trelogan
Mostyn
Glan-y-don
Whitford
Lloc
Gorsedd
Carmel
Greenfield
Basingwerk Abbey
Greenfield Valley
Holywell
(Treffynnon)
Point of Ayr
River Dee
Prestatyn
Minirature Railway
Offa's Dyke
Winifrede's
Pantasaph
Calcot
Brynford
Dolphin
Flint
Moel Ffenna
Tremeirchion

0 1 2 3 4 miles
0 1 2 3 4 5 kilometres

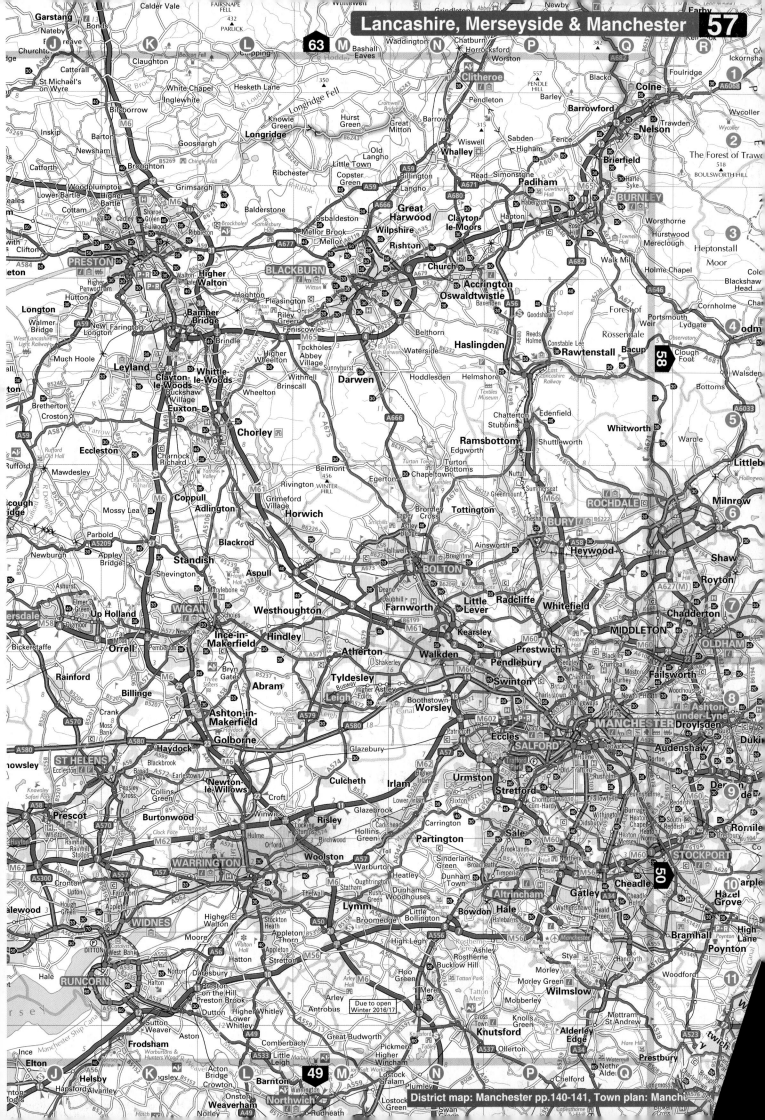

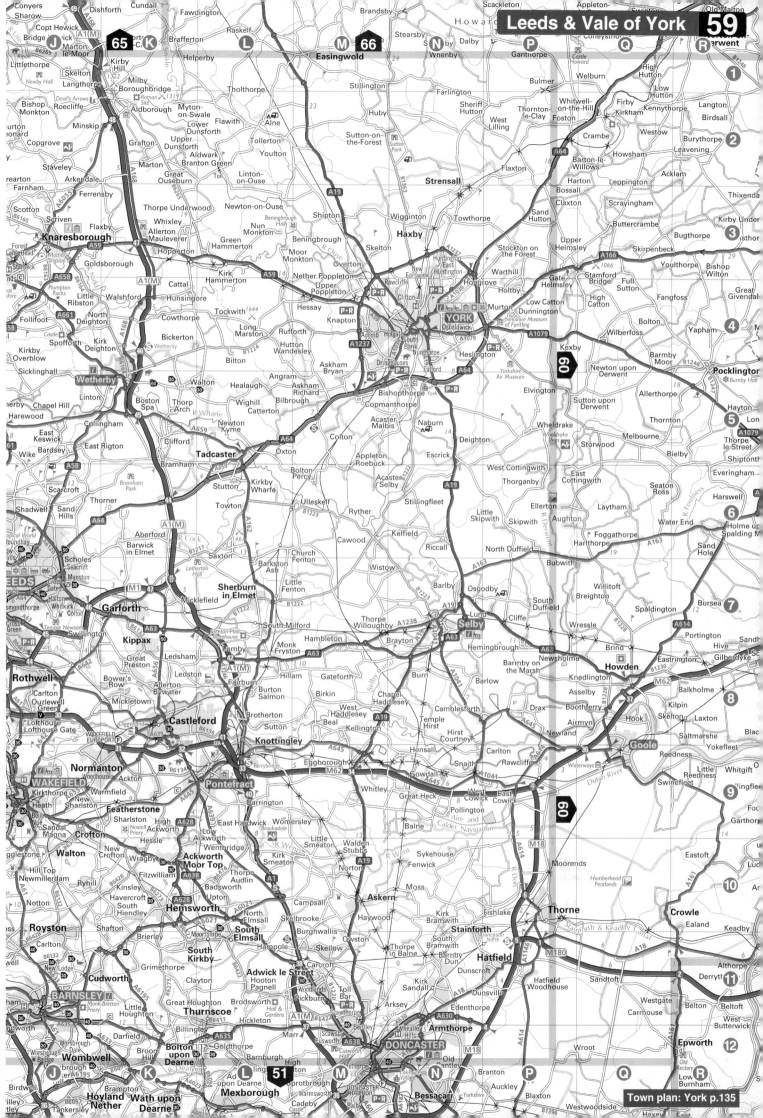

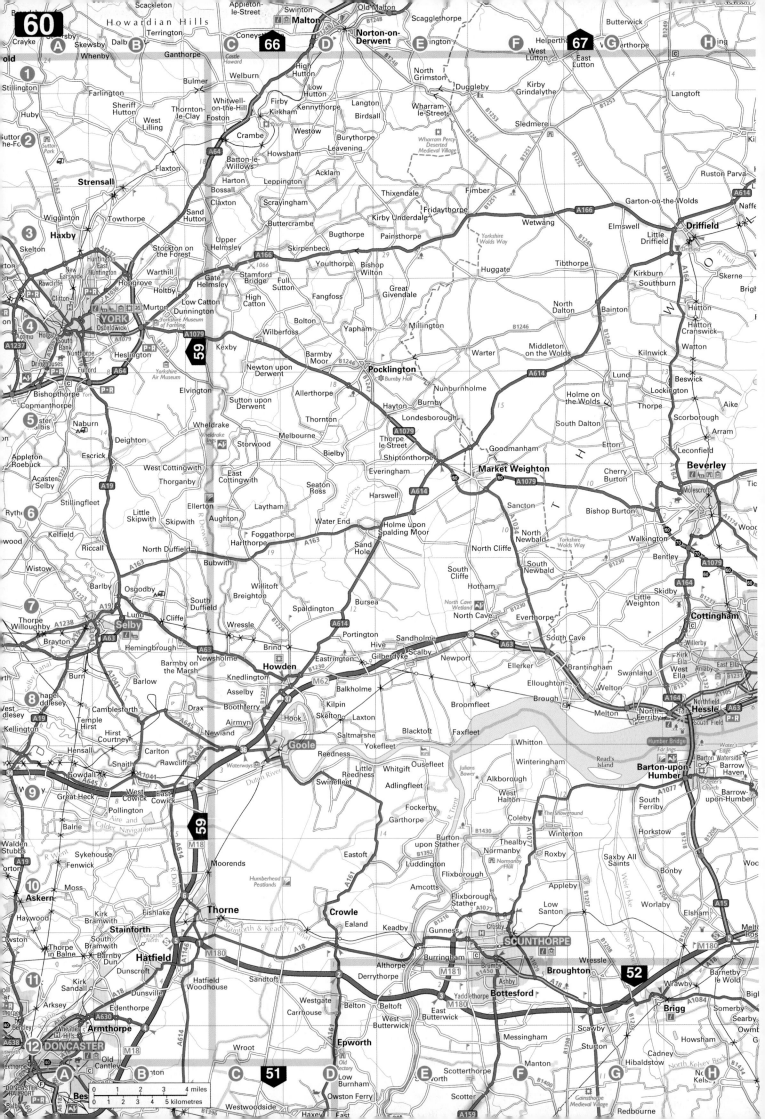

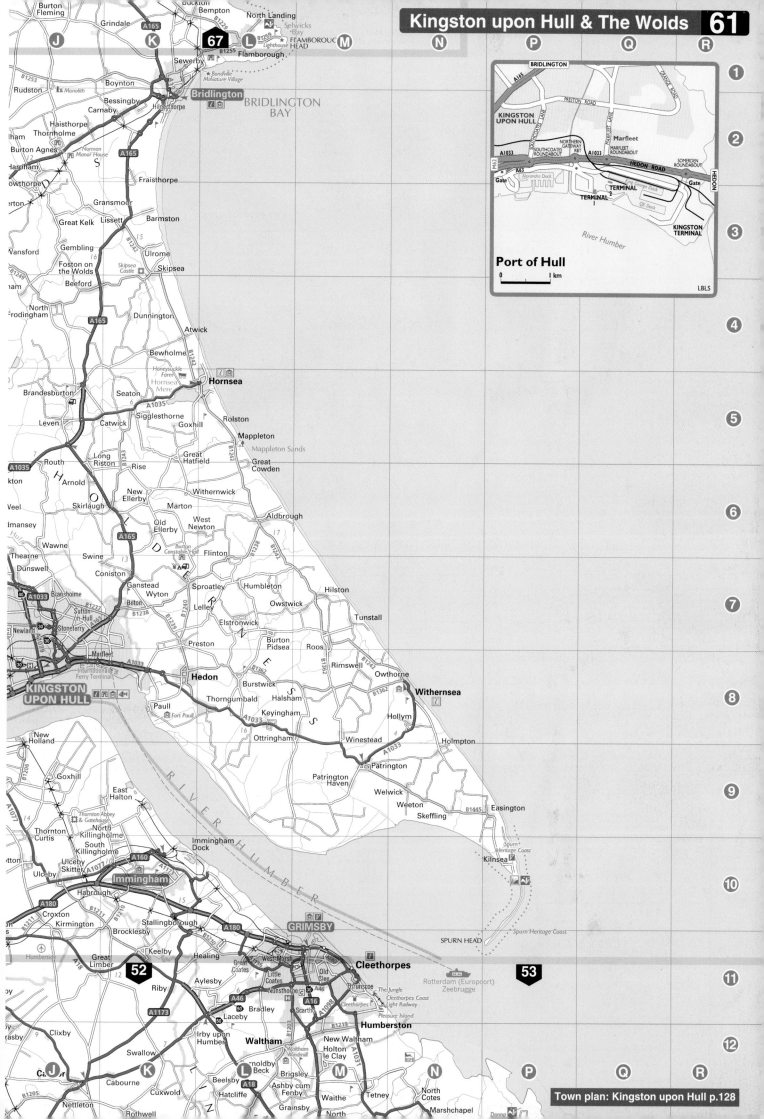

Town plan: Kingston upon Hull p.128

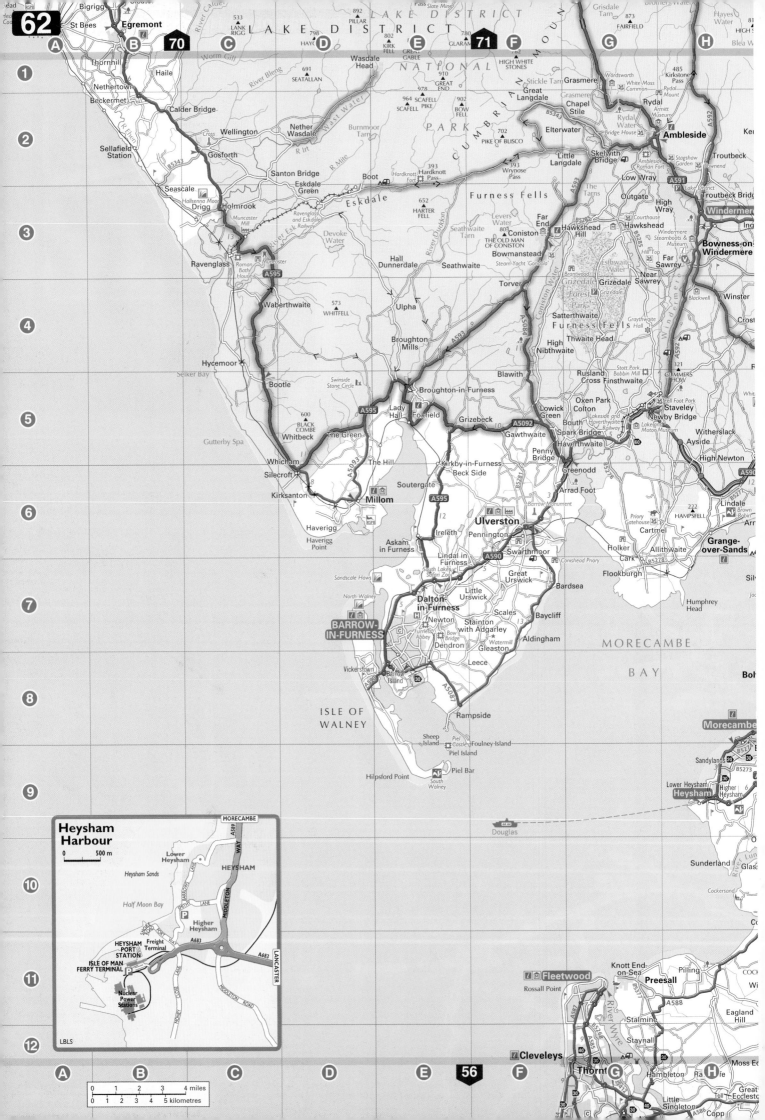

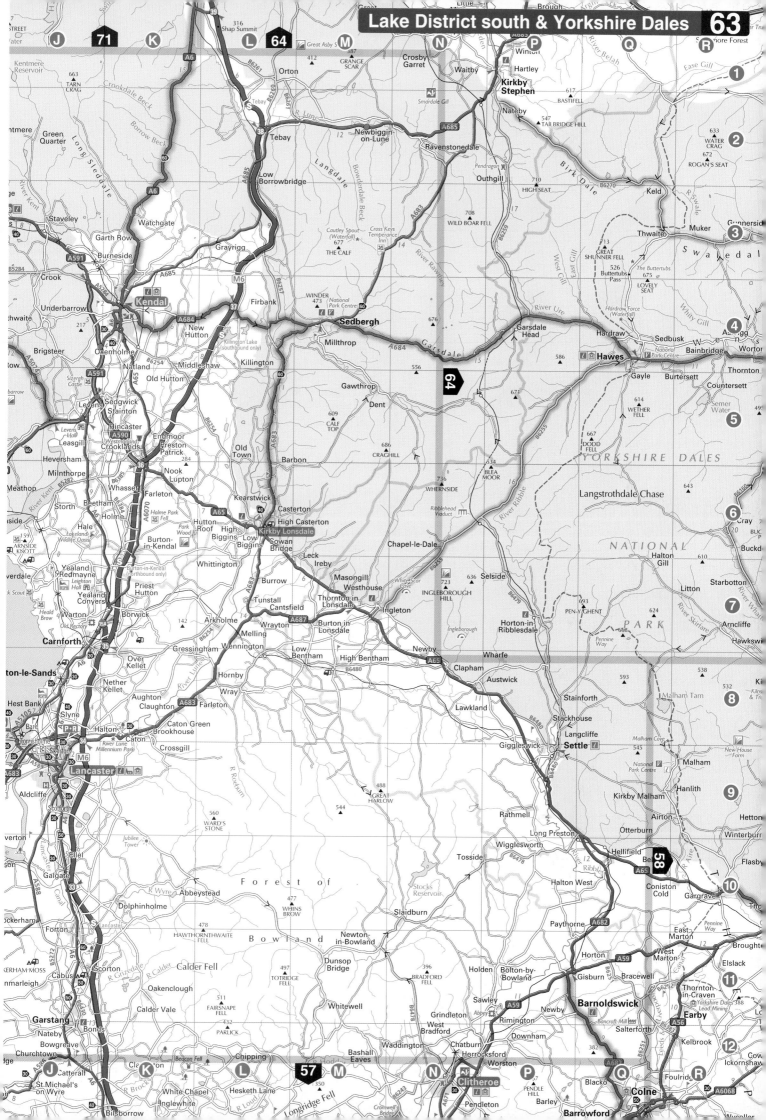

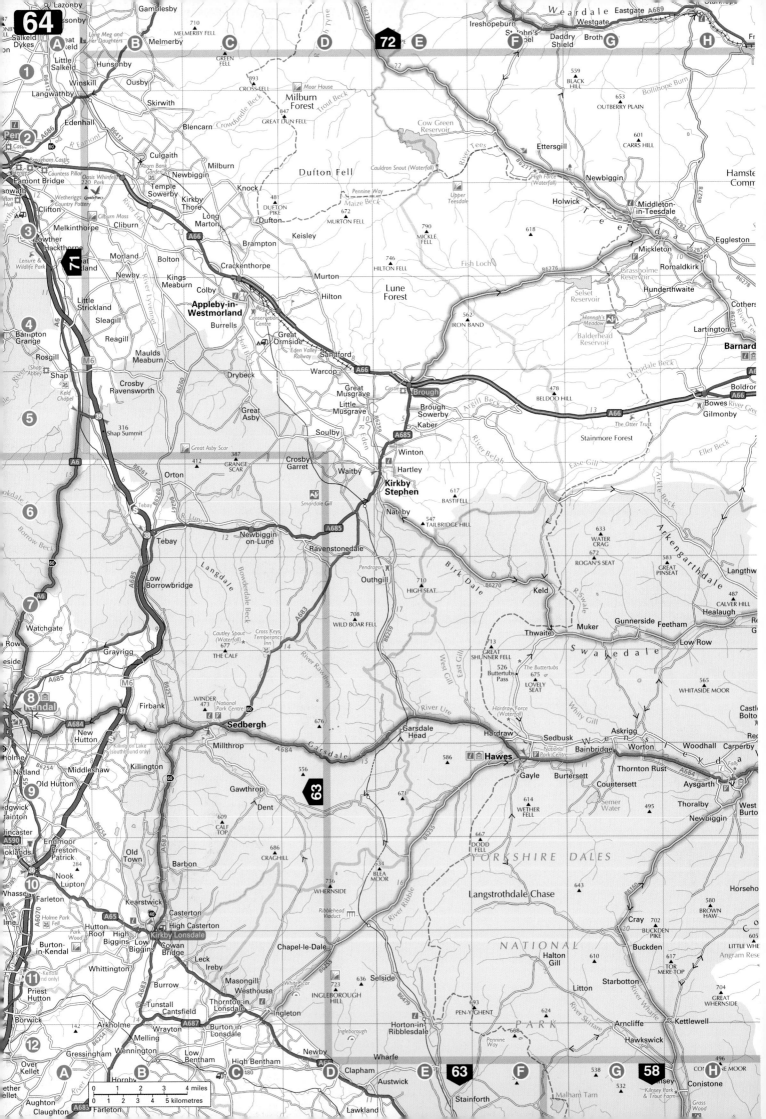

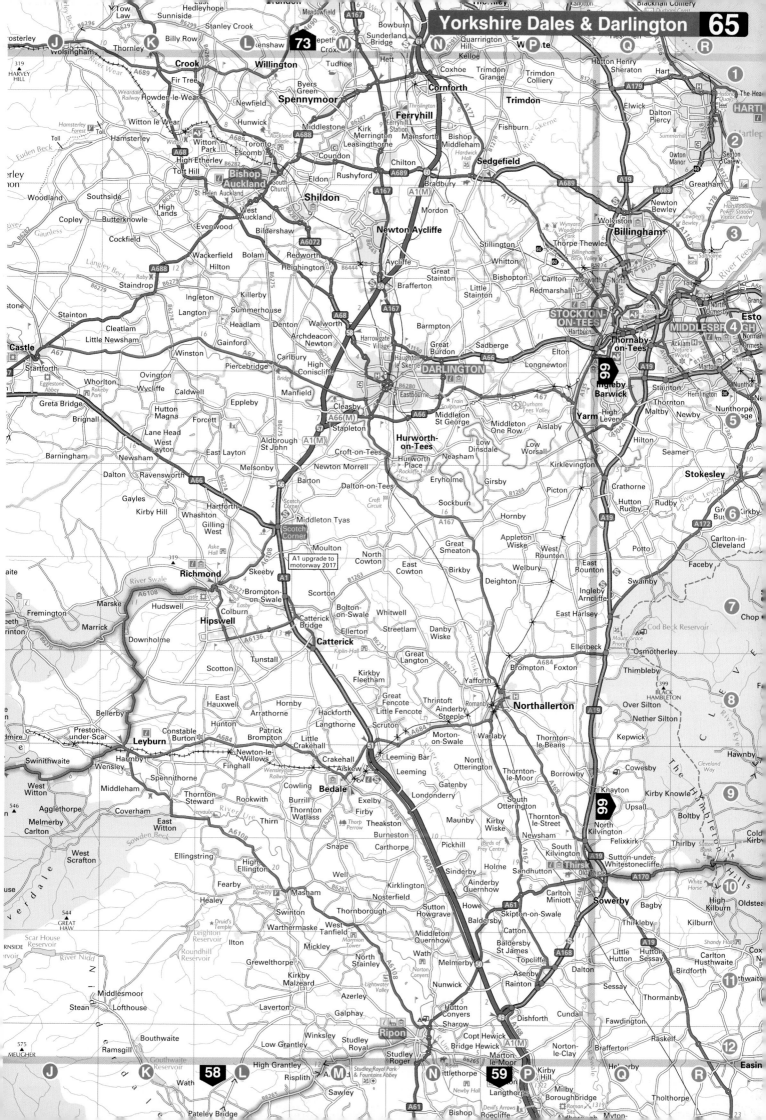

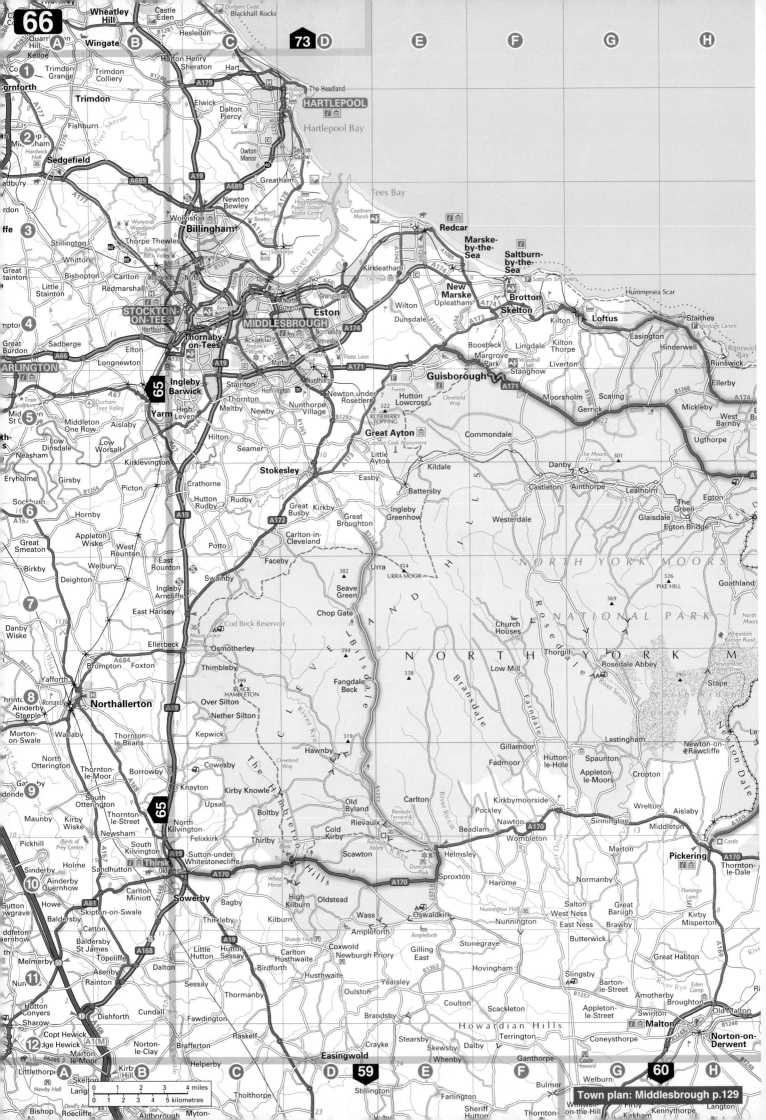

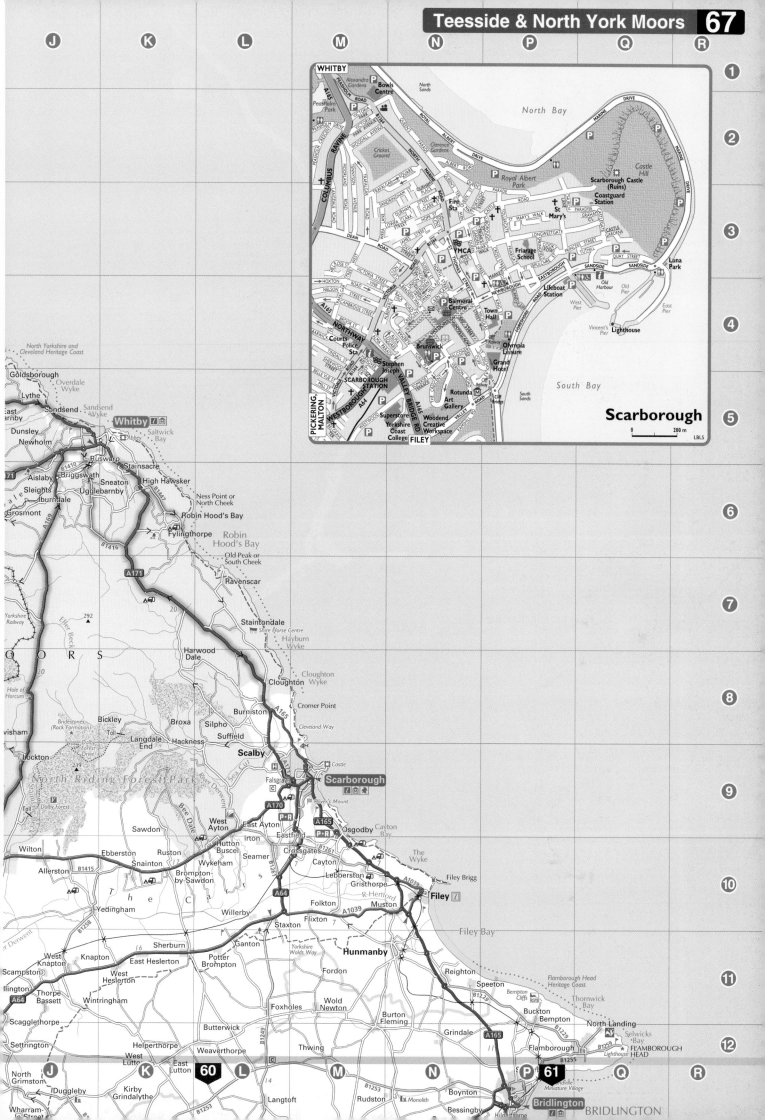

Grid references (top): J K L M N P Q R

Grid references (side): 1 2 3 4 5 6 7 8 9 10 11 12

**WHITBY** (inset map)

North Bay
Alexandra Gardens
Bowls Centre
North Sands
Peasholm Park
Peasholm Drive
RAVINE
COLUMBUS
MOORLAND ROAD
Victoria Park
Cricket Ground
Woodall Avenue
Queens Parade
Royal Albert Drive
Clarence Gardens
NORTH
Castle Hill
Scarborough Castle (Ruins)
Royal Albert Park
Coastguard Station
St Mary's
CASTLE GARDENS
Fire Sta
YMCA
Friarage School
LONGWESTGATE
EASTBOROUGH
NEWBOROUGH
SANDSIDE
QUAY STREET
Luna Park
Old Harbour
Old Pier
East Pier
Balmoral Centre
Town Hall
Lifeboat Station
West Pier
Vincent's Pier
Lighthouse
Courts
Police Sta
Stephen Joseph
Brunswick
Olympia Leisure
Grand Hotel
South Bay
NORTHWAY
SCARBOROUGH STATION
WESTBOROUGH
VALLEY BRIDGE RD
Rotunda Art Gallery
Woodend Creative Workspace
South Sands
Superstore
Yorkshire Coast College
**Scarborough**
0   200 m
LBLS

**PICKERING, MALTON** / **FILEY** (inset borders)

North Yorkshire and Cleveland Heritage Coast
Goldsborough
Overdale Wyke
Lythe
East Barnby
Sandsend
Sandsend Wyke
Dunsley
Newholm
**Whitby**
Abbey
Saltwick Bay
Ruswarp
Aislaby
Briggswath
Sneaton
Stainsacre
High Hawsker
B1410
Sleights
Ugglebarnby
B1447
Iburndale
Ness Point or North Cheek
Grosmont
**Robin Hood's Bay**
A169
Fylingthorpe
Robin Hood's Bay
B1416
Old Peak or South Cheek
**A171**
Ravenscar
20
Yorkshire Railway
292
Staintondale
Shire Horse Centre
Hayburn Wyke
MOORS
Harwood Dale
Cloughton Wyke
Eller Beck
Cloughton
20
Hole of Horcum
Burniston
A165
Cromer Point
Bridestones (Rock Formation)
Bickley
Broxa
Silpho
Cleveland Way
visham
Toll
Hackness
Suffield
Langdale End
**Scalby**
Dolby Forest Drive
239
Castle
Lockton
Sea Cut
North Riding Forest Park
Falsgrave
**Scarborough**
Toll
Dolby Forest
River Derwent
Oliver's Mount
**A170**
West Ayton
East Ayton
P+R
Sawdon
Irton
Eastfield
P+R
Osgodby
Cayton Bay
Hutton Buscel
Wilton
Ebberston
Ruston
Wykeham
Seamer
Crossgates
B1261
The Wyke
Allerston
B1415
Snainton
Brompton-by-Sawdon
Cayton
B1261
Filey Brigg
Lebberston
Gristhorpe
A1039
**Filey**
Yedingham
The Ca
Willerby
A64
Folkton
R. Hertford
Muston
Filey Bay
B1258
Sherburn
Ganton
A1039
Flixton
Staxton
West Knapton
Knapton
Potter Brompton
Fordon
**Hunmanby**
Scampston
East Heslerton
Yorkshire Wolds Way
Illington
Thorpe Bassett
West Heslerton
Foxholes
Wold Newton
Reighton
Speeton
Flamborough Head Heritage Coast
A64
Wintringham
Burton Fleming
Bempton Cliffs
Thornwick Bay
Scagglethorpe
Butterwick
B1249
Grindale
A165
Buckton
Bempton
North Landing
Settrington
Helperthorpe
Weaverthorpe
Thwing
Selwicks Bay
B1259
**FLAMBOROUGH HEAD**
North Grimston
West Lutton
East Lutton
**60**
Langtoft
B1229
Flamborough
Lighthouse
B1255
Duggleby
Kirby Grindalythe
B1253
Rudston
Monolith
Boynton
**61**
Wharram-le-Street
Langtoft
B1253
Bessingby
**Bridlington**
BRIDLINGTON

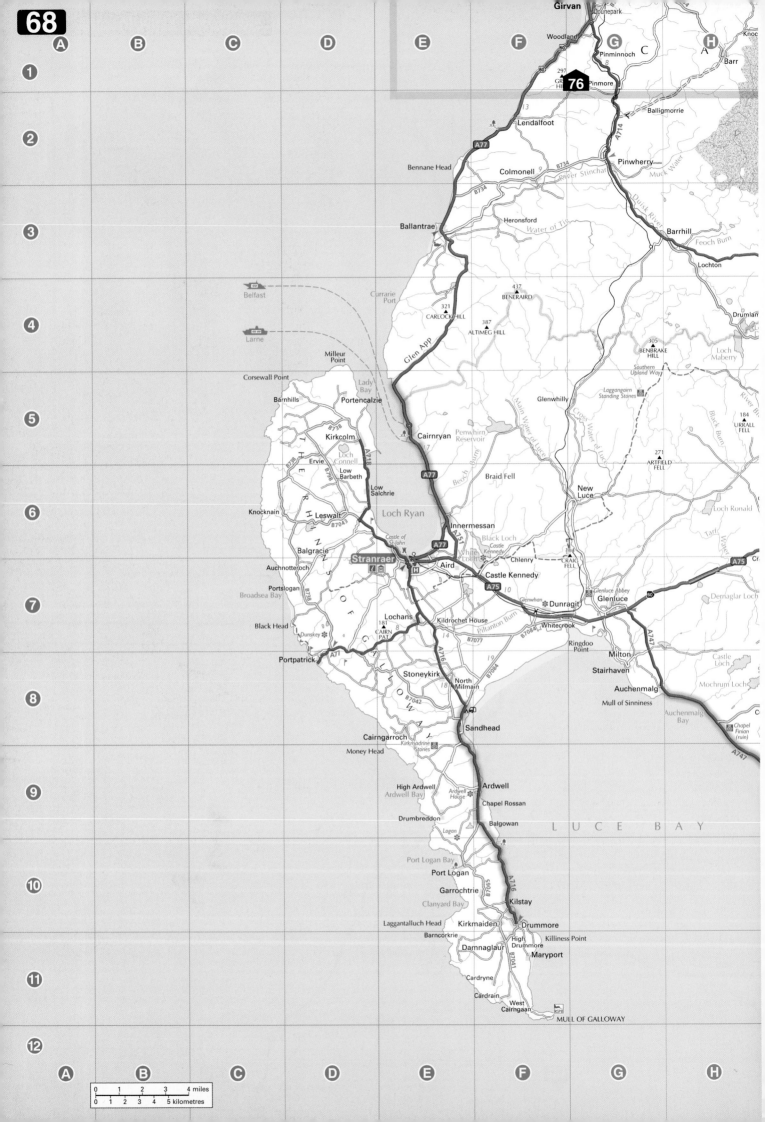

A  B  C  D  E  F  G  H

1
2
3
4
5
6
7
8
9
10
11
12

**Girvan**
Dounepark
Woodland
Pinminnoch
C
50
60
297
GR
HILL
**76**
Pinmore
Knoc
Barr
A714
Balligmorrie

Lendalfoot
A77
Bennane Head
Colmonell
B734
River Stinchar
Pinwherry
Muck Water
Duisk River

B734
Heronsford
Ballantrae
Water of Tig
Barrhill
Feoch Burn
Lochton

Belfast
Currarie Port
437
BENERAIRD
CARLOCK HILL
321
Drumlan
Larne
387
ALTIMEG HILL
305
BENBRAKE
HILL
Loch
Maberry

Milleur Point
Lady Bay
Glen App
Southern
Upland Way

Corsewall Point
Laggangairn
Standing Stones
184
URRALL FELL
Barnhills
Portencalzie
A718
B738
Glenwhilly
Cross Water of Luce
Black Burn

Kirkcolm
Cairnryan
A77
Penwhirn Reservoir
271
ARTFIELD FELL
Loch Connell
Ervie
B738
Low Barbeth
Braid Fell
Beoch Burn
New Luce
Loch Ronald

Knocknain
Leswalt
B7043
Low Salchrie
Loch Ryan
Main Water of Luce
Tarf

A75
Cr.
Balgracie
Castle of St John
Innermessan
A77
Black Loch
Castle Kennedy
Chlenry
CRAIG FELL
104

**Stranraer**
Aird
Castle Kennedy
A75
10
Glenwhan
Dunragit
Glenluce Abbey
Glenluce
60
Demaglar Loch

Auchnotteroch
White Loch
Kildrochet House
Piltanton Burn
B7084
Whitecrook
B7084
Ringdoo Point

Portslogan
B738
Broadsea Bay
Lochans
CAIRN PAT
181
8
A716
14
B7077
19
Milton
Stairhaven
Castle Loch

Black Head
Dunskey
Stoneykirk
North Milmain
18
Auchenmalg
Mull of Sinniness
Mochrum Lochs

Portpatrick
A77
B7042
B7084
Auchenmalg Bay
A747
Chapel Finian (ruin)

Cairngarroch
Kirkmadrine Stones
Sandhead

Money Head

High Ardwell
Ardwell Bay
Ardwell House
Ardwell
Chapel Rossan

Drumbreddon
Logan
Balgowan
L U C E   B A Y

Port Logan Bay
Port Logan
Garrochtrie
B7065
A716

Clanyard Bay
Kilstay

Laggantalluch Head
Kirkmaiden
Drummore
Killiness Point
Barncorkrie
Damnaglaur
High Drummore
Maryport
B7041

Cardryne
Cardrain
West Cairngaan
MULL OF GALLOWAY

A  B  C  D  E  F  G  H

0    1    2    3    4 miles
0  1  2  3  4  5 kilometres

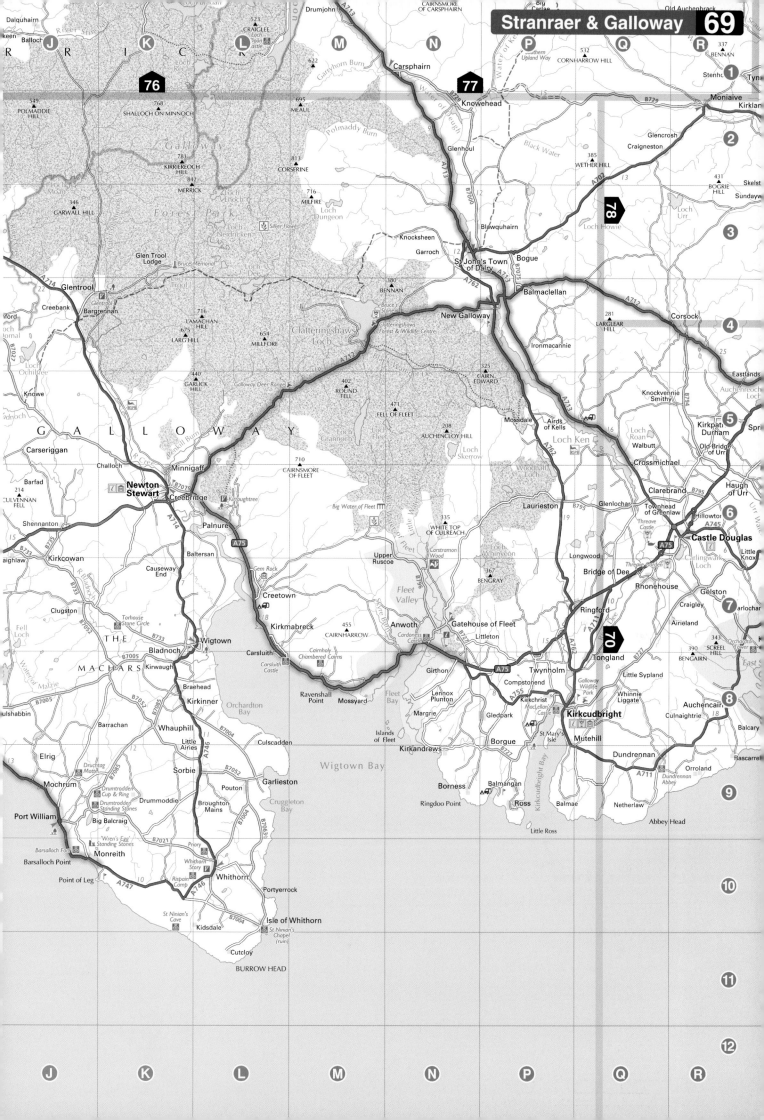

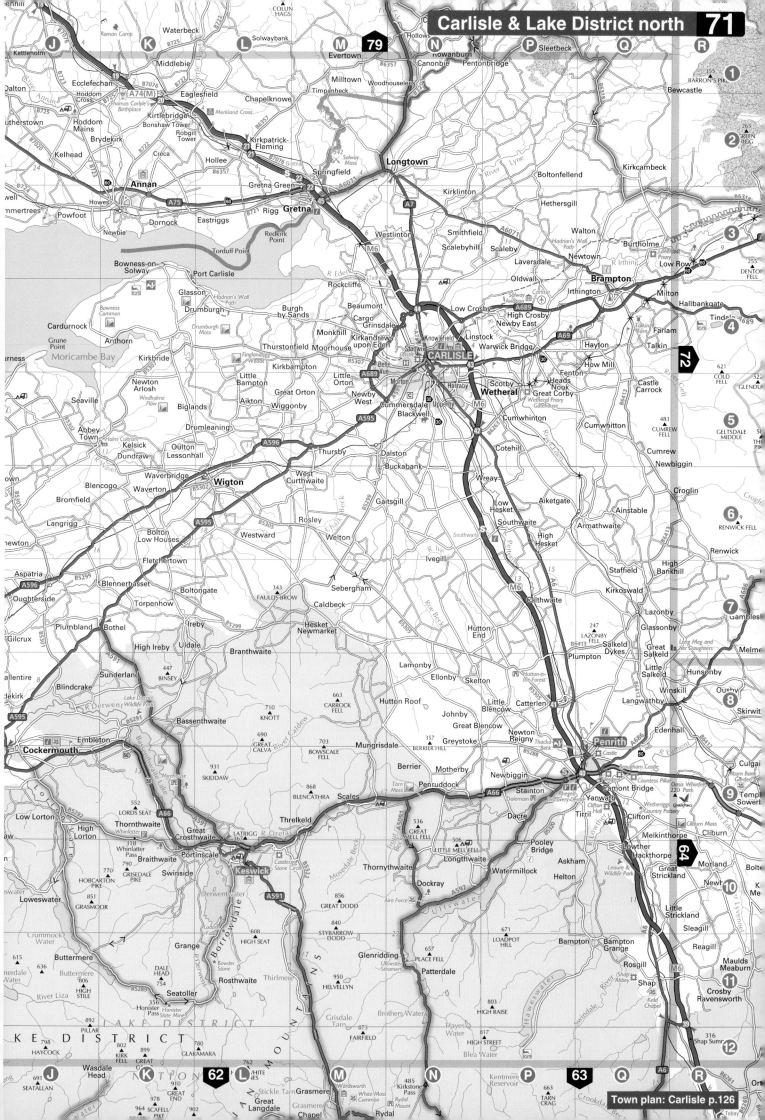

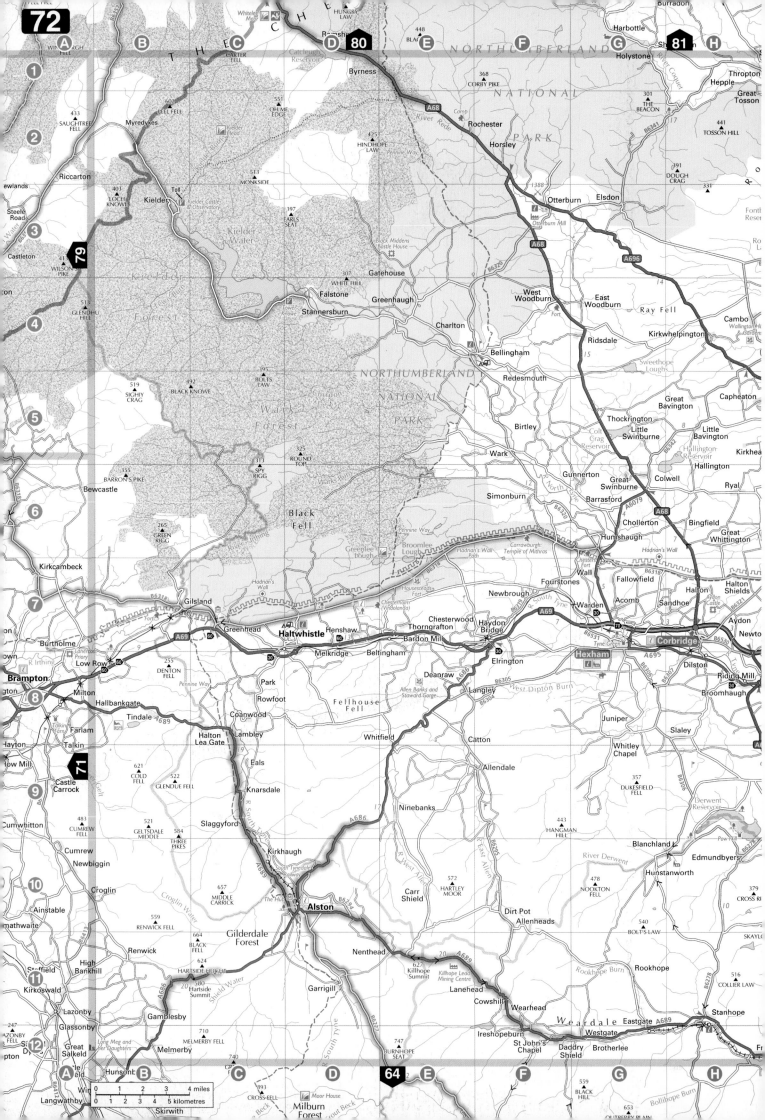

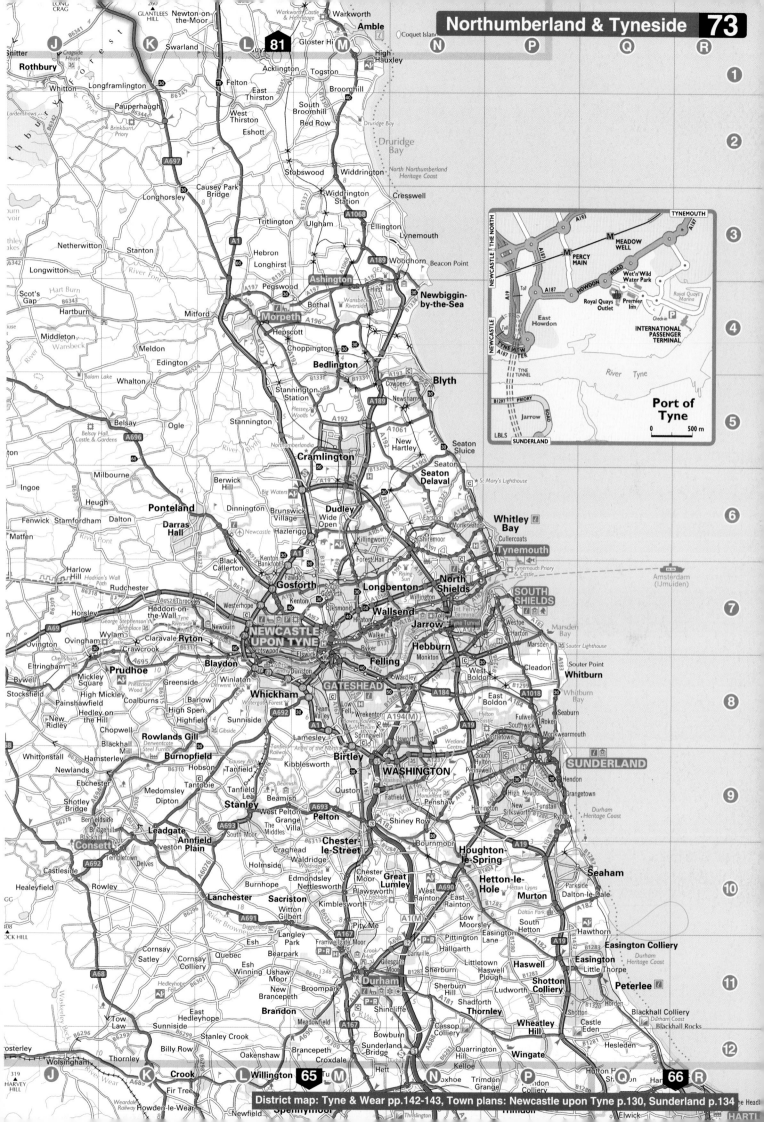

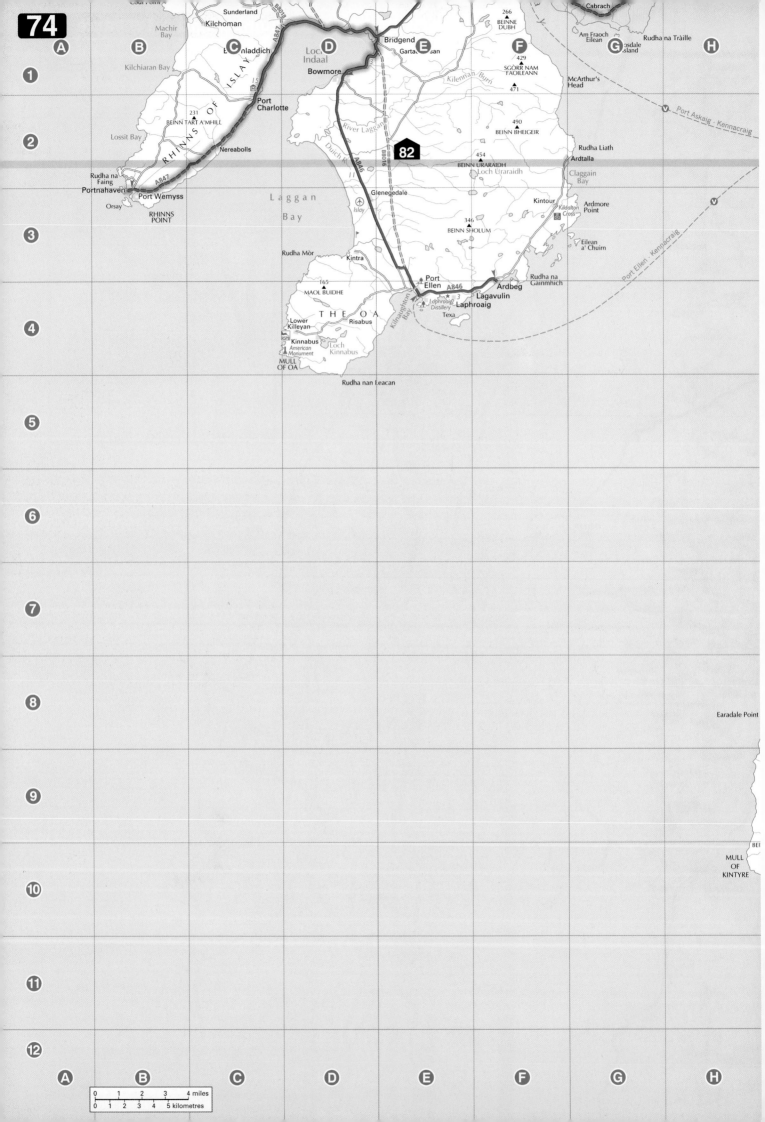

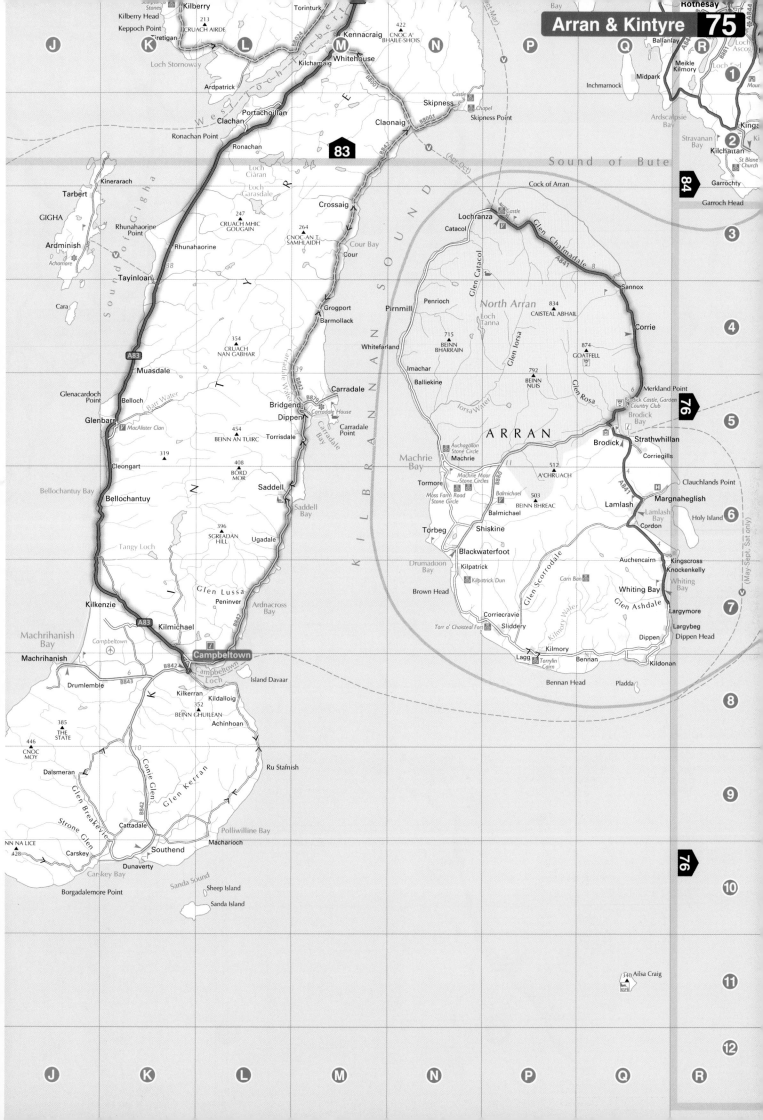

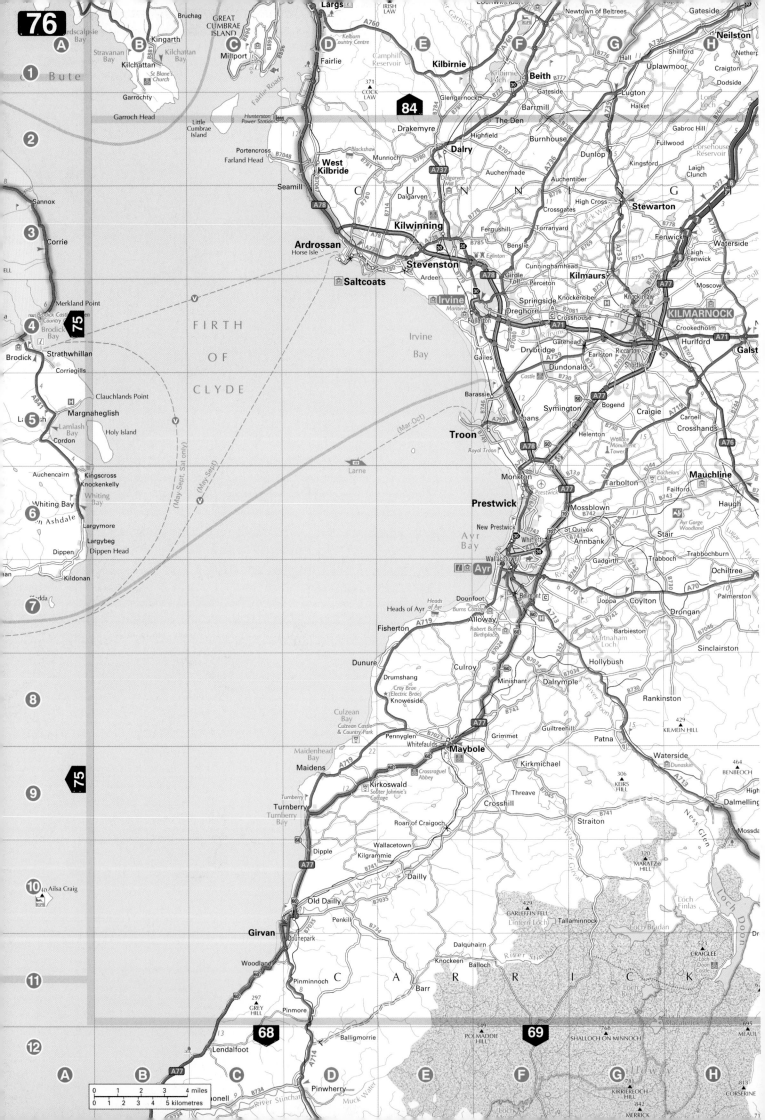

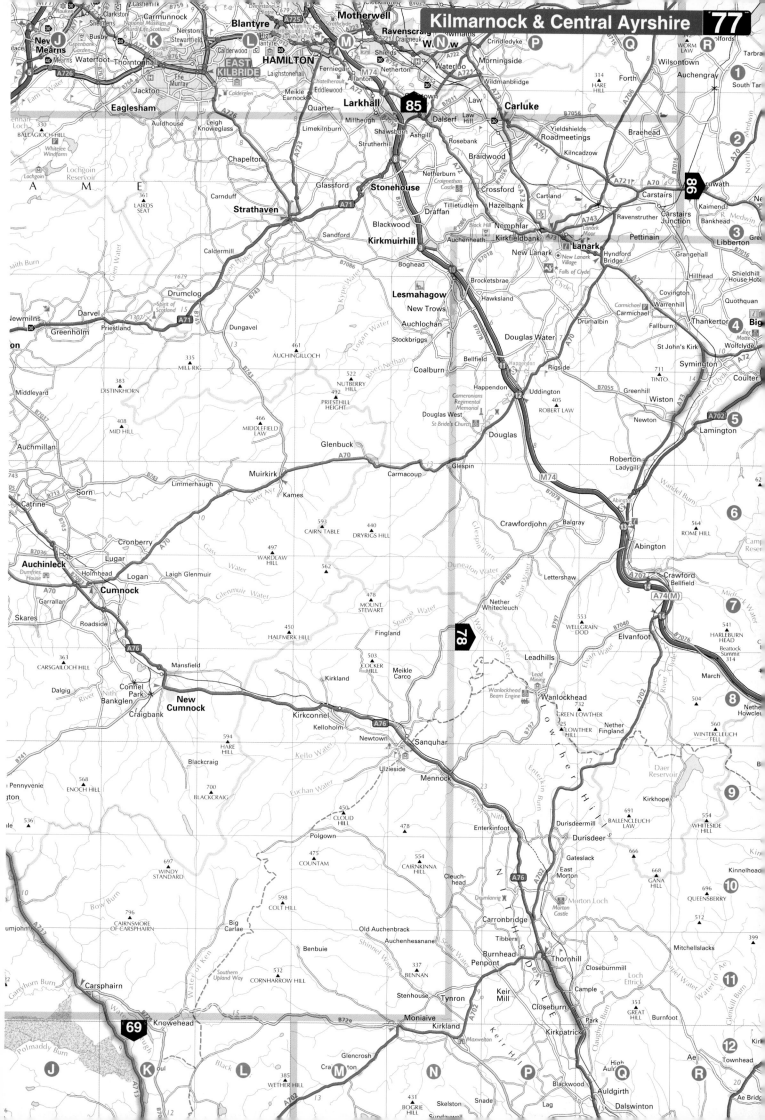

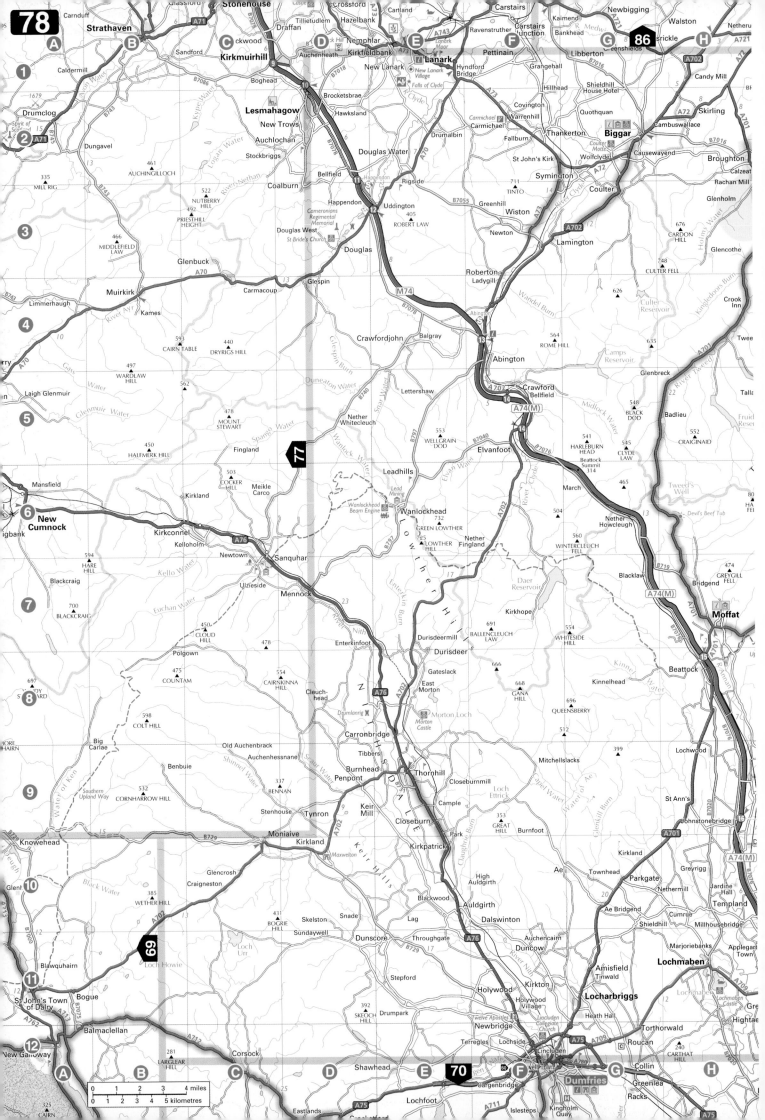

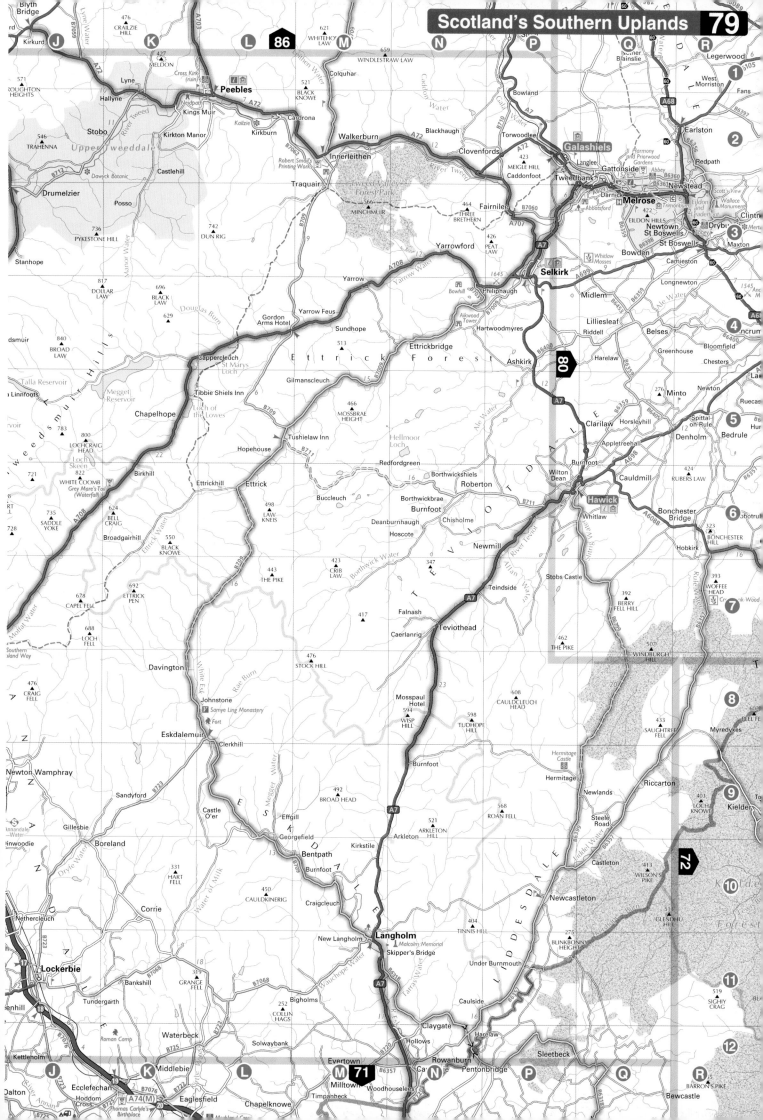

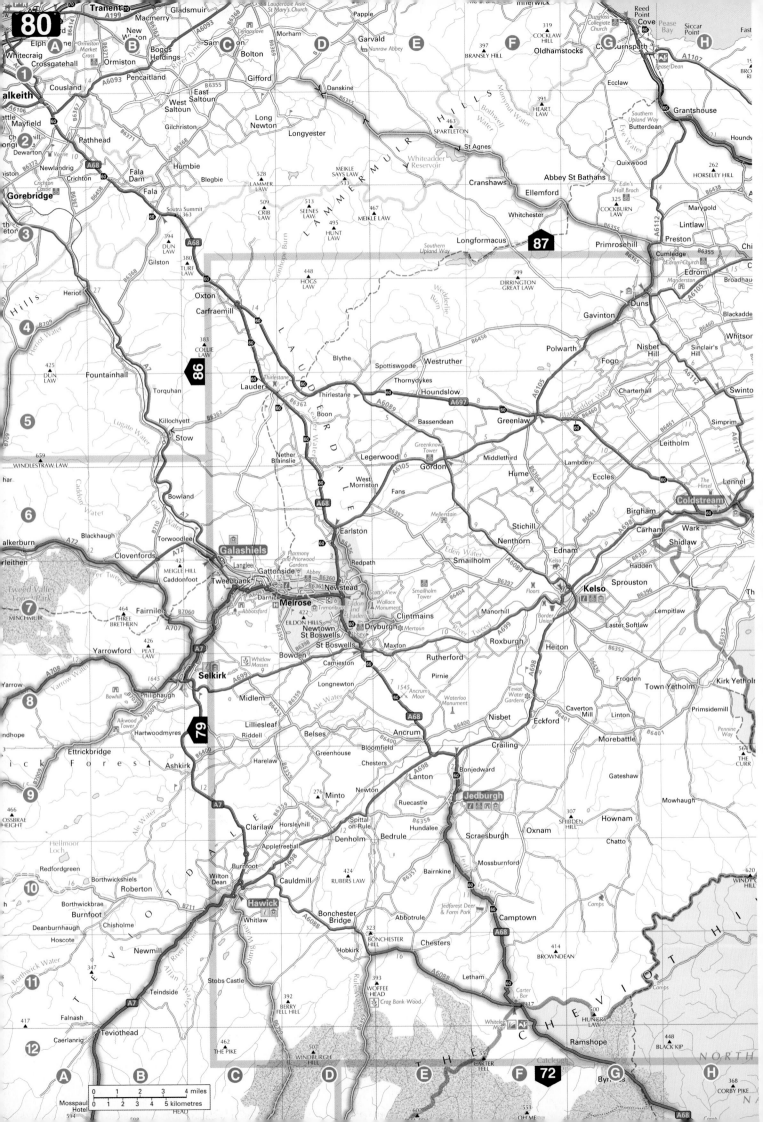

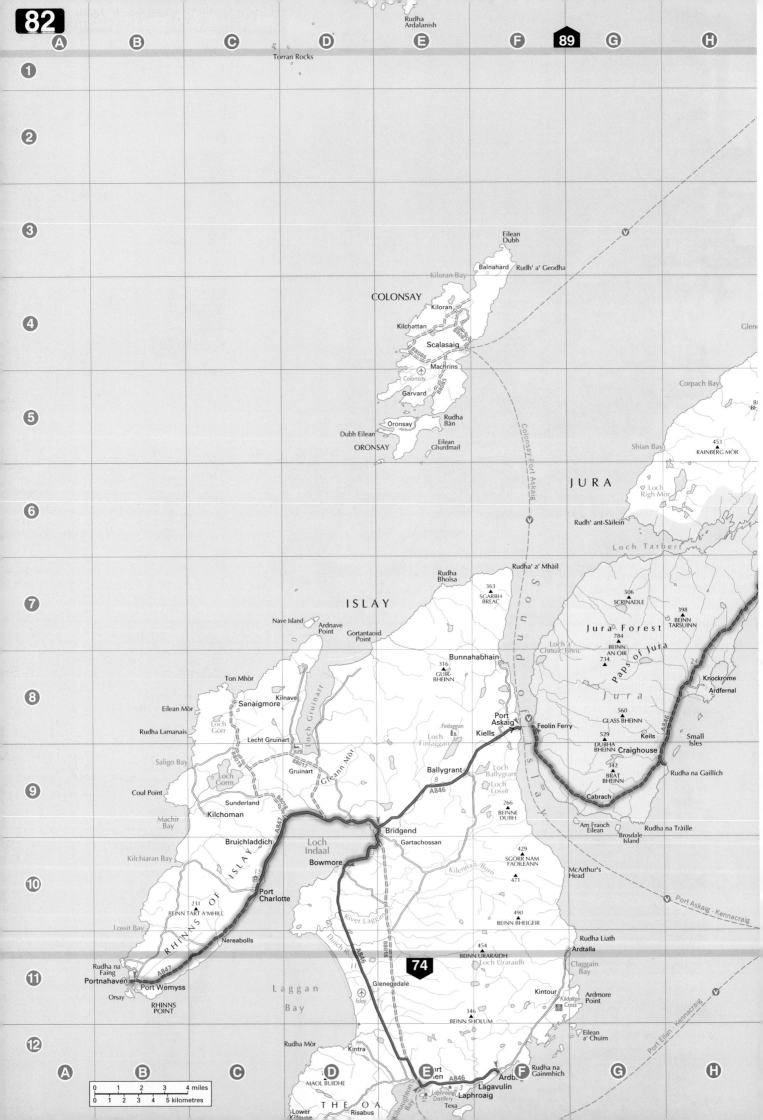

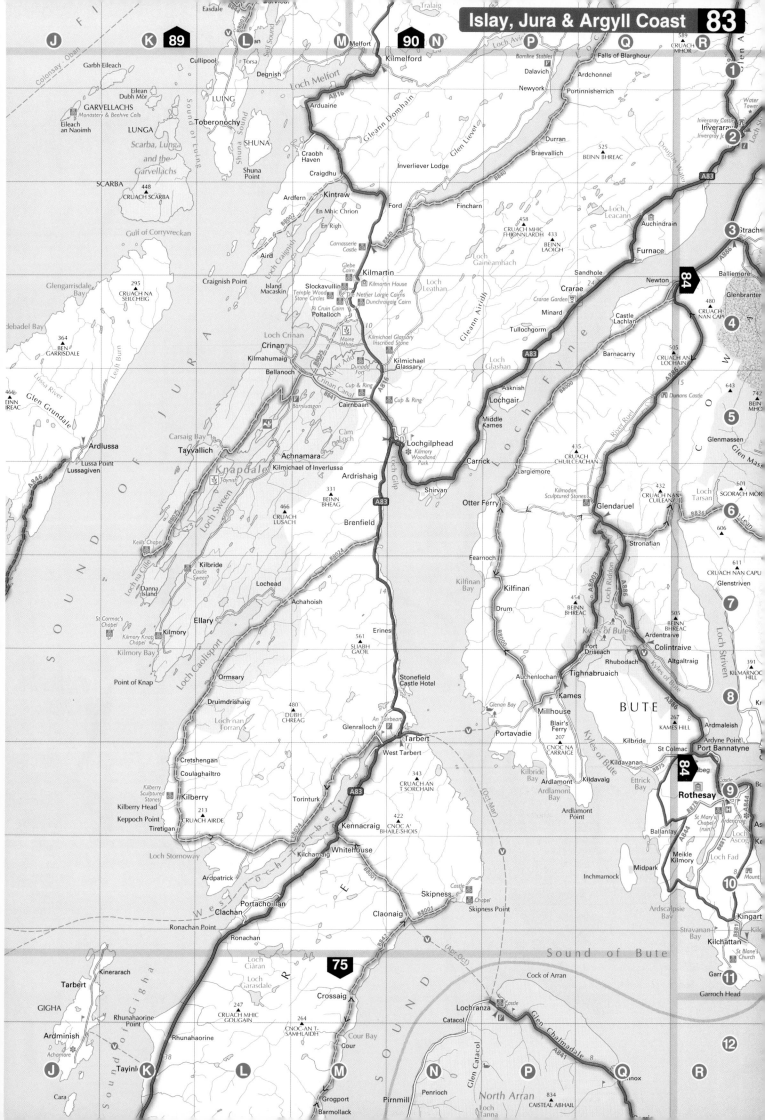

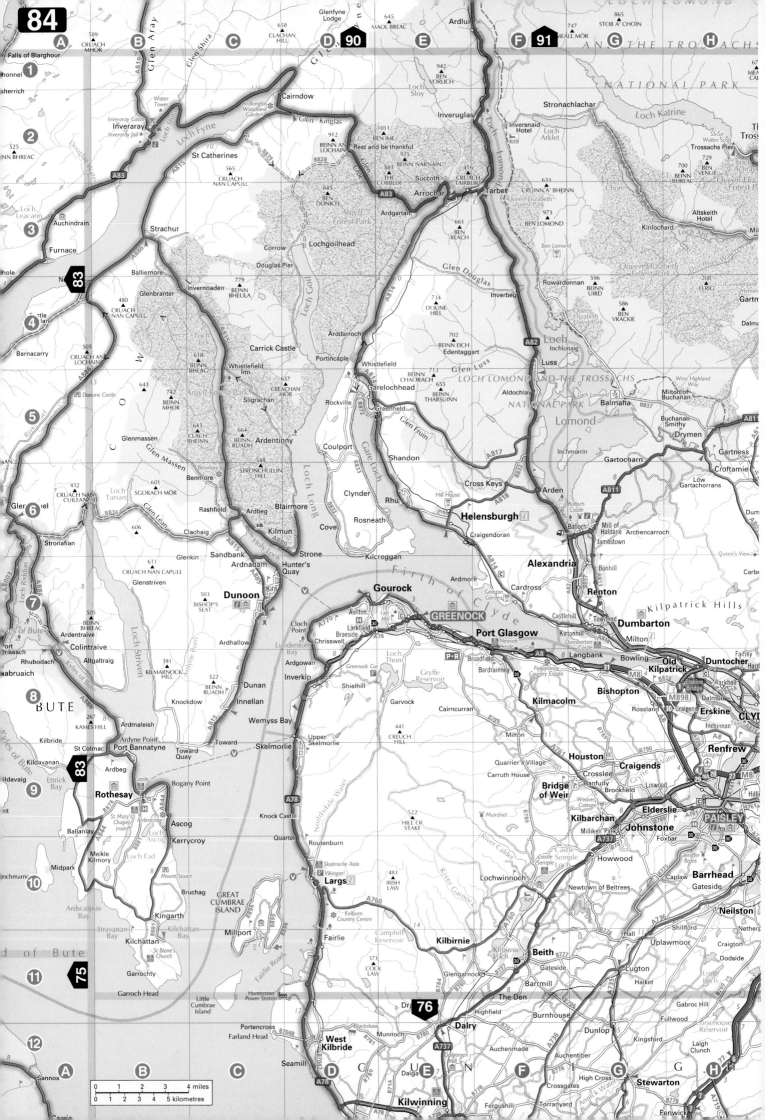

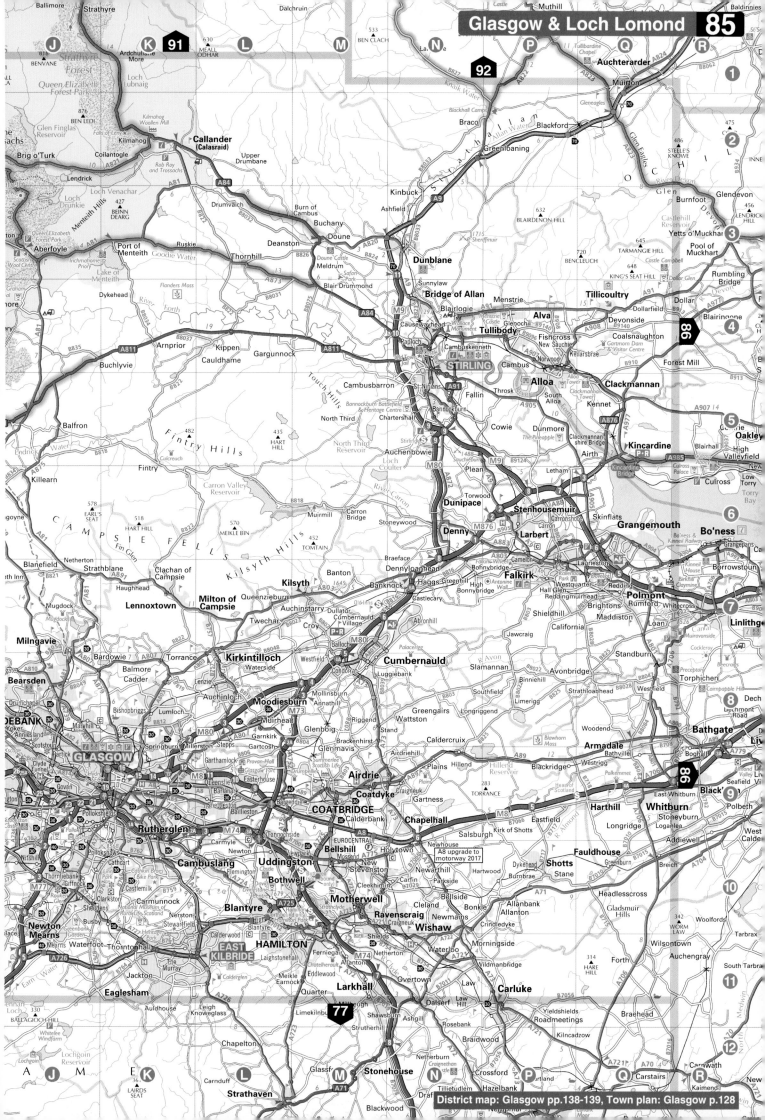

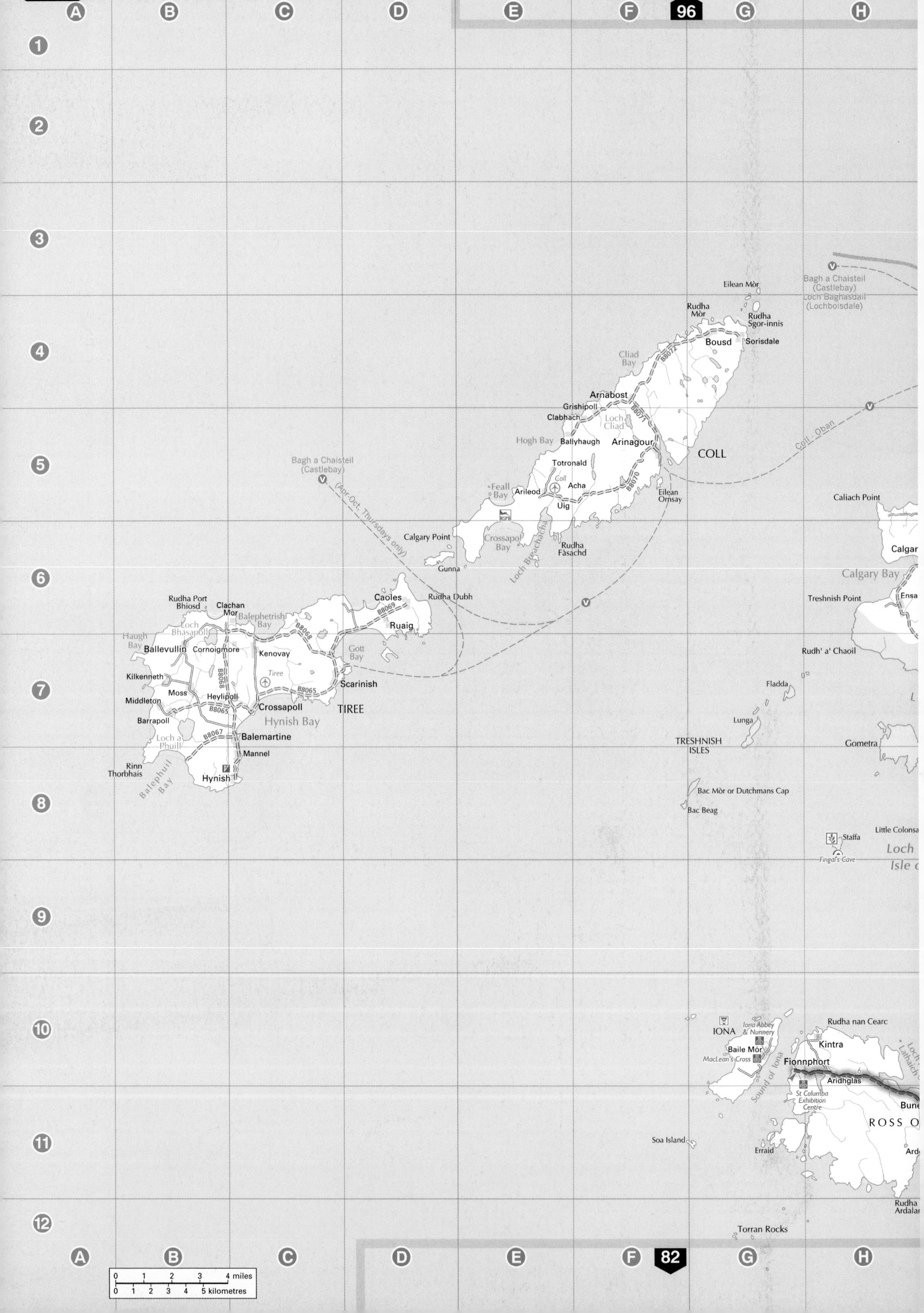

Eilean Mòr

Bagh a Chaisteil
(Castlebay)
Loch Baghasdail
(Lochboisdale)

Rudha
Mòr

Rudha
Sgor-innis

Bousd
Sorisdale

Cliad
Bay

Coll - Oban

Arnabost

Grishipoll
Clabhach
Loch
Cliad

Hogh Bay
Ballyhaugh
Arinagour

COLL

Totronald

Bagh a Chaisteil
(Castlebay)

Feall
Bay

Coll
Acha
Arileod

Uig

Eilean
Ornsay

Caliach Point

(Apr.-Oct. Thursdays only)

Calgary Point

Crossapoll
Bay

Rudha
Fàsachd

Calgar

Gunna

Loch Breachacha

Calgary Bay

Rudha Port
Bhiosd
Clachan
Mor

Caoles
B8069
Rudha Dubh

Treshnish Point
Ensa

Balephetrish
Bay
Ruaig

Loch
Bhasapoll
B8068

Rudh' a' Chaoil

Haugh
Bay
Ballevullin
Cornoigmore
Kenovay

Tiree

Gott
Bay

Fladda

Kilkenneth
B8068

Moss
Heylipoll
Crossapoll
B8065
Scarinish

Lunga

Middleton
B8065
TIREE

TRESHNISH
ISLES

Gometra

Barrapoll
Hynish Bay
B8067
Balemartine

Loch a'
Phuill
Mannel

Rinn
Thorbhais
Hynish

Balephuil
Bay

Bac Mòr or Dutchmans Cap

Bac Beag

Staffa

Little Colonsa

Fingal's Cave

Loch

Isle o

IONA
Iona Abbey
& Nunnery

Rudha nan Cearc

Baile Mòr
Kintra

MacLean's Cross
Fionnphort

Aridhglas

Sound of Iona
St Columba
Exhibition
Centre

Bune

Soa Island

Erraid

ROSS O

Ard

Rudha
Ardalan

Torran Rocks

0   1   2   3   4 miles
0  1  2  3  4  5 kilometres

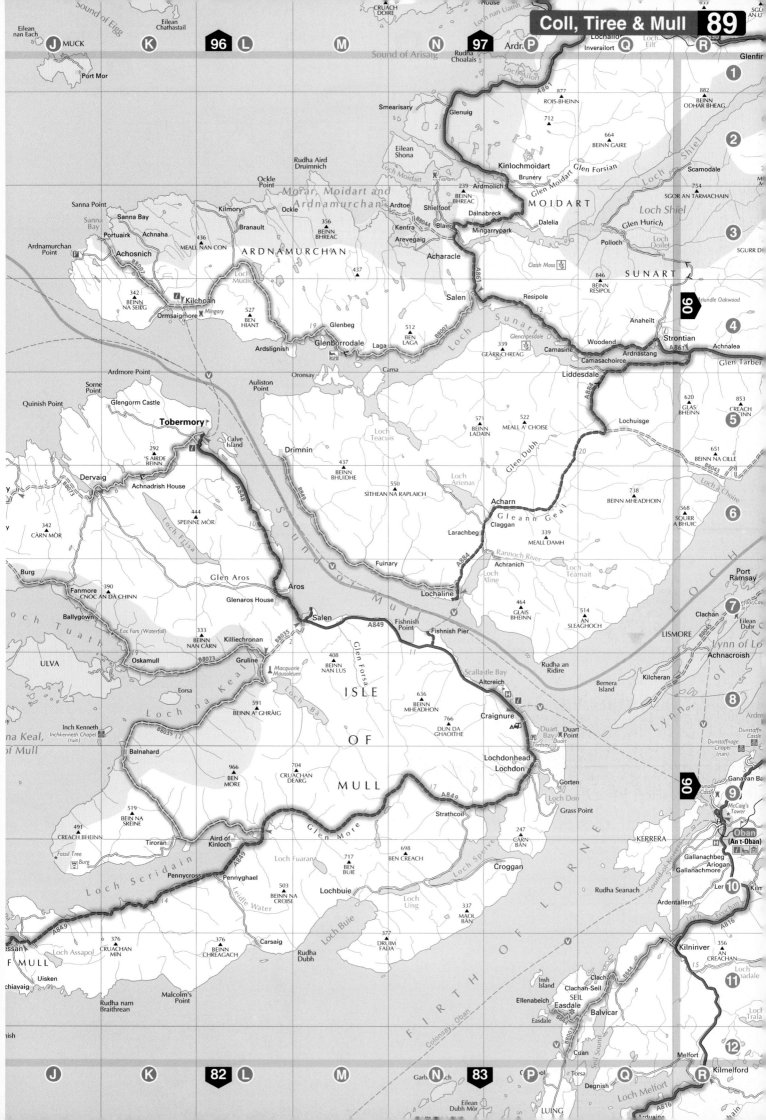

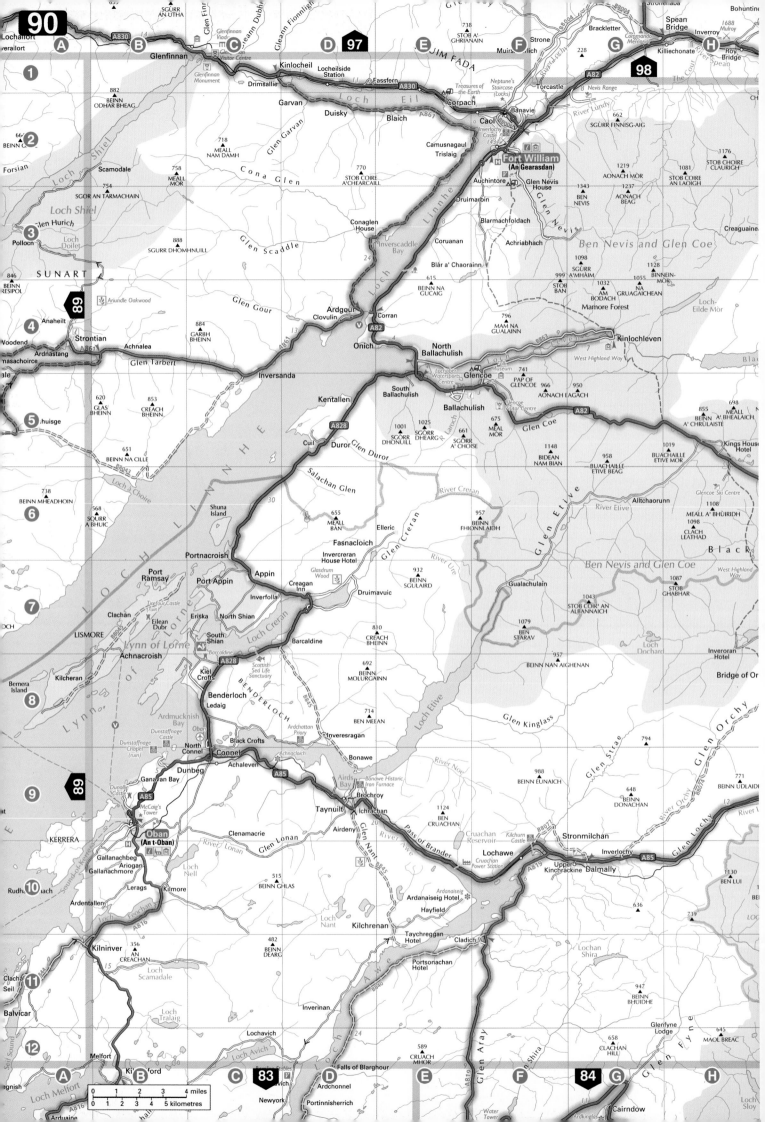

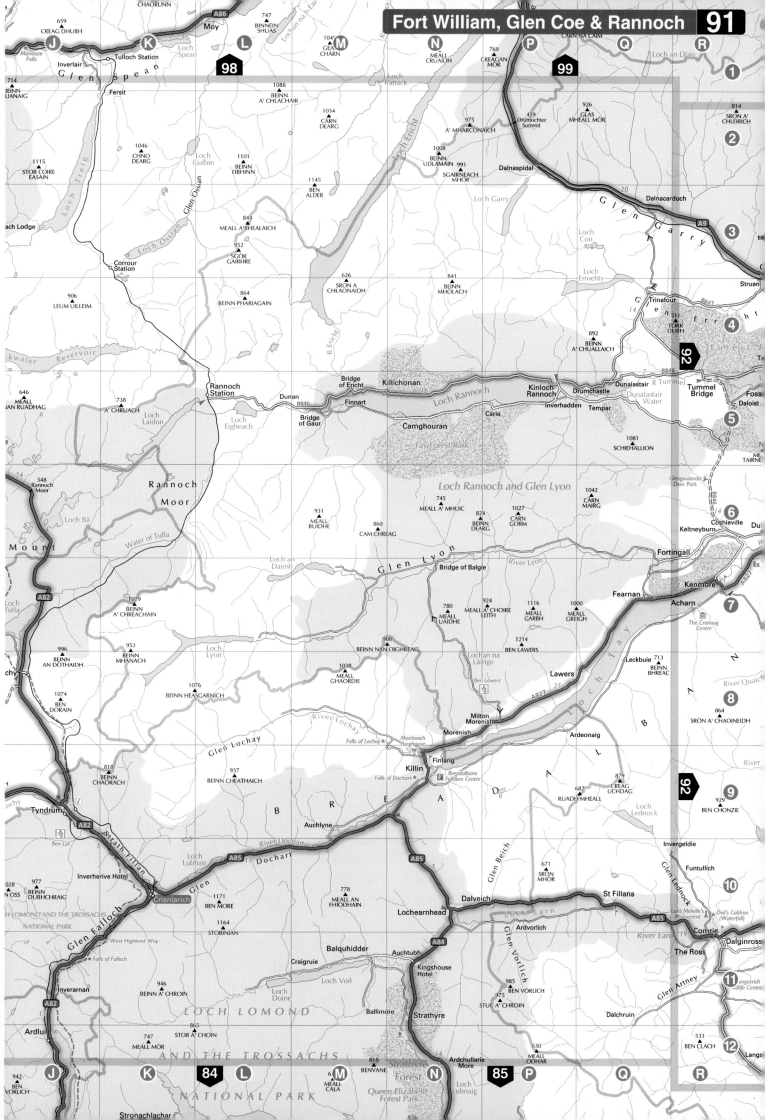

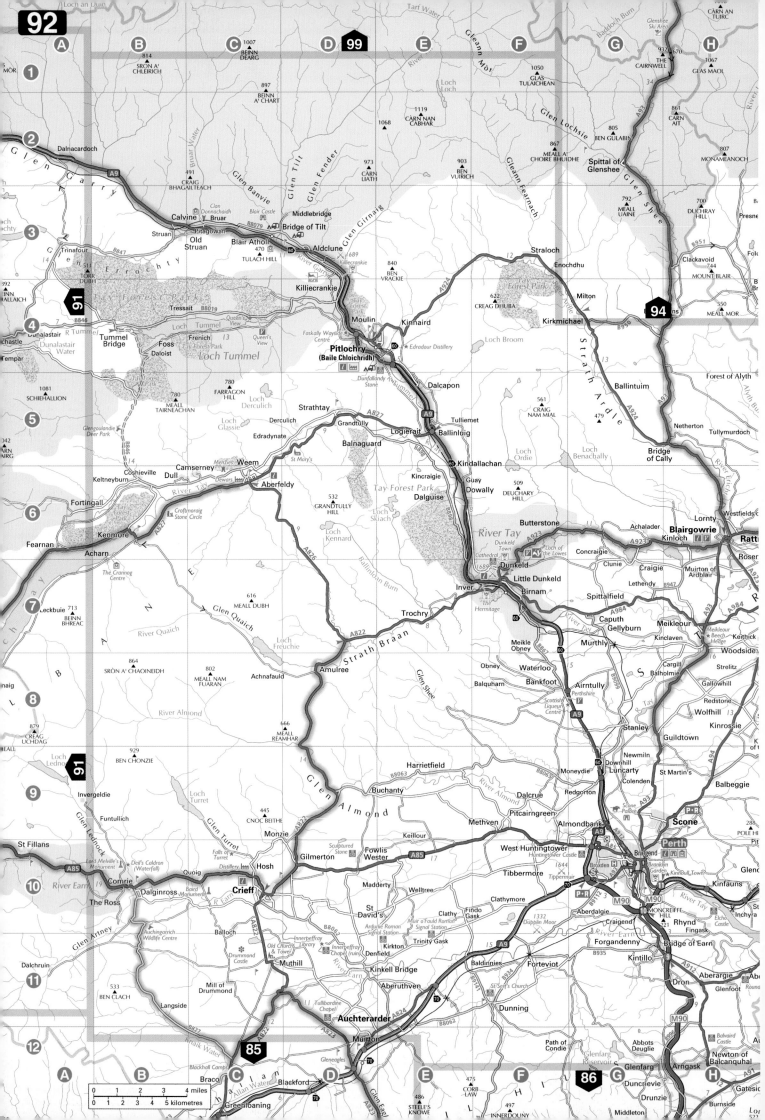

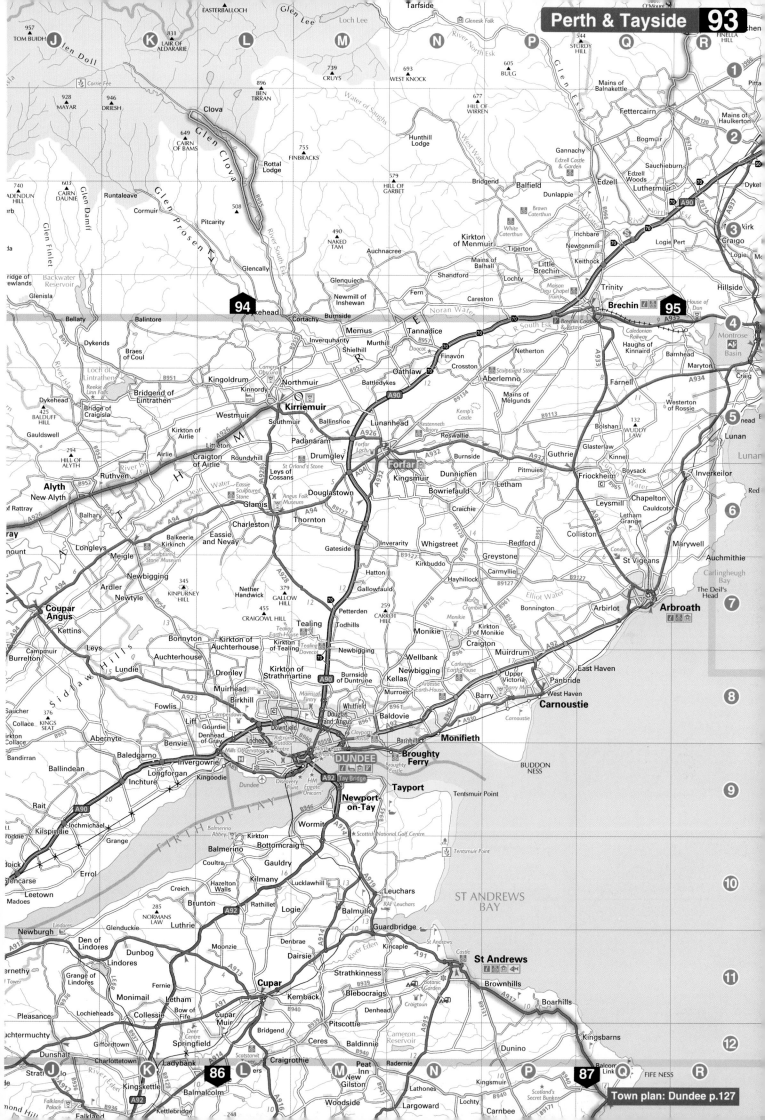

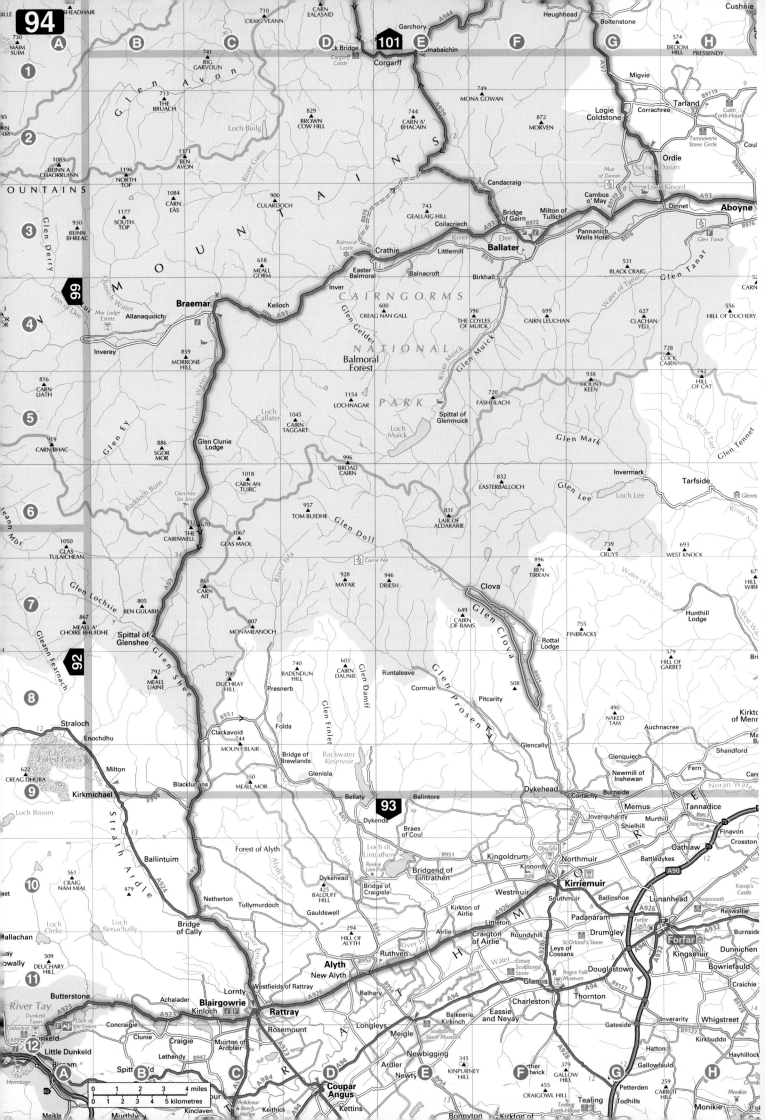

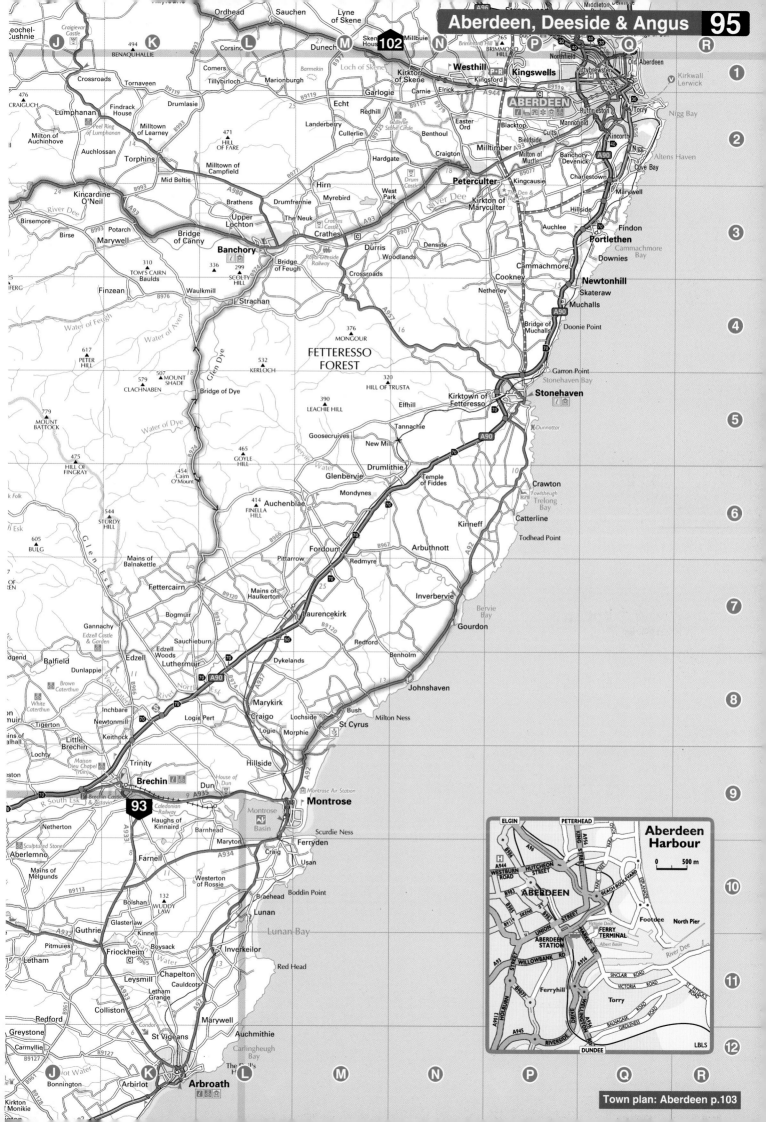

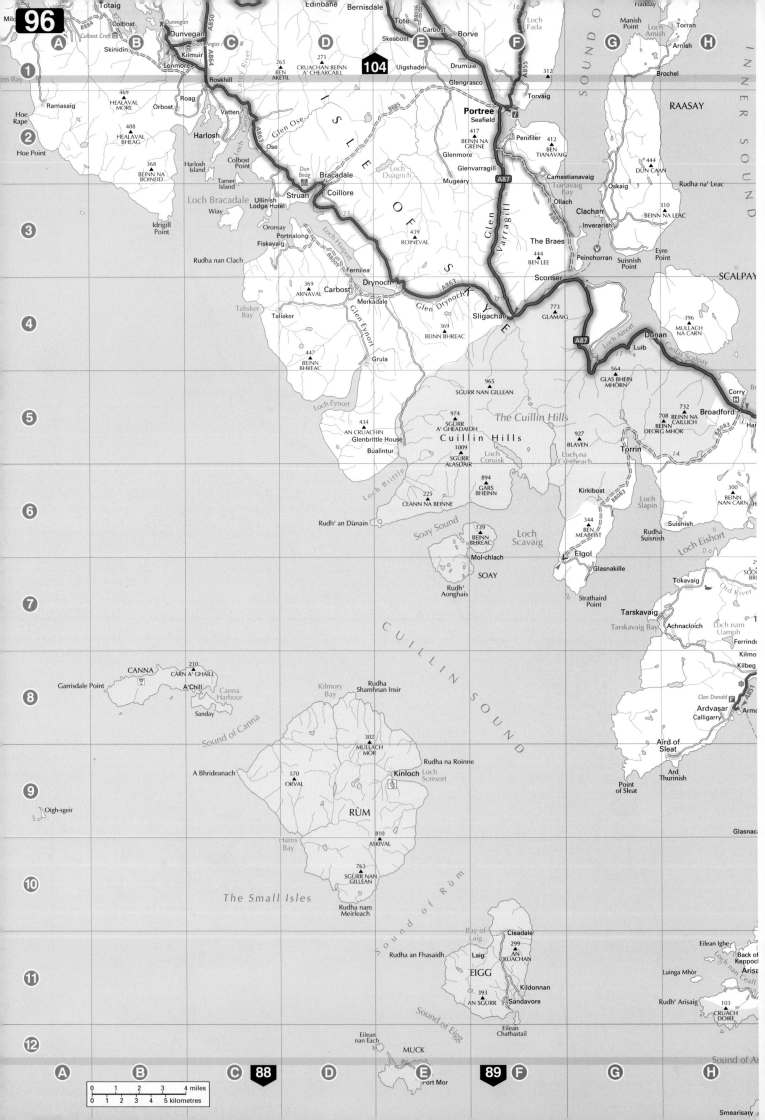

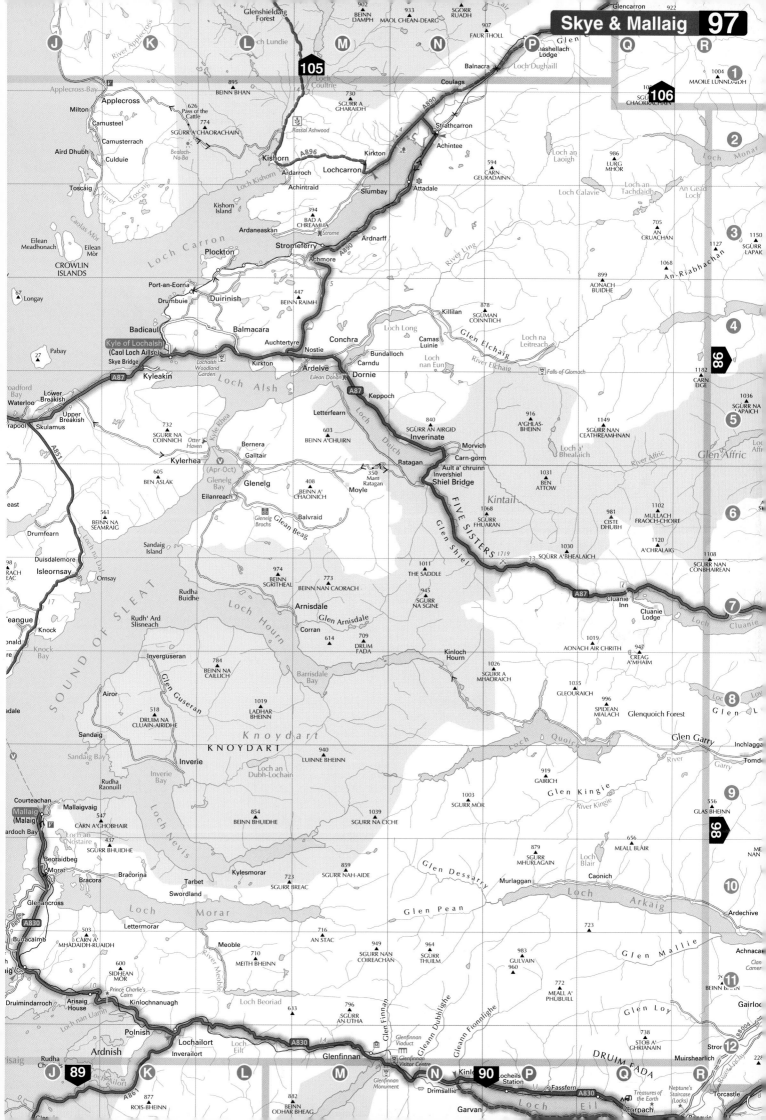

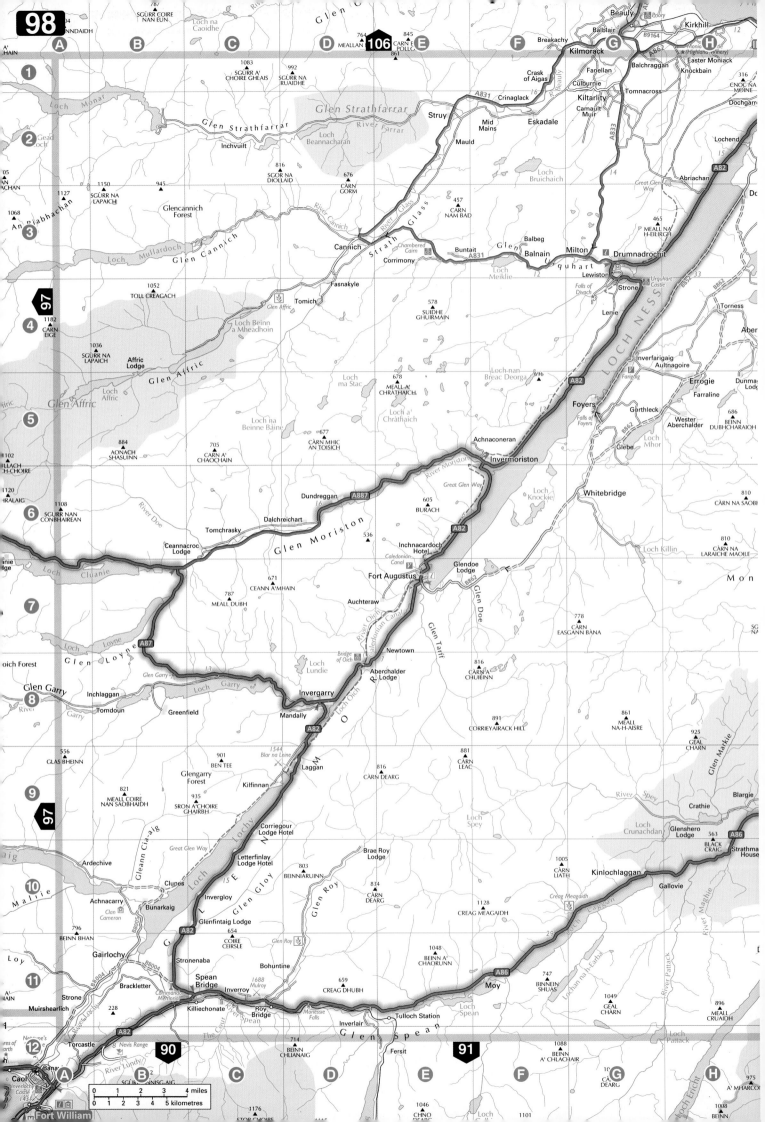

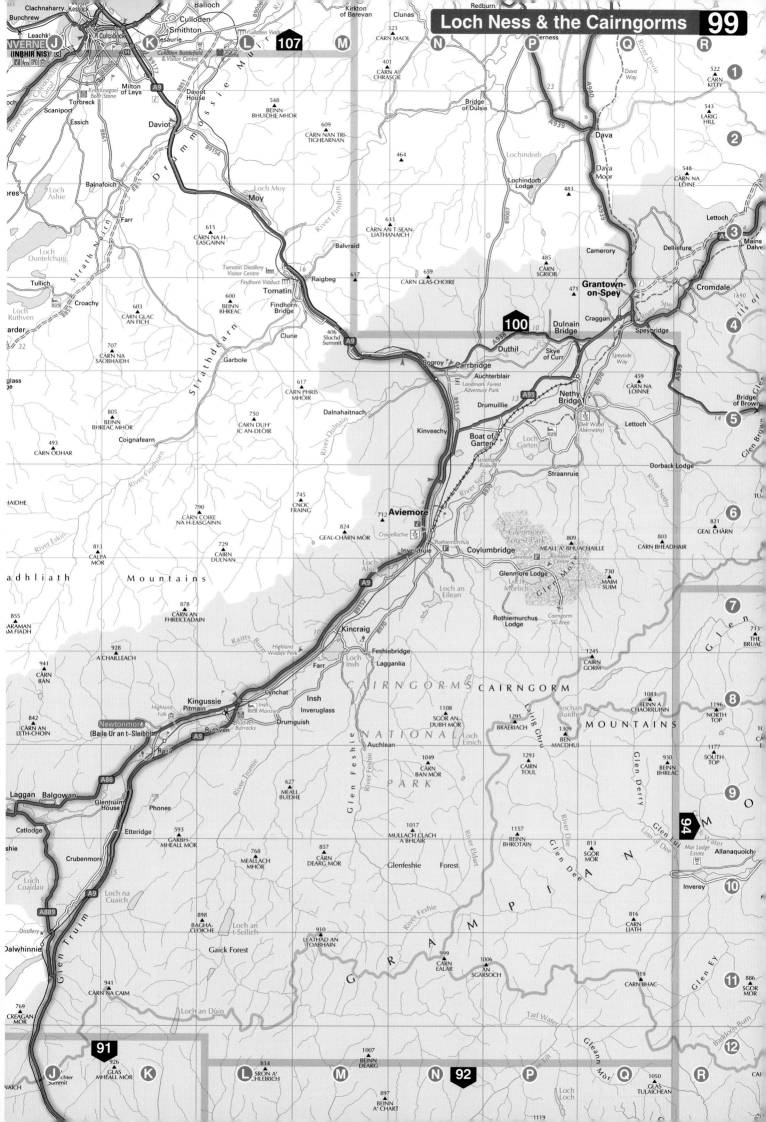

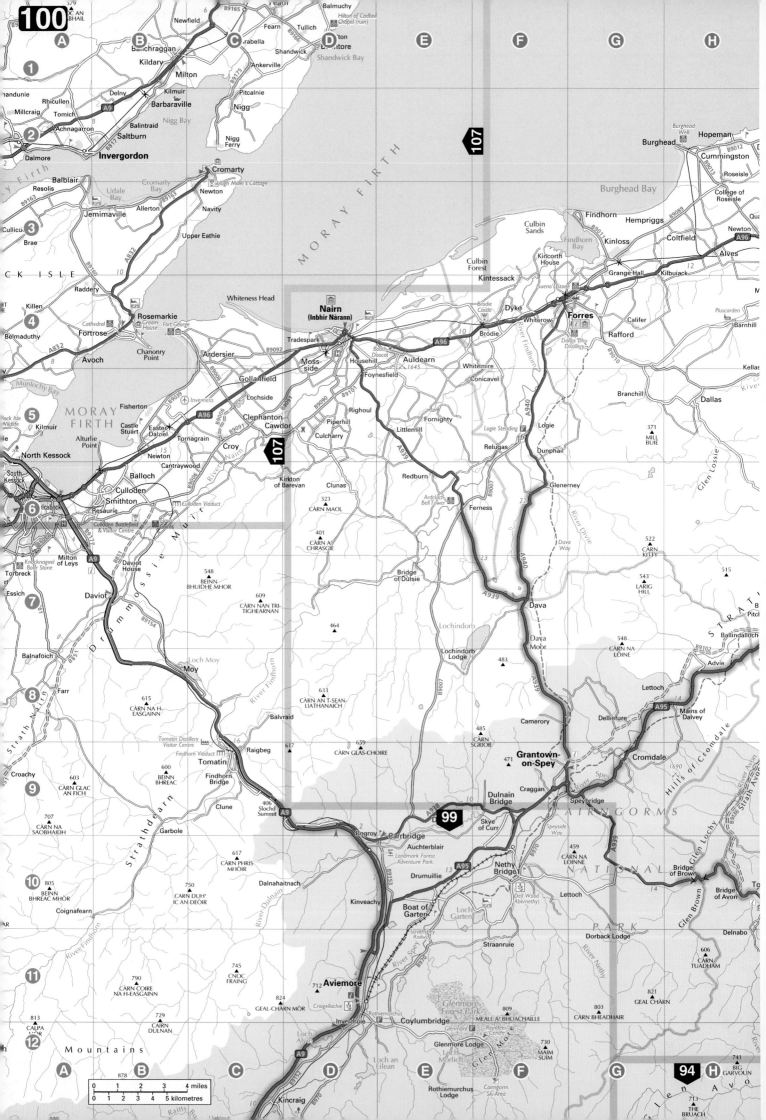

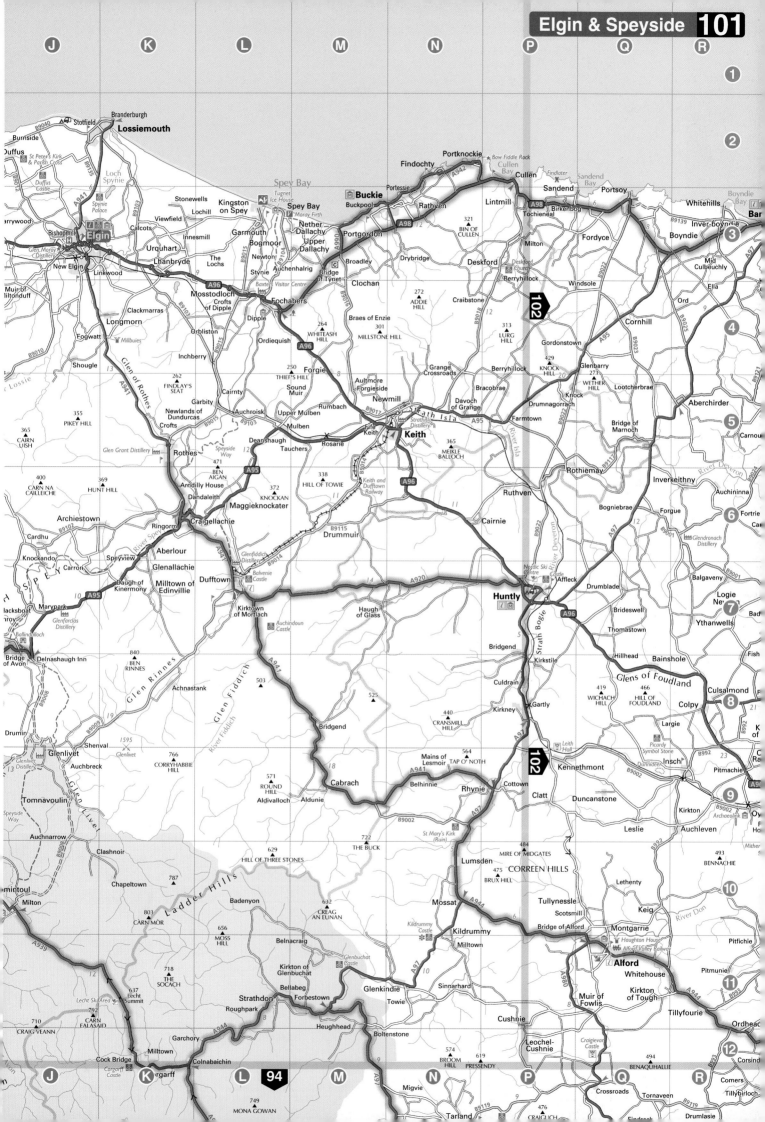

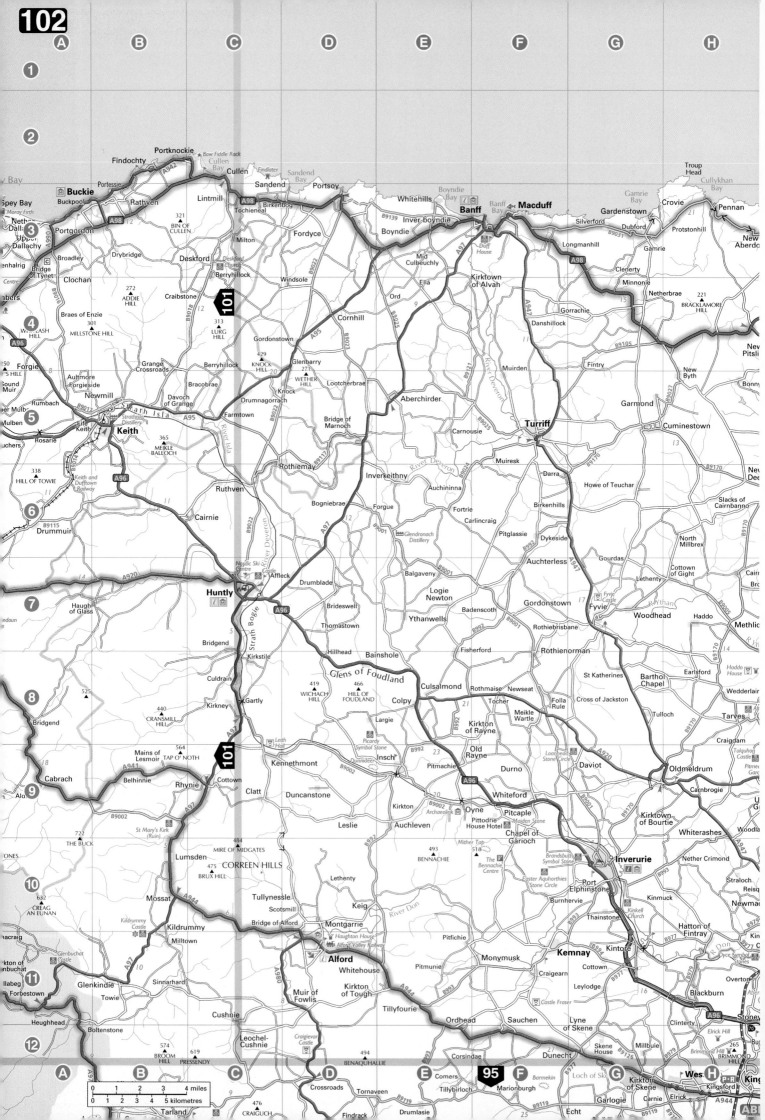

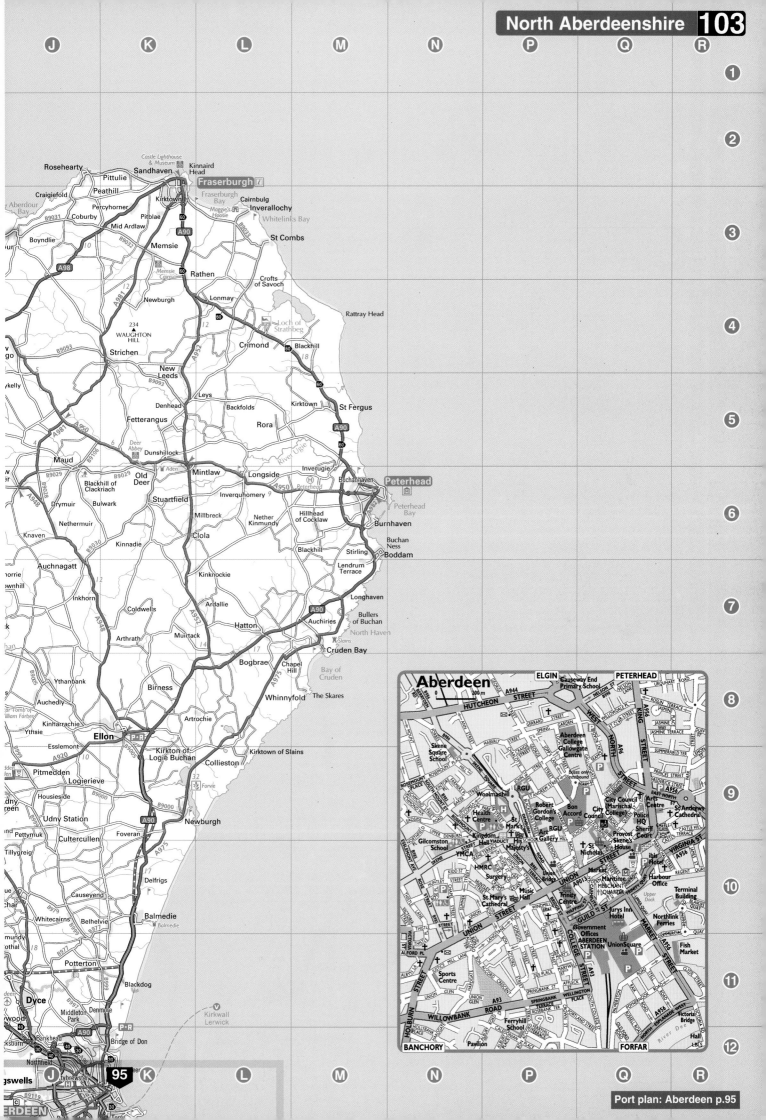

Rosehearty · Pittulie · Sandhaven · Castle Lighthouse & Museum · Kinnaird Head
Craigiefold · Peathill · Kirktown · Fraserburgh · Fraserburgh Bay · Maggie's Hoosie · Cairnbulg · Inverallochy
Aberdour Bay · Coburby · Percyhorner · Pitblae · Mid Ardlaw · Whitelinks Bay
Boyndlie · Memsie · Rathen · St Combs
Memsie Cairn
Newburgh · Lonmay · Crofts of Savoch
234 WAUGHTON HILL · Strichen · Loch of Strathbeg · Rattray Head
New Leeds · Crimond · Blackhill
Denhead · Leys · Backfolds · Kirktown · St Fergus
Fetterangus · Rora
Maud · Deer Abbey · Dunshillock · Mintlaw · Longside · Inverugie · Buchanhaven · Peterhead
Blackhill of Clackriach · Old Deer · Aden · Peterhead · Peterhead Bay
Drymuir · Bulwark · Stuartfield · Inverquhomery
Nethermuir · Millbreck · Nether Kinmundy · Hillhead of Cocklaw · Burnhaven
Knaven · Kinnadie · Clola · Blackhill · Buchan Ness · Boddam
Auchnagatt · Stirling
Kinknockie · Lendrum Terrace
Inkhorn · Coldwells · Ardallie · Longhaven
Arthrath · Muirtack · Hatton · Auchiries · Bullers of Buchan · North Haven
Bogbrae · Slains · Cruden Bay
Birness · Chapel Hill · Bay of Cruden
Ythanbank · Whinnyfold · The Skares
Auchedly · Artrochie
Kinharrachie · Ellon · Esslemont · Kirkton of Logie Buchan · Kirktown of Slains
Ythsie · Collieston
Pitmedden · Logierieve · Forvie
Housieside · Udny Station · Newburgh
Pettymuk · Cultercullen · Foveran
Tillygreig · Delfrigs
Causeyend
Whitecairns · Belhelvie · Balmedie
Potterton
Blackdog
Dyce · Middleton Park · Denmore · Kirkwall Lerwick
Bridge of Don
Bankhead · Northfield

---

**Aberdeen** inset map:

ELGIN · Causeway End Primary School · PETERHEAD · URQUHART ROAD
HUTCHEON STREET · WEST NORTH STREET · ROSLIN TERRACE · Jasmine
Skene Square School · Aberdeen College Gallowgate Centre · KING STREET · St Andrews Cathedral
RGU · Woolmanhill · Buses only eastbound
Health Centre · Robert Gordon's College · Bon Accord · City Council (Marischal College) · Arts Centre
Gilcomston School · St Mark's · Art Gallery · City Council · Police HQ · Sheriff Court
Kingdom Hall · His Majesty's · St Nicholas · Provost Skene's House · ibis Hotel
YMCA · HMRC · Union Bridge · Maritime · Harbour Office
Surgery · Music Hall · Trinity Centre · MERCHANT QUARTER · Terminal Building · Northlink Ferries
St Mary's Cathedral · Jurys Inn Hotel · UNION STREET · GUILD STREET · Upper Dock
Sports Centre · Government Offices · ABERDEEN STATION · Union Square · Fish Market
HOLBURN STREET · UNION STREET · COLLEGE STREET · MARKET STREET
WILLOWBANK ROAD · Ferryhill School · Victoria Bridge
BANCHORY · Pavilion · FORFAR · River Dee

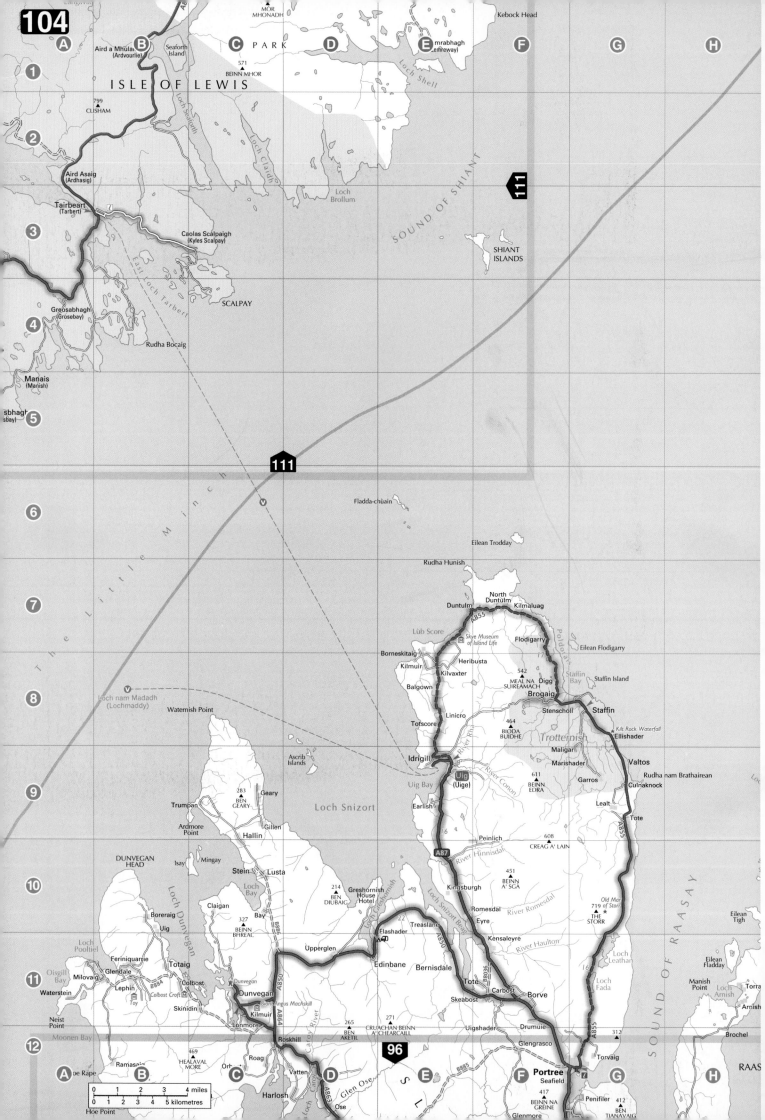

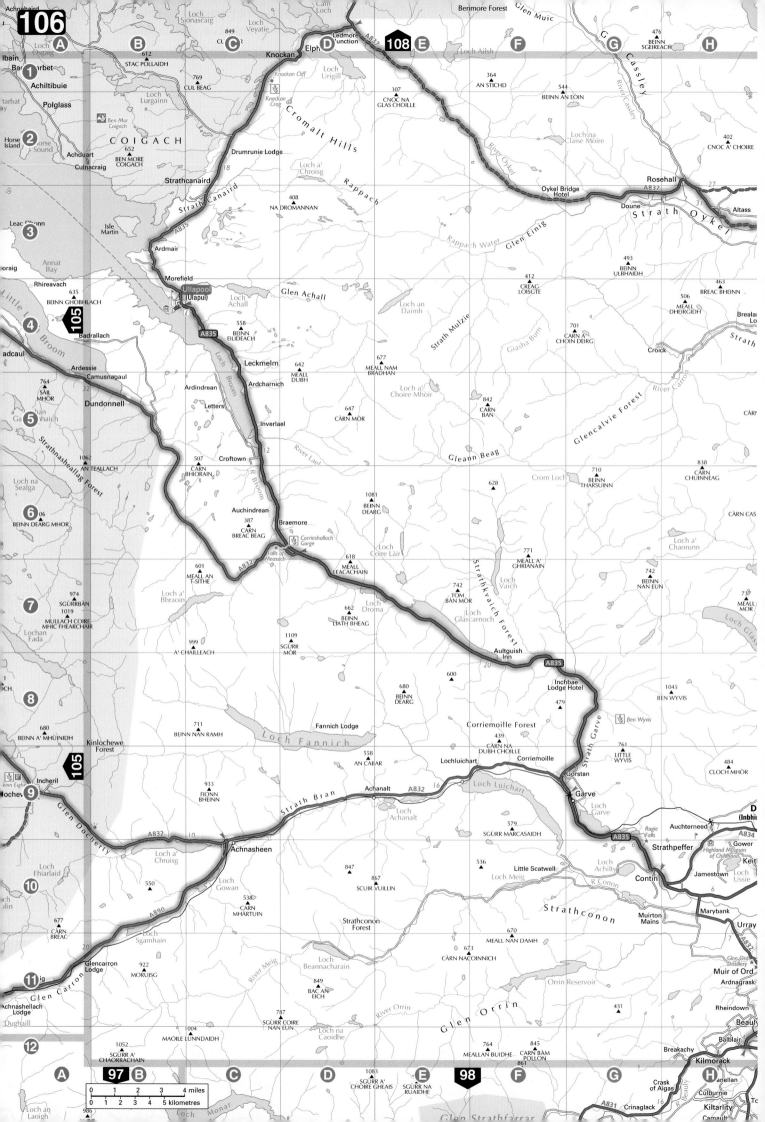

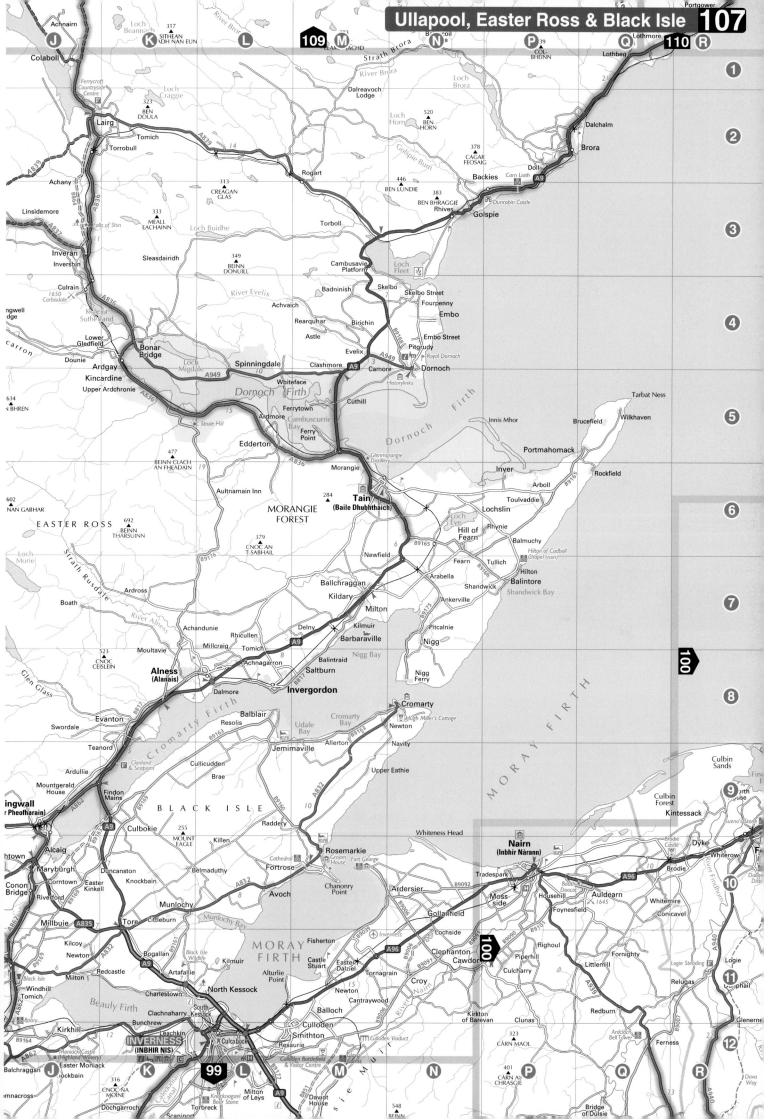

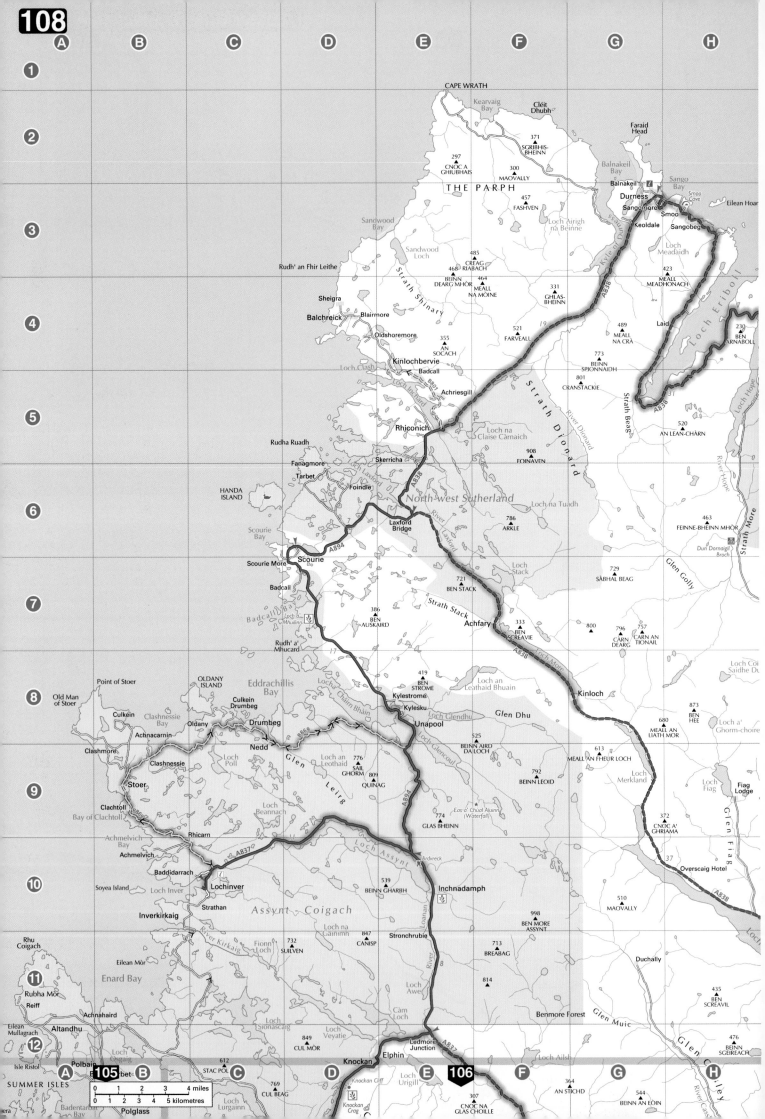

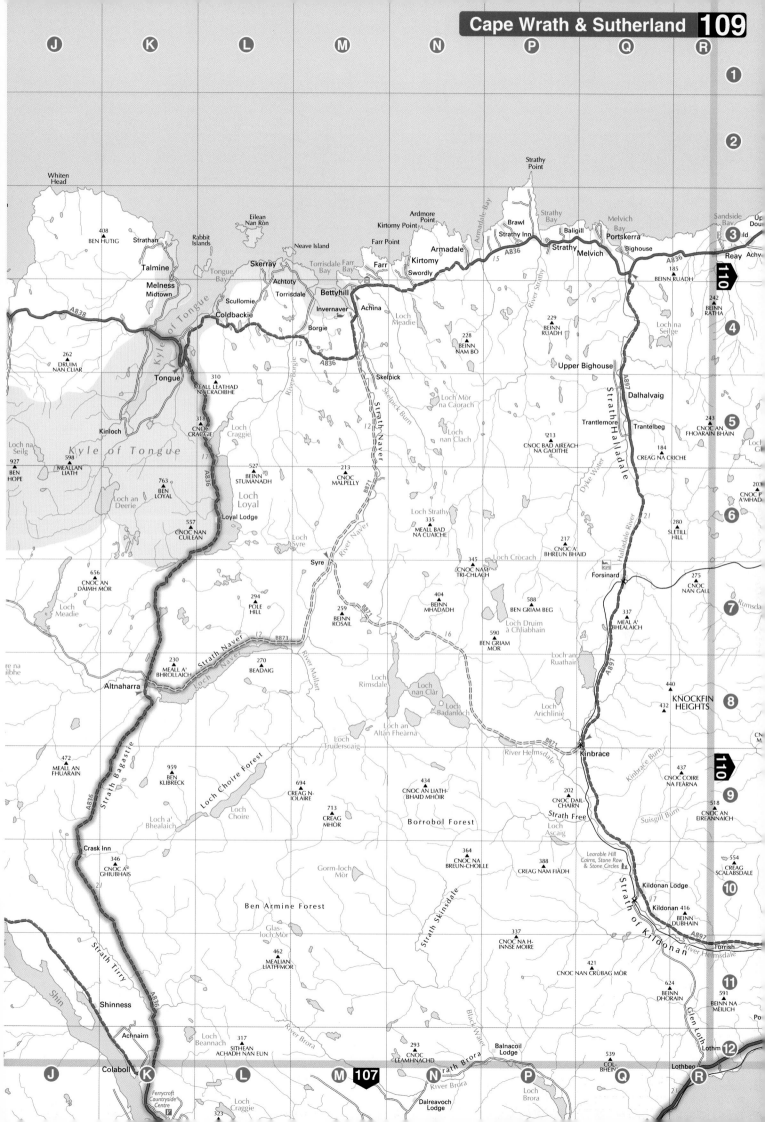

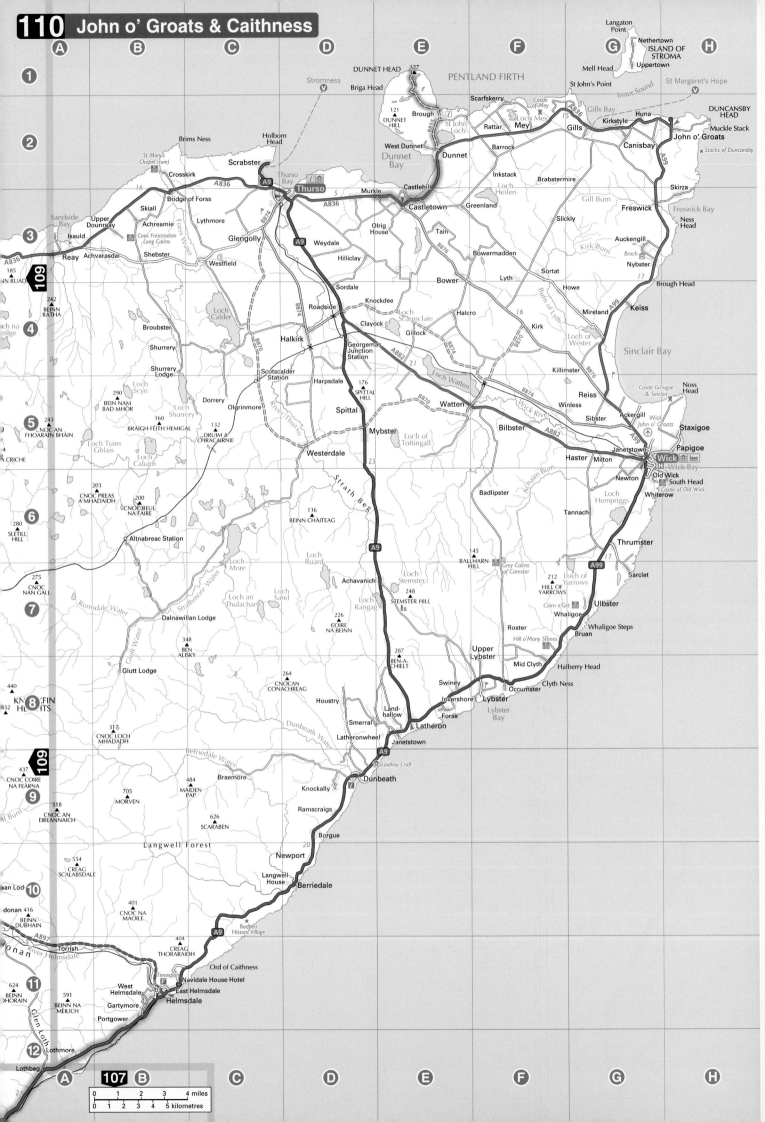

A B C D E F G H

1

2

3

4

5

6

7

8

9

10

11

12

**109**

**109**

PENTLAND FIRTH

ISLAND OF STROMA

Langaton Point
Netherton
Mell Head
Uppertown

St Margaret's Hope
Inner Sound

DUNCANSBY HEAD
Muckle Stack
John o' Groats
Stacks of Duncansby
Skirza
Freswick
Freswick Bay
Ness Head
Brough Head
Keiss
Sinclair Bay
Noss Head
Castle Girnigoe & Sinclair
Ackergill
Wick
Staxigoe
Papigoe
Wick Bay
Old Wick
Castle of Old Wick
South Head
Whiterow
Thrumster
Sarclet
Ulbster
Whaligoe Steps
Bruan
Clyth Ness
Halberry Head
Mid Clyth
Occumster
Lybster
Lybster Bay
Forse
Clyth Ness

DUNNET HEAD
Stromness
Briga Head
Brough
DUNNET HILL
DUNNET
West Dunnet
Dunnet
Dunnet Bay
Castlehill
Castletown
Scarfskerry
Castle of Mey
Mey
St John's Loch
Rattar
Barrock
Greenland
Inkstack
Brabstermire
Loch Heilen
Gill Burn
Kirk Burn
Slickly
Bowermadden
Sortat
Howe
Mireland
Gill Burn
Canisbay
St John's Point
Gills Bay
Gills
Kirkstyle
Huna
Nybster
Auckengill
Broch
Reiss
Killimster
Loch of Wester
Winless
Sibster
Janetstown
Milton
Newton
Tannach
Loch Hempriggs
Badlipster
Haster
Loch of Yarrows
HILL OF YARROWS
Cairn o' Get
Roster
Hill o' Many Stones
Upper Lybster
Swiney
Invershore
Land-hallow
Smerral
Houstry
Latheronwheel
Latheron
Janetstown
Dunbeath
Laidhay Croft
Knockally
Ramscraigs
Borgue
Newport
Langwell House
Berriedale
Ord of Caithness
Navidale House Hotel
West Helmsdale
East Helmsdale
Helmsdale
Gartymore
Portgower
Lothmore
Lothbeg
Torrish
River Helmsdale
Glen Loth

Brims Ness
St Mary's Chapel (ruin)
Holborn Head
Scrabster
Thurso Bay
Thurso
Crosskirk
Bridge of Forss
Upper Dounreay
Achreamie
Lythmore
Cnoc Freiceadain Long Cairns
Weydale
Hilliclay
Olrig House
Tain
Bower
Lyth
Halcro
Kirk
Sandside Bay
Isauld
Reay
Achvarasdal
Shebster
Westfield
Glengolly
Sordale
Roadside
Knockdee
Clayock
Gillock
Loch Scarmclate
Loch Watten
Watten
Wick River
Bilbster
Bower
Broubster
Shurrery
Shurrery Lodge
Dorrery
Olgrinmore
Halkirk
Scotscalder Station
Georgemas Junction Station
Harpsdale
Spittal
SPITTAL HILL
Spittal
Westerdale
Mybster
Loch of Toftingall
Loch Calder
Loch Scye
BEIN NAM BAD MHOR
Loch Shurrery
DRUIM A' CHRACAIRNIE
BEINN CHÀITEAG
Strath Beg
River Thurso
Loch More
Loch Ruard
Loch Sand
Loch Rangag
Loch Stemster
Achavanich
STEMSTER HILL
BALLHARN HILL
Grey Cairns of Camster
CNOC NAN GALL
CNOC PREAS A'MHADAIDH
CNOC BEUL NA FAIRE
COIRE NA BEINN
Dalnawillan Lodge
Altnabreac Station
SLETILL HILL
CNOC AN FHOARAIN BHÀIN
Loch Tuim Ghlais
Loch Caluim
Rumsdale Water
Strathmore Water
Loch an Thulachan
BEN ALISKY
CNOCAN CONACHREAG
Glutt Water
Glutt Lodge
Dunbeath Water
KNOCKFIN HEIGHTS
CNOC LOCH MHADADH
CNOC COIRE NA FEÀRNA
CNOC AN EIREANNAICH
Berriedale Water
Braemore
MAIDEN PAP
MORVEN
SCARABEN
Langwell Forest
CREAG SCALABSDALE
CNOC NA MAOILE
CREAG THORARAIDH
Badbea Historic Village
BEINN DUBHAIN
BEINN NA MEILICH
BEINN DHORAIN

A836
A9
B874
A882
B876
B870
A99
A836
B855
A897
A9

185 CNOC NA RUADH
242 BEINN RATHA
290
203
200
280
275
348 BEN ALISKY
226 COIRE NA BEINN
264 CNOCAN CONACHREAG
136
176
160
132
248 STEMSTER HILL
212
145
287 BEN-A-CHIELT
317
440
437
518 CNOC AN EIREANNAICH
705 MORVEN
626 SCARABEN
484 MAIDEN PAP
554 CREAG SCALABSDALE
401 CNOC NA MAOILE
404 CREAG THORARAIDH
624 BEINN DUBHAIN
591 BEINN NA MEILICH
243

0 1 2 3 4 miles
0 1 2 3 4 5 kilometres

A B C D E F G H

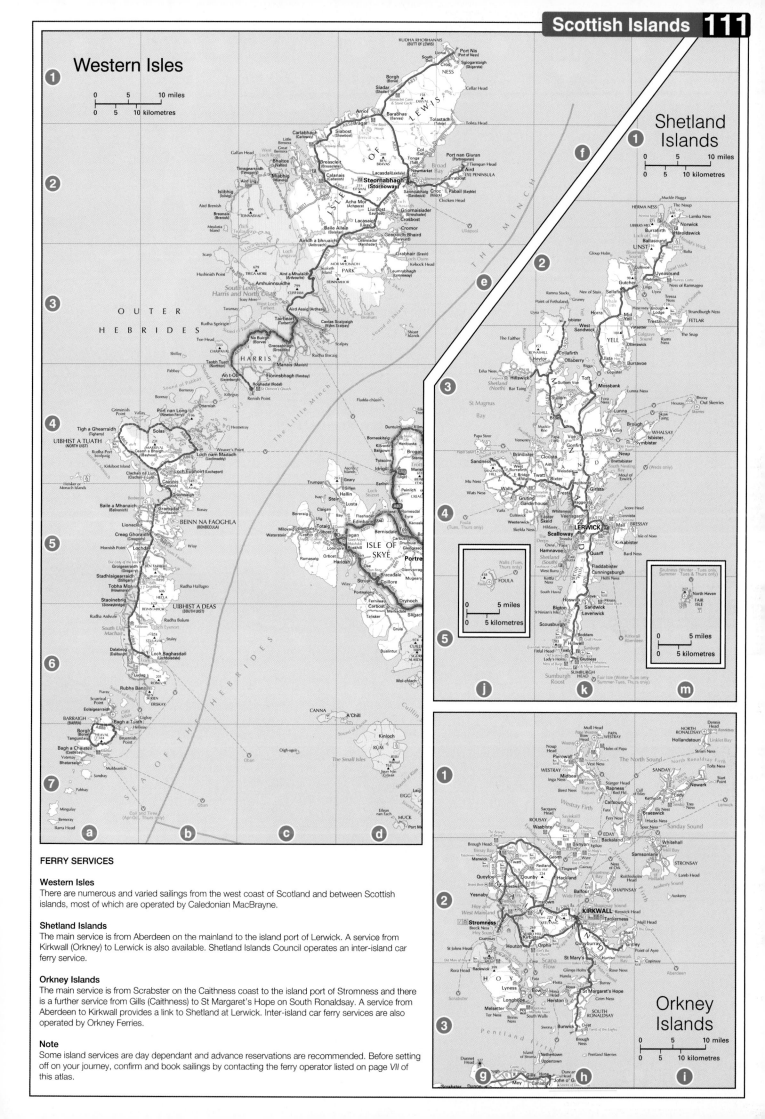

## Western Isles

## Shetland Islands

## Orkney Islands

## FERRY SERVICES

### Western Isles

There are numerous and varied sailings from the west coast of Scotland and between Scottish islands, most of which are operated by Caledonian MacBrayne.

### Shetland Islands

The main service is from Aberdeen on the mainland to the island port of Lerwick. A service from Kirkwall (Orkney) to Lerwick is also available. Shetland Islands Council operates an inter-island car ferry service.

### Orkney Islands

The main service is from Scrabster on the Caithness coast to the island port of Stromness and there is a further service from Gills (Caithness) to St Margaret's Hope on South Ronaldsay. A service from Aberdeen to Kirkwall provides a link to Shetland at Lerwick. Inter-island car ferry services are also operated by Orkney Ferries.

### Note

Some island services are day dependant and advance reservations are recommended. Before setting off on your journey, confirm and book sailings by contacting the ferry operator listed on page VII of this atlas.

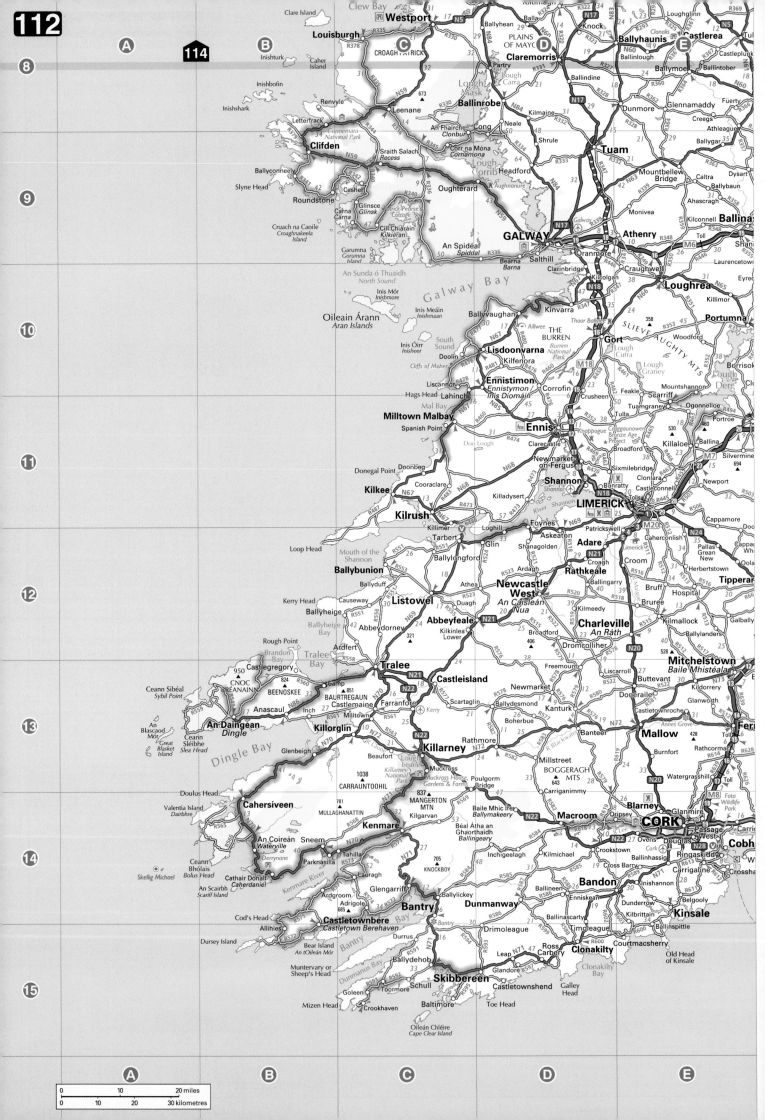

Key / Legend:

|  |  |
|---|---|
| M1 | Toll-free motorway |
| M1 Toll | Toll motorway and plaza |
| 3 | Motorway junctions with and without number |
| 3 | Restricted motorway junctions |
| S Gorey | Motorway service area |
| N7 | National primary route (Republic of Ireland) |
| N81 | National secondary route (Republic of Ireland) |
| R116 | Regional road (Republic of Ireland) |
| 7 | Distance in kilometres between symbols (Republic of Ireland) |
| A2 | Primary route (Northern Ireland) |
| A42 | A road (Northern Ireland) |
| B176 | B road (Northern Ireland) |
| 7 | Distance in miles between symbols (Northern Ireland) |
| | Minor road |
| | Road under construction |
| | Scenic route |
| | International boundary |
| Roscoff | Vehicle ferry |
| Troon | Fast vehicle ferry or catamaran |
| | National Park |
| | Gaeltacht (Irish language area) |

To reflect the distances shown on road signs, distances are shown in miles in Northern Ireland and kilometres in the Republic of Ireland.

16 kilometres = 10 miles

For key to touring information see page 1

# Ireland index

Abbeydorney ... C12
Abbeyfeale ... D12
Abbeyleix ... G11
Adamstown ... H12
Adare ... D12
Adrigole ... C14
Aghadowey ... H4
Ahascragh ... E9
Aghoghill ... J4
Allihies ... B15
Anascaul ... B13
An Bun Beag ... E4
An Charraig ... E5
An Clochán Liath ... E4
An Coireán ... B14
An Daingean ... B13
An Fhairche ... C9
Annalong ... J7
Annestown ... G13
An Rinn ... G13
An Spidéal ... D9
Antrim ... J5
Ardagh ... D12
Ardara ... E5
Ardee ... H8
Ardfert ... C12
Ardfinnan ... F12
Ardglass ... K6
Ardgroom ... B14
Ardmore ... F14
Arklow ... J11
Arless ... H11
Armagh ... H6
Armoy ... J3
Arthurstown ... H13
Arvagh ... G7
Ashbourne ... J9
Ashford ... J10
Askeaton ... D12
Athboy ... H8
Athea ... D12
Athenry ... E9
Athleague ... E8
Athlone ... F9
Athy ... H10
Augher ... G6
Aughnacloy ... H6
Aughrim ... J11
Avoca ... J11

Bagenalstown ... H11
Baile Mhic Íre ... D14
Bailieborough ... H7
Balbriggan ... J8
Balla ... D8
Ballaghaderreen ... E7
Ballina ... D7
Ballina ... E11
Ballinafad ... E7
Ballinagh ... G7
Ballinakill ... G11
Ballinalee ... F8
Ballinamallard ... G6
Ballinamore ... F7
Ballinascarty ... D14
Ballinasloe ... E9
Ballindine ... D8
Ballineen ... D14
Ballingarry ... D12
Ballingarry ... G12
Ballingeary ... D14
Ballinhassig ... E14
Ballinlough ... E8
Ballinrobe ... D8
Ballinspittle ... E15
Ballintober ... E8
Ballintra ... F5
Ballivor ... H9
Ballon ... H11
Ballybaun ... E9
Ballybay ... H7
Ballybofey ... F5
Ballybunion ... C12
Ballycanew ... J11
Ballycarry ... K5
Ballycastle ... J3
Ballycastle ... C6
Ballyclare ... J5
Ballycolla ... G11
Ballyconneely ... B9
Ballyconnell ... G7
Ballycotton ... F14
Ballycumber ... F9
Ballydehob ... C15
Ballydesmond ... D13
Ballyduff ... C12
Ballyduff ... F13
Ballyfarnan ... E7
Ballygalley ... J4
Ballygar ... E9
Ballygawley ... E6
Ballygawley ... H6
Ballygowan ... K5
Ballyhack ... H13
Ballyhaise ... G7
Ballyhale ... G12
Ballyhaunis ... E8
Ballyhean ... D8
Ballyheige ... C12
Ballyjamesduff ... G8
Ballykeeran ... F9
Ballylanders ... E12
Ballylickey ... C14
Ballyliffin ... G3
Ballylongford ... C12
Ballylooby ... F12
Ballylynan ... H10
Ballymacarbry ... F13
Ballymahon ... F8
Ballymakeery ... D14
Ballymena ... J4
Ballymoe ... E8
Ballymoney ... H4
Ballymore ... F9
Ballymore Eustace ... H10
Ballymote ... E7
Ballynahinch ... J6
Ballynure ... J5

Ballyporeen ... F13
Ballyragget ... G11
Ballyroan ... G10
Ballyronan ... H5
Ballysadare ... E6
Ballyshannon ... F5
Ballyvaughan ... D10
Ballywalter ... K5
Balrothery ... J8
Baltinglass ... H10
Baltimore ... C15
Banagher ... F10
Banbridge ... J6
Bandon ... E14
Bangor ... K5
Bangor Erris ... C7
Bansha ... F12
Banteer ... D13
Bantry ... C14
Barna ... D9
Béal an Mhuirthead ... B6
Béal Átha an Ghaorthaidh ... D14
Bearna ... D9
Beaufort ... C13
Belcoo ... F6
Belfast ... J5
Belgooly ... E14
Bellaghy ... H4
Belleek ... F6
Belmullet ... B6
Belturbet ... G7
Benburb ... H6
Bennettsbridge ... G12
Beragh ... G5
Bettystown ... J8
Birr ... F10
Blacklion ... F6
Blackwater ... J12
Blarney ... E14
Blessington ... H10
Boherbue ... D13
Borris ... H12
Borris-in-Ossory ... F10
Borrisokane ... F10
Borrisoleigh ... F11
Boyle ... E7
Bracknagh ... G10
Bray ... J10
Brittas ... J9
Broadford ... E11
Broadford ... D12
Broughshane ... J4
Bruff ... E12
Bruree ... E12
Bunbeg ... E4
Bunclody ... H11
Buncrana ... G3
Bundoran ... E6
Bunmahon ... G13
Bunnahowen ... C6
Bunnyconnellan ... D7
Bunratty ... D11
Burnfort ... E13
Bushmills ... H3
Buttevant ... E13

Cadamstown ... F10
Caherconlish ... E12
Caherdaniel ... B14
Cahersiveen ... B14
Cahir ... F12
Caledon ... H6
Callan ... G12
Caltra ... E9
Camp ... B13
Campile ... H13
Cappagh White ... F12
Cappamore ... E11
Cappoquin ... F13
Carlanstown ... H8
Carlingford ... J7
Carlow ... H11
Carna ... C9
Carndonagh ... G3
Carnew ... J11
Carnlough ... J4
Carracastle ... E7
Carraig Airt ... F3
Carrick ... E5
Carrickfergus ... K5
Carrickmacross ... H7
Carrickmore ... G5
Carrick-on-Shannon ... F7
Carrick-on-Suir ... G12
Carrigahorig ... F10
Carrigaline ... E14
Carrigallen ... F7
Carriganimmy ... D14
Carrigans ... G4
Carrigart ... F3
Carrigtohill ... E14
Carryduff ... J5
Cashel ... C9
Cashel ... F12
Castlebar ... D8
Castlebellingham ... J7
Castleblayney ... H7
Castlebridge ... J12
Castlecomer ... G11
Castleconnell ... E11
Castlederg ... G5
Castledermot ... H11
Castlegregory ... B13
Castleisland ... C13
Castlemaine ... C13
Castlemartyr ... F14
Castleplunket ... E8
Castlepollard ... G8
Castlerea ... E8
Castlerock ... H3
Castleshane ... H6
Castletown ... G8
Castletownbere ... B15

Castletownroche ... E13
Castletownshend ... D15
Castlewellan ... J6
Cathair Dónall ... B14
Causeway ... C12
Cavan ... G7
Celbridge ... H9
Charlestown ... D7
Charleville ... E12
Cheekpoint ... H13
Cill Charthaigh ... E5
Cill Chiaráin ... C9
Clady ... G5
Clane ... H9
Clara ... G9
Clarecastle ... D11
Claremorris ... D8
Clarinbridge ... D10
Claudy ... G4
Clifden ... B9
Cliffony ... E6
Clogh ... G11
Cloghan ... F10
Clogheen ... F12
Clogher ... G6
Clohamon ... H11
Clonakilty ... D15
Clonard ... H9
Clonaslee ... G10
Clonbulloge ... G9
Clonbur ... C9
Clondalkin ... J9
Clones ... G7
Clonlara ... E11
Clonmany ... G3
Clonmel ... F12
Clonmellon ... H8
Clonmore ... H11
Clonony ... F10
Clonoulty ... F12
Clonroche ... H12
Clontibret ... H6
Cloondara ... F8
Clough ... K6
Cloughjordan ... F10
Cloyne ... F14
Coagh ... H5
Coalisland ... H5
Cobh ... E14
Coleraine ... H3
Collinstown ... G8
Collon ... H8
Collooney ... E6
Comber ... K5
Cong ... D9
Conna ... F13
Cookstown ... H5
Coole ... G8
Cooraclare ... C11
Cootehill ... G7
Cork ... E14
Cornamona ... C9
Corr na Móna ... C9
Corrofin ... D10
Courtmacsherry ... E15
Courtown ... J11
Craigavon ... J6
Craughwell ... E10
Crawfordsburn ... K5
Creegs ... E8
Creeslough ... F4
Croagh ... D12
Croithlí ... E4
Crolly ... E4
Crookedwood ... G8
Crookhaven ... C15
Crookstown ... D14
Croom ... E12
Crossakeel ... H8
Cross Barry ... E14
Crosshaven ... E14
Crossmaglen ... H7
Crossmolina ... D7
Crumlin ... J5

Crusheen ... D10
Culdaff ... G3
Cullybackey ... J4
Curracloe ... J12
Curraghboy ... F9
Curry ... E7
Cushendall ... J4
Cushendun ... J3

Daingean ... G9
Delgany ... J10
Delvin ... G8
Derry ... G4
Derrygonnelly ... F6
Derrylin ... G6
Dervock ... H3
Dingle ... B13
Doagh ... J5
Donaghadee ... K5
Donaghmore ... G11
Donard ... H10
Donegal ... F5
Doneraile ... E13
Doolin ... C10
Doon ... E12
Doonbeg ... C11
Doon Cross Roads ... F9
Douglas ... E14
Downpatrick ... K6
Dowra ... F6
Draperstown ... H5
Drimoleague ... D15
Dripsey ... E14
Drogheda ... J8
Dromahair ... E6
Dromcolliher ... D12
Dromore ... J6
Dromore ... G5
Dromore West ... D6
Drumcliff ... E6
Drumcondra ... H8
Drumkeeran ... F7
Drumlish ... F8
Drumod ... F8
Drumshanbo ... F7
Drumsna ... F7
Duagh ... C12
Dublin ... J9
Duleek ... J8
Dunboyne ... J9
Duncormick ... H13
Dundalk ... J7
Dunderrow ... E14
Dundonald ... K5
Dundrum ... K6
Dundrum ... F12
Dunfanaghy ... F3
Dungannon ... H5
Dungarvan ... G12
Dungarvan ... G13
Dungiven ... H4
Dunglow ... E4
Dungourney ... F14
Dunkineely ... E5
Dún Laoghaire ... J9
Dunlavin ... H10
Dunleer ... J8
Dunloy ... J4
Dunmanway ... D14
Dunmore ... E8
Dunmore East ... H13
Dunmurry ... J6
Dunshaughlin ... H9
Durrow ... G11
Durrus ... C15
Dysart ... E9

Easky ... D6
Edenderry ... H9
Edgeworthstown ... G8
Eglinton ... G4
Elphin ... E7
Emyvale ... H6
Enfield ... H9

Ennis ... D11
Enniscorthy ... H12
Enniscrone ... D6
Enniskean ... D14
Enniskillen ... F6
Ennistimon ... D10
Eyrecourt ... F10

Fahan ... G4
Farranfore ... C13
Feakle ... E10
Fenagh ... F7
Ferbane ... F9
Fermoy ... E13
Ferns ... J12
Fethard ... F12
Fethard ... H13
Finnea ... G8
Fintona ... G6
Fivemiletown ... G6
Fontstown ... H10
Foulksmill ... H13
Foxford ... D7
Foynes ... D11
Freemount ... D13
Frenchpark ... E8
Freshford ... G11
Fuerty ... E8

Galbally ... E12
Galway ... D9
Garrison ... F6
Garristown ... J8
Garryvoe ... F14
Garvagh ... H4
Geashill ... G10
Gilford ... J6
Glandore ... D15
Glanmire ... E14
Glanworth ... E13
Glaslough ... H6
Glassan ... F9
Gleann Cholm Cille ... E5
Glenarm ... J4
Glenavy ... J5
Glenbeigh ... B13
Glencolumbkille ... E5
Glenealy ... J10
Glengarriff ... C14
Glenmore ... H12
Glennamaddy ... E8
Glenties ... E5
Glin ... D12
Glinsce ... C9
Glinsk ... C9
Golden ... F12
Goleen ... C15
Goresbridge ... H11
Gorey ... J11
Gort ... D10
Gortin ... G5
Gowran ... H11
Graiguenamanagh ... H12
Granard ... G8
Grange ... E6
Greenore ... J7
Greyabbey ... K5
Greystones ... J10
Gulladuff ... H4

Hacketstown ... H11
Headford ... D9
Herbertstown ... E12
Hillsborough ... J6
Hilltown ... J6
Holycross ... F11
Holywood ... K5
Horseleap ... G9
Hospital ... E12
Howth ... J9

Inch ... B13
Inchigeelagh ... D14
Inishannon ... E14
Inishcrone ... D6

Inistioge ... H12
Irvinestown ... F6

Johnstown ... G11

Kanturk ... D13
Keadew ... F7
Keady ... H6
Keel ... B7
Keenagh ... F8
Kells ... J4
Kells ... H8
Kenmare ... C14
Kesh ... F5
Kilbeggan ... G9
Kilberry ... H8
Kilbrittain ... E14
Kilcar ... E5
Kilcock ... H9
Kilcolgan ... D10
Kilconnell ... E9
Kilcoole ... J10
Kilcormac ... F10
Kilcullen ... H10
Kilcurry ... J7
Kildavin ... H11
Kildorrery ... E13
Kilfenora ... D10
Kilgarvan ... C14
Kilkee ... C11
Kilkeel ... J7
Kilkelly ... D7
Kilkenny ... G11
Kilkieran ... C9
Kilkinlea Lower ... C12
Kill ... H9
Kill ... G13
Killadysert ... D11
Killala ... D6
Killaloe ... E11
Killarney ... C13
Killashandra ... G7
Killeagh ... F14
Killeigh ... G10
Killenaule ... F12
Killimer ... C11
Killimor ... E10
Killiney ... J9
Killinick ... J13
Killorglin ... C13
Killough ... K6
Killucan ... G9
Killybegs ... E5
Killyleagh ... K6
Kilmacanoge ... J10
Kilmacrenan ... F4
Kilmacthomas ... G13
Kilmaganny ... G12
Kilmaine ... D8
Kilmallock ... E12
Kilmanagh ... G11
Kilmeadan ... G13
Kilmeage ... H9
Kilmeedy ... D12
Kilmichael ... D14
Kilmore Quay ... H13
Kilmuckridge ... J12
Kilnaleck ... G8
Kilrea ... H4
Kilrush ... C11
Kilsheelan ... G12
Kiltamagh ... D8
Kiltealy ... H12
Kiltegan ... H11
Kiltoom ... F9
Kingscourt ... H7
Kinlough ... E6
Kinnegad ... G9
Kinnitty ... F10
Kinsale ... E14
Kinvarra ... D10
Kircubbin ... K5
Knock ... D8
Knockcroghery ... F8

Knocklofty ... F12
Knocktopher ... G12

Lahinch ... C10
Lanesborough ... F8
Laragh ... J10
Larne ... K4
Lauragh ... C14
Laurencetown ... F10
Leap ... D15
Leenane ... C8
Leighlinbridge ... H11
Leitrim ... F7
Leixlip ... H9
Lemybrien ... G13
Letterfrack ... B8
Letterkenny ... F4
Lifford ... G4
Limavady ... H4
Limerick ... E11
Lisbellaw ... G6
Lisburn ... J5
Liscannor ... C10
Liscarroll ... D13
Lisdoonvarna ... D10
Lismore ... F13
Lisnaskea ... G6
Lisryan ... G8
Listowel ... C12
Loghill ... D12
Londonderry ... G4
Longford ... F8
Loughbrickland ... J6
Loughgall ... H6
Loughglinn ... E8
Loughrea ... E10

Louisburgh ... C8
Lucan ... J9
Lurgan ... J6
Lusk ... J9

Machair Loiscthe ... F3
Macroom ... D14
Maghera ... J6
Maghera ... H4
Magherafelt ... H5
Maguiresbridge ... G6
Malahide ... J9
Málainn Mhóir ... E5
Malin ... G3
Malin More ... E5
Mallow ... E13
Manorhamilton ... F6
Markethill ... H6
Martinstown ... J4
Maynooth ... H9
Mazetown ... J5
Middletown ... H6
Midleton ... F14
Milford ... F4
Millstreet ... D13
Milltown ... C13
Milltown Malbay ... C11
Mitchelstown ... E13
Moate ... F9
Mohill ... F7
Monaghan ... H6
Monasterevin ... G10
Moneygall ... F11
Moneymore ... H5
Monivea ... E9
Mooncoin ... G13

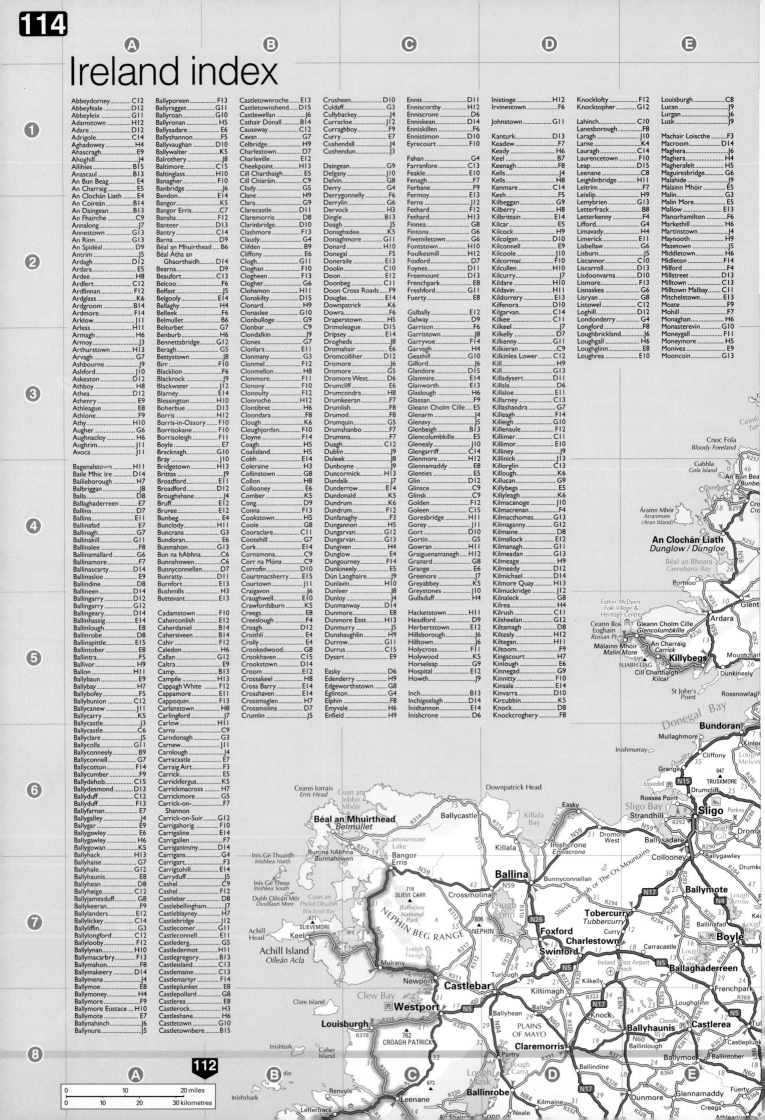

112

| 0 | 10 | 20 miles |
| 0 | 10 | 20 | 30 kilometres |

F · G · H · J · K

Moorfields ..................... J4
Mountbellew Bridge ... E9
Mountcharles ............... F5
Mountmellick ............... G10
Mountrath .................... G10
Mountshannon ........... E10
Moville ......................... G3
Moynalty ...................... H8
Moyvore ....................... F9
Muckross ..................... C13
Muff ............................. G4
Mullaghmore .............. E6
Mullinavat ................... G12
Mullingar ..................... G9
Mulrany ....................... C7
Myshall ........................ H11

Naas ............................ H10
Naul ............................. J8
Navan .......................... H8
Neale ........................... D8
Nenagh ....................... E11
Newbliss ...................... G7
Newbridge ................... H10
Newcastle .................... J6

Newcastle West ........... D12
Newinn ........................ F12
Newmarket .................. D13
Newmarket-on-
  Fergus ...................... D11
Newport ...................... C7
Newport ...................... E11
New Ross ..................... H12
Newry .......................... H7
Newtown ..................... G11
Newtownabbey ........... J5
Newtownards .............. K5
Newtownbutler ........... G7
Newtown Forbes ........ F8
Newtownhamilton ....... H6
Newtownmount-
  kennedy ................... J10
Newtownstewart ........ G5
Nobber ........................ H8

Ogonnelloe ................. E11
Oilgate ......................... H12
Oldcastle ..................... G8
Omagh ......................... G5
Omeath ........................ J7
Oola ............................. E12

Oranmore .................... D9
Oughterard .................. D9
Ovens .......................... E14

Pallas Green New ....... E12
Parknasilla .................. B14
Partry ........................... D8
Passage East ............. H13
Passage West ............. E14
Patrickswell ................ E12
Paulstown ................... H11
Pettigo ........................ F5
Plumbridge ................. G5
Pomeroy ...................... H5
Portadown ................... H6
Portaferry .................... K6
Portarlington .............. G10
Portavogie ................... K6
Portballintrae .............. H3
Portglenone ................ H4
Portlaoise ................... G10
Portmarnock ............... J9
Portnoo ....................... E4
Portraine ..................... J9
Portroe ........................ E11
Portrush ...................... H3

Portstewart ................. H3
Portumna ..................... E10
Poulgorm Bridge ........ C13
Poyntz Pass ................ J6

Raharney ..................... G9
Randalstown ............... J5
Rasharkin .................... H4
Rathangan ................... H10
Rathcoole .................... J9
Rathcormack ............... E13
Rathdowney ................ G11
Rathdrum .................... J10
Rathfriland ................... H6
Rathkeale .................... D12
Rathmelton .................. F4
Rathmolyon ................. H9
Rathmore ..................... D13
Rathmullan .................. G4
Rathnew ...................... J10
Rathowen ..................... G8
Rathvilly ...................... H11
Ratoath ........................ J9
Ray ............................... G4
Recess ........................ C9
Renvyle ....................... B8

Ringaskiddy ................ E14
Ringville ...................... G13
Rockcorry .................... H7
Roosky ......................... F8
Rosapenna .................. F3
Rosbercon ................... H12
Roscommon ................ F8
Roscrea ....................... F10
Ross Carbery .............. D15
Rosses Point ............... E6
Rosslare ...................... J13
Rosslare Harbour ....... J13
Rosslea ........................ G6
Rossnowlagh ............... F5
Rostrevor ..................... J7
Roundstone ................. B9
Roundwood ................. J10
Rush ............................ J9

Saintfield ..................... K6
St Johnston ................. G4
Sallins ......................... H9
Salthill ......................... D9
Scarriff ........................ E11
Scartaglin .................... C13
Scarva ......................... J6

Schull .......................... C15
Scramoge ..................... F8
Seskinore ..................... G5
Shanagarry .................. F14
Shanagolden ............... D12
Shankill ........................ J9
Shannon ...................... D11
Shannonbridge ........... F9
Shercock ...................... H7
Shillelagh ..................... H11
Shinrone ...................... F10
Shrule .......................... D9
Silvermines ................. E11
Sion Mills .................... G5
Sixmilebridge .............. D11
Skerries ....................... J8
Skibbereen ................... D15
Slane ........................... H8
Sligo ............................ E6
Smithborough .............. G6
Sneem ......................... B14
Spanish Point ............. C11
Spiddal ........................ D9
Sraith Salach .............. C9
Stewartstown .............. H5
Stillorgan .................... J9

Stonyford .................... G12
Strabane ...................... G4
Stradbally ..................... G10
Stradone ...................... G7
Straffan ....................... H9
Strandhill ..................... E6
Strangford .................... K6
Stranorlar ..................... F5
Strokestown ................ F8
Summerhill .................. H9
Swanlinbar ................... F6
Swatragh ..................... H4
Swinford ...................... D7
Swords ........................ J9

Taghmon ...................... H12
Tagoat ......................... J13
Tahilla ......................... C14
Tallaght ....................... J9
Tallow .......................... F13
Tallowbridge ............... F13
Tandragee .................... J6
Tang ............................. F9
Tarbert ......................... C12
Templemore ................ F11
Templetouhy ............... F11
Termonfeckin .............. J8
Termon Rock ............... G5
Thomastown ............... G12
Thurles ........................ F11
Timahoe ...................... G10
Timoleague .................. D15
Tinahely ....................... J11
Tipperary ..................... F12

Tobercurry ................... E7
Tobermore ................... H4
Toomyvara ................... F11
Toormore ..................... C15
Tralee .......................... C13
Tramore ....................... G13
Trim ............................. H8
Tuam ............................ D9
Tuamgraney ................ E11
Tubbercurry ................. E7
Tulla ............................ D11
Tullamore ..................... G9
Tullow .......................... H11
Tulsk ............................ E8
Turlough ...................... D7
Tyrrellspass ................ G9

Urlingford ................... G11

Virginia ....................... G8

Warrenpoint ................ J7
Waterford ..................... G13
Watergrasshill ............ E13
Waterville .................... B14
Westport ...................... C8
Wexford ....................... J12
Whitegate ..................... E14
Whitehead .................... K5
Wicklow ....................... J10
Woodenbridge ............. J11
Woodford ..................... E10

Youghal ....................... F14

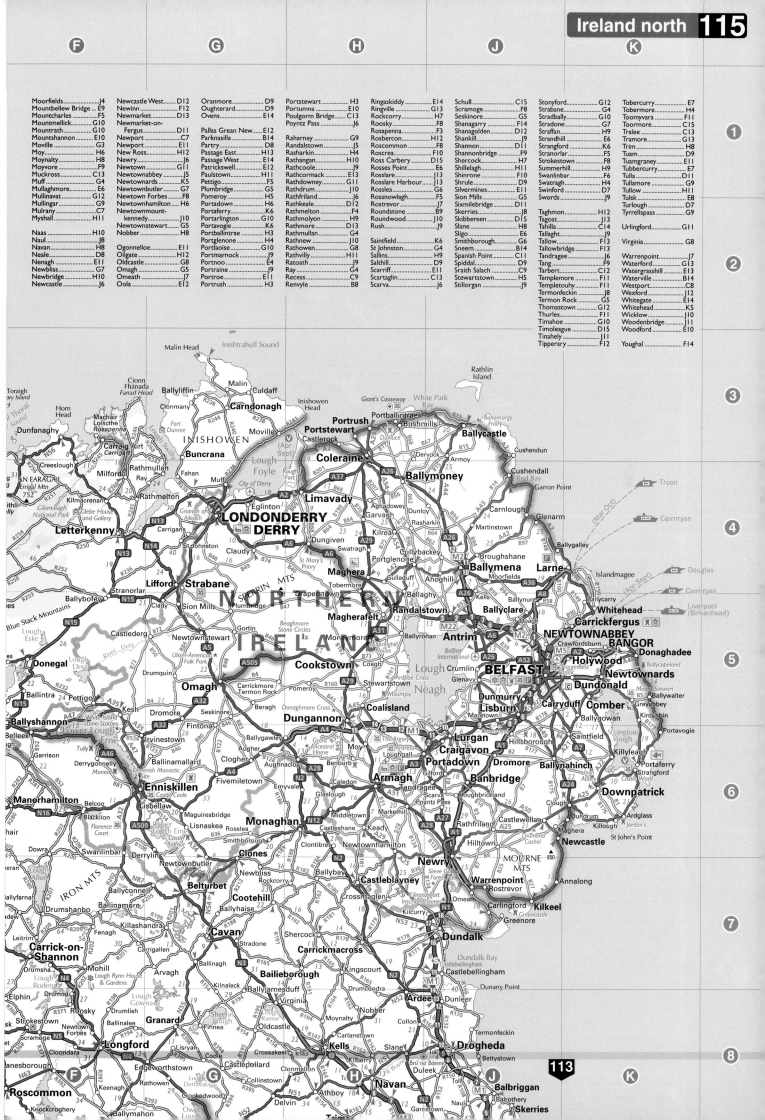

F · G · H · J · K

# Restricted junctions

Motorway and Primary Route junctions which have access or exit restrictions are shown on the map pages thus:

## M1 London - Leeds

**Northbound**
Access only from A1
(northbound)

**Southbound**
Exit only to A1
(southbound)

**Northbound**
Access only from A41
(northbound)

**Southbound**
Exit only to A41
(southbound)

**Northbound**
Access only from M25
(no link from A405)

**Southbound**
Exit only to M25 (no link from A405)

**Northbound**
Access only from A414

**Southbound**
Exit only to A414

**Northbound**
Exit only to M45

**Southbound**
Access only from M45

**Northbound**
Exit only to M6
(northbound)

**Southbound**
Exit only to A14
(southbound)

**Northbound**
Exit only, no access

**Southbound**
Access only, no exit

**Northbound**
Access only from A42

**Southbound**
No restriction

**Northbound**
No exit, access only

**Southbound**
Exit only, no access

**Northbound**
Exit only, no access

**Southbound**
Access only, no exit

**Northbound**
Exit only to M621

**Southbound**
Access only from M621

**Northbound**
Exit only to A1(M)
(northbound)

**Southbound**
Access only from A1(M)
(southbound)

## M2 Rochester - Faversham

**Westbound**
No exit to A2
(eastbound)

**Eastbound**
No access from A2
(westbound)

## M3 Sunbury - Southampton

**Northeastbound**
Access only from A303,
no exit

**Southwestbound**
Exit only to A303,
no access

**Northbound**
Exit only, no access

**Southbound**
Access only, no exit

**Northeastbound**
Access from M27 only.
No exit

**Southwestbound**
No access to M27
(westbound)

## M4 London - South Wales

**Westbound**
Access only from A4
(westbound)

**Eastbound**
Exit only to A4
(eastbound)

**Westbound**
Exit only to M48

**Eastbound**
Access only from M48

**Westbound**
Access only from M48

**Eastbound**
Exit only to M48

**Westbound**
Exit only, no access

**Eastbound**
Access only, no exit

**Westbound**
Exit only, no access

**Eastbound**
Access only, no exit

**Westbound**
Exit only to A48(M)

**Eastbound**
Access only from A48(M)

**Westbound**
Exit only, no access

**Eastbound**
No restriction

**Westbound**
Access only, no exit

**Eastbound**
No access or exit

## M5 Birmingham - Exeter

**Northeastbound**
Access only, no exit

**Southwestbound**
Exit only, no access

**Northeastbound**
Access only from A417
(westbound)

**Southwestbound**
Exit only to A417
(eastbound)

**Northeastbound**
Exit only to M49

**Southwestbound**
Access only from M49

**Northeastbound**
No access, exit only

**Southwestbound**
No exit, access only

## M6 Toll Motorway

See M6 Toll Motorway map on page 121

## M6 Rugby - Carlisle

**Northbound**
Exit only to M6 Toll

**Southbound**
Access only from M6 Toll

**Northbound**
Access only from M42
(southbound)

**Southbound**
Exit only to M42

**Northbound**
Exit only, no access

**Southbound**
Access only, no exit

**Northbound**
Exit only to M54

**Southbound**
Access only from M54

**Northbound**
Access only from M6 Toll

**Southbound**
Exit only to M6 Toll

**Northbound**
No restriction

**Southbound**
Access only from M56
(eastbound)

**Northbound**
Exit only to M56
(westbound)

**Southbound**
Access only from M56
(eastbound)

**Northbound**
Access only, no exit

**Southbound**
Exit only, no access

**Northbound**
Exit only, no access

**Southbound**
Access only, no exit

*Northbound*
Access only from M61

*Southbound*
Exit only to M61

*Northbound*
Exit only, no access

*Southbound*
Access only, no exit

*Northbound*
Exit only, no access

*Southbound*
Access only, no exit

### M8 Edinburgh - Bishopton

See Glasgow District map on pages 138-139

### M9 Edinburgh - Dunblane

*Northwestbound*
Access only, no exit

*Southeastbound*
Exit only, no access

*Northwestbound*
Exit only, no access

*Southeastbound*
Access only, no exit

*Northwestbound*
Access only, no exit

*Southeastbound*
Exit only to A905

*Northwestbound*
Exit only to M876
(southwestbound)

*Southeastbound*
Access only from M876
(northeastbound)

### M11 London - Cambridge

*Northbound*
Access only from A406
(eastbound)

*Southbound*
Exit only to A406

*Northbound*
Exit only, no access

*Southbound*
Access only, no exit

*Northbound*
Exit only, no access

*Southbound*
No direct access,
use jct 8

*Northbound*
Exit only to A11

*Southbound*
Access only from A11

*Northbound*
Exit only, no access

*Southbound*
Access only, no exit

*Northbound*
Exit only, no access

*Southbound*
Access only, no exit

### M20 Swanley - Folkestone

*Northwestbound*
Staggered junction; follow
signs - access only

*Southeastbound*
Staggered junction; follow
signs - exit only

*Northwestbound*
Exit only to M26
(westbound)

*Southeastbound*
Access only from M26
(eastbound)

*Northwestbound*
Access only from A20

*Southeastbound*
For access follow signs -
exit only to A20

*Northwestbound*
No restriction

*Southeastbound*
For exit follow signs

*Northwestbound*
Access only, no exit

*Southeastbound*
Exit only, no access

### M23 Hooley - Crawley

*Northbound*
Exit only to A23
(northbound)

*Southbound*
Access only from A23
(southbound)

*Northbound*
Access only, no exit

*Southbound*
Exit only, no access

### M25 London Orbital Motorway

See M25 London Orbital Motorway map on
page 120


### M26 Sevenoaks - Wrotham

*Westbound*
Exit only to clockwise M25
(westbound)

*Eastbound*
Access only from anti-
clockwise M25
(eastbound)

*Westbound*
Access only from M20
(northwestbound)

*Eastbound*
Exit only to M20
(southeastbound)

### M27 Cadnam - Portsmouth

*Westbound*
Staggered junction; follow
signs - access only from
M3 (southbound). Exit only
to M3 (northbound)

*Eastbound*
Staggered junction; follow
signs - access only from
M3 (southbound). Exit only
to M3 (northbound)

*Westbound*
Exit only, no access

*Eastbound*
Access only, no exit

*Westbound*
Staggered junction; follow
signs - exit only to M275
(southbound)

*Eastbound*
Staggered junction; follow
signs - access only from
M275 (northbound)

### M40 London - Birmingham

*Northwestbound*
Exit only, no access

*Southeastbound*
Access only, no exit

*Northwestbound*
Exit only, no access

*Southeastbound*
Access only, no exit

*Northwestbound*
Exit only to M40/A40

*Southeastbound*
Access only from
M40/A40

*Northwestbound*
Exit only, no access

*Southeastbound*
Access only, no exit

*Northwestbound*
Access only, no exit

*Southeastbound*
Exit only, no access

*Northwestbound*
Access only, no exit

*Southeastbound*
Access only, no access

### M42 Bromsgrove - Measham

See Birmingham District map on pages
136-137

### M45 Coventry - M1

*Westbound*
Access only from A45
(northbound)

*Eastbound*
Exit only, no access

*Westbound*
Access only from M1
(northbound)

*Eastbound*
Exit only to M1
(southbound)

### M53 Mersey Tunnel - Chester

*Northbound*
Access only from M56
(westbound). Exit only to
M56 (eastbound)

*Southbound*
Access only from M56
(westbound). Exit only to
M56 (eastbound)

### M54 Telford - Birmingham

*Westbound*
Access only from M6
(northbound)

*Eastbound*
Exit only to M6
(southbound)

### M56 Chester - Manchester

For junctions 1,2,3,4 & 7 see Manchester
District map on pages 140-141

*Westbound*
Access only, no exit

*Eastbound*
No access or exit

*Westbound*
No exit to M6
(southbound)

*Eastbound*
No access from M6
(northbound)

*Westbound*
Exit only to M53

*Eastbound*
Access only from M53

*Westbound*
No access or exit

*Eastbound*
No restriction

## M57 Liverpool Outer Ring Road

*Northwestbound*
Access only, no exit

*Southeastbound*
Exit only, no access

*Northwestbound*
Access only from A580 (westbound)

*Southeastbound*
Exit only, no access

## M58 Liverpool - Wigan

*Westbound*
Exit only, no access

*Eastbound*
Access only, no exit

## M60 Manchester Orbital

See Manchester District map on pages 140-141

## M61 Manchester - Preston

*Northwestbound*
No access or exit

*Southeastbound*
Exit only, no access

*Northwestbound*
Exit only to M6 (northbound)

*Southeastbound*
Access only from M6 (southbound)

## M62 Liverpool - Kingston upon Hull

*Westbound*
Access only, no exit

*Eastbound*
Exit only, no access

*Westbound*
No access to A1(M) (southbound)

*Eastbound*
No restriction

## M65 Preston - Colne

*Northeastbound*
Exit only, no access

*Southwestbound*
Access only, no exit

*Northeastbound*
Access only, no exit

*Southwestbound*
Exit only, no access

## M66 Bury

*Northbound*
Exit only to A56 (northbound)

*Southbound*
Access only from A56 (southbound)

*Northbound*
Exit only, no access

*Southbound*
Access only, no exit

## M67 Hyde Bypass

*Westbound*
Access only, no exit

*Eastbound*
Exit only, no access

*Westbound*
Exit only, no access

*Eastbound*
Access only, no exit

*Westbound*
Exit only, no access

*Eastbound*
No restriction

## M69 Coventry - Leicester

*Northbound*
Access only, no exit

*Southbound*
Exit only, no access

## M73 East of Glasgow

*Northbound*
No access from or exit to A89. No access from M8 (eastbound)

*Southbound*
No access from or exit to A89. No exit to M8 (westbound)

## M74 and A74(M) Glasgow - Gretna

*Northbound*
Exit only, no access

*Southbound*
Access only, no exit

*Northbound*
Access only, no exit

*Southbound*
Exit only, no access

*Northbound*
Access only, no exit

*Southbound*
Exit only, no access

## M77 Glasgow - Kilmarnock

*Northbound*
No exit to M8 (westbound)

*Southbound*
No access from M8 (eastbound)

*Northbound*
Access only, no exit

*Southbound*
Exit only, no access

*Northbound*
Access only, no exit

*Southbound*
Exit only, no access

*Northbound*
Access only, no exit

*Southbound*
No restriction

## M80 Glasgow - Stirling

For junctions 1 & 4 see Glasgow District map on pages 138-139

*Northbound*
Exit only, no access

*Southbound*
Access only, no exit

*Northbound*
Access only, no exit

*Southbound*
Exit only, no access

*Northbound*
Access only, no exit

*Southbound*
Exit only, no access

*Northbound*
No access or exit

*Southbound*
Access only, no exit

*Northbound*
Access only, no exit

*Southbound*
Exit only, no access

*Northbound*
Exit only, no access

*Southbound*
Access only, no exit

*Northbound*
Access only, no exit

*Southbound*
No restriction

*Northbound*
Access only, no exit

*Southbound*
Exit only, no access

*Northbound*
Exit only, no access

*Southbound*
Access only, no exit

*Northbound*
No restriction

*Southbound*
Exit only, no access

*Northbound*
Access only, no exit

*Southbound*
Exit only, no access

*Northbound*
Exit only to M876 (northeastbound)

*Southbound*
Access only from M876 (southwestbound)

## M90 Edinburgh - Perth

*Northbound*
No exit, access only

*Southbound*
Exit only to A90 (eastbound)

*Northbound*
Exit only to A92 (eastbound)

*Southbound*
Access only from A92 (westbound)

*Northbound*
Access only, no exit

*Southbound*
Exit only, no access

*Northbound*
Exit only, no access

*Southbound*
Access only, no exit

*Northbound*
No access from A912 No exit to A912 (southbound)

*Southbound*
No access from A912 (northbound). No exit to A912

## M180 Doncaster - Grimsby

*Westbound*
Access only, no exit

*Eastbound*
Exit only, no access

## M606 Bradford Spur

*Northbound*
Exit only, no access

*Southbound*
No restriction

## M621 Leeds - M1

*Clockwise*
Access only, no exit

*Anticlockwise*
Exit only, no access

*Clockwise*
No exit or access

*Anticlockwise*
No restriction

*Clockwise*
Access only, no exit

*Anticlockwise*
Exit only, no access

*Clockwise*
Exit only, no access

*Anticlockwise*
Access only, no exit

*Clockwise*
Exit only to M1 (southbound)

*Anticlockwise*
Access only from M1 (northbound)

### M876 Bonnybridge - Kincardine Bridge

*Northeastbound*
Access only from M80 (northbound)

*Southwestbound*
Exit only to M80 (southbound)

*Northeastbound*
Exit only to M9 (eastbound)

*Southwestbound*
Access only from M9 (westbound)

### A1(M) South Mimms - Baldock

*Northbound*
Exit only, no access

*Southbound*
Access only, no exit

*Northbound*
No restriction

*Southbound*
Exit only, no access

*Northbound*
Access only, no exit

*Southbound*
No access or exit

### A1(M) Pontefract - Bedale

*Northbound*
No access to M62 (eastbound)

*Southbound*
No restriction

*Northbound*
Access only from M1 (northbound)

*Southbound*
Exit only to M1 (southbound)

### A1(M) Scotch Corner - Newcastle upon Tyne

*Northbound*
Exit only to A66(M) (eastbound)

*Southbound*
Access only from A66(M) (westbound)

*Northbound*
No access. Exit only to A194(M) & A1 (northbound)

*Southbound*
No exit. Access only from A194(M) & A1 (southbound)

### A3(M) Horndean - Havant

*Northbound*
Access only from A3

*Southbound*
Exit only to A3

*Northbound*
Exit only, no access

*Southbound*
Access only, no exit

### A48(M) Cardiff Spur

*Westbound*
Access only from M4 (westbound)

*Eastbound*
Exit only to M4 (eastbound)

*Westbound*
Exit only to A48 (westbound)

*Eastbound*
Access only from A48 (eastbound)

### A66(M) Darlington Spur

*Westbound*
Exit only to A1(M) (southbound)

*Eastbound*
Access only from A1(M) (northbound)

### A194(M) Newcastle upon Tyne

*Northbound*
Access only from A1(M) (northbound)

*Southbound*
Exit only to A1(M) (southbound)

### A12 M25 - Ipswich

*Northeastbound*
Access only, no exit

*Southwestbound*
No restriction

*Northeastbound*
Exit only, no access

*Southwestbound*
Access only, no exit

*Northeastbound*
Exit only, no access

*Southwestbound*
Access only, no exit

*Northeastbound*
Access only, no exit

*Southwestbound*
Exit only, no access

*Northeastbound*
No restriction

*Southwestbound*
Access only, no exit

*Northeastbound*
Exit only, no access

*Southwestbound*
Access only, no exit

*Northeastbound*
Access only, no exit

*Southwestbound*
Exit only, no access

*Northeastbound*
Exit only, no access

*Southwestbound*
Access only, no exit

*Northeastbound*
Exit only (for Stratford St Mary and Dedham)

*Southwestbound*
Access only

### A14 M1 - Felixstowe

*Westbound*
Exit only to M6 & M1 (northbound)

*Eastbound*
Access only from M6 & M1 (southbound)

*Westbound*
Exit only, no access

*Eastbound*
Access only, no exit

*Westbound*
Exit onlt to M11 (for London)

*Eastbound*
Access only, no exit

*Westbound*
Exit only to A14 (northbound)

*Eastbound*
Access only, no exit

*Westbound*
Access only, no exit

*Eastbound*
Exit only, no access

*Westbound*
Exit only to A11
Access only from A1303

*Eastbound*
Access only from A11

*Westbound*
Access only from A11

*Eastbound*
Exit only to A11

*Westbound*
Exit only, no access

*Eastbound*
Access only, no exit

*Westbound*
Access only, no exit

*Eastbound*
Exit only, no access

### A55 Holyhead - Chester

*Westbound*
Exit only, no access

*Eastbound*
Access only, no exit

*Westbound*
Access only, no exit

*Eastbound*
Exit only, no access

*Westbound*
Exit only, no access

*Eastbound*
No access or exit

*Westbound*
No restriction

*Eastbound*
No access or exit

*Westbound*
Exit only, no access

*Eastbound*
No access or exit

*Westbound*
Exit only, no access

*Eastbound*
Access only, no exit

*Westbound*
Exit only to A5104

*Eastbound*
Access only from A5104

# M25 London Orbital motorway

Refer also to atlas pages 20–21

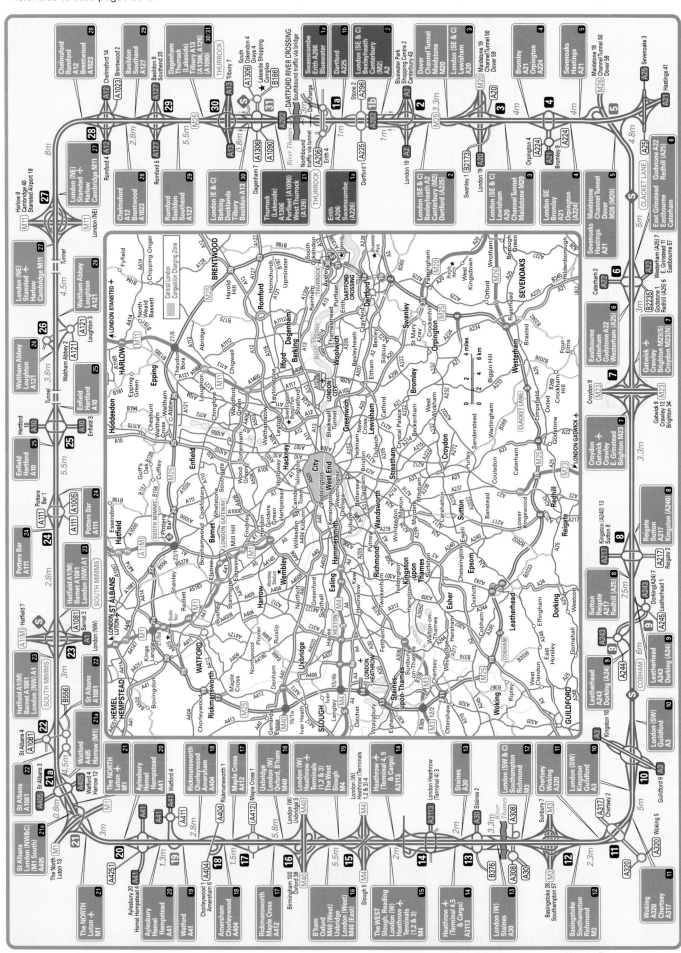

Refer also to atlas page 40

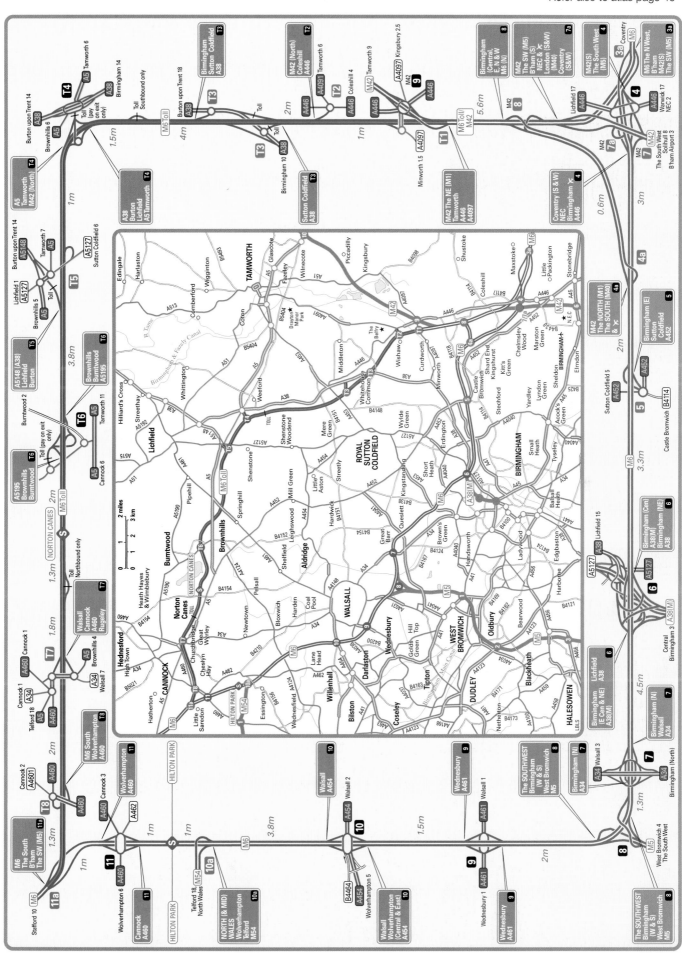

# Street map symbols

## Town and port plans

| | | | |
|---|---|---|---|
| Motorway and junction | One-way, gated/closed road | Railway station | P Car park |
| Primary road single/dual carriageway | Restricted access road | Light rapid transit system station | P+R Park and Ride (at least 6 days per week) |
| A road single/dual carriageway | Pedestrian area | Level crossing | Bus/coach station |
| B road single/dual carriageway | Footpath | Tramway | H Hospital |
| Local road single/dual carriageway | Road under construction | Ferry route | H 24-hour Accident & Emergency hospital |
| Other road single/dual carriageway, minor road | Road tunnel | Airport, heliport | Petrol station, 24 hour Major suppliers only |
| Building of interest | M Museum | R Railair terminal | City wall |
| Ruined building | Castle | Theatre or performing arts centre | Escarpment |
| i Tourist Information Centre | Castle mound | Cinema | Cliff lift |
| V Visitor or heritage centre | Monument, statue | † Abbey, chapel, church | River/canal, lake |
| World Heritage Site (UNESCO) | Post Office | Synagogue | Lock, weir |
| English Heritage site | Public library | Mosque | Park/sports ground |
| Historic Scotland site | Shopping centre | Golf course | Cemetery |
| Cadw (Welsh heritage) site | Shopmobility | Racecourse | Woodland |
| National Trust site | Viewpoint | Nature reserve | Built-up area |
| National Trust Scotland site | Toilet, with facilities for the less able | Aquarium | Beach |

## Central London street map (see pages 148–157)

| | | |
|---|---|---|
| 30 Safety camera site (fixed location) with speed limit in mph | London Underground station | Docklands Light Railway (DLR) station |
| 40 Section of road with two or more fixed camera sites; speed limit in mph | London Overground station | Central London Congestion Charging Zone |
| 50→ ←50 Average speed (SPECS™) camera system with speed limit in mph | Rail interchange | |

**Royal Parks**

| | |
|---|---|
| Green Park | Park open 24 hours. Constitution Hill and The Mall closed to traffic Sundays and public holidays |
| Hyde Park | Park open 5am–midnight. Park roads closed to traffic midnight–5am. |
| Kensington Gardens | Park open 6am–dusk. |
| Regent's Park | Park open 5am–dusk. Park roads closed to traffic midnight–7am. |
| St James's Park | Park open 5am–midnight. The Mall closed to traffic Sundays and public holidays. |

Traffic regulations in the City of London include security checkpoints and restrict the number of entry and exit points.

**Note:** Oxford Street is closed to through-traffic (except buses & taxis) 7am–7pm Monday–Saturday.

**Central London Congestion Charging Zone**

The daily charge for driving or parking a vehicle on public roads in the Congestion Charging Zone (CCZ), during operating hours, is £11.50 per vehicle per day in advance or on the day of travel. Alternatively you can pay £10.50 by registering with CC Auto Pay, an automated payment system. Drivers can also pay the next charging day after travelling in the zone but this will cost £14. Payment permits entry, travel within and exit from the CCZ by the vehicle as often as required on that day.

The CCZ operates between 7am and 6pm, Mon–Fri only. There is no charge at weekends, on public holidays or between 25th Dec and 1st Jan inclusive.

For up to date information on the CCZ, exemptions, discounts or ways to pay, visit tfl.gov.uk/modes/driving/congestion-charge or write to Congestion Charging, P.O. Box 4782, Worthing BN11 9PS. Textphone users can call 020 7649 9123.

# Town and port plans

## Town plans

Aberdeen ....................103
Aberystwyth .................36
Basingstoke..................123
Bath ..........................123
Birmingham ................124
Blackpool ..................124
Bournemouth ..............124
Bradford.....................124
Brighton .....................125
Bristol ........................125
Cambridge .................125
Canterbury .................125
Cardiff .......................126
Carlisle.......................126
Chester ......................126
Coventry ....................126
Derby .........................127
Dundee ......................127
Edinburgh ..................127
Exeter ........................127
Glasgow .....................128
Ipswich ......................128
Kingston upon Hull......128
Leeds .........................128
Leicester ....................129
Liverpool ...................129
LONDON ...........148–157
Manchester .................129
Middlesbrough ............129
Milton Keynes .............130
Newcastle upon Tyne ...........130
Newquay ......................3

Norwich......................130
Nottingham ................130
Oxford........................131
Peterborough ..............131
Plymouth ...................131
Portsmouth .................131
Ramsgate ....................23
Reading ......................132
Royal Tunbridge Wells .........132
Salisbury....................132
Scarborough ................67
Sheffield.....................132
Shrewsbury .................133
Southampton ...............133
Stoke-on-Trent (Hanley).......133
Stratford-upon-Avon ....133
Sunderland .................134
Swansea .....................134
Taunton......................134
Warwick .....................134
Watford ......................135
Winchester ..................135
Worcester....................135
York ...........................135

## Ferry Ports

Aberdeen Harbour.................95
Dover, Port of ......................12
Fishguard Harbour .................24
Harwich International Port....35
Heysham Harbour ................62
Holyhead Harbour ...............54
Hull, Port of .........................61
Liverpool Docks ...................56
Newhaven Harbour ...............11
Pembroke Dock ....................24
Plymouth, Port of...................4
Port of Tyne ..........................73
Portsmouth Harbour............10

## Channel Tunnel

Folkestone Terminal...............13
Calais / Coquelles Terminal....13

## Central London

**Basingstoke**
**Bath**

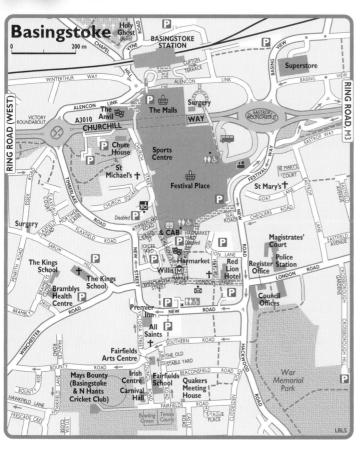

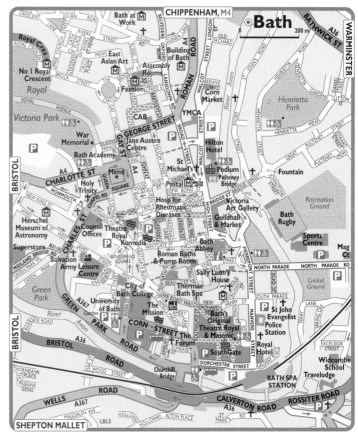

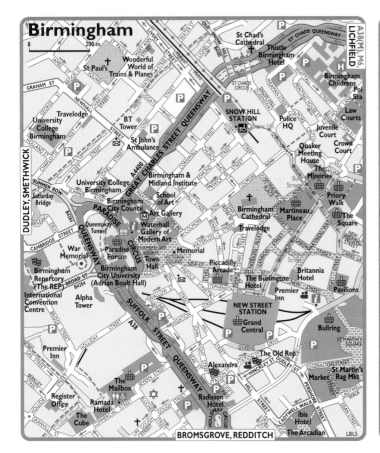

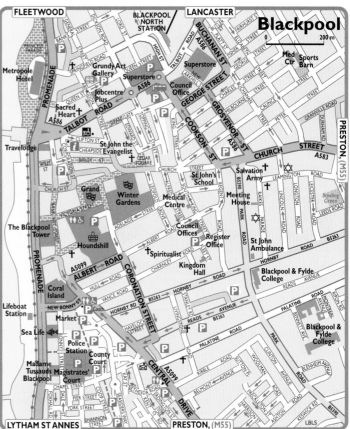

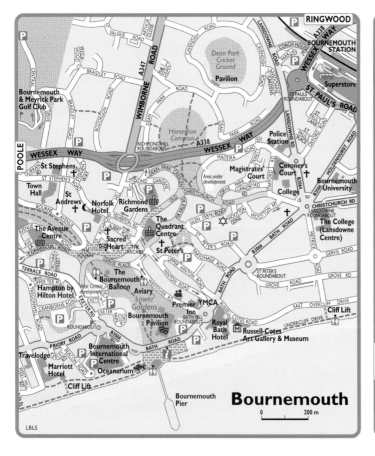

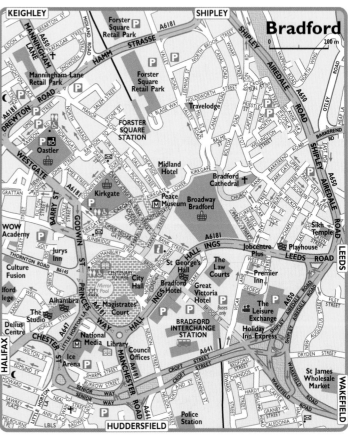

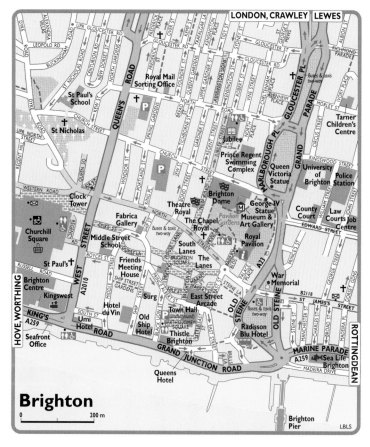

**Brighton**

LONDON, CRAWLEY · LEWES

0    200 m

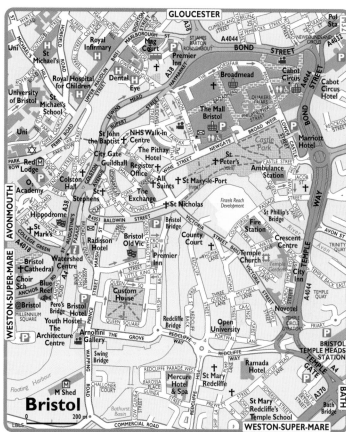

**Bristol**

GLOUCESTER

0    200 m

WESTON-SUPER-MARE

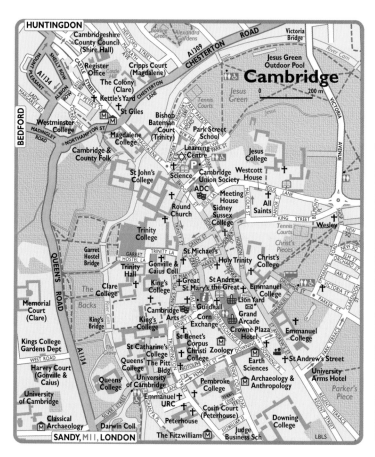

**Cambridge**

HUNTINGDON

0    200 m

SANDY, M11, LONDON

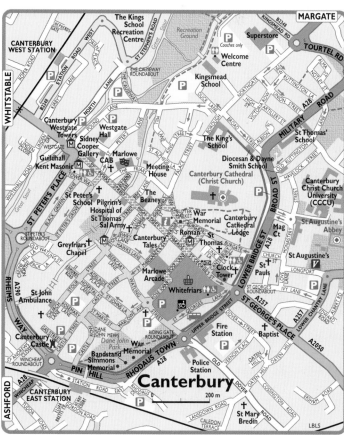

**Canterbury**

MARGATE

0    200 m

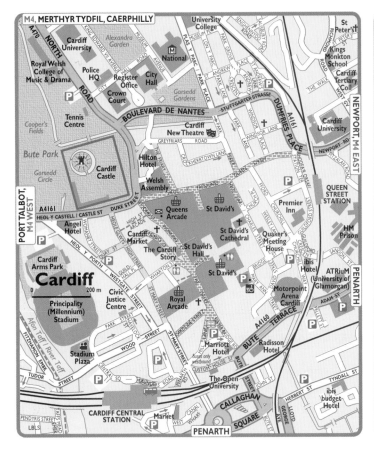

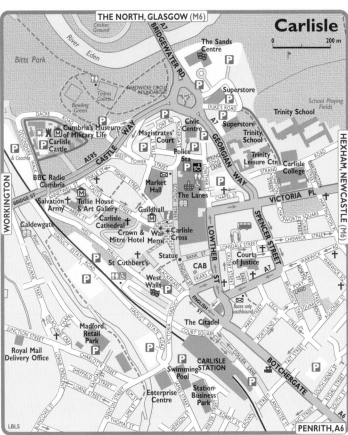

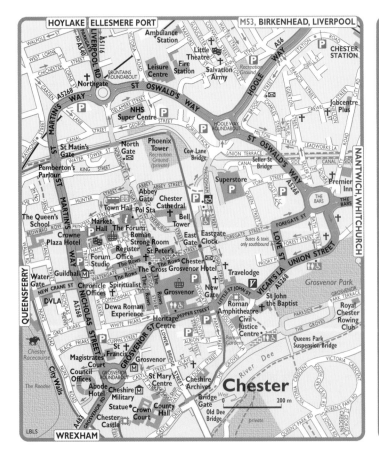

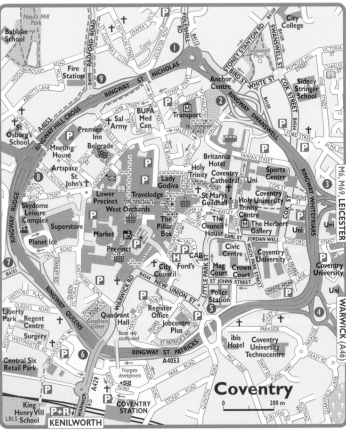

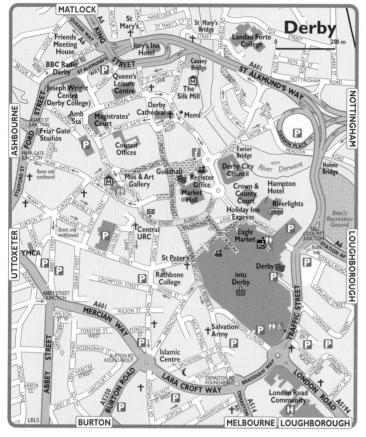

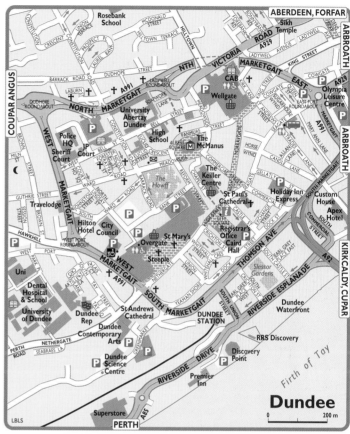

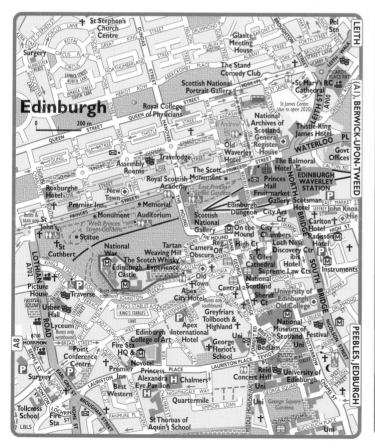

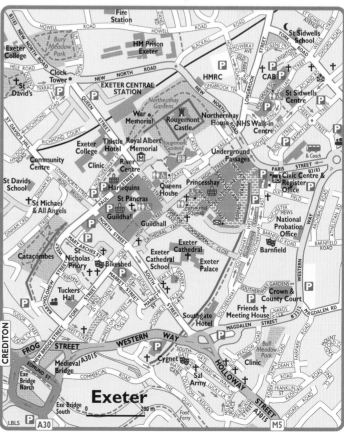

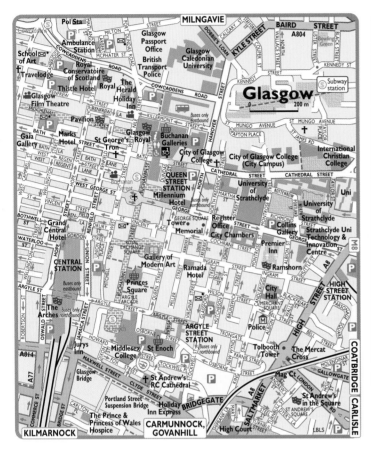

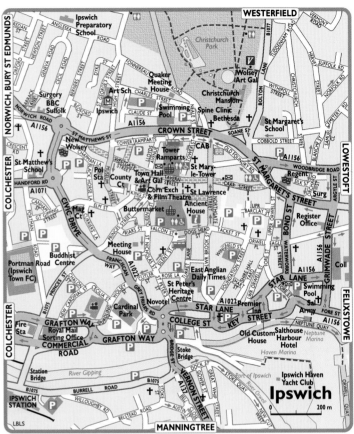

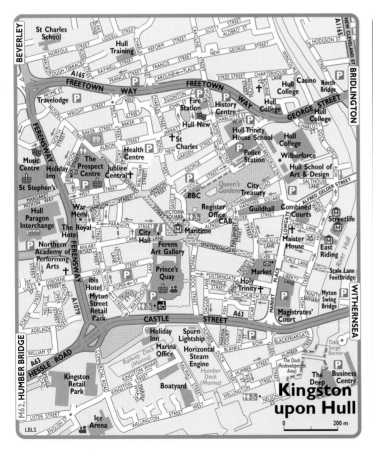

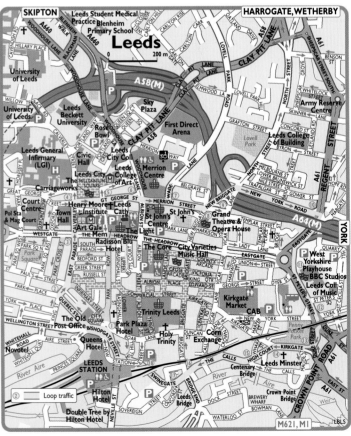

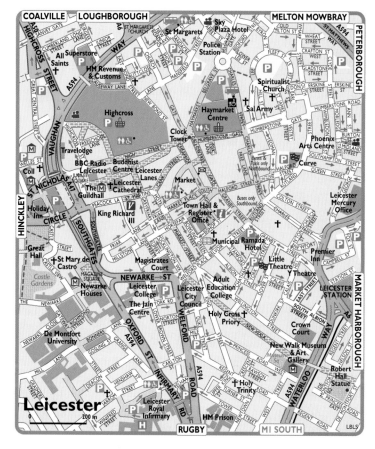

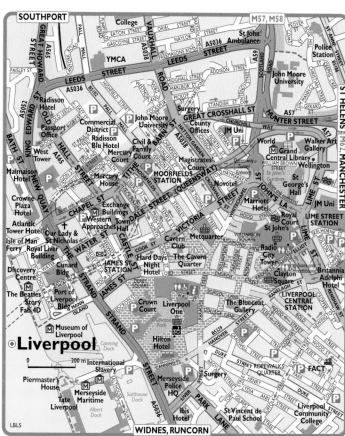

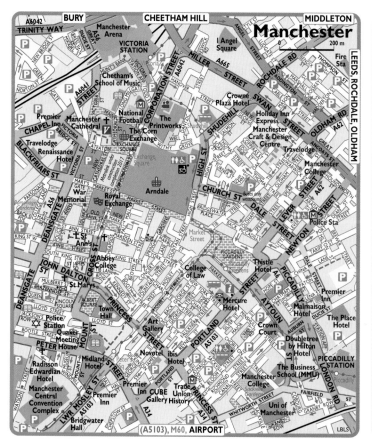

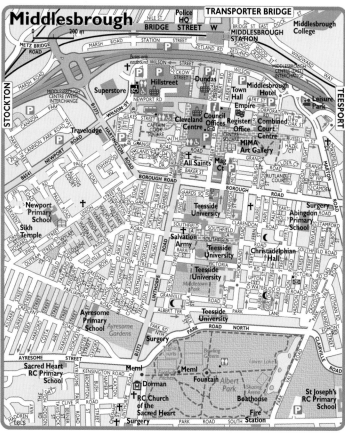

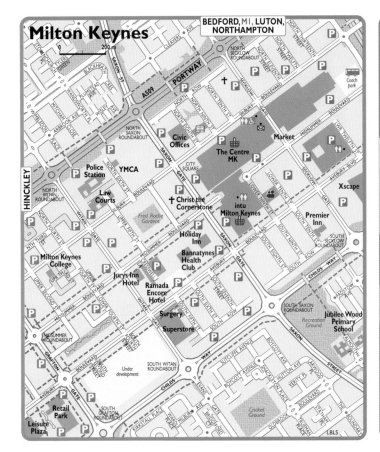

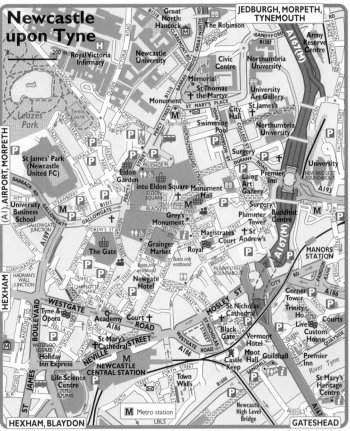

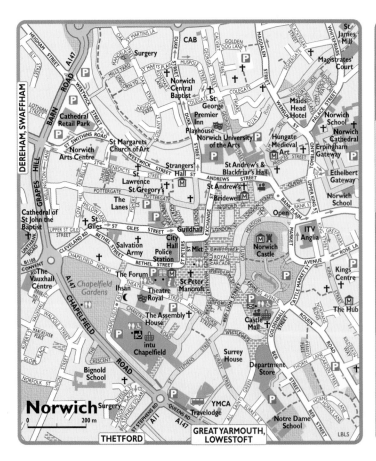

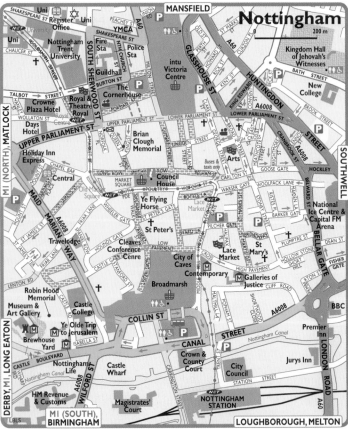

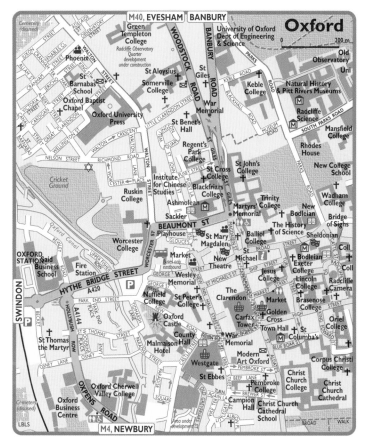

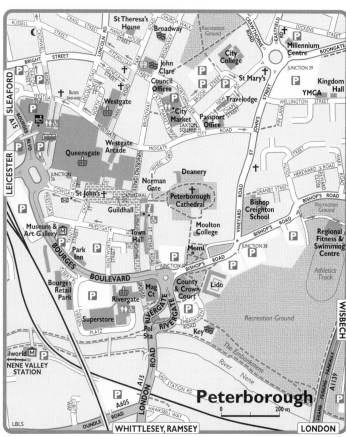

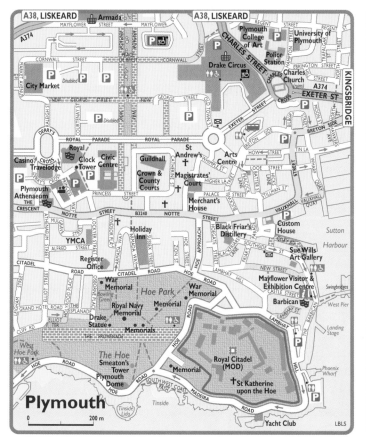

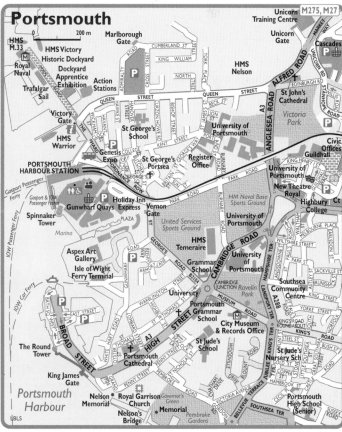

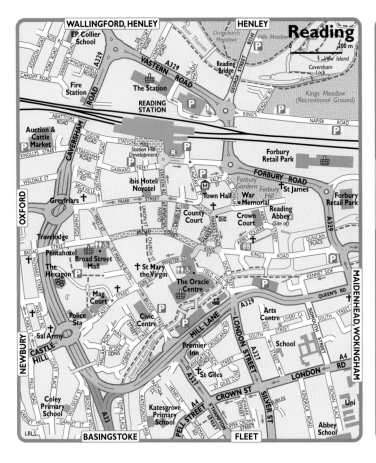

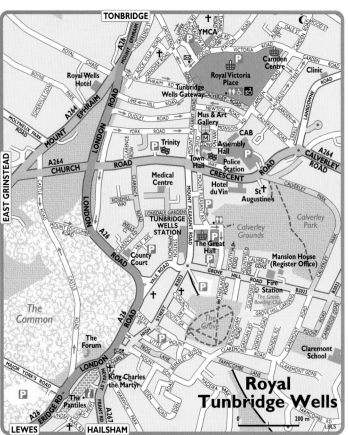

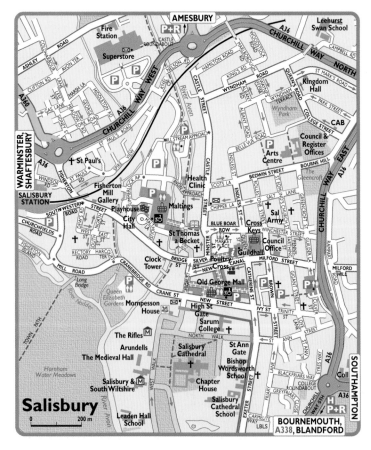

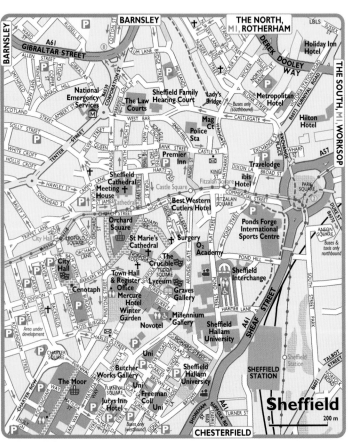

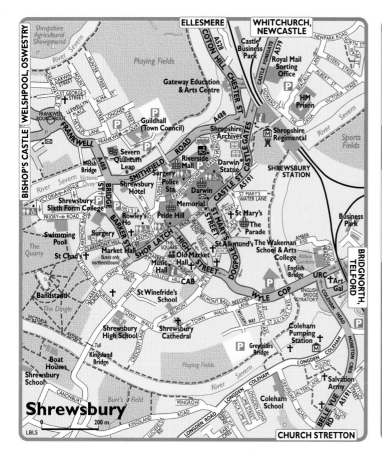

# Shrewsbury

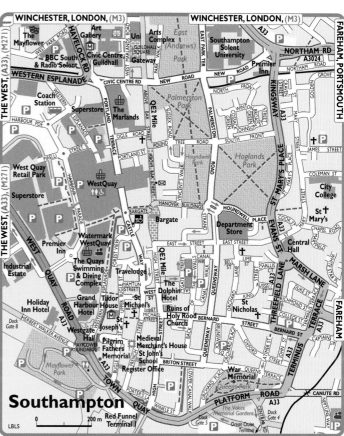

# Southampton

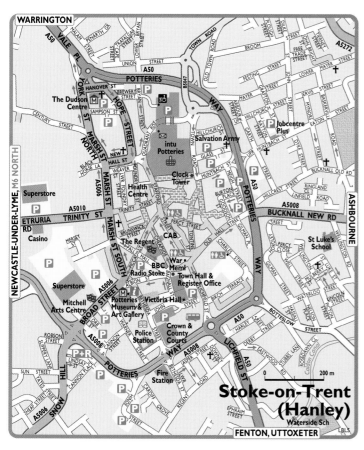

# Stoke-on-Trent (Hanley)

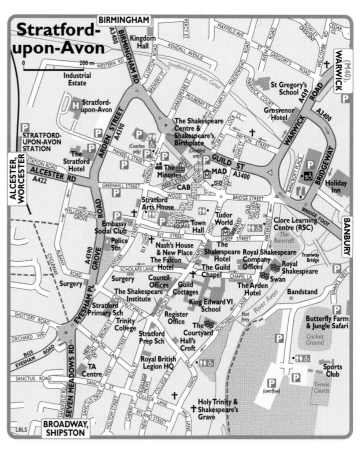

# Stratford-upon-Avon

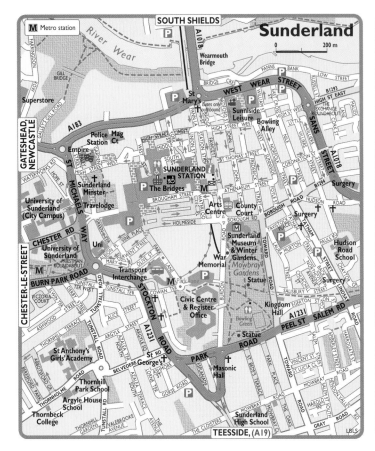

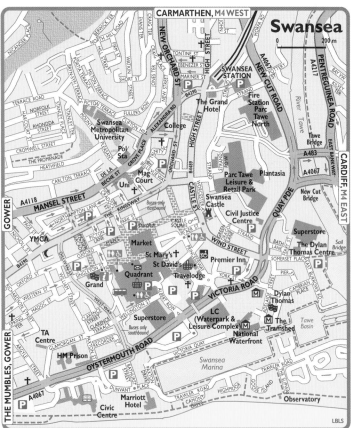

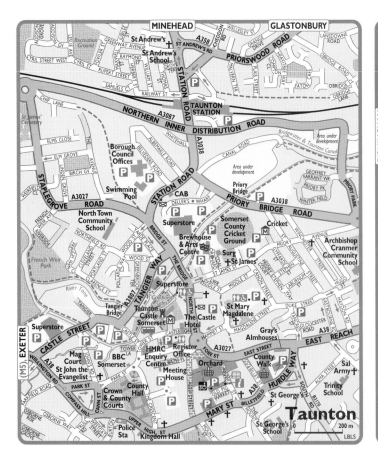

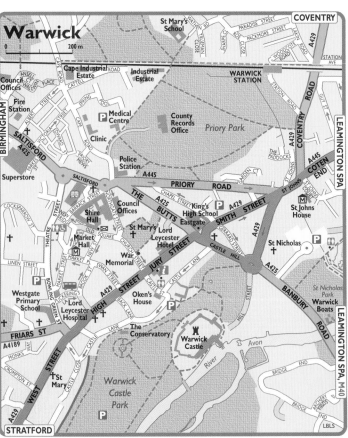

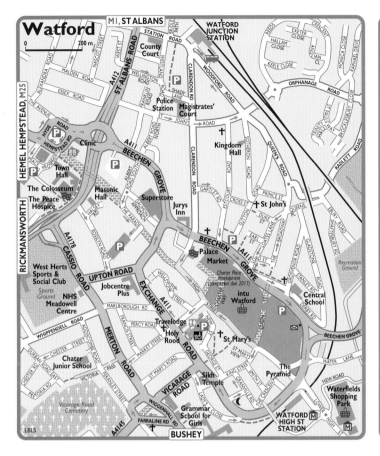

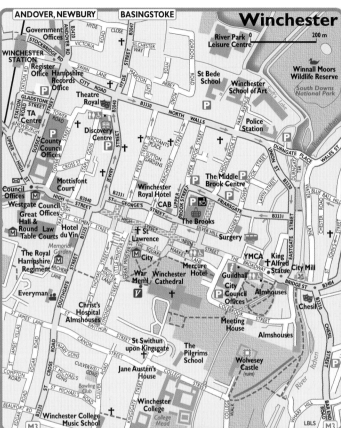

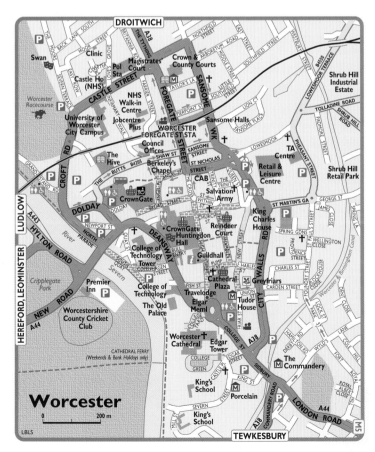

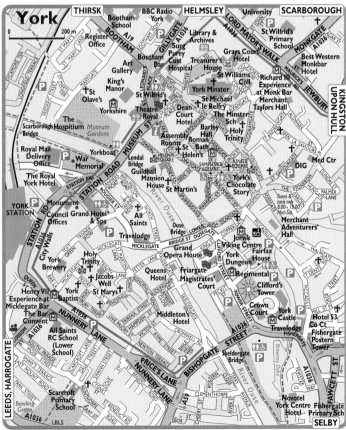

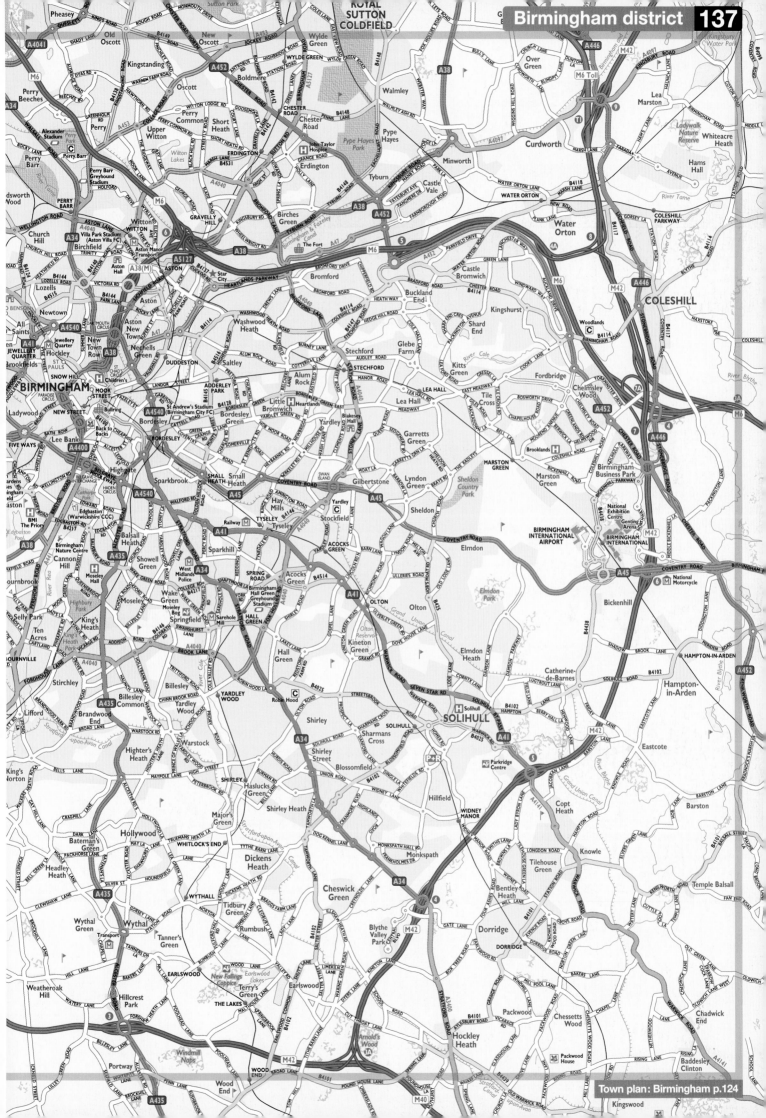

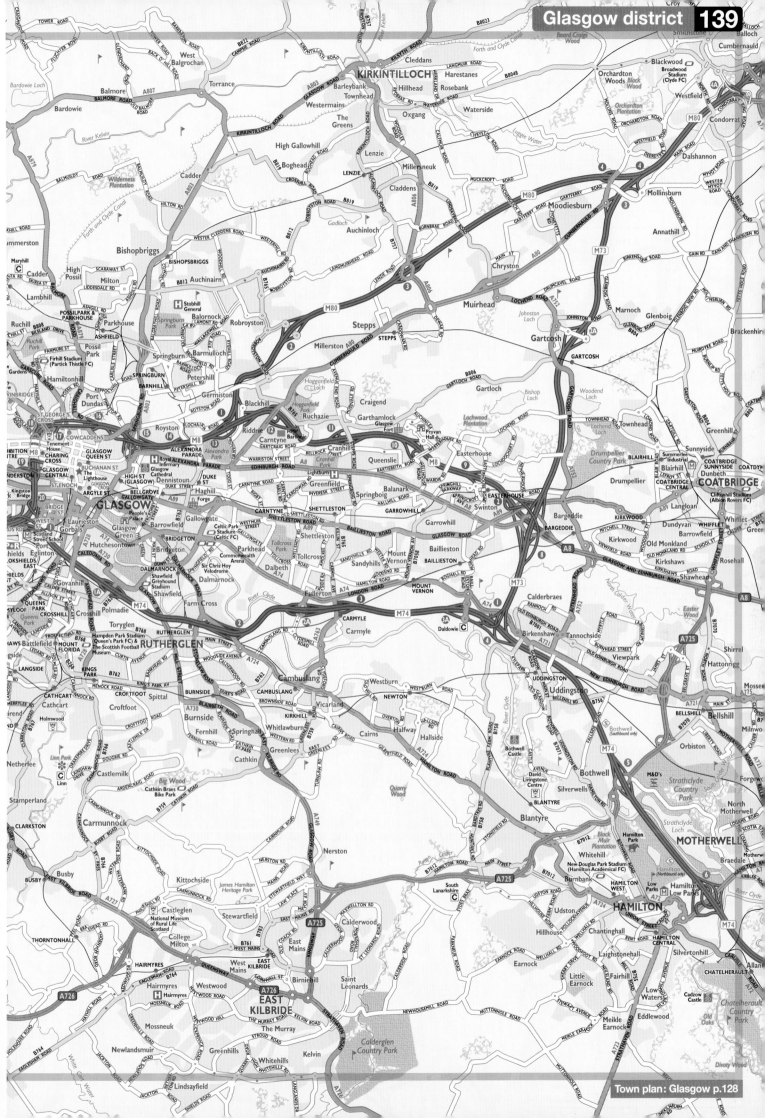

Town plan: Manchester p.129

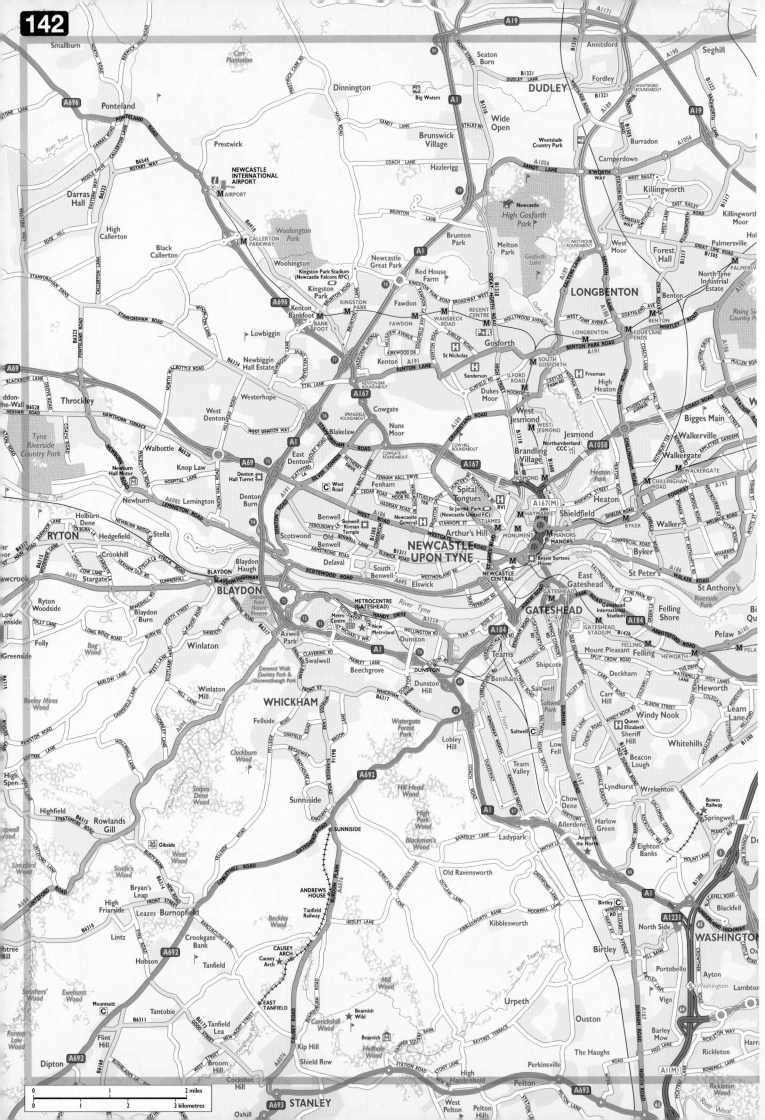

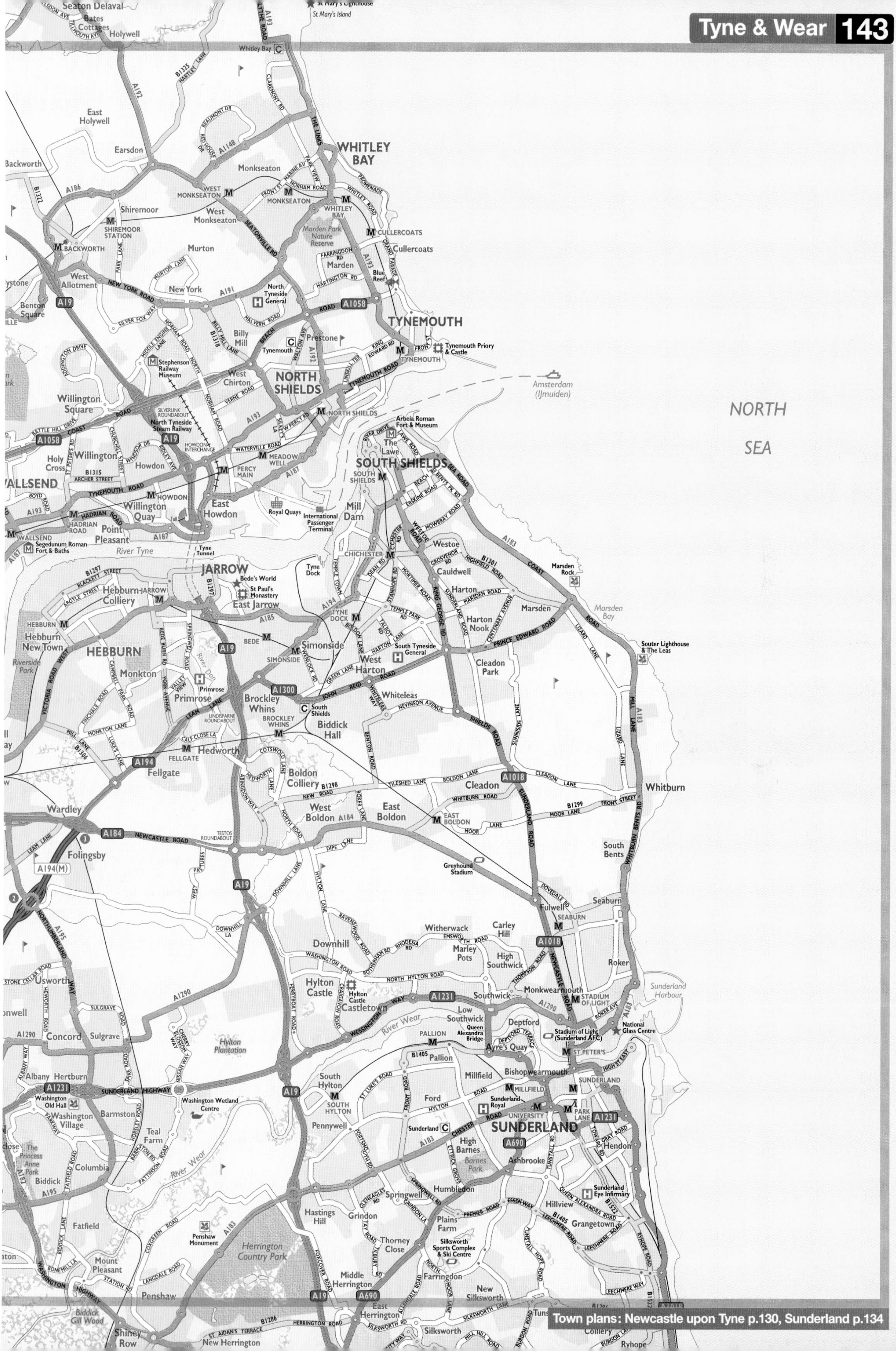

**NORTH SEA**

**WHITLEY BAY**

**TYNEMOUTH**

**NORTH SHIELDS**

**SOUTH SHIELDS**

**WALLSEND**

**JARROW**

**HEBBURN**

**SUNDERLAND**

Amsterdam (IJmuiden)

Marsden Bay

Souter Lighthouse & The Leas

Marsden Rock

Stadium of Light (Sunderland AFC)

National Glass Centre

Sunderland Harbour

St Mary's Lighthouse
St Mary's Island

Tynemouth Priory & Castle

Arbeia Roman Fort & Museum

Royal Quays

International Passenger Terminal

Tyne Tunnel

Segedunum Roman Fort & Baths

Stephenson Railway Museum

North Tyneside Steam Railway

Marden Park Nature Reserve

Blue Reef

North Tyneside General

South Tyneside General

Bede's World
St Paul's Monastery

Penshaw Monument

Herrington Country Park

Washington Wetland Centre

Washington Old Hall

Hylton Castle

Greyhound Stadium

Queen Alexandra Bridge

Sunderland Royal

Sunderland Eye Infirmary

Silksworth Sports Complex & Ski Centre

The Princess Anne Park

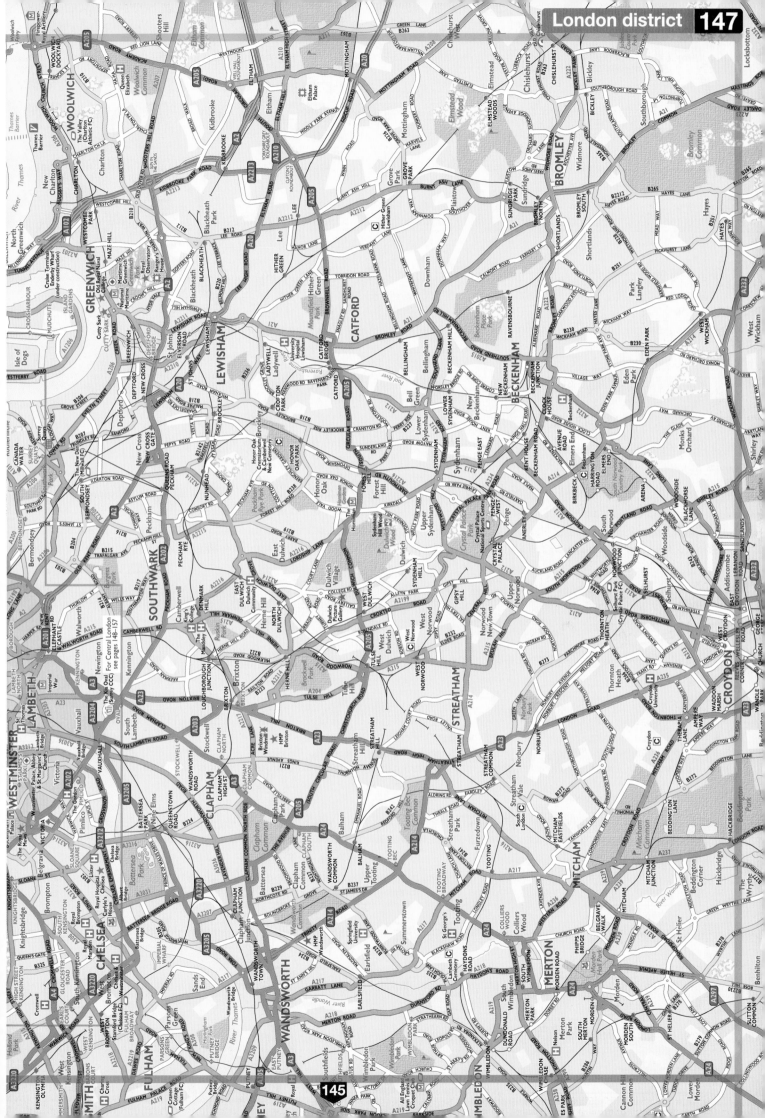

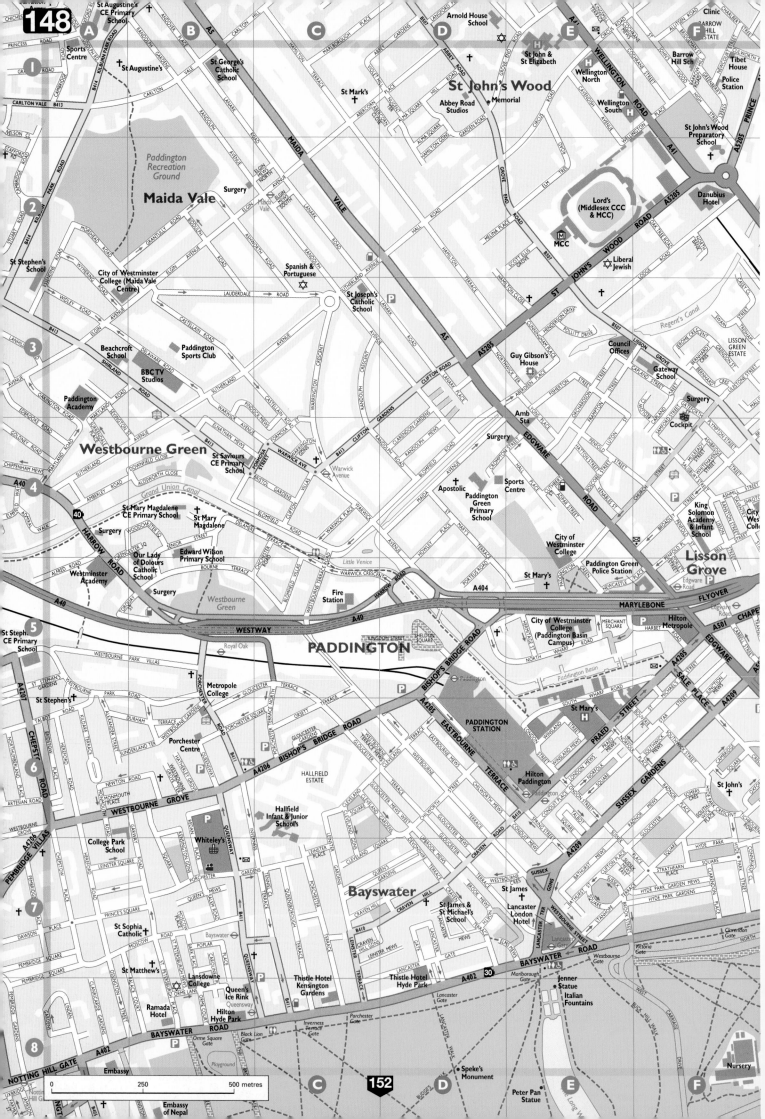

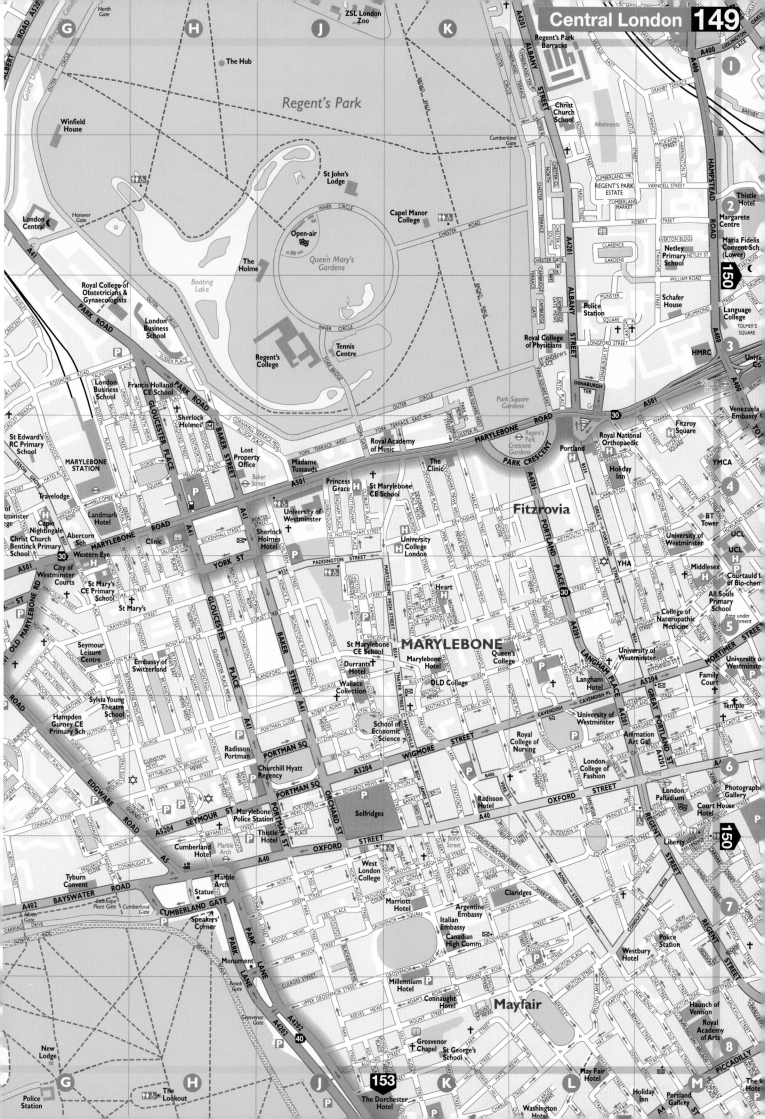

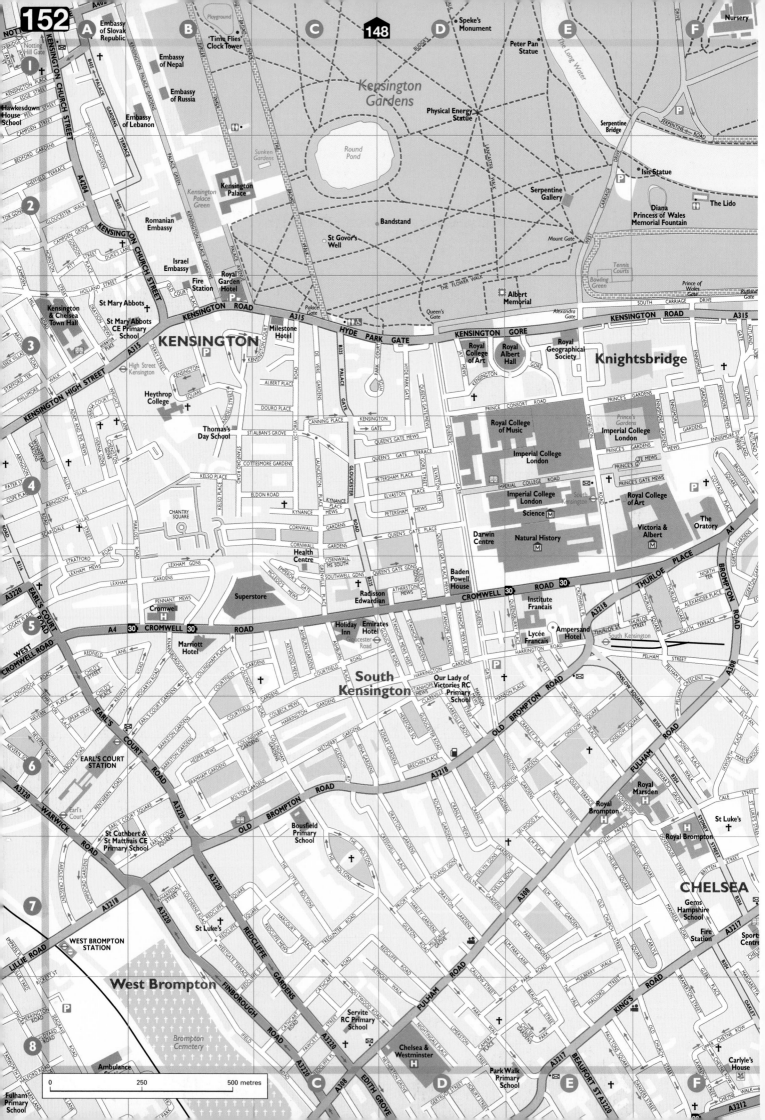

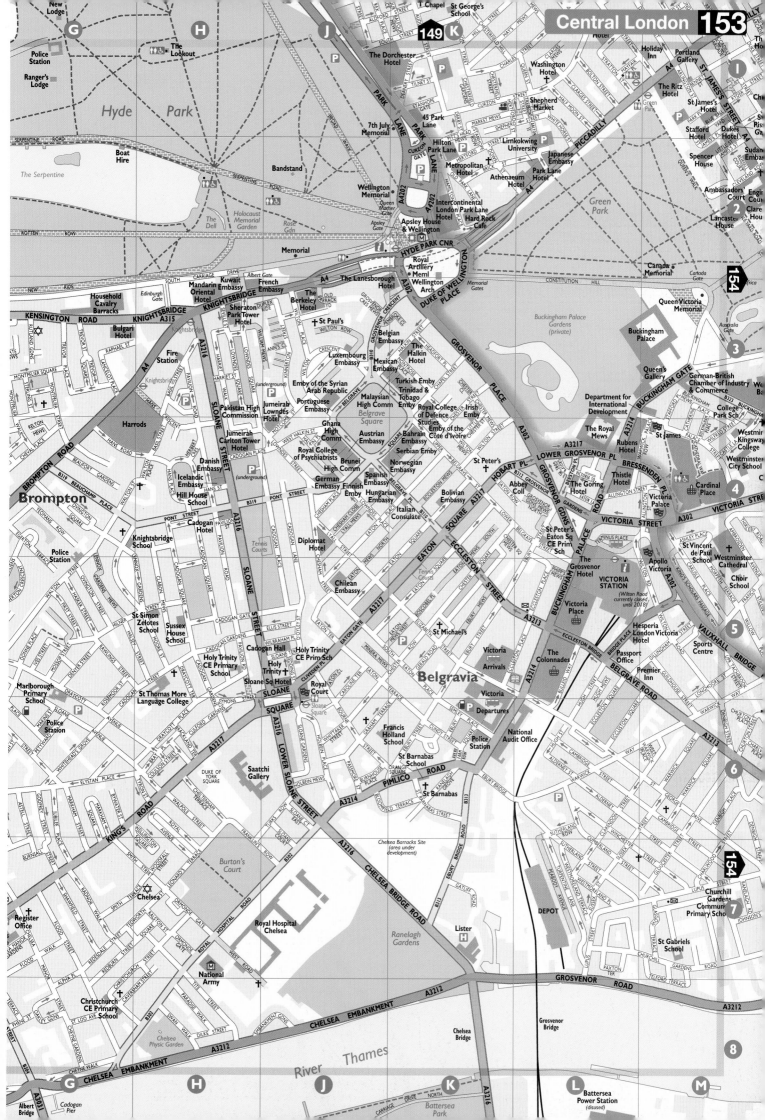

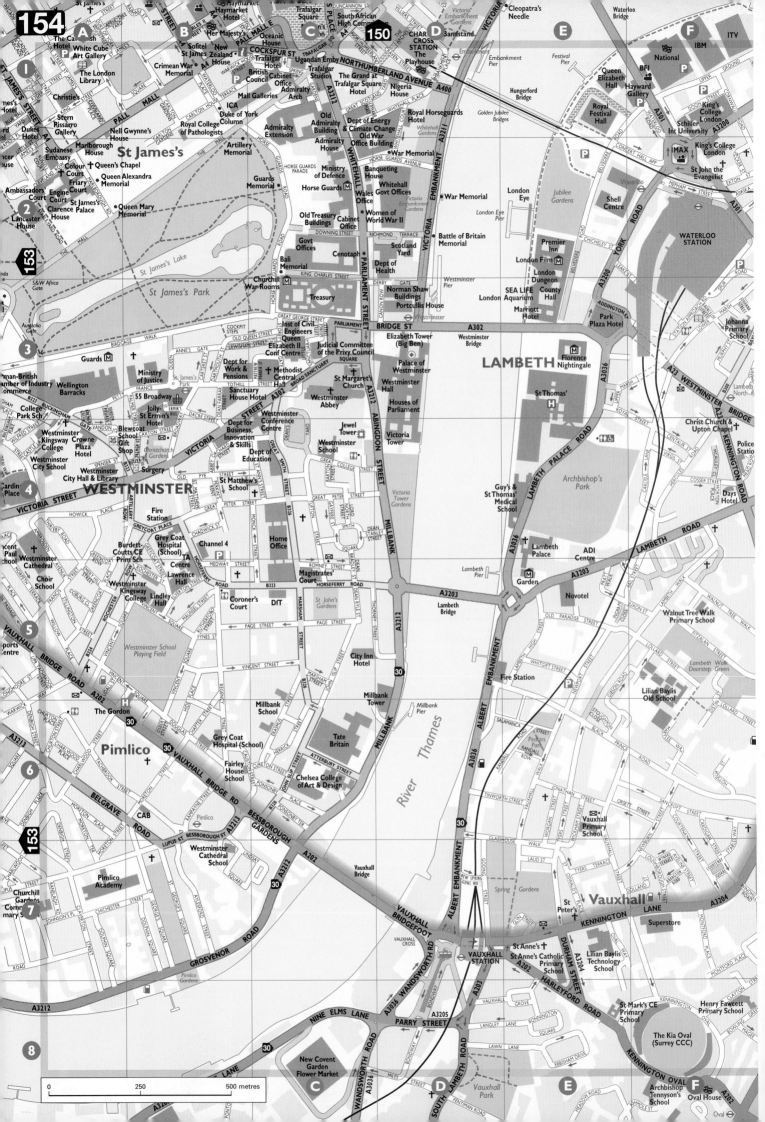

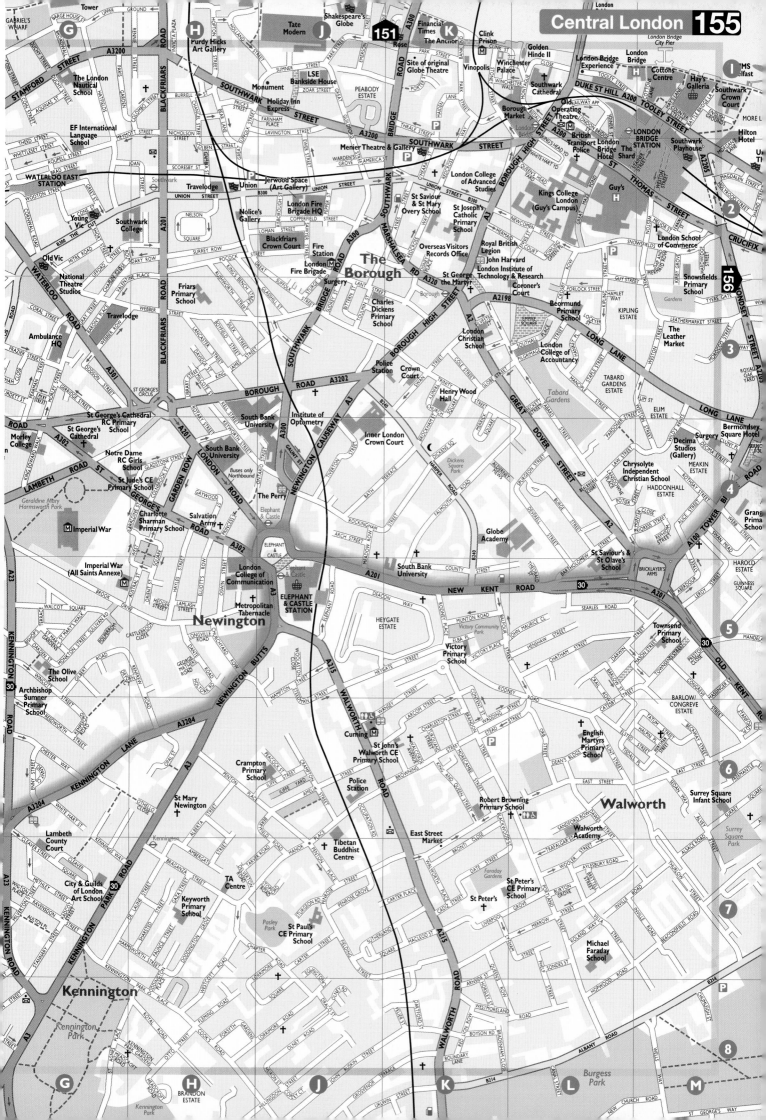

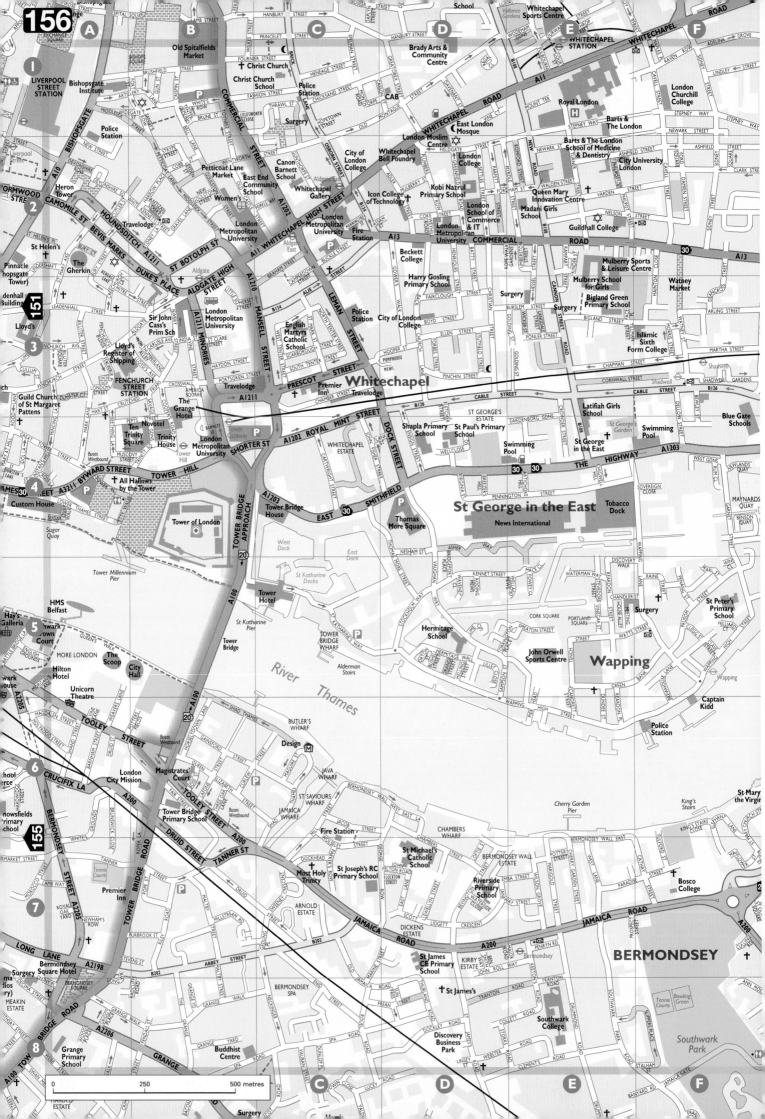

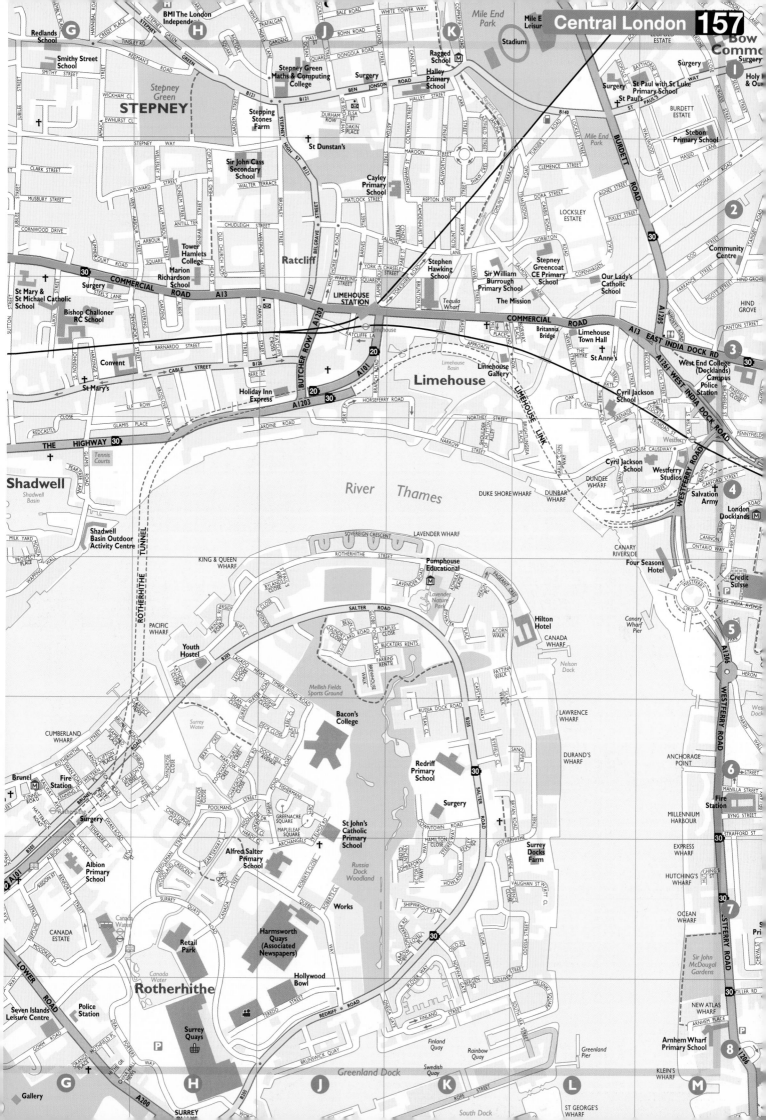

# Central London index

This index lists street and station names, and top places of tourist interest shown in **red**. Names are listed in alphabetical order and written in full, but may be abbreviated on the map. Each entry is followed by its Postcode District and then the page number and grid reference to the square in which the name is found. Names are asterisked (*) in the index where there is insufficient space to show them on the map.

### A

Abbey Gardens NW8 ......... 148 C1
Abbey Orchard Street SW1P .. 154 B4
Abbey Road NW8 ............ 148 D1
Abbey Street SE1 ........... 156 B7
Abchurch Lane EC4N ........ 151 L7
Abercorn Close NW8 ........ 148 C1
Abercorn Place NW8 ........ 148 C1
Aberdeen Street SE1 ........ 155 M5
Abingdon Road W8 .......... 152 A4
Abingdon Street SW1P ...... 154 C4
Abingdon Villas W8 ......... 152 A4
Ackroyd Drive E3 ........... 157 L1
Acorn Walk SE16 ........... 157 K5
Acton Street WC1X .......... 150 E2
Adam and Eve Mews W8 ..... 152 A3
Adam's Row W1K ........... 149 K8
Adam Street WC2N .......... 150 D8
Addle Hill EC4V ............ 151 H7
Adelina Grove E1 ........... 156 F1
Adeline Place WC1B ........ 150 B5
Adler Street E1 ............ 156 D2
Admiral Place SE16 ......... 157 K5
Admiral Walk W9 ........... 148 A4
Adpar Street W2 ........... 148 E4
Agar Street WC2N .......... 150 D8
Agdon Street EC1V ......... 151 H3
Agnes Street E14 ........... 157 L2
Ainsty Street SE16 ......... 157 G6
Air Street W1B ............. 150 A8
Alaska Street SE1 .......... 154 F2
Albany Road SE5 ........... 155 L8
Albany Street NW1 ......... 149 L1
Albemarle Street W1S ....... 149 L8
Albemarle Way EC1V ........ 151 H4
Alberta Street SE1 ......... 155 H6
Albert Bridge SW3 ......... 153 G8
Albert Embankment SE1 ..... 154 D7
Albert Gardens E1 ......... 157 H3
Albert Gate SW1X .......... 153 H2
Albert Place W8 ........... 152 C3
Albion Gate W2 ............ 149 G7
Albion Place EC1M ......... 151 H4
Albion Place SE16 ......... 157 G7
Albion Street SE16 ......... 157 G7
Albion Street W2 ........... 149 G7
Aldenham Street NW1 ....... 150 A1
Aldermanbury EC2V ........ 151 K6
Alderney Mews SE1 ......... 155 K4
Alderney Street SW1V ....... 153 L6
Aldersgate Street EC1A ...... 151 J4
Aldford Street W1K ......... 149 J8
Aldgate EC3M .............. 156 B3
Aldgate ⊖ EC3N ........... 156 B3
Aldgate East ⊖ E1 ......... 156 C2
Aldgate High Street EC3N .... 156 B3
Aldsworth Close W9 ........ 148 B4
Aldwych WC2E .............. 150 E7
Alexander Place SW7 ........ 152 F5
Alexander Street W2 ........ 148 A6
Alexandra Gate SW7 ........ 152 E3
Alfred Mews WC1E ......... 150 B4
Alfred Place WC1E ......... 150 B4
Alfred Road W2 ............ 148 A5
Alice Street SE1 ........... 156 A6
Alie Street E1 ............. 156 C3
Allen Street W8 ........... 152 A4
Allhallows Lane EC4R ....... 151 L8
Allington Street SW1E ...... 153 L4
Allitsen Road NW8 ......... 148 F1
Allsop Place NW1 .......... 149 H4
Alma Square NW8 .......... 148 D1
Alpha Place SW3 ........... 153 G8
Alsace Road SE17 .......... 155 M7
Alscot Road SE1 ........... 156 C8
Alvey Street SE17 .......... 155 M6
Ambergate Street SE17 ...... 155 H7
Amberley Road W9 ......... 148 A4
Ambrosden Avenue SW1P ..... 154 A4
Amelia Street SE17 ......... 155 J6
America Square EC3N ....... 156 B3
America Street SE1 ......... 155 J2
Ampton Street WC1X ........ 150 E2
Amwell Street EC1R ........ 150 F2
Anchorage Point E14 ....... 157 M6
Andover Place NW6 ......... 148 B1
Angel ⊖ N1 ............... 151 G1
Angel Junction N1 ......... 151 G1
Angel Lane EC4R ........... 151 L8
Angel Street EC1A ......... 151 J6
Ann Moss Way SE16 ........ 156 F8
Ann's Close SW1X .......... 153 J3
Ansdell Street W8 ......... 152 A3
Antill Terrace E1 .......... 157 H2
Antizan Street E1 ......... 156 B2
Apple Tree Yard SW1Y ...... 150 A8
Appold Street EC2A ........ 151 M4
Apsley Gate W1J ........... 153 J2
Apsley House & Wellington
    Museum W1J ........... 153 K2
Aquinas Street SE1 ......... 155 G1
Arbour Square E1 .......... 157 H2
Archangels SE16 ........... 157 J7
Archer Street W1B .......... 150 B7
Arch Street SE1 ........... 155 J4
Arden Estate N1 ........... 151 M1
Argyle Square WC1H ........ 150 D2
Argyle Street WC1H ......... 150 D2
Argyll Road W8 ............ 152 A3
Argyll Street W1F .......... 149 M6
Arlington Street SW1A ...... 153 M1
Arlington Way EC1R ......... 151 G2
Arne Street WC2H .......... 150 D6
Arnhem Place E14 .......... 157 M8
Arnold Estate SE1 ......... 156 C7
Arnside Street SE17 ........ 155 K8

Artesian Road W11 ......... 148 A6
Arthur Street EC4V ......... 151 L7
Artichoke Hill E1W ......... 156 E4
Artillery Lane E1 .......... 156 A1
Artillery Row SW1P ........ 154 B4
Arundel Street WC2R ....... 150 F7
Ashbridge Street NW8 ...... 148 F4
Ashburn Gardens SW7 ...... 152 C5
Ashburn Place SW7 ........ 152 C5
Ashby Street EC1V ......... 151 H2
Ashby Street SE1 .......... 155 L3
Ashfield Street E1 ......... 156 E2
Ashford Street N1 ......... 151 M2
Ashley Place SW1P ......... 153 M4
Ashmill Street NW1 ........ 148 F4
Ashmole Street SW8 ........ 154 F8
Ashworth Road W9 ......... 148 B2
Assam Street E1 ........... 156 C2
Assembly Place E1 ......... 157 G1
Astell Street SW3 ......... 153 G6
Astwood Mews SW7 ........ 152 C5
Atherstone Mews SW7 ...... 152 D5
Atterbury Street SW1P ...... 154 C6
Attneave Street WC1X ...... 150 F3
Augustus Street NW1 ....... 149 L1
Aulton Place SE11 ......... 155 G7
Austin Friars EC2N ......... 151 L6
Australia Gate SW1A ....... 153 M3
Austral Street SE11 ........ 155 H5
Aveline Street SE11 ........ 154 F7
Avenue Dock Hill SE16 ...... 157 J6
Avery Farm Row SW1W ...... 153 K6
Avery Row W1K ............ 149 L7
Aybrook Street W1U ........ 149 J5
Aylesbury Road SE17 ....... 155 L7
Aylesbury Street EC1R ...... 151 H4
Aylesford Street SW1V ...... 154 B7
Aylward Street E1 ......... 157 G2
Ayres Street SE1 .......... 155 K2

### B

Babmaes Street SW1Y ....... 150 B8
Bache's Street N1 ......... 151 L2
Back Church Lane E1 ....... 156 D3
Back Hill EC1R ............ 151 G4
Bacon Grove SE1 .......... 156 B8
Bainbridge Street WC1A ..... 150 C6
Bakers Mews W1U .......... 149 J6
Baker's Row EC1R ......... 151 G4
Baker Street NW1 ......... 149 H4
Baker Street W1U .......... 149 J5
Baker Street ⊖ NW1 ....... 149 H4
Balcombe Street NW1 ...... 149 G3
Balderton Street W1K ...... 149 J7
Baldwin's Gardens EC1N ..... 150 F5
Baldwin Street EC1V ....... 151 L2
Bale Road E1 ............. 157 J1
Balfe Street N1 ........... 150 D1
Balfour Mews W1K ......... 149 K8
Balfour Place W1K ......... 149 J8
Balfour Street SE17 ....... 155 K5
Baltic Street East EC1Y ..... 151 J3
Baltic Street West EC1Y ..... 151 J4
Bank ⊖ EC2R ............. 151 L6
Bank End SE1 ............. 155 K1
Bankside SE1 ............. 155 J1
Banner Street EC1Y ........ 151 K3
Banqueting House SW1A ..... 154 C2
Banyard Road SE16 ........ 156 E8
Barbara Brosnan Court
    NW8 .................. 148 D2
Barbican EC2A ............ 151 J4
Barbican Estate EC2Y ...... 151 J5
Barge House Street SE1 ..... 155 G1
Bark Place W2 ............ 148 B7
Barkston Gardens SW5 ...... 152 B6
Barley Corn Way E14 ....... 157 L4
Barlow/Congreve
    Estate SE17 ........... 155 M5
Barlow Place W1J ......... 149 L7
Barlow Street SE17 ........ 155 L5
Barnardo Street E1 ........ 157 H3
Barnby Street NW1 ........ 150 A1
Barnes Street E14 ......... 157 J2
Barnham Street SE1 ........ 156 A6
Baron's Place SE1 ......... 155 G3
Baron Street N1 .......... 151 G1
Barrett Street W1U ........ 149 K6
Barrow Hill Estate NW8 ..... 148 F1
Barrow Hill Road NW8 ...... 148 F1
Barter Street WC1A ........ 150 D5
Bartholomew Close EC1A .... 151 J5
Bartholomew Lane EC2R ..... 151 L6
Bartholomew Street SE1 ..... 155 L5
Bartlett Court EC4A ........ 151 G6
Barton Street SW1P ........ 154 C4
Basil Street SW3 .......... 153 H4
Basin Approach E14 ....... 157 K3
Basinghall Lane EC2V ...... 151 K6
Basinghall Street EC2V ...... 151 K5
Bastwick Street EC1V ....... 151 J3
Bateman's Buildings W1D .... 150 B6
Bateman Street W1D ....... 150 B6
Bath Street EC1V .......... 151 K2
Bath Terrace SE1 ......... 155 J4
Bathurst Mews W2 ........ 148 E7
Bathurst Street W2 ........ 148 E7
Battle Bridge Lane SE1 ..... 155 M1
Batty Street E1 ........... 156 D2
Bayley Street WC1B ........ 150 B5
Baylis Road SE1 .......... 154 F3
Bayswater ⊖ W2 .......... 148 B7
Bayswater Road W2 ........ 148 D7
Baythorne Street E3 ....... 157 L1
Beaconsfield Road SE17 ..... 155 M7

Beak Street W1F .......... 150 A7
Bear Gardens SE1 ......... 155 J1
Bear Lane SE1 ............ 155 H1
Beauchamp Place SW3 ...... 153 G4
Beaufort Gardens SW3 ...... 153 G4
Beaufort Street SW3 ....... 152 E8
Beaumont Place W1T ....... 150 A3
Beaumont Street W1G ...... 149 K4
Beccles Street E14 ........ 157 K4
Beckett Street SE1 ........ 155 L3
Beckway Street SE17 ....... 155 M6
Bedale Street SE1 ......... 155 L1
Bedford Avenue WC1B ...... 150 C5
Bedfordbury WC2N ........ 150 C7
Bedford Gardens W8 ....... 152 A2
Bedford Place WC1N ....... 150 D4
Bedford Row WC1R ........ 150 E4
Bedford Square WC1B ...... 150 B5
Bedford Street WC2E ...... 150 D7
Bedford Way WC1H ........ 150 C3
Bedlow Close NW8 ........ 148 F3
Beech Street EC2Y ........ 151 J4
Beeston Place SW1W ...... 153 L4
Belgrave Mews North * SW1X . 153 J3
Belgrave Mews South * SW1X . 153 J3
Belgrave Place SW1X ....... 153 J4
Belgrave Road SW1V ....... 153 L5
Belgrave Road SW1V ....... 154 A6
Belgrave Square SW1X ...... 153 J3
Belgrave Street E1 ........ 157 J2
Belgrove Street WC1H ...... 150 D2
Bell Lane E1 ............. 156 B1
Bell Street NW1 .......... 148 F4
Bell Yard WC2A ........... 150 F6
Belvedere Road SE1 ....... 154 E2
Benjamin Street EC1M ...... 151 H4
Ben Jonson Road E1 ....... 157 J1
Bennett Street SW1A ....... 153 M1
Ben Smith Way SE16 ....... 156 D7
Benson Quay E1W ......... 156 F4
Bentinck Mews W1U ....... 149 K6
Bentinck Street W1U ....... 149 K6
Bere Street E1W .......... 157 H3
Bergen Square SE16 ....... 157 K8
Berkeley Mews W1H ....... 149 H6
Berkeley Square W1J ....... 149 L8
Berkeley Street W1J ....... 149 L8
Bermondsey ⊖ ⊖ SE16 .... 156 E7
Bermondsey Spa SE16 ...... 156 C8
Bermondsey Square SE1 ..... 156 A8
Bermondsey Street SE1 ..... 156 A6
Bermondsey Wall East SE16 .. 156 E7
Bermondsey Wall
    Estate SE16 ........... 156 D7
Bermondsey Wall West SE16 .. 156 C6
Bernard Street WC1N ...... 150 D4
Berners Mews W1T ........ 150 A5
Berners Place W1F ........ 150 A6
Berners Street W1T ........ 150 A5
Bernhardt Crescent NW8 .... 148 F3
Berryfield Road SE17 ...... 155 J6
Berry Street EC1V ......... 151 H3
Berwick Street W1F ........ 150 A6
Bessborough Gardens SW1V .. 154 B6
Bessborough Street SW1V ... 154 B6
Betterton Street WC2H ..... 150 D6
Bevenden Street N1 ....... 151 L2
Bevin Close SE16 ......... 157 J5
Bevington Street SE16 ...... 156 D7
Bevin Way WC1X .......... 150 F1
Bevis Marks EC3A ......... 156 A2
Bewley Street E1 ......... 156 F3
Bickenhall Street W1U ...... 149 H4
Bidborough Street WC1H .... 150 C2
Biddulph Road W9 ........ 148 B2
Big Ben (Elizabeth
    Tower) SW1A ........... 154 D3
Bigland Street E1 ......... 156 E3
Billiter Square EC3M ...... 156 A3
Billiter Street EC3M ....... 156 A3
Bina Gardens SW5 ......... 152 C6
Bingham Place W1U ....... 149 J4
Binney Street W1K ......... 149 K7
Birchfield Street E14 ...... 157 M3
Birchin Lane EC3V ........ 151 L7
Birdcage Walk SW1H ....... 154 A3
Birde Lane EC4Y .......... 151 H6
Bird Street W1C .......... 149 K6
Birkenhead Street N1 ...... 150 D1
Bishop's Bridge Road W2 .... 148 C6
Bishopsgate EC2M ......... 156 A2
Bishops Square E1 ........ 156 B1
Bishop's Terrace SE11 ...... 155 G5
Bittern Street SE1 ......... 155 J3
Blackall Street EC2A ....... 151 M3
Blackburne's Mews W1K ..... 149 J7
Blackfriars ⇌ ⊖ EC4V ..... 151 H7
Blackfriars Bridge SE1 ..... 151 H8
Black Friars Lane EC4V ..... 151 H7
Blackfriars Road SE1 ...... 155 H3
Blackhorse Court SE1 ...... 155 L4
Black Lion Gate W2 ....... 148 B8
Black Prince Road SE1 ..... 154 E6
Blackwood Street SE17 ..... 155 K6
Blandford Street W1U ...... 149 H5
Blenheim Street W1S ....... 149 L7
Bletchley Street N1 ....... 151 K1
Blomfield Road W9 ........ 148 C4
Blomfield Street EC2M ...... 151 M5
Blomfield Villas W2 ........ 148 C5
Bloomfield Terrace SW1W ... 153 J6
Bloomsbury Square WC1A .... 150 D5
Bloomsbury Street WC1B .... 150 C5
Bloomsbury Way WC1A ...... 150 D6
Blount Street E14 ......... 157 K2
Blue Ball Yard SW1A ....... 153 M1
Bohn Road E1 ............ 157 J1
Bolsover Street W1W ...... 149 L4

Bolton Gardens SW5 ....... 152 B6
Bolton Street W1J ......... 153 L1
Bond Street ⊖ W1C ....... 149 K6
Bondway SW8 ............. 154 D8
Bonhill Street EC2A ....... 151 L4
Bonnington Square SW8 ..... 154 E8
Boot Street N1 ........... 151 M2
Borough ⊖ SE1 ........... 155 K3
Borough High Street SE1 .... 155 K3
Borough Road SE1 ........ 155 H3
Boscobel Place SW1W ...... 153 K5
Boscobel Street NW8 ...... 148 E4
Boss Street SE1 .......... 156 B6
Boston Place NW1 ........ 149 G3
Botolph Lane EC3R ........ 151 M7
Boundary Lane SE17 ....... 155 K8
Boundary Row SE1 ........ 155 G2
Bourdon Street W1K ....... 149 L7
Bourlet Close W1W ........ 149 M5
Bourne Estate EC1N ....... 150 F4
Bourne Street SW1W ....... 153 J6
Bourne Terrace W2 ........ 148 B5
Bouverie Place W2 ........ 148 F6
Bouverie Street EC4Y ...... 151 G6
Bowland Yard * SW1X ...... 153 J3
Bow Lane EC4M ........... 151 K6
Bowling Green Lane EC1R ... 151 G3
Bowling Green Place SE1 .... 155 L2
Bowling Green Street SE11 .. 154 F8
Bowling Green Walk N1 ..... 151 M2
Bowsell Street WC1N ...... 150 D4
Bow Street WC2E .......... 150 D7
Boyd Street E1 ........... 156 D3
Boyfield Street SE1 ....... 155 H3
Boyle Street W1S ......... 149 M7
Boyson Road SE17 ........ 155 K8
Brackland Terrace SW3 ..... 153 H6
Brackley Street EC1Y ...... 151 J4
Bradenham Close SE17 ..... 155 K8
Brad Street SE1 .......... 155 G2
Braganza Street SE17 ...... 155 H7
Braham Street E1 ......... 156 C3
Bramerton Street SW3 ..... 152 F7
Bramham Gardens SW5 ..... 152 B6
Branch Road E14 ......... 157 J3
Brandon Estate SE17 ...... 155 H8
Brandon Street SE17 ...... 155 K6
Brangton Road SE11 ....... 154 F7
Bray Crescent SE16 ....... 157 H6
Bray Place SW3 .......... 153 H6
Bread Street EC4M ........ 151 K7
Bream's Buildings EC4A ..... 150 F6
Brechin Place SW7 ........ 152 D6
Breezer's Hill E1W ........ 156 D4
Brendon Street W1H ....... 149 G5
Bressenden Place SW1W .... 153 L4
Brettell Street SE17 ...... 155 L7
Brewers Green SW1H ....... 154 A3
Brewer Street W1F ........ 150 A7
Brewhouse Lane E1W ...... 156 F6
Brewhouse Walk SE16 ...... 157 J5
Brick Court WC2R ......... 150 F7
Brick Lane E1 ............ 156 C1
Brick Street W1J .......... 153 K2
Bridewell Place EC4V ...... 151 H7
Bridgeman Street NW8 ..... 148 F1
Bridge Place SW1V ........ 153 L5
Bridgeport Place E1W ...... 156 D4
Bridge Street SW1A ....... 154 D3
Bridgewater Street EC2Y .... 151 J4
Bridgeway Street NW1 ...... 150 A1
Bridle Lane W1F .......... 150 A7
Bridstow Place W2 ........ 148 A6
Brightlingsea Place E14 .... 157 L4
Brill Place NW1 .......... 150 C1
Briset Street EC1M ........ 151 H4
Bristol Gardens W9 ....... 148 B4
Britannia Street WC1X ...... 150 E2
Britannia Walk N1 ........ 151 L2
Britannia Way N1 ......... 151 K1
British Museum WC1B ...... 150 C5
Britten Street SW3 ........ 152 F7
Britton Street EC1M ....... 151 H4
Broadbent Street W1K ...... 149 L7
Broadgate Circle EC2M ..... 151 M5
Broadley Street NW8 ...... 148 F4
Broadley Terrace NW1 ..... 148 F4
Broadstone Place W1U ...... 149 J5
Broad Walk NW1 .......... 149 K1
Broad Walk W2 ........... 149 H7
Broadwall SE1 ............ 155 G1
Broadway SW1H .......... 154 B4
Broadwick Street W1F ...... 150 A7
Brockham Street SE1 ...... 155 K4
Brodlove Lane E1W ....... 157 H3
Bromley Street E1 ......... 157 J2
Brompton Road SW3 ....... 153 G4
Brompton Road SW3 ....... 153 G4
Brompton Square SW3 ...... 152 F4
Bronti Close SE17 ......... 155 K6
Brook Drive SE11 ......... 155 G5
Brooke Street EC1N ....... 150 F5
Brook Gate W2 ........... 149 H8
Brook Mews North W2 ...... 148 D7
Brook's Mews W1K ........ 149 K7
Brook Street W1K ......... 149 K7
Brook Street W2 .......... 148 E7
Brown Heart Gardens W1K ... 149 K7
Browning Mews W1G ....... 149 K5
Browning Street SE17 ...... 155 K6
Brownlow Mews WC1N ...... 150 E3
Brownlow Street WC1V ...... 150 E5
Brown Street W1H ......... 149 G6
Brunel Road SE16 ......... 157 G6
Brune Street E1 .......... 156 B1
Brunswick Close SE1 ...... 156 A6

Brunswick Place N1 ....... 151 L2
Brunswick Quay SE16 ...... 157 J8
Brunswick Square WC1N .... 150 D3
Brunswick Street WC1N .... 150 D3
Brunton Place E14 ........ 157 K3
Brushfield Street E1 ....... 156 B1
Bruton Lane W1J .......... 149 L7
Bruton Place W1J ......... 149 L7
Bruton Street W1J ........ 149 L8
Bryan Road SE16 ......... 157 K6
Bryanstone Mews West W1H .. 149 G5
Bryanston Mews East W1H ... 149 H5
Bryanston Place W1H ...... 149 G5
Bryanston Square W1H ..... 149 H5
Bryanston Street W1C ...... 149 H7
Buck Hill Walk W2 ........ 148 E8
Buckingham Gate SW1E .... 153 L3
Buckingham Mews SW1E .... 153 M3
Buckingham Palace SW1A ... 153 L3
Buckingham Palace
    Road SW1W ........... 153 L5
Buckingham Place SW1E .... 153 M4
Buckland Street N1 ....... 151 L1
Buckle Street E1 ......... 156 C2
Bucknall Street WC2H ...... 150 C6
Buckters Rents SE16 ....... 157 J5
Budge's Walk W2 ......... 152 D2
Bulleid Way SW1V ......... 153 L5
Bulstrode Street W1U ...... 149 K5
Bunhill Row EC1Y ......... 151 L3
Burdett Estate E14 ........ 157 M1
Burdett Road E14 ......... 157 L2
Burdett Street SE1 ....... 155 F3
Burgess Street E14 ....... 157 M1
Burge Street SE1 ......... 155 L4
Burlington Arcade W1J ..... 149 M8
Burlington Gardens W1S .... 149 M8
Burnhouse Place SW1W ..... 153 J6
Burnsall Street SW3 ...... 153 G7
Burnside Close SE16 ...... 157 J5
Burrell Street SE1 ........ 155 H1
Burslem Street E1 ........ 156 D3
Burton Grove SE17 ....... 155 L7
Burton Street WC1H ....... 150 C3
Burwood Place W2 ........ 149 G6
Bury Close SE16 .......... 157 H5
Bury Court EC3A .......... 156 A2
Bury Place WC1A .......... 150 D5
Bury Street EC3A ......... 156 A2
Bury Street SW1Y ......... 154 A1
Bury Walk SW3 ........... 152 F6
Bushell Street E1W ....... 156 D5
Bush Lane EC4V .......... 151 L7
Butcher Row E14 ......... 157 J3
Bute Street SW7 .......... 152 E5
Butler Place SW1H ........ 154 B4
Butler's Wharf SE1 ....... 156 C6
Buttesland Street N1 ...... 151 L2
Byefield Close SE16 ....... 157 K6
Bylands Close SE16 ....... 157 J5
Byng Place WC1E ......... 150 B4
Byng Street E14 .......... 157 M6
Byward Street EC3R ....... 156 A4
Bywater Place SE16 ....... 157 K5
Bywater Street SW3 ....... 153 G6

### C

Cabbell Street NW1 ....... 148 F5
Cable Street E1 ........... 156 F3
Cadiz Street SE17 ........ 155 K7
Cadogan Gardens SW3 ..... 153 H5
Cadogan Gate SW1X ....... 153 H5
Cadogan Lane SW1X ....... 153 J4
Cadogan Place SW1X ...... 153 J4
Cadogan Square SW1X ..... 153 H5
Cadogan Street SW3 ...... 153 G6
Caledonian Road N1 ...... 150 D1
Caledonia Street N1 ...... 150 D1
Cale Street SW3 .......... 152 F6
Callow Street SW3 ........ 152 D7
Calshot Street N1 ........ 150 E1
Calthorpe Street WC1X ..... 150 E3
Cambridge Circus WC2H .... 150 C7
Cambridge Gardens NW6 ... 148 A1
Cambridge Gate NW1 ...... 149 L3
Cambridge Road NW6 ...... 148 A1
Cambridge Road NW6 ...... 148 A2
Cambridge Square W2 ...... 148 F6
Cambridge Street SW1V .... 153 L6
Cambridge Terrace NW1 .... 149 L2
Cambridge Terrace
    Mews NW1 ............ 149 L3
Camdenhurst Street E14 .... 157 K2
Camera Place SW10 ....... 152 D8
Camomile Street EC3A ..... 156 A2
Campden Grove W8 ....... 152 A2
Campden Hill Road W8 ..... 152 A2
Campden Street W8 ....... 152 A2
Camperdown Street E1 ..... 156 C3
Canada Estate SE16 ....... 157 G7
Canada Gate SW1A ....... 153 M3
Canada Street SE16 ....... 157 H7
Canada Water ⊖ ⊖ SE16 ... 157 H7
Canada Wharf SE16 ....... 157 L5
Canal Street SE5 ......... 155 L8
Canary Riverside E14 ...... 157 L4
Candle Street E1 ......... 157 K1
Canning Place W8 ........ 152 C4
Cannon Drive E14 ........ 157 M4
Cannon Street EC4N ...... 151 K7
Cannon Street ⊖ ⊖ EC4R .. 151 K7
Cannon Street Road E1 ..... 156 E3
Canon Beck Road SE16 ..... 157 G6
Canon Row SW1A ......... 154 D3
Canton Street E14 ........ 157 M3

Capeners Close * SW1X ............153 J3
Capland Street NW8 ............148 E3
Capper Street WC1E ............150 A4
Capstan Way SE16 ............157 K5
Carbis Road E14 ............157 L2
Carburton Street W1W ............149 L4
Cardigan Street SE11 ............154 F6
Cardington Street NW1 ............150 A2
Carey Street WC2A ............150 F6
Carlisle Avenue EC3N ............156 B3
Carlisle Lane SE1 ............154 F4
Carlisle Place SW1P ............153 M5
Carlisle Street W1D ............150 B6
Carlos Place W1K ............149 K7
Carlton Gardens SW1Y ............154 B2
Carlton Hill NW6 ............148 B1
Carlton House Terrace SW1Y ............154 B1
Carlton Street W1J ............153 L1
Carlton Vale NW6 ............148 A1
Carlton Vale NW6 ............148 B1
Carlyle Square SW3 ............152 F7
Carmelite Street EC4Y ............151 G7
Carnaby Street W1F ............149 M7
Caroline Place W2 ............148 B7
Caroline Street E1 ............157 H3
Caroline Terrace SW1W ............153 J5
Carpenter Street W1K ............149 K7
Carrington Street W1J ............153 L1
Carr Street E14 ............157 H1
Carteret Street SW1H ............154 B3
Carter Lane EC4V ............151 H7
Carter Place SE17 ............155 K7
Carter Street SE17 ............155 J7
Carthusian Street EC1M ............151 J4
Carting Lane WC2R ............150 D8
Cartwright Gardens WC1H ............150 C2
Cartwright Street E1 ............156 C4
Casey Close NW8 ............148 F3
Casson Street E1 ............156 C1
Castellain Road W9 ............148 B3
Castlebrook Close SE11 ............155 G5
Castle Lane SW1E ............153 M4
Catesby Street SE17 ............155 L6
Cathay Street SE16 ............156 F7
Cathcart Road SW10 ............152 C8
Cathedral Walk SW1E ............153 M4
Catherine Place SW1E ............153 M4
Catherine Street WC2E ............150 D7
Cato Street W1H ............149 G5
Causton Street SW1P ............154 B6
Cavell Street E1 ............156 F1
Cavendish Avenue NW8 ............148 E1
Cavendish Place W1G ............149 L6
Cavendish Square W1G ............149 L6
Cavendish Street N1 ............151 L1
Caversham Street SW3 ............153 G8
Caxton Street SW1H ............154 B4
Cayton Street EC1V ............151 K2
Centaur Street SE1 ............154 F4
Central Street EC1V ............151 J2
Chadwell Street EC1R ............151 G1
Chadwick Street SW1P ............154 B4
Chagford Street NW1 ............149 H4
Chalton Street NW1 ............150 B1
Chambers Street SE16 ............156 D7
Chamber Street E1 ............156 C4
Chambers Wharf SE16 ............156 D6
Chancel Street SE1 ............155 H1
Chancery Lane WC2A ............151 F5
Chancery Lane ⊖ WC1V ............150 F5
Chandos Place WC2N ............150 C8
Chandos Street W1G ............149 L5
Chantry Square W8 ............152 B4
Chapel Market N1 ............150 F1
Chapel Street NW1 ............148 F5
Chapel Street SW1X ............153 K3
Chaplin Close SE1 ............155 G3
Chapman Street E1 ............156 E3
Chapter Road SE17 ............155 H7
Chapter Street SW1P ............154 B6
Chargrove Close SE16 ............157 H6
Charing Cross ⇌ ⊖ WC2N ............154 D1
Charing Cross Road WC2H ............150 B6
Charing Cross Road WC2N ............150 C8
Charlbert Street NW8 ............148 F1
Charles II Street SW1Y ............150 B8
Charles Square N1 ............151 M2
Charles Street W1J ............153 K1
Charleston Street SE17 ............155 K6
Charlotte Road EC2A ............151 M3
Charlotte Street W1T ............150 A4
Charlwood Place SW1V ............154 A6
Charlwood Street SW1V ............153 M7
Charlwood Street SW1V ............154 A6
Charrington Street NW1 ............150 B1
Charterhouse Square EC1M ............151 H4
Charterhouse Street EC1M ............151 H5
Chart Street N1 ............151 L2
Chaseley Street E14 ............157 J2
Chatham Street SE17 ............155 L5
Cheapside EC2V ............151 K6
Chelsea Bridge SW1W ............153 K8
Chelsea Bridge Road SW1W ............153 J7
Chelsea Embankment SW3 ............153 G8
Chelsea Manor Gardens SW3 ............152 F7
Chelsea Manor Street SW3 ............153 G7
Chelsea Park Gardens SW3 ............152 E8
Chelsea Physic Garden SW3 ............153 H8
Chelsea Square SW3 ............152 F7
Cheltenham Terrace SW3 ............153 H6
Chenies Mews WC1E ............150 B4
Chenies Street WC1E ............150 B4
Cheniston Gardens W8 ............152 A4
Chepstow Place W2 ............148 A7
Chepstow Road W2 ............148 A6
Chequer Street EC1Y ............151 K3
Cherbury Street N1 ............151 L1
Cherry Garden Street SE16 ............156 E7
Chesham Close SW1X ............153 J4
Chesham Place SW1X ............153 J4
Chesham Street SW1X ............153 J4
Chester Close SW1X ............153 K3
Chester Close North NW1 ............149 L2
Chester Close South NW1 ............149 L2
Chesterfield Gardens W1J ............153 K1
Chesterfield Hill W1J ............149 K8
Chesterfield Street W1J ............153 K1
Chester Gate NW1 ............149 L2
Chester Mews SW1X ............153 K3
Chester Place NW1 ............149 L1
Chester Road NW1 ............149 L2
Chester Row SW1W ............153 K5
Chester Square SW1W ............153 K5
Chester Square Mews SW1W ............153 K4
Chester Street SW1X ............153 K4
Chester Terrace NW1 ............149 L2
Chester Way SE11 ............155 G6
Cheval Place SW7 ............153 G4
Cheval Street E14 ............157 M7
Cheyne Gardens SW3 ............153 G8
Cheyne Row SW3 ............152 F8

Cheyne Walk SW3 ............152 F8
Chicheley Street SE1 ............154 E2
Chichester Road NW6 ............148 A1
Chichester Road W2 ............148 C5
Chichester Street SW1V ............154 A7
Chicksand Street E1 ............156 C1
Chigwell Hill E1W ............156 E4
Child's Place SW5 ............152 A5
Child's Street SW5 ............152 A5
Chiltern Street W1U ............149 J4
Chilworth Mews W2 ............148 D6
Chilworth Street W2 ............148 D6
China Hall Mews SE16 ............157 G8
Chinatown W1D ............150 B7
Chippenham Mews W9 ............148 A4
Chiswell Street EC1Y ............151 K4
Chitty Street W1T ............150 A4
Christchurch Street SW3 ............153 G8
Christian Street E1 ............156 D3
Christina Street EC2A ............151 M3
Christopher Close SE16 ............157 H6
Christopher Street EC2A ............151 L4
Chudleigh Street E1 ............157 H2
Chumleigh Street SE5 ............155 M8
Churchill Gardens
    Road SW1V ............153 L7
Churchill War Rooms SW1A ............154 C3
Church Street NW8 ............148 F4
Church Way NW1 ............150 B2
Churchyard Row SE1 ............155 H5
Churton Place SW1V ............154 A6
Churton Street SW1V ............154 A6
Circus Road NW8 ............148 E1
Cirencester Square W2 ............148 A5
City Garden Row N1 ............151 J1
City Road EC1V ............151 J1
City Road EC1Y ............151 L3
City Thameslink ⇌ EC4M ............151 H6
Clabon Mews SW1X ............153 H5
Clack Street SE16 ............157 G7
Clanricarde Gardens W2 ............148 A8
Claremont Square N1 ............150 F1
Clarence Gardens NW1 ............149 L2
Clarence Mews SE16 ............157 G6
Clarendon Gardens W9 ............148 D4
Clarendon Gate W2 ............148 F7
Clarendon Place W2 ............148 F7
Clarendon Street SW1V ............153 L6
Clareville Grove SW7 ............152 D6
Clareville Street SW7 ............152 D6
Clarges Mews W1J ............153 L1
Clarges Street W1J ............153 L1
Clark Street E1 ............156 F2
Claverton Street SW1V ............154 A7
Clave Street E1W ............156 F5
Clay Street W1U ............149 H5
Clayton Street SE11 ............154 F8
Cleaver Square SE11 ............155 G7
Cleaver Street SE11 ............155 G7
Clegg Street E1W ............156 F5
Clemence Street E14 ............157 L2
Clements Lane EC4N ............151 L7
Clement's Road SE16 ............156 E8
Clenston Mews W1H ............149 H6
Clere Street EC2A ............151 L3
Clerkenwell Close EC1R ............151 G3
Clerkenwell Green EC1R ............151 G4
Clerkenwell Road EC1M ............151 G4
Cleveland Gardens W2 ............148 C6
Cleveland Mews W1T ............149 M4
Cleveland Place SW1Y ............154 A1
Cleveland Row SW1A ............154 A2
Cleveland Square W2 ............148 C6
Cleveland Street W1T ............149 M4
Cleveland Terrace W2 ............148 D6
Clifford Street W1S ............149 M7
Clifton Gardens W9 ............148 C4
Clifton Place SE16 ............157 G6
Clifton Place W2 ............148 E7
Clifton Road W9 ............148 D3
Clifton Street EC2A ............151 M3
Clifton Villas W9 ............148 C4
Clink Street SE1 ............155 K1
Clipper Close SE16 ............157 H6
Clipstone Mews W1W ............149 M4
Clipstone Street W1W ............149 L4
Cliveden Place SW1W ............153 J5
Cloak Lane EC4R ............151 K7
Cloth Fair EC1A ............151 J5
Cloth Street EC1A ............151 J5
Cluny Place SE1 ............156 A5
Cobb Street E1 ............156 B2
Cobourg Street NW1 ............150 A2
Coburg Close SW1P ............154 A5
Cochrane Mews NW8 ............148 E1
Cochrane Street NW8 ............148 E1
Cock Lane EC1A ............151 H5
Cockspur Street SW1Y ............154 C1
Codling Close * E1W ............156 D5
Coin Street SE1 ............155 G1
Colbeck Mews SW7 ............152 C6
Colebrook Row N1 ............151 H1
Coleherne Road SW10 ............152 B7
Coleman Street EC2R ............151 L6
Cole Street SE1 ............155 K3
Coley Street WC1X ............150 F3
College Hill EC4R ............151 K7
College Street EC4R ............151 K7
Collett Road SE16 ............156 D8
Collier Street N1 ............150 E1
Collingham Gardens SW5 ............152 B6
Collingham Place SW5 ............152 B5
Collingham Road SW5 ............152 B5
Colnbrook Street SE1 ............155 H4
Colombo Street SE1 ............155 H1
Colonnade WC1N ............150 D4
Coltman Street E14 ............157 K2
Commercial Road E1 ............156 D2
Commercial Road E14 ............157 K3
Commercial Street E1 ............156 B3
Compton Street EC1V ............151 H3
Concert Hall
    Approach SE1 ............154 E2
Conder Street E14 ............157 K2
Conduit Mews W2 ............148 E6
Conduit Place W2 ............148 E6
Conduit Street W1S ............149 L7
Congreve Street SE17 ............155 M5
Connaught Close W2 ............148 F7
Connaught Place W2 ............149 G7
Connaught Square W2 ............149 G6
Connaught Street W2 ............149 G6
Cons Street SE1 ............155 G2
Constitution Hill SW1A ............153 L3
Content Street SE17 ............155 K5
Conway Street W1T ............149 M4
Cookham Crescent SE16 ............157 H6
Cook's Road SE17 ............155 H8
Coombs Street N1 ............151 J1
Cooper's Lane Estate NW1 ............150 B1

Cooper's Road EC3N ............156 B3
Copenhagen Place E14 ............157 L2
Cope Place W8 ............152 A4
Copley Court SE17 ............155 J8
Copley Street E1 ............157 H2
Copperfield Road E3 ............157 K1
Copperfield Street SE1 ............155 J2
Copthall Avenue EC2R ............151 L6
Coptic Street WC1A ............150 C5
Coral Street SE1 ............155 G3
Coram Street WC1H ............150 C3
Cork Square E1W ............156 E5
Cork Street W1S ............149 M8
Cornhill EC3V ............151 L6
Cornwall Gardens SW7 ............152 C4
Cornwall Mews South SW7 ............152 C5
Cornwall Road SE1 ............155 F1
Cornwall Road SE1 ............155 G2
Cornwall Street E1 ............156 E3
Cornwall Terrace
    Mews NW1 ............149 H4
Cornwood Drive E1 ............157 G2
Coronet Street N1 ............151 M2
Corporation Row EC1R ............151 G3
Corsham Street N1 ............151 L2
Cosser Street SE1 ............154 F4
Cosway Street NW1 ............149 G4
Cottage Place SW3 ............152 F4
Cottesmore Gardens W8 ............152 B4
Cottons Lane SE1 ............155 M1
Coulson Street SW3 ............153 H6
Counter Street SE1 ............155 M1
County Street SE1 ............155 K5
Courtenay Square SE11 ............154 F7
Courtenay Street SE11 ............154 F6
Courtfield Gardens SW5 ............152 B5
Courtfield Road SW7 ............152 C5
Court Street E1 ............156 F1
Cousin Lane SE1 ............151 K8
Covent Garden ⊖ WC2E ............150 D7
Covent Garden WC2E ............150 D7
Coventry Street W1D ............150 B8
Cowcross Street EC1M ............151 H4
Cowper Street EC2A ............151 L3
Crail Row SE17 ............155 L5
Cramer Street W1U ............149 J5
Crampton Street SE17 ............155 J6
Cranbourn Street WC2H ............150 C7
Cranleigh Street NW1 ............150 A1
Cranley Gardens SW7 ............152 D6
Cranley Mews SW7 ............152 D6
Cranley Place SW7 ............152 E6
Cranston Estate N1 ............151 L1
Cranwood Street EC1V ............151 L2
Craven Hill W2 ............148 D7
Craven Hill W2 ............148 D7
Craven Hill Gardens W2 ............148 C6
Craven Road W2 ............148 D7
Craven Street WC2N ............154 D1
Craven Terrace W2 ............148 D7
Crawford Passage EC1R ............151 G3
Crawford Place W1H ............149 G5
Crawford Street W1H ............149 G5
Creechurch Lane EC3A ............156 A3
Creed Lane EC4V ............151 H7
Cresswell Place SW10 ............152 D6
Cressy Place E1 ............157 G1
Crestfield Street WC1H ............150 D2
Crimscott Street SE1 ............156 B4
Crispin Street E1 ............156 B1
Cromer Street WC1H ............150 D2
Crompton Street W2 ............148 D4
Cromwell Place SW7 ............152 E5
Cromwell Road SW5 ............152 B5
Cromwell Road SW7 ............152 E5
Crondall Court N1 ............151 M1
Crondall Street N1 ............151 L1
Cropley Street N1 ............151 K1
Crosby Row SE1 ............155 L3
Cross Lane EC3R ............156 A4
Crosswall EC3N ............156 B3
Crowder Street E1 ............156 E3
Crucifix Lane SE1 ............156 A6
Cruikshank Street WC1X ............150 F1
Crutched Friars EC3N ............156 A3
Cuba Street E14 ............157 M6
Cubitt Street WC1X ............150 E2
Culford Gardens SW3 ............153 H6
Culling Road SE16 ............156 F7
Cullum Street EC3M ............151 M7
Culross Street W1K ............149 J8
Culworth Street NW8 ............148 F1
Cumberland Gardens WC1X ............150 F2
Cumberland Gate W2 ............149 H7
Cumberland Market NW1 ............149 L2
Cumberland Street SW1V ............153 L6
Cumberland Terrace NW1 ............149 K1
Cumberland Terrace
    Mews NW1 ............149 L1
Cumberland Wharf SE16 ............157 G6
Cumming Street N1 ............150 E1
Cundy Street SW1W ............153 K6
Cunningham Place NW8 ............148 E3
Cureton Street SW1P ............154 C6
Curlew Street SE1 ............156 B6
Cursitor Street EC4A ............150 F6
Curtain Road EC2A ............151 M3
Curtain Road EC2A ............151 M4
Curzon Gate W2 ............153 K2
Curzon Street W1J ............153 K1
Cuthbert Street W2 ............148 E4
Cutler Street EC3A ............156 A2
Cynthia Street N1 ............150 F1
Cypress Place W1T ............150 A4
Cyrus Street EC1V ............151 H3

### D

Dacre Street SW1H ............154 B3
Dakin Place E1 ............157 J1
Dallington Street EC1V ............151 H3
Damien Street E1 ............156 F2
Dane Street WC1R ............150 E5
Dansey Place W1D ............150 B7
Dante Road SE11 ............155 H5
Danvers Street SW3 ............152 F8
D'Arblay Street W1F ............150 A6
Dartford Street SE17 ............155 K8
Dartmouth Street SW1H ............154 B3
Darwin Street SE17 ............155 L5
Date Street SE17 ............155 K7
Davenant Street E1 ............156 D1
Daventry Street NW1 ............148 F4
Davidge Street SE1 ............155 H3
Davies Mews W1K ............149 K7
Davies Street W1K ............149 K7
Dawes Street SE17 ............155 L6
Dawson Place W2 ............148 A7

Deacon Way SE17 ............155 J5
Deal Porters Way SE16 ............157 G8
Dean Bradley Street SW1P ............154 C4
Dean Street E1 ............156 D1
Deancross Street E1 ............156 F3
Deanery Street W1K ............153 K1
Dean Farrar Street SW1H ............154 B3
Dean Ryle Street SW1P ............154 C5
Dean's Buildings SE17 ............155 L5
Dean Stanley Street SW1P ............154 C4
Dean's Yard SW1P ............154 C4
Decima Street SE1 ............155 M4
Deck Close SE16 ............157 J6
Defoe Close SE16 ............157 K7
Delamere Terrace W2 ............148 B4
De Laune Street SE17 ............155 H7
Delaware Road W9 ............148 B3
Dellow Street E1 ............156 E3
Delverton Road SE17 ............155 H7
Denbigh Place SW1V ............153 M6
Denman Street W1D ............150 B7
Denmark Street WC2H ............150 C6
Denny Close SE11 ............155 G6
Denyer Street SW3 ............153 G5
Derby Gate SW1A ............154 D3
Derby Street W1J ............153 K1
Derry Street W1S ............149 L6
Derry Street W8 ............152 B3
De Vere Gardens W8 ............152 C3
Deverell Street SE1 ............155 L4
Devonport Street E1 ............157 G3
Devonshire Close W1G ............149 K4
Devonshire Mews
    South W1G ............149 K4
Devonshire Mews
    West W1G ............149 K4
Devonshire Place W1G ............149 K4
Devonshire Place
    Mews W1G ............149 K4
Devonshire Row EC2M ............156 A2
Devonshire Square EC2M ............156 A2
Devonshire Terrace W2 ............148 D7
De Walden Street W1G ............149 K5
Dickens Estate SE16 ............156 D7
Dickens Square SE1 ............155 K4
Dilke Street SW3 ............153 H8
Dingley Place EC1V ............151 K2
Dingley Road EC1V ............151 J2
Discovery Walk E1W ............156 E5
Disney Place SE1 ............155 K2
Distaff Lane EC4V ............151 J7
Distin Street SE11 ............154 F6
Dockhead SE1 ............156 C7
Dockley Road SE16 ............156 D8
Dock Street E1 ............156 D4
Doddington Grove SE17 ............155 H7
Doddington Place SE17 ............155 H8
Dodson Street SE1 ............155 G3
Dod Street E14 ............157 M2
Dolben Street SE1 ............155 H2
Dolland Street SE11 ............154 E7
Dolphin Square SW1V ............154 A7
Dolphin Square SW1V ............154 B7
Dombey Street WC1N ............150 E4
Dominion Street EC2A ............151 L5
Donegal Street N1 ............150 F1
Dongola Road E1 ............157 J1
Donne Place SW3 ............153 G5
Doon Street SE1 ............154 F1
Dora Street E14 ............157 L2
Doric Way NW1 ............150 B2
Dorset Rise EC4Y ............151 G7
Dorset Square NW1 ............149 H4
Dorset Street W1U ............149 H5
Doughty Mews WC1N ............150 E3
Doughty Street WC1N ............150 E3
Douglas Street SW1P ............154 B6
Douro Place W8 ............152 C3
Douthwaite Square * E1W ............156 D5
Dovehouse Street SW3 ............152 E6
Dover Street W1J ............153 L1
Dover Street W1S ............149 L8
Dowgate Hill EC4R ............151 K7
Downfield Close W9 ............148 B4
Downing Street SW1A ............154 C2
Down Street W1J ............153 K2
Downtown Road SE16 ............157 K6
D'Oyley Street SW1X ............153 J5
Draco Street SE17 ............155 J8
Drake Close SE16 ............157 H6
Draycott Avenue SW3 ............153 G5
Draycott Place SW3 ............153 H6
Draycott Terrace SW3 ............153 H5
Drayson Mews W8 ............152 A3
Drayton Gardens SW10 ............152 D6
Druid Street SE1 ............156 A6
Druid Street SE1 ............156 B6
Drummond Crescent NW1 ............150 B2
Drummond Road SE16 ............156 E8
Drummond Street NW1 ............150 A3
Drury Lane WC2B ............150 D6
Dryden Court SE11 ............155 G5
Dryden Street WC2B ............150 D6
Duchess Mews W1G ............149 L5
Duchess Street W1B ............149 L5
Duchy Street SE1 ............155 G1
Duckett Street E1 ............157 J1
Duck Lane W1F ............150 B6
Dufferin Street EC1Y ............151 K4
Duke of Wellington
    Place SW1W ............153 K3
Duke of York Square SW3 ............153 H6
Duke of York Street SW1Y ............150 A8
Duke Shore Wharf E14 ............157 K4
Duke's Lane W8 ............152 A2
Duke's Place EC3A ............156 B2
Duke's Road WC1H ............150 C2
Duke Street W1K ............149 K7
Duke Street W1U ............149 J6
Duke Street
    St James's SW1Y ............154 A1
Dunbar Wharf E14 ............157 L4
Duncannon Street WC2N ............150 C8
Duncan Terrace N1 ............151 H1
Dundee Street E1W ............156 F5
Dundee Wharf E14 ............157 L4
Dunelm Street E1 ............157 H2
Dunraven Street W1K ............149 H7
Dunster Court EC3R ............156 A3
Duplex Ride SW1X ............153 H3
Durand's Wharf SE16 ............157 L6
Durham Row E1 ............157 J1
Durham Street SE11 ............154 E7
Durham Terrace W2 ............148 A6
Dyott Street WC1A ............150 C6
Dysart Street EC2A ............151 M4

### E

Eagle Close EC1M ............151 H4
Eagle Street WC1R ............150 E5
Eardley Crescent SW5 ............152 A7
Earlham Street WC2H ............150 C7
Earl's Court ⇌ ⊖ SW5 ............152 A6
Earl's Court Gardens SW5 ............152 B6
Earl's Court Road SW5 ............152 A6
Earl's Court Square SW5 ............152 A6
Earlstoke Street EC1V ............151 H2
Earl Street EC2A ............151 M4
Earnshaw Street WC2H ............150 C6
East Arbour Street E1 ............157 H2
Eastbourne Mews W2 ............148 D6
Eastbourne Terrace W2 ............148 D6
Eastcastle Street W1W ............150 A6
Eastcheap EC3M ............151 M7
Eastfield Street E14 ............157 K1
East India Dock Road E14 ............157 M3
East Lane SE16 ............156 D6
Easton Street WC1X ............150 F3
East Poultry Avenue EC1A ............151 H5
East Road N1 ............151 L2
East Smithfield E1W ............156 C4
East Street SE17 ............155 L6
Eaton Close SW1W ............153 J5
Eaton Gate SW1W ............153 J5
Eaton Lane SW1W ............153 L4
Eaton Mews North SW1W ............153 J5
Eaton Mews South SW1W ............153 K5
Eaton Mews West SW1W ............153 K5
Eaton Place SW1X ............153 J4
Eaton Row SW1W ............153 K4
Eaton Square SW1W ............153 K5
Eaton Terrace SW1W ............153 J5
Ebbisham Drive SW8 ............154 E8
Ebury Bridge SW1W ............153 K6
Ebury Bridge Road SW1W ............153 K6
Ebury Mews SW1W ............153 K5
Ebury Square SW1W ............153 K5
Ebury Street SW1W ............153 K5
Eccleston Bridge SW1W ............153 L5
Eccleston Mews SW1X ............153 K4
Eccleston Place SW1W ............153 L5
Eccleston Square SW1V ............153 L5
Eccleston Street SW1X ............153 K4
Edbrooke Road W9 ............148 A3
Edge Street W8 ............152 A1
Edgware Road W2 ............148 F5
Edgware Road ⊖ NW1 ............148 F5
Edinburgh Gate SW1X ............153 H3
Edith Grove SW10 ............152 C8
Edwards Mews W1H ............149 J6
Egerton Crescent SW3 ............152 F5
Egerton Gardens SW3 ............152 F5
Egerton Terrace SW3 ............153 G4
Eglington Court SE17 ............155 J7
Elba Place SE17 ............155 K5
Eldon Place EC2M ............151 L5
Eldon Road W8 ............152 B4
Eleanor Close SE16 ............157 H6
Elephant & Castle SE1 ............155 J4
Elephant & Castle ⇌ ⊖ SE1 ............155 J5
Elephant Lane SE16 ............156 F6
Elephant Road SE17 ............155 J5
Elf Row E1W ............157 G3
Elgar Street SE16 ............157 K7
Elgin Avenue W9 ............148 B2
Elgin Mews North W9 ............148 C2
Elgin Mews South W9 ............148 C2
Elia Mews N1 ............151 H1
Elia Street N1 ............151 H1
Elim Estate SE1 ............155 M3
Elim Street SE1 ............155 M3
Elizabeth Street SW1W ............153 K5
Ellen Street E1 ............156 D3
Elliott's Row SE11 ............155 H5
Ellis Street SW1X ............153 J5
Elmfield Way W9 ............148 A4
Elm Park Gardens SW10 ............152 E7
Elm Park Lane SW3 ............152 E7
Elm Park Road SW3 ............152 E8
Elm Place SW7 ............152 E7
Elms Mews W2 ............148 D7
Elm Street WC1X ............150 F4
Elm Tree Road NW8 ............148 E2
Elnathan Mews W9 ............148 B4
Elsa Street E1 ............157 J1
Elsted Street SE17 ............155 L6
Elvaston Mews SW7 ............152 D4
Elvaston Place SW7 ............152 D4
Elverton Street SW1P ............154 B5
Ely Place EC1N ............151 G5
Elystan Place SW3 ............153 G6
Elystan Street SW3 ............152 F6
Embankment ⊖ WC2N ............154 D1
Embankment Gardens SW3 ............153 H8
Embankment Place WC2N ............154 D1
Emba Street SE16 ............156 D7
Emerald Street WC1N ............150 E4
Emerson Street SE1 ............155 J1
Emery Hill Street SW1P ............154 A5
Emery Street SE1 ............155 G3
Emperor's Gate SW7 ............152 C5
Empire Square SE1 ............155 L3
Empress Place SW6 ............152 A7
Endell Street WC2H ............150 C6
Endsleigh Gardens WC1H ............150 B3
Endsleigh Place WC1H ............150 B3
Endsleigh Street WC1H ............150 B3
Enford Street W1H ............149 G5
English Grounds SE1 ............155 M1
Enid Street SE16 ............156 C8
Ennismore Gardens SW7 ............152 F3
Ennismore Gardens
    Mews SW7 ............152 F3
Ennismore Mews SW7 ............152 F3
Ennismore Street SW7 ............152 F4
Enny Street SE11 ............155 G6
Ensign Street E1 ............156 D4
Epworth Street EC2A ............151 L3
Erasmus Street SW1P ............154 C6
Errol Street EC1Y ............151 K4
Essendine Road W9 ............148 A3
Essex Street WC2R ............150 F7
Essex Villas W8 ............152 A3
Europa Place EC1V ............151 J2
Euston ⇌ ⊖ NW1 ............150 B2
Euston Road NW1 ............150 B3
Euston Square NW1 ............150 A3
Euston Square ⊖ NW1 ............150 A3
Euston Street NW1 ............150 A3
Evelyn Gardens SW7 ............152 D7
Evelyn Way N1 ............151 L1
Eversholt Street NW1 ............150 A1
Everton Buildings NW1 ............149 M2
Ewer Street SE1 ............155 J2
Ewhurst Close E1 ............157 G1
Exchange Square EC2A ............151 M4

Exeter Street WC2E ............ 150 D7
Exhibition Road SW7 ......... 152 E3
Exmouth Market EC1R ....... 151 G3
Exon Street SE17 ............... 155 M6
Exton Street SE1 ............... 154 F2
Eyre Street Hill EC1R ......... 150 F4

**F**

Fairclough Street E1 .......... 156 D3
Fair Street SE1 .................. 156 B6
Falmouth Road SE1 ........... 155 K4
Fann Street EC1M .............. 151 J4
Fanshaw Street N1 ............ 151 M1
Fareham Street W1D .......... 150 B6
Farmer Street W8 .............. 152 A1
Farm Lane SW6 .................. 152 A8
Farm Street W1K ............... 149 K8
Farnham Place SE1 ............ 155 J1
Farrance Street E14 ........... 157 M3
Farringdon ⇌ EC1M .......... 151 G4
Farringdon Lane EC1R ....... 151 G4
Farringdon Road EC1R ....... 150 F3
Farringdon Street EC1M ..... 151 H5
Farrins Rents SE16 ............ 157 J5
Farrow Place SE16 ............. 157 K7
Farthing Fields * E1W ........ 156 F5
Fashion Street E1 .............. 156 B1
Faunce Street SE17 ........... 155 H7
Fawcett Street SW10 ......... 152 C8
Featherstone Street EC1Y ... 151 L3
Fenchurch Avenue EC3M .... 156 A3
Fenchurch Buildings EC3M .. 156 A3
Fenchurch Place EC3M ....... 156 A3
Fenchurch Street EC3M ...... 156 A3
Fenchurch Street ⇌ EC3M .. 156 A3
Fendall Street SE1 ............. 156 B8
Fenning Street SE1 ............ 155 M2
Fentiman Road SW8 .......... 154 D8
Fernsbury Street WC1X ...... 150 F2
Fetter Lane EC4A ............... 151 G6
Fieldgate Street E1 ............ 156 D2
Fielding Street SE17 .......... 155 J7
Field Street WC1X .............. 150 E1
Finborough Road SW10 ...... 152 B8
Finch Lane EC3V ............... 151 L6
Finland Street SE16 ........... 157 K8
Finsbury Circus EC2M ........ 151 L5
Finsbury Estate EC1R ......... 151 G3
Finsbury Market EC2A ........ 151 M4
Finsbury Square EC2A ........ 151 L4
Finsbury Street EC2Y ......... 151 L4
First Street SW3 ................ 153 G5
Fishermans Drive SE16 ....... 157 J6
Fisher Street WC1R ............ 150 D5
Fisherton Street NW8 ........ 148 E3
Fish Street Hill EC3R .......... 151 L7
Fitzalan Street SE11 ........... 154 F5
Fitzhardinge Street W1H ..... 149 J6
Fitzroy Square W1T ............ 149 M4
Fitzroy Street W1T ............. 149 M4
Flamborough Street E14 ..... 157 J3
Flank Street E1 .................. 156 C4
Flaxman Terrace WC1H ....... 150 C3
Fleet Street EC4A ............... 151 G6
Fleming Road SE17 ............ 155 H8
Fletcher Street E1 .............. 156 D3
Flint Street SE17 ............... 155 L6
Flitcroft Street WC2H ......... 150 C6
Flockton Street SE16 .......... 156 D7
Flood Street SW3 ............... 153 G7
Flood Walk SW3 ................. 153 G7
Floral Street WC2E ............. 150 D7
Foley Street W1W .............. 149 M5
Forbes Street E1 ................ 156 D3
Fordham Street E1 ............. 156 D2
Ford Square E1 .................. 156 F2
Fore Street EC2Y ............... 151 K5
Formosa Street W9 ............ 148 C4
Forset Street W1H ............. 149 G6
Forsyth Gardens SE17 ........ 155 H8
Fort Street E1 ................... 156 B1
Fortune Street EC1Y .......... 151 K4
Foster Lane EC2V ............... 151 J6
Foulis Terrace SW7 ............ 152 E6
Foundry Close SE16 ........... 157 J6
Fournier Street E1 ............. 156 B1
Fowey Close E1W ............... 156 E5
Frampton Street NW8 ........ 148 E4
Francis Street SW1P .......... 154 A4
Frankland Close SE16 ......... 156 F8
Franklin's Row SW3 ........... 153 H6
Frazier Street SE1 .............. 155 G3
Frean Street SE16 .............. 156 C8
Frederick Close W2 ............ 149 G7
Frederick Street WC1X ....... 150 E2
Frederic Mews * SW1X ....... 153 J3
Freemantle Street SE17 ...... 155 M6
Friend Street EC1V ............ 151 H2
Frith Street W1D ............... 150 B6
Fulbourne Street E1 ........... 156 E1
Fulford Street SE16 ............ 156 F7
Fulham Road SW10 ............ 152 D8
Fulham Road SW3 .............. 152 F6
Furnival Street EC4A .......... 150 F5
Fynes Street SW1P ............. 154 B4

**G**

Gabriel's Wharf SE1 ........... 155 G1
Gainsford Street SE1 .......... 156 B6
Galleon Close SE16 ............ 157 G6
Galsworthy Avenue E14 ...... 157 K2
Galway Street EC1V ........... 151 K2
Gambia Street SE1 ............. 155 H2
Garden Road NW8 ............. 148 D1
Garden Row SE1 ................ 155 H4
Garden Street E1 ............... 157 H1
Garden Walk EC2A ............. 151 M3
Gard Street EC1V ............... 151 J2
Garford Street E14 ............. 157 M4
Garnault Place EC1R .......... 151 G3
Garnet Street E1W ............. 156 F3
Garrett Street EC1Y ........... 151 K3
Garrick Street WC2E .......... 150 C7
Garterway SE16 ................. 157 H7
Garway Road W2 ............... 148 B6
Gataker Street * SE16 ........ 156 E8
Gate Mews SW7 ................ 152 F3
Gateforth Street NW8 ........ 148 F3
Gate Mews NW1 ................ 149 G4
Gatesborough Street * EC2A 151 M3
Gate Street WC2A .............. 150 E5
Gatliff Road SW1W ............ 153 K7
Gaunt Street SE1 ............... 155 J4
Gayfere Street SW1P .......... 154 C4
Gaywood Street SE1 .......... 155 H4

Gaza Street SE17 ............... 155 H7
Gedling Place SE1 .............. 156 C7
Gee Street EC1V ................ 151 J3
George Mathers Road SE11 . 155 H5
George Row SE16 .............. 156 C7
George Street W1H ............ 149 H6
George Yard W1K ............... 149 K7
Geraldine Street SE1 .......... 155 H4
Gerald Road SW1W ............ 153 K5
Gerrard Street W1D ........... 150 B7
Gerridge Street SE1 ........... 155 G3
Gertrude Street SW10 ........ 152 D8
Gibson Road SE11 .............. 154 E5
Gilbert Place WC1A ............ 150 C5
Gilbert Road SE11 .............. 155 G5
Gilbert Street W1K ............. 149 K7
Gildea Street W1W ............. 149 L5
Gillingham Street SW1V ...... 153 M5
Gill Street E14 .................. 157 L3
Gilston Road SW10 ............ 152 D7
Giltspur Street EC1A ........... 151 H5
Gladstone Street SE1 ......... 155 H4
Glamis Place E1W .............. 157 G4
Glamis Road E1W .............. 157 G4
Glasgow Terrace SW1V ....... 153 M7
Glasshill Street SE1 ........... 155 J3
Glasshouse Street W1B ....... 150 A8
Glasshouse Walk SE11 ....... 154 D7
Glebe Place SW3 ............... 152 F7
Gledhow Road SW5 ........... 152 C6
Glentworth Street NW1 ...... 149 H4
Globe Pond Road SE16 ....... 157 J5
Globe Street SE1 ............... 155 K3
Gloucester Court * EC3R ..... 156 A4
Gloucester Gardens W2 ...... 148 C6
Gloucester Mews W2 .......... 148 D6
Gloucester Mews West W2 .. 148 C6
Gloucester Place NW1 ........ 149 H3
Gloucester Place W1U ........ 149 H5
Gloucester Place Mews W1U 149 H5
Gloucester Road SW7 ......... 152 C4
Gloucester Road SE16 ........ 156 D8
Gloucester Road ⇌ SW7 .... 152 C5
Gloucester Square W2 ........ 148 F6
Gloucester Street SW1V ...... 153 M7
Gloucester Terrace W2 ....... 148 B5
Gloucester Terrace W2 ....... 148 D6
Gloucester Walk W8 ........... 152 A2
Gloucester Way EC1R ......... 151 G2
Glyn Street SE11 ................ 154 E7
Godfrey Street SW3 ........... 153 G6
Goding Street SE11 ............ 154 D7
Godliman Street EC4V ........ 151 J7
Godwin Close N1 ............... 151 K1
Golden Hinde II SE1 ........... 155 L1
Golden Jubilee Bridge WC2N 154 D1
Golden Lane EC1Y .............. 151 J4
Golden Square W1F ........... 150 A7
Golding Street E1 .............. 156 E3
Goldney Road W9 .............. 148 A4
Goldsmith Street EC2V ....... 151 K6
Gomm Road SE16 ............. 157 G8
Goodge Place W1T ............. 150 A5
Goodge Street W1T ............ 150 A5
Goodge Street ⇌ W1T ....... 150 B5
Goodwin Close SE16 .......... 156 C8
Gordon Place W8 ............... 152 A2
Gordon Square WC1H ......... 150 B3
Gordon Street WC1H .......... 150 B3
Gore Street SW7 ................ 152 D4
Goring Street * EC3A .......... 156 A2
Gosfield Street W1W .......... 149 L5
Goslett Yard WC2H ............ 150 B6
Goswell Road EC1V ............ 151 H1
Gough Street WC1X ........... 150 F3
Goulston Street E1 ............. 156 B2
Gower Mews WC1E ............ 150 B5
Gower Place NW1 .............. 150 A3
Gower Street WC1E ............ 150 B3
Gower's Walk E1 ............... 156 D2
Gracechurch Street EC3V .... 151 M7
Grafton Place NW1 ............ 150 B2
Grafton Street W1S ............ 149 L8
Grafton Way W1T ............... 150 A4
Graham Street N1 .............. 151 J1
Graham Terrace SW1W ....... 153 J6
Granby Terrace NW1 .......... 149 M1
Grand Avenue EC1A ........... 151 H5
Grange Road SE1 ............... 156 B8
Grange Walk SE1 ............... 156 B8
Grange Yard SE1 ............... 156 B8
Grantully Road W9 ............. 148 B2
Granville Place W1H ........... 149 J6
Granville Road NW6 ........... 148 A1
Granville Square WC1X ....... 150 F2
Grape Street WC2H ............ 150 C6
Gravel Lane E1 .................. 156 B2
Gray's Inn Road WC1X ....... 150 D2
Gray's Inn Square WC1R ..... 150 F5
Gray Street SE1 ................. 155 G3
Great Castle Street W1G ..... 149 L6
Great Central Street NW1 ... 149 G4
Great Chapel Street W1D .... 150 B6
Great College Street SW1P .. 154 C4
Great Cumberland
    Place W1H ..................... 149 H6
Great Dover Street SE1 ....... 155 K3
Great Eastern Street EC2A .. 151 M3
Great George Street SW1A .. 154 C3
Great Guildford Street SE1 .. 155 J1
Great James Street WC1N ... 150 E4
Great Marlborough
    Street W1F ..................... 149 M7
Great Maze Pond SE1 ......... 155 L2
Great New Portland
    Street WC2H .................. 150 C7
Greatorex Street E1 ........... 156 D1
Great Ormond Street WC1N . 150 D4
Great Percy Street WC1X ..... 150 F2
Great Peter Street SW1P ..... 154 B4
Great Portland Street W1W .. 149 L4
Great Portland
    Street ⇌ W1W ................ 149 L4
Great Pulteney Street W1F .. 150 A7
Great Queen Street WC2B ... 150 D6
Great Russell Street WC1B .. 150 C5
Great Scotland Yard SW1A .. 154 C1
Great Smith Street SW1P .... 154 C4
Great Suffolk Street SE1 ..... 155 H2
Great Sutton Street EC1V .... 151 H4
Great Swan Alley EC2R ....... 151 L6
Great Titchfield Street W1W 149 M4
Great Tower Street EC3M .... 151 M7
Great Tower Street EC3R ..... 156 A4
Great Winchester
    Street EC2N ................... 151 L6
Great Windmill Street W1D .. 150 B7
Greek Street W1D ............... 150 B6
Greenacre Square SE16 ...... 157 J6
Green Bank E1W ................ 156 E5
Greenberry Street NW8 ...... 148 F1

Greencoat Place SW1P ....... 154 A5
Green Coat Row SW1P ........ 154 A4
Greenfield Road E1 ............ 156 D2
Greenham Close SE1 .......... 154 F3
Green Park ⇌ SW1J ........... 153 M1
Green Street W1K .............. 149 J7
Greenwell Street W1W ....... 149 L4
Greet Street SE1 ............... 155 G2
Grenade Street E14 ............ 157 L4
Grendon Street NW8 .......... 148 F4
Grenville Place SW7 ........... 152 C5
Gresham Street EC2V ......... 151 J6
Gresse Street W1T ............. 150 B5
Greville Street EC1N .......... 151 G5
Greycoat Place SW1P ......... 154 B4
Greycoat Street SW1P ........ 154 B4
Grigg's Place SE1 .............. 156 A8
Grosvenor Bridge SW1 ....... 153 L8
Grosvenor Crescent SW1X ... 153 J3
Grosvenor Crescent
    Mews SW1X ................... 153 J3
Grosvenor Gardens SW1W .. 153 L4
Grosvenor Gardens Mews
    East SW1W ..................... 153 L4
Grosvenor Gardens Mews
    North SW1W ................... 153 L4
Grosvenor Gardens Mews
    South * SW1W ................ 153 L4
Grosvenor Gate W2 ........... 149 H8
Grosvenor Hill W1K ........... 149 L7
Grosvenor Place SW1X ....... 153 K3
Grosvenor Road SW1V ........ 153 L8
Grosvenor Square W1K ....... 149 J7
Grosvenor Street W1K ........ 149 K7
Grosvenor Terrace SE5 ....... 155 J8
Grove End Road NW8 ......... 148 D2
Guildhouse Street SW1V ..... 153 M5
Guilford Street WC1N ......... 150 D4
Guinness Square SE1 .......... 155 M5
Gulliver Street SE16 ........... 157 K8
Gunpowder Square EC4A .... 151 G6
Gun Street E1 ................... 156 B1
Gunthorpe Street E1 .......... 156 C2
Gutter Lane EC2V .............. 151 J6
Guy Street SE1 .................. 155 L3

**H**

Haberdasher Street N1 ....... 151 L2
Haddonhall Estate SE1 ....... 155 M4
Hainton Close E1 ............... 156 F3
Halcrow Street * E1 ........... 156 E2
Half Moon Street W1J ......... 153 L1
Halford Road SW6 ............. 152 A8
Halkin Place SW1X ............. 153 J4
Halkin Street SW1X ............ 153 K3
Hallam Street W1W ........... 149 L5
Halley Street E14 ............... 157 K1
Hallfield Estate W2 ............ 148 C6
Hall Place W2 .................... 148 E4
Hall Road NW8 .................. 148 D2
Hall Street EC1V ................ 151 H2
Halpin Place SE17 .............. 155 M6
Halsey Street SW3 ............. 153 G5
Hamilton Close NW8 .......... 148 D2
Hamilton Close SE16 .......... 157 K7
Hamilton Gardens NW8 ...... 148 D2
Hamilton Place W1J ........... 153 K2
Hamilton Terrace NW8 ....... 148 C1
Hamlet Way SE1 ............... 155 L3
Hammett Street EC3N ........ 156 B4
Hampden Close NW1 ......... 150 B1
Hampden Gurney Street W2 149 H6
Hampstead Road NW1 ........ 149 M2
Hampton Street SE17 ......... 155 J6
Hanbury Street E1 ............. 156 C1
Hand Court WC1V .............. 150 E5
Handel Street WC1N .......... 150 D3
Hankey Place SE1 .............. 155 L3
Hannibal Road E1 .............. 157 G1
Hanover Square W1S ......... 149 L6
Hanover Street W1S ........... 149 L7
Hans Crescent SW3 ........... 153 H3
Hanson Street W1W ........... 149 M4
Hans Place SW1X ............... 153 H4
Hans Road SW3 ................ 153 H4
Hans Street SW1X ............. 153 H4
Hanway Place W1T ............. 150 B6
Hanway Street W1T ............ 150 B6
Harbet Road W2 ................ 148 F5
Harbour Street WC1N ......... 150 E4
Harcourt Street W1H .......... 149 G5
Harcourt Terrace SW10 ...... 152 C7
Hardinge Street E1W .......... 157 G3
Hardwick Street EC1R ........ 151 G2
Hardwidge Street SE1 ........ 155 M2
Hardy Close SE16 .............. 157 H6
Harewood Place W1G ......... 149 L6
Harewood Row NW1 .......... 149 G4
Harewoood Avenue NW1 .... 149 G4
Harford Street E1 .............. 157 J1
Harleyford Road SE11 ........ 154 E8
Harley Gardens SW10 ........ 152 D7
Harley Street W1G ............. 149 K4
Harmsworth Street SE17 ..... 155 G7
Harold Estate SE1 .............. 156 A8
Harper Road SE1 ............... 155 K4
Harriet Street SW1X ........... 153 H3
Harriet Walk SW1X ............ 153 H3
Harrington Gardens SW7 .... 152 C6
Harrington Road SW7 ......... 152 E5
Harrington Square NW1 ...... 149 M1
Harrington Street NW1 ....... 149 M2
Harrison Street WC1H ........ 150 D2
Harrods SW1X .................. 153 G4
Harrowby Street W1H ......... 149 G6
Harrow Place E1 ................ 156 B2
Harrow Road W2 ............... 148 A4
Hart Street EC3R ............... 156 A3
Hasker Street SW3 ............ 153 G5
Hastings Street WC1H ........ 150 C2
Hatfields SE1 .................... 155 G1
Hatherley Grove W2 ........... 148 B6
Hatteraick Road SE16 ......... 157 G6
Hatton Garden EC1N .......... 151 G4
Hatton Street W2 ............... 148 E4
Hatton Wall EC1N .............. 151 G4
Havering Street E1 ............. 157 H3
Haverstock Street N1 ......... 151 J1
Hawke Place * SE16 ........... 157 H6
Haydon Street EC3N .......... 156 B3
Hayes Place NW1 .............. 149 G4
Hay Hill W1J ..................... 149 L8
Hayles Street SE11 ............ 155 H5
Haymarket SW1Y ............... 150 B8
Hayne Street EC1A ............. 151 J4
Hay's Lane SE1 ................. 155 M1
Hay's Mews W1J ................ 149 L8
Haywood Place EC1R ......... 151 J4

Headfort Place SW1X ......... 153 K3
Head Street E1 .................. 157 H2
Hearnshaw Street E14 ........ 157 K2
Hearn Street EC2A ............. 151 M4
Heathcote Street WC1N ...... 150 E3
Heddon Street W1B ............ 149 M7
Hedger Street W1S ............. 150 A7
Hedger Street SE11 ............ 155 H5
Heiron Street SE17 ............ 155 J8
Hellings Street E1W ........... 156 D5
Helmet Row EC1V .............. 151 K3
Helsinki Square SE16 ......... 157 L8
Henderson Drive NW8 ........ 148 E3
Heneage Lane EC3A ........... 156 A3
Heneage Street E1 ............. 156 C1
Henrietta Place W1G .......... 149 L6
Henrietta Street WC2E ....... 150 D7
Henriques Street E1 ........... 156 D2
Henshaw Street SE17 ......... 155 L5
Herbal Hill EC1R ............... 151 G4
Herbert Crescent SW1X ...... 153 H4
Herbrand Street WC1H ....... 150 C3
Hercules Road SE1 ............. 154 F4
Hereford Road W2 ............. 148 A6
Hereford Square SW7 ........ 152 D6
Hermitage Street W2 ......... 148 E5
Hermitage Wall E1W .......... 156 D5
Hermit Street EC1V ............ 151 H2
Heron Quay E14 ................ 157 M5
Herrick Street SW1P .......... 154 C6
Hertford Street W1J ........... 153 K2
Hertsmere Road E14 .......... 157 M4
Hesper Mews SW5 ............. 152 B6
Hessel Street E1 ............... 156 E3
Hewett Street EC2A ........... 151 M3
Heygate Estate SE17 .......... 155 J5
Heygate Street SE17 .......... 155 J5
Hide Place SW1P ............... 154 B6
High Holborn WC1V ........... 150 E5
High Street
    Kensington ⇌ W8 .......... 152 A3
Hildyard Road SW6 ............ 152 A8
Hilliards Court E1W ............ 156 F5
Hillingdon Street SE17 ....... 155 J8
Hill Road NW8 .................. 148 D1
Hills Place W1F ................. 149 M6
Hill Street W1J .................. 149 K8
Hinde Street W1U .............. 149 K6
Hind Grove E14 ................. 157 M3
Hindgrove Area E14 ........... 157 M3
Hithe Grove SE16 .............. 157 G8
HMS Belfast SE1 ............... 156 A5
Hobart Place SW1W ........... 153 K4
Hobury Street SW10 .......... 152 D8
Hogarth Road SW5 ............ 152 B6
Holbein Mews SW1W ......... 153 J6
Holbein Place SW1W .......... 153 J6
Holborn EC1N ................... 151 G5
Holborn ⇌ WC2B ............. 150 E5
Holborn Circus EC1N ......... 151 G5
Holborn Viaduct EC1A ........ 151 G5
Holford Street WC1X .......... 150 F2
Holland Street SE1 ............. 155 H1
Holland Street W8 ............. 152 A3
Hollen Street W1F ............. 150 A6
Holles Street W1C .............. 149 L6
Hollywood Road SW10 ....... 152 C8
Holyoak Road SE11 ............ 155 H5
Holyrood Street SE1 ........... 155 M2
Holyrood Street SE1 ........... 156 A6
Holywell Row EC2A ............ 151 M4
Homefield Street * N1 ........ 151 M1
Homer Row W1H ............... 149 G5
Homer Street W1H ............. 149 G5
Hooper Street E1 ............... 156 D3
Hopetown Street E1 ........... 156 C1
Hopkins Street W1F ........... 150 A7
Hopton Street SE1 ............. 155 H1
Hopwood Road SE17 ......... 155 L8
Hornton Place W8 ............. 152 A3
Hornton Street W8 ............ 152 A2
Horse & Dolphin Yard W1D . 150 B7
Horseferry Road E14 .......... 157 J3
Horseferry Road SW1P ....... 154 B4
Horse Guards Avenue SW1A 154 C2
Horse Guards Parade SW1A . 154 C2
Horse Guards Road SW1A ... 154 C2
Horselydown Lane SE1 ....... 156 B6
Horsley Street SE17 ........... 155 K8
Hosier Lane EC1A .............. 151 H5
Hothfield Place SE16 .......... 157 G8
Hotspur Street SE11 .......... 154 F6
Houghton Street WC2A ...... 150 E6
Houndsditch EC3A ............. 156 A2
Houses of Parliament SW1A 154 D3
Howick Place SW1P ........... 154 A4
Howland Street W1T ........... 150 A4
Howland Way SE16 ............ 157 K7
Howley Place W2 ............... 148 D4
Hoxton Square N1 ............. 151 M2
Hoxton Street N1 .............. 151 M1
Hugh Mews SW1V .............. 153 L6
Hugh Street SW1V ............. 153 L6
Hugh Street SW1V ............. 153 L6
Hull Close SE16 ................ 157 J6
Hull Street EC1V ............... 151 J2
Hungerford Bridge SE1 ....... 154 E1
Hunter Close SE1 .............. 155 M4
Hunter Street WC1N .......... 150 D3
Huntley Street WC1E .......... 150 A4
Huntsman Street SE17 ....... 155 M6
Huntsworth Mews NW1 ...... 149 H3
Hurley Crescent SE16 ......... 157 H6
Hutching's Street E14 ........ 157 M7
Hutton Street EC4Y ........... 151 G7
Hyde Park W2 ................... 153 G1
Hyde Park Corner SW1X ..... 153 K2
Hyde Park Corner ⇌ W1J ... 153 K2
Hyde Park Court SW7 ......... 152 D3
Hyde Park Crescent W2 ...... 148 F6
Hyde Park Gardens W2 ....... 148 F7
Hyde Park Gardens Mews W2 148 F7
Hyde Park Gate SW7 ......... 152 C3
Hyde Park Gate SW7 ......... 152 D3
Hyde Park Square W2 ........ 148 F7
Hyde Park Street W2 .......... 148 F7

**I**

Idol Lane EC3R .................. 151 M7
Ifield Road SW10 .............. 152 B8
Iliffe Street SE17 ............... 155 J6
Iliffe Yard SE17 ................. 155 J6
Imperial College Road SW7 . 152 D4
Imperial War Museum SE1 .. 155 G4
India Street EC3N .............. 156 B3
Ingestre Place W1F ............ 150 A7
Inglebert Street EC1R ........ 150 F2

Ingram Close SE11 ............ 154 E5
Inner Circle NW1 ............... 149 J2
Inverness Terrace W2 ........ 148 B6
Inverness Terrace Gate W2 . 148 C8
Invicta Plaza SE1 ............... 155 H1
Ironmonger Lane EC2V ....... 151 K6
Ironmonger Row EC1V ....... 151 K2
Irving Street WC2N ............ 150 C8
Isambard Place SE16 ......... 157 G6
Island Row E14 ................. 157 K3
Iverna Court W8 ............... 152 A4
Iverna Gardens W8 ........... 152 A4
Ives Street SW3 ................ 153 G5
Ivor Place NW1 ................. 149 G4
Ixworth Place SW3 ............ 152 F6

**J**

Jacob Street SE1 ............... 156 C6
Jamaica Gate SE16 ............ 156 F8
Jamaica Road SE1 ............. 156 C7
Jamaica Road SE16 ............ 156 E7
Jamaica Street E1 .............. 157 G2
Jamaica Wharf SE1 ............ 156 C6
James Street W1U ............. 149 K6
James Street WC2E ............ 150 D7
Jameson Street W8 ........... 152 A1
Jamuna Close E14 .............. 157 K1
Janeway Street SE16 .......... 156 D7
Jardine Road E1W .............. 157 J4
Java Wharf SE1 ................. 156 C6
Jay Mews SW7 .................. 152 D3
Jermyn Street SW1Y .......... 150 A8
Jerome Crescent NW8 ........ 148 F3
Jewery Street EC3N ........... 156 B3
Joan Street SE1 ................ 155 G2
Jockey's Fields WC1R ......... 150 E4
Johanna Street SE1 ........... 154 F3
John Adam Street WC2N ..... 150 D8
John Carpenter Street EC4Y 151 G7
John Felton Road SE16 ....... 156 D7
John Fisher Street E1 ......... 156 C4
John Islip Street SW1P ....... 154 C5
John Prince's Street W1G .... 149 L6
John Roll Way SE16 ........... 156 D7
John Ruskin Street SE5 ...... 155 J8
John Slip Street SW1P ........ 154 C6
John's Mews WC1N ........... 150 E4
Johnson's Place SW1V ........ 154 A7
Johnson Street E1 ............. 157 G3
John Street WC1N .............. 150 E4
Joiner Street SE1 ............... 155 L1
Jonathan Street SE11 ......... 154 E6
Jubilee Place SW3 ............. 153 G6
Jubilee Street E1 ............... 157 G2
Jubilee Walk SE1 ............... 152 B1
Judd Street WC1H ............. 150 C2
Junction Mews W2 ............. 148 F5
Juxton Street SE11 ............ 154 E5

**K**

Katherine Close SE16 ......... 157 H5
Kean Street WC2B ............. 150 E6
Keel Close SE16 ................ 157 J6
Keeley Street WC2B ........... 150 E6
Keeton's Road SE16 .......... 156 E7
Kell Street SE1 .................. 155 H3
Kelso Place W8 ................. 152 B4
Kemble Street WC2B .......... 150 E6
Kempsford Gardens SW5 .... 152 A7
Kempsford Road SE11 ........ 155 G6
Kendall Place W1U ............ 149 J5
Kendal Street W2 .............. 149 G6
Kennet Street E1W ............ 156 D5
Kenning Street SE16 .......... 157 G6
Kennings Way SE11 ........... 155 G7
Kennington ⇌ SE11 .......... 155 H7
Kennington Lane SE11 ........ 154 E7
Kennington Oval SE11 ........ 154 E8
Kennington Park
    Gardens SE11 ................ 155 G8
Kennington Park Place SE11 155 G7
Kennington Park Road SE11 155 G7
Kennington Road SE1 ......... 154 F4
Kennington Road SE11 ....... 155 G5
Kennington Oval SE11 ........ 154 F8
Kennnington Oval SE11 ...... 154 F8
Kenrick Place W1U ............ 149 J5
Kensington Church Street W8 152 A1
Kensington Gardens W2 ..... 152 C1
Kensington Gardens
    Square W2 .................... 148 B6
Kensington Gate W8 .......... 152 C4
Kensington Gore SW7 ........ 152 D3
Kensington High Street W8 . 152 A4
Kensington Palace W8 ........ 152 B2
Kensington Palace
    Gardens W8 .................. 152 B1
Kensington Palace
    Gardens W8 .................. 152 B2
Kensington Place W8 ......... 152 A1
Kensington Road SW7 ........ 153 G3
Kensington Road W8 ......... 152 B3
Kensington Square W8 ....... 152 B3
Kenton Street WC1H .......... 150 C3
Kenway Road SW5 ............. 152 A6
Keystone Close N1 ............ 150 D1
Keyworth Street SE1 .......... 155 H4
Kilburn Park Road NW6 ...... 148 A2
Kildare Terrace W2 ............ 148 A6
Killick Street N1 ................ 150 E1
Kinburn Street SE16 .......... 157 H6
Kinder Street E1 ............... 156 E2
King & Queen Wharf SE16 .. 157 H5
King and Queen Street SE17 155 K6
King Charles Street SW1A ... 154 C2
Kingdom Street W2 ........... 148 C5
King Edward Street EC1A .... 151 J6
King Edward Walk SE1 ........ 155 G4
King James Street SE1 ....... 155 H3
Kingly Street W1F .............. 149 M7
King's Arms Yard EC2R ...... 151 L6
King's Bench Street SE1 ..... 155 H2
Kingscote Street EC4V ....... 151 H7
King's Cross ⇌ N1 ............ 150 D1
King's Cross Road WC1X .... 150 E2
King's Cross St
    Pancras ⇌ N1C ............. 150 D1
King's Head Yard SE1 ........ 155 L1
King's Mews WC1N ............ 150 E4
Kingsmill Terrace NW8 ....... 148 E1
King Square EC1V .............. 151 J2
King's Road SW3 ............... 152 E8
King's Scholars
    Passage SW1P .............. 153 M5

King's Stairs Close - Paddington Street 161


King's Stairs Close SE16 156 F6
King Street WC2E 150 D7
King Street SW1Y 154 A1
King Street EC2V 151 K6
Kingsway WC2B 150 E6
King William Street EC4N 151 L7
Kinnerton Place North * SW1X 153 J3
Kinnerton Place South * SW1X 153 J3
Kinnerton Street SW1X 153 J3
Kinnerton Yard * SW1X 153 J3
Kipling Estate SE1 155 L3
Kipling Street SE1 155 L3
Kirby Estate SE16 156 D7
Kirby Grove SE1 155 M3
Kirby Street EC1N 151 G4
Knaresborough Place SW5 152 B5
Knightrider Street EC4V 151 H7
Knightsbridge SW1X 153 H3
Knightsbridge ⊖ SW3 153 H3
Knox Street W1H 149 H4
Kynance Mews SW7 152 C4
Kynance Place SW7 152 C4

## L

Lackington Street EC2A 151 L4
Lafone Street SE1 156 B6
Lagado Mews SE16 157 H5
Lambeth Bridge SW1P 154 D5
Lambeth High Street SE1 154 E5
Lambeth Hill EC4V 151 J7
Lambeth North ⊖ SE1 154 F3
Lambeth Palace Road SE1 154 E4
Lambeth Road SE1 154 F4
Lambeth Walk SE11 154 F5
Lamb's Conduit Street WC1N 150 E4
Lamb's Passage EC1Y 151 K4
Lamb Street E1 156 B1
Lamb Way SE1 156 A7
Lamlash Street SE11 155 H5
Lanark Place W9 148 D3
Lanark Road W9 148 B1
Lancaster Gate W2 148 D7
Lancaster Gate W2 148 D8
Lancaster Gate ⊖ W2 148 E7
Lancaster Mews W2 148 D7
Lancaster Place WC2E 150 E7
Lancaster Street SE1 155 H3
Lancaster Terrace W2 148 E7
Lancaster Walk W2 148 D8
Lancelot Place SW7 153 G3
Lancing Street NW1 150 B2
Lanesborough Place * SW1X 153 J3
Langdale Street E1 156 E3
Langford Place NW8 148 D1
Langham Place W1B 149 L5
Langham Street W1W 149 L5
Langham Street W1W 149 M5
Langley Lane SW8 154 D8
Langley Street WC2H 150 C7
Langton Close WC1X 150 E3
Lanhill Road W9 148 A3
Lansdowne Place SE1 155 L4
Lant Street SE1 155 J3
Larcom Street SE17 155 K6
Lauderdale Road W9 148 B3
Laud Street SE11 154 E7
Launcelot Street SE1 154 F3
Launceston Place W8 152 C4
Laurence Pountney Lane EC4V 151 L7
Lavender Road SE16 157 K5
Lavender Wharf SE16 157 K4
Lavington Street SE1 155 J1
Lawn Lane SW8 154 D8
Lawrence Street SW3 152 F8
Lawrence Wharf SE16 157 L6
Law Street SE1 155 L4
Laxton Place NW1 149 L3
Laystall Street EC1R 150 F4
Leadenhall Street EC3A 156 A3
Leadenhall Street EC3V 151 M6
Leake Street SE1 154 E2
Leather Lane EC1N 151 G4
Leathermarket Street SE1 155 M3
Leeke Street WC1X 150 E2
Lees Place W1K 149 J7
Leicester Square ⊖ WC2H 150 C7
Leicester Square WC2H 150 C7
Leicester Street WC2H 150 B7
Leigh Street WC1H 150 C3
Leinster Gardens W2 148 C6
Leinster Mews W2 148 C7
Leinster Place W2 148 C7
Leinster Square W2 148 A7
Leinster Terrace W2 148 C7
Leman Street E1 156 C3
Lennox Gardens SW1X 153 G4
Lennox Gardens Mews SW1X 153 G5
Leonard Street EC2A 151 L3
Leopold Estate E3 157 M1
Leopold Street E3 157 L1
Leroy Street SE1 155 M5
Lever Street EC1V 151 J2
Lewisham Street SW1H 154 B3
Lexham Gardens W8 152 A5
Lexham Mews W8 152 A5
Lexington Street W1F 150 A7
Leyden Street E1 156 B2
Leydon Close SE16 157 H5
Library Street SE1 155 H3
Lidlington Place NW1 150 A1
Lilestone Street NW8 148 F3
Lilley Close E1W 156 D5
Lillie Road SW6 152 A7
Lillie Yard SW6 152 A7
Limeburner Lane EC4M 151 H6
Lime Close E1W 156 D5
Limehouse Causeway E14 157 L4
Limehouse Link E14 157 L3
Limehouse ⇌ ⊖ E14 157 J3
Limerston Street SW10 152 D8
Lime Street EC3M 151 M7
Lincoln's Inn Fields WC2A 150 E6
Linden Gardens W2 148 A8
Lindley Street E1 156 F1
Lindsay Square SW1V 154 B7
Lindsey Street EC1A 151 H4
Linhope Street NW1 149 G3
Linsey Street SE16 156 D8
Lisle Street WC2H 150 B7
Lisson Green Estate NW8 148 F3
Lisson Grove NW1 149 G4
Lisson Grove NW8 148 F3
Lisson Street NW1 148 F4
Litchfield Street WC2H 150 C7
Little Argyll Street W1F 149 M6
Little Britain EC1A 151 J5
Little Chester Street SW1X 153 K4
Little George Street SW1P 154 C3
Little Marlborough Street W1F 150 A7
Little New Street EC4A 151 G6
Little Portland Street W1G 149 L6
Little Russell Street WC1A 150 C5
Little St James's Street SW1A 153 M2
Little Sanctuary SW1A 154 C3
Little Somerset Street E1 156 B3
Little Titchfield Street W1W 149 M5
Liverpool Grove SE17 155 K7
Liverpool Street EC2M 151 M5
Liverpool Street ⇌ ⊖ EC2M 151 M5
Lizard Street EC1V 151 K3
Llewellyn Street SE16 156 D7
Lloyd Baker Street WC1X 150 F2
Lloyd's Avenue EC3N 156 B3
Lloyd Square WC1X 150 F2
Lloyds Row EC1R 151 G2
Lloyd's Street WC1X 150 F2
Locksley Estate E14 157 L2
Locksley Street E14 157 L1
Lockyer Street SE1 155 L3
Lodge Road NW8 148 F3
Loftie Street SE16 156 D7
Logan Place W8 152 A5
Lolesworth Close E1 156 B1
Lollard Street SE11 154 F5
Lollard Street SE11 154 F6
Loman Street SE1 155 J2
Lomas Street E1 156 D1
Lombard Lane EC4Y 151 G6
Lombard Street EC3V 151 L7
London Bridge EC4R 151 L8
London Bridge ⇌ ⊖ SE1 155 L1
London Bridge Street SE1 155 L1
London Dungeon SE1 154 E2
London Eye SE1 154 E2
London Mews W2 148 E6
London Road SE1 155 H4
London Street EC3R 156 A3
London Street W2 148 E6
London Transport Museum WC2E 150 D7
London Wall EC2M 151 K5
London Zoo ZSL NW1 149 J1
Long Acre WC2E 150 D7
Longford Street NW1 149 L3
Long Lane EC1A 151 J5
Long Lane SE1 155 L3
Longmoore Street SW1V 153 M5
Longridge Road SW5 152 A5
Longville Road SE11 155 H5
Long Walk SE1 156 A8
Long Yard WC1N 150 E4
Lord North Street SW1P 154 C4
Lord's Cricket Ground NW8 148 E2
Lorenzo Street WC1X 150 E1
Lorrimore Road SE17 155 J8
Lorrimore Square SE17 155 H8
Lothbury EC2R 151 L6
Loughborough Street SE11 154 F7
Lovat Lane EC3R 151 M7
Love Lane EC2V 151 K6
Lovell Place SE16 157 K7
Lowell Street E14 157 K2
Lower Belgrave Street SW1W 153 K4
Lower Grosvenor Place SW1W 153 L4
Lower James Street W1F 150 A7
Lower John Street W1F 150 A7
Lower Marsh SE1 154 F3
Lower Road SE16 157 G7
Lower Sloane Street SW1W 153 J6
Lower Thames Street EC3R 156 A4
Lowndes Close * SW1X 153 J4
Lowndes Place SW1X 153 J4
Lowndes Square SW1X 153 H3
Lowndes Street SW1X 153 J4
Lucan Place SW3 152 F5
Lucey Road SE16 156 C8
Ludgate Circus EC4M 151 H6
Ludgate Hill EC4M 151 H6
Luke Street EC2A 151 M3
Lukin Street E1 157 G3
Lumley Street W1K 149 K7
Lupus Street SW1V 153 L7
Lupus Street SW1V 154 B7
Luton Street NW8 148 E4
Luxborough Street W1U 149 J4
Lyall Mews SW1X 153 J4
Lyall Street SW1X 153 J4
Lyons Place NW8 148 E3
Lytham Street SE17 155 K7

## M

Macclesfield Road EC1V 151 J2
Macclesfield Street * W1D 150 B7
Mace Close E1W 156 E5
Macklin Street WC2B 150 D6
Mackworth Street NW1 149 M2
Macleod Street SE17 155 K7
Madame Tussauds NW1 149 J4
Maddox Street W1S 149 M7
Magdalen Street SE1 155 M2
Magee Street SE11 154 F8
Maguire Street SE1 156 C6
Maida Avenue W9 148 D4
Maida Vale W9 148 C2
Maida Vale ⊖ W9 148 C2
Maiden Lane SE1 155 K1
Maiden Lane WC2E 150 D7
Major Road SE16 156 D7
Makins Street SW3 153 G6
Malet Street WC1E 150 B4
Mallord Street SW3 152 E8
Mallory Street NW8 148 F3
Mallow Street EC1Y 151 L3
Malta Street EC1V 151 H3
Maltby Street SE1 156 B7
Manchester Square W1U 149 J6
Manchester Street W1U 149 J5
Manciple Street SE1 155 L3
Mandeville Place W1U 149 K6
Manette Street W1D 150 B6
Manilla Street E14 157 M6
Manningford Close EC1V 151 H2
Manor Place SE17 155 J7
Manresa Road SW3 152 F7
Mansell Street E1 156 C3
Mansfield Mews W1G 149 K5
Mansfield Street W1G 149 L5
Mansion House ⊖ EC4V 151 K7
Manson Mews SW7 152 D5
Manson Place SW7 152 D6
Mapleleaf Square SE16 157 J6
Maples Place E1 156 F1
Maple Street W1T 149 M4
Marble Arch ⊖ W1C 149 H7
Marchmont Street WC1H 150 C3
Margaret Street W1W 149 L6
Margaretta Terrace SW3 152 F7
Margery Street WC1X 150 F3
Marigold Street SE16 156 E7
Marine Street SE16 156 C7
Market Mews W1J 153 K1
Market Place W1W 149 M6
Markham Square SW3 153 G6
Markham Street SW3 153 G6
Mark Lane EC3R 156 A4
Marlborough Gate W2 148 E7
Marlborough Place NW8 148 C1
Marlborough Road SW1A 154 A2
Marlborough Street SW3 152 F6
Marloes Road W8 152 B4
Marlow Way SE16 157 H6
Maroon Street E14 157 K2
Marshall Street W1F 150 A7
Marshalsea Road SE1 155 J2
Marsham Street SW1P 154 C5
Marsh Wall E14 157 M5
Martha's Buildings EC1V 151 K3
Martha Street E1 156 F3
Martin Lane EC4V 151 L7
Maryland Road W9 148 A4
Marylands Road W9 148 A4
Marylebone ⇌ ⊖ NW1 149 G4
Marylebone Flyover W2 148 E5
Marylebone High Street W1U 149 K5
Marylebone Lane W1U 149 K6
Marylebone Road NW1 149 G4
Marylebone Street W1G 149 K5
Marylee Way SE11 154 F6
Masjid Lane E14 157 M2
Mason Street SE17 155 M5
Massinger Street SE17 155 M6
Masters Street E1 157 J1
Matlock Street E14 157 J2
Matthew Parker Street SW1H 154 C3
Maunsel Street SW1P 154 B5
Mayfair Place W1J 153 L1
Mayflower Street SE16 156 F7
Mayford Estate NW1 150 A1
Maynards Quay E1W 156 F4
May's Street WC2N 150 C8
McAuley Close SE1 154 F4
McLeod's Mews SW7 152 C5
Meadcroft Road SE11 155 G8
Meadcroft Road SE11 155 H8
Meadow Road SW8 154 E8
Meadow Row SE1 155 J5
Mead Row SE1 154 F4
Meakin Estate SE1 155 M4
Mecklenburgh Square WC1N 150 E3
Medway Street SW1P 154 B5
Meeting House Alley E1W 156 E5
Melcombe Place NW1 149 G4
Melcombe Street W1U 149 H4
Melina Place NW8 148 D2
Melior Street SE1 155 M2
Melton Street NW1 150 A2
Memorial Gates SW1W 153 K3
Mepham Street SE1 154 F2
Mercer Street WC2H 150 C7
Merchant Square W2 148 E5
Merlin Street EC1R 150 F2
Mermaid Court SE1 155 K2
Merrick Square SE1 155 K4
Merrington Road SW6 152 A8
Merrow Street SE17 155 L7
Methley Street SE11 155 G7
Meymott Street SE1 155 G2
Micawber Street N1 151 K1
Micklethwaite Lane SW6 152 A8
Middlesex Street E1 156 A1
Middlesex Street E1 156 B2
Middle Street EC1A 151 J5
Middle Temple WC2R 150 F7
Middle Temple Lane EC4Y 150 F7
Middleton Drive SE16 157 H6
Midland Road NW1 150 C1
Midship Close SE16 157 H6
Milborne Grove SW10 152 D7
Milcote Street SE1 155 H3
Miles Street SW8 154 D8
Milford Lane WC2R 150 F7
Milk Street EC2V 151 K6
Milk Yard E1W 157 G4
Millbank SW1P 154 D4
Millennium Bridge SE1 151 J8
Millennium Harbour E14 157 M6
Milligan Street E14 157 L4
Millman Mews WC1N 150 E4
Millman Street WC1N 150 E4
Mill Place E14 157 K3
Millstream Road SE1 156 B7
Mill Street SE1 156 C6
Mill Street W1S 149 L7
Milner Street SW3 153 G5
Milton Street EC2Y 151 K4
Milverton Street SE11 155 G7
Mincing Lane EC3M 156 A4
Minera Mews SW1W 153 J5
Minories EC3N 156 B3
Mitchell Street EC1V 151 J3
Mitre Road SE1 155 G2
Mitre Street EC3A 156 A3
Molyneux Street W1H 149 G5
Monck Street SW1P 154 C4
Monkton Street SE11 155 G5
Monkwell Square EC2Y 151 K5
Monmouth Place W2 148 A6
Monmouth Road W2 148 A6
Monmouth Street WC2H 150 C6
Montague Close SE1 155 L1
Montague Place EC3R 150 C5
Montague Street WC1B 150 C5
Montagu Mansions W1U 149 H5
Montagu Mews North W1H 149 H5
Montagu Mews West W1H 149 H6
Montagu Place W1H 149 H5
Montagu Row W1U 149 H5
Montagu Square W1H 149 H5
Montagu Street W1H 149 H6
Montford Place SE11 154 F7
Monthorpe Road E1 156 C1
Montpelier Square SW7 153 G3
Montpelier Street SW7 153 G3
Montpelier Walk SW7 152 G3
Montrose Place SW1X 153 K3
Monument ⊖ EC4R 151 L7
Monument Street EC3R 151 L7
Monument Street EC3R 151 M7
Monza Street E1W 157 G4
Moodkee Street SE16 157 G7
Moore Street SW3 153 H5
Moorfields EC2Y 151 L5
Moorgate EC2R 151 L6
Moorgate ⇌ ⊖ EC2Y 151 L5
Moor Lane EC2Y 151 K5
Moor Street W1D 150 C7
Mora Street EC1V 151 K2
Morecambe Street SE17 155 K6
Moreland Street EC1V 151 H2
More London SE1 156 A5
Moreton Place SW1V 154 A6
Moreton Street SW1V 154 B6
Moreton Terrace SW1V 154 A6
Morgan's Lane SE1 155 M2
Morgan's Lane SE1 156 A5
Morley Street SE1 155 G3
Mornington Crescent NW1 149 M1
Mornington Place NW1 149 L1
Mornington Terrace NW1 149 L1
Morocco Street SE1 156 A7
Morpeth Terrace SW1P 153 M5
Morris Street E1 156 F3
Morshead Road W9 148 A2
Mortimer Market WC1E 150 A4
Mortimer Street W1T 150 A5
Mortimer Street W1W 149 M5
Morton Place SE1 154 F4
Morwell Street WC1B 150 B5
Moscow Place W2 148 B7
Moscow Road W2 148 B7
Mossop Street SW3 153 G5
Motcomb Street SW1X 153 J4
Mount Gate W2 152 E2
Mount Mills EC1V 151 J3
Mount Pleasant WC1X 150 F4
Mount Row W1K 149 K8
Mount Street W1K 149 K8
Mount Street Mews W1K 149 K8
Mount Terrace E1 156 E1
Moxon Street W1U 149 J5
Mulberry Street E1 156 D2
Mulberry Walk SW3 152 E8
Mulready Street NW8 148 F4
Mundy Street N1 151 M2
Munster Square NW1 149 L3
Munton Road SE17 155 K5
Murphy Street SE1 154 F3
Murray Grove N1 151 K1
Musbury Street E1 157 G2
Muscovy Street EC3N 156 A4
Museum of London EC2Y 151 J5
Museum Street WC1A 150 C5
Myddelton Passage EC1R 151 G2
Myddelton Square EC1R 151 G1
Myddelton Street EC1R 151 G3
Myrdle Street E1 156 D2

## N

Naoroji Street WC1X 150 F2
Napier Grove N1 151 K1
Narrow Street E14 157 K4
Nash Street NW1 149 L2
Nassau Street W1W 149 M5
Nathaniel Close * E1 156 C2
National Portrait Gallery WC2H 150 C8
Natural History Museum SW7 152 E4
Neal Street WC2H 150 C6
Neckinger SE1 156 C8
Needleman Street SE16 157 H7
Nelson Close NW6 148 A1
Nelson Place N1 151 H1
Nelson's Column WC2N 150 C8
Nelson Square SE1 155 H2
Nelson Street E1 156 E2
Nelson Terrace N1 151 H1
Neptune Street SE16 157 G7
Nesham Street E1W 156 D4
Netherton Grove SW10 152 D8
Netley Street NW1 149 M2
Nevern Place SW5 152 A6
Nevern Square SW5 152 A6
Neville Street SW7 152 E6
Newark Street E1 156 E2
New Atlas Wharf E14 157 M8
New Bond Street W1S 149 L7
New Bond Street W1S 149 L8
New Bridge Street EC4V 151 H6
New Broad Street EC2M 151 M5
New Burlington Street W1S 149 M7
Newburn Street SE11 154 F7
Newbury Street EC1A 151 J5
Newcastle Place W2 148 E5
New Cavendish Street W1G 149 K5
New Change EC4M 151 J6
New Church Road SE5 155 L8
Newcomen Street SE1 155 K2
New Compton Street WC2H 150 C6
Newcourt Street NW8 148 F1
Newell Street E14 157 L3
New Fetter Lane EC4A 151 G6
Newgate Street WC1A 151 H6
New Goulston Street E1 156 B2
Newham's Row SE1 156 A7
Newington Butts SE1 155 H6
Newington Causeway SE1 155 J4
New Kent Road SE1 155 K5
Newlands Quay E1W 156 F4
Newman Street W1T 150 A5
New North Place EC2A 151 M3
New North Road N1 151 L1
New North Street WC1N 150 D4
New Oxford Street WC1A 150 C6
Newport Street SE11 154 E5
New Quebec Street W1H 149 H6
New Ride SW7 152 E3
New Road E1 156 E2
New Row WC2N 150 C7
New Spring Gardens Walk SE1 154 D7
New Square WC2A 150 F6
New Street EC2M 156 A2
New Street Square EC4A 151 G6
Newton Road W2 148 A6
Newton Street WC2B 150 D5
New Union Street EC2Y 151 K5
Nicholas Lane EC3V 151 L7
Nicholson Street SE1 155 H1
Nightingale Place SW10 152 D8
Nile Street N1 151 K2
Nine Elms Lane SW8 154 C8
Noble Street EC2V 151 J6
Noel Road N1 151 J1
Noel Street W1F 150 A6
Norbiton Road E14 157 L2
Norfolk Crescent W2 149 G6
Norfolk Place W2 148 E6
Norfolk Square W2 148 E6
Norman Street EC1V 151 J3
Norris Street SW1Y 150 B8
Northampton Road EC1R 151 G3
Northampton Square EC1V 151 H2
North Audley Street W1K 149 J7
North Bank NW8 148 F2
Northburgh Street EC1V 151 H3
North Carriage Drive W2 148 F7
Northdown Street N1 150 D1
Northey Street E14 157 K4
North Gower Street NW1 150 A2
Northington Street WC1N 150 E4
North Mews WC1N 150 E4
North Ride W2 149 G7
North Row W1K 149 J7
North Tenter Street E1 156 C3
North Terrace SW3 152 F5
Northumberland Alley EC3N 156 B3
Northumberland Avenue WC2N 154 C1
Northumberland Place W2 148 A6
Northumberland Street WC2N 154 C1
North Wharf Road W2 148 E5
Northwick Terrace NW8 148 D3
Norway Gate SE16 157 K7
Norway Place E14 157 L3
Norwich Street EC4A 150 F5
Nottingham Place W1U 149 J4
Nottingham Street W1U 149 J4
Notting Hill Gate W11 148 A8
Notting Hill Gate ⊖ W11 152 A1
Nugent Terrace NW8 148 D1
Nutford Place W1H 149 G6

## O

Oakden Street SE11 155 G5
Oakington Road W9 148 A3
Oak Lane E14 157 L3
Oakley Close EC1V 151 H1
Oakley Gardens SW3 153 G8
Oakley Square NW1 150 A1
Oakley Street SW3 152 F8
Oak Tree Road NW8 148 F2
Oat Lane EC2V 151 J5
Occupation Road SE17 155 J6
Ocean Square E1 157 J1
Odessa Street SE16 157 L7
Ogle Street W1W 149 M5
Old Bailey EC4M 151 H6
Old Barrack Yard SW1X 153 J3
Old Bond Street W1S 149 M8
Old Broad Street EC2N 151 M6
Old Brompton Road SW5 152 B6
Old Brompton Road SW7 152 D6
Old Burlington Street W1S 149 M7
Oldbury Place W1U 149 J4
Old Castle Street E1 156 B2
Old Cavendish Street W1G 149 L6
Old Church Road E1 157 H2
Old Church Street SW3 152 E7
Old Compton Street W1D 150 B7
Old Court Place W8 152 B3
Old Gloucester Street WC1N 150 D4
Old Jamaica Road SE16 156 C7
Old Jewry EC2R 151 K6
Old Kent Road SE1 155 M5
Old Marylebone Road NW1 149 G5
Old Montague Street E1 156 C1
Old North Street WC1X 150 E5
Old Paradise Street SE11 154 E5
Old Park Lane W1J 153 K2
Old Pye Street SW1P 154 B4
Old Queen Street SW1H 154 B3
Old Square WC2A 150 F6
Old Street EC1V 151 J3
Old Street ⇌ ⊖ EC1Y 151 L3
Old Street Junction EC1Y 151 L3
Oliver's Yard EC1Y 151 L3
Olney Road SE17 155 J8
O'Meara Street SE1 155 K2
Omega Place N1 150 D1
Onega Gate SE16 157 J8
Ongar Road SW6 152 A8
Onslow Gardens SW7 152 D6
Onslow Square SW7 152 E5
Onslow Square SW7 152 E6
Ontario Street SE1 155 J4
Ontario Way E14 157 M4
Opal Street SE1 155 H6
Orange Place SE16 157 G8
Orange Square SW1W 153 K6
Orange Street E1W 156 D5
Orange Street WC2H 150 B8
Orb Street SE17 155 L6
Orchardson Street NW8 148 E4
Orchard Street W1H 149 J6
Ordehall Street WC1N 150 E4
Orient Street SE11 155 H5
Orme Court W2 148 B8
Orme Lane W2 148 B8
Orme Square Gate W2 148 B8
Ormond Close WC1N 150 D4
Ormonde Gate SW3 153 H7
Ormond Yard SW1Y 150 A8
Orsett Street SE11 154 E6
Orsett Terrace W2 148 C6
Orton Street E1W 156 D5
Osbert Street SW1V 154 B6
Osborn Street E1 156 C2
Oslo Square SE16 157 K7
Osnaburgh Street NW1 149 L3
Osnaburgh Terrace NW1 149 L3
Ossington Buildings W1U 149 J5
Ossington Street W2 148 A7
Ossulston Street NW1 150 B1
Oswin Street SE11 155 H5
Othello Close SE1 155 H6
Otto Street SE17 155 H8
Outer Circle NW1 149 H3
Outer Circle NW1 149 K1
Oval ⊖ SE11 154 F8
Oval Way SE11 154 E7
Ovington Square SW3 153 G4
Ovington Street SW3 153 G5
Owen Street EC1V 151 G1
Oxendon Street SW1Y 150 B8
Oxford Circus ⊖ W1B 149 M6
Oxford Road NW6 148 A1
Oxford Square W2 148 F6
Oxford Street W1C 149 L6
Oxford Street WC1A 150 A6

## P

Pace Place E1 156 E3
Pacific Wharf SE16 157 H5
Paddington ⇌ ⊖ W2 148 D6
Paddington Green W2 148 E4
Paddington Street W1U 149 J5

162 Pageant Crescent - Stainer Street


Pageant Crescent SE16 157 K5
Page Street SW1P 154 B5
Paget Street EC1V 151 H2
Pakenham Street WC1X 150 E3
Palace Avenue W8 152 B2
Palace Court W2 148 A7
Palace Gardens Terrace W8 152 A1
Palace Gate W8 152 C3
Palace Green W8 152 B2
Palace Place SW1E 153 M4
Palace Street SW1E 153 M4
Pall Mall SW1Y 154 A1
Pall Mall East SW1Y 154 B1
Palmer Street SW1H 154 B3
Pancras Lane EC4N 151 K6
Pancras Road N1C 150 C1
Panton Street SW1Y 150 B8
Paradise Street SE16 156 F7
Paradise Walk SW3 153 H8
Pardoner Street SE1 155 L4
Pardon Street EC1V 151 H3
Parfett Street E1 156 D2
Paris Garden SE1 155 G1
Park Crescent W1B 149 K4
Parker's Row SE1 156 C7
Parker Street WC2B 150 D6
Park Lane W1K 149 H7
Park Lane W2 153 J1
Park Place SW1A 153 M1
Park Road NW1 149 H3
Park Square East NW1 149 L3
Park Square Mews NW1 149 K3
Park Square West NW1 149 K3
Park Street SE1 155 K1
Park Street W1K 149 J7
Park Village East NW1 149 L1
Park Walk SW10 152 D8
Park West Place W2 149 G6
Parliament Street SW1A 154 C2
Parry Street SW8 154 D8
Passmore Street SW1W 153 J6
Paternoster Square 151 J6
Pater Street W8 152 A4
Pattina Walk SE16 157 K5
Paul Street EC2A 151 M3
Paultons Square SW3 152 E8
Paveley Street NW1 149 G3
Pavilion Road SW1X 153 H3
Pavilion Street SW1X 153 H4
Paxton Terrace SW1V 153 L7
Peabody Avenue SW1V 153 L7
Peabody Estate SE1 155 J1
Peacock Street SE17 155 J6
Pearl Street E1W 156 F5
Pearman Street SE1 155 G3
Pear Tree Court EC1R 151 G3
Peartree Lane E1W 157 G4
Pear Tree Street EC1V 151 J3
Peel Street W8 152 A1
Peerless Street EC1V 151 K2
Pelham Crescent SW7 152 F6
Pelham Place SW7 152 F5
Pelham Street SW7 152 F5
Pelier Street SE17 155 K8
Pemberton Row EC4A 151 G6
Pembridge Gardens W2 148 A8
Pembridge Place W2 148 A7
Pembridge Square W2 148 A7
Pembridge Villas W11 148 A7
Pembroke Close SW1X 153 J3
Penang Street E1W 156 F5
Penfold Place NW8 148 F5
Penfold Street NW8 148 E4
Pennant Mews W8 152 B5
Pennington Street E1W 156 D4
Pennyfields E14 157 M4
Penrose Grove SE17 155 J7
Penrose Street SE17 155 J7
Penryn Road SE16 156 E7
Penton Place SE17 155 H6
Penton Rise WC1X 150 E2
Penton Street N1 150 F1
Pentonville Road N1 150 E1
Penywern Road SW5 152 A6
Pepper Street SE1 155 J2
Pepys Street EC3N 156 A4
Percival Street EC1V 151 H3
Percy Circus WC1X 150 F2
Percy Street W1T 150 B5
Perkin's Rent SW1P 154 B4
Petersham Mews SW7 152 D4
Petersham Place SW7 152 C4
Peter Street W1F 150 B7
Peto Place NW1 149 L3
Petticoat Lane E1 156 B2
Petty France SW1H 154 A3
Petty Wales EC3R 156 A4
Petyward SW3 153 G6
Phelp Street SE17 155 L7
Phene Street SW3 153 G8
Phillimore Walk W8 152 A3
Philpot Lane EC3M 151 M7
Philpot Street E1 156 E2
Phipp's Mews SW1W 153 L5
Phipp Street EC2A 151 M3
Phoenix Place WC1X 150 F3
Phoenix Road NW1 150 B1
Phoenix Street WC2H 150 C6
Piccadilly W1J 153 L2
Piccadilly Arcade SW1Y 153 M1
Piccadilly Circus W1B 150 A8
Piccadilly Circus ⊖ W1J 150 B8
Pickard Street EC1V 151 J2
Picton Place W1U 149 K6
Pier Head E1W 156 E6
Pigott Street E14 157 M3
Pilgrimage Street SE1 155 L3
Pimlico ⊖ SW1V 154 B6
Pimlico Road SW1W 153 J6
Pinchin Street E1 156 D3
Pindar Street EC2A 151 M4
Pindock Mews W9 148 B3
Pine Street EC1R 150 F3
Pitfield Street N1 151 M1
Pitsea Street E1 157 H3
Pitt's Head Mews W1J 153 K2
Pitt Street W8 152 A2
Pixley Street E14 157 L2
Platina Street * EC2A 151 L3
Plover Way SE16 157 K8
Plumbers Row E1 156 D2
Plumtree Court EC4A 151 G5
Plympton Street NW8 148 F4
Pocock Street SE1 155 H2
Poland Street W1F 150 A6
Pollen Street W1S 149 L7
Pollitt Drive NW8 148 E3
Polperrom SE11 155 G5
Polygon Road NW1 150 B1
Pond Place SW3 152 F6
Ponler Street E1 156 E3
Ponsonby Place SW1P 154 C6
Ponsonby Terrace SW1P 154 C6
Ponton Road SW1V 154 B8
Pont Street SW1X 153 H4
Poolmans Street SE16 157 H6
Pope Street SE1 156 B7
Poplar Place W2 148 B7
Poppin's Court EC4A 151 H6
Porchester Gardens W2 148 B7
Porchester Gate W2 148 C8
Porchester Place W2 149 G6
Porchester Road W2 148 B5
Porchester Square W2 148 B6
Porchester Terrace W2 148 C7
Porchester Terrace North W2 148 C6
Porlock Street SE1 155 L3
Porter Street NW1 149 H4
Porteus Road W2 148 D5
Portland Place W1B 149 L4
Portland Place W1B 149 L5
Portland Square E1W 156 E5
Portland Street SE17 155 L7
Portman Close W1H 149 J6
Portman Mews South W1H 149 J6
Portman Square W1H 149 J6
Portman Street W1H 149 J6
Portpool Lane EC1N 150 F4
Portsea Place W2 149 G6
Portsmouth Street WC2A 150 E6
Portsoken Street E1 156 B3
Portugal Street WC2A 150 E6
Potier Street SE1 155 L4
Potters Fields SE1 156 B6
Pottery Street SE16 156 E7
Poultry EC2V 151 K6
Powis Place WC1N 150 D4
Praed Mews W2 148 E6
Praed Street W2 148 E6
Pratt Walk SE1 154 E5
Premier Place E14 157 M4
Prescot Street E1 156 C3
Preston Close SE1 155 M5
Price's Street SE1 155 H1
Prideaux Place WC1X 150 F2
Primrose Street EC2A 156 A1
Prince Albert Road NW8 148 F1
Prince Consort Road SW7 152 D3
Princelet Street E1 156 C1
Prince of Wales Gate SW7 152 F3
Princes Arcade SW1Y 150 A8
Prince's Gardens SW7 152 E3
Prince's Gate Mews SW7 152 E4
Princes Riverside Road SE16 157 H5
Prince's Square W2 148 A7
Princess Road NW6 148 A1
Princess Street SE1 155 H4
Princes Street W1B 149 L6
Prince's Street EC2R 151 L6
Princeton Street WC1R 150 E5
Prioress Street SE1 155 L4
Priory Green Estate N1 150 E1
Priory Walk SW10 152 D7
Proctor Street WC1V 150 E5
Prospect Place E1W 157 G5
Prospect Street SE16 156 E7
Provident Court W1K 149 J7
Provost Street N1 151 L1
Prusom Street E1W 156 F5
Pudding Lane EC3R 151 M7
Pumphouse Mews E1 156 D3
Purbrook Street SE1 156 A7
Purcell Street N1 151 M1
Purchese Street NW1 150 B1


## Q


Quebec Way SE16 157 J7
Queen Anne's Gate SW1H 154 B3
Queen Anne Street W1G 149 K5
Queen Elizabeth Street SE1 156 B6
Queen Mother Gate W2 153 J2
Queensborough Terrace W2 148 C7
Queensburry Place SW7 152 E5
Queen's Gardens W2 148 C7
Queen's Gate SW7 152 D3
Queen's Gate SW7 152 D4
Queen's Gate Gardens SW7 152 D5
Queen's Gate Mews SW7 152 D4
Queen's Gate Place SW7 152 D4
Queen's Gate Place Mews SW7 152 D4
Queen's Gate Terrace SW7 152 C4
Queen's Head Yard SE1 155 L2
Queen's Mews W2 148 B7
Queen Square WC1N 150 D4
Queen's Row SE17 155 K7
Queen Street EC4N 151 K7
Queen Street W1J 153 L1
Queen Street Place EC4R 151 K7
Queen's Walk SE1 156 A5
Queen's Walk SW1A 153 M2
Queensway W2 148 B6
Queensway ⊖ W2 148 B8
Queen Victoria Street EC4V 151 J7
Quick Street N1 151 H1


## R


Raby Street E14 157 K2
Radcliffe Road SE1 156 B8
Radcot Street SE11 155 G7
Radnor Mews W2 148 E6
Radnor Place W2 148 F6
Radnor Street EC1V 151 K3
Radnor Walk SW3 153 G7
Railway Approach SE1 155 L1
Railway Avenue SE16 157 G6
Railway Street N1 150 D1
Raine Street E1W 156 F5
Ralston Street SW3 153 H7
Ramillies Place W1F 149 M6
Ramillies Street W1F 149 M6
Rampart Street E1 156 E2
Rampayne Street SW1V 154 B6
Randall Road SE11 154 D6
Randall Row SE11 154 E6
Randolph Avenue W9 148 B1
Randolph Crescent W9 148 C3
Randolph Gardens NW6 148 B1
Randolph Mews W9 148 D4
Randolph Road W9 148 C4
Ranelagh Grove SW1W 153 K6
Ranelagh Road SW1V 154 A7
Rangoon Street * EC3N 156 B3
Ranston Street NW8 148 F4
Raphael Street SW7 153 G3
Ratcliffe Cross Street E1W 157 J3
Ratcliffe Lane E14 157 J3
Rathbone Place W1T 150 B5
Rathbone Street W1T 150 A5
Raven Row E1 156 F1
Ravensdon Street SE11 155 G7
Ravey Street EC2A 151 M3
Rawlings Street SW3 153 G5
Rawstone Street EC1V 151 H2
Ray Street EC1R 151 G4
Reardon Place E1W 156 E5
Reardon Street E1W 156 E5
Rectory Square E1 157 H1
Redan Place W2 148 B6
Redburn Street SW3 153 G7
Redcastle Close E1W 157 G4
Redcliffe Gardens SW10 152 B7
Redcliffe Mews SW10 152 C7
Redcliffe Place SW10 152 C8
Redcliffe Road SW10 152 D7
Redcliffe Square SW10 152 B7
Redcliffe Street SW10 152 B8
Redcross Way SE1 155 K2
Redesdale Street SW3 153 G7
Redfield Lane SW5 152 A5
Redhill Street NW1 149 L1
Red Lion Row SE5 155 K8
Red Lion Square WC1R 150 E5
Red Lion Street WC2B 150 E5
Redman's Road E1 157 G1
Red Place W1K 149 J7
Redriff Road SE16 157 J8
Reedworth Street SE11 155 G6
Reeves Mews W1K 149 J8
Regal Close E1 156 D1
Regan Way N1 151 M1
Regency Street SW1P 154 B5
Regent Place W1B 150 A7
Regent's Park ⊖ W1B 149 L4
Regent's Park NW1 149 J1
Regent's Park Estate NW1 149 L2
Regent Square WC1H 150 D2
Regent Street SW1Y 150 B8
Regent Street W1S 149 M7
Relton Mews SW7 153 G4
Remington Street N1 151 H1
Remnant Street WC2A 150 E6
Renforth Street SE16 157 G7
Renfrew Road SE11 155 H5
Rennie Street SE1 155 H1
Rephidim Street SE1 155 M4
Repton Street E14 157 K2
Reveley Square SE16 157 K7
Rex Place W1K 149 J8
Rhodeswell Road E14 157 L2
Rich Street E14 157 M3
Rickett Street SW6 152 A8
Ridgemount Street WC1E 150 B4
Ridgemount Gardens WC1E 150 B4
Riding House Street W1W 149 M5
Riley Road SE1 156 B7
Ripley's Believe It or Not! W1J 150 B8
Risborough Street SE1 155 J2
Risdon Street SE16 157 G7
Rissinghill Street N1 150 F1
River Street EC1R 150 F2
Rivington Street EC2A 151 M3
Robert Adam Street W1U 149 J6
Roberts Close SE16 157 J7
Robert Street NW1 149 L2
Rochester Row SW1P 154 A5
Rochester Street SW1P 154 B5
Rockingham Street SE1 155 J4
Rocliffe Street N1 151 H1
Roding Mews E1W 156 D5
Rodmarton Street W1U 149 H5
Rodney Place SE17 155 K5
Rodney Road SE17 155 K5
Rodney Street N1 150 E1
Roger Street WC1N 150 E4
Roland Gardens SW7 152 D6
Roland Way SE17 155 L7
Romford Street E1 156 E2
Romilly Street W1D 150 B7
Romney Street SW1P 154 C5
Rood Lane EC3M 151 M7
Ropemaker Road SE16 157 K7
Ropemaker Street EC2Y 151 L4
Roper Lane SE1 156 B7
Rope Street SE16 157 K8
Rope Walk Gardens E1 156 E2
Rosary Gardens SW7 152 D6
Roscoe Street EC1Y 151 K3
Rose Alley SE1 151 K8
Rosebery Avenue EC1R 150 F3
Rosemoor Street SW3 153 G6
Rose Street WC2E 150 C7
Rossmore Road NW1 149 G3
Rotary Street SE1 155 H3
Rotherhithe ⊖ SE16 157 G6
Rotherhithe Street SE16 157 G6
Rotherhithe Street SE16 157 J4
Rotherhithe Tunnel SE16 157 H5
Rothsay Street SE1 155 M4
Rotten Row W2 152 F2
Rouel Road SE16 156 C8
Roupell Street SE1 155 G2
Royal Albert Hall SW7 152 E3
Royal Avenue SW3 153 H6
Royal Hospital Road SW3 153 H7
Royal Mint Street E1 156 C4
Royal Oak ⊖ W2 148 B5
Royal Oak Yard SE1 156 A7
Royal Opera House WC2E 150 D7
Royal Road SE17 155 H8
Royal Street SE1 154 E3
Rudolph Road NW6 148 A1
Rugby Street WC1N 150 E4
Rum Close E1W 156 F4
Rupack Street SE16 156 F7
Rupert Street W1D 150 B7
Rushworth Street SE1 155 H2
Russell Court SW1A 154 A2
Russell Square WC1B 150 C4
Russell Square ⊖ WC1B 150 D4
Russell Street WC2B 150 D7
Russia Dock Road SE16 157 K6
Rutherford Street SW1P 154 B5
Rutland Gardens SW7 153 G3
Rutland Gate SW7 152 F3
Rutland Mews SW7 152 F4
Rutland Street SW7 152 F4
Ryder Street SW1Y 154 A1


## S


Sackville Street W1S 150 A8
Saffron Hill EC1N 151 G4
Saffron Street EC1N 151 G4
Sail Street SE11 154 F5
St Agnes Place SE11 155 G8
St Alban's Grove W8 152 B4
St Alban's Street SW1Y 150 B8
St Alphage Garden EC2Y 151 K5
St Andrews Hill EC4V 151 H7
St Andrew's Place NW1 149 L3
St Andrew Street EC4A 151 G5
St Anne's Court W1F 150 B6
St Ann's Street SW1P 154 C4
St Anselm's Place W1K 149 K7
St Barnabas Street SW1W 153 K6
St Botolph Street EC3N 156 B2
St Bride Street EC4A 151 G6
St Chad's Street WC1H 150 D2
St Clare Street EC3N 156 B3
St Clements Lane WC2A 150 E6
St Cross Street EC1N 151 G4
St Dunstan's Hill EC3R 151 M8
St Dunstan's Lane EC3R 151 M7
St Elmos Road SE16 157 J7
St Ermin's Hill SW1H 154 B3
St George's Circus SE1 155 H3
St George's Drive SW1V 153 M6
St George's Estate E1 156 D3
St George's Lane * EC3R 151 M7
St George's Road SE1 155 G4
St George's Square SW1V 154 B7
St George Street W1S 149 L7
St Giles High Street WC2H 150 C6
St Helen's Place EC3A 151 M6
St James Market * SW1Y 150 B8
St James's Park ⊖ SW1H 154 B3
St James's Park SW1A 154 B3
St James's Place SW1A 153 M2
St James's Road SE16 156 D8
St James's Square SW1Y 154 A1
St James's Street SW1A 153 M1
St James Walk EC1R 151 G3
St John's Lane EC1M 151 H4
St John's Place EC1M 151 H4
St John's Square EC1V 151 H4
St John Street EC1V 151 H2
St John's Wood High Street NW8 148 F1
St John's Wood Road NW8 148 E3
St Katharine's Way E1W 156 C5
St Leonard's Terrace SW3 153 H7
St Loo Avenue SW3 153 G8
St Luke's Close EC1V 151 K3
St Luke's Street SW3 152 F6
St Manningtree E1 156 C2
St Mark Street E1 156 C3
St Martin's Lane WC2N 150 C7
St Martin's le Grand EC1A 151 J6
St Mary at Hill EC3R 151 M8
St Mary Axe EC3A 156 A3
St Mary Church Street SE16 156 F7
St Mary's Gardens SE11 155 G5
St Mary's Terrace W2 148 D4
St Mary's Walk SE11 155 G5
St Matthew Street SW1P 154 B4
St Michael's Street W2 148 F6
St Olav's Square SE16 156 F7
St Oswald's Place SE11 154 E7
St Pancras International ⇌ N1C 150 C1
St Paul's ⊖ EC1A 151 J6
St Paul's Avenue SE16 157 J5
St Paul's Cathedral EC4M 151 J6
St Paul's Churchyard EC4M 151 J6
St Paul's Way E3 157 L1
St Petersburgh Mews W2 148 B7
St Petersburgh Place W2 148 B7
St Saviours Wharf SE1 156 C6
St Stephen's Gardens W2 148 A5
St Swithin's Lane EC4N 151 L7
St Thomas Street SE1 155 L2
St Vincent Street W1U 149 J5
Salamanca Street SE1 154 D6
Salem Road W2 148 B7
Sale Place W2 148 F5
Salisbury Court EC4Y 151 G6
Salisbury Place W1H 149 H4
Salisbury Street NW8 148 F4
Salmon Lane E14 157 J2
Salter Road SE16 157 J5
Salter Street E14 157 M4
Samford Street NW8 148 F4
Sampson Street E1W 156 D5
Sancroft Street SE11 154 F6
Sandford Row SE17 155 L6
Sandland Street WC1R 150 E5
Sandpiper Close SE16 157 L6
Sandwich Street WC1H 150 C2
Sandy's Row E1 156 B1
Sans Walk EC1R 151 G3
Sardinia Street WC2A 150 E6
Savage Gardens EC3N 156 B3
Savile Row W1S 149 M7
Savoy Hill WC2R 150 E8
Savoy Place WC2R 150 D8
Savoy Street WC2E 150 E7
Sawyer Street SE1 155 J2
Scala Street W1T 150 A5
Scandrett Street E1W 156 E5
Scarborough Street E1 156 C3
Scarsdale Villas W8 152 A4
Schooner Close * SE16 157 H6
Science Museum SW7 152 E4
Scoresby Street SE1 155 H2
Scotch House Junction SW1X 153 H3
Scotland Place SW1A 154 C1
Scott Ellis Grove NW8 148 E2
Scott Lidgett Crescent SE16 156 D7
Scrutton Street EC2A 151 M3
Seaford Street WC1H 150 D2
Seagrave Road SW6 152 A8
Sea Life London Aquarium SE1 154 E3
Searles Road SE1 155 L5
Sebastian Street EC1V 151 H2
Secker Street SE1 154 F2
Sedan Way SE17 155 M6
Sedding Street SW1X 153 J5
Seddon Street WC1X 150 E3
Seething Lane EC3N 156 A4
Sekforde Street EC1R 151 H3
Selfridges W1A 149 J6
Selsey Street E14 157 M1
Selwood Place SW7 152 E6
Semley Place SW1W 153 K6
Senior Street W2 148 B4
Senrab Street E1 157 H2
Serle Street WC2A 150 F6
Serpentine Bridge W2 152 E1
Serpentine Road W2 152 F2
Seth Street SE16 157 G7
Settles Street E1 156 D2
Seven Dials WC2H 150 C6
Seville Street SW1X 153 H3
Sevington Street W9 148 A3
Seward Street EC1V 151 J3
Seymour Mews W1H 149 J6
Seymour Place W1H 149 G5
Seymour Street W1H 149 H6
Seymour Street W2 149 G7
Seymour Walk SW10 152 C7
Shad Thames SE1 156 B6
Shad Thames SE1 156 C6
Shadwell ⊖ ⊖ E1 156 F3
Shadwell Gardens E1 156 F3
Shaftesbury Avenue W1D 150 B7
Shaftesbury Avenue WC2H 150 C6
Shaftesbury Street N1 151 K1
Shakespeare's Globe SE1 151 J8
Shand Street SE1 156 A6
Sharsted Street SE17 155 H7
Shaw Crescent E14 157 K2
Shawfield Street SW3 153 G7
Sheffield Terrace W8 152 A2
Sheldon Square W2 148 D5
Shelmerdine Close E3 157 M1
Shelton Street WC2H 150 D6
Shepherdess Walk N1 151 K1
Shepherd Street W1J 153 K1
Sheraton Street W1F 150 B6
Sherborne Lane EC4N 151 L7
Ship and Mermaid Row SE1 155 M2
Shipwright Road SE16 157 K7
Shirland Road W9 148 A3
Shoe Lane EC4A 151 G5
Shorter Street EC3N 156 B4
Shorts Gardens WC2H 150 C6
Short Street SE1 155 G2
Shoulder of Mutton Alley E14 157 K4
Shouldham Street W1H 149 G5
Shroton Street NW1 148 F4
Siddons Lane W1H 149 H4
Sidmouth Street WC1N 150 D3
Sidney Square E1 156 F2
Sidney Street E1 156 F1
Silex Street SE1 155 H3
Silk Street EC2Y 151 K4
Silver Walk SE16 157 K5
Silvester Street SE1 155 K3
Singer Street EC2A 151 L3
Sir John Soane's Museum WC2A 150 E5
Skinner Place * SW1W 153 J6
Skinners Lane EC4V 151 K7
Skinner Street EC1R 151 G3
Slippers Place SE16 156 F8
Sloane Avenue SW3 153 G6
Sloane Court SW3 153 J6
Sloane Court East SW3 153 J6
Sloane Gardens SW1W 153 J6
Sloane Square SW1W 153 J5
Sloane Square ⊖ SW1W 153 J6
Sloane Street SW1X 153 H3
Sloane Terrace SW1X 153 J5
Smeaton Street E1W 156 E5
Smithfield Street EC1A 151 H5
Smith Square SW1P 154 C4
Smith Street SW3 153 G7
Smith Terrace SW3 153 G7
Smithy Street E1 157 G1
Snowden Street EC2A 151 M4
Snow Hill EC1A 151 H5
Snowsfields SE1 155 L2
Soho Square W1D 150 B6
Soho Street W1D 150 B6
Somerford Way SE16 157 K7
Somers Crescent W2 148 F6
Somerset House WC2R 150 E7
Somerstown Estate NW1 150 A1
Sondes Street SE17 155 L7
South & West Africa Gate SW1A 154 A3
Southall Place SE1 155 L3
Southampton Buildings WC2A 150 F5
Southampton Place WC1A 150 D5
Southampton Row WC1B 150 D4
Southampton Street WC2E 150 D7
South Audley Street W1K 149 K8
South Carriage Drive SW1X 153 H3
South Carriage Drive SW7 152 F3
South Eaton Place SW1W 153 J5
Southern Street N1 150 E1
South Kensington ⊖ SW7 152 E4
South Kensington ⊖ SW7 152 E5
South Lambeth Road SW8 154 D8
South Molton Lane W1K 149 K7
South Molton Street W1K 149 K7
South Parade SW3 152 E7
South Place EC2M 151 L5
South Sea Street SE16 157 L8
South Square WC1R 150 F5
South Street W1K 153 J1
South Tenter Street E1 156 C3
South Terrace SW7 152 F5
Southwark ⊖ SE1 155 H2
Southwark Bridge SE1 151 K8
Southwark Bridge Road SE1 155 J3
Southwark Park Road SE16 156 E8
Southwark Street SE1 155 H1
Southwell Gardens SW7 152 C5
South Wharf Road W2 148 E6
Southwick Mews W2 148 F6
Southwick Place W2 148 F6
Southwick Street W2 148 F6
Sovereign Close E1W 156 F4
Sovereign Crescent SE16 157 J4
Spanish Place W1U 149 J5
Spa Road SE16 156 C8
Spear Mews SW5 152 A6
Spelman Street E1 156 C1
Spence Close SE16 157 K7
Spencer Street EC1V 151 H2
Spenser Street SW1E 154 A4
Spert Street E14 157 J4
Spital Square E1 156 A1
Spring Gardens SW1A 154 C1
Spring Street W2 148 E6
Spurgeon Street SE1 155 L4
Spur Road SE1 154 F3
Stables Way SE11 154 F7
Stable Yard Road SW1A 154 A2
Stacey Street WC2H 150 C6
Stafford Place SW1E 153 M3
Stafford Road NW6 148 A2
Stafford Street W1S 149 M8
Stafford Terrace W8 152 A3
Stainer Street SE1 155 L2

Stainsby Road E14 ............ 157 M2
Stalham Street SE16 ......... 156 F8
Stamford Street SE1 .......... 155 G1
Stanford Place SE1 ........... 155 M6
Stanford Road W8 ............ 152 B4
Stanhope Close * SE16 ...... 157 H6
Stanhope Gardens SW7 ...... 152 D5
Stanhope Gate W1K .......... 153 K1
Stanhope Mews SW7 ......... 152 D5
Stanhope Mews East SW7 ... 152 D5
Stanhope Mews West SW7 ... 152 D5
Stanhope Place W2 ........... 149 G7
Stanhope Place Gate W2 ..... 149 G7
Stanhope Row W1J ........... 153 K1
Stanhope Street NW1 ........ 149 M1
Stanhope Terrace W2 ........ 148 E7
Stannary Street SE11 ........ 155 G7
Staples Close SE16 .......... 157 J5
Staple Street SE1 ............ 155 L3
Starcross Street NW1 ....... 150 A2
Star Street W2 ............... 148 F6
Station Approach Road SE1 . 154 F3
Stave Yard Road SE16 ....... 157 J5
Stead Street SE17 ........... 155 K6
Steedman Street SE17 ....... 155 J5
Steel's Lane E1 .............. 157 G3
Steeres Way SE16 ........... 157 K7
Stephenson Way NW1 ........ 150 A3
Stephen Street W1T .......... 150 B5
Stepney Green E1 ............ 157 H1
Stepney High Street E1 ...... 157 J1
Stepney Way E1 .............. 156 F1
Sterling Street SW7 ......... 153 G3
Stevedore Street E1W ....... 156 E5
Stevens Street SE1 .......... 156 A7
Steward Street * E1 .......... 156 B1
Stewart's Grove SW3 ........ 152 F6
Stew Lane EC4V .............. 151 J7
Stillington Street SW1P ...... 154 A5
Stockholm Way E1W ......... 156 D5
Stocks Place E14 ............. 157 M3
Stone Buildings WC2A ....... 150 F5
Stonecutter Street EC4A ..... 151 G6
Stoney Lane E1 .............. 156 B2
Stoney Street SE1 ........... 155 K1
Stopford Road SE17 ......... 155 J7
Store Street WC1E ........... 150 B5
Storey's Gate SW1H ......... 154 C3
Storks Road SE16 ........... 156 D8
Stoughton Close SE11 ....... 154 E6
Stourcliffe Street W1H ....... 149 G6
Strafford Street E14 ......... 157 M6
Strand WC2R ................ 150 D8
Stratford Place W1C ......... 149 K6
Stratford Road W8 ........... 152 A5
Strathearn Place W2 ......... 148 F7
Stratton Street W1J .......... 153 L1
Strype Street E1 ............. 156 B2
Stuart Road NW6 ............ 148 A2
Stukeley Street WC2B ........ 150 D6
Sturgeon Road SE17 ......... 155 J7
Sturge Street SE1 ........... 155 J3
Sturt Street N1 ............... 151 K1
Stutfield Street E1 ........... 156 D3
Sudley Street N1 ............. 151 H1
Sudrey Street SE1 ........... 155 J3
Suffolk Lane EC4V ........... 151 L7
Suffolk Street SW1Y ......... 150 B8
Sugar Quay Walk EC3R ...... 156 A4
Sullivan Road SE11 .......... 155 G5
Summercourt Road E1 ....... 157 G2
Summer Place SW7 .......... 152 E6
Summers Street EC1R ....... 150 F4
Sumner Street SE1 .......... 155 J1
Sunderland Terrace W2 ...... 148 A6
Sun Passage SE16 ........... 156 D8
Sun Street EC2M ............. 151 M4
Surrendale Place W9 ........ 148 A4
Surrey Quays Road SE16 .... 157 H7
Surrey Row SE1 .............. 155 H2
Surrey Square SE17 ......... 155 M6
Surrey Street WC2E ......... 150 E7
Surrey Water Road SE16 .... 157 H6
Sussex Gardens W2 ......... 148 E6
Sussex Mews East W2 ...... 148 E7
Sussex Place NW1 ........... 149 H3
Sussex Place W2 ............ 148 E6
Sussex Square W2 ........... 148 E7
Sussex Street SW1V ......... 153 L7
Sutherland Avenue W9 ...... 148 A4
Sutherland Row SW1V ....... 153 L6
Sutherland Square SE17 ..... 155 J7
Sutherland Street SW1V ..... 153 L7
Sutton Row W1D ............. 150 B6
Sutton Street E1 ............. 157 G3
Suttons Way EC1Y ........... 151 K4
Swain Street NW8 ........... 148 F3
Swallow Place W1B .......... 149 L6
Swallow Street W1B ......... 150 A8
Swan Lane EC4R ............. 151 L8
Swan Mead SE1 .............. 155 M4
Swan Road SE16 ............. 157 G6
Swan Street SE1 ............. 155 K3
Swan Walk SW3 .............. 153 H8
Swedenborg Gardens E1 ..... 156 E4
Sweeney Crescent SE1 ...... 156 C7
Swinton Street WC1X ........ 150 E2
Sydney Street SW3 .......... 152 F6
Symons Street SW3 ......... 153 H6

T

Tabard Gardens Estate SE1 . 155 L3
Tabard Street SE1 ........... 155 L3
Tabernacle Street EC2A ...... 151 L3
Tachbrook Street SW1V ...... 154 A6
Talbot Road W2 .............. 148 A6
Talbot Square W2 ............ 148 E6
Tallis Street EC4Y ........... 151 G7
Tamworth Street SW6 ....... 152 A8
Tanner Street SE1 ........... 156 A7
Taplow Street N1 ............ 151 K1
Tarling Street E1 ............. 156 F3
Tarver Road SE17 ........... 155 H7
Tate Britain SW1P ........... 154 C6
Tate Modern SE1 ............ 151 J8
Tatum Street SE17 .......... 155 M6
Taunton Place NW1 ......... 149 G3
Tavistock Place WC1H ....... 150 C3
Tavistock Square WC1H ..... 150 C3
Tavistock Street WC2E ...... 150 D7
Taviton Street WC1H ........ 150 B3
Teak Close SE16 ............. 157 K6
Tedworth Square SW3 ....... 153 G7
Telford Terrace SW1V ....... 153 M7
Temeraire Street SE16 ...... 157 G6
Temple ⊖ WC2R ............. 150 F7
Temple Avenue EC4Y ........ 151 G7
Temple Lane EC4Y ........... 151 G7

Temple Place WC2R ......... 150 F7
Templeton Place SW5 ....... 152 A5
Tench Street E1W ........... 156 E5
Tenniel Close W2 ............ 148 C7
Tennis Street SE1 ........... 155 L2
Tenterden Street W1S ....... 149 L6
Tenterground E1 ............. 156 B1
Teredo Street SE16 .......... 157 J8
Terminus Place SW1V ....... 153 L4
Thame Road SE16 ........... 157 H6
Thanet Street WC1H ......... 150 C2
Thavies Inn EC4A ............ 151 G6
Thayer Street W1U .......... 149 K5
The Arches WC2N ........... 150 D8
The Boltons SW10 ........... 152 C7
The British Library NW1 ..... 150 C2
The Broad Walk W2 ......... 148 B8
The Broad Walk W8 ......... 152 C2
The Cut SE1 ................. 155 G2
Theed Street SE1 ........... 155 G2
The Flower Walk W2 ........ 152 D3
The Grange SE1 ............. 156 B8
The Highway E1W ........... 156 E4
The Little Boltons SW10 ..... 152 C7
The Mall SW1A .............. 154 B2
The Mitre E14 ............... 157 L3
The Monument EC3R ........ 151 L7
The National Gallery WC2N . 150 C8
Theobald's Road WC1X ...... 150 E4
Theobald Street SE1 ........ 155 L5
The Oval (Surrey County
  Cricket Ground) SE11 ... 154 F8
The Shard SE1 ............... 155 L2
The Vale SW3 ............... 152 E8
Thirleby Road SW1P ......... 154 A4
Thomas More Street E1W .... 156 D4
Thomas Road E14 ........... 157 M2
Thoresby Street N1 ......... 151 K1
Thorney Street SW1P ....... 154 C5
Thornton Place W1H ......... 149 H4
Thrale Street SE1 ........... 155 K1
Thrawl Street E1 ............. 156 C1
Threadneedle Street EC2R .. 151 L6
Three Colt Street E14 ....... 157 L3
Three Oak Lane SE1 ........ 156 B6
Throgmorton Avenue EC2N . 151 L6
Throgmorton Street EC2N ... 151 L6
Thurland Road SE16 ........ 156 D8
Thurloe Place SW7 .......... 152 F5
Thurloe Square SW7 ........ 152 F5
Thurloe Street SW7 ......... 152 E5
Thurlow Street SE17 ........ 155 M7
Tichbourne Row W2 ......... 148 F6
Tiller Road E14 .............. 157 M8
Tillman Street E1 ............ 156 E3
Tilney Street W1J ............ 153 K1
Timber Pond Road SE16 .... 157 J6
Tinsley Road E1 ............. 157 G1
Tinworth Street SE11 ....... 154 D6
Tisdall Place SE17 ........... 155 L6
Tite Street SW3 ............. 153 H8
Tiverton Street SE1 ......... 155 J4
Token House Yard EC2R ..... 151 L6
Tolmer's Square NW1 ....... 150 A3
Tomlin's Terrace E14 ........ 157 K2
Tonbridge Street WC1H ..... 150 D2
Tooley Street SE1 ........... 155 L1
Tooley Street SE1 ........... 156 B6
Tor Gardens W8 ............. 152 A2
Torquay Street W2 .......... 148 A5
Torrens Street EC1V ........ 151 G1
Torrington Place SE1 ........ 156 D5
Torrington Place W1E ....... 150 B4
Torrington Square WC1E .... 150 B4
Tothill Street SW1H ......... 154 B3
Tottenham Court Road W1T . 150 A4
Tottenham Court
  Road ⊖ W1D .............. 150 B6
Tottenham Street W1T ...... 150 A5
Toulmin Street SE1 .......... 155 J3
Tower Bridge EC3N .......... 156 B5
Tower Bridge
  Approach EC3N .......... 156 B5
Tower Bridge Road SE1 ..... 156 A7
Tower Bridge Wharf E1W .... 156 C5
Tower Gateway ⊖ EC3N ..... 156 B4
Tower Hill EC3N ............. 156 B4
Tower Hill ⊖ EC3N .......... 156 B4
Tower of London EC3N ...... 156 B4
Tower Place EC3R ........... 156 A4
Tower Street WC2H ......... 150 C7
Toynbee Street E1 .......... 156 B1
Trafalgar Gardens E1 ....... 157 H1
Trafalgar Square WC2N ..... 150 C8
Trafalgar Street SE17 ....... 155 L7
Transept Street NW1 ....... 148 F5
Trebeck Street W1J ......... 153 L1
Trebovir Road SW5 ......... 152 A6
Tregunter Road SW10 ....... 152 C7
Trenton Road SE16 ......... 156 E8
Tresham Crescent NW8 ..... 148 F3
Trevor Place SW7 ........... 153 G3
Trevor Square SW7 ......... 153 G3
Trevor Street SW7 .......... 153 G3
Trinidad Street E14 ......... 157 M4
Trinity Church Square SE1 .. 155 K3
Trinity Square EC3N ........ 156 B4
Trinity Street SE1 ........... 155 K3
Trump Street EC2V .......... 151 K6
Tudor Street EC4Y .......... 151 G7
Tufton Street SW1P ......... 154 C4
Tunnel Road SE16 .......... 157 G6
Turks Row SW3 ............. 153 J6
Turner's Road E3 ............ 157 L2
Turner Street E1 ............ 156 E2
Turnmill Street EC1N ........ 151 G4
Turpentine Lane SW1V ...... 153 L7
Turquand Street SE17 ....... 155 K6
Tyers Gate SE1 ............. 155 M3
Tyers Street SE11 ........... 154 E7
Tyers Terrace SE11 ......... 154 E7
Tyron Street SW3 ........... 153 H6
Tysoe Street EC1R .......... 151 G3

U

Udall Street SW1P ........... 154 A5
Ufford Street SE1 ........... 155 G3
Ulster Place NW1 ........... 149 K4
Umberston Street E1 ........ 156 E2
Underwood Road E1 ........ 156 D1
Underwood Street N1 ....... 151 K1
Union Street SE1 ............ 155 H2
University Street WC1E ..... 150 A4
Upbrook Mews W2 .......... 148 D6
Upper Belgrave Street SW1X 153 K4
Upper Berkeley Street W1H . 149 H6

Upper Brook Street W1K .... 149 J7
Upper Cheyne Row SW3 .... 152 F8
Upper Grosvenor Street W1K 149 J8
Upper Ground SE1 .......... 154 F1
Upper Harley Street NW1 ... 149 K3
Upper James Street W1F .... 150 A7
Upper John Street W1F ..... 150 A7
Upper Marsh SE1 ........... 154 E3
Upper Montagu Street W1H . 149 H5
Upper St Martin's WC2H .... 150 C7
Upper Tachbrook
  Street SW1V ............. 154 A5
Upper Thames Street EC4V . 151 J7
Upper Wimpole Street W1G . 149 K4
Upper Woburn Place WC1H . 150 B2
Urlwin Street SE5 ........... 155 J8
Uxbridge Street W8 ......... 152 A1

V

Valentine Place SE1 ........ 155 G3
Vandon Passage SW1H ..... 154 A3
Vandon Street SW1H ....... 154 A4
Vandy Street EC2A .......... 151 M4
Varden Street E1 ............ 156 E2
Varndell Street NW1 ........ 149 M2
Vaughan Street SE16 ....... 157 L7
Vaughan Way E1W .......... 156 D5
Vauxhall ⊖ ⊕ SW8 ......... 154 D7
Vauxhall Bridge SE1 ........ 154 D7
Vauxhall Bridgefoot SE1 .... 154 D7
Vauxhall Bridge Road SW1V 153 M5
Vauxhall Cross SE1 ......... 154 D8
Vauxhall Grove SW8 ........ 154 D8
Vauxhall Street SE11 ....... 154 E6
Vauxhall Walk SE11 ........ 154 E6
Venables Street W2 ........ 148 E4
Vere Street W1G ........... 149 K6
Vernon Place WC1A ........ 150 D5
Vernon Rise WC1X ......... 150 F2
Verulam Street WC1X ...... 150 F4
Vestry Street N1 ........... 151 L2
Victoria ⊖ ⊕ SW1V ......... 153 L5
Victoria & Albert
  Museum SW7 ............. 152 F4
Victoria Embankment SW1A . 154 D2
Victoria Embankment WC2R . 150 F7
Victoria Gate W2 ........... 148 E7
Victoria Road W8 ........... 152 C4
Victoria Square SW1V ...... 153 L4
Victoria Street SW1E ....... 153 L4
Victoria Place SE17 ......... 155 K5
Victory Place SE17 ......... 155 K5
Victory Way SE16 .......... 157 K7
Vigo Street W1S ............ 149 M8
Villa Street SE17 ........... 155 L7
Villiers Street WC2N ........ 150 D8
Vincent Close SE16 ......... 157 K7
Vincent Square SW1P ...... 154 B5
Vincent Street SW1P ....... 154 B5
Vincent Terrace N1 ......... 151 H1
Vince Street EC1V .......... 151 L2
Vine Court E1 .............. 156 D1
Vinegar Street E1W ........ 156 E5
Vine Hill EC1R ............. 150 F4
Vine Lane SE1 ............. 156 A6
Vine Street EC3N .......... 156 B3
Violet Hill NW8 ............ 148 C1
Virgil Street SE1 ........... 154 F4
Virginia Street E1W ........ 156 D4
Viscount Street EC2Y ...... 151 J4

W

Wadding Street SE17 ....... 155 K6
Wakefield Street WC1H ..... 150 D3
Wakeling Street E14 ........ 157 J3
Wakley Street EC1V ........ 151 H2
Walbrook EC4N ............ 151 L7
Walcorde Avenue SE17 ..... 155 K6
Walcot Square SE11 ........ 155 G5
Walden Street E1 ........... 156 E2
Wallwood Street E14 ....... 157 M1
Walnut Tree Walk SE11 ..... 154 F5
Walpole Street SW3 ........ 153 H6
Walter Terrace E1 .......... 157 H2
Walton Place SW3 ......... 153 H4
Walton Street SW3 ......... 153 G4
Walworth Place SE17 ....... 155 K7
Walworth Road SE17 ....... 155 J5
Wandsworth Road SW8 ..... 154 C8
Wansey Street SE17 ........ 155 J6
Wapping ⊖ E1W ............ 156 F5
Wapping High Street E1W ... 156 E6
Wapping Lane E1W ......... 156 F4
Wapping Wall E1W ......... 157 G5
Warden's Grove SE1 ....... 155 J2
Wardour Street W1F ........ 150 B6
Warner Street EC1R ........ 150 F4
Warren Street W1T ......... 149 M4
Warren Street ⊖ NW1 ...... 149 M3
Warrington Crescent W9 .... 148 C3
Warrington Gardens W9 .... 148 C4
Warwick Avenue W9 ........ 148 B3
Warwick Avenue ⊖ W9 ..... 148 C4
Warwick Crescent W2 ...... 148 C5
Warwick House Street SW1Y 154 B1
Warwick Lane EC4M ........ 151 H6
Warwick Place W9 ......... 148 C4
Warwick Road SW5 ........ 152 A6
Warwick Row SW1E ........ 153 L4
Warwick Square SW1V ..... 153 M6
Warwick Street W1B ........ 150 A7
Warwick Way SW1V ........ 153 L7
Waterhouse Square EC1N .. 151 G5
Waterloo ⊖ ⊕ SE1 ......... 155 M3
Waterloo Bridge SE1 ....... 154 E1
Waterloo Bridge WC2R ..... 150 E8
Waterloo East ⊖ SE1 ....... 155 G2
Waterloo Place SW1Y ...... 154 B1
Waterloo Road SE1 ........ 154 F1
Waterloo Road SE1 ........ 155 G2
Waterman Way E1W ....... 156 E5
Waterside Close SE16 ...... 156 D7
Watling Street EC4N ....... 151 K7
Watney Street E1 .......... 156 F3
Waveney Close E1W ....... 156 D5
Waverton Street W1J ...... 149 K8
Weavers Lane SE1 ........ 156 A6
Webber Row SE1 .......... 155 G3
Webber Street SE1 ........ 155 H3
Webb Street SE1 .......... 156 A8
Webster Road SE16 ....... 156 D8
Weigh House Street W1K ... 149 K7
Welbeck Street W1G ...... 149 K5
Welbeck Way W1G ........ 149 K6

Welland Mews E1W ........ 156 E5
Wellclose Square E1 ....... 156 D4
Wellesley Street E1 ........ 157 H2
Wellesley Terrace N1 ...... 151 K2
Wellington Arch W1J ....... 153 K2
Wellington Place NW8 ..... 148 E2
Wellington Road NW8 ..... 148 E1
Wellington Square SW3 .... 153 H6
Wellington Street WC2E ... 150 D7
Wells Mews W1T .......... 150 A5
Wells Street W1T .......... 150 A5
Wells Way SE5 ............ 155 M8
Wenlock Road N1 ......... 151 K1
Wenlock Street N1 ........ 151 K1
Wentworth Street E1 ...... 156 B2
Werrington Street NW1 .... 150 A1
Wesley Street W1G ....... 149 K5
West Arbour Street E1 .... 157 G2
Westbourne Crescent W2 .. 148 D7
Westbourne Gardens W2 .. 148 B6
Westbourne Gate W2 ..... 148 E7
Westbourne Grove W2 .... 148 A6
Westbourne Grove
  Terrace W2 .............. 148 B6
Westbourne Park Road W2 . 148 A5
Westbourne Park Villas W2 . 148 A5
Westbourne Street W2 .... 148 E7
Westbourne Terrace W2 ... 148 D6
Westbourne Terrace
  Mews W2 ................ 148 C6
Westbourne Terrace
  Road W2 ................ 148 C5
West Brompton ⊖ ⊕ SW5 .. 152 A7
West Carriage Drive W2 ... 152 E2
Westcott Road SE17 ....... 155 H8
West Cromwell Road SW5 . 152 A5
Western Place SE16 ....... 157 G6
Westferry ⊖ E14 .......... 157 M4
Westferry Circus E14 ...... 157 M5
Westferry Road E14 ....... 157 M5
West Gardens E1W ....... 156 F4
Westgate Terrace SW10 ... 152 B7
West Halkin Street SW1X .. 153 J4
West India Avenue E14 .... 157 M5
West India Dock Road E14 . 157 M3
Westland Place N1 ........ 151 K2
West Lane SE16 .......... 156 E7
Westminster ⊖ SW1A ..... 154 D3
Westminster Abbey SW1P .. 154 C3
Westminster Bridge SE1 ... 154 D3
Westminster Bridge
  Road SE1 ............... 154 F3
Westmoreland Place SW1V . 153 L7
Westmoreland Road SE17 .. 155 K8
Westmoreland Street W1G . 149 K5
Westmoreland Terrace SW1V 153 L7
Weston Rise WC1X ........ 150 E1
Weston Street SE1 ........ 155 M2
Weston Street SE1 ........ 156 A7
Westport Street E1 ........ 157 H2
West Poultry Avenue EC1A . 151 H5
West Road SW3 ........... 153 H7
West Smithfield EC1A ..... 151 H5
West Square SE11 ........ 155 H4
West Street WC2H ........ 150 C7
West Tenter Street E1 ..... 156 C3
West Warwick Place SW1V . 153 M6
Westway W2 .............. 148 B5
Wetherby Gardens SW5 ... 152 C6
Weyhill Road E1 .......... 156 D2
Weymouth Mews W1G .... 149 L5
Weymouth Street W1G .... 149 K5
Wharfdale Road N1 ....... 150 D1
Wharfedale Street SW10 .. 152 B7
Wharf Road N1 ........... 151 J1
Wharton Street WC1X ..... 150 F2
Wheatley Street W1G ..... 149 K5
Whetstone Park WC2A .... 150 E5
Whidborne Street WC1H ... 150 D2
Whiskin Street EC1R ...... 151 G2
Whitcomb Street WC2H ... 150 B8
Whitechapel ⊖ ⊕ E1 ...... 156 E1
Whitechapel Estate E1 .... 156 C4
Whitechapel High Street E1 . 156 C2
Whitechapel Road E1 ..... 156 D1
Whitecross Street EC1Y ... 151 K3
Whitefriars Street EC4Y ... 151 G6
Whitehall SW1A ........... 154 C2
Whitehall Court SW1A ..... 154 D2
Whitehall Place SW1A ..... 154 D1
Whitehaven Street NW8 ... 148 F4
Whitehead's Grove SW3 ... 153 G6
White Horse Lane E1 ...... 157 H1
Whitehorse Road E1 ...... 157 J1
Whitehorse Road E1 ...... 157 J3
White Horse Street W1J ... 153 L1
White Kennett Street E1 ... 156 B2
White Lion Hill EC4V ...... 151 H7
White Lion Street N1 ...... 150 F1
White's Grounds SE1 ..... 156 A7
White's Row E1 ........... 156 B1
White Tower Way E1 ...... 157 J1
Whitfield Place W1T ....... 150 A4
Whitfield Street W1T ...... 150 A4
Whitgift Street SE11 ...... 154 E5
Whittaker Street SW1W ... 153 J6
Whittlesey Street SE1 ..... 155 G2
Wicker Street E1 .......... 156 E3
Wickham Close E1 ........ 157 G1
Wickham Street SE11 ..... 154 E7
Wicklow Street WC1X ..... 150 E2
Widegate Street E1 ....... 156 A1
Widley Road W9 .......... 148 A3
Wigmore Place W1G ...... 149 K5
Wigmore Street W1U ..... 149 K6
Wigton Place SE11 ....... 155 G7
Wilbraham Place SW1X ... 153 J5
Wild Court WC2B ......... 150 E6
Wild's Rents SE1 ......... 155 M4
Wild Street WC2B ........ 150 D6
Wilfred Street SW1E ...... 153 M4
Wilkes Street E1 .......... 156 B1
William IV Street WC2N ... 150 C8
William Mews SW1X ...... 153 H3
William Road NW1 ........ 149 M3
Willow Place SW1P ....... 154 A5
Willow Street EC2A ....... 151 M3
Wilmington Square WC1X . 150 F3
Wilmington Street WC1X .. 150 F2
Wilson Grove SE16 ....... 156 E7
Wilson Street EC2A ....... 151 L4
Wilton Crescent SW1X .... 153 J3
Wilton Mews SW1X ....... 153 K4
Wilton Place SW1X ....... 153 J3
Wilton Road SW1V ....... 153 L4
Wilton Row SW1X ........ 153 J3
Wilton Street SW1X ...... 153 K4
Wimpole Mews W1G ...... 149 K5
Wimpole Street W1G ..... 149 K5

Winchester Street SW1V .. 153 L6
Winchester Walk SE1 ..... 155 K1
Wincott Street SE11 ...... 155 G5
Windmill Road SE11 ...... 154 F7
Windmill Walk SE1 ....... 150 B5
Windrose Close SE16 ..... 157 H6
Windsor Terrace N1 ...... 151 K1
Wine Close E1W .......... 156 F5
Winnett Street W1D ...... 150 B7
Winsland Mews W2 ...... 148 E6
Winsland Street W2 ...... 148 E6
Winsley Street W1W ..... 150 A6
Winthrop Street E1 ...... 156 E1
Woburn Place WC1H ..... 150 C3
Woburn Square WC1H ... 150 C4
Wodeham Gardens E1 ... 156 E1
Wolfe Crescent SE16 .... 157 H7
Wolseley Street SE1 .... 156 C6
Woodbridge Street EC1R . 151 G3
Woodchester Square W9 . 148 A4
Woodfall Street SW3 .... 153 H7
Woodland Crescent SE16 . 157 H7
Woodseer Street E1 ..... 156 C1
Woods Mews W1K ...... 149 J7
Woods Place SE1 ....... 156 A8
Woodstock Street W1C .. 149 K6
Wood Street EC2V ...... 151 K6
Woolaston Close SE1 ... 155 J5
Wooler Street SE17 ..... 155 L7
Wooton Street SE1 ..... 155 G2
Worgan Street SE11 .... 154 E6
Worgan Street SE16 .... 157 H8
Wormwood Street EC2M . 151 M5
Worship Street EC2A ... 151 M4
Wren Street WC1X ..... 150 E3
Wright's Lane W8 ...... 152 A3
Wyatt Close SE16 ..... 157 L7
Wyclif Street EC1V .... 151 H2
Wymering Road W9 ... 148 A2
Wynard Street SE11 ... 154 F7
Wyndham Place W1H .. 149 H5
Wyndham Street W1H . 149 G4
Wynnstay Gardens W8 . 152 A4
Wynyat Street EC1V ... 151 H2
Wythburn Place W1H .. 149 H6

Y

Yalding Road SE16 ...... 156 C8
Yardley Street WC1X .... 150 F2
Yeomans Row SW3 ...... 153 G4
York Boulevard WC2N ... 150 D8
York Bridge NW1 ........ 149 J3
York Gate NW1 .......... 149 J4
York Road SE1 .......... 154 E2
York Street W1H ........ 149 G5
Yorkshire Road E14 ..... 157 K3
York Square E14 ........ 157 J2
York Street W1H ........ 149 G5
York Terrace East NW1 .. 149 J4
York Terrace West NW1 . 149 J4
York Way N1 ........... 150 D1

Z

Zoar Street SE1 ......... 155 J1
ZSL London Zoo NW1 ... 149 J1

# Index to place names

This index lists places appearing in the main-map section of the atlas in alphabetical order. The reference following each name gives the atlas page number and grid reference of the square in which the place appears. The map shows counties, unitary authorities and administrative areas, together with a list of the abbreviated name forms used in the index. The top 100 places of tourist interest are indexed in **red**, World Heritage sites in **green**, motorway service areas in **blue**, airports in blue *italic* and National Parks in green *italic*.

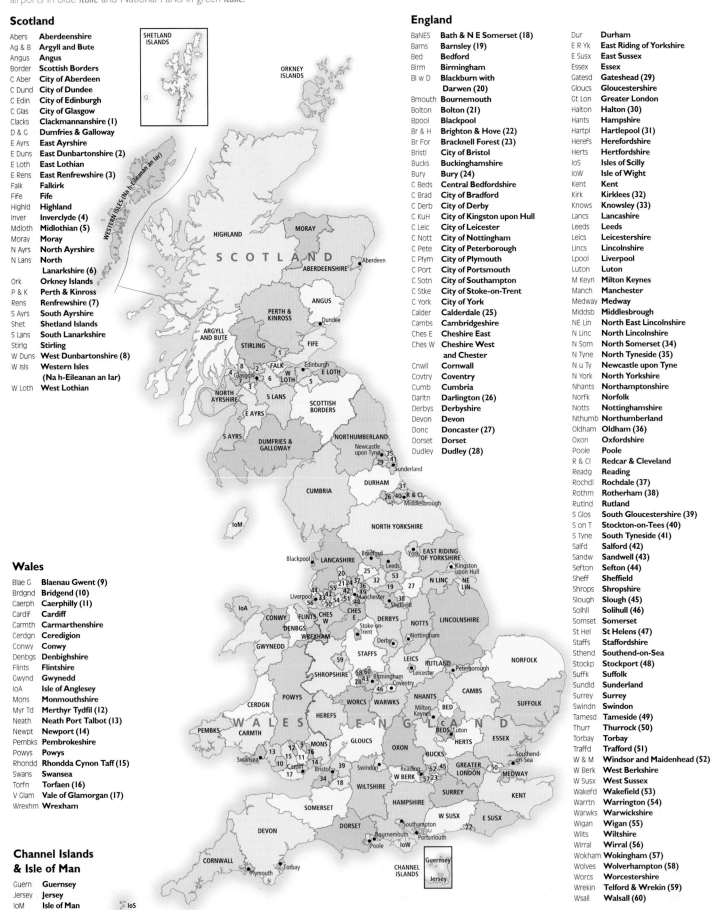

## Scotland

| | |
|---|---|
| Abers | **Aberdeenshire** |
| Ag & B | **Argyll and Bute** |
| Angus | **Angus** |
| Border | **Scottish Borders** |
| C Aber | **City of Aberdeen** |
| C Dund | **City of Dundee** |
| C Edin | **City of Edinburgh** |
| C Glas | **City of Glasgow** |
| Clacks | **Clackmannanshire (1)** |
| D & G | **Dumfries & Galloway** |
| E Ayrs | **East Ayrshire** |
| E Duns | **East Dunbartonshire (2)** |
| E Loth | **East Lothian** |
| E Rens | **East Renfrewshire (3)** |
| Falk | **Falkirk** |
| Fife | **Fife** |
| Highld | **Highland** |
| Inver | **Inverclyde (4)** |
| Mdloth | **Midlothian (5)** |
| Moray | **Moray** |
| N Ayrs | **North Ayrshire** |
| N Lans | **North Lanarkshire (6)** |
| Ork | **Orkney Islands** |
| P & K | **Perth & Kinross** |
| Rens | **Renfrewshire (7)** |
| S Ayrs | **South Ayrshire** |
| Shet | **Shetland Islands** |
| S Lans | **South Lanarkshire** |
| Stirlg | **Stirling** |
| W Duns | **West Dunbartonshire (8)** |
| W Isls | **Western Isles (Na h-Eileanan an Iar)** |
| W Loth | **West Lothian** |

## Wales

| | |
|---|---|
| Blae G | **Blaenau Gwent (9)** |
| Brdgnd | **Bridgend (10)** |
| Caerph | **Caerphilly (11)** |
| Cardif | **Cardiff** |
| Carmth | **Carmarthenshire** |
| Cerdgn | **Ceredigion** |
| Conwy | **Conwy** |
| Denbgs | **Denbighshire** |
| Flints | **Flintshire** |
| Gwynd | **Gwynedd** |
| IoA | **Isle of Anglesey** |
| Mons | **Monmouthshire** |
| Myr Td | **Merthyr Tydfil (12)** |
| Neath | **Neath Port Talbot (13)** |
| Newpt | **Newport (14)** |
| Pembks | **Pembrokeshire** |
| Powys | **Powys** |
| Rhondd | **Rhondda Cynon Taff (15)** |
| Swans | **Swansea** |
| Torfn | **Torfaen (16)** |
| V Glam | **Vale of Glamorgan (17)** |
| Wrexhm | **Wrexham** |

## Channel Islands & Isle of Man

| | |
|---|---|
| Guern | **Guernsey** |
| Jersey | **Jersey** |
| IoM | **Isle of Man** |

## England

| | |
|---|---|
| BaNES | **Bath & N E Somerset (18)** |
| Barns | **Barnsley (19)** |
| Bed | **Bedford** |
| Birm | **Birmingham** |
| Bl w D | **Blackburn with Darwen (20)** |
| Bmouth | **Bournemouth** |
| Bolton | **Bolton (21)** |
| Bpool | **Blackpool** |
| Br & H | **Brighton & Hove (22)** |
| Br For | **Bracknell Forest (23)** |
| Bristl | **City of Bristol** |
| Bucks | **Buckinghamshire** |
| Bury | **Bury (24)** |
| C Beds | **Central Bedfordshire** |
| C Brad | **City of Bradford** |
| C Derb | **City of Derby** |
| C KuH | **City of Kingston upon Hull** |
| C Leic | **City of Leicester** |
| C Nott | **City of Nottingham** |
| C Pete | **City of Peterborough** |
| C Plym | **City of Plymouth** |
| C Port | **City of Portsmouth** |
| C Sotn | **City of Southampton** |
| C Stke | **City of Stoke-on-Trent** |
| C York | **City of York** |
| Calder | **Calderdale (25)** |
| Cambs | **Cambridgeshire** |
| Ches E | **Cheshire East** |
| Ches W | **Cheshire West and Chester** |
| Cnwll | **Cornwall** |
| Covtry | **Coventry** |
| Cumb | **Cumbria** |
| Darltn | **Darlington (26)** |
| Derbys | **Derbyshire** |
| Devon | **Devon** |
| Donc | **Doncaster (27)** |
| Dorset | **Dorset** |
| Dudley | **Dudley (28)** |

| | |
|---|---|
| Dur | **Durham** |
| E R Yk | **East Riding of Yorkshire** |
| E Susx | **East Sussex** |
| Essex | **Essex** |
| Gatesd | **Gateshead (29)** |
| Gloucs | **Gloucestershire** |
| Gt Lon | **Greater London** |
| Halton | **Halton (30)** |
| Hants | **Hampshire** |
| Hartpl | **Hartlepool (31)** |
| Herefs | **Herefordshire** |
| Herts | **Hertfordshire** |
| IoS | **Isles of Scilly** |
| IoW | **Isle of Wight** |
| Kent | **Kent** |
| Kirk | **Kirklees (32)** |
| Knows | **Knowsley (33)** |
| Lancs | **Lancashire** |
| Leeds | **Leeds** |
| Leics | **Leicestershire** |
| Lincs | **Lincolnshire** |
| Lpool | **Liverpool** |
| Luton | **Luton** |
| M Keyn | **Milton Keynes** |
| Manch | **Manchester** |
| Medway | **Medway** |
| Middsb | **Middlesbrough** |
| NE Lin | **North East Lincolnshire** |
| N Linc | **North Lincolnshire** |
| N Som | **North Somerset (34)** |
| N Tyne | **North Tyneside (35)** |
| N u Ty | **Newcastle upon Tyne** |
| N York | **North Yorkshire** |
| Nhants | **Northamptonshire** |
| Norfk | **Norfolk** |
| Notts | **Nottinghamshire** |
| Nthumb | **Northumberland** |
| Oldham | **Oldham (36)** |
| Oxon | **Oxfordshire** |
| Poole | **Poole** |
| R & Cl | **Redcar & Cleveland** |
| Readg | **Reading** |
| Rochdl | **Rochdale (37)** |
| Rothm | **Rotherham (38)** |
| Rutlnd | **Rutland** |
| S Glos | **South Gloucestershire (39)** |
| S on T | **Stockton-on-Tees (40)** |
| S Tyne | **South Tyneside (41)** |
| Salfd | **Salford (42)** |
| Sandw | **Sandwell (43)** |
| Sefton | **Sefton (44)** |
| Sheff | **Sheffield** |
| Shrops | **Shropshire** |
| Slough | **Slough (45)** |
| Solhll | **Solihull (46)** |
| Somset | **Somerset** |
| St Hel | **St Helens (47)** |
| Staffs | **Staffordshire** |
| Sthend | **Southend-on-Sea** |
| Stockp | **Stockport (48)** |
| Suffk | **Suffolk** |
| Sundld | **Sunderland** |
| Surrey | **Surrey** |
| Swindn | **Swindon** |
| Tamesd | **Tameside (49)** |
| Thurr | **Thurrock (50)** |
| Torbay | **Torbay** |
| Traffd | **Trafford (51)** |
| W & M | **Windsor and Maidenhead (52)** |
| W Berk | **West Berkshire** |
| W Susx | **West Sussex** |
| Wakefd | **Wakefield (53)** |
| Warrtn | **Warrington (54)** |
| Warwks | **Warwickshire** |
| Wigan | **Wigan (55)** |
| Wilts | **Wiltshire** |
| Wirral | **Wirral (56)** |
| Wokham | **Wokingham (57)** |
| Wolves | **Wolverhampton (58)** |
| Worcs | **Worcestershire** |
| Wrekin | **Telford & Wrekin (59)** |
| Wsall | **Walsall (60)** |

**A**

Abbas Combe Somset ......... 17 Q10
Abberley Worcs ......... 39 N8
Abberley Common Worcs ... 39 N8
Abberton Essex ......... 34 G11
Abberton Worcs ......... 30 C4
Abbess Roding Essex ......... 22 C2
Abbeydale Sheff ......... 50 H4
Abbey Dore Herefs ......... 28 D3
Abbey Green Staffs ......... 50 C8
Abbey St Bathans Border ... 87 P9
Abbeystead Lancs ......... 63 K10
Abbey Town Cumb ......... 71 J5
Abbey Valley
    Crematorium Derbys .. 51 K9
Abbey Village Lancs ......... 57 M4
Abbey Wood Gt Lon ......... 21 P7
Abbotrule Border ......... 80 E10
Abbots Bickington Devon .. 14 G9
Abbots Bromley Staffs ...... 40 E3
Abbotsbury Dorset ......... 7 N6
Abbots Deuglie P & K ...... 92 G12
Abbotsham Devon ......... 14 H6
Abbotskerswell Devon ...... 6 B8
Abbots Langley Herts ...... 20 H3
Abbots Leigh N Som ......... 17 M2
Abbotsley Cambs ......... 32 H5
Abbots Morton Worcs ...... 30 D3
Abbots Ripton Cambs ...... 32 H2
Abbot's Salford Warwks .... 30 E4
Abbots Worthy Hants ...... 9 N2
Abbotts Ann Hants ......... 19 K11
Abbott Street Dorset ...... 8 E7
Abdon Shrops ......... 39 L5
Aberaeron Cerdgn ......... 36 G7
Aberaman Rhondd ......... 27 L8
Aberangell Gwynd ......... 47 N8
Aberarder Highld ......... 99 J4
Aberargie P & K ......... 92 H11
Aberarth Cerdgn ......... 36 H7
Aberavon Neath ......... 26 G10
Abercanaid Myr Td ......... 27 M7
Abercarn Caerph ......... 27 P9
Abercastle Pembks ......... 24 F3
Abercegir Powys ......... 47 N10
Aberchalder Lodge Highld .. 98 D8
Aberchirder Abers ......... 102 E5
Abercraf Powys ......... 26 H4
Abercregan Neath ......... 26 H9
Abercwmboi Rhondd ......... 27 L8
Abercych Pembks ......... 36 D11
Abercynon Rhondd ......... 27 M9
Aberdalgie P & K ......... 92 G10
Aberdare Rhondd ......... 27 L8
Aberdaron Gwynd ......... 46 C6
Aberdeen C Aber ......... 95 Q1
Aberdeen Airport C Aber ... 103 J11
Aberdeen Crematorium
    C Aber ......... 95 P2
Aberdour Fife ......... 86 E5
Aberdulais Neath ......... 26 G8
Aberdyfi Gwynd ......... 47 K11
Aberedw Powys ......... 38 C11
Abereiddy Pembks ......... 24 E3
Abererch Gwynd ......... 46 G4
Aberfan Myr Td ......... 27 M8
Aberfeldy P & K ......... 92 C6
Aberffraw IoA ......... 54 E7
Aberford Leeds ......... 59 K6
Aberfoyle Stirlg ......... 85 J3
Abergavenny Mons ......... 28 C6
Abergele Conwy ......... 55 P6
Abergorlech Carmth ......... 26 C2
Abergwesyn Powys ......... 37 P9
Abergwili Carmth ......... 25 Q5
Abergwynfi Neath ......... 27 J9
Abergwyngregyn Gwynd .... 55 J7
Abergynolwyn Gwynd ...... 47 L9
Aberkenfig Brdgnd ......... 27 J11
Aberlady E Loth ......... 87 J6
Aberlemno Angus ......... 93 N5
Aberllefenni Gwynd ......... 47 M8
Aberllynfi Powys ......... 27 N2
Aberlour Moray ......... 101 K6
Abermule Powys ......... 38 D4
Abernant Carmth ......... 25 N4
Aber-nant Rhondd ......... 27 L7
Abernethy P & K ......... 92 H11
Abernyte P & K ......... 93 J8
Aberporth Cerdgn ......... 36 D9
Abersoch Gwynd ......... 46 E6
Abersychan Torfn ......... 28 B7
Aberthin V Glam ......... 16 E2
Abertillery Blae G ......... 27 P7
Abertridwr Caerph ......... 27 N10
Abertridwr Powys ......... 48 B10
Aberuthven P & K ......... 92 E11
Aberystwyth Cerdgn ...... 37 J4
Aberystwyth
    Crematorium Cerdgn .. 37 K4
Abingdon-on-Thames
    Oxon ......... 19 N2
Abinger Common Surrey ... 10 H2
Abinger Hammer Surrey ... 10 H1
Afton IoW ......... 9 ⸱
Abington Nhants ......... 32 A5
Abington S Lans ......... 78 F4
Abington Pigotts Cambs ... 33 K7
Abington Services S Lans .. 78 F4
Abingworth W Susx ......... 10 H6
Ab Kettleby Leics ......... 41 Q3
Ablington Gloucs ......... 30 E11
Abney Derbys ......... 50 G5
Aboyne Abers ......... 95 J3
Abram Wigan ......... 57 L8
Abriachan Highld ......... 98 H2
Abridge Essex ......... 21 P4
Abronhill N Lans ......... 85 N7
Abson S Glos ......... 17 Q2
Abthorpe Nhants ......... 31 N5
Aby Lincs ......... 53 L7
Acaster Malbis C York ...... 59 N5
Acaster Selby N York ...... 59 M6
Accrington Lancs ......... 57 N3
Accrington
    Crematorium Lancs ... 57 N3
Acha Ag & B ......... 88 F5
Achahoish Ag & B ......... 83 L5
Achalader P & K ......... 92 G6
Achaleven Ag & B ......... 90 C9
Acha Mor W Isls ......... 111 c2
Achanalt Highld ......... 106 D9
Achandunie Highld ......... 107 K7
Achany Highld ......... 107 J3
Acharacle Highld ......... 89 N3
Acharn Highld ......... 89 P6

Acharn P & K ......... 92 B6
Achavanich Highld ......... 110 E7
Achduart Highld ......... 105 Q2
Achfary Highld ......... 108 F7
A'Chill Highld ......... 96 C8
Achiltibuie Highld ......... 105 Q1
Achina Highld ......... 109 M4
Achinhoan Ag & B ......... 75 L4
Achintee Highld ......... 97 N2
Achintraid Highld ......... 97 L2
Achmelvich Highld ......... 108 B10
Achmore Highld ......... 97 M3
Achmore W Isls ......... 111 c2
Achnacarnin Highld ......... 108 B8
Achnacarry Highld ......... 98 B10
Achnacloich Highld ......... 96 H7
Achnaconeran Highld ...... 98 F5
Achnacroish Ag & B ......... 90 B7
Achnadrish House Ag & B .. 89 K6
Achnafauld P & K ......... 92 D8
Achnagarron Highld ......... 107 L8
Achnaha Highld ......... 89 K3
Achnahaird Highld ......... 108 A11
Achnairn Highld ......... 109 K12
Achnalea Highld ......... 90 B4
Achnamara Ag & B ......... 83 L5
Achnasheen Highld ......... 106 C10
Achnashellach Lodge
    Highld ......... 105 Q11
Achnastank Moray ......... 101 K8
Achosnich Highld ......... 89 K3
Achranich Highld ......... 89 P6
Achreamie Highld ......... 110 B3
Achriabhach Highld ......... 90 F3
Achriesgill Highld ......... 108 E5
Achtoty Highld ......... 109 M3
Achurch Nhants ......... 42 E12
Achvaich Highld ......... 107 L4
Achvarasdal Highld ......... 110 B3
Ackergill Highld ......... 110 G5
Acklam Middsb ......... 66 C4
Acklam N York ......... 60 D2
Ackleton Shrops ......... 39 P3
Acklington Nthumb ......... 73 M1
Ackton Wakefd ......... 59 K9
Ackworth Moor Top
    Wakefd ......... 59 K10
Acle Norfk ......... 45 N7
Acock's Green Birm ......... 40 E10
Acol Kent ......... 23 P9
Acomb C York ......... 59 M4
Acomb Nthumb ......... 72 G7
Aconbury Herefs ......... 28 F3
Acton Ches E ......... 49 L5
Acton Gt Lon ......... 21 K7
Acton Staffs ......... 49 P7
Acton Suffk ......... 34 E7
Acton Beauchamp Herefs .. 39 M11
Acton Bridge Ches W ...... 49 L1
Acton Burnell Shrops ...... 39 K2
Acton Green Herefs ......... 39 M11
Acton Park Wrexhm ......... 48 G5
Acton Round Shrops ...... 39 L3
Acton Scott Shrops ......... 39 J4
Acton Trussell Staffs ...... 40 C4
Acton Turville S Glos ...... 18 B5
Adbaston Staffs ......... 49 N9
Adber Dorset ......... 17 N11
Adbolton Notts ......... 51 N12
Adderbury Oxon ......... 31 L7
Adderley Shrops ......... 49 M7
Addiewell W Loth ......... 86 B9
Addingham C Brad ......... 58 E4
Addington Bucks ......... 31 Q8
Addington Gt Lon ......... 21 M9
Addington Kent ......... 22 D10
Addinston Border ......... 87 J7
Addiscombe Gt Lon ......... 21 M9
Addlestone Surrey ......... 20 G9
Addlethorpe Lincs ......... 53 N9
Adeyfield Herts ......... 20 H2
Adfa Powys ......... 38 C2
Adforton Herefs ......... 38 H7
Adisham Kent ......... 23 N11
Adlestrop Gloucs ......... 30 G8
Adlingfleet E R Yk ......... 60 E9
Adlington Lancs ......... 57 L6
Admaston Staffs ......... 40 D3
Admaston Wrekin ......... 49 L11
Adpar Cerdgn ......... 36 E11
Adsborough Somset ......... 16 H9
Adscombe Somset ......... 16 G8
Adstock Bucks ......... 31 Q7
Adstone Nhants ......... 31 N4
Adversane W Susx ......... 10 H5
Advie Highld ......... 100 H8
Adwick le Street Donc ...... 59 M11
Adwick upon Dearne
    Donc ......... 51 L1
Ae D & G ......... 78 G10
Ae Bridgend D & G ......... 78 G10
Afan Forest Park Neath ... 26 H8
Affleck Abers ......... 102 D7
Affpuddle Dorset ......... 8 B8
Affric Lodge Highld ......... 98 B5
Afon-wen Flints ......... 48 D2
Afton IoW ......... 9 ⸱
Agecroft Crematorium
    Salfd ......... 57 P8
Agglethorpe N York ......... 65 J9
Aigburth Lpool ......... 56 H10
Aike E R Yk ......... 60 H5
Aiketgate Cumb ......... 71 P6
Aikton Cumb ......... 71 L5
Ailsworth C Pete ......... 42 G9
Ainderby Quernhow
    N York ......... 65 N10
Ainderby Steeple N York .. 65 N8
Aingers Green Essex ...... 35 J11
Ainsdale Sefton ......... 56 F6
Ainstable Cumb ......... 71 Q6
Ainsworth Bury ......... 57 N6
Ainthorpe N York ......... 66 G6
Aintree Sefton ......... 56 H8
Ainville W Loth ......... 86 D9
Aird Ag & B ......... 83 L3
Aird D & G ......... 68 E7
Aird W Isls ......... 111 e2
Aird a Mhulaidh W Isls ... 111 c3
Aird Asaig W Isls ......... 111 c3
Aird Dhubh Highld ......... 97 J2
Airdeny Ag & B ......... 90 D9
Aird of Kinloch Ag & B .... 89 L9
Aird of Sleat Highld ...... 96 H9
Airdrie N Lans ......... 85 N9
Airdriehill N Lans ......... 85 N9
Airds of Kells D & G ...... 69 P5
Aird Uig W Isls ......... 111 c2

Airidh a bhruaich W Isls .. 111 c3
Airieland D & G ......... 70 C4
Airlie Angus ......... 93 K5
Airmyn E R Yk ......... 60 C9
Airntully P & K ......... 92 G8
Airor Highld ......... 97 J8
Airth Falk ......... 85 Q5
Airton N York ......... 58 B3
Aisby Lincs ......... 42 E3
Aisby Lincs ......... 52 C5
Aish Devon ......... 5 N7
Aish Devon ......... 6 A10
Aisholt Somset ......... 16 G8
Aiskew N York ......... 65 M9
Aislaby N York ......... 66 H9
Aislaby N York ......... 67 J6
Aislaby S on T ......... 65 P5
Aisthorpe Lincs ......... 52 D7
Aith Shet ......... 111 k4
Akeld Nthumb ......... 81 K8
Akeley Bucks ......... 31 P6
Akenham Suffk ......... 35 J7
Albaston Cnwll ......... 5 J6
Alberbury Shrops ......... 48 G11
Albourne W Susx ......... 11 K6
Albrighton Shrops ......... 39 P2
Albrighton Shrops ......... 49 J10
Alburgh Norfk ......... 45 L11
Albury Herts ......... 33 M10
Albury Surrey ......... 10 G1
Albury Heath Surrey ...... 10 G2
Alcaig Highld ......... 107 J10
Alcaston Shrops ......... 39 J5
Alcester Warwks ......... 30 E3
Alcester Lane End Birm ... 40 E10
Alciston E Susx ......... 11 P8
Alcombe Somset ......... 16 C7
Alconbury Cambs ......... 32 H2
Alconbury Weston Cambs .. 32 H1
Aldborough N York ......... 59 K2
Aldborough Norfk ......... 45 K4
Aldbourne Wilts ......... 19 J5
Aldbrough E R Yk ......... 61 L6
Aldbrough St John N York .. 65 L5
Aldbury Herts ......... 20 F2
Aldcliffe Lancs ......... 63 J9
Aldclune P & K ......... 92 D3
Aldeburgh Suffk ......... 35 P5
Aldeby Norfk ......... 45 P10
Aldenham Herts ......... 21 J4
Alderbury Wilts ......... 8 H2
Alderford Norfk ......... 45 J6
Alderholt Dorset ......... 8 G5
Alderley Gloucs ......... 29 K10
Alderley Edge Ches E ...... 57 Q12
Aldermans Green Covtry ... 41 J10
Aldermaston W Berk ...... 19 P7
Alderminster Warwks ...... 30 G4
Aldershot Hants ......... 20 D12
Alderton Gloucs ......... 30 D7
Alderton Nhants ......... 31 Q5
Alderton Suffk ......... 35 M8
Alderton Wilts ......... 18 C4
Aldfield N York ......... 58 H1
Aldford Ches W ......... 48 H4
Aldgate Rutlnd ......... 42 E8
Aldham Essex ......... 34 F10
Aldham Suffk ......... 34 H7
Aldingbourne W Susx ...... 10 E8
Aldingham Cumb ......... 62 F7
Aldington Kent ......... 13 K3
Aldington Worcs ......... 30 E5
Aldington Corner Kent ..... 13 K3
Aldivalloch Moray ......... 101 M9
Aldochlay Ag & B ......... 84 F5
Aldreth Cambs ......... 33 M3
Aldridge Wsall ......... 40 D7
Aldringham Suffk ......... 35 P5
Aldsworth Gloucs ......... 30 F11
Aldunie Moray ......... 101 M9
Aldwark Derbys ......... 50 G8
Aldwark N York ......... 59 L2
Aldwick W Susx ......... 10 E9
Aldwincle Nhants ......... 32 F1
Aldworth W Berk ......... 19 P5
Alexandria W Duns ......... 84 G7
Aley Somset ......... 16 G8
Alfington Devon ......... 6 F4
Alfold Surrey ......... 10 G4
Alfold Crossways Surrey ... 10 G3
Alford Abers ......... 102 D11
Alford Lincs ......... 53 M8
Alford Somset ......... 17 N9
Alford Crematorium Lincs .. 53 M8
Alfreton Derbys ......... 51 K9
Alfrick Worcs ......... 39 N10
Alfrick Pound Worcs ...... 39 N10
Alfriston E Susx ......... 11 P9
Algarkirk Lincs ......... 43 J3
Alhampton Somset ......... 17 P8
Alkborough N Linc ......... 60 F9
Alkham Kent ......... 13 N2
Alkmonton Derbys ......... 50 F12
Allaleigh Devon ......... 5 Q9
Allanaquoich Abers ......... 94 B4
Allanbank N Lans ......... 85 P10
Allanton Border ......... 81 J4
Allanton N Lans ......... 85 P10
Allanton S Lans ......... 85 M11
Allaston Gloucs ......... 28 H7
Allbrook Hants ......... 9 M4
All Cannings Wilts ......... 18 F8
Allendale Nthumb ......... 72 F9
Allenheads Nthumb ......... 72 F10
Allen's Green Herts ......... 33 M12
Allensmore Herefs ......... 28 F2
Allenton C Derb ......... 41 J2
Aller Devon ......... 15 N7
Aller Somset ......... 17 L9
Allerby Cumb ......... 70 H7
Allercombe Devon ......... 6 E4
Allerford Somset ......... 16 B6
Allerston N York ......... 67 J10
Allerthorpe E R Yk ......... 60 D5
Allerton C Brad ......... 58 E7
Allerton Highld ......... 107 M8
Allerton Lpool ......... 56 H10
Allerton Bywater Leeds .... 59 K8
Allerton Mauleverer
    N York ......... 59 K3
Allesley Covtry ......... 40 H10
Allestree C Derb ......... 51 J11
Allexton Leics ......... 42 B9
Allgreave Ches E ......... 50 C7
Allhallows Medway ......... 22 H7
Alligin Shuas Highld ...... 105 M10
Allington Dorset ......... 7 L4

Allington Lincs ......... 42 C3
Allington Wilts ......... 18 D5
Allington Wilts ......... 18 F8
Allington Wilts ......... 18 H11
Allithwaite Cumb ......... 62 H6
Alloa Clacks ......... 85 P4
Allonby Cumb ......... 70 H7
Alloway S Ayrs ......... 76 F7
Allowenshay Somset ...... 17 K12
All Stretton Shrops ......... 39 J3
Alltchaorunn Highld ...... 90 G6
Alltwalis Carmth ......... 25 Q3
Alltwen Neath ......... 26 G7
Alltyblaca Cerdgn ......... 36 H10
Allweston Dorset ......... 17 P12
Almeley Herefs ......... 38 G11
Almington Staffs ......... 49 N8
Almondbank P & K ......... 92 F9
Almondbury Kirk ......... 58 F10
Almondsbury S Glos ...... 28 H11
Alne N York ......... 59 L2
Alness Highld ......... 107 L8
Alnham Nthumb ......... 81 L11
Alnmouth Nthumb ......... 81 P11
Alnwick Nthumb ......... 81 P10
Alperton Gt Lon ......... 21 J6
Alphamstone Essex ......... 34 E9
Alpheton Suffk ......... 34 E6
Alphington Devon ......... 6 C5
Alport Derbys ......... 50 G7
Alpraham Ches E ......... 49 L4
Alresford Essex ......... 34 H11
Alrewas Staffs ......... 40 F5
Alsager Ches E ......... 49 P4
Alsop en le Dale Derbys .. 50 F9
Alston Cumb ......... 72 D10
Alston Devon ......... 7 J3
Alstone Gloucs ......... 29 N3
Alstonefield Staffs ......... 50 F9
Alston Sutton Somset ...... 17 K6
Alswear Devon ......... 15 M7
Altandhu Highld ......... 108 A12
Altarnun Cnwll ......... 4 F4
Altass Highld ......... 106 H3
Altcreich Ag & B ......... 89 N8
Altgaltraig Ag & B ......... 83 Q8
Althorne Essex ......... 22 H4
Althorpe N Linc ......... 60 E11
Altnabreac Station Highld .. 110 B6
Altnaharra Highld ......... 109 K8
Alton Derbys ......... 51 J7
Alton Hants ......... 10 B3
Alton Staffs ......... 50 E11
Alton Barnes Wilts ......... 18 G8
Alton Pancras Dorset ...... 7 Q3
Alton Priors Wilts ......... 18 G8
Alton Towers Staffs ...... 50 E11
Altrincham Traffd ......... 57 P10
Altrincham
    Crematorium Traffd .. 57 N10
Altskeith Hotel Stirlg ...... 84 H3
Alva Clacks ......... 85 P4
Alvanley Ches W ......... 49 J1
Alvaston C Derb ......... 41 K2
Alvechurch Worcs ......... 40 D11
Alvecote Warwks ......... 40 G6
Alvediston Wilts ......... 8 E3
Alveley Shrops ......... 39 N5
Alverdiscott Devon ......... 15 J7
Alverstoke Hants ......... 9 P7
Alverstone IoW ......... 9 P10
Alverthorpe Wakefd ...... 58 H9
Alverton Notts ......... 42 B2
Alves Moray ......... 100 H3
Alvescot Oxon ......... 30 H12
Alveston S Glos ......... 28 H10
Alveston Warwks ......... 30 G3
Alvingham Lincs ......... 53 K5
Alvington Gloucs ......... 28 H8
Alwalton C Pete ......... 42 G10
Alwinton Nthumb ......... 81 J11
Alwoodley Leeds ......... 58 H6
Alyth P & K ......... 93 J6
Ambergate Derbys ......... 51 J9
Amberley Gloucs ......... 29 L8
Amberley W Susx ......... 10 G7
Amble Nthumb ......... 81 Q12
Amblecote Dudley ......... 40 B9
Ambler Thorn C Brad ...... 58 E8
Ambleside Cumb ......... 62 G2
Ambleston Pembks ......... 24 H4
Ambrosden Oxon ......... 31 N9
Amcotts N Linc ......... 60 E10
Amersham Bucks ......... 20 F4
Amersham Common
    Bucks ......... 20 F4
Amersham Old Town
    Bucks ......... 20 F4
Amersham on the Hill
    Bucks ......... 20 F4
Amerton Railway &
    Farm Staffs ......... 40 C2
Amesbury Wilts ......... 18 H11
Amhuinnsuidhe W Isls ..... 111 c3
Amington Staffs ......... 40 G6
Amisfield D & G ......... 78 G11
Amlwch IoA ......... 54 F3
Ammanford Carmth ......... 26 E6
Amotherby N York ......... 66 G11
Ampfield Hants ......... 9 L3
Ampleforth N York ......... 66 E10
Ampney Crucis Gloucs ..... 18 F1
Ampney St Mary Gloucs .. 18 G1
Ampney St Peter Gloucs .. 18 F1
Amport Hants ......... 19 K11
Ampthill C Beds ......... 32 E8
Ampton Suffk ......... 34 E3
Amroth Pembks ......... 25 K7
Amulree P & K ......... 92 D8
Amwell Herts ......... 21 J2
Anaheilt Highld ......... 89 Q4
Ancaster Lincs ......... 42 E2
Ancroft Nthumb ......... 81 L5
Anderby Lincs ......... 53 N8
Andover Hants ......... 19 L10
Andoversford Gloucs ...... 30 D9
Andreas IoM ......... 56 d2
Anerley Gt Lon ......... 21 M9
Anfield Lpool ......... 56 H9
Anfield Crematorium
    Lpool ......... 56 G9
Angarrack Cnwll ......... 2 E7
Angelbank Shrops ......... 39 L6
Angle Pembks ......... 24 F7
Anglesey IoA ......... 54 F5
Anglesey Abbey Cambs ... 33 N4

Angmering W Susx ......... 10 H8
Angram N York ......... 59 M5
Ankerville Highld ......... 107 N7
Anlaby E R Yk ......... 60 H8
Anmer Norfk ......... 44 C4
Anmore Hants ......... 9 Q5
Annan D & G ......... 71 K3
Annandale Water
    Services D & G ......... 78 H9
Annat Highld ......... 105 N10
Annathill N Lans ......... 85 M8
Anna Valley Hants ......... 19 L11
Annbank S Ayrs ......... 76 G6
Anne Hathaway's
    Cottage Warwks ...... 30 F3
Annfield Plain Dur ......... 73 L9
Anniesland C Glas ......... 85 J8
Ansdell Lancs ......... 56 G3
Ansford Somset ......... 17 P9
Ansley Warwks ......... 40 H8
Anslow Staffs ......... 40 G3
Anslow Gate Staffs ...... 40 G3
Anstey Herts ......... 33 L9
Anstey Leics ......... 41 M6
Anstruther Fife ......... 87 L2
Ansty W Susx ......... 11 K6
Ansty Warwks ......... 41 K10
Ansty Wilts ......... 8 E3
Anthorn Cumb ......... 71 K4
Antingham Norfk ......... 45 L4
An t-Ob W Isls ......... 111 c4
Antonine Wall Falk ......... 85 P7
Anton's Gowt Lincs ......... 43 J1
Antony Cnwll ......... 5 J8
Antrobus Ches W ......... 57 M11
Anwick Lincs ......... 52 G12
Anwoth D & G ......... 69 N7
Aperfield Gt Lon ......... 21 N10
Apethorpe Nhants ......... 42 E10
Apley Lincs ......... 52 G8
Apperknowle Derbys ...... 51 J5
Apperley Gloucs ......... 29 M3
Appin Ag & B ......... 90 C7
Appleby N Linc ......... 60 G10
Appleby-in-
    Westmorland Cumb ... 64 C4
Appleby Magna Leics ...... 40 H5
Appleby Parva Leics ...... 40 H6
Applecross Highld ......... 97 J2
Appledore Devon ......... 14 H6
Appledore Devon ......... 16 E12
Appledore Kent ......... 13 J4
Appleford Oxon ......... 19 N3
Applegarth Town D & G .. 78 H11
Appleshaw Hants ......... 19 K10
Appleton Halton ......... 57 K11
Appleton Oxon ......... 19 M1
Appleton Warrtn ......... 57 L11
Appleton-le-Moors N York .. 66 G9
Appleton-le-Street N York .. 66 G11
Appleton Roebuck N York .. 59 M6
Appleton Thorn Warrtn .... 57 M11
Appleton Wiske N York .... 65 P6
Appletreehall Border ...... 80 C10
Appletreewick N York ...... 58 D3
Appley Somset ......... 16 E10
Appley Bridge Lancs ...... 57 K7
Apse Heath IoW ......... 9 P10
Apsley End C Beds ......... 32 G9
Apuldram W Susx ......... 10 D9
Arabella Highld ......... 107 N7
Arbirlot Angus ......... 93 Q7
Arboll Highld ......... 107 P6
Arborfield Wokham ......... 20 C9
Arborfield Cross Wokham .. 20 C9
Arbourthorne Sheff ...... 51 J4
Arbroath Angus ......... 93 Q7
Arbuthnott Abers ......... 95 N6
Archddu Carmth ......... 25 Q8
Archdeacon Newton
    Darltn ......... 65 M4
Archencarroch W Duns .... 84 G6
Archiestown Moray ...... 101 J6
Arclid Green Ches E ...... 49 P3
Ardallie Abers ......... 103 L7
Ardanaiseig Hotel Ag & B .. 90 E10
Ardaneaskan Highld ...... 97 L3
Ardarroch Highld ......... 97 L2
Ardbeg Ag & B ......... 84 F4
Ardbeg Ag & B ......... 84 B9
Ardbeg Ag & B ......... 84 C6
Ardcharnich Highld ...... 106 C5
Ardchiavaig Ag & B ...... 89 J11
Ardchonnel Ag & B ...... 83 P1
Ardchullarie More Stirlg ... 85 K1
Arddarroch Ag & B ...... 84 D4
Arddleen Powys ......... 48 F11
Ardechive Highld ......... 98 A10
Ardeer N Ayrs ......... 76 E4
Ardeley Herts ......... 33 K10
Ardelve Highld ......... 97 M4
Arden Ag & B ......... 84 F6
Ardens Grafton Warwks ... 30 E4
Ardentallen Ag & B ...... 90 B10
Ardentinny Ag & B ...... 84 D5
Ardentraive Ag & B ...... 83 Q7
Ardeonaig Stirlg ......... 91 P8
Ardersier Highld ......... 107 N10
Ardessie Highld ......... 105 Q5
Ardfern Ag & B ......... 83 M3
Ardfernal Ag & B ......... 82 H8
Ardgartan Ag & B ......... 84 E3
Ardgay Highld ......... 107 K4
Ardgour Highld ......... 90 D4
Ardgowan Inver ......... 84 D8
Ardhallow Ag & B ......... 84 C7
Ardhasig W Isls ......... 111 c3
Ardheslaig Highld ......... 105 L10
Ardindrean Highld ...... 106 C5
Ardingly W Susx ......... 11 M4
Ardington Oxon ......... 19 M3
Ardlamont Ag & B ......... 83 P9
Ardleigh Essex ......... 34 H10
Ardleigh Heath Essex ..... 34 H10
Ardler P & K ......... 93 J7
Ardley Oxon ......... 31 M8
Ardlui Ag & B ......... 91 J12
Ardlussa Ag & B ......... 83 J5
Ardmair Highld ......... 106 B3
Ardmaleish Ag & B ......... 84 B8
Ardminish Ag & B ......... 75 J3
Ardmolich Highld ......... 89 P2
Ardmore Ag & B ......... 84 F7
Ardmore Highld ......... 107 L5
Ardnadam Ag & B ......... 84 C7
Ardnagrask Highld ......... 106 H11
Ardnamurchan Highld .... 89 L3

Ardnarff Highld ....97 M3
Ardnastang Highld ....89 Q4
Ardpatrick Ag & B ....83 L10
Ardrishaig Ag & B ....83 M6
Ardross Highld ....107 K7
Ardrossan N Ayrs ....76 D3
Ardsley East Leeds ....58 H8
Ardslignish Highld ....89 L4
Ardtalla Ag & B ....82 G11
Ardtoe Highld ....89 M3
Arduaine Ag & B ....83 M2
Ardullie Highld ....107 J9
Ardvasar Highld ....96 H8
Ardvorlich P & K ....91 P10
Ardvourlie W Isls ....111 c3
Ardwell D & G ....68 F9
Ardwick Manch ....57 Q9
Areley Kings Worcs ....39 P7
Arevegaig Highld ....89 N3
Arford Hants ....10 D3
Argoed Caerph ....27 N8
Argyll Forest Park Ag & B ....84 D3
Aribruach W Isls ....111 c3
Aridhglas Ag & B ....88 H10
Arileod Ag & B ....88 E5
Arinagour Ag & B ....88 F5
Ariogan Ag & B ....90 B10
Arisaig Highld ....97 J11
Arisaig House Highld ....97 J11
Arkendale N York ....59 K2
Arkesden Essex ....33 M9
Arkholme Lancs ....63 L7
Arkleton D & G ....79 N10
Arkley Gt Lon ....21 K4
Arksey Donc ....59 M11
Arkwright Town Derbys ....51 K6
Arle Gloucs ....29 N4
Arlecdon Cumb ....70 G10
Arlesey C Beds ....32 H9
Arleston Wrekin ....49 M12
Arley Ches E ....57 M11
Arley Warwks ....40 H8
Arlingham Gloucs ....29 J6
Arlington Devon ....15 K4
Arlington E Susx ....12 B8
Armadale Highld ....96 H8
Armadale Highld ....109 N3
Armadale W Loth ....85 Q8
Armathwaite Cumb ....71 Q6
Arminghall Norfk ....45 L8
Armitage Staffs ....40 E4
Armley Leeds ....58 H7
Armscote Warwks ....30 G5
Armthorpe Donc ....59 N12
Arnabost Ag & B ....88 H8
Arncliffe N York ....64 G12
Arncroach Fife ....87 K2
Arndilly House Moray ....101 K6
Arne Dorset ....8 E9
Arnesby Leics ....41 N8
Arngask P & K ....92 H12
Arnisdale Highld ....97 L7
Arnish Highld ....104 H11
Arniston Mdloth ....86 G9
Arnol W Isls ....111 d1
Arnold E R Yk ....61 J6
Arnold Notts ....51 N11
Arnprior Stirlg ....85 K4
Arnside Cumb ....63 J6
Aros Ag & B ....89 L7
Arrad Foot Cumb ....62 F6
Arram E R Yk ....60 H5
Arran N Ayrs ....75 P5
Arrathorne N York ....65 L8
Arreton IoW ....9 N9
Arrina Highld ....105 L10
Arrington Cambs ....33 K6
Arrochar Ag & B ....84 E3
Arrow Warwks ....30 E3
Arscott Shrops ....38 H1
Artafallie Highld ....107 K11
Arthington Leeds ....58 H5
Arthingworth Nhants ....41 Q10
Arthrath Abers ....103 K7
Artrochie Abers ....103 L8
Arundel W Susx ....10 G8
Asby Cumb ....70 H10
Ascog Ag & B ....84 B9
Ascot W & M ....20 E9
Ascott-under-
　　Wychwood Oxon ....30 H9
Asenby N York ....65 P11
Asfordby Leics ....41 P4
Asfordby Hill Leics ....41 Q4
Asgarby Lincs ....42 G2
Ash Kent ....22 C9
Ash Kent ....23 P10
Ash Somset ....17 L11
Ash Surrey ....20 E12
Ashampstead W Berk ....19 P5
Ashbocking Suffk ....35 K6
Ashbourne Derbys ....50 F10
Ashbrittle Somset ....16 E11
Ashburton Devon ....5 P6
Ashbury Devon ....15 J11
Ashbury Oxon ....19 J4
Ashby N Linc ....52 C2
Ashby by Partney Lincs ....53 L9
Ashby cum Fenby NE Lin ....53 J4
Ashby de la Launde Lincs ....52 F11
Ashby-de-la-Zouch Leics ....41 J4
Ashby Folville Leics ....41 P5
Ashby Magna Leics ....41 M9
Ashby Parva Leics ....41 M9
Ashby Puerorum Lincs ....53 K8
Ashby St Ledgers Nhants ....31 M1
Ashby St Mary Norfk ....45 M9
Ashchurch Gloucs ....29 N3
Ashcombe Devon ....6 C6
Ashcombe N Som ....17 J4
Ashcott Somset ....17 L8
Ashdon Essex ....33 P8
Ashdown Forest E Susx ....11 P4
Ashe Hants ....19 N10
Asheldham Essex ....23 J3
Ashen Essex ....34 C8
Ashendon Bucks ....31 P10
Asheridge Bucks ....20 F3
Ashfield Stirlg ....85 N3
Ashfield cum Thorpe
　　Suffk ....35 K4
Ashfield Green Suffk ....35 L3
Ashford Devon ....5 N9
Ashford Derbys ....15 J3
Ashford Kent ....13 J2
Ashford Surrey ....20 H8
Ashford Bowdler Shrops ....39 K7

Ashford Carbonell Shrops ....39 K7
Ashford Hill Hants ....19 P8
Ashford in the Water
　　Derbys ....50 G6
Ashgill S Lans ....77 N2
Ash Green Surrey ....20 E12
Ash Green Warwks ....41 J9
Ashill Devon ....6 E1
Ashill Norfk ....44 E8
Ashill Somset ....17 J11
Ashingdon Essex ....22 G5
Ashington Nthumb ....73 M4
Ashington Somset ....17 N11
Ashington W Susx ....11 J7
Ashkirk Border ....79 P4
Ashleworth Gloucs ....29 L4
Ashleworth Quay Gloucs ....29 L4
Ashley Cambs ....34 B5
Ashley Ches E ....57 P11
Ashley Devon ....15 L9
Ashley Gloucs ....29 N9
Ashley Hants ....9 J8
Ashley Hants ....9 L2
Ashley Kent ....13 P1
Ashley Nhants ....42 B11
Ashley Staffs ....49 N7
Ashley Wilts ....18 B7
Ashley Green Bucks ....20 F3
Ash Magna Shrops ....49 K7
Ashmansworth Hants ....19 M8
Ashmansworthy Devon ....14 F8
Ash Mill Devon ....15 N7
Ashmore Dorset ....8 D4
Ashmore Green W Berk ....19 N6
Ashorne Warwks ....30 H3
Ashover Derbys ....51 J8
Ashow Warwks ....40 H12
Ashperton Herefs ....28 H1
Ashprington Devon ....5 Q8
Ash Priors Somset ....16 F9
Ashreigney Devon ....15 L9
Ash Street Suffk ....34 G7
Ashtead Surrey ....21 J10
Ash Thomas Devon ....6 D1
Ashton Ches W ....49 J2
Ashton Cnwll ....2 F9
Ashton Devon ....6 B6
Ashton Herefs ....39 K8
Ashton Inver ....84 D7
Ashton Nhants ....31 Q4
Ashton Nhants ....42 F11
Ashton Common Wilts ....18 D8
Ashton-in-Makerfield
　　Wigan ....57 L8
Ashton Keynes Wilts ....18 F2
Ashton under Hill Worcs ....30 C6
Ashton-under-Lyne
　　Tamesd ....50 C2
Ashurst Hants ....9 K5
Ashurst Kent ....11 P3
Ashurst Lancs ....57 J7
Ashurst W Susx ....11 J6
Ashurstwood W Susx ....11 N3
Ash Vale Surrey ....20 E11
Ashwater Devon ....5 J2
Ashwell Herts ....33 J8
Ashwell Rutlnd ....42 C7
Ashwell End Herts ....33 J8
Ashwellthorpe Norfk ....45 J9
Ashwick Somset ....17 P6
Ashwicken Norfk ....44 B6
Askam in Furness Cumb ....62 E6
Askern Donc ....59 M10
Askerswell Dorset ....7 M4
Askett Bucks ....20 D3
Askham Cumb ....71 Q10
Askham Notts ....51 Q6
Askham Bryan C York ....59 M5
Askham Richard C York ....59 M5
Asknish Ag & B ....83 P5
Askrigg N York ....64 G8
Askwith N York ....58 F5
Aslackby Lincs ....42 F4
Aslacton Norfk ....45 J11
Aslockton Notts ....51 Q11
Aspatria Cumb ....71 J7
Aspenden Herts ....33 K10
Aspley Guise C Beds ....32 D9
Aspley Heath C Beds ....32 D9
Aspull Wigan ....57 L7
Asselby E R Yk ....60 C8
Assington Suffk ....34 F8
Assington Green Suffk ....34 C6
Astbury Ches E ....49 Q3
Astcote Nhants ....31 P4
Asterby Lincs ....53 J7
Asterley Shrops ....38 G1
Asterton Shrops ....38 H4
Asthall Oxon ....30 H10
Asthall Leigh Oxon ....30 H10
Astle Highld ....107 M4
Astley Shrops ....49 K10
Astley Warwks ....40 H9
Astley Wigan ....57 M8
Astley Worcs ....39 P8
Astley Abbots Shrops ....39 N3
Astley Bridge Bolton ....57 N6
Astley Cross Worcs ....39 P8
Aston Birm ....40 E9
Aston Ches E ....49 L6
Aston Ches W ....57 K12
Aston Derbys ....50 F4
Aston Flints ....48 F3
Aston Herts ....33 J11
Aston Oxon ....31 J12
Aston Rothm ....51 L4
Aston Shrops ....39 P4
Aston Shrops ....49 K9
Aston Staffs ....40 N8
Aston Staffs ....49 N7
Aston Wokham ....20 C6
Aston Wrekin ....49 L12
Aston Abbotts Bucks ....32 C11
Aston Botterell Shrops ....39 L5
Aston-by-Stone Staffs ....40 B2
Aston Cantlow Warwks ....30 F3
Aston Clinton Bucks ....20 E2
Aston Crews Herefs ....29 J4
Aston End Herts ....33 J11
Aston Fields Worcs ....40 C12
Aston Flamville Leics ....41 L8
Aston Ingham Herefs ....29 J4
Aston le Walls Nhants ....31 L4
Aston Magna Gloucs ....30 G4
Aston Munslow Shrops ....39 K5
Aston on Clun Shrops ....38 H6
Aston Pigott Shrops ....38 G2

Aston Rogers Shrops ....38 G2
Aston Rowant Oxon ....20 B4
Aston Somerville Worcs ....30 D6
Aston-sub-Edge Gloucs ....30 F6
Aston Tirrold Oxon ....19 P4
Aston-upon-Trent Derbys ....41 K2
Aston Upthorpe Oxon ....19 P4
Astwick C Beds ....33 H8
Astwood M Keyn ....32 D7
Astwood Worcs ....30 C2
Astwood Bank Worcs ....30 D2
Aswarby Lincs ....42 F3
Aswardby Lincs ....53 L9
Atcham Shrops ....39 K1
Athelhampton Dorset ....8 B8
Athelington Suffk ....35 K3
Athelney Somset ....17 J9
Athelstaneford E Loth ....87 K6
Atherington Devon ....15 K7
Atherstone Warwks ....40 H7
Atherstone on Stour
　　Warwks ....30 G4
Atherton Wigan ....57 M8
Atlow Derbys ....50 G10
Attadale Highld ....97 N3
Atterby Lincs ....52 E5
Attercliffe Sheff ....51 J3
Atterton Leics ....41 J7
Attingham Park Shrops ....49 K12
Attleborough Norfk ....44 H10
Attleborough Warwks ....41 J8
Attlebridge Norfk ....45 J6
Attleton Green Suffk ....34 C6
Atwick E R Yk ....61 K4
Atworth Wilts ....18 C7
Aubourn Lincs ....52 D10
Auchbreck Moray ....101 J9
Auchedly Abers ....103 J8
Auchenblae Abers ....95 M6
Auchenbowie Stirlg ....85 N5
Auchencairn D & G ....70 D5
Auchencairn D & G ....78 F11
Auchencairn N Ayrs ....75 Q6
Auchencrow Border ....87 Q9
Auchendinny Mdloth ....86 F9
Auchengray S Lans ....86 B10
Auchenhalrig Moray ....101 M3
Auchenheath S Lans ....77 N3
Auchenhessnane D & G ....77 N11
Auchenlochan Ag & B ....83 P8
Auchenmade N Ayrs ....76 F2
Auchenmalg D & G ....68 G8
Auchentiber N Ayrs ....76 F2
Auchindrain Ag & B ....83 Q3
Auchindrean Highld ....106 C6
Auchininna Abers ....102 E6
Auchinleck E Ayrs ....77 J7
Auchinloch N Lans ....85 L8
Auchinstarry N Lans ....85 M7
Auchintore Highld ....90 F2
Auchiries Abers ....103 M7
Auchlean Highld ....99 M9
Auchlee Abers ....95 P3
Auchleven Abers ....102 E9
Auchlochan S Lans ....77 N4
Auchlossan Abers ....95 J2
Auchlyne Stirlg ....91 M9
Auchmillan E Ayrs ....77 J5
Auchmithie Angus ....93 R6
Auchmuirbridge Fife ....86 E3
Auchnacree Angus ....94 H8
Auchnagatt Abers ....103 J7
Auchnarrow Moray ....101 J9
Auchnotteroch D & G ....68 D7
Auchroisk Moray ....101 L5
Auchterarder P & K ....92 E12
Auchteraw Highld ....98 E7
Auchterblair Highld ....99 N5
Auchtercairn Highld ....105 M7
Auchterderran Fife ....86 E3
Auchterhouse Angus ....93 L8
Auchterless Abers ....102 F7
Auchtermuchty Fife ....93 J12
Auchterneed Highld ....106 H9
Auchtertool Fife ....86 E4
Auchtertyre Highld ....97 L4
Auchtubh Stirlg ....91 N11
Auckengill Highld ....110 G3
Auckley Donc ....51 P1
Audenshaw Tamesd ....50 B2
Audlem Ches E ....49 M6
Audley Staffs ....49 P5
Audley End Essex ....33 N8
Audley End House &
　　Gardens Essex ....33 N8
Audnam Dudley ....40 B9
Aughton E R Yk ....60 C6
Aughton Lancs ....56 H7
Aughton Lancs ....63 K8
Aughton Rothm ....51 L4
Aughton Wilts ....19 J9
Aughton Park Lancs ....56 H7
Auldearn Highld ....100 E4
Aulden Herefs ....39 J10
Auldgirth D & G ....78 E10
Auldhouse S Lans ....77 K2
Ault a' chruinn Highld ....97 N5
Aultbea Highld ....105 N5
Aultgrishin Highld ....105 L5
Aultguish Inn Highld ....106 F8
Ault Hucknall Derbys ....51 L7
Aultmore Moray ....101 M5
Aultnagoire Highld ....98 H4
Aultnamain Inn Highld ....107 L6
Aunsby Lincs ....42 F3
Aust S Glos ....28 G10
Austerfield Donc ....51 P2
Austrey Warwks ....40 H6
Austwick N York ....63 N8
Authorpe Lincs ....53 L7
Avebury Wilts ....18 G6
Avebury Wilts ....18 G6
Aveley Thurr ....22 C7
Avening Gloucs ....29 M8
Averham Notts ....51 Q9
Aveton Gifford Devon ....5 N10
Aviemore Highld ....99 N6
Avington W Berk ....19 L7
Avoch Highld ....107 L10
Avon Hants ....8 G7
Avonbridge Falk ....85 Q8
Avon Dassett Warwks ....31 K4
Avonmouth Bristl ....28 F12
Avonwick Devon ....5 P8
Awbridge Hants ....9 K3
Awliscombe Devon ....6 F3
Awre Gloucs ....29 J7

Awsworth Notts ....51 L11
Axbridge Somset ....17 L5
Axford Hants ....19 Q11
Axford Wilts ....19 J6
Axminster Devon ....6 H3
Axmouth Devon ....6 H5
Aycliffe Dur ....65 M3
Aydon Nthumb ....72 H7
Aylburton Gloucs ....28 H8
Aylesbeare Devon ....6 D4
Aylesbury Bucks ....20 D1
Aylesbury Crematorium
　　Bucks ....32 B12
Aylesby NE Lin ....52 H3
Aylesford Kent ....22 E10
Aylesham Kent ....23 N11
Aylestone C Leic ....41 M7
Aylestone Park C Leic ....41 N7
Aylmerton Norfk ....45 K3
Aylsham Norfk ....45 K5
Aylton Herefs ....28 H2
Aylworth Gloucs ....30 E9
Aymestrey Herefs ....38 H8
Aynho Nhants ....31 L7
Ayot St Lawrence Herts ....32 H12
Ayr S Ayrs ....76 F7
Aysgarth N York ....64 H9
Ayshford Devon ....16 E11
Ayside Cumb ....62 H5
Ayston Rutlnd ....42 C9
Ayton Border ....81 J3
Azerley N York ....65 M11

Babbacombe Torbay ....6 C9
Babbs Green Herts ....33 L12
Babcary Somset ....17 N9
Babraham Cambs ....33 N6
Babworth Notts ....51 P5
Backaland Ork ....111 h1
Backfolds Abers ....103 L5
Backford Ches W ....48 H2
Backies Highld ....107 N3
Back of Keppoch Highld ....97 J11
Backwell N Som ....17 L3
Baconsthorpe Norfk ....45 J3
Bacton Herefs ....28 D3
Bacton Norfk ....45 M4
Bacton Suffk ....34 H4
Bacup Lancs ....57 Q4
Badachro Highld ....105 L7
Badbury Swindn ....18 H5
Badby Nhants ....31 M3
Badcall Highld ....108 D3
Badcall Highld ....108 E5
Badcaul Highld ....105 Q4
Baddeley Edge C Stke ....50 B9
Baddeley Green C Stke ....50 B9
Baddesley Clinton Warwks ....40 G11
Baddesley Ensor Warwks ....40 H7
Baddidarrach Highld ....108 C10
Baddinsgill Border ....86 D10
Badenscoth Abers ....102 F7
Badentarbet Highld ....105 Q1
Badenyon Abers ....101 L10
Badger Shrops ....39 N3
Badgeworth Gloucs ....29 M5
Badgworth Somset ....17 K5
Badicaul Highld ....97 K4
Badingham Suffk ....35 M3
Badlesmere Kent ....23 J11
Badlieu Border ....78 H5
Badlipster Highld ....110 F6
Badluarach Highld ....105 P4
Badninish Highld ....107 M4
Badrallach Highld ....105 Q4
Badsey Worcs ....30 E5
Badshot Lea Surrey ....10 D1
Badsworth Wakefd ....59 L10
Badwell Ash Suffk ....34 G3
Bagber Dorset ....17 Q12
Bagendon Gloucs ....30 D11
Bag Enderby Lincs ....53 K8
Bagh a Chaisteil W Isls ....111 a7
Bagh a Tuath W Isls ....111 a7
Bagillt Flints ....48 E1
Baginton Warwks ....41 J11
Baglan Neath ....26 G9
Bagley Shrops ....48 H9
Bagley Somset ....17 L7
Bagnall Staffs ....50 B10
Bagshot Surrey ....20 E10
Bagstone S Glos ....29 J10
Bagworth Leics ....41 K6
Bagwy Llydiart Herefs ....28 E4
Baildon C Brad ....58 F6
Baildon Green C Brad ....58 F6
Baile Ailein W Isls ....111 d2
Baile a Mhanaich W Isls ....111 b5
Baile Mór Ag & B ....88 G10
Baillieston C Glas ....85 L9
Bainbridge N York ....64 G9
Bainshole Abers ....102 D8
Bainton C Pete ....42 F8
Bainton E R Yk ....60 G4
Bairnkine Border ....80 E10
Bakewell Derbys ....50 G7
Bala Gwynd ....47 Q4
Balallan W Isls ....111 d2
Balbeg Highld ....98 F3
Balbeggie P & K ....92 H9
Balblair Highld ....106 H12
Balblair Highld ....107 L8
Balby Donc ....51 M1
Balcary D & G ....70 D5
Balchraggan Highld ....98 G1
Balchreick Highld ....108 D4
Balcombe W Susx ....11 L4
Balcomie Links Fife ....87 M1
Baldersby N York ....65 N10
Baldersby St James
　　N York ....65 P11
Balderstone Lancs ....57 L3
Balderton Notts ....52 B12
Baldinnie Fife ....93 M12
Baldinnies P & K ....92 F11
Baldock Herts ....33 J9
Baldock Services Herts ....32 H9
Baldovie C Dund ....93 M8
Baldrine IoM ....56 d5
Baldslow E Susx ....12 F7
Bale Norfk ....44 G3

Baledgarno P & K ....93 K9
Balemartine Ag & B ....88 C7
Balerno C Edin ....86 D8
Balfarg Fife ....86 F2
Balfield Angus ....95 J8
Balfour Ork ....111 h2
Balfron Stirlg ....85 J5
Balgaveny Abers ....102 E7
Balgonar Fife ....86 B4
Balgowan D & G ....68 F9
Balgowan Highld ....99 J9
Balgown Highld ....104 E8
Balgracie D & G ....68 D7
Balgray S Lans ....78 E4
Balhary P & K ....93 J6
Baligill Highld ....109 P3
Balintore Angus ....93 K4
Balintore Highld ....107 P7
Balintraid Highld ....107 M8
Balivanich W Isls ....111 b5
Balkeerie Angus ....93 K6
Balkholme E R Yk ....60 D8
Ballachulish Highld ....90 D4
Ballajora IoM ....56 e4
Ballanlay Ag & B ....83 Q9
Ballantrae S Ayrs ....68 E3
Ballasalla IoM ....56 b6
Ballater Abers ....94 F3
Ballaugh IoM ....56 c3
Ballchraggan Highld ....107 M7
Ballencrieff E Loth ....87 J6
Ballevullin Ag & B ....88 B7
Ball Green C Stke ....50 B9
Ballidon Derbys ....50 G9
Balliekine N Ayrs ....75 N5
Balliemore Ag & B ....84 B3
Balligmorrie S Ayrs ....68 G2
Ballimore Stirlg ....91 M11
Ballindean P & K ....93 J9
Ballindalloch Moray ....101 J7
Ballinger Common Bucks ....20 E3
Ballingham Herefs ....28 G3
Ballingry Fife ....86 E3
Ballinluig P & K ....92 E5
Ballinshoe Angus ....93 M5
Ballintuim P & K ....92 G5
Balloch Highld ....107 M11
Balloch N Lans ....85 M7
Balloch P & K ....92 C10
Balloch S Ayrs ....76 F11
Balloch W Duns ....84 G6
Balls Cross W Susx ....10 F5
Balls Green E Susx ....11 P3
Ballygown Ag & B ....89 J7
Ballygrant Ag & B ....82 E9
Ballyhaugh Ag & B ....88 E5
Balmaclellan D & G ....69 P4
Balmacqueen Highld ....104 F7
Balmae D & G ....69 P9
Balmaha Stirlg ....84 G5
Balmalcolm Fife ....86 G1
Balmangan D & G ....69 P9
Balmedie Abers ....103 K10
Balmerino Fife ....93 L10
Balmichael N Ayrs ....75 P5
Balmore E Duns ....85 K8
Balmuchy Highld ....107 P6
Balmule Fife ....86 E5
Balmullo Fife ....93 M10
Balnacoil Lodge Highld ....109 P12
Balnacra Highld ....105 P12
Balnacroft Abers ....94 E3
Balnafoich Highld ....99 K2
Balnaguard P & K ....92 E5
Balnahard Ag & B ....82 F3
Balnahard Ag & B ....89 K9
Balnain Highld ....98 F3
Balnakeil Highld ....108 G3
Balne N York ....59 N9
Balquharn P & K ....92 F9
Balquhidder Stirlg ....91 M11
Balsall Common Solhll ....40 G10
Balsall Heath Birm ....40 E9
Balscote Oxon ....31 K6
Balsham Cambs ....33 P6
Baltasound Shet ....111 m2
Baltersan D & G ....69 K6
Baltonsborough Somset ....17 M8
Balvicar Ag & B ....89 Q11
Balvraid Highld ....97 M6
Balvraid Highld ....99 M3
Bamber Bridge Lancs ....57 K4
Bamber's Green Essex ....33 P11
Bamburgh Nthumb ....81 N7
Bamburgh Castle Nthumb ....81 N7
Bamford Derbys ....50 G4
Bampton Cumb ....71 Q10
Bampton Devon ....16 C10
Bampton Oxon ....30 H12
Bampton Grange Cumb ....71 Q11
Banavie Highld ....90 F2
Banbury Oxon ....31 L6
Banbury Crematorium
　　Oxon ....31 L5
Bancffosfelen Carmth ....26 C6
Banchory Abers ....95 L3
Banchory-Devenick Abers ....95 P2
Bancycapel Carmth ....25 P6
Bancyfelin Carmth ....25 N5
Bandirran P & K ....93 J9
Banff Abers ....102 F3
Bangor Gwynd ....54 H7
Bangor Crematorium
　　Gwynd ....54 H7
Bangor-on-Dee Wrexhm ....48 H7
Bangors Cnwll ....14 D11
Banham Norfk ....44 H11
Bank Hants ....9 K6
Bankend D & G ....70 D2
Bankfoot P & K ....92 F8
Bankglen E Ayrs ....77 K8
Bankhead C Aber ....103 J12
Bankhead S Lans ....86 B12
Banknock Falk ....85 N7
Banks Lancs ....56 H5
Bankshill D & G ....79 K11
Banningham Norfk ....45 K4
Bannister Green Essex ....34 B11
Bannockburn Stirlg ....85 N5
Banstead Surrey ....21 K10
Bantham Devon ....5 N10
Banton N Lans ....85 M7
Banwell N Som ....17 K4
Bapchild Kent ....22 H10
Bapton Wilts ....18 E12
Barabhas W Isls ....111 d1

Barassie - Binfield 167


Barassie S Ayrs 76 F5
Barbaraville Highld 107 M7
Barbieston S Ayrs 76 G7
Barbon Cumb 63 L6
Barbrook Devon 15 M3
Barby Nhants 41 M12
Barcaldine Ag & B 90 D7
Barcombe E Susx 11 N7
Barcombe Cross E Susx 11 N6
Barden Park Kent 12 C2
Bardfield End Green Essex 33 Q9
Bardfield Saling Essex 34 B10
Bardney Lincs 52 G9
Bardon Leics 41 K5
Bardon Mill Nthumb 72 E7
Bardowie E Duns 85 K8
Bardrainney Inver 84 F8
Bardsea Cumb 62 F7
Bardsey Leeds 59 J5
Bardsey Island Gwynd 46 B7
Bardwell Suffk 34 F3
Bare Lancs 63 J8
Barfad D & G 69 J6
Barford Norfk 45 J8
Barford Warwks 30 H2
Barford St John Oxon 31 K7
Barford St Martin Wilts 8 F2
Barford St Michael Oxon 31 K7
Barfrestone Kent 23 N12
Bargeddie N Lans 85 L9
Bargoed Caerph 27 N8
Bargrennan D & G 69 J4
Barham Cambs 32 G2
Barham Kent 23 N12
Barham Suffk 35 J6
Barham Crematorium Kent 13 N1
Bar Hill Cambs 33 L4
Barholm Lincs 42 F7
Barkby Leics 41 N5
Barkby Thorpe Leics 41 N5
Barkestone-le-Vale Leics 41 R1
Barkham Wokham 20 C9
Barking Gt Lon 21 N6
Barking Suffk 34 H6
Barkingside Gt Lon 21 N5
Barking Tye Suffk 34 H6
Barkisland Calder 58 D9
Barkla Shop Cnwll 2 H5
Barkston Lincs 42 D2
Barkston Ash N York 59 L7
Barkway Herts 33 L9
Barlanark C Glas 85 L9
Barlaston Staffs 50 B11
Barlavington W Susx 10 F6
Barlborough Derbys 51 L5
Barlby N York 59 N7
Barlestone Leics 41 K6
Barley Herts 33 L8
Barley Lancs 57 P1
Barleythorpe Rutlnd 42 C8
Barling Essex 22 H5
Barlings Lincs 52 F8
Barlochan D & G 70 D4
Barlow Derbys 51 J6
Barlow Gatesd 73 K8
Barlow N York 59 N8
Barmby Moor E R Yk 60 D4
Barmby on the Marsh E R Yk 59 P8
Barmollack Ag & B 75 M4
Barmouth Gwynd 47 K7
Barmpton Darltn 65 N4
Barmston E R Yk 61 K3
Barnacarry Ag & B 83 Q4
Barnack C Pete 42 F8
Barnard Castle Dur 65 J4
Barnard Gate Oxon 31 K11
Barnardiston Suffk 34 B7
Barnbarroch D & G 70 D4
Barnburgh Donc 59 L12
Barnby Suffk 45 P11
Barnby Dun Donc 59 N11
Barnby in the Willows Notts 52 C11
Barnby Moor Notts 51 P4
Barncorkrie D & G 68 E11
Barnes Gt Lon 21 K7
Barnes Street Kent 12 D1
Barnet Gt Lon 21 K4
Barnetby le Wold N Linc 52 F2
Barney Norfk 44 G4
Barnham Suffk 34 E2
Barnham W Susx 10 F8
Barnham Broom Norfk 44 H8
Barnhead Angus 93 R4
Barnhill C Dund 93 N8
Barnhill Moray 100 H4
Barnhills D & G 68 D5
Barningham Dur 65 J5
Barningham Suffk 34 F2
Barnoldby le Beck NE Lin 52 H3
Barnoldswick Lancs 63 Q11
Barns Green W Susx 10 H5
Barnsley Barns 59 J11
Barnsley Gloucs 30 E12
Barnsley Crematorium Barns 59 J12
Barnstaple Devon 15 K5
Barnston Essex 33 Q11
Barnston Wirral 56 F11
Barnstone Notts 41 Q1
Barnt Green Worcs 40 D11
Barnton C Edin 86 E7
Barnton Ches W 49 L1
Barnwell All Saints Nhants 42 F12
Barnwell St Andrew Nhants 42 F12
Barnwood Gloucs 29 M5
Barr S Ayrs 76 E11
Barra W Isls 111 a7
*Barra Airport W Isls 111 a6*
Barrachan D & G 69 J8
Barraigh W Isls 111 a7
Barrapoll Ag & B 88 B7
Barrasford Nthumb 72 G6
Barrhead E Rens 84 H10
Barrhill S Ayrs 68 H3
Barrington Cambs 33 L6
Barrington Somset 17 K11
Barripper Cnwll 2 F7
Barrmill N Ayrs 84 F11
Barrock Highld 110 F2
Barrow Gloucs 29 M4
Barrow Lancs 57 N2
Barrow Rutlnd 42 C7
Barrow Somset 17 Q9
Barrow Suffk 34 C4
Barrowby Lincs 42 C3
Barrowden Rutlnd 42 D9
Barrowford Lancs 57 Q2
Barrow Gurney N Som 17 M3
Barrow Haven N Linc 60 H9
Barrow-in-Furness Cumb 62 E8
Barrow Island Cumb 62 E8
Barrow-upon-Humber N Linc 60 H9
Barrow upon Soar Leics 41 M4
Barrow upon Trent Derbys 41 J2
Barry Angus 93 P8
Barry V Glam 16 F3
Barry Island V Glam 16 F3
Barsby Leics 41 P5
Barsham Suffk 45 N11
Barston Solhll 40 G10
Bartestree Herefs 28 G1
Barthol Chapel Abers 102 H8
Bartholomew Green Essex 34 C11
Barthomley Ches E 49 N5
Bartley Hants 9 K5
Bartley Green Birm 40 D10
Bartlow Cambs 33 P7
Barton Cambs 33 L5
Barton Ches W 49 J5
Barton Gloucs 30 E8
Barton Lancs 56 G7
Barton Lancs 57 K2
Barton N York 65 M6
Barton Oxon 31 M11
Barton Torbay 6 C8
Barton Bendish Norfk 44 B8
Barton End Gloucs 29 L8
Barton Hartshorn Bucks 31 N7
Barton in Fabis Notts 41 M2
Barton in the Beans Leics 41 K6
Barton-le-Clay C Beds 32 F9
Barton-le-Street N York 66 G11
Barton-le-Willows N York 60 C2
Barton Mills Suffk 34 C3
Barton-on-Sea Hants 9 J8
Barton-on-the-Heath Warwks 30 G7
Barton St David Somset 17 M9
Barton Seagrave Nhants 32 C2
Barton Stacey Hants 19 M11
Barton Town Devon 15 L4
Barton Turf Norfk 45 M5
Barton-under-Needwood Staffs 40 F4
Barton-upon-Humber N Linc 60 H9
Barton Waterside N Linc 60 H9
Barvas W Isls 111 d1
Barway Cambs 33 N2
Barwell Leics 41 K8
Barwick Devon 15 K10
Barwick Somset 17 M12
Barwick in Elmet Leeds 59 K6
Baschurch Shrops 48 H10
Bascote Warwks 31 K2
Bashall Eaves Lancs 63 M12
Basildon Essex 22 E5
Basildon & District Crematorium Essex 22 E6
Basingstoke Hants 19 Q9
Basingstoke Crematorium Hants 19 P10
Baslow Derbys 50 G6
Bason Bridge Somset 17 J7
Bassaleg Newpt 28 C10
Bassendean Border 80 E5
Bassenthwaite Cumb 71 K8
Bassett C Sotn 9 M4
Bassingbourn-cum-Kneesworth Cambs 33 K7
Bassingham Lincs 52 C10
Bassingthorpe Lincs 42 D5
Bassus Green Herts 33 K10
Baston Lincs 42 G7
Bastwick Norfk 45 N6
Batchworth Herts 20 G5
Batcombe Dorset 7 N3
Batcombe Somset 17 Q8
Batford Herts 21 J1
Bath BaNES 17 Q4
Bathampton BaNES 18 B7
Bath, City of BaNES 17 Q3
Bathealton Somset 16 E10
Batheaston BaNES 18 B7
Bathford BaNES 18 B7
Bathgate W Loth 86 B8
Bathley Notts 51 Q8
Bathpool Cnwll 4 G5
Bathpool Somset 16 H10
Bath Side Essex 35 L9
Bathville W Loth 85 Q9
Bathway Somset 17 N6
Batley Kirk 58 G8
Batsford Gloucs 30 F7
Battersby N York 66 E6
Battersea Gt Lon 21 L7
Battisford Tye Suffk 34 G6
Battle E Susx 12 E7
Battle Powys 27 L3
Battledykes Angus 93 M5
Battlesbridge Essex 22 F5
Battleton Somset 16 C10
Baughton Worcs 29 M1
Baughurst Hants 19 P8
Baulds Abers 95 K4
Baulking Oxon 19 K3
Baumber Lincs 52 H8
Baunton Gloucs 30 D12
Baverstock Wilts 8 F2
Bawburgh Norfk 45 J8
Bawdeswell Norfk 44 H6
Bawdrip Somset 17 J8
Bawdsey Suffk 35 M8
Bawtry Donc 51 P3
Baxenden Lancs 57 P4
Baxterley Warwks 40 H7
Bay Highld 104 C10
Bayble W Isls 111 e2
Baybridge Hants 9 N3
Baycliff Cumb 62 F7
Baydon Wilts 19 K5
Bayford Herts 21 L2
Bayford Somset 17 Q9
Bayhead W Isls 111 a4
Baylham Suffk 34 H6
Baysham Herefs 28 G4
Bayston Hill Shrops 39 J1
Baythorne End Essex 34 C8
Bayton Worcs 39 M7
Bayworth Oxon 19 N1
Beachampton Bucks 31 Q6
Beachamwell Norfk 44 C8
Beachy Head E Susx 12 C10
Beacon Devon 6 G2
Beacon End Essex 34 F10
Beacon Hill Notts 52 B11
Beacon Hill Surrey 10 E3
Beacon's Bottom Bucks 20 C4
Beaconsfield Bucks 20 F5
*Beaconsfield Services Bucks 20 F5*
Beadlam N York 66 F9
Beadlow C Beds 32 F8
Beadnell Nthumb 81 P8
Beaford Devon 15 K8
Beal N York 59 M8
Beal Nthumb 81 M6
Bealsmill Cnwll 4 H5
Beaminster Dorset 7 L3
Beamish Dur 73 L9
*Beamish Museum Dur 73 L9*
Beamsley N York 58 E4
Beanacre Wilts 18 D7
Beanley Nthumb 81 M9
Beardon Devon 5 L4
Beare Green Surrey 11 J2
Bearley Warwks 30 F3
Bearpark Dur 73 M11
Bearsden E Duns 85 J8
Bearsted Kent 22 F11
Bearstone Shrops 49 N7
Bearwood Birm 40 D9
Bearwood Herefs 38 H10
Bearwood Poole 8 F7
Beattock D & G 78 H8
Beauchamp Roding Essex 22 C2
Beaufort Blae G 27 N6
Beaulieu Hants 9 L7
Beauly Highld 107 J11
Beaumaris IoA 54 H6
Beaumaris Castle IoA 54 H6
Beaumont Cumb 71 M4
Beaumont Essex 35 J10
Beaumont Jersey 7 b2
Beausale Warwks 40 G12
Beauworth Hants 9 P3
Beaworthy Devon 14 H11
Beazley End Essex 34 C10
Bebington Wirral 56 G11
Beccles Suffk 45 N11
Becconsall Lancs 57 J4
Beckbury Shrops 39 N2
Beckenham Gt Lon 21 M9
Beckenham Crematorium Gt Lon 21 M9
Beckermet Cumb 62 B2
Beckfoot Cumb 70 H5
Beckford Worcs 29 N2
Beckhampton Wilts 18 G7
Beckingham Lincs 52 C11
Beckingham Notts 51 R3
Beckington Somset 18 B9
Beckjay Shrops 38 H6
Beckley E Susx 12 G5
Beckley Oxon 31 M10
Beck Row Suffk 34 B2
Beck Side Cumb 62 E6
Beckton Gt Lon 21 N7
Beckwithshaw N York 58 H4
Becontree Gt Lon 21 P6
Bedale N York 65 M9
Bedchester Dorset 8 C4
Beddau Rhondd 27 M10
Beddgelert Gwynd 54 H11
Beddingham E Susx 11 N8
Beddington Gt Lon 21 L9
Beddington Corner Gt Lon 21 L9
Bedfield Suffk 35 K4
Bedford Bed 32 F6
Bedford Crematorium Bed 32 F6
Bedhampton Hants 10 B8
Bedingfield Suffk 35 K3
Bedlam N York 58 H2
Bedlington Nthumb 73 M5
Bedlinog Myr Td 27 M8
Bedminster Bristl 17 N2
Bedminster Down Bristl 17 N3
Bedmond Herts 20 H3
Bednall Staffs 40 C4
Bedrule Border 80 E10
Bedstone Shrops 38 G7
Bedwas Caerph 27 N10
Bedwellty Caerph 27 N8
Bedworth Warwks 41 J9
Beeby Leics 41 P6
Beech Hants 10 B3
Beech Staffs 49 Q7
Beech Hill W Berk 20 B9
Beechingstoke Wilts 18 G8
Beedon W Berk 19 N5
Beeford E R Yk 61 J4
Beeley Derbys 50 H7
Beelsby NE Lin 52 H3
Beenham W Berk 19 P7
Beer Devon 6 G5
Beer Somset 17 K9
Beercrocombe Somset 17 J11
Beer Hackett Dorset 7 N1
Beesands Devon 5 Q11
Beesby Lincs 53 M7
Beeson Devon 5 Q11
Beeston C Beds 32 G7
Beeston Ches W 49 K4
Beeston Leeds 58 H7
Beeston Norfk 44 E7
Beeston Notts 51 M12
Beeston Regis Norfk 45 J2
Beeswing D & G 70 E2
Beetham Cumb 63 J6
Beetham Somset 6 H1
Beetley Norfk 44 F6
Begbroke Oxon 31 L10
Begelly Pembks 25 K7
Beguildy Powys 38 E6
Beighton Norfk 45 N8
Beighton Sheff 51 K4
Beinn Na Faoghla W Isls 111 b5
Beith N Ayrs 84 F11
Bekesbourne Kent 23 M11
Belaugh Norfk 45 L6
Belbroughton Worcs 40 B11
Belchalwell Dorset 8 B5
Belchamp Otten Essex 34 D8
Belchamp St Paul Essex 34 D8
Belchamp Walter Essex 34 D8
Belchford Lincs 53 J8
Belford Nthumb 81 M7
Belgrave C Leic 41 N6
Belhaven E Loth 87 M6
Belhelvie Abers 103 K10
Belhinnie Abers 101 N9
Bellabeg Abers 101 L11
Bellanoch Ag & B 83 M5
Bellaty Angus 93 J4
Bell Busk N York 58 B3
Belleau Lincs 53 L7
Bell End Worcs 40 C11
Bellerby N York 65 K8
Belle Vue Cumb 71 M4
Belle Vue Wakefd 59 J9
Bellfield S Lans 78 D2
Bellfield S Lans 78 F5
Bellingdon Bucks 20 F3
Bellingham Nthumb 72 F4
Belloch Ag & B 75 K5
Bellochantuy Ag & B 75 K6
Bell o' th' Hill Ches W 49 K6
Bellshill N Lans 85 M10
Bellside N Lans 85 N10
Bellsquarry W Loth 86 C8
Bells Yew Green E Susx 12 C3
Belluton BaNES 17 N4
Belmaduthy Highld 107 K10
Belmont Bl w D 57 M6
Belmont Gt Lon 21 K10
Belmont S Ayrs 76 F7
Belmont Shet 111 m2
Belnacraig Abers 101 M11
Belper Derbys 51 J10
Belsay Nthumb 73 K5
Belses Border 80 D8
Belsford Devon 5 P8
Belsize Herts 20 G4
Belstead Suffk 35 J8
Belstone Devon 5 M2
Belthorn Lancs 57 N4
Beltinge Kent 23 M9
Beltingham Nthumb 72 E7
Beltoft N Linc 52 B3
Belton Leics 41 K4
Belton Lincs 42 D3
Belton N Linc 52 B3
Belton Norfk 45 P9
Belton Rutlnd 42 B9
*Belton House Lincs 42 D3*
Belvedere Gt Lon 21 P7
Belvoir Leics 42 B4
Bembridge IoW 9 Q9
Bemerton Wilts 8 G2
Bempton E R Yk 67 P12
Benacre Suffk 45 Q12
Benbecula W Isls 111 b5
*Benbecula Airport W Isls 111 b5*
Benbuie D & G 77 M11
Benderloch Ag & B 90 C8
Benenden Kent 12 F4
Benfieldside Dur 73 J9
Bengeo Herts 21 L1
Bengeworth Worcs 30 D5
Benhall Green Suffk 35 N5
Benhall Street Suffk 35 M5
Benholm Abers 95 N7
Beningbrough N York 59 M3
Benington Herts 33 J11
Benington Lincs 43 L2
Benllech IoA 54 G5
Benmore Ag & B 84 C6
Bennan N Ayrs 75 Q8
Ben Nevis Highld 90 G3
Benniworth Lincs 52 H7
Benover Kent 12 E1
Ben Rhydding C Brad 58 F5
Benslie N Ayrs 76 F3
Benson Oxon 19 Q3
Benthoul C Aber 95 N2
Bentley Donc 59 M11
Bentley E R Yk 60 H7
Bentley Hants 10 C2
Bentley Suffk 35 J8
Bentley Warwks 40 H8
Bentley Crematorium Essex 22 C4
Bentpath D & G 79 M10
Bentwichen Devon 15 M5
Bentworth Hants 19 Q11
Benvie Angus 93 K8
Benville Dorset 7 M3
Benwick Cambs 43 K11
Beoley Worcs 40 E12
Beoraidbeg Highld 97 J10
Bepton W Susx 10 D6
Berden Essex 33 M10
Berea Pembks 24 E3
Bere Alston Devon 5 J6
Bere Ferrers Devon 5 K7
Bere Regis Dorset 8 C8
Bergh Apton Norfk 45 M9
Berinsfield Oxon 19 P2
Berkeley Gloucs 29 J8
Berkhamsted Herts 20 F2
Berkley Somset 18 B10
Berkswell Solhll 40 G10
Bermondsey Gt Lon 21 M7
Bernera Highld 97 L5
Bernisdale Highld 104 E11
Berrick Prior Oxon 19 Q2
Berrick Salome Oxon 19 Q3
Berriedale Highld 110 D10
Berrier Cumb 71 N9
Berriew Powys 38 E2
Berrington Shrops 39 K2
Berrington Worcs 39 L8
Berrington Green Worcs 39 L8
Berrow Somset 16 H6
Berrow Green Worcs 39 N9
Berryhillock Moray 101 P3
Berryhillock Moray 101 P5
Berrynarbor Devon 15 K3
Berry Pomeroy Devon 5 Q7
Bersham Wrexhm 48 F6
Berwick E Susx 11 P8
Berwick Bassett Wilts 18 G6
Berwick Hill Nthumb 73 K6
Berwick St James Wilts 18 F11
Berwick St John Wilts 8 D3
Berwick St Leonard Wilts 8 D2
Berwick-upon-Tweed Nthumb 81 L4
Bescar Lancs 56 H6
Besford Worcs 30 B5
Bessacarr Donc 51 N1
Bessingby E R Yk 61 K2
Bessingham Norfk 45 J3
Besthorpe Norfk 44 H10
Besthorpe Notts 52 B9
Bestwood Village Notts 51 M10
Beswick E R Yk 60 H5
Betchworth Surrey 21 K12
Bethel Gwynd 54 G8
Bethel IoA 54 E7
Bethersden Kent 12 H3
Bethesda Gwynd 55 J8
Bethesda Pembks 25 J5
Bethlehem Carmth 26 F4
Bethnal Green Gt Lon 21 M6
Betley Staffs 49 N6
Betsham Kent 22 C8
Betteshanger Kent 23 P11
Bettiscombe Dorset 7 K3
Bettisfield Wrexhm 49 J8
Bettws Newpt 28 C10
Bettws Cedewain Powys 38 D3
Bettws Evan Cerdgn 36 E10
Bettws-Newydd Mons 28 D7
Bettyhill Highld 109 M4
Betws Brdgnd 27 J10
Betws Bledrws Cerdgn 37 K9
Betws Gwerfil Goch Denbgs 48 B6
Betws-y-Coed Conwy 55 L9
Betws-yn-Rhos Conwy 55 N6
Beulah Cerdgn 36 E10
Beulah Powys 37 Q9
Bevercotes Notts 51 P6
Beverley E R Yk 60 H6
Beverston Gloucs 29 M9
Bewcastle Cumb 71 Q1
Bewdley Worcs 39 P7
Bewerley N York 58 F2
Bewholme E R Yk 61 K4
Bexhill E Susx 12 E8
Bexley Gt Lon 21 P8
Bexleyheath Gt Lon 21 P8
Bexwell Norfk 43 Q9
Beyton Suffk 34 F4
Beyton Green Suffk 34 F4
Bhaltos W Isls 111 c2
Bhatarsaigh W Isls 111 a7
Bibury Gloucs 30 E11
Bicester Oxon 31 N9
Bickenhill Solhll 40 F10
Bicker Lincs 42 H3
Bickerstaffe Lancs 57 J7
Bickerton N York 59 K4
Bickford Staffs 40 B5
Bickington Devon 5 Q6
Bickington Devon 15 J6
Bickleigh Devon 5 L7
Bickleigh Devon 6 C2
Bickley Ches W 49 K6
Bickley Gt Lon 21 N9
Bickley N York 67 K8
Bicknacre Essex 22 F3
Bicknoller Somset 16 F8
Bicknor Kent 22 G10
Bicton Shrops 38 F5
Bicton Shrops 49 J11
Bidborough Kent 12 C2
Biddenden Kent 12 G3
Biddenham Bed 32 E6
Biddestone Wilts 18 C6
Biddisham Somset 17 K5
Biddlesden Bucks 31 N6
Biddulph Staffs 50 B8
Biddulph Moor Staffs 50 B8
Bideford Devon 14 H6
Bidford-on-Avon Warwks 30 E4
Bielby E R Yk 60 D5
Bieldside C Aber 95 P2
Bierley IoW 9 N10
Bierton Bucks 20 D1
Big Balcraig D & G 69 K9
Bigbury Devon 5 N10
Bigbury-on-Sea Devon 5 N10
Bigby Lincs 52 F3
Big Carlae D & G 77 L10
Biggar S Lans 78 G2
Biggin Derbys 50 F8
Biggin Hill Gt Lon 21 N10
*Biggin Hill Airport Gt Lon 21 N10*
Biggleswade C Beds 32 H7
Bigholms D & G 79 M11
Bighouse Highld 109 Q3
Bighton Hants 9 Q1
Biglands Cumb 71 L5
Bignor W Susx 10 F7
Bigrigg Cumb 70 G11
Big Sand Highld 105 L6
Bigton Shet 111 k5
Bilborough C Nott 51 M11
Bilbrook Somset 16 D7
Bilbrough N York 59 M5
Bilbster Highld 110 F5
Bildershaw Dur 65 L3
Bildeston Suffk 34 G6
Billericay Essex 22 D5
Billesdon Leics 41 Q7
Billesley Warwks 30 F3
Billingborough Lincs 42 G4
Billinge St Hel 57 K8
Billingford Norfk 35 J2
Billingford Norfk 44 G6
Billingham S on T 66 C3
Billinghay Lincs 52 G11
Billingley Barns 59 K12
Billingshurst W Susx 10 H5
Billingsley Shrops 39 N5
Billington C Beds 32 D11
Billington Lancs 57 N2
Billockby Norfk 45 N7
Billy Row Dur 73 L12
Bilsborrow Lancs 57 K2
Bilsby Lincs 53 M8
Bilsham W Susx 10 F9
Bilsington Kent 13 K3
Bilsthorpe Notts 51 N8
Bilston Mdloth 86 F8
Bilston Wolves 40 C8
Bilstone Leics 41 J6
Bilton E R Yk 61 K7
Bilton N York 58 H3
Bilton N York 59 L4
Bilton Warwks 41 L11
Binbrook Lincs 52 H5
Bincombe Dorset 7 P6
Binegar Somset 17 N6
Binfield Br For 20 D8

168 Binfield Heath - Bracorina


Binfield Heath Oxon 20 C7
Bingfield Nthumb 72 H6
Bingham Notts 51 P11
Bingley C Brad 58 E6
Binham Norfk 44 G3
Binley Covtry 41 J10
Binley Hants 19 M9
Binley Woods Warwks 41 K11
Binnegar Dorset 8 C9
Binniehill Falk 85 P8
Binscombe Surrey 10 F2
Binstead IoW 9 P8
Binsted Hants 10 C2
Binsted W Susx 10 F8
Binton Warwks 30 F4
Bintree Norfk 44 G5
Birch Essex 34 F11
Bircham Newton Norfk 44 C4
Bircham Tofts Norfk 44 C4
Birchanger Essex 33 N11
Birchanger Green Services Essex 33 N11
Birch Cross Staffs 40 E2
Bircher Herefs 39 J8
Birchfield Birm 40 E8
Birch Green Essex 34 F11
Birchgrove Cardif 27 N11
Birchgrove Swans 26 F8
Birchgrove W Susx 11 N4
Birchington Kent 23 P9
Birchley Heath Warwks 40 H8
Birchover Derbys 50 G8
Birch Services Rochdl 57 Q7
Birch Vale Derbys 50 D4
Birchwood Lincs 52 D9
Birch Wood Somset 16 H12
Birchwood Warrtn 57 M9
Bircotes Notts 51 N3
Birdbrook Essex 34 B8
Birdforth N York 66 C11
Birdham W Susx 10 D9
Birdingbury Warwks 31 K1
Birdlip Gloucs 29 N6
Birdsall N York 60 E2
Birds Edge Kirk 58 G11
Birds Green Essex 22 C2
Birdsgreen Shrops 39 P5
Birdsmoorgate Dorset 7 K3
Birdwell Barns 51 J1
Birgham Border 80 G6
Birichin Highld 107 M4
Birkby N York 65 N7
Birkdale Sefton 56 G6
Birkenbog Abers 102 C3
Birkenhead Wirral 56 G10
Birkenhills Abers 102 F6
Birkenshaw Kirk 58 G8
Birkhall Abers 94 F4
Birkhill Angus 93 L8
Birkhill D & G 79 K6
Birkin N York 59 M8
Birley Herefs 39 J10
Birley Carr Sheff 51 J3
Birling Kent 22 D10
Birlingham Worcs 30 C5
Birmingham Birm 40 E9
Birmingham Airport Solhll 40 F10
Birnam P & K 92 F7
Birness Abers 103 K8
Birse Abers 95 J3
Birsemore Abers 95 J3
Birstall Kirk 58 G8
Birstall Leics 41 N5
Birstwith N York 58 G3
Birtley Gatesd 73 M9
Birtley Herefs 38 G8
Birtley Nthumb 72 F5
Birtley Crematorium Gatesd 73 M9
Birts Street Worcs 29 K2
Bisbrooke Rutlnd 42 C9
Biscathorpe Lincs 52 H6
Bisham W & M 20 D6
Bishampton Worcs 30 C4
Bish Mill Devon 15 M7
Bishop Auckland Dur 65 L2
Bishopbridge Lincs 52 E5
Bishopbriggs E Duns 85 K8
Bishop Burton E R Yk 60 G6
Bishop Middleham Dur 65 N2
Bishopmill Moray 101 J3
Bishop Monkton N York 59 J2
Bishop Norton Lincs 52 E5
Bishopsbourne Kent 23 M11
Bishops Cannings Wilts 18 F7
Bishop's Castle Shrops 38 G4
Bishop's Caundle Dorset 17 Q12
Bishop's Cleeve Gloucs 29 N4
Bishop's Frome Herefs 39 M11
Bishop's Green Essex 33 Q12
Bishop's Hull Somset 16 G10
Bishop's Itchington Warwks 31 K3
Bishops Lydeard Somset 16 G9
Bishop's Norton Gloucs 29 L4
Bishop's Nympton Devon 15 N7
Bishop's Offley Staffs 49 P9
Bishop's Stortford Herts 33 M11
Bishop's Sutton Hants 9 Q2
Bishop's Tachbrook Warwks 30 H2
Bishop's Tawton Devon 15 K6
Bishopsteignton Devon 6 B7
Bishopstoke Hants 9 M4
Bishopston Swans 26 D10
Bishopstone Bucks 20 C2
Bishopstone E Susx 11 P9
Bishopstone Herefs 38 H12
Bishopstone Kent 23 N9
Bishopstone Swindn 19 J4
Bishopstone Wilts 8 F3
Bishopstrow Wilts 18 D11
Bishop Sutton BaNES 17 N4
Bishop's Waltham Hants 9 P4
Bishopswood Somset 6 H1
Bishop's Wood Staffs 49 Q12
Bishopsworth Bristl 17 N3
Bishop Thornton N York 58 H2
Bishopthorpe C York 59 N5
Bishopton Darltn 65 P4
Bishopton Rens 84 G8
Bishop Wilton E R Yk 60 D3
Bishton Newpt 28 D10
Bishton Staffs 40 D4
Bisley Gloucs 29 M7
Bisley Surrey 20 F10
Bissoe Cnwll 2 H7
Bisterne Hants 8 G7
Bitchfield Lincs 42 E4
Bittadon Devon 15 J4
Bittaford Devon 5 N8
Bitterley Shrops 39 K6
Bitterne C Sotn 9 M5
Bitteswell Leics 41 M9
Bitton S Glos 17 P3
Bix Oxon 20 B6
Bixter Shet 111 k4
Blaby Leics 41 M7
Blackadder Border 80 H4
Blackawton Devon 5 Q9
Blackborough Devon 6 E2
Blackborough End Norfk 43 Q7
Black Bourton Oxon 30 H12
Blackboys E Susx 11 Q6
Blackbrook Derbys 51 J10
Blackbrook St Hel 57 K9
Blackbrook Staffs 49 N7
Blackburn Abers 102 H11
Blackburn Bl w D 57 M4
Blackburn W Loth 86 B8
Blackburn with Darwen Services Bl w D 57 M4
Black Callerton N u Ty 73 L7
Blackcraig E Ayrs 77 K9
Black Crofts Ag & B 90 C8
Blackdog Abers 103 K11
Black Dog Devon 15 N9
Blackdown Dorset 7 K3
Blacker Hill Barns 51 J1
Blackfen Gt Lon 21 P8
Blackfield Hants 9 M7
Blackford P & K 85 P2
Blackford Somset 17 K6
Blackford Somset 17 P10
Blackfordby Leics 41 J4
Blackhall C Edin 86 E7
Blackhall Colliery Dur 73 Q11
Blackhall Mill Gatesd 73 K9
Blackhaugh Border 79 N2
Blackheath Gt Lon 21 M7
Blackheath Sandw 40 C9
Blackheath Suffk 35 N2
Blackheath Surrey 10 G2
Blackhill Abers 103 M4
Blackhill Abers 103 M6
Blackhill Dur 73 J9
Blackhill of Clackriach Abers 103 J6
Blackhorse Devon 6 D4
Blacklaw D & G 78 G7
Blackley Manch 57 Q8
Blackley Crematorium Manch 57 Q7
Blacklunans P & K 94 C9
Blackmarstone Herefs 28 F2
Blackmill Brdgnd 27 K10
Blackmoor Hants 10 C4
Blackmoor N Som 17 L4
Blackmoorfoot Kirk 58 E10
Blackmore Essex 22 C3
Blackmore End Essex 34 C9
Black Mountains 27 Q4
Blackness Falk 86 C6
Blacknest Hants 10 C2
Black Notley Essex 34 C11
Blacko Lancs 57 Q1
Black Pill Swans 26 E10
Blackpool Bpool 56 F2
Blackpool Devon 6 B12
Blackpool Airport Lancs 56 G3
Blackridge W Loth 85 P9
Blackrod Bolton 57 L6
Blacksboat Moray 101 J7
Blackshaw D & G 70 G3
Blackshaw Head Calder 58 C8
Blackstone W Susx 11 K6
Black Street Suffk 45 Q11
Blackthorn Oxon 31 N9
Blackthorpe Suffk 34 E4
Blacktoft E R Yk 60 E8
Blacktop C Aber 95 P2
Black Torrington Devon 14 H10
Blackwall Derbys 50 G10
Blackwater Cnwll 2 H6
Blackwater Hants 20 D10
Blackwater IoW 9 N9
Blackwater Somset 16 H11
Blackwaterfoot N Ayrs 75 N6
Blackwell Cumb 71 N5
Blackwell Derbys 50 E6
Blackwell Derbys 51 K8
Blackwell Warwks 30 G5
Blackwell Worcs 40 C11
Blackwood Caerph 27 N8
Blackwood D & G 78 E10
Blackwood S Lans 77 N3
Blacon Ches W 48 H2
Bladnoch D & G 69 K8
Bladon Oxon 31 K10
Blaenannerch Cerdgn 36 D10
Blaenau Ffestiniog Gwynd 47 L3
Blaenavon Torfn 27 Q7
Blaenavon Industrial Landscape Torfn 27 P7
Blaenffos Pembks 25 L2
Blaengarw Brdgnd 27 J9
Blaengwrach Neath 27 J7
Blaengwynfi Neath 27 J9
Blaenpennal Cerdgn 37 K7
Blaenplwyf Cerdgn 37 J5
Blaenporth Cerdgn 36 D10
Blaenrhondda Rhondd 27 K8
Blaenwaun Carmth 25 L4
Blaen-y-Coed Carmth 25 N4
Blaen-y-cwm Rhondd 27 K8
Blagdon N Som 17 M4
Blagdon Somset 16 G11
Blagdon Torbay 6 B9
Blagdon Hill Somset 16 G11
Blaich Highld 90 E2
Blain Highld 89 N3
Blaina Blae G 27 P7
Blair Atholl P & K 92 C3
Blair Drummond Stirlg 85 M3
Blairgowrie P & K 92 H6
Blairhall Fife 86 B5
Blairingone P & K 86 B3
Blairlogie Stirlg 85 N4
Blairmore Ag & B 84 D6
Blairmore Highld 108 D4
Blair's Ferry Ag & B 83 P8
Blaisdon Gloucs 29 J5
Blakebrook Worcs 39 P6
Blakedown Worcs 39 Q6
Blake End Essex 34 B11
Blakemere Ches W 49 K2
Blakemere Herefs 28 D1
Blakenall Heath Wsall 40 D7
Blakeney Gloucs 29 J7
Blakeney Norfk 44 G2
Blakenhall Ches E 49 N6
Blakenhall Wolves 40 B7
Blakesley Nhants 31 N4
Blanchland Nthumb 72 H10
Blandford Forum Dorset 8 C6
Blandford St Mary Dorset 8 C6
Blanefield Stirlg 85 J7
Blankney Lincs 52 F10
Blantyre S Lans 85 L10
Blar a' Chaorainn Highld 90 F3
Blargie Highld 98 H9
Blarmachfoldach Highld 90 F3
Blaston Leics 42 B10
Blatherwycke Nhants 42 D10
Blawith Cumb 62 F5
Blawquhairn D & G 69 P3
Blaxhall Suffk 35 M5
Blaxton Donc 51 P2
Blaydon Gatesd 73 L8
Bleadney Somset 17 L7
Bleadon N Som 17 J5
Blean Kent 23 L10
Bleasby Notts 51 Q10
Blebocraigs Fife 93 M11
Bleddfa Powys 38 E8
Bledington Gloucs 30 G9
Bledlow Bucks 20 C3
Bledlow Ridge Bucks 20 C4
Blegbie E Loth 87 J9
Blencarn Cumb 64 B2
Blencogo Cumb 71 K6
Blendworth Hants 10 B7
Blenheim Palace Oxon 31 K10
Blennerhasset Cumb 71 J7
Bletchingdon Oxon 31 L9
Bletchingley Surrey 21 M12
Bletchley M Keyn 32 C9
Bletchley Shrops 49 L8
Bletherston Pembks 25 J5
Bletsoe Bed 32 E5
Blewbury Oxon 19 N4
Blickling Norfk 45 K4
Blidworth Notts 51 N9
Blidworth Bottoms Notts 51 N9
Blindcrake Cumb 71 J8
Blindley Heath Surrey 11 M2
Blisland Cnwll 4 D5
Blissford Hants 8 H5
Bliss Gate Worcs 39 N7
Blisworth Nhants 31 Q4
Blithbury Staffs 40 E4
Blockley Gloucs 30 F7
Blofield Norfk 45 M8
Blofield Heath Norfk 45 M7
Blo Norton Norfk 34 G2
Bloomfield Border 80 D8
Blore Staffs 50 F10
Bloxham Oxon 31 K7
Bloxholm Lincs 52 F11
Bloxwich Wsall 40 D7
Bloxworth Dorset 8 C8
Blubberhouses N York 58 F3
Blue Anchor Somset 16 D7
Blue Bell Hill Kent 22 E10
Blue John Cavern Derbys 50 F4
Blundellsands Sefton 56 F8
Blundeston Suffk 45 Q10
Blunham C Beds 32 G6
Blunsdon St Andrew Swindn 18 G3
Bluntington Worcs 40 B11
Bluntisham Cambs 33 K2
Blurton C Stke 50 B11
Blyborough Lincs 52 D5
Blyford Suffk 35 N2
Blymhill Staffs 49 P11
Blyth Notts 51 N4
Blyth Nthumb 73 N5
Blyth Bridge Border 86 D12
Blythburgh Suffk 35 P2
Blyth Crematorium Nthumb 73 N5
Blythe Border 80 D4
Blyton Lincs 52 C5
Boarhills Fife 93 P11
Boarhunt Hants 9 P6
Boarstall Bucks 31 N10
Boath Highld 107 J7
Boat of Garten Highld 99 P5
Bobbing Kent 22 H9
Bobbington Staffs 39 P4
Bocking Essex 34 C11
Bocking Churchstreet Essex 34 C10
Boddam Abers 103 M6
Boddam Shet 111 k5
Boddington Gloucs 29 M4
Bodedern IoA 54 D5
Bodelwyddan Denbgs 55 Q6
Bodenham Herefs 39 K11
Bodenham Wilts 8 H3
Bodenham Moor Herefs 39 K11
Bodewryd IoA 54 E4
Bodfari Denbgs 48 C2
Bodffordd IoA 54 F6
Bodfuan Gwynd 46 E4
Bodham Norfk 45 J3
Bodiam E Susx 12 F5
Bodicote Oxon 31 L6
Bodinnick Cnwll 4 E9
Bodle Street Green E Susx 12 D7
Bodmin Cnwll 3 N3
Bodmin Moor Cnwll 4 F5
Bodsham Kent 13 L2
Bodwen Cnwll 3 M4
Bogallan Highld 107 K11
Bogbrae Abers 103 L8
Bogend S Ayrs 76 G5
Boggs Holdings E Loth 87 J7
Boghall Mdloth 86 F8
Boghall W Loth 86 B8
Boghead S Lans 77 N3
Bogmoor Moray 101 L3
Bogmuir Abers 95 K7
Bogniebrae Abers 102 D6
Bognor Regis W Susx 10 E9
Bogroy Highld 99 N4
Bogue D & G 69 P3
Bohortha Cnwll 3 J8
Bohuntine Highld 98 D11
Bolam Dur 65 L3
Bolberry Devon 5 N11
Boldmere Birm 40 E8
Boldre Hants 9 K7
Boldron Dur 65 J5
Bole Notts 52 B6
Bolehill Derbys 50 H9
Bolham Devon 16 C12
Bolham Water Devon 6 F1
Bolingey Cnwll 2 H5
Bollington Ches E 50 C5
Bolney W Susx 11 L5
Bolnhurst Bed 32 F5
Bolnore W Susx 11 M5
Bolshan Angus 93 Q5
Bolsover Derbys 51 L6
Bolsterstone Sheff 50 H2
Boltby N York 66 C9
Boltenstone Abers 101 M12
Bolton Bolton 57 N7
Bolton Cumb 64 B3
Bolton E Loth 87 K8
Bolton E R Yk 60 D4
Bolton Nthumb 81 M10
Bolton Abbey N York 58 E4
Bolton-by-Bowland Lancs 63 P11
Boltonfellend Cumb 71 P2
Boltongate Cumb 71 K7
Bolton-le-Sands Lancs 63 J8
Bolton Low Houses Cumb 71 K6
Bolton-on-Swale N York 65 M7
Bolton Percy N York 59 M6
Bolton upon Dearne Barns 51 L1
Bolventor Cnwll 4 E5
Bomere Heath Shrops 49 J10
Bonar Bridge Highld 107 K4
Bonawe Ag & B 90 D9
Bonby N Linc 60 G10
Boncath Pembks 25 L2
Bonchester Bridge Border 80 D10
Bondleigh Devon 15 L10
Bonds Lancs 63 J12
Bo'ness Falk 86 B6
Boney Hay Staffs 40 D5
Bonhill W Duns 84 G7
Boningale Shrops 39 P2
Bonjedward Border 80 E9
Bonkle N Lans 85 P10
Bonnington Angus 93 P7
Bonnington Kent 13 K3
Bonnybank Fife 86 G2
Bonnybridge Falk 85 N7
Bonnykelly Abers 102 H5
Bonnyrigg Mdloth 86 G8
Bonnyton Angus 93 L7
Bonsall Derbys 50 H8
Bonshaw Tower D & G 71 K2
Bont-Dolgadfan Powys 47 P10
Bont-goch Cerdgn 37 L4
Bontnewydd Cerdgn 37 K7
Bontnewydd Gwynd 54 G9
Bontuchel Denbgs 48 C4
Bonvilston V Glam 16 E2
Boode Devon 15 J5
Booker Bucks 20 D5
Boon Border 80 D5
Boosbeck R & Cl 66 F4
Boose's Green Essex 34 E9
Boot Cumb 62 D3
Booth Calder 58 D8
Boothby Graffoe Lincs 52 E10
Boothby Pagnell Lincs 42 D4
Boothferry E R Yk 60 C8
Boothstown Salfd 57 N8
Bootle Cumb 62 C5
Bootle Sefton 56 G9
Boraston Shrops 39 L8
Bordeaux Guern 6 c1
Borden Kent 22 G10
Borders Crematorium Border 80 D7
Boreham Essex 22 F2
Boreham Wilts 18 D11
Boreham Street E Susx 12 D7
Borehamwood Herts 21 J4
Boreland D & G 79 J10
Boreraig Highld 104 B10
Borgh W Isls 111 a7
Borgh W Isls 111 d1
Borgie Highld 109 M4
Borgue D & G 69 P9
Borgue Highld 110 D9
Borley Essex 34 E7
Borneskitaig Highld 104 E7
Borness D & G 69 N9
Boroughbridge N York 59 K2
Borough Green Kent 22 C11
Borrowash Derbys 41 K1
Borrowby N York 65 Q9
Borrowstoun Falk 86 B6
Borstal Medway 22 E9
Borth Cerdgn 37 K3
Borthwickbrae Border 79 N6
Borthwickshiels Border 79 N6
Borth-y-Gest Gwynd 47 J4
Borve Highld 104 F11
Borve W Isls 111 a7
Borve W Isls 111 c3
Borve W Isls 111 d1
Borwick Lancs 63 K7
Bosbury Herefs 39 M12
Boscastle Cnwll 4 D3
Boscombe Bmouth 8 G8
Boscombe Wilts 18 H11
Bosham W Susx 10 D8
Bosherston Pembks 24 G9
Bosley Ches E 50 B7
Bossall N York 60 C3
Bossiney Cnwll 4 D3
Bossingham Kent 13 M1
Bossington Somset 16 B6
Bostock Green Ches W 49 M2
Boston Lincs 43 K2
Boston Crematorium Lincs 43 K2
Boston Spa Leeds 59 K5
Boswinger Cnwll 3 L7
Botallack Cnwll 2 B8
Botany Bay Gt Lon 21 L4
Botesdale Suffk 34 H2
Bothal Nthumb 73 M4
Bothamsall Notts 51 P6
Bothel Cumb 71 K7
Bothenhampton Dorset 7 L5
Bothwell S Lans 85 L10
Bothwell Services S Lans 85 M10
Botley Bucks 20 F3
Botley Hants 9 N5
Botley Oxon 31 L11
Botolph Claydon Bucks 31 Q8
Botolphs W Susx 11 J8
Bottesford Leics 42 B3
Bottesford N Linc 52 C3
Bottisham Cambs 33 N5
Bottomcraig Fife 93 L10
Bottoms Calder 58 B9
Botusfleming Cnwll 5 J7
Botwnnog Gwynd 46 D5
Bough Beech Kent 11 P1
Boughrood Powys 27 N2
Boughton Nhants 31 Q2
Boughton Norfk 44 B9
Boughton Notts 51 P7
Boughton Aluph Kent 13 K1
Boughton Green Kent 22 F12
Boughton Monchelsea Kent 22 F12
Boughton Street Kent 23 K10
Bouldon Shrops 39 K5
Boulmer Nthumb 81 Q10
Boultham Lincs 52 D9
Bourn Cambs 33 K5
Bourne Lincs 42 F6
Bournebridge Essex 21 P5
Bournebrook Birm 40 D10
Bourne End Bucks 20 E6
Bourne End C Beds 32 D7
Bourne End Herts 20 G3
Bournemouth Bmouth 8 G8
Bournemouth Airport Dorset 8 G7
Bournemouth Crematorium Bmouth 8 G8
Bournes Green Sthend 22 H6
Bournheath Worcs 40 C11
Bournmoor Dur 73 N9
Bournville Birm 40 D10
Bourton Dorset 8 B2
Bourton Oxon 19 J4
Bourton Shrops 39 L3
Bourton Wilts 18 F7
Bourton on Dunsmore Warwks 41 K12
Bourton-on-the-Hill Gloucs 30 F7
Bourton-on-the-Water Gloucs 30 F9
Bousd Ag & B 88 G4
Bouth Cumb 62 G5
Bouthwaite N York 65 K12
Boveridge Dorset 8 F4
Bovey Tracey Devon 5 Q5
Bovingdon Herts 20 G3
Bow Devon 15 M10
Bow Gt Lon 21 M6
Bow Ork 111 h3
Bow Brickhill M Keyn 32 C9
Bowbridge Gloucs 29 M7
Bowburn Dur 73 N12
Bowcombe IoW 9 M9
Bowd Devon 6 F5
Bowden Border 80 D7
Bowden Hill Wilts 18 D7
Bowdon Traffd 57 N10
Bower Highld 110 E3
Bowerchalke Wilts 8 F3
Bowermadden Highld 110 F3
Bowers Staffs 49 P8
Bowers Gifford Essex 22 E6
Bowershall Fife 86 C4
Bower's Row Leeds 59 K8
Bowes Dur 64 H5
Bowgreave Lancs 63 J12
Bowhouse D & G 70 G3
Bowland Border 79 P2
Bowley Herefs 39 K10
Bowlhead Green Surrey 10 E3
Bowling C Brad 58 F7
Bowling W Duns 84 G8
Bowmanstead Cumb 62 F3
Bowmore Ag & B 82 D10
Bowness-on-Solway Cumb 71 K3
Bowness-on-Windermere Cumb 62 H3
Bow of Fife Fife 93 K12
Bowriefauld Angus 93 N6
Bowsden Nthumb 81 L6
Bow Street Cerdgn 37 K4
Box Gloucs 29 M8
Box Wilts 18 C7
Boxford Suffk 34 F8
Boxford W Berk 19 M6
Boxgrove W Susx 10 E8
Boxley Kent 22 F10
Boxmoor Herts 20 G3
Boxted Essex 34 G9
Boxted Essex 34 G9
Boxted Suffk 34 D6
Boxted Cross Essex 34 G9
Boxworth Cambs 33 K4
Boyden Gate Kent 23 N9
Boylestone Derbys 40 F1
Boyndie Abers 102 E3
Boyndlie Abers 103 J3
Boynton E R Yk 61 K1
Boysack Angus 93 Q6
Boyton Cnwll 4 H2
Boyton Suffk 35 N7
Boyton Wilts 18 D11
Boyton Cross Essex 22 D2
Boyton End Suffk 34 C7
Bozeat Nhants 32 C5
Brabourne Kent 13 L2
Brabourne Lees Kent 13 L3
Brabstermire Highld 110 G2
Bracadale Highld 96 D2
Braceborough Lincs 42 F7
Bracebridge Heath Lincs 52 E9
Bracebridge Low Fields Lincs 52 D9
Braceby Lincs 42 E3
Bracewell Lancs 63 Q11
Brackenfield Derbys 51 J8
Brackenhirst N Lans 85 M8
Bracklesham W Susx 10 D10
Brackletter Highld 98 B11
Brackley Nhants 31 N6
Bracknell Br For 20 E9
Braco P & K 85 N2
Bracobrae Moray 101 P5
Bracon Ash Norfk 45 K9
Bracora Highld 97 K10
Bracorina Highld 97 K10

Bradbourne - Buckland 169

Bradbourne Derbys 50 G9
Bradbury Dur 65 N2
Bradden Nhants 31 N5
Bradeley C Stke 49 Q5
Bradenham Bucks 20 D4
Bradenstoke Wilts 18 E5
Bradfield Devon 6 E2
Bradfield Essex 35 J9
Bradfield Norfk 45 L4
Bradfield Sheff 50 H3
Bradfield W Berk 19 P6
Bradfield Combust Suffk 34 E5
Bradfield Green Ches E 49 M4
Bradfield Heath Essex 35 J10
Bradfield St Clare Suffk 34 E5
Bradfield St George Suffk 34 E5
Bradford C Brad 58 F7
Bradford Devon 14 G10
Bradford Abbas Dorset 17 N12
Bradford Leigh Wilts 18 C8
Bradford-on-Avon Wilts 18 C8
Bradford-on-Tone Somset 16 G10
Bradford Peverell Dorset 7 P4
Bradiford Devon 15 K5
Brading IoW 9 Q9
Bradley Derbys 50 G10
Bradley Hants 19 Q11
Bradley NE Lin 53 J3
Bradley Staffs 49 Q11
Bradley Wolves 40 C8
Bradley Worcs 30 C2
Bradley Green Worcs 30 C2
Bradley in the Moors Staffs 50 D11
Bradley Stoke S Glos 28 H11
Bradmore Notts 41 N2
Bradninch Devon 6 D3
Bradnop Staffs 50 D9
Bradpole Dorset 7 L4
Bradshaw Calder 58 E8
Bradstone Devon 4 H4
Bradwall Green Ches E 49 N3
Bradwell Derbys 50 F5
Bradwell Essex 34 D11
Bradwell M Keyn 32 B8
Bradwell Norfk 45 Q8
Bradwell Crematorium Staffs 49 Q5
Bradwell-on-Sea Essex 23 J3
Bradwell Waterside Essex 23 J2
Bradworthy Devon 14 F8
Brae Highld 107 L9
Brae Shet 111 k3
Braeface Falk 85 N7
Braehead Angus 95 L10
Braehead D & G 69 K8
Braehead S Lans 77 Q2
Braemar Abers 94 C4
Braemore Highld 106 C6
Braemore Highld 110 C9
Brae Roy Lodge Highld 98 D10
Braeside Inver 84 D7
Braes of Coul Angus 93 K4
Braes of Enzie Moray 101 M4
Braeswick Ork 111 i1
Braevallich Ag & B 83 P2
Brafferton Darltn 65 N4
Brafferton N York 66 B12
Brafield-on-the-Green Nhants 32 B5
Bragar W Isls 111 d1
Bragbury End Herts 33 J11
Braidwood S Lans 77 P2
Brailsford Derbys 50 G11
Braintree Essex 34 C11
Braiseworth Suffk 35 J3
Braishfield Hants 9 L3
Braithwaite Cumb 71 K10
Braithwell Donc 51 M2
Bramber W Susx 11 J7
Bramcote Warwks 41 K9
Bramcote Crematorium Notts 51 L11
Bramdean Hants 9 Q2
Bramerton Norfk 45 L8
Bramfield Herts 33 J12
Bramfield Suffk 35 N3
Bramford Suffk 35 J7
Bramhall Stockp 50 B4
Bramham Leeds 59 K5
Bramhope Leeds 58 G5
Bramley Hants 19 Q8
Bramley Leeds 58 G7
Bramley Rothm 51 L3
Bramley Surrey 10 G2
Bramley Corner Hants 19 Q8
Bramling Kent 23 N11
Brampford Speke Devon 6 C3
Brampton Cambs 32 H3
Brampton Cumb 64 C3
Brampton Cumb 71 Q4
Brampton Lincs 52 B7
Brampton Norfk 45 K5
Brampton Rothm 51 K1
Brampton Suffk 35 P1
Brampton Abbotts Herefs 28 H4
Brampton Ash Nhants 42 B11
Brampton Bryan Herefs 38 G7
Brampton-en-le-Morthen Rothm 51 L4
Bramshall Staffs 40 D2
Bramshaw Hants 9 J4
Bramshott Hants 10 D4
Bramwell Somset 17 L9
Branault Highld 89 L3
Brancaster Norfk 44 C2
Brancaster Staithe Norfk 44 D2
Brancepeth Dur 73 L12
Branchill Moray 100 G5
Branderburgh Moray 101 K2
Brandesburton E R Yk 61 J5
Brandeston Suffk 35 L5
Brandiston Norfk 45 J6
Brandon Dur 73 M11
Brandon Lincs 42 C1
Brandon Suffk 44 D11
Brandon Warwks 41 K11
Brandon Parva Norfk 44 H8
Brandsby N York 66 E11
Brandy Wharf Lincs 52 E4
Bran End Essex 33 Q10
Branksome Poole 8 F8
Branksome Park Poole 8 F8
Bransbury Hants 19 M11
Bransby Lincs 52 C7
Branscombe Devon 6 G5
Bransford Worcs 39 P10
Bransgore Hants 8 H7
Bransholme C KuH 61 J7
Bransley Shrops 39 M7
Branston Leics 42 B4
Branston Lincs 52 E9
Branston Staffs 40 G4
Branston Booths Lincs 52 F9
Branstone IoW 9 P10
Brant Broughton Lincs 52 D11
Brantham Suffk 35 J9
Branthwaite Cumb 70 H9
Branthwaite Cumb 71 L7
Brantingham E R Yk 60 G8
Branton Donc 51 N1
Branton Nthumb 81 L10
Branton Green N York 59 K2
Branxton Nthumb 81 J6
Brassington Derbys 50 G9
Brasted Kent 21 P11
Brasted Chart Kent 21 P11
Brathens Abers 95 L3
Bratoft Lincs 53 M9
Brattleby Lincs 52 D7
Bratton Wilts 18 D9
Bratton Wrekin 49 L11
Bratton Clovelly Devon 5 K2
Bratton Fleming Devon 15 L5
Bratton Seymour Somset 17 P9
Braughing Herts 33 L10
Braunston Nhants 31 M2
Braunston Rutlnd 42 B8
Braunton Devon 14 H5
Brawby N York 66 G11
Brawl Highld 109 P3
Bray W & M 20 E7
Braybrooke Nhants 41 Q9
Brayford Devon 15 M5
Bray Shop Cnwll 4 H5
Brayton N York 59 N7
Braywick W & M 20 E7
Breachwood Green Herts 32 G11
Breadsall Derbys 51 J11
Breadstone Gloucs 29 J8
Breage Cnwll 2 F9
Breakachy Highld 106 H12
Breakspear Crematorium Gt Lon 20 H5
Brealangwell Lodge Highld 106 H4
Bream Gloucs 28 H7
Breamore Hants 8 H4
Brean Somset 16 H5
Breanais W Isls 111 b2
Brearton N York 58 H3
Breascleit W Isls 111 c2
Breasclete W Isls 111 c2
Breaston Derbys 41 L2
Brechfa Carmth 26 C3
Brechin Angus 95 K9
Breckles Norfk 44 F10
Brecon Powys 27 L3
*Brecon Beacons National Park* 27 L4
Bredbury Stockp 50 B3
Brede E Susx 12 G6
Bredenbury Herefs 39 L10
Bredfield Suffk 35 L6
Bredgar Kent 22 G10
Bredhurst Kent 22 F10
Bredon Worcs 29 N2
Bredon's Hardwick Worcs 29 M2
Bredon's Norton Worcs 29 N2
Bredwardine Herefs 38 G12
Breedon on the Hill Leics 41 K3
Breich W Loth 85 Q10
Breightmet Bolton 57 N7
Breighton E R Yk 60 C7
Breinton Herefs 28 F2
Bremhill Wilts 18 E6
Brenchley Kent 12 D2
Brendon Devon 15 N3
Brenfield Ag & B 83 M6
Brenish W Isls 111 b2
Brent Cross Gt Lon 21 K6
Brent Eleigh Suffk 34 F7
Brentford Gt Lon 21 J7
Brentingby Leics 42 B6
Brent Knoll Somset 17 J6
Brent Mill Devon 5 N8
Brent Pelham Herts 33 M10
Brentwood Essex 22 C5
Brenzett Kent 13 J5
Brenzett Green Kent 13 J4
Brereton Staffs 40 D4
Brereton Green Ches E 49 P3
Bressay Shet 111 k4
Bressingham Norfk 34 H1
Bretby Derbys 40 H3
Bretby Crematorium Derbys 40 H3
Bretford Warwks 41 K11
Bretforton Worcs 30 E5
Bretherton Lancs 57 J5
Brettabister Shet 111 k4
Brettenham Norfk 44 F12
Brettenham Suffk 34 F6
Bretton Flints 48 G3
Brewood Staffs 40 B6
Briantspuddle Dorset 8 B8
Brickendon Herts 21 L2
Bricket Wood Herts 20 H3
Brick Houses Sheff 50 H5
Bricklehampton Worcs 29 N1
Bride IoM 56 e2
Bridekirk Cumb 71 J8
Bridestowe Devon 5 L3
Brideswell Abers 102 D7
Bridford Devon 5 Q3
Bridge Kent 23 M11
Bridgehampton Somset 17 N10
Bridge Hewick N York 65 N12
Bridgehill Dur 73 K9
Bridgemary Hants 9 P6
Bridgend Abers 101 P7
Bridgend Ag & B 75 M5
Bridgend Ag & B 82 E9
Bridgend Angus 95 J8
Bridgend Brdgnd 27 J11
Bridgend D & G 78 H7
Bridgend Devon 5 L9
Bridgend Fife 93 L12
Bridgend Moray 101 M8
Bridgend P & K 92 G10
Bridgend W Loth 86 C7
Bridgend of Lintrathen Angus 93 K5
Bridge of Alford Abers 102 D10
Bridge of Allan Stirlg 85 N4
Bridge of Avon Moray 100 H10
Bridge of Avon Moray 101 J7
Bridge of Balgie P & K 91 N7
Bridge of Brewlands Angus 94 C9
Bridge of Brown Highld 100 H10
Bridge of Cally P & K 92 H5
Bridge of Canny Abers 95 K3
Bridge of Craigisla Angus 93 J5
Bridge of Dee D & G 70 C4
Bridge of Don C Aber 103 K12
Bridge of Dulsie Highld 100 E7
Bridge of Dye Abers 95 K5
Bridge of Earn P & K 92 G11
Bridge of Ericht P & K 91 M5
Bridge of Feugh Abers 95 L3
Bridge of Forss Highld 110 B3
Bridge of Gairn Abers 94 F3
Bridge of Gaur P & K 91 M5
Bridge of Marnoch Abers 102 D5
Bridge of Muchalls Abers 95 P4
Bridge of Orchy Ag & B 91 J8
Bridge of Tilt P & K 92 D3
Bridge of Tynet Moray 101 M3
Bridge of Walls Shet 111 j4
Bridge of Weir Rens 84 G9
Bridgerule Devon 14 E10
Bridge Sollers Herefs 28 E1
Bridge Street Suffk 34 E6
Bridgetown Somset 16 C9
Bridge Trafford Ches W 49 J2
Bridgham Norfk 44 F11
Bridgnorth Shrops 39 N4
Bridgwater Somset 16 H8
Bridgwater Services Somset 17 J8
Bridlington E R Yk 61 K2
Bridport Dorset 7 L4
Bridstow Herefs 28 G4
Brierfield Lancs 57 Q2
Brierley Barns 59 K11
Brierley Gloucs 28 H6
Brierley Hill Dudley 40 B9
Brigg N Linc 52 E3
Briggate Norfk 45 M5
Briggswath N York 67 J6
Brigham Cumb 70 H9
Brigham E R Yk 61 J4
Brighouse Calder 58 F9
Brighstone IoW 9 M10
Brighthampton Oxon 31 K12
Brightley Devon 15 K11
Brightling E Susx 12 D6
Brightlingsea Essex 34 H12
Brighton Br & H 11 L8
Brighton le Sands Sefton 56 F8
Brightons Falk 85 Q7
Brightwalton W Berk 19 M5
Brightwell Suffk 35 L7
Brightwell Baldwin Oxon 19 Q2
Brightwell-cum-Sotwell Oxon 19 P3
Brightwell Upperton Oxon 19 Q2
Brignall Dur 65 J5
Brig o'Turk Stirlg 85 J2
Brigsley NE Lin 53 J3
Brigsteer Cumb 63 J4
Brigstock Nhants 42 D11
Brill Bucks 31 P10
Brill Cnwll 2 G9
Brilley Herefs 38 F11
Brimfield Herefs 39 K8
Brimfield Cross Herefs 39 K8
Brimington Derbys 51 K6
Brimley Devon 5 Q5
Brimpsfield Gloucs 29 N6
Brimpton W Berk 19 P7
Brimscombe Gloucs 29 M8
Brimstage Wirral 56 F11
Brincliffe Sheff 51 J4
Brind E R Yk 60 C7
Brindister Shet 111 j4
Brindle Lancs 57 L4
Brineton Staffs 49 P11
Bringhurst Leics 42 B10
Bringsty Common Herefs 39 M10
Brington Cambs 32 F2
Briningham Norfk 44 G4
Brinkhill Lincs 53 L8
Brinkley Cambs 33 Q6
Brinklow Warwks 41 K10
Brinkworth Wilts 18 E4
Brinscall Lancs 57 L5
Brinsley Notts 51 L10
Brinsworth Rothm 51 K3
Brinton Norfk 44 G3
Brinyan Ork 111 h2
Brisley Norfk 44 F6
Brislington Bristl 17 N3
Brissenden Green Kent 12 H3
Bristol Bristl 17 N2
*Bristol Airport N Som* 17 M3
Bristol Zoo Gardens Bristl 17 N2
Briston Norfk 44 H4
Britford Wilts 8 H2
Brithdir Caerph 27 N8
Brithdir Gwynd 47 M7
British Legion Village Kent 22 E11
Briton Ferry Neath 26 G9
Britwell Salome Oxon 19 R3
Brixham Torbay 6 C10
Brixton Devon 5 L9
Brixton Gt Lon 21 L8
Brixton Deverill Wilts 18 C11
Brixworth Nhants 41 Q12
Brize Norton Oxon 30 H11
*Brize Norton Airport Oxon* 30 H11
Broad Alley Worcs 30 B1
Broad Blunsdon Swindn 18 G3
Broadbottom Tamesd 50 C3
Broadbridge W Susx 10 D8
Broadbridge Heath W Susx 11 J4
Broad Campden Gloucs 30 F6
Broad Carr Calder 58 E9
Broad Chalke Wilts 8 F3
Broadclyst Devon 6 D4
Broadfield Inver 84 F8
Broadford Highld 96 H5
Broadford Bridge W Susx 10 H6
Broadgairhill Border 79 K6
Broad Green Worcs 39 P10
Broadhaugh Border 81 J4
Broad Haven Pembks 24 F6
Broadheath Traffd 57 N10
Broadhembury Devon 6 E2
Broadhempston Devon 5 Q7
Broad Hinton Wilts 18 G5
Broadland Row E Susx 12 G6
Broad Layings Hants 19 M8
Broadley Moray 101 M3
Broad Marston Worcs 30 F5
Broadmayne Dorset 7 Q5
Broad Meadow Staffs 49 Q6
Broadmoor Pembks 25 J7
Broadoak Dorset 7 L4
Broad Oak E Susx 12 C5
Broad Oak E Susx 12 G6
Broad Oak Herefs 28 F5
Broad Oak Kent 23 M10
Broad Oak St Hel 57 K9
Broad's Green Essex 22 E2
Broadstairs Kent 23 Q9
Broadstone Poole 8 E8
Broadstone Shrops 39 K4
Broad Street E Susx 12 G6
Broad Street Kent 22 G11
Broad Town Wilts 18 G5
Broadwas Worcs 39 N10
Broadwater Herts 33 J11
Broadwater W Susx 11 J8
Broadwaters Worcs 39 Q6
Broadway Pembks 24 F6
Broadway Somset 17 J11
Broadway Worcs 30 E6
Broadwell Gloucs 28 G6
Broadwell Gloucs 30 G8
Broadwell Oxon 30 G12
Broadwell Warwks 31 L2
Broadwindsor Dorset 7 L3
Broadwood Kelly Devon 15 K10
Broadwoodwidger Devon 5 J3
Brochel Highld 104 H12
Brochroy Ag & B 90 D9
Brockamin Worcs 39 P10
Brockbridge Hants 9 Q4
Brockdish Norfk 35 K2
Brockenhurst Hants 9 K7
Brocketsbrae S Lans 78 D2
Brockford Street Suffk 35 J4
Brockhall Nhants 31 N2
Brockham Surrey 21 K12
Brockhampton Gloucs 30 D9
Brockhampton Hants 10 B8
Brockhampton Herefs 28 H3
Brockholes Kirk 58 F11
Brocklesby Lincs 61 K11
Brockley N Som 17 L3
Brockley Suffk 34 D3
Brockley Green Suffk 34 C7
Brockley Green Suffk 34 D6
Brockmoor Dudley 40 B9
Brockton Shrops 38 G2
Brockton Shrops 38 G5
Brockton Shrops 39 L4
Brockweir Gloucs 28 G8
Brockworth Gloucs 29 M5
Brocton Staffs 40 C4
Brodick N Ayrs 75 Q5
Brodie Moray 100 F4
Brodsworth Donc 59 L11
Brogaig Highld 104 F8
Brokenborough Wilts 18 D3
Broken Cross Ches E 50 B6
Brokerswood Wilts 18 C9
Bromborough Wirral 56 G11
Brome Suffk 35 J2
Brome Street Suffk 35 J2
Bromeswell Suffk 35 M6
Bromfield Cumb 71 J6
Bromfield Shrops 39 J6
Bromham Bed 32 E6
Bromham Wilts 18 E7
Bromley Dudley 40 B9
Bromley Gt Lon 21 N9
Bromley Shrops 39 N3
Bromley Cross Bolton 57 N6
Brompton Medway 22 F9
Brompton N York 65 P8
Brompton-by-Sawdon N York 67 K10
Brompton-on-Swale N York 65 L7
Brompton Ralph Somset 16 E9
Brompton Regis Somset 16 C9
Bromsberrow Gloucs 29 K3
Bromsberrow Heath Gloucs 29 K3
Bromsgrove Worcs 40 C12
Bromyard Herefs 39 M10
Bronant Cerdgn 37 K7
Brongest Cerdgn 36 E10
Bronington Wrexhm 49 J7
Bronllys Powys 27 N2
Bronwydd Carmth 25 P4
Bronygarth Shrops 48 F7
Brook Hants 9 J5
Brook IoW 9 L9
Brook Kent 13 K2
Brook Surrey 10 E3
Brooke Norfk 45 L9
Brooke Rutlnd 42 C8
Brookenby Lincs 52 H4
Brookfield Rens 84 G9
Brookhampton Somset 17 P9
Brook Hill Hants 9 J5
Brookhouse Lancs 63 K8
Brookhouse Rothm 51 L3
Brookhouse Green Ches E 49 P4
Brookhouses Derbys 50 D3
Brookland Kent 13 J5
Brooklands Traffd 57 P10
Brookmans Park Herts 21 K3
Brook Street Essex 22 C5
Brook Street Kent 12 H4
Brookthorpe Gloucs 29 L6
Brookwood Surrey 20 F11
Broom C Beds 32 G8
Broom Rothm 51 K3
Broom Warwks 30 E4
Broome Norfk 45 M10
Broome Shrops 38 H6
Broome Worcs 40 B10
Broomedge Warrtn 57 N10
Broomfield Essex 22 E2
Broomfield Kent 22 G11
Broomfield Kent 23 M9
Broomfield Somset 16 G9
Broomfleet E R Yk 60 F8
Broomhaugh Nthumb 72 H8
Broom Hill Barns 59 K12
Broom Hill Notts 51 M10
Broomhill Nthumb 73 M1
Broompark Dur 73 M11
Brora Highld 107 P2
Broseley Shrops 39 M2
Brotherlee Dur 72 G12
Brotherton N York 59 L8
Brotton R & Cl 66 F4
Broubster Highld 110 B4
Brough Cumb 64 E5
Brough E R Yk 60 F8
Brough Highld 110 E2
Brough Notts 52 B10
Brough Shet 111 m3
Broughall Shrops 49 K7
Brough Lodge Shet 111 m2
Brough Sowerby Cumb 64 E5
Broughton Border 78 H2
Broughton Cambs 33 J2
Broughton Flints 48 G3
Broughton Hants 9 K2
Broughton Lancs 57 K2
Broughton M Keyn 32 C8
Broughton N Linc 52 D2
Broughton N York 58 C4
Broughton N York 66 H11
Broughton Nhants 32 B2
Broughton Oxon 31 K6
Broughton Salfd 57 P8
Broughton V Glam 16 C3
Broughton Astley Leics 41 M8
Broughton Gifford Wilts 18 C7
Broughton Green Worcs 30 C2
Broughton Hackett Worcs 30 B3
Broughton-in-Furness Cumb 62 E5
Broughton Mains D & G 69 L9
Broughton Mills Cumb 62 E4
Broughton Moor Cumb 70 H8
Broughton Poggs Oxon 30 G12
Broughty Ferry C Dund 93 N9
Brown Candover Hants 19 P11
Brown Edge Staffs 50 B9
Brownhill Abers 102 H7
Brownhills Fife 93 P11
Brownhills Wsall 40 D6
Browninghill Green Hants 19 P8
Brown Lees Staffs 49 Q4
Brownsea Island Dorset 8 F9
Brown's Green Birm 40 D8
Browns Hill Gloucs 29 M8
Brownston Devon 5 N9
Broxa N York 67 K8
Broxbourne Herts 21 M3
Broxburn E Loth 87 N6
Broxburn W Loth 86 C7
Broxted Essex 33 P10
Bruan Highld 110 G7
Bruar P & K 92 C3
Brucefield Highld 107 Q5
Bruchag Ag & B 84 B10
Bruichladdich Ag & B 82 C10
Bruisyard Suffk 35 M4
Bruisyard Street Suffk 35 M4
Brumby N Linc 52 C2
Brund Staffs 50 E8
Brundall Norfk 45 M8
Brundish Suffk 35 L3
Brundish Street Suffk 35 L3
Brunery Highld 89 P2
Brunswick Village N u Ty 73 M6
Brunthwaite C Brad 58 D5
Bruntingthorpe Leics 41 N9
Brunton Fife 93 K10
Brunton Wilts 19 J9
Brushford Devon 15 L9
Brushford Somset 16 C10
Bruton Somset 17 P8
Bryan's Green Worcs 30 B1
Bryanston Dorset 8 C6
Brydekirk D & G 71 K2
Bryher IoS 2 b2
Brympton Somset 17 M11
Bryn Carmth 26 D8
Bryn Neath 26 H9
Brynamman Carmth 26 F6
Brynberian Pembks 25 J2
Bryncir Gwynd 46 H3
Bryn-côch Neath 26 G8
Bryncroes Gwynd 46 D5
Bryncrug Gwynd 47 K9
Bryneglwys Denbgs 48 D6
Brynford Flints 48 D1
Bryn Gates Wigan 57 L8
Bryngwran IoA 54 D6
Bryngwyn Mons 28 D7
Bryngwyn Powys 38 E11
Bryn-Henllan Pembks 24 H2
Brynhoffnant Cerdgn 36 E9
Brynmawr Blae G 27 P6
Bryn-mawr Gwynd 46 D5
Brynmenyn Brdgnd 27 J10
Brynmill Swans 26 E9
Brynna Rhondd 27 L11
Brynrefail Gwynd 54 H8
Brynsadler Rhondd 27 L11
Bryn Saith Marchog Denbgs 48 C5
Brynsiencyn IoA 54 F7
Brynteg IoA 54 G5
Bryn-y-Maen Conwy 55 M6
Bualintur Highld 96 E5
Bubbenhall Warwks 41 J11
Bubwith E R Yk 60 C7
Buccleuch Border 79 M6
Buchanan Smithy Stirlg 84 H5
Buchanhaven Abers 103 M6
Buchanty P & K 92 D9
Buchany Stirlg 85 M3
Buchlyvie Stirlg 85 J4
Buckabank Cumb 71 M6
Buckden Cambs 32 H4
Buckden N York 64 G11
Buckenham Norfk 45 M8
Buckerell Devon 6 F3
Buckfast Devon 5 P6
Buckfastleigh Devon 5 P7
Buckhaven Fife 86 G3
Buckholt Mons 28 F5
Buckhorn Weston Dorset 17 R10
Buckhurst Hill Essex 21 N5
Buckie Moray 101 M3
Buckingham Bucks 31 P7
Buckland Bucks 20 E2
Buckland Devon 5 N10
Buckland Gloucs 30 E7
Buckland Herts 33 K9

Buckland Kent ........... 13 P2
Buckland Oxon ........... 19 K2
Buckland Surrey ........... 21 K12
Buckland Brewer Devon.... 14 G7
Buckland Common Bucks.. 20 E3
Buckland Dinham Somset.. 17 R6
Buckland Filleigh Devon... 14 H9
Buckland in the Moor
　Devon.............................. 5 P5
Buckland Monachorum
　Devon.............................. 5 K6
Buckland Newton Dorset.. 7 P2
Buckland Ripers Dorset.... 7 P6
Buckland St Mary Somset.. 16 H12
Buckland-Tout-Saints
　Devon.............................. 5 P10
Bucklebury W Berk........ 19 P6
Bucklers Hard Hants........ 9 L11
Bucklesham Suffk.......... 35 L8
Buckley Flints.............. 48 F3
Bucklow Hill Ches E....... 57 N11
Buckminster Leics......... 42 C5
Bucknall C Stke............ 50 B10
Bucknall Lincs.............. 52 G9
Bucknell Oxon.............. 31 M8
Bucknell Shrops............ 38 G7
Buckpool Moray............ 101 M3
Bucksburn C Aber.......... 103 J12
Buck's Cross Devon........ 14 F7
Bucks Green W Susx....... 10 H4
Buckshaw Village Lancs... 57 K5
Bucks Horn Oak Hants..... 10 D2
Buck's Mills Devon......... 14 F7
Buckton E R Yk............. 67 P11
Buckton Nthumb........... 81 M6
Buckworth Cambs.......... 32 G2
Budby Notts................ 51 N6
Bude Cnwll................. 14 D10
Budge's Shop Cnwll....... 4 H8
Budleigh Salterton Devon.. 6 E6
Budock Water Cnwll....... 2 H9
Buerton Ches E............. 49 M6
Bugbrooke Nhants......... 31 P3
Bugle Cnwll................ 3 M4
Bugley Dorset.............. 8 B3
Bugthorpe E R Yk.......... 60 D3
Buildwas Shrops........... 39 L2
Builth Wells Powys........ 38 B11
Bulbridge Wilts............ 8 G2
Bulford Wilts.............. 18 H11
Bulkeley Ches E............ 49 K5
Bulkington Warwks........ 41 K9
Bulkington Wilts........... 18 D8
Bulkworthy Devon......... 14 G8
Bullamore N York.......... 65 N6
Bullbrook Br For........... 20 E9
Bullington Hants........... 19 M11
Bullington Lincs........... 52 F7
Bulmer Essex.............. 34 D8
Bulmer N York............. 60 C1
Bulmer Tye Essex.......... 34 D8
Bulphan Thurr............. 22 D6
Bulverhythe E Susx....... 12 F8
Bulwark Abers............. 103 J6
Bulwell C Nott............. 51 M11
Bulwick Nhants............ 42 D10
Bumble's Green Essex..... 21 N3
Bunacaimb Highld......... 97 J11
Bunarkaig Highld.......... 98 B10
Bunbury Ches E............ 49 K4
Bunchrew Highld.......... 107 K12
Bundalloch Highld......... 97 M4
Bunessan Ag & B........... 89 J11
Bungay Suffk.............. 45 M11
Bunnahabhain Ag & B..... 82 C8
Bunny Notts............... 41 N2
Buntait Highld............. 98 E3
Buntingford Herts.......... 33 K10
Bunwell Norfk.............. 45 J10
Burbage Leics.............. 41 K8
Burbage Wilts............. 19 J8
Burchett's Green W & M... 20 D7
Burcombe Wilts............ 8 F2
Burcott Bucks.............. 32 C11
Burcott Bucks.............. 19 Q7
Burdale N York............. ... ...
Bures Essex................ 34 E9
Burford Oxon.............. 30 G10
Burford Shrops............ 39 L8
Burg Ag & B................ 89 J7
Burgates Hants............ 10 C4
Burgess Hill W Susx....... 11 L6
Burgh Suffk................ 35 L5
Burgh by Sands Cumb..... 71 M4
Burgh Castle Norfk........ 45 P8
Burghclere Hants.......... 19 M8
Burghead Moray........... 100 H2
Burghfield W Berk......... 19 Q7
Burghfield Common
　W Berk.......................... 19 Q7
Burgh Heath Surrey....... 21 K10
Burghill Herefs............ 39 J12
Burgh Island Devon....... 5 M10
Burgh le Marsh Lincs...... 53 N9
Burgh next Aylsham
　Norfk............................ 45 K5
Burgh on Bain Lincs....... 52 H6
Burgh St Margaret Norfk.. 45 P7
Burgh St Peter Norfk...... 45 P10
Burghwallis Donc.......... 59 M10
Burham Kent............... 22 E10
Buriton Hants.............. 10 C6
Burland Ches E............. 49 L5
Burlawn Cnwll............. 3 M2
Burleigh Gloucs............ 29 M8
Burlescombe Devon....... 16 E11
Burleston Dorset........... 8 B8
Burley Hants............... 8 H6
Burley Rutlnd.............. 42 C7
Burleydam Ches E......... 49 L7
Burley Gate Herefs........ 39 L11
Burley in Wharfedale
　C Brad.......................... 58 F5
Burley Street Hants....... 8 H6
Burley Wood Head C Brad.. 58 F5
Burlton Shrops............. 49 J9
Burmarsh Kent............. 13 L4
Burmington Warwks....... 30 H6
Burn N York............... 59 N8
Burnage Manch............ 57 Q9
Burnaston Derbys......... 40 H2
Burnbrae N Lans........... 85 P10
Burnby E R Yk............. 60 E5
Burneside Cumb........... 63 J3
Burneston N York......... 65 N9
Burnett BaNES............. 17 P3
Burnfoot Border........... 79 N6
Burnfoot Border........... 80 C10
Burnfoot D & G............ 78 F9
Burnfoot D & G............ 79 M10
Burnfoot D & G............ 79 N9

Burnfoot P & K............. 86 B2
Burnham Bucks............ 20 E7
Burnham Deepdale Norfk.. 44 D2
Burnham Market Norfk.... 44 D2
Burnham Norton Norfk.... 44 D2
Burnham-on-Crouch
　Essex............................ 23 J4
Burnham-on-Sea Somset.. 17 J6
Burnham Overy Norfk..... 44 D2
Burnham Overy Staithe
　Norfk............................ 44 D2
Burnham Thorpe Norfk.... 44 E2
Burnhaven Abers.......... 103 M6
Burnhead D & G............ 78 E9
Burnhervie Abers.......... 102 F10
Burnhill Green Staffs...... 39 P3
Burnhope Dur.............. 73 L10
Burnhouse N Ayrs......... 76 G2
Burniston N York.......... 67 L8
Burnley Lancs.............. 57 Q3
Burnley Crematorium
　Lancs............................ 57 P3
Burnmouth Border........ 81 K3
Burn of Cambus Stirlg.... 85 M3
Burnopfield Dur........... 73 L9
Burnsall N York........... 58 D2
Burnside Angus............ 93 M4
Burnside Angus............ 93 N5
Burnside Fife.............. 86 D1
Burnside Moray............ 101 J2
Burnside W Loth.......... 86 C7
Burnside of Duntrune
　Angus............................ 93 M8
Burntisland Fife............ 86 F5
Burntwood Staffs......... 40 D5
Burntwood Green Staffs.. 40 D5
Burnt Yates N York........ 58 G2
Burnworthy Somset....... 16 G11
Burpham Surrey........... 20 G11
Burpham W Susx.......... 10 G8
Burradon Nthumb......... 81 K11
Burrafirth Shet............ 111 m2
Burravoe Shet............. 111 k3
Burrells Cumb............. 64 C4
Burrelton P & K............ 92 H8
Burridge Devon........... 7 J2
Burridge Hants............ 9 N5
Burrill N York.............. 65 M9
Burringham N Linc........ 52 B2
Burrington Devon......... 15 L8
Burrington Herefs......... 38 H7
Burrington N Som......... 17 L4
Burrough Green Cambs... 33 Q6
Burrough on the Hill Leics.. 41 Q5
Burrow Lancs.............. 63 L7
Burrow Somset............ 16 C7
Burrow Bridge Somset.... 17 J9
Burrowhill Surrey......... 20 F10
Burry Green Swans....... 26 B9
Burry Port Carmth......... 25 Q8
Burscough Lancs.......... 56 H6
Burscough Bridge Lancs... 57 J6
Bursea E R Yk.............. 60 D7
Burshill E R Yk............ 61 J5
Bursledon Hants.......... 9 N5
Burslem C Stke............ 50 B10
Burstall Suffk.............. 34 H7
Burstock Dorset........... 7 K3
Burston Norfk............. 45 J12
Burstow Surrey............ 11 L2
Burstwick E R Yk.......... 61 L8
Burtersett N York......... 64 F9
Burtholme Cumb........... 71 Q3
Burthorpe Green Suffk.... 34 C4
Burtoft Lincs.............. 43 J3
Burton Ches W............. 48 G1
Burton Ches W............. 49 K3
Burton Dorset............. 8 H8
Burton Lincs............... 52 D8
Burton Pembks............ 24 H7
Burton Somset............ 16 G7
Burton Wilts............... 18 B5
Burton Agnes E R Yk...... 61 J2
Burton Bradstock Dorset.. 7 L5
Burton Coggles Lincs..... 42 E5
Burton End Essex.......... 33 N11
Burton Fleming E R Yk.... 67 M12
Burton Hastings Warwks.. 41 K9
Burton-in-Kendal Cumb... 63 K7
Burton-in-Kendal
　Services Cumb................. 63 K7
Burton in Lonsdale N York.. 63 M7
Burton Joyce Notts....... 51 N11
Burton Latimer Nhants... 32 C2
Burton Lazars Leics....... 41 Q4
Burton Leonard N York... 59 J2
Burton on the Wolds Leics.. 41 N4
Burton Overy Leics........ 41 P7
Burton Pedwardine Lincs.. 42 G2
Burton Pidsea E R Yk...... 61 L7
Burton Salmon N York.... 59 L8
Burton's Green Essex..... 34 D10
Burton upon Stather
　N Linc........................... 60 E10
Burton upon Trent Staffs.. 40 G3
Burton Waters Lincs...... 52 D8
Burtonwood Warrtn...... 57 K9
Burtonwood Services
　Warrtn........................... 57 L9
Burwardsley Ches W...... 49 K4
Burwarton Shrops........ 39 L5
Burwash E Susx........... 12 D5
Burwash Common E Susx.. 12 D5
Burwash Weald E Susx.... 12 D5
Burwell Cambs............ 33 P4
Burwell Lincs.............. 53 K7
Burwen IoA................ 54 F3
Burwick Ork............... 111 h3
Bury Bury................. 57 P6
Bury Cambs............... 43 J12
Bury Somset............... 16 C10
Bury W Susx.............. 10 G7
Bury Green Herts.......... 33 M11
Bury St Edmunds Suffk... 34 E4
Burythorpe N York....... 60 D2
Busby E Rens.............. 85 J10
Buscot Oxon............... 19 J2
Bush Abers................ 95 M8
Bush Bank Herefs......... 39 J10
Bushbury Wolves......... 40 B7
Bushbury Crematorium
　Wolves.......................... 40 B6
Bushey Herts.............. 21 J4
Bushey Heath Herts....... 21 J5
Bush Hill Park Gt Lon..... 21 M4
Bushley Worcs............. 29 M2
Bushmoor Shrops......... 38 H5
Bushton Wilts............. 18 F5
Bussage Gloucs............ 29 M7

Bussex Somset............ 17 J8
Butcombe N Som.......... 17 M4
Bute Ag & B................ 83 Q8
Butleigh Somset........... 17 M9
Butleigh Wootton Somset.. 17 M8
Butlers Marston Warwks.. 30 H4
Butley Suffk............... 35 N6
Buttercrambe N York..... 60 C3
Butterdean Border........ 87 P8
Butterknowle Dur......... 65 K3
Butterleigh Devon......... 6 D2
Buttermere Cumb......... 71 J11
Buttershaw C Brad........ 58 F8
Butterstone P & K......... 92 F6
Butterton Staffs........... 49 P7
Butterton Staffs........... 50 E9
Butterwick Lincs.......... 43 L2
Butterwick N York........ 66 G11
Butterwick N York........ 67 L12
Buttington Powys......... 38 F1
Buttonoak Shrops......... 39 N6
Buxhall Suffk.............. 34 G5
Buxted E Susx............. 11 P5
Buxton Derbys............ 50 D6
Buxton Norfk.............. 45 K5
Buxton Heath Norfk...... 45 K6
Bwlch Powys.............. 27 N4
Bwlchgwyn Wrexhm...... 48 F5
Bwlchllan Cerdgn......... 37 J8
Bwlchtocyn Gwynd....... 46 E6
Bwlch-y-cibau Powys..... 48 D11
Bwlch-y-ffridd Powys..... 38 C3
Bwlch-y-groes Pembks.... 25 M2
Bwlch-y-sarnau Powys.... 38 B7
Byers Green Dur........... 65 L2
Byfield Nhants............ 31 M4
Byfleet Surrey............. 20 G10
Byford Herefs............. 38 H12
Byker N u Ty.............. 73 M7
Bylchau Conwy........... 55 P8
Byley Ches W.............. 49 N2
Byrness Nthumb.......... 72 D1
Bystock Devon............ 6 D6
Bythorn Cambs........... 32 F2
Byton Herefs.............. 38 G8
Bywell Nthumb........... 73 J8
Byworth W Susx.......... 10 F6

## C

Cabourne Lincs............ 52 G3
Cabrach Ag & B............ 82 G9
Cabrach Moray............ 101 M9
Cabus Lancs............... 63 J11
Cadbury Devon............ 6 C2
Cadbury World Birm....... 40 D10
Cadder E Duns............ 85 K8
Caddington C Beds........ 32 F11
Caddonfoot Border....... 79 P2
Cadeby Donc.............. 51 L1
Cadeby Leics.............. 41 K7
Cadeleigh Devon.......... 6 C2
Cade Street E Susx........ 12 C6
Cadgwith Cnwll........... 2 G11
Cadham Fife............... 86 F2
Cadishead Salfd........... 57 N9
Cadle Swans............... 26 E9
Cadley Lancs.............. 57 K3
Cadley Wilts.............. 18 H7
Cadley Wilts.............. 19 J9
Cadmore End Bucks...... 20 C5
Cadnam Hants............ 9 K5
Cadney N Linc............. 52 E3
Cadoxton V Glam......... 16 F3
Cadoxton Juxta-Neath
　Neath............................ 26 G8
Caeathro Gwynd.......... 54 G8
Caenby Lincs.............. 52 E5
Caeo Carmth.............. 37 L11
Caerau Brdgnd............ 27 J9
Caerau Cardif............. 16 F2
Caer Farchell Pembks..... 24 E4
Caergeiliog IoA............ 54 D6
Caergwrle Flints........... 48 F4
Caerlanrig Border......... 79 N7
Caerleon Newpt........... 28 D10
Caernarfon Gwynd....... 54 F8
Caernarfon Castle Gwynd.. 54 F8
Caerphilly Caerph......... 27 N10
Caersws Powys........... 38 B4
Caerwedros Cerdgn...... 36 F9
Caerwent Mons........... 28 F10
Caerwys Flints............ 48 D2
Cairinis W Isls............. 111 b5
Cairnbaan Ag & B......... 83 M5
Cairnbulg Abers........... 103 L3
Cairncross Border......... 81 J2
Cairncurran Inver......... 84 F8
Cairndow Ag & B.......... 84 C2
Cairneyhill Fife............ 86 C5
Cairngarroch D & G....... 68 E8
Cairngorms National Park.. 99 N8
Cairnie Abers............. 101 N6
Cairnorrie Abers.......... 102 H7
Cairnryan D & G........... 68 E5
Cairnty Moray............. 101 L5
Caister-on-Sea Norfk..... 45 Q7
Caistor Lincs.............. 52 G3
Caistor St Edmund Norfk.. 45 K8
Calanais W Isls............ 111 c2
Calbourne IoW............ 9 M9
Calcot Flints.............. 48 D1
Calcot Gloucs............. 30 E11
Calcot Row W Berk....... 19 R6
Calcots Moray............. 101 K3
Caldbeck Cumb........... 71 M7
Caldecote Cambs......... 33 K5
Caldecote Cambs......... 42 G11
Caldecote Highfields
　Cambs........................... 33 K5
Caldecott Nhants......... 32 E3
Caldecott Oxon............ 19 N2
Caldecott Rutlnd.......... 42 C10
Calderbank N Lans........ 85 M9
Calder Bridge Cumb...... 62 B2
Caldercruix N Lans........ 85 N9
Calder Grove Wakefd..... 58 H10
Caldermill S Lans......... 77 L3
Calder Vale Lancs......... 63 K11
Calderwood S Lans....... 85 L11
Caldey Island Pembks.... 25 L9
Caldicot Mons............. 28 F10
Caldmore Wsall........... 40 D7
Caldwell N York........... 65 L5
Calf of Man IoM........... 56 a7

Calfsound Ork............. 111 h1
Calgary Ag & B............ 89 J6
Califer Moray.............. 100 G4
California Falk............. 85 Q7
California Norfk........... 45 Q7
Calke Derbys.............. 41 J3
Calke Abbey Derbys...... 41 J3
Callakille Highld........... 105 K10
Callander Stirlg............ 85 K2
Callanish W Isls........... 111 c2
Callestick Cnwll........... 2 H6
Calligarry Highld.......... 96 H8
Callington Cnwll.......... 4 H6
Callow Herefs............. 28 F2
Callow End Worcs......... 39 Q11
Callow Hill Wilts.......... 18 F4
Calmore Hants............ 9 K5
Calmsden Gloucs.......... 30 D11
Calne Wilts............... 18 E6
Calshot Hants............. 9 N7
Calstock Cnwll............ 5 J6
Calstone Wellington Wilts.. 18 F7
Calthorpe Norfk.......... 45 K4
Calthorpe Street Norfk... 45 N5
Calthwaite Cumb.......... 71 P7
Calton Staffs.............. 50 E10
Calveley Ches E........... 49 L4
Calver Derbys............. 50 G6
Calverhall Shrops......... 49 L7
Calverleigh Devon........ 16 C12
Calverton M Keyn......... 32 B8
Calverton Notts........... 51 N10
Calvine P & K.............. 92 B3
Calzeat Border............ 78 H2
Cam Gloucs............... 29 K8
Camasachoire Highld..... 89 Q4
Camasine Highld.......... 89 P4
Camas Luinie Highld...... 97 N4
Camastianavaig Highld... 96 F2
Camault Muir Highld..... 98 G2
Camber E Susx............ 13 J6
Camberley Surrey......... 20 E10
Camberwell Gt Lon....... 21 L7
Cambesforth N York...... 59 N8
Cambo Nthumb........... 72 H4
Camborne Cnwll.......... 2 F7
Camborne and Redruth
　Mining District Cnwll........ 2 F7
Cambourne Cambs........ 33 K5
Cambridge Cambs........ 33 M5
Cambridge Gloucs........ 29 K7
Cambridge Airport Cambs.. 33 M5
Cambridge City
　Crematorium Cambs.......... 33 L4
Cambrose Cnwll........... 2 G6
Cambus Clacks............ 85 P4
Cambusavie Platform
　Highld........................... 107 M3
Cambusbarron Stirlg...... 85 N5
Cambuskenneth Stirlg.... 85 N4
Cambuslang S Lans....... 85 L10
Cambus o' May Abers..... 94 G3
Cambuswallace S Lans... 78 G2
Camden Town Gt Lon..... 21 L6
Cameley BaNES............ 17 N5
Camelford Cnwll.......... 4 D4
Camelon Falk.............. 85 P6
Camerory Highld.......... 100 F8
Camerton BaNES.......... 17 P5
Camerton Cumb........... 70 G8
Camghouran P & K........ 91 N5
Camieston Border......... 80 D8
Cammachmore Abers..... 95 P3
Cammeringham Lincs..... 52 D7
Camore Highld............ 107 N4
Campbeltown Ag & B..... 75 K8
Campbeltown Airport
　Ag & B........................... 75 K7
Cample D & G.............. 78 E9
Campmuir P & K........... 93 J7
Camps W Loth............ 86 C8
Campsall Donc............ 59 M10
Campsea Ash Suffk....... 35 M5
Campton C Beds........... 32 G8
Camptown Border........ 80 F10
Camrose Pembks.......... 24 G5
Camserney P & K.......... 92 C7
Camusnagaul Highld..... 90 E2
Camusnagaul Highld..... 105 Q5
Camusteel Highld......... 97 J2
Camusterrach Highld..... 97 J2
Canada Highld............. 9 K4
Candacraig Abers......... 94 F3
Candlesby Lincs........... 53 M9
Candy Mill Border........ 78 H1
Cane End Oxon............ 20 B7
Canewdon Essex.......... 22 H5
Canford Cliffs Poole...... 8 F9
Canford Crematorium
　Brstl............................. 28 G12
Canford Heath Poole..... 8 F8
Canisbay Highld........... 110 G2
Canley Covtry............. 40 H11
Canley Crematorium
　Covtry........................... 40 H11
Cann Dorset............... 8 C3
Canna Highld.............. 96 B8
Cann Common Dorset.... 8 C4
Cannich Highld............ 98 D3
Cannington Somset....... 16 H8
Canning Town Gt Lon.... 21 N7
Cannock Staffs............ 40 C5
Cannock Chase Staffs.... 40 C4
Cannon Bridge Herefs.... 28 E1
Canonbie D & G........... 71 N1
Canon Frome Herefs...... 39 M12
Canon Pyon Herefs....... 39 J11
Canons Ashby Nhants.... 31 M4
Canonstown Cnwll........ 2 D8
Canterbury Kent.......... 23 M10
Canterbury Cathedral
　Kent............................. 23 M10
Cantley Norfk............. 45 N8
Canton Cardif............. 16 F2
Cantraywood Highld..... 107 N11
Cantsfield Lancs.......... 63 L7
Canvey Island Essex...... 22 F6
Canwick Lincs............. 52 D9
Canworthy Water Cnwll.. 4 F2
Caol Highld............... 90 F2
Caolas Scalpaigh W Isls.. 111 c3
Caoles Ag & B............. 88 C6
Caonich Highld........... 97 Q10
Capel Kent................ 12 D2
Capel Surrey.............. 11 J2
Capel Bangor Cerdgn..... 37 K5
Capel Coch IoA........... 54 F5

Capel Curig Conwy....... 55 K9
Capel Dewi Carmth....... 26 C5
Capel Dewi Cerdgn....... 36 G11
Capel-Dewi Cerdgn....... 37 K4
Capel Garmon Conwy..... 55 M9
Capel Hendre Carmth..... 26 E6
Capel Iwan Carmth....... 25 M2
Capel le Ferne Kent....... 13 N3
Capel Parc IoA............ 54 F4
Capel St Andrew Suffk... 35 N7
Capel St Mary Suffk...... 34 H8
Capel Seion Cerdgn....... 37 K5
Capelulo Conwy........... 55 L6
Capenhurst Ches W....... 48 G2
Cape Wrath Highld........ 108 E1
Capheaton Nthumb....... 73 J5
Caplaw E Rens............ 84 G10
Cappercleuch Border..... 79 K4
Capton Devon............. 5 Q9
Caputh P & K.............. 92 G7
Caradon Mining District
　Cnwll............................ 4 G5
Carbeth Inn Stirlg......... 85 J7
Carbis Bay Cnwll.......... 2 D7
Carbost Highld............ 96 D6
Carbost Highld............ 104 F11
Carbrook Sheff............ 51 J3
Carbrooke Norfk.......... 44 F9
Car Colston Notts......... 51 N11
Carcroft Donc............. 59 M11
Cardenden Fife............ 86 E4
Cardhu Moray............. 101 J6
Cardiff Cardif............. 16 G2
Cardiff & Glamorgan
　Crematorium Cardif.......... 27 N11
Cardiff Gate Services
　Cardif........................... 27 P11
Cardiff West Services
　Cardif........................... 27 M11
Cardigan Cerdgn.......... 36 C10
Cardington Bed........... 32 F7
Cardington Shrops........ 39 J3
Cardinham Cnwll.......... 4 D6
Cardrain D & G............ 68 F11
Cardrona Border.......... 79 L2
Cardross Ag & B........... 84 F7
Cardross Crematorium
　Ag & B........................... 84 F7
Cardryne D & G........... 68 F11
Cardurnock Cumb........ 71 J4
Careby Lincs.............. 42 E6
Careston Angus........... 95 J9
Carew Pembks............ 24 H7
Carew Cheriton Pembks.. 24 H8
Carew Newton Pembks... 24 H7
Carey Herefs.............. 28 G3
Carfin N Lans............. 85 N10
Carfraemill Border........ 80 C4
Cargate Green Norfk..... 45 N7
Cargenbridge D & G...... 70 F1
Cargill P & K.............. 92 H8
Cargo Cumb.............. 71 M4
Cargreen Cnwll........... 5 J7
Carham Nthumb.......... 80 H6
Carhampton Somset...... 16 D7
Carharrack Cnwll......... 2 G7
Carie P & K............... 91 P5
Carinish W Isls............ 111 b5
Carisbrooke IoW......... 9 N9
Cark Cumb................ 62 G6
Carkeel Cnwll............. 5 J7
Carlabhagh W Isls........ 111 c2
Carlbury Darltn........... 65 L4
Carlby Lincs.............. 42 F7
Carleen Cnwll............. 2 F9
Carleton N York.......... 58 C4
Carleton Crematorium
　Bpool............................ 56 G2
Carleton Forehoe Norfk.. 44 H8
Carleton Rode Norfk...... 44 H10
Carleton St Peter Norfk... 45 M9
Carlincraig Abers......... 102 E6
Carlingcott BaNES........ 17 Q5
Carlisle Cumb............. 71 N4
Carlisle Airport Cumb.... 71 P4
Carlisle Crematorium
　Cumb............................ 71 N5
Carlops Border............ 86 D10
Carloway W Isls........... 111 c2
Carlton Barns............. 59 J11
Carlton Bed............... 32 D6
Carlton Cambs............ 33 Q6
Carlton Leeds............. 59 J8
Carlton Leics............. 41 K6
Carlton N York............ 59 N9
Carlton N York............ 65 J9
Carlton N York............ 66 E9
Carlton Notts............. 51 N11
Carlton S on T............ 65 P3
Carlton Suffk............. 35 N4
Carlton Colville Suffk.... 45 Q11
Carlton Curlieu Leics..... 41 P7
Carlton Green Cambs..... 33 Q6
Carlton Husthwaite
　N York........................... 66 C11
Carlton-in-Cleveland
　N York........................... 66 C6
Carlton in Lindrick Notts.. 51 N4
Carlton-le-Moorland Lincs.. 52 C10
Carlton Miniott N York... 65 P10
Carlton-on-Trent Notts.. 52 B10
Carlton Scroop Lincs..... 42 D2
Carluke S Lans............ 77 P2
Carmacoup S Lans....... 77 N6
Carmarthen Carmth...... 25 P5
Carmel Carmth............ 26 D5
Carmel Flints............. 56 D12
Carmel Gwynd............ 54 G9
Carmichael S Lans........ 78 F2
Carmountside
　Crematorium C Stke.......... 50 B10
Carmunnock C Glas....... 85 K10
Carmyle C Glas........... 85 L9
Carmyllie Angus.......... 93 P7
Carnaby E R Yk........... 61 K2
Carnbee Fife.............. 87 K2
Carnbo P & K............. 86 C2
Carn Brea Cnwll.......... 2 G7
Carnbrogie Abers......... 102 H9
Carndu Highld............ 97 M4
Carnduff S Lans........... 77 L3
Carnell E Ayrs............. 76 H5
Carnforth Lancs........... 63 J7
Carn-gorm Highld........ 97 N5
Carnhell Green Cnwll..... 2 F8
Carnie Abers.............. 95 N2

Carnkie - Churt 171


**Carnkie** Cnwll 2 G7
**Carnkie** Cnwll 2 G8
**Carno** Powys 47 Q11
**Carnock** Fife 86 C4
**Carnon Downs** Cnwll 3 J7
**Carnousie** Abers 102 E5
**Carnoustie** Angus 93 P8
**Carnwath** S Lans 86 B11
**Carol Green** Solhll 40 H11
**Carperby** N York 64 H9
**Carradale** Ag & B 75 M5
**Carrbridge** Highld 99 N4
**Carrefour** Jersey 7 b1
**Carreglefn** IoA 54 E4
**Carr Gate** Wakefd 58 H8
**Carrhouse** N Linc 60 D11
**Carrick** Ag & B 83 N5
**Carrick Castle** Ag & B 84 D4
**Carriden** Falk 86 B6
**Carrington** Mdloth 86 G9
**Carrington** Traffd 57 N9
**Carrog** Denbgs 48 C6
**Carron** Falk 85 P6
**Carron** Moray 101 J7
**Carronbridge** D & G 78 E8
**Carron Bridge** Stirlg 85 M6
**Carronshore** Falk 85 P6
**Carr Shield** Nthumb 72 E10
**Carrutherstown** D & G 70 H2
**Carruth House** Inver 84 F9
**Carrville** Dur 73 N11
**Carsaig** Ag & B 89 L11
**Carseriggan** D & G 69 J5
**Carsethorn** D & G 70 G4
**Carshalton** Gt Lon 21 L9
**Carsington** Derbys 50 G9
**Carskey** Ag & B 75 J10
**Carsluith** D & G 69 L8
**Carsphairn** D & G 77 J11
**Carstairs** S Lans 77 Q3
**Carstairs Junction** S Lans 77 Q3
**Carterton** Oxon 30 H11
**Carthew** Cnwll 3 M5
**Carthorpe** N York 65 N10
**Cartland** S Lans 77 P3
**Cartmel** Cumb 62 H6
**Carway** Carmth 26 C7
**Cashe's Green** Gloucs 29 L7
**Cassington** Oxon 31 L11
**Cassop Colliery** Dur 73 N12
**Castel** Guern 6 b2
**Casterton** Cumb 63 L6
**Castle Acre** Norfk 44 D7
**Castle Ashby** Nhants 32 C5
**Castlebay** W Isls 111 a7
**Castle Bolton** N York 65 J8
**Castle Bromwich** Solhll 40 F9
**Castle Bytham** Lincs 42 E6
**Castlebythe** Pembks 24 H3
**Castle Caereinion** Powys 38 D2
**Castle Camps** Cambs 33 P8
**Castle Carrock** Cumb 71 Q5
**Castlecary** Falk 85 N7
**Castle Cary** Somset 17 P9
**Castle Combe** Wilts 18 C5
**Castle Donington** Leics 41 K3
**Castle Douglas** D & G 70 C3
**Castle Eaton** Swindn 18 G2
**Castle Eden** Dur 73 Q12
**Castleford** Wakefd 59 K8
**Castle Frome** Herefs 39 M11
**Castle Gresley** Derbys 40 H4
**Castle Hedingham** Essex 34 D9
**Castlehill** Border 79 K2
**Castlehill** Highld 110 E3
**Castle Hill** Suffk 35 J7
**Castlehill** W Duns 84 G7
Castle Howard N York 66 G12
**Castle Kennedy** D & G 68 F7
**Castle Lachlan** Ag & B 83 Q4
**Castlemartin** Pembks 24 F8
**Castlemilk** C Glas 85 K10
**Castlemorton** Worcs 29 L2
**Castlemorton Common** Worcs 29 K2
**Castle O'er** D & G 79 L9
**Castle Pulverbatch** Shrops 38 H2
**Castle Rising** Norfk 43 Q5
**Castleside** Dur 73 J10
**Castle Stuart** Highld 107 M11
**Castlethorpe** M Keyn 32 B7
**Castleton** Border 79 Q10
**Castleton** Derbys 50 F4
**Castleton** N York 66 F6
**Castleton** Newpt 27 Q11
**Castleton** Rochdl 58 B11
**Castletown** Highld 110 E3
**Castletown** IoM 56 b7
**Castletown** Sundld 73 P8
**Castley** N York 58 H5
**Caston** Norfk 44 F9
**Castor** C Pete 42 G9
**Catacol** N Ayrs 75 N3
**Catcliffe** Rothm 51 K3
**Catcomb** Wilts 18 E5
**Catcott** Somset 17 K8
**Catcott Burtle** Somset 17 K7
**Caterham** Surrey 21 M11
**Catfield** Norfk 45 N6
**Catford** Gt Lon 21 M8
**Catforth** Lancs 57 J2
**Cathcart** C Glas 85 K10
**Cathedine** Powys 27 N4
**Catherington** Hants 10 B7
**Catherston Leweston** Dorset 7 K4
**Catisfield** Hants 9 P6
**Catlodge** Highld 99 J9
**Catmere End** Essex 33 M8
**Catmore** W Berk 19 M5
**Caton** Lancs 63 K8
**Caton Green** Lancs 63 K8
**Catrine** E Ayrs 77 J6
**Catsfield** E Susx 12 E7
**Catsgore** Somset 17 M10
**Catshill** Worcs 40 C11
**Cattadale** Ag & B 75 K9
**Cattal** N York 59 K4
**Cattawade** Suffk 34 H9
**Catterall** Lancs 57 J1
**Catterick** N York 65 M7
**Catterick Bridge** N York 65 M7
**Catterlen** Cumb 71 P8
**Catterline** Abers 95 P6
**Catterton** N York 59 L5
**Catteshall** Surrey 10 F2
**Catthorpe** Leics 41 M10
**Cattistock** Dorset 7 N3
**Catton** N York 65 P11
**Catton** Nthumb 72 E8
**Catwick** E R Yk 61 J5
**Catworth** Cambs 32 F3
**Caudle Green** Gloucs 29 N6
**Caulcott** Oxon 31 L8
**Cauldcots** Angus 93 Q6
**Cauldhame** Stirlg 85 L4
**Cauldmill** Border 80 C10
**Cauldon** Staffs 50 E10
**Cauldwell** Derbys 40 G4
**Caulkerbush** D & G 70 F4
**Caulside** D & G 79 P11
**Caundle Marsh** Dorset 17 P12
**Caunton** Notts 51 Q8
**Causeway End** D & G 69 K7
**Causeway End** Essex 34 B11
**Causewayend** S Lans 78 G2
**Causewayhead** Stirlg 85 N4
**Causeyend** Abers 103 K10
**Causey Park Bridge** Nthumb 73 L2
**Cavendish** Suffk 34 D7
**Cavenham** Suffk 34 C3
**Caversfield** Oxon 31 M8
**Caversham** Readg 20 B8
**Caverswall** Staffs 50 C11
**Caverton Mill** Border 80 G8
**Cawdor** Highld 100 D5
**Cawood** N York 59 M6
**Cawsand** Cnwll 5 J9
**Cawston** Norfk 45 J5
**Cawthorne** Barns 58 H11
**Caxton** Cambs 33 K5
**Caynham** Shrops 39 K7
**Caythorpe** Lincs 42 D1
**Caythorpe** Notts 51 P10
**Cayton** N York 67 M10
**Ceann a Bhaigh** W Isls 111 a4
**Ceannacroc Lodge** Highld 98 C6
**Cearsiadar** W Isls 111 d2
**Cefn** Newpt 28 C10
**Cefn-brith** Conwy 55 N10
**Cefn-bryn-brain** Carmth 26 G6
**Cefn Cribwr** Brdgnd 27 J11
**Cefneithin** Carmth 26 D6
**Cefngorwydd** Powys 37 P10
**Cefn-mawr** Wrexhm 48 F7
**Cefn-y-pant** Carmth 25 L4
**Cellardyke** Fife 87 L2
**Cellarhead** Staffs 50 C10
**Cemaes** IoA 54 E3
**Cemmaes** Powys 47 N9
**Cemmaes Road** Powys 47 N9
**Cenarth** Cerdgn 36 E11
**Ceres** Fife 93 M12
**Cerne Abbas** Dorset 7 P3
**Cerney Wick** Gloucs 18 F2
**Cerrigydrudion** Conwy 55 P11
**Ceunant** Gwynd 54 G8
**Chaceley** Gloucs 29 M3
**Chacewater** Cnwll 2 H6
**Chackmore** Bucks 31 P7
**Chacombe** Nhants 31 L5
**Chadbury** Worcs 30 D5
**Chadderton** Oldham 58 B12
**Chaddesden** C Derb 51 J12
**Chaddesley Corbett** Worcs 40 B11
**Chaddlehanger** Devon 5 K5
**Chaddleworth** W Berk 19 M5
**Chadlington** Oxon 31 J9
**Chadshunt** Warwks 31 J4
**Chadwell** Leics 42 B5
**Chadwell Heath** Gt Lon 21 P6
**Chadwell St Mary** Thurr 22 D7
**Chadwick** Worcs 39 Q8
**Chadwick End** Solhll 40 G11
**Chaffcombe** Somset 7 J2
**Chagford** Devon 5 N3
**Chailey** E Susx 11 N6
**Chainhurst** Kent 12 E1
**Chaldon** Surrey 21 L11
**Chale** IoW 9 N11
**Chale Green** IoW 9 N10
**Chalfont Common** Bucks 20 G5
**Chalfont St Giles** Bucks 20 F5
**Chalfont St Peter** Bucks 20 G5
**Chalford** Gloucs 29 M8
**Chalford** Wilts 18 C10
**Chalgrove** Oxon 19 Q2
**Chalk** Kent 22 D8
**Chalkwell** Kent 22 H10
**Challacombe** Devon 15 M4
**Challoch** D & G 69 K5
**Challock** Kent 23 J12
**Chalton** C Beds 32 E10
**Chalton** Hants 10 B6
**Chalvey** Slough 20 F7
**Chalvington** E Susx 11 P8
**Chandler's Cross** Herts 20 H4
**Chandler's Ford** Hants 9 M4
**Channel Tunnel Terminal** Kent 13 M3
**Chanterlands Crematorium** C KuH 61 J7
**Chantry** Somset 17 Q6
**Chantry** Suffk 35 J7
**Chapel** Fife 86 F4
**Chapel Allerton** Leeds 58 H6
**Chapel Allerton** Somset 17 K6
**Chapel Amble** Cnwll 3 M1
**Chapel Brampton** Nhants 31 Q2
**Chapel Chorlton** Staffs 49 P7
**Chapelend Way** Essex 34 B8
**Chapel-en-le-Frith** Derbys 50 D5
**Chapel Green** Warwks 31 L3
**Chapel Haddlesey** N York 59 M8
**Chapelhall** N Lans 85 N9
**Chapel Hill** Abers 103 L8
**Chapel Hill** Lincs 52 H11
**Chapel Hill** Mons 28 G8
**Chapel Hill** N York 59 J5
**Chapelhope** Border 79 K5
**Chapelknowe** D & G 71 M2
**Chapel Lawn** Shrops 38 G6
**Chapel-le-Dale** N York 64 D11
**Chapel Leigh** Somset 16 F9
**Chapel of Garioch** Abers 102 F9
**Chapel Rossan** D & G 68 F9
**Chapel Row** W Berk 19 P6
**Chapel St Leonards** Lincs 53 N8
**Chapel Stile** Cumb 62 G2
**Chapelton** Angus 93 Q6
**Chapelton** Devon 15 K6
**Chapelton** S Lans 77 L2
**Chapeltown** Bl w D 57 N6
**Chapeltown** Moray 101 K10
**Chapeltown** Sheff 51 J2
**Chapmanslade** Wilts 18 C10
**Chapmans Well** Devon 4 H2
**Chapmore End** Herts 33 K12
**Chappel** Essex 34 E10
**Chard** Somset 7 J2
**Chard Junction** Somset 7 J2
**Chardleigh Green** Somset 7 J1
**Chardstock** Devon 7 J2
**Charfield** S Glos 29 J9
**Charing** Kent 23 J12
**Charing Crematorium** Kent 13 J1
**Charingworth** Gloucs 30 G6
**Charlbury** Oxon 31 J9
**Charlcombe** BaNES 17 Q3
**Charlcutt** Wilts 18 E5
**Charlecote** Warwks 30 H3
**Charlemont** Sandw 40 D8
**Charles** Devon 15 M5
**Charleston** Angus 93 L6
**Charlestown** C Aber 95 Q2
**Charlestown** C Brad 58 F6
**Charlestown** Calder 58 C8
**Charlestown** Cnwll 3 M5
Charlestown Cnwll 3 M5
**Charlestown** Fife 86 C5
**Charlestown** Highld 105 M7
**Charlestown** Highld 107 K11
**Charlestown** Salfd 57 P8
**Charles Tye** Suffk 34 G6
**Charlesworth** Derbys 50 D3
**Charlinch** Somset 16 H8
**Charlottetown** Fife 93 K12
**Charlton** Gt Lon 21 N7
**Charlton** Nhants 31 M7
**Charlton** Nthumb 72 E4
**Charlton** Oxon 19 L3
**Charlton** Somset 16 H10
**Charlton** Somset 17 P6
**Charlton** W Susx 10 E7
**Charlton** Wilts 8 D3
**Charlton** Wilts 18 E3
**Charlton** Worcs 30 D5
**Charlton** Wrekin 49 L12
**Charlton Abbots** Gloucs 30 D8
**Charlton Adam** Somset 17 M9
**Charlton All Saints** Wilts 8 H3
**Charlton Down** Dorset 7 P4
**Charlton Horethorne** Somset 17 P10
**Charlton Kings** Gloucs 29 N5
**Charlton Mackrell** Somset 17 M9
**Charlton Marshall** Dorset 8 D6
**Charlton Musgrove** Somset 17 Q9
**Charlton-on-Otmoor** Oxon 31 M10
**Charlton on the Hill** Dorset 8 D6
**Charlton St Peter** Wilts 18 G9
**Charlwood** Hants 10 A4
**Charlwood** Surrey 11 K2
**Charminster** Dorset 7 P4
**Charmouth** Dorset 7 J4
**Charndon** Bucks 31 P8
**Charney Bassett** Oxon 19 L2
**Charnock Richard** Lancs 57 K6
**Charnock Richard Crematorium** Lancs 57 K5
Charnock Richard Services Lancs 57 K6
**Charsfield** Suffk 35 L5
**Charter Alley** Hants 19 P8
**Charterhall** Border 80 G5
**Charterhouse** Somset 17 M5
**Chartershall** Stirlg 85 N5
**Chartham** Kent 23 L11
**Chartham Hatch** Kent 23 L11
**Chartridge** Bucks 20 E3
**Chart Sutton** Kent 22 F12
**Charvil** Wokham 20 C8
**Charwelton** Nhants 31 M3
**Chase Terrace** Staffs 40 D5
**Chasetown** Staffs 40 D6
**Chastleton** Oxon 30 G8
**Chasty** Devon 14 F10
**Chatburn** Lancs 63 P12
**Chatcull** Staffs 49 P8
**Chatham** Medway 22 F9
**Chatham Green** Essex 22 E1
**Chathill** Nthumb 81 P8
Chatsworth House Derbys 50 H6
**Chattenden** Medway 22 F8
**Chatteris** Cambs 43 L11
**Chatterton** Lancs 57 P5
**Chattisham** Suffk 34 H8
**Chatto** Border 80 G10
**Chatton** Nthumb 81 M8
**Chawleigh** Devon 15 M9
**Chawton** Hants 10 B3
**Cheadle** Staffs 50 D11
**Cheadle** Stockp 57 Q10
**Cheadle Hulme** Stockp 57 Q10
**Cheam** Gt Lon 21 K10
**Chearsley** Bucks 31 Q11
**Chebsey** Staffs 49 Q9
**Checkendon** Oxon 19 Q4
**Checkley** Ches E 49 N6
**Checkley** Staffs 50 D12
**Chedburgh** Suffk 34 D5
**Cheddar** Somset 17 L5
**Cheddington** Bucks 32 D12
**Cheddleton** Staffs 50 C9
**Cheddon Fitzpaine** Somset 16 H9
**Chedgrave** Norfk 45 M9
**Chedington** Dorset 7 L2
**Chediston** Suffk 35 M2
**Chedworth** Gloucs 30 D10
**Chedzoy** Somset 17 J8
**Cheetham Hill** Manch 57 Q8
**Cheldon** Devon 15 M9
**Chelford** Ches E 49 P1
**Chellaston** C Derb 41 J2
**Chellington** Bed 32 D5
**Chelmarsh** Shrops 39 N5
**Chelmondiston** Suffk 35 K8
**Chelmorton** Derbys 50 E6
**Chelmsford** Essex 22 E3
**Chelmsford Crematorium** Essex 22 E3
**Chelmsley Wood** Solhll 40 F9
**Chelsea** Gt Lon 21 L7
**Chelsfield** Gt Lon 21 P9
**Chelsworth** Suffk 34 G7
**Cheltenham** Gloucs 29 N4
**Cheltenham Crematorium** Gloucs 29 N4
**Chelveston** Nhants 32 E3
**Chelvey** N Som 17 L3
**Chelwood** BaNES 17 P4
**Chelwood Gate** E Susx 11 N4
**Cheney Longville** Shrops 38 H5
**Chenies** Bucks 20 G4
**Chepstow** Mons 28 G9
**Cherhill** Wilts 18 F6
**Cherington** Gloucs 29 M8
**Cherington** Warwks 30 H6
**Cheriton** Hants 9 P2
**Cheriton** Kent 13 M3
**Cheriton** Swans 26 B9
**Cheriton Bishop** Devon 5 P2
**Cheriton Fitzpaine** Devon 15 P10
**Cheriton or Stackpole Elidor** Pembks 24 H8
**Cherrington** Wrekin 49 M10
**Cherry Burton** E R Yk 60 G6
**Cherry Hinton** Cambs 33 M5
**Cherry Orchard** Worcs 39 Q10
**Cherry Willingham** Lincs 52 E8
**Chertsey** Surrey 20 G9
Cherwell Valley Services Oxon 31 M8
**Cheselbourne** Dorset 8 B7
**Chesham** Bucks 20 F3
**Chesham** Bury 57 P6
**Chesham Bois** Bucks 20 F4
Cheshire Farm Ice Cream Ches W 49 J4
**Cheshunt** Herts 21 M3
**Chesil Beach** Dorset 7 N6
**Cheslyn Hay** Staffs 40 C6
**Chessetts Wood** Warwks 40 F11
**Chessington** Gt Lon 21 J10
Chessington World of Adventures Gt Lon 21 J10
**Chester** Ches W 48 H3
**Chesterblade** Somset 17 P7
**Chester Crematorium** Ches W 48 H2
**Chesterfield** Derbys 51 J6
**Chesterfield Crematorium** Derbys 51 K6
**Chesterhill** Mdloth 86 H8
**Chester-le-Street** Dur 73 M9
**Chester Moor** Dur 73 M10
**Chesters** Border 80 E11
**Chesters** Border 80 E9
Chester Services Ches W 49 J1
**Chesterton** Cambs 33 M5
**Chesterton** Cambs 42 G10
**Chesterton** Gloucs 18 E1
**Chesterton** Oxon 31 M9
**Chesterton** Shrops 39 P3
**Chesterton** Staffs 49 P5
**Chesterton Green** Warwks 31 J3
**Chesterwood** Nthumb 72 E7
Chester Zoo Ches W 48 H2
**Chestfield** Kent 23 L9
**Cheston** Devon 5 N8
**Cheswardine** Shrops 49 N9
**Cheswick** Nthumb 81 L5
**Chetnole** Dorset 7 N2
**Chettisham** Cambs 43 N12
**Chettle** Dorset 8 D5
**Chetton** Shrops 39 M4
**Chetwynd** Wrekin 49 N10
**Chetwynd Aston** Wrekin 49 N11
**Cheveley** Cambs 34 B5
**Chevening** Kent 21 P11
**Chevington** Suffk 34 D5
**Cheviot Hills** 80 G11
**Chevithorne** Devon 16 D11
**Chew Magna** BaNES 17 N4
**Chew Stoke** BaNES 17 M4
**Chewton Keynsham** BaNES 17 P3
**Chewton Mendip** Somset 17 N5
**Chicheley** M Keyn 32 C7
**Chichester** W Susx 10 D8
**Chichester Crematorium** W Susx 10 E8
**Chickerell** Dorset 7 P6
**Chicklade** Wilts 8 D1
**Chidden** Hants 9 Q4
**Chiddingfold** Surrey 10 F3
**Chiddingly** E Susx 12 B7
**Chiddingstone** Kent 11 P2
**Chiddingstone Causeway** Kent 11 Q1
**Chideock** Dorset 7 K4
**Chidham** W Susx 10 C8
**Chidswell** Kirk 58 H9
**Chieveley** W Berk 19 M6
Chieveley Services W Berk 19 N6
**Chignall St James** Essex 22 D2
**Chignall Smealy** Essex 22 D2
**Chigwell** Essex 21 N5
**Chigwell Row** Essex 21 P5
**Chilbolton** Hants 19 L11
**Chilcomb** Hants 9 N2
**Chilcombe** Dorset 7 M5
**Chilcompton** Somset 17 P6
**Chilcote** Leics 40 H5
**Childer Thornton** Ches W 56 G12
**Child Okeford** Dorset 8 C5
**Childrey** Oxon 19 L3
**Child's Ercall** Shrops 49 M9
**Childswickham** Worcs 30 E6
**Childwall** Lpool 56 H10
**Chilfrome** Dorset 7 N3
**Chilgrove** W Susx 10 D7
**Chilham** Kent 23 K11
**Chillaton** Devon 5 J4
**Chillenden** Kent 23 N11
**Chillerton** IoW 9 N10
**Chillesford** Suffk 35 N6
**Chillington** Devon 5 Q10
**Chillington** Somset 7 K1
**Chilmark** Wilts 8 E2
**Chilmington Green** Kent 13 J3
**Chilson** Oxon 30 H9
**Chilsworthy** Cnwll 5 J6
**Chilsworthy** Devon 14 F10
**Chiltern Hills** 20 C4
**Chilterns Crematorium** Bucks 20 F4
**Chilthorne Domer** Somset 17 M11
**Chilton** Bucks 31 P10
**Chilton** Dur 65 M2
**Chilton** Oxon 19 N4
**Chilton Candover** Hants 19 P11
**Chilton Cantelo** Somset 17 N10
**Chilton Foliat** Wilts 19 K6
**Chilton Polden** Somset 17 K7
**Chilton Street** Suffk 34 C7
**Chilton Trinity** Somset 16 H8
**Chilwell** Notts 41 L1
**Chilworth** Hants 9 L4
**Chilworth** Surrey 10 G1
**Chimney** Oxon 19 L1
**Chineham** Hants 19 Q9
**Chingford** Gt Lon 21 M5
**Chinley** Derbys 50 D4
**Chinnor** Oxon 20 C3
**Chipnall** Shrops 49 N8
**Chippenham** Cambs 33 Q3
**Chippenham** Wilts 18 D6
**Chipperfield** Herts 20 G3
**Chipping** Herts 33 K9
**Chipping** Lancs 63 L12
**Chipping Campden** Gloucs 30 F6
**Chipping Norton** Oxon 30 H8
**Chipping Ongar** Essex 22 B3
**Chipping Sodbury** S Glos 29 K11
**Chipping Warden** Nhants 31 L5
**Chipstable** Somset 16 E10
**Chipstead** Kent 21 P11
**Chipstead** Surrey 21 L11
**Chirbury** Shrops 38 F3
**Chirk** Wrexhm 48 F7
**Chirnside** Border 81 J3
**Chirnsidebridge** Border 80 H3
**Chirton** Wilts 18 F8
**Chisbury** Wilts 19 J7
**Chiselborough** Somset 17 L12
**Chiseldon** Swindn 18 H5
**Chiselhampton** Oxon 19 P2
**Chisholme** Border 79 N6
**Chislehurst** Gt Lon 21 N9
**Chislet** Kent 23 N9
**Chisley** Calder 58 D8
**Chiswell Green** Herts 21 J3
**Chiswick** Gt Lon 21 K7
**Chisworth** Derbys 50 C3
**Chithurst** W Susx 10 D5
**Chittering** Cambs 33 M3
**Chitterne** Wilts 18 E11
**Chittlehamholt** Devon 15 L7
**Chittlehampton** Devon 15 L7
**Chittoe** Wilts 18 E7
**Chivelstone** Devon 5 Q11
**Chivenor** Devon 15 J5
**Chlenry** D & G 68 F6
**Chobham** Surrey 20 F10
**Cholderton** Wilts 19 J11
**Cholesbury** Bucks 20 E3
**Chollerton** Nthumb 72 G6
**Cholsey** Oxon 19 P4
**Cholstrey** Herefs 39 J9
**Chop Gate** N York 66 D7
**Choppington** Nthumb 73 M4
**Chopwell** Gatesd 73 K8
**Chorley** Ches E 49 K5
**Chorley** Lancs 57 L5
**Chorley** Shrops 39 M5
**Chorleywood** Herts 20 G4
**Chorleywood West** Herts 20 G4
**Chorlton** Ches E 49 N5
**Chorlton-cum-Hardy** Manch 57 P9
**Chorlton Lane** Ches W 49 J6
**Choulton** Shrops 38 H5
**Chrishall** Essex 33 M8
**Chrisswell** Inver 84 D7
**Christchurch** Cambs 43 M10
**Christchurch** Dorset 8 H8
**Christchurch** Newpt 28 D10
**Christian Malford** Wilts 18 E5
**Christon** N Som 17 K5
**Christon Bank** Nthumb 81 P9
**Christow** Devon 5 Q4
**Chudleigh** Devon 6 B6
**Chudleigh Knighton** Devon 6 B7
**Chulmleigh** Devon 15 M8
**Church** Lancs 57 N3
**Churcham** Gloucs 29 K5
**Church Aston** Wrekin 49 N11
**Church Brampton** Nhants 31 Q2
**Church Broughton** Derbys 40 G2
**Church Cove** Cnwll 2 G12
**Church Crookham** Hants 20 D12
**Churchdown** Gloucs 29 M5
**Church Eaton** Staffs 49 Q11
**Church End** C Beds 32 H8
**Churchend** Essex 23 J5
**Church End** Essex 34 C10
**Church End** Gt Lon 21 K5
**Church Enstone** Oxon 31 J8
**Church Fenton** N York 59 L6
**Churchfield** Sandw 40 D8
**Church Green** Devon 6 G4
**Church Hanborough** Oxon 31 K10
**Church Houses** N York 66 F7
**Churchill** Devon 6 H3
**Churchill** N Som 17 L4
**Churchill** Oxon 30 H8
**Churchill** Worcs 30 B4
**Churchill** Worcs 39 Q6
**Churchinford** Somset 6 G1
**Church Knowle** Dorset 8 D10
**Church Langton** Leics 41 Q8
**Church Lawford** Warwks 41 L11
**Church Leigh** Staffs 40 D1
**Church Lench** Worcs 30 D4
**Church Mayfield** Staffs 50 F11
**Church Minshull** Ches E 49 M4
**Church Norton** W Susx 10 E10
**Churchover** Warwks 41 L10
**Church Preen** Shrops 39 K3
**Church Pulverbatch** Shrops 38 H2
**Churchstanton** Somset 16 G12
**Churchstoke** Powys 38 F4
**Churchstow** Devon 5 P10
**Church Stowe** Nhants 31 N3
**Church Street** Kent 22 E8
**Church Stretton** Shrops 39 J4
**Churchtown** Cnwll 4 D5
**Churchtown** Derbys 50 H8
**Churchtown** IoM 56 d3
**Churchtown** Lancs 63 J12
**Church Village** Rhondd 27 M10
**Church Warsop** Notts 51 M7
**Churston Ferrers** Torbay 6 B10
**Churt** Surrey 10 D3

172 Churton - Corton


Churton Ches W 48 H4
Churwell Leeds 58 H8
Chwilog Gwynd 46 G4
Chyandour Cnwll 2 D9
Cilcain Flints 48 D3
Cilcennin Cerdgn 36 H8
Cilfrew Neath 26 G8
Cilfynydd Rhondd 27 M9
Cilgerran Pembks 36 C11
Cilmaengwyn Neath 26 G7
Cilmery Powys 38 B11
Cilsan Carmth 26 E4
Ciltalgarth Gwynd 47 P4
Cilycwm Carmth 37 M11
Cimla Neath 26 G9
Cinderford Gloucs 28 H6
Cinder Hill Wolves 40 B8
Cippenham Slough 20 F7
Cirencester Gloucs 18 F1
City Gt Lon 21 M7
City Airport Gt Lon 21 N7
City of London Crematorium Gt Lon 21 N6
Clabhach Ag & B 88 F5
Clachaig Ag & B 84 B6
Clachan Ag & B 83 L10
Clachan Ag & B 89 Q11
Clachan Ag & B 90 B7
Clachan Highld 96 G3
Clachan-a-Luib W Isls 111 b4
Clachan Mor Ag & B 88 C6
Clachan na Luib W Isls 111 b4
Clachan of Campsie E Duns 85 K7
Clachan-Seil Ag & B 89 Q11
Clachnaharry Highld 107 K11
Clachtoll Highld 108 B9
Clackavoid P & K 94 C8
Clacket Lane Services Surrey 21 N11
Clackmannan Clacks 85 Q5
Clackmannanshire Bridge Fife 85 Q5
Clackmarras Moray 101 K4
Clacton-on-Sea Essex 23 M1
Cladich Ag & B 90 F11
Cladswell Worcs 30 D3
Claggan Highld 89 P6
Claigan Highld 104 C10
Clanfield Hants 10 B6
Clanfield Oxon 19 K1
Clanville Hants 19 K10
Clanville Somset 17 P9
Claonaig Ag & B 83 N10
Clapgate Herts 33 M10
Clapham Bed 32 E6
Clapham Gt Lon 21 L8
Clapham N York 63 N8
Clapham W Susx 10 H8
Clapton Somset 7 K2
Clapton Somset 17 P5
Clapton-in-Gordano N Som 17 L2
Clapton-on-the-Hill Gloucs 30 F9
Claravale Gatesd 73 K7
Clarbeston Pembks 25 J5
Clarbeston Road Pembks 24 H5
Clarborough Notts 51 Q4
Clare Suffk 34 C7
Clarebrand D & G 70 C3
Clarencefield D & G 70 H2
Clarilaw Border 80 C9
Clarkston E Rens 85 J10
Clashmore Highld 107 M5
Clashmore Highld 108 B9
Clashnessie Highld 108 B9
Clashnoir Moray 101 J10
Clathy P & K 92 E10
Clathymore P & K 92 F10
Clatt Abers 102 C9
Clatter Powys 38 B4
Clatworthy Somset 16 E9
Claughton Lancs 57 K1
Claughton Lancs 63 K8
Claughton Wirral 56 F10
Claverdon Warwks 30 G2
Claverham N Som 17 L3
Clavering Essex 33 M9
Claverley Shrops 39 P4
Claverton BaNES 18 B7
Clawdd-coch V Glam 27 M12
Clawdd-newydd Denbgs 48 C5
Clawton Devon 14 F11
Claxby Lincs 52 G5
Claxton N York 59 P3
Claxton Norfk 45 M9
Claybrooke Magna Leics 41 L9
Clay Coton Nhants 41 N11
Clay Cross Derbys 51 K8
Claydon Oxon 31 L4
Claydon Suffk 35 J6
Claygate D & G 79 N11
Claygate Kent 12 E2
Claygate Surrey 21 J10
Clayhall Gt Lon 21 N5
Clayhanger Devon 16 D10
Clayhidon Devon 16 F11
Clayhill E Susx 12 G5
Clayock Highld 110 D4
Claypits Gloucs 29 K7
Claypole Lincs 42 C1
Clayton C Brad 58 E7
Clayton Donc 59 L11
Clayton W Susx 11 L7
Clayton-le-Moors Lancs 57 N3
Clayton-le-Woods Lancs 57 K4
Clayton West Kirk 58 H11
Clayworth Notts 51 Q4
Cleadale Highld 96 F11
Cleadon S Tyne 73 P8
Clearbrook Devon 5 L7
Clearwell Gloucs 28 G7
Cleasby N York 65 M5
Cleat Ork 111 h3
Cleatlam Dur 65 K4
Cleator Cumb 70 G11
Cleator Moor Cumb 70 G11
Cleckheaton Kirk 58 F8
Cleehill Shrops 39 L7
Cleekhimin N Lans 85 M10
Clee St Margaret Shrops 39 K5
Cleethorpes NE Lin 53 K2
Cleeton St Mary Shrops 39 L6
Cleeve N Som 17 L3
Cleeve Oxon 19 Q5
Cleeve Hill Gloucs 29 N4
Cleeve Prior Worcs 30 E4
Cleghornie E Loth 87 L5
Clehonger Herefs 28 E2
Cleish P & K 86 C3
Cleland N Lans 85 N10
Clenamacrie Ag & B 90 C9
Clenchwarton Norfk 43 P6
Clenerty Abers 102 G3
Clent Worcs 40 B10
Cleobury Mortimer Shrops 39 M7
Cleobury North Shrops 39 L5
Cleongart Ag & B 75 K5
Clephanton Highld 107 N11
Clerkhill D & G 79 L8
Cleuch-head D & G 78 D8
Clevancy Wilts 18 F6
Clevedon N Som 17 K2
Cleveleys Lancs 62 G12
Cleverton Wilts 18 E4
Clewer Somset 17 L6
Cley next the Sea Norfk 44 H2
Cliburn Cumb 64 B3
Cliddesden Hants 19 Q10
Cliffe Medway 22 E7
Cliffe N York 59 P7
Cliff End E Susx 12 H7
Cliffe Woods Medway 22 E8
Clifford Herefs 38 E11
Clifford Leeds 59 K5
Clifford Chambers Warwks 30 G4
Clifford's Mesne Gloucs 29 J4
Clifton Bristl 17 N2
Clifton C Beds 32 G8
Clifton C Nott 41 M1
Clifton C York 59 N4
Clifton Calder 58 F9
Clifton Cumb 71 Q9
Clifton Derbys 50 F11
Clifton Devon 15 K4
Clifton Donc 51 M2
Clifton Lancs 57 J3
Clifton N York 58 F5
Clifton Oxon 31 L7
Clifton Worcs 39 Q11
Clifton Campville Staffs 40 G5
Clifton Hampden Oxon 19 P2
Clifton Reynes M Keyn 32 C6
Clifton upon Dunsmore Warwks 41 M11
Clifton upon Teme Worcs 39 N9
Cliftonville Kent 23 Q8
Climping W Susx 10 F9
Clink Somset 18 B10
Clint N York 58 H3
Clinterty C Aber 102 H11
Clint Green Norfk 44 G7
Clintmains Border 80 E7
Clippesby Norfk 45 N7
Clipsham Rutlnd 42 D6
Clipston Nhants 41 Q10
Clipston Notts 41 N1
Clipstone C Beds 32 D10
Clitheroe Lancs 57 N1
Clive Shrops 49 K9
Cliveden Bucks 20 E6
Clixby Lincs 52 F3
Cloatley Wilts 29 N10
Clocaenog Denbgs 48 C5
Clochan Moray 101 M3
Clodock Herefs 28 C4
Clola Abers 103 K6
Clophill C Beds 32 F8
Clopton Nhants 32 F1
Clopton Suffk 35 K6
Clopton Corner Suffk 35 K6
Clos du Valle Guern 6 c1
Closeburn D & G 78 E9
Closeburnmill D & G 78 E9
Closworth Somset 7 N2
Clothall Herts 33 J9
Clotton Ches W 49 K3
Clough Foot Calder 58 B9
Clough Head Calder 58 E9
Cloughton N York 67 L8
Clousta Shet 111 k4
Clova Angus 94 F7
Clovelly Devon 14 F7
Clovenfords Border 79 P2
Clovulin Highld 90 D4
Clowne Derbys 51 L6
Clows Top Worcs 39 N7
Cluanie Inn Highld 97 Q7
Cluanie Lodge Highld 97 Q7
Clugston D & G 69 J7
Clun Shrops 38 F6
Clunas Highld 100 D6
Clunbury Shrops 38 G6
Clunderwen Carmth 25 K5
Clune Highld 99 L4
Clunes Highld 98 B10
Clungunford Shrops 38 H6
Clunie P & K 92 G6
Clunton Shrops 38 G6
Cluny Fife 86 F3
Clutton BaNES 17 N4
Clutton Ches W 49 J5
Clutton Hill BaNES 17 P4
Clydach Mons 27 P6
Clydach Swans 26 F8
Clydach Vale Rhondd 27 K9
Clydebank W Duns 84 H8
Clydebank Crematorium W Duns 84 H8
Clyffe Pypard Wilts 18 F5
Clynder Ag & B 84 D6
Clyne Neath 26 H8
Clynnog-fawr Gwynd 54 E10
Clyro Powys 38 E12
Clyst Honiton Devon 6 D4
Clyst Hydon Devon 6 D3
Clyst St George Devon 6 D5
Clyst St Lawrence Devon 6 D3
Clyst St Mary Devon 6 C5
Cnoc W Isls 111 d2
Cnwch Coch Cerdgn 37 L5
Coad's Green Cnwll 4 G5
Coalburn S Lans 78 D2
Coalburns Gatesd 73 K8
Coaley Gloucs 29 K8
Coalhill Essex 22 F4
Coalpit Heath S Glos 29 J11
Coal Pool Wsall 40 D7
Coalport Wrekin 39 M2
Coalsnaughton Clacks 85 Q4
Coaltown of Balgonie Fife 86 G3
Coaltown of Wemyss Fife 86 G3
Coalville Leics 41 K5
Coanwood Nthumb 72 C8
Coat Somset 17 L11
Coatbridge N Lans 85 M9
Coatdyke N Lans 85 M9
Coate Swindn 18 H4
Coate Wilts 18 F8
Coates Cambs 43 K9
Coates Gloucs 29 N8
Coates Lincs 52 C6
Coates W Susx 10 F6
Cobbaton Devon 15 K6
Coberley Gloucs 29 N5
Cobham Kent 22 D9
Cobham Surrey 20 H10
Cobham Services Surrey 20 H11
Cobnash Herefs 39 J9
Cobo Guern 6 b1
Cobridge C Stke 49 Q5
Coburby Abers 103 J3
Cockayne Hatley C Beds 33 J6
Cock Bridge Abers 101 K12
Cockburnspath Border 87 P7
Cock Clarks Essex 22 F3
Cockenzie and Port Seton E Loth 86 H7
Cockerham Lancs 63 J10
Cockermouth Cumb 71 J9
Cockernhoe Herts 32 G11
Cockett Swans 26 E9
Cockfield Dur 65 K3
Cockfield Suffk 34 E6
Cockfosters Gt Lon 21 L4
Cock Green Essex 34 B11
Cocking W Susx 10 E6
Cocking Causeway W Susx 10 E6
Cockington Torbay 6 B9
Cocklake Somset 17 L6
Cockley Cley Norfk 44 D8
Cock Marling E Susx 12 G6
Cockpole Green Wokham 20 C7
Cockshutt Shrops 48 H9
Cockthorpe Norfk 44 G2
Cockwood Devon 6 D6
Cockyard Derbys 50 D5
Coddenham Suffk 35 J6
Coddington Herefs 29 J1
Coddington Notts 52 B11
Codford St Mary Wilts 18 E11
Codford St Peter Wilts 18 E11
Codicote Herts 32 H11
Codmore Hill W Susx 10 G6
Codnor Derbys 51 K10
Codrington S Glos 29 K11
Codsall Staffs 39 Q2
Codsall Wood Staffs 39 Q2
Coedpoeth Wrexhm 48 F5
Coed Talon Flints 48 F4
Coed-y-paen Mons 28 D8
Coffinswell Devon 6 B8
Cofton Devon 6 C6
Cofton Hackett Worcs 40 D11
Cogan V Glam 16 G2
Cogenhoe Nhants 32 B5
Coggeshall Essex 34 E11
Coignafearn Highld 99 K5
Coilacriech Abers 94 E3
Coilantogle Stirlg 85 K2
Coillore Highld 96 D3
Coity Brdgnd 27 K11
Col W Isls 111 d2
Colaboll Highld 107 J1
Colan Cnwll 3 K4
Colaton Raleigh Devon 6 E5
Colbost Highld 104 B11
Colburn N York 65 L7
Colby Cumb 64 C4
Colby IoM 56 b6
Colchester Essex 34 G10
Colchester Crematorium Essex 34 G11
Colchester Zoo Essex 34 F11
Cold Ash W Berk 19 N6
Cold Ashby Nhants 41 P11
Cold Ashton S Glos 17 Q2
Cold Aston Gloucs 30 F9
Coldbackie Highld 109 L4
Cold Brayfield M Keyn 32 D6
Coldean Br & H 11 M8
Coldeast Devon 5 Q5
Colden Calder 58 C8
Colden Common Hants 9 N3
Cold Hanworth Lincs 52 E6
Coldharbour Surrey 11 J2
Cold Higham Nhants 31 P4
Coldingham Border 81 J2
Cold Kirby N York 66 D10
Coldmeece Staffs 49 Q8
Cold Norton Essex 22 G4
Cold Overton Leics 42 B7
Coldred Kent 13 P1
Coldridge Devon 15 M10
Coldstream Border 80 H6
Coldwaltham W Susx 10 G6
Coldwell Herefs 28 E2
Coldwells Abers 103 K7
Cole Somset 17 P9
Colebatch Shrops 38 G5
Colebrook Devon 6 D2
Colebrooke Devon 15 N11
Coleby Lincs 52 D10
Coleby N Linc 60 F9
Coleford Devon 15 N11
Coleford Gloucs 28 G6
Coleford Somset 17 P6
Colegate End Norfk 45 K11
Colehill Dorset 8 F7
Coleman's Hatch E Susx 11 N4
Colemere Shrops 48 H8
Colemore Hants 10 B4
Colenden P & K 92 G9
Colerne Wilts 18 B6
Colesbourne Gloucs 30 D10
Coleshill Bucks 20 F4
Coleshill Oxon 19 J3
Coleshill Warwks 40 G9
Coley BaNES 17 N5
Colgate W Susx 11 K4
Colinsburgh Fife 87 J2
Colinton C Edin 86 E8
Colintraive Ag & B 83 Q7
Colkirk Norfk 44 F5
Coll Ag & B 88 F5
Coll W Isls 111 d2
Collace P & K 93 J8
Collafirth Shet 111 k3
Coll Airport Ag & B 88 E5
Collaton Devon 5 P11
Collaton St Mary Torbay 6 B10
College of Roseisle Moray 100 H3
College Town Br For 20 D10
Collessie Fife 93 K11
Collier Row Gt Lon 21 P5
Collier's End Herts 33 L11
Collier Street Kent 12 E2
Collieston Abers 103 L9
Collin D & G 70 G1
Collingbourne Ducis Wilts 19 J9
Collingbourne Kingston Wilts 19 J9
Collingham Leeds 59 K5
Collingham Notts 52 B10
Collington Herefs 39 M9
Collingtree Nhants 31 Q3
Collins Green Warrtn 57 K9
Colliston Angus 93 Q6
Colliton Devon 6 E2
Collyweston Nhants 42 E9
Colmonell S Ayrs 68 F2
Colmworth Bed 32 F5
Colnabaichin Abers 101 K12
Colnbrook Slough 20 G7
Colne Cambs 33 L2
Colne Lancs 58 B6
Colne Engaine Essex 34 E10
Colney Norfk 45 K8
Colney Heath Herts 21 K3
Coln Rogers Gloucs 30 E11
Coln St Aldwyns Gloucs 30 F12
Coln St Dennis Gloucs 30 E11
Colonsay Ag & B 82 E4
Colonsay Airport Ag & B 82 E5
Colpy Abers 102 E8
Colquhar Border 79 M1
Colsterworth Lincs 42 D5
Colston Bassett Notts 41 P2
Coltfield Moray 100 H3
Coltishall Norfk 45 L6
Colton Cumb 62 G5
Colton Leeds 59 J7
Colton N York 59 M5
Colton Norfk 44 H7
Colton Staffs 40 D4
Colt's Hill Kent 12 D2
Colvend D & G 70 E5
Colwall Herefs 29 K1
Colwell Nthumb 72 G6
Colwich Staffs 40 D4
Colwinston V Glam 16 C2
Colworth W Susx 10 E9
Colwyn Bay Conwy 55 M6
Colwyn Bay Crematorium Conwy 55 M6
Colyford Devon 6 H4
Colyton Devon 6 H4
Combe Oxon 31 K10
Combe W Berk 19 L8
Combe Down BaNES 18 B8
Combe Fishacre Devon 6 A9
Combe Florey Somset 16 F9
Combe Hay BaNES 17 Q4
Combeinteignhead Devon 6 B8
Combe Martin Devon 15 K3
Combe Raleigh Devon 6 F3
Comberbach Ches W 57 M12
Comberford Staffs 40 F6
Comberton Cambs 33 L5
Comberton Herefs 39 J8
Combe St Nicholas Somset 7 J1
Combrook Warwks 30 H4
Combs Derbys 50 D5
Combs Suffk 34 H5
Combs Ford Suffk 34 H5
Combwich Somset 16 H7
Comers Abers 95 L1
Comhampton Worcs 39 Q8
Commins Coch Powys 47 N10
Commondale N York 66 F5
Common End Cumb 70 G10
Common Moor Cnwll 4 F6
Compstall Stockp 50 C3
Compstonend D & G 69 P8
Compton Devon 6 B9
Compton Hants 9 M3
Compton Staffs 39 P5
Compton Surrey 10 F1
Compton W Berk 19 N5
Compton W Susx 10 C7
Compton Wilts 18 G9
Compton Abbas Dorset 8 C4
Compton Abdale Gloucs 30 D10
Compton Bassett Wilts 18 F6
Compton Beauchamp Oxon 19 J4
Compton Bishop Somset 17 K5
Compton Chamberlayne Wilts 8 F2
Compton Dando BaNES 17 P4
Compton Dundon Somset 17 L9
Compton Durville Somset 17 K11
Compton Greenfield S Glos 28 G11
Compton Martin BaNES 17 M5
Compton Pauncefoot Somset 17 P10
Compton Valence Dorset 7 N4
Comrie Fife 86 B4
Comrie P & K 92 B10
Conaglen House Highld 90 E3
Conchra Highld 97 M4
Concraigie P & K 92 G6
Conderton Worcs 29 N2
Condicote Gloucs 30 F8
Condorrat N Lans 85 M8
Condover Shrops 39 J2
Coney Hill Gloucs 29 L5
Coneyhurst Common W Susx 10 H5
Coneysthorpe N York 66 G12
Coney Weston Suffk 34 F2
Congerstone Leics 41 J6
Congham Norfk 44 B5
Congleton Ches E 49 Q3
Congresbury N Som 17 L4
Conheath D & G 70 G2
Conicavel Moray 100 F5
Coningsby Lincs 52 H11
Conington Cambs 33 K4
Conington Cambs 42 H11
Conisbrough Donc 51 L2
Conisholme Lincs 53 L4
Coniston Cumb 62 F3
Coniston E R Yk 61 K7
Coniston Cold N York 58 B3
Conistone N York 58 C1
Connah's Quay Flints 48 F2
Connel Ag & B 90 C9
Connel Park E Ayrs 77 K8
Connor Downs Cnwll 2 E7
Conon Bridge Highld 107 J10
Cononley N York 58 C5
Consall Staffs 50 C10
Consett Dur 73 K10
Constable Burton N York 65 L8
Constable Lee Lancs 57 P4
Constantine Cnwll 2 G9
Constantine Bay Cnwll 3 K2
Contin Highld 106 G10
Conwy Conwy 55 L6
Conwy Castle Conwy 55 L6
Conyer's Green Suffk 34 E3
Cooden E Susx 12 E8
Cookbury Devon 14 G10
Cookham W & M 20 E6
Cookham Dean W & M 20 D6
Cookham Rise W & M 20 E6
Cookhill Worcs 30 D3
Cookley Suffk 35 M2
Cookley Worcs 39 Q6
Cookley Green Oxon 20 B5
Cookney Abers 95 P4
Cook's Green Essex 35 K11
Cooks Green Suffk 34 G6
Cooksmill Green Essex 22 D3
Coolham W Susx 10 H5
Cooling Medway 22 F8
Coombe Cnwll 3 L5
Coombe Devon 6 C7
Coombe Devon 6 E4
Coombe Gloucs 29 K9
Coombe Hants 9 Q4
Coombe Abbey Warwks 41 K10
Coombe Bissett Wilts 8 G3
Coombe Cellars Devon 6 B8
Coombe Hill Gloucs 29 M4
Coombe Keynes Dorset 8 C9
Coombe Pafford Torbay 6 C9
Coombes W Susx 11 J8
Coombes-Moor Herefs 38 G9
Coombeswood Dudley 40 C9
Coopersale Common Essex 21 P3
Copdock Suffk 35 J8
Copford Green Essex 34 F11
Copgrove N York 59 J2
Copister Shet 111 k3
Cople Bed 32 F7
Copley Dur 65 J3
Copmanthorpe C York 59 M5
Copmere End Staffs 49 P9
Copp Lancs 56 H2
Coppenhall Staffs 40 B4
Copperhouse Cnwll 2 E8
Coppingford Cambs 32 G2
Copplestone Devon 15 N10
Coppull Lancs 57 K6
Copsale W Susx 11 J5
Copster Green Lancs 57 M3
Copston Magna Warwks 41 L9
Cop Street Kent 23 P10
Copt Hewick N York 65 N12
Copthorne W Susx 11 L3
Copt Oak Leics 41 L5
Copythorne Hants 9 K5
Corbets Tey Gt Lon 22 C6
Corbière Jersey 7 a2
Corbridge Nthumb 72 H7
Corby Nhants 42 C11
Corby Glen Lincs 42 E5
Cordon N Ayrs 75 Q6
Coreley Shrops 39 L7
Corfe Somset 16 G11
Corfe Castle Dorset 8 E10
Corfe Mullen Dorset 8 E8
Corfton Shrops 39 J5
Corgarff Abers 94 E1
Corhampton Hants 9 Q4
Corley Warwks 40 H9
Corley Services Warwks 40 H9
Cormuir Angus 94 E8
Cornard Tye Suffk 34 E8
Cornforth Dur 65 N1
Cornhill Abers 102 D4
Cornhill-on-Tweed Nthumb 81 J6
Cornholme Calder 58 B8
Cornoigmore Ag & B 88 C7
Cornsay Dur 73 K11
Cornsay Colliery Dur 73 L11
Corntown Highld 107 J10
Corntown V Glam 27 J12
Cornwell Oxon 30 H8
Cornwood Devon 5 M8
Cornworthy Devon 5 Q8
Corpach Highld 90 F2
Corpusty Norfk 45 J4
Corrachree Abers 94 H2
Corran Highld 90 D4
Corran Highld 97 M7
Corrie D & G 79 K10
Corrie N Ayrs 75 Q4
Corriecravie N Ayrs 75 P7
Corriegills N Ayrs 75 Q5
Corriegour Lodge Hotel Highld 98 C9
Corriemoille Highld 106 F9
Corrimony Highld 98 E3
Corringham Lincs 52 C5
Corringham Thurr 22 E6
Corris Gwynd 47 M9
Corris Uchaf Gwynd 47 M9
Corrow Ag & B 84 D3
Corry Highld 96 H5
Corscombe Devon 15 L11
Corscombe Dorset 7 M2
Corse Gloucs 29 K3
Corse Lawn Gloucs 29 L3
Corsham Wilts 18 C6
Corsindae Abers 102 F12
Corsley Wilts 18 C10
Corsley Heath Wilts 18 B10
Corsock D & G 78 C12
Corston BaNES 17 Q3
Corston Wilts 18 D4
Corstorphine C Edin 86 E7
Cortachy Angus 94 F9
Corton Suffk 45 Q10
Corton Wilts 18 D11

Corton Denham Somset ... 17 P10
Coruanan Highld ... 90 E3
Corwen Denbgs ... 48 C6
Coryton Devon ... 5 K4
Coryton Thurr ... 22 E6
Cosby Leics ... 41 M8
Coseley Dudley ... 40 C8
Cosgrove Nhants ... 32 B8
Cosham C Port ... 9 N6
Cosheston Pembks ... 24 H7
Coshieville P & K ... 92 B6
Cossall Notts ... 51 L11
Cossington Leics ... 41 N5
Cossington Somset ... 17 L8
Costessey Norfk ... 45 K7
Costock Notts ... 41 M3
Coston Leics ... 42 B6
Coston Norfk ... 44 H8
Cote Oxon ... 19 L1
Cotebrook Ches W ... 49 L3
Cotehill Cumb ... 71 P5
Cotes Leics ... 41 M4
Cotesbach Leics ... 41 M10
Cotford St Luke Somset ... 16 G9
Cotgrave Notts ... 41 N1
Cothal Abers ... 102 H11
Cotham Notts ... 42 B1
Cotherstone Dur ... 64 H4
Cothill Oxon ... 19 M2
Cotleigh Devon ... 6 G3
Cotmanhay Derbys ... 51 L11
Coton Cambs ... 33 L5
Coton Nhants ... 41 P12
Coton Staffs ... 49 P10
Coton Clanford Staffs ... 49 Q10
Coton Hill Shrops ... 49 J11
Coton in the Elms Derbys ... 40 G4
Cotswolds ... 30 C11
Cotswold Wildlife Park
& Gardens Oxon ... 30 G11
Cott Devon ... 5 Q7
Cottam Lancs ... 57 J3
Cottam Notts ... 52 B7
Cottenham Cambs ... 33 M4
Cottered Herts ... 33 K10
Cotteridge Birm ... 40 D10
Cotterstock Nhants ... 42 F11
Cottesbrooke Nhants ... 41 P11
Cottesmore Rutlnd ... 42 C7
Cottingham E R Yk ... 60 H7
Cottingham Nhants ... 42 B11
Cottingley C Brad ... 58 E6
Cottingley Hall
Crematorium Leeds ... 58 H7
Cottisford Oxon ... 31 N7
Cotton Suffk ... 34 H4
Cottown Abers ... 101 P9
Cottown Abers ... 102 C11
Cottown of Gight Abers ... 102 H7
Cotts Devon ... 5 J7
Coughton Warwks ... 30 E3
Coulaghailtro Ag & B ... 83 K9
Coulags Highld ... 97 N1
Coull Abers ... 94 H2
Coulport Ag & B ... 84 D5
Coulsdon Gt Lon ... 21 L10
Coulston Wilts ... 18 D9
Coulter S Lans ... 78 G3
Coulton N York ... 66 E11
Coultra Fife ... 93 L10
Cound Shrops ... 39 K2
Coundon Dur ... 65 M2
Countersett N York ... 64 G9
Countess Wear Devon ... 6 C5
Countesthorpe Leics ... 41 N8
Countisbury Devon ... 15 M3
Coupar Angus P & K ... 93 J7
Coupland Nthumb ... 81 K7
Cour Ag & B ... 75 M3
Courteachan Highld ... 97 J9
Courteenhall Nhants ... 31 Q4
Court Henry Carmth ... 26 D4
Courtsend Essex ... 23 K5
Courtway Somset ... 16 G8
Cousland Mdloth ... 86 H8
Cousley Wood E Susx ... 12 D4
Cove Ag & B ... 84 D6
Cove Border ... 87 P3
Cove Devon ... 16 C11
Cove Hants ... 20 D11
Cove Highld ... 105 M4
Cove Bay C Aber ... 95 Q2
Covehithe Suffk ... 35 Q1
Coven Staffs ... 40 B6
Coveney Cambs ... 33 M1
Covenham St
Bartholomew Lincs ... 53 K5
Covenham St Mary Lincs ... 53 K5
Coventry Covtry ... 41 J10
Coventry Airport Warwks ... 41 J11
Coverack Cnwll ... 2 H11
Coverack Bridges Cnwll ... 2 G9
Coverham N York ... 65 K9
Covington Cambs ... 32 F3
Covington S Lans ... 78 F2
Cowan Bridge Lancs ... 63 L7
Cowbeech E Susx ... 12 C7
Cowbit Lincs ... 43 J6
Cowbridge V Glam ... 16 D2
Cowden Kent ... 11 P3
Cowdenbeath Fife ... 86 D4
Cowers Lane Derbys ... 50 H10
Cowes IoW ... 9 N8
Cowesby N York ... 66 C9
Cowfold W Susx ... 11 K5
Cowhill S Glos ... 28 H9
Cowie Stirlg ... 85 P5
Cowley Devon ... 6 B4
Cowley Gloucs ... 29 N6
Cowley Gt Lon ... 20 G7
Cowley Oxon ... 31 M12
Cowling Lancs ... 57 L5
Cowling N York ... 58 C5
Cowling N York ... 65 M9
Cowlinge Suffk ... 34 B6
Cowpen Nthumb ... 73 N5
Cowplain Hants ... 10 B7
Cowshill Dur ... 72 F11
Cowthorpe N York ... 59 K4
Coxbank Ches E ... 49 M7
Coxbench Derbys ... 51 J11
Coxford Cnwll ... 14 C11
Coxford Norfk ... 44 E4
Coxheath Kent ... 22 E12
Coxhoe Dur ... 65 N1
Coxley Somset ... 17 M7

Coxley Wick Somset ... 17 M7
Coxtie Green Essex ... 22 C4
Coxwold N York ... 66 D11
Coychurch Brdgnd ... 27 K11
Coychurch
Crematorium Brdgnd ... 27 K11
Coylton S Ayrs ... 76 G7
Coylumbridge Highld ... 99 N7
Coytrahen Brdgnd ... 27 J10
Crabbs Cross Worcs ... 30 D2
Crabtree W Susx ... 11 K5
Crackenthorpe Cumb ... 64 C3
Crackington Haven Cnwll ... 14 C11
Crackley Staffs ... 49 Q5
Crackleybank Shrops ... 49 N12
Cracoe N York ... 58 C3
Craddock Devon ... 6 E1
Cradley Dudley ... 40 C9
Cradley Herefs ... 39 N11
Cradley Heath Sandw ... 40 C9
Cradoc Powys ... 27 L3
Crafthole Cnwll ... 4 H4
Craggan Highld ... 100 F9
Craghead Dur ... 73 L10
Cragside House &
Garden Nthumb ... 73 J1
Crai Powys ... 27 J4
Craibstone Moray ... 101 P4
Craichie Angus ... 93 N6
Craig Angus ... 95 L10
Craig Highld ... 105 Q11
Craigbank E Ayrs ... 77 K8
Craigburn Border ... 86 F10
Craigcleuch D & G ... 79 M10
Craigdam Abers ... 102 H8
Craigdhu Ag & B ... 83 M2
Craigearn Abers ... 102 F11
Craigellachie Moray ... 101 K6
Craigend P & K ... 92 G10
Craigend Rens ... 84 H8
Craigends Rens ... 84 G9
Craighlaw D & G ... 69 J6
Craighouse Ag & B ... 82 G9
Craigie P & K ... 92 G7
Craigie S Ayrs ... 76 G5
Craigiefold Abers ... 103 J3
Craigley D & G ... 70 C4
Craig Llangiwg Neath ... 26 C7
Craiglockhart C Edin ... 86 E7
Craigmillar C Edin ... 86 G7
Craigneston D & G ... 78 C10
Craigneuk N Lans ... 85 N10
Craigneuk N Lans ... 85 N9
Craignure Ag & B ... 89 P8
Craigo Angus ... 95 L8
Craigrothie Fife ... 93 L12
Craigruie Stirlg ... 91 M11
Craigton Angus ... 93 N7
Craigton C Aber ... 95 N2
Craigton E Rens ... 84 H11
Craigton Crematorium
C Glas ... 85 J9
Craigton of Airlie Angus ... 93 K5
Crail Fife ... 87 L1
Crailing Border ... 80 F8
Craiselound N Linc ... 51 Q2
Crakehall N York ... 65 M9
Crambe N York ... 60 C2
Cramlington Nthumb ... 73 M5
Cramond C Edin ... 86 E7
Cramond Bridge C Edin ... 86 E7
Cranage Ches E ... 49 N2
Cranberry Staffs ... 49 P8
Cranborne Dorset ... 8 F5
Cranbourne Br For ... 20 E8
Cranbrook Devon ... 6 D4
Cranbrook Kent ... 12 F3
Cranfield C Beds ... 32 D8
Cranford Gt Lon ... 20 H7
Cranford St Andrew
Nhants ... 32 D2
Cranford St John Nhants ... 32 D2
Cranham Gloucs ... 29 M6
Crank St Hel ... 57 J8
Cranleigh Surrey ... 10 G3
Cranmore Somset ... 17 P7
Cranoe Leics ... 41 Q8
Cransford Suffk ... 35 M4
Cranshaws Border ... 87 N9
Crantock Cnwll ... 2 H4
Cranwell Lincs ... 52 E12
Cranwich Norfk ... 44 C10
Cranworth Norfk ... 44 G8
Craobh Haven Ag & B ... 83 M2
Crarae Ag & B ... 83 Q4
Crask Inn Highld ... 109 J10
Crask of Aigas Highld ... 98 F1
Craster Nthumb ... 81 Q9
Cratfield Suffk ... 35 M2
Crathes Abers ... 95 M3
Crathes Crematorium
Abers ... 95 M3
Crathie Abers ... 94 E3
Crathie Highld ... 98 H9
Crathorne N York ... 66 B6
Craven Arms Shrops ... 38 H5
Crawcrook Gatesd ... 73 K8
Crawford S Lans ... 78 F5
Crawfordjohn S Lans ... 78 E4
Crawley Hants ... 9 M1
Crawley Oxon ... 31 J10
Crawley W Susx ... 11 L3
Crawley Down W Susx ... 11 M3
Crawton Abers ... 95 P6
Cray N York ... 64 G10
Crayford Gt Lon ... 21 P8
Crayke N York ... 66 D12
Crays Hill Essex ... 22 H5
Creacombe Devon ... 15 P8
Creagan Inn Ag & B ... 90 D7
Creag Ghoraidh W Isls ... 111 b5
Creagorry W Isls ... 111 b5
Creaguaineach Lodge
Highld ... 91 J3
Creaton Nhants ... 41 P12
Creca D & G ... 71 K2
Credenhill Herefs ... 39 J12
Crediton Devon ... 15 P11
Creebank D & G ... 69 J4
Creebridge D & G ... 69 K6
Creech Heathfield Somset ... 16 H10
Creech St Michael Somset ... 16 H10
Creed Cnwll ... 3 L6
Creekmouth Gt Lon ... 21 P7
Creeting St Mary Suffk ... 34 H5
Creeton Lincs ... 42 E6

Creetown D & G ... 69 L7
Cregneash IoM ... 56 a7
Creich Fife ... 93 K10
Creigiau Cardif ... 27 M11
Cremyll Cnwll ... 5 K9
Cressage Shrops ... 39 L2
Cressbrook Derbys ... 50 F6
Cresselly Pembks ... 25 J7
Cressex Bucks ... 20 D5
Cressing Essex ... 34 D11
Cresswell Nthumb ... 73 N3
Cresswell Pembks ... 25 J7
Cresswell Staffs ... 50 C11
Creswell Derbys ... 51 M6
Cretingham Suffk ... 35 K5
Cretshengan Ag & B ... 83 K9
Crewe Ches E ... 49 N4
Crewe-by-Farndon
Ches W ... 48 H5
Crewe Crematorium
Ches E ... 49 N4
Crewe Green Ches E ... 49 N5
Crew Green Powys ... 48 G11
Crewkerne Somset ... 7 L2
Crewton C Derb ... 41 J2
Crianlarich Stirlg ... 91 K10
Cribyn Cerdgn ... 36 H9
Criccieth Gwynd ... 46 H4
Crich Derbys ... 51 J9
Crichton Mdloth ... 86 H9
Crick Nhants ... 41 N11
Crickadarn Powys ... 27 M1
Cricket St Thomas Somset ... 7 L2
Crickhowell Powys ... 27 P5
Cricklade Wilts ... 18 G3
Cricklewood Gt Lon ... 21 K6
Crieff P & K ... 92 C10
Criggion Powys ... 48 F11
Crigglestone Wakefd ... 58 H10
Crimond Abers ... 103 L4
Crimplesham Norfk ... 43 Q8
Crimscote Warwks ... 30 G5
Crinaglack Highld ... 98 F2
Crinan Ag & B ... 83 L4
Crindledyke N Lans ... 85 N10
Cringleford Norfk ... 45 K8
Crinow Pembks ... 25 K6
Croachy Highld ... 99 J4
Crockenhill Kent ... 21 P9
Crocker End Oxon ... 20 B6
Crockernwell Devon ... 5 P2
Crockerton Wilts ... 18 C11
Crocketford D & G ... 70 D2
Crockham Hill Kent ... 21 N12
Croeserw Neath ... 27 J9
Croes-goch Pembks ... 24 E3
Croes-lan Cerdgn ... 36 F10
Croesor Gwynd ... 47 K3
Croesyceiliog Carmth ... 25 P5
Croesyceiliog Torfn ... 28 C9
Croft Leics ... 41 L8
Croft Lincs ... 53 N10
Croft Warrtn ... 57 L9
Croftamie Stirlg ... 84 H6
Crofton Wakefd ... 59 J9
Croft-on-Tees N York ... 65 M5
Croftown Highld ... 106 C5
Crofts Moray ... 101 K5
Crofts of Dipple Moray ... 101 L4
Crofts of Savoch Abers ... 103 L4
Crofty Swans ... 26 C9
Croggan Ag & B ... 89 P10
Croglin Cumb ... 71 R6
Croick Highld ... 106 H4
Cromarty Highld ... 107 N8
Crombie Fife ... 86 C5
Cromdale Highld ... 100 G9
Cromer Herts ... 33 J10
Cromer Norfk ... 45 K2
Cromford Derbys ... 50 H9
Cromhall S Glos ... 29 J10
Cromor W Isls ... 111 d2
Crompton Moor Oldham ... (not shown)
Cromwell Notts ... 52 B10
Cronberry E Ayrs ... 77 K6
Crondall Hants ... 10 C1
Cronton Knows ... 57 J10
Crook Cumb ... 63 J3
Crook Dur ... 65 L1
Crookedholm E Ayrs ... 76 H4
Crookham Nthumb ... 81 J6
Crookham W Berk ... 19 P7
Crookham Village Hants ... 20 C11
Crook Inn Border ... 78 H4
Crooklands Cumb ... 63 K5
Crook of Devon P & K ... 86 C3
Cropredy Oxon ... 31 L5
Cropston Leics ... 41 M5
Cropthorne Worcs ... 30 D5
Cropton N York ... 66 G9
Cropwell Bishop Notts ... 41 P1
Cropwell Butler Notts ... 51 P12
Cros W Isls ... 111 e1
Crosbost W Isls ... 111 d2
Crosby Cumb ... 70 H7
Crosby IoM ... 56 c5
Crosby N Linc ... 60 F10
Crosby Sefton ... 56 G8
Crosby Garret Cumb ... 63 N1
Crosby Ravensworth
Cumb ... 64 B5
Croscombe Somset ... 17 N7
Cross Somset ... 17 K5
Crossaig Ag & B ... 75 M3
Crossapoll Ag & B ... 88 C7
Cross Ash Mons ... 28 E5
Cross-at-Hand Kent ... 12 F2
Crosscanonby Cumb ... 70 H7
Crossdale Street Norfk ... 45 K3
Cross Flatts C Brad ... 58 E6
Crossford Fife ... 86 C5
Crossford S Lans ... 77 N3
Crossgatehall E Loth ... 86 H8
Crossgates E Ayrs ... 76 H3
Crossgates Fife ... 86 D5
Cross Gates Leeds ... 59 J7
Crossgates N York ... 67 M10
Crossgill Lancs ... 63 K9
Cross Green Leeds ... 59 J7
Cross Green Suffk ... 34 E5
Cross Green Suffk ... 34 G6
Cross Hands Carmth ... 26 D6
Crosshands E Ayrs ... 76 H5
Crosshill Fife ... 86 E3
Crosshill S Ayrs ... 76 F9
Crosshouse E Ayrs ... 76 G4
Cross Houses Shrops ... 39 K1
Cross in Hand E Susx ... 12 C6

Cross Inn Cerdgn ... 36 F8
Cross Keys Ag & B ... 84 F6
Crosskeys Caerph ... 27 P9
Crosskirk Highld ... 110 B2
Cross Lane IoW ... 9 N9
Cross Lane Head Shrops ... 39 N3
Crosslee Rens ... 84 G9
Crossmichael D & G ... 70 C3
Cross of Jackston Abers ... 102 G8
Cross o' th' hands Derbys ... 50 H10
Crossroads Abers ... 95 J1
Crossroads Abers ... 95 M3
Cross Street Suffk ... 35 K2
Crosston Angus ... 93 N5
Cross Town Ches E ... 57 N12
Crossway Green Worcs ... 39 Q8
Crossways Dorset ... 8 B9
Crosswell Pembks ... 25 K2
Crosthwaite Cumb ... 62 H4
Croston Lancs ... 57 J5
Crostwick Norfk ... 45 L7
Crouch End Gt Lon ... 21 L6
Croucheston Wilts ... 8 F3
Crouch Hill Dorset ... 7 P2
Croughton Nhants ... 31 M7
Crovie Abers ... 102 H3
Crowan Cnwll ... 2 F8
Crowborough E Susx ... 11 P4
Crowcombe Somset ... 16 F8
Crowdecote Derbys ... 50 E7
Crowden Derbys ... 50 E2
Crow Edge Barns ... 58 F12
Crowell Oxon ... 20 C4
Crowfield Suffk ... 35 J5
Crowhill E Loth ... 87 N17
Crow Hill Herefs ... 28 H4
Crowhurst E Susx ... 12 F7
Crowhurst Surrey ... 11 M1
Crowland Lincs ... 43 J7
Crowland Lincs ... 34 G3
Crowlas Cnwll ... 2 D8
Crowle N Linc ... 60 D10
Crowle Worcs ... 30 B3
Crowle Green Worcs ... 30 B3
Crowmarsh Gifford Oxon ... 19 Q3
Crownhill C Plym ... 5 K8
Crownhill Crematorium
M Keyn ... 32 B8
Crownthorpe Norfk ... 44 H9
Crowntown Cnwll ... 2 F9
Crows-an-Wra Cnwll ... 2 B9
Crowthorne Wokham ... 20 D9
Crowton Ches W ... 49 L1
Croxdale Dur ... 73 M12
Croxden Staffs ... 50 E11
Croxley Green Herts ... 20 H4
Croxteth Lpool ... 56 H9
Croxton Cambs ... 33 J5
Croxton N Linc ... 61 J10
Croxton Norfk ... 44 E11
Croxton Norfk ... 44 G4
Croxton Staffs ... 49 P8
Croxton Kerrial Leics ... 42 B4
Croy Highld ... 107 N11
Croy N Lans ... 85 M7
Croyde Devon ... 14 H4
Croydon Cambs ... 33 K6
Croydon Gt Lon ... 21 L9
Croydon Crematorium
Gt Lon ... 21 L9
Crubenmore Highld ... 99 K10
Cruckmeole Shrops ... 38 H1
Cruckton Shrops ... 48 H12
Cruden Bay Abers ... 103 M7
Crudgington Wrekin ... 49 L11
Crudwell Wilts ... 29 N9
Crug Powys ... 38 C6
Crulabhig W Isls ... (not shown)
Crumlin Caerph ... 27 P8
Crumplehorn Cnwll ... 4 F9
Crumpsall Manch ... 57 Q8
Crundale Kent ... 13 K1
Crunwear Pembks ... 25 L6
Crux Easton Hants ... 19 M9
Crwbin Carmth ... 26 C6
Cryers Hill Bucks ... 20 E4
Crymych Pembks ... 25 L2
Crynant Neath ... 26 H7
Crystal Palace Gt Lon ... 21 M8
Cuaig Highld ... 105 K10
Cuan Ag & B ... 89 P12
Cubert Cnwll ... 2 H4
Cublington Bucks ... 32 B11
Cublington Herefs ... 28 E2
Cuckfield W Susx ... 11 L5
Cucklington Somset ... 17 R10
Cuckney Notts ... 51 M6
Cuddesdon Oxon ... 31 N12
Cuddington Bucks ... 31 Q11
Cuddington Ches W ... 49 L1
Cuddington Heath
Ches W ... 49 J6
Cudham Gt Lon ... 21 N10
Cudliptown Devon ... 5 L4
Cudnell Bmouth ... 8 F7
Cudworth Barns ... 59 K11
Cudworth Somset ... 7 K1
Cuffley Herts ... 21 L3
Cuil Highld ... 90 D5
Culbokie Highld ... 107 K9
Culburnie Highld ... 98 G1
Culcabock Highld ... 107 L12
Culcharry Highld ... 100 D5
Culcheth Warrtn ... 57 M9
Culdrain Abers ... 101 P8
Culduie Highld ... 97 K2
Culford Suffk ... 34 D3
Culfordheath Suffk ... (not shown)
Culgaith Cumb ... 64 B2
Culham Oxon ... 19 N2
Culkein Highld ... 108 B8
Culkein Drumbeg Highld ... 108 C7
Culkerton Gloucs ... 29 N9
Cullen Moray ... 101 P2
Cullercoats N Tyne ... 73 P6
Cullerlie Abers ... 95 M2
Cullicudden Highld ... 107 K9
Cullingworth C Brad ... 58 E6
Cuillin Hills Highld ... 96 F5
Cullipool Ag & B ... 83 L1
Cullivoe Shet ... 111 m2
Culloden Highld ... 107 M12
Cullompton Devon ... 6 D2
Cullompton Services
Devon ... 6 D2
Culm Davy Devon ... 16 F12
Culmington Shrops ... 39 J6
Culmstock Devon ... 16 E12
Culnacraig Highld ... 106 A2

Culnaightrie D & G ... 70 C5
Culnaknock Highld ... 104 G9
Culrain Highld ... 107 J4
Culross Fife ... 86 B5
Culroy S Ayrs ... 76 F8
Culsalmond Abers ... 102 E8
Culscadden D & G ... 69 L8
Culshabbin D & G ... 69 J8
Culswick Shet ... 111 j4
Cultercullen Abers ... 103 J9
Cults C Aber ... 95 P2
Culverstone Green Kent ... 22 D10
Culverthorpe Lincs ... 42 E3
Culworth Nhants ... 31 M5
Culzean Castle &
Country Park S Ayrs ... 76 D8
Cumbernauld N Lans ... 85 M7
Cumbernauld Village
N Lans ... 85 M7
Cumberworth Lincs ... 53 N8
Cuminestown Abers ... 102 G5
Cumledge Border ... 80 G3
Cummersdale Cumb ... 71 N5
Cummertrees D & G ... 71 J3
Cummingston Moray ... 100 H2
Cumnock E Ayrs ... 77 J7
Cumnor Oxon ... 31 L12
Cumrew Cumb ... 71 Q5
Cumrue D & G ... 78 H10
Cumwhinton Cumb ... 71 P5
Cumwhitton Cumb ... 71 Q5
Cundall N York ... 65 Q11
Cunninghamhead N Ayrs ... 76 F3
Cunningsburgh Shet ... 111 k4
Cupar Fife ... 93 L11
Cupar Muir Fife ... 93 L11
Curbar Derbys ... 50 G6
Curbridge Hants ... 9 N5
Curbridge Oxon ... 31 J11
Curdridge Hants ... 9 N5
Curdworth Warwks ... 40 F8
Curland Somset ... 16 H11
Curridge W Berk ... 19 N6
Currie C Edin ... 86 E8
Curry Mallet Somset ... 17 J10
Curry Rivel Somset ... 17 K10
Curtisden Green Kent ... 12 E3
Curtisknowle Devon ... 5 P9
Cury Cnwll ... 2 G10
Cushnie Abers ... 102 C11
Cusworth Donc ... 59 M12
Cutcloy D & G ... 69 L11
Cutcombe Somset ... 16 C8
Cuthill Highld ... 107 M5
Cutnall Green Worcs ... 39 Q8
Cutsdean Gloucs ... 30 E7
Cutthorpe Derbys ... 51 J6
Cuxham Oxon ... 19 Q2
Cuxton Medway ... 22 E9
Cuxwold Lincs ... 52 G4
Cwm Denbgs ... 56 C12
Cwmaman Rhondd ... 27 L8
Cwmbach Carmth ... 25 M4
Cwmbach Powys ... 27 N2
Cwmbach Rhondd ... 27 L8
Cwmbach Llechrhyd
Powys ... 38 B10
Cwmbran Torfn ... 28 C9
Cwmcarn Caerph ... 27 P9
Cwmcarvan Mons ... 28 F7
Cwm-cou Cerdgn ... 36 E11
Cwm Crawnon Powys ... 27 N5
Cwmdare Rhondd ... 27 L7
Cwmdu Powys ... 27 P4
Cwmdu Swans ... 26 E9
Cwmduad Carmth ... 25 P3
Cwmfelin Brdgnd ... 27 J10
Cwmfelin Myr Td ... 27 M8
Cwmfelin Boeth Carmth ... 25 L5
Cwmfelinfach Caerph ... 27 P9
Cwmffrwd Carmth ... 25 P5
Cwmgiedd Powys ... 26 H6
Cwmgorse Carmth ... 26 F6
Cwmgwili Carmth ... 26 D6
Cwmhiraeth Carmth ... 25 N2
Cwm Llinau Powys ... 47 N9
Cwmllynfell Neath ... 26 G6
Cwmmawr Carmth ... 26 D6
Cwmparc Rhondd ... 27 K9
Cwmpengraig Carmth ... 25 N2
Cwmtillery Blae G ... 27 P7
Cwm-twrch Isaf Powys ... 26 G6
Cwm-twrch Uchaf Powys ... 26 G6
Cwm-y-glo Gwynd ... 54 H8
Cwmystwyth Cerdgn ... 37 N6
Cwrt-newydd Cerdgn ... 36 H10
Cyfarthfa Castle
Museum Myr Td ... 27 L7
Cylibebyll Neath ... 26 G7
Cymer Neath ... 27 J9
Cymmer Rhondd ... 27 L10
Cynghordy Carmth ... 37 N11
Cynonville Neath ... 26 H9
Cynwyd Denbgs ... 48 C6
Cynwyl Elfed Carmth ... 25 P4

**D**

Daccombe Devon ... 6 B8
Dacre Cumb ... 71 P9
Dacre N York ... 58 F3
Dacre Banks N York ... 58 G2
Daddry Shield Dur ... 72 F12
Dadford Bucks ... 31 P6
Dadlington Leics ... 41 K7
Dagenham Gt Lon ... 21 P6
Daglingworth Gloucs ... 30 C12
Dagnall Bucks ... 32 E12
Dailly S Ayrs ... 76 E10
Dairsie Fife ... 93 M11
Dalabrog W Isls ... 111 a6
Dalavich Ag & B ... 83 P1
Dalbeattie D & G ... 70 C4
Dalby IoM ... 56 b5
Dalby N York ... 66 F12
Dalcapon P & K ... 92 E5
Dalchalm Highld ... 107 Q2
Dalchreichart Highld ... 98 D6
Dalchruin P & K ... 91 Q11
Dalcrue P & K ... 92 F9
Daiditch Devon ... 6 E6
Daldowie Crematorium
C Glas ... 85 L9
Dale Derbys ... 51 K12

| Place | County | Page | Grid |
|---|---|---|---|
| **Dale** Pembks | | 24 | E7 |
| Dalelia Highld | | 89 | P3 |
| Dalgarven N Ayrs | | 76 | E3 |
| Dalgety Bay Fife | | 86 | E5 |
| Dalgig E Ayrs | | 77 | J8 |
| Dalginross P & K | | 92 | B10 |
| Dalguise P & K | | 92 | E6 |
| Dalhalvaig Highld | | 109 | Q5 |
| Dalham Suffk | | 34 | C4 |
| Daliburgh W Isls | | 111 | a6 |
| Dalkeith Mdloth | | 86 | G8 |
| Dallas Moray | | 100 | H5 |
| Dallinghoo Suffk | | 35 | L6 |
| Dallington E Susx | | 12 | D6 |
| Dallington Nhants | | 31 | Q2 |
| Dalmally Ag & B | | 90 | G10 |
| Dalmary Stirlg | | 85 | J4 |
| Dalmellington E Ayrs | | 76 | H9 |
| Dalmeny C Edin | | 86 | D6 |
| Dalmore Highld | | 107 | L8 |
| Dalmuir W Duns | | 84 | H8 |
| Dalnabreck Highld | | 89 | P3 |
| Dalnacardoch P & K | | 91 | Q3 |
| Dalnahaitnach Highld | | 99 | M5 |
| Dalnaspidal P & K | | 91 | P2 |
| Dalnawillan Lodge Highld | | 110 | B7 |
| Daloist P & K | | 92 | B4 |
| Dalqueich P & K | | 86 | C2 |
| Dalquhairn S Ayrs | | 76 | F11 |
| Dalreavoch Lodge Highld | | 107 | M1 |
| Dalry N Ayrs | | 76 | E2 |
| Dalrymple E Ayrs | | 76 | F8 |
| Dalserf S Lans | | 77 | N2 |
| Dalsmeran Ag & B | | 75 | J9 |
| Dalston Cumb | | 71 | M5 |
| Dalston Gt Lon | | 21 | M6 |
| Dalswinton D & G | | 78 | F10 |
| Dalton D & G | | 70 | H2 |
| Dalton N York | | 65 | K6 |
| Dalton N York | | 66 | B11 |
| Dalton Nthumb | | 73 | K6 |
| Dalton-in-Furness Cumb | | 62 | E7 |
| Dalton-le-Dale Dur | | 73 | P10 |
| Dalton-on-Tees N York | | 65 | N6 |
| Dalton Piercy Hartpl | | 66 | C2 |
| Dalveich Stirlg | | 91 | P10 |
| Dalwhinnie Highld | | 99 | J11 |
| Dalwood Devon | | 6 | H3 |
| Damerham Hants | | 8 | G4 |
| Damgate Norfk | | 45 | N8 |
| Damnaglaur D & G | | 68 | F11 |
| Danbury Essex | | 22 | F3 |
| Danby N York | | 66 | G6 |
| Danby Wiske N York | | 65 | N7 |
| Dandaleith Moray | | 101 | K6 |
| Danderhall Mdloth | | 86 | G8 |
| Dane End Herts | | 33 | K11 |
| Danehill E Susx | | 11 | N5 |
| Dane Hills C Leic | | 41 | M6 |
| Dane Street Kent | | 23 | K11 |
| Danshillock Abers | | 102 | F4 |
| Danskine E Loth | | 87 | L8 |
| Darenth Kent | | 22 | C8 |
| Daresbury Halton | | 57 | L11 |
| Darfield Barns | | 59 | K12 |
| Dargate Kent | | 23 | L10 |
| Darite Cnwll | | 4 | G6 |
| Darlaston Wsall | | 40 | C7 |
| Darlaston Green Wsall | | 40 | C7 |
| Darley N York | | 58 | G3 |
| Darley Abbey C Derb | | 51 | J12 |
| Darley Bridge Derbys | | 50 | H8 |
| Darley Dale Derbys | | 50 | H7 |
| Darley Green Solhll | | 40 | F11 |
| Darleyhall Herts | | 32 | G11 |
| Darley Head N York | | 58 | G3 |
| Darlingscott Warwks | | 30 | G6 |
| Darlington Darltn | | 65 | M5 |
| Darlington Crematorium Darltn | | 65 | M5 |
| Darlton Notts | | 51 | Q6 |
| Darnick Border | | 80 | D7 |
| Darowen Powys | | 47 | N10 |
| Darra Abers | | 102 | F6 |
| Darracott Devon | | 14 | E8 |
| Darracott Devon | | 14 | H4 |
| Darras Hall Nthumb | | 73 | K6 |
| Darrington Wakefd | | 59 | L9 |
| Darsham Suffk | | 35 | N3 |
| Darshill Somset | | 17 | N7 |
| Dartford Kent | | 22 | B8 |
| Dartford Crossing Kent | | 22 | C8 |
| Dartington Devon | | 5 | Q7 |
| Dartmoor National Park Devon | | 5 | N4 |
| Dartmouth Devon | | 6 | B11 |
| Darton Barns | | 58 | H11 |
| Darvel E Ayrs | | 77 | J4 |
| Darwen Bl w D | | 57 | M4 |
| Datchet W & M | | 20 | F7 |
| Datchworth Herts | | 33 | J11 |
| Daubhill Bolton | | 57 | M7 |
| Daugh of Kinermony Moray | | 101 | K7 |
| Dauntsey Wilts | | 18 | E4 |
| Dava Highld | | 100 | F7 |
| Davenham Ches W | | 49 | M2 |
| Daventry Nhants | | 31 | M2 |
| Davidson's Mains C Edin | | 86 | E7 |
| Davidstow Cnwll | | 4 | E3 |
| Davington D & G | | 79 | K8 |
| Davington Hill Kent | | 23 | J10 |
| Daviot Abers | | 102 | G9 |
| Daviot Highld | | 99 | K2 |
| Daviot House Highld | | 99 | K2 |
| Davoch of Grange Moray | | 101 | N5 |
| Daw End Wsall | | 40 | D7 |
| Dawesgreen Surrey | | 11 | K1 |
| Dawley Wrekin | | 39 | M1 |
| Dawlish Devon | | 6 | C7 |
| Dawlish Warren Devon | | 6 | D7 |
| Daybrook Notts | | 51 | M10 |
| Daylesford Gloucs | | 30 | G8 |
| Deal Kent | | 23 | Q11 |
| Dean Cumb | | 70 | H9 |
| Dean Devon | | 5 | P7 |
| Dean Devon | | 15 | M3 |
| Dean Hants | | 9 | P4 |
| Dean Oxon | | 31 | J9 |
| Dean Somset | | 17 | P7 |
| Dean Bottom Kent | | 22 | C9 |
| Deanburnhaugh Border | | 79 | N6 |
| Deancombe Devon | | 5 | P7 |
| Dean Court Oxon | | 31 | L11 |
| Deane Bolton | | 57 | M7 |
| Deane Hants | | 19 | P10 |
| Deanhead Kirk | | 58 | D10 |
| Deanland Dorset | | 8 | E4 |
| Dean Prior Devon | | 5 | P7 |
| Deanraw Nthumb | | 72 | E8 |
| Deans W Loth | | 86 | B8 |
| Deanscales Cumb | | 70 | H9 |
| Deanshanger Nhants | | 31 | Q6 |
| Deanshaugh Moray | | 101 | L2 |
| Deanston Stirlg | | 85 | M3 |
| Dearham Cumb | | 70 | H8 |
| Debach Suffk | | 35 | L5 |
| Debden Essex | | 21 | N4 |
| Debden Essex | | 33 | N9 |
| Debenham Suffk | | 35 | K4 |
| Deblin's Green Worcs | | 39 | P11 |
| Dechmont W Loth | | 86 | C7 |
| Dechmont Road W Loth | | 86 | B8 |
| Deddington Oxon | | 31 | L7 |
| Dedham Essex | | 34 | H9 |
| Dedworth W & M | | 20 | F8 |
| Deene Nhants | | 42 | D10 |
| Deenethorpe Nhants | | 42 | D10 |
| Deepcar Sheff | | 50 | H2 |
| Deeping Gate C Pete | | 42 | G8 |
| Deeping St James Lincs | | 42 | G8 |
| Deeping St Nicholas Lincs | | 42 | H7 |
| Deerhurst Gloucs | | 29 | M3 |
| Defford Worcs | | 30 | B5 |
| Defynnog Powys | | 27 | K4 |
| Deganwy Conwy | | 55 | L6 |
| Degnish Ag & B | | 83 | L1 |
| Deighton C York | | 59 | N5 |
| Deighton N York | | 65 | P7 |
| Deiniolen Gwynd | | 54 | H8 |
| Delabole Cnwll | | 4 | D4 |
| Delamere Ches W | | 49 | K2 |
| Delfrigs Abers | | 103 | K10 |
| Delliefure Highld | | 100 | F7 |
| Dell Quay W Susx | | 10 | D9 |
| Delnabo Moray | | 100 | H4 |
| Delnashaugh Inn Moray | | 101 | J8 |
| Delny Highld | | 107 | M7 |
| Delph Oldham | | 58 | C11 |
| Delves Dur | | 73 | K10 |
| Dembleby Lincs | | 42 | E3 |
| Denaby Donc | | 51 | L2 |
| Denbigh Denbgs | | 48 | C3 |
| Denbighshire Crematorium Denbgs | | 55 | Q6 |
| Denbrae Fife | | 93 | L11 |
| Denbury Devon | | 5 | Q6 |
| Denby Derbys | | 51 | K10 |
| Denby Dale Kirk | | 58 | G11 |
| Denchworth Oxon | | 19 | L3 |
| Dendron Cumb | | 62 | E7 |
| Denfield P & K | | 92 | E11 |
| Denford Nhants | | 32 | E2 |
| Dengie Essex | | 23 | J3 |
| Denham Bucks | | 20 | G6 |
| Denham Suffk | | 34 | C5 |
| Denham Suffk | | 35 | L4 |
| Denham Green Bucks | | 20 | G6 |
| Denhead Abers | | 103 | K5 |
| Denhead Fife | | 93 | N11 |
| Denhead of Gray C Dund | | 93 | L8 |
| Denholm Border | | 80 | D9 |
| Denholme C Brad | | 58 | E7 |
| Denmead Hants | | 9 | Q5 |
| Denmore C Aber | | 103 | K11 |
| Dennington Suffk | | 35 | L4 |
| Denny Falk | | 85 | N6 |
| Dennyloanhead Falk | | 85 | N6 |
| Den of Lindores Fife | | 93 | J11 |
| Denshaw Oldham | | 58 | C11 |
| Denside Abers | | 95 | N3 |
| Densole Kent | | 13 | N2 |
| Denston Suffk | | 34 | C6 |
| Denstone Staffs | | 50 | E11 |
| Denstroude Kent | | 23 | L10 |
| Dent Cumb | | 63 | N5 |
| Denton Cambs | | 42 | G11 |
| Denton Darltn | | 65 | L4 |
| Denton E Susx | | 11 | P9 |
| Denton Kent | | 13 | N1 |
| Denton Lincs | | 42 | C4 |
| Denton N York | | 58 | F4 |
| Denton Nhants | | 32 | B5 |
| Denton Norfk | | 45 | L11 |
| Denton Tamesd | | 50 | B2 |
| Denver Norfk | | 43 | P9 |
| Denwick Nthumb | | 81 | P10 |
| Deopham Norfk | | 44 | H9 |
| Deopham Green Norfk | | 44 | H9 |
| Depden Suffk | | 34 | C5 |
| Deptford Gt Lon | | 21 | M7 |
| Deptford Wilts | | 18 | E12 |
| Derby C Derb | | 41 | J1 |
| Derby Devon | | 15 | K5 |
| Derbyhaven IoM | | 56 | b7 |
| Derculich P & K | | 92 | D5 |
| Dereham Norfk | | 44 | G7 |
| Deri Caerph | | 27 | N8 |
| Derringstone Kent | | 23 | M12 |
| Derrington Staffs | | 40 | B3 |
| Derry Hill Wilts | | 18 | E6 |
| Derrythorpe N Linc | | 52 | B2 |
| Dersingham Norfk | | 44 | B4 |
| Dervaig Ag & B | | 89 | J6 |
| Derwen Denbgs | | 48 | C5 |
| Derwenlas Powys | | 47 | L10 |
| Derwent Valley Mills Derbys | | 50 | H9 |
| Derwentwater Cumb | | 71 | L10 |
| Desborough Nhants | | 42 | B12 |
| Desford Leics | | 41 | L6 |
| Deskford Moray | | 101 | P3 |
| Detling Kent | | 22 | F10 |
| Deuxhill Shrops | | 39 | M4 |
| Devauden Mons | | 28 | F9 |
| Devil's Bridge Cerdgn | | 37 | M5 |
| Devizes Wilts | | 18 | E8 |
| Devonport C Plym | | 5 | K8 |
| Devonside Clacks | | 85 | Q4 |
| Devoran Cnwll | | 2 | H7 |
| Devoran & Perran Cnwll | | 2 | H7 |
| Dewarton Mdloth | | 86 | H9 |
| Dewlish Dorset | | 8 | B7 |
| Dewsbury Kirk | | 58 | G9 |
| Dewsbury Moor Crematorium Kirk | | 58 | G9 |
| Deytheur Powys | | 48 | E11 |
| Dibden Hants | | 9 | L6 |
| Dibden Purlieu Hants | | 9 | M6 |
| Dickleburgh Norfk | | 35 | J1 |
| Didbrook Gloucs | | 30 | D7 |
| Didcot Oxon | | 19 | N3 |
| Diddington Cambs | | 32 | H4 |
| Diddlebury Shrops | | 39 | K5 |
| Didling W Susx | | 10 | D6 |
| Didmarton Gloucs | | 18 | B4 |
| Didsbury Manch | | 57 | Q9 |
| Digby Lincs | | 52 | F11 |
| Digg Highld | | 104 | F8 |
| Diggle Oldham | | 58 | D11 |
| Digmoor Lancs | | 57 | J7 |
| Dihewyd Cerdgn | | 36 | H9 |
| Dilham Norfk | | 45 | M5 |
| Dilhorne Staffs | | 50 | C11 |
| Dill Hall Lancs | | 57 | N3 |
| Dillington Cambs | | 32 | G4 |
| Dilston Nthumb | | 72 | H8 |
| Dilton Wilts | | 18 | C10 |
| Dilton Marsh Wilts | | 18 | C10 |
| Dilwyn Herefs | | 38 | H10 |
| Dinas Gwynd | | 46 | E4 |
| Dinas Pembks | | 24 | H2 |
| Dinas-Mawddwy Gwynd | | 47 | P8 |
| Dinas Powys V Glam | | 16 | F2 |
| Dinder Somset | | 17 | N7 |
| Dinedor Herefs | | 28 | G2 |
| Dingestow Mons | | 28 | E6 |
| Dingle Lpool | | 56 | G10 |
| Dingley Nhants | | 41 | Q9 |
| Dingwall Highld | | 107 | J9 |
| Dinnet Abers | | 94 | H3 |
| Dinnington N u Ty | | 73 | L6 |
| Dinnington Rothm | | 51 | M4 |
| Dinnington Somset | | 17 | K12 |
| Dinorwic Gwynd | | 54 | H8 |
| Dinton Bucks | | 31 | Q11 |
| Dinton Wilts | | 8 | E2 |
| Dinwoodie D & G | | 78 | H10 |
| Dinworthy Devon | | 14 | F8 |
| Dipford Somset | | 16 | G10 |
| Dippen Ag & B | | 75 | M5 |
| Dippen N Ayrs | | 75 | Q7 |
| Dippertown Devon | | 5 | J4 |
| Dipple Moray | | 101 | L4 |
| Dipple S Ayrs | | 76 | D10 |
| Diptford Devon | | 5 | P8 |
| Dipton Dur | | 73 | K9 |
| Dirleton E Loth | | 87 | K5 |
| Dirt Pot Nthumb | | 72 | F10 |
| Diseworth Leics | | 41 | L3 |
| Dishforth N York | | 65 | P11 |
| Disley Ches E | | 50 | C4 |
| Diss Norfk | | 35 | J1 |
| Distington Cumb | | 70 | G10 |
| Distington Hall Crematorium Cumb | | 70 | G10 |
| Ditchampton Wilts | | 8 | E2 |
| Ditcheat Somset | | 17 | P8 |
| Ditchingham Norfk | | 45 | M11 |
| Ditchling E Susx | | 11 | M7 |
| Ditherington Shrops | | 49 | J11 |
| Ditteridge Wilts | | 18 | B6 |
| Dittisham Devon | | 6 | B10 |
| Ditton Kent | | 22 | E10 |
| Ditton Green Cambs | | 33 | Q5 |
| Ditton Priors Shrops | | 39 | L4 |
| Dixton Mons | | 28 | F6 |
| Dobcross Oldham | | 58 | C11 |
| Dobwalls Cnwll | | 4 | F7 |
| Doccombe Devon | | 5 | Q3 |
| Dochgarroch Highld | | 99 | J2 |
| Docking Norfk | | 44 | C3 |
| Docklow Herefs | | 39 | K10 |
| Dockray Cumb | | 71 | N10 |
| Doddinghurst Essex | | 22 | C4 |
| Doddington Cambs | | 43 | L11 |
| Doddington Kent | | 22 | H11 |
| Doddington Lincs | | 52 | C9 |
| Doddington Nthumb | | 81 | L7 |
| Doddington Shrops | | 39 | L6 |
| Doddiscombsleigh Devon | | 6 | B5 |
| Dodd's Green Ches E | | 49 | L6 |
| Dodford Nhants | | 31 | N3 |
| Dodford Worcs | | 40 | C11 |
| Dodington S Glos | | 29 | K11 |
| Dodington Somset | | 16 | G7 |
| Dodleston Ches W | | 48 | G4 |
| Dodside E Rens | | 84 | H11 |
| Dod's Leigh Staffs | | 40 | D1 |
| Dodworth Barns | | 58 | H12 |
| Doe Bank Birm | | 40 | E7 |
| Dogdyke Lincs | | 52 | H11 |
| Dogmersfield Hants | | 20 | C11 |
| Dolanog Powys | | 48 | C11 |
| Dolbenmaen Gwynd | | 46 | H3 |
| Dolfach Powys | | 47 | P10 |
| Dolfor Powys | | 38 | C5 |
| Dolgarrog Conwy | | 55 | L7 |
| Dolgellau Gwynd | | 47 | M7 |
| Doll Highld | | 107 | P2 |
| Dollar Clacks | | 85 | Q4 |
| Dollarfield Clacks | | 85 | Q4 |
| Dolphin Flints | | 48 | E2 |
| Dolphinholme Lancs | | 63 | K10 |
| Dolphinton S Lans | | 86 | D11 |
| Dolton Devon | | 15 | K9 |
| Dolwen Conwy | | 55 | N6 |
| Dolwyddelan Conwy | | 55 | K10 |
| Domgay Powys | | 48 | F10 |
| Doncaster Donc | | 59 | M12 |
| Doncaster North Services Donc | | 59 | P11 |
| Donhead St Andrew Wilts | | 8 | D3 |
| Donhead St Mary Wilts | | 8 | D3 |
| Donibristle Fife | | 86 | E5 |
| Doniford Somset | | 16 | E7 |
| Donington Lincs | | 42 | H3 |
| Donington on Bain Lincs | | 52 | H7 |
| Donington Park Services Leics | | 41 | L3 |
| Donisthorpe Leics | | 40 | H5 |
| Donnington Gloucs | | 30 | F8 |
| Donnington Herefs | | 39 | L1 |
| Donnington W Berk | | 19 | M7 |
| Donnington W Susx | | 10 | D9 |
| Donnington Wrekin | | 49 | N11 |
| Donnington Wood Wrekin | | 49 | N11 |
| Donyatt Somset | | 17 | J12 |
| Doonfoot S Ayrs | | 76 | F7 |
| Dorback Lodge Highld | | 100 | G11 |
| Dorchester Dorset | | 7 | Q5 |
| Dorchester Oxon | | 19 | P2 |
| Dordon Warwks | | 40 | H7 |
| Dores Highld | | 98 | H3 |
| Dorking Surrey | | 11 | J2 |
| Dormansland Surrey | | 11 | N2 |
| Dormington Herefs | | 28 | G2 |
| Dormston Worcs | | 30 | C3 |
| Dorney Bucks | | 20 | E7 |
| Dornie Highld | | 97 | M3 |
| Dornoch Highld | | 107 | N4 |
| Dornock D & G | | 71 | K3 |
| Dorrery Highld | | 110 | C5 |
| Dorridge Solhll | | 40 | F11 |
| Dorrington Lincs | | 52 | F11 |
| Dorrington Shrops | | 39 | J2 |
| Dorrington Shrops | | 49 | N7 |
| Dorsington Warwks | | 30 | F4 |
| Dorstone Herefs | | 28 | C1 |
| Dorton Bucks | | 31 | P10 |
| Douglas IoM | | 56 | d6 |
| Douglas S Lans | | 78 | D3 |
| Douglas and Angus C Dund | | 93 | M8 |
| Douglas Crematorium IoM | | 56 | d5 |
| Douglas Pier Ag & B | | 84 | D3 |
| Douglastown Angus | | 93 | M6 |
| Douglas Water S Lans | | 78 | E2 |
| Douglas West S Lans | | 78 | D3 |
| Doulting Somset | | 17 | P7 |
| Dounby Ork | | 111 | g2 |
| Doune Highld | | 106 | G3 |
| Doune Stirlg | | 85 | M3 |
| Dounepark S Ayrs | | 76 | D11 |
| Dounie Highld | | 107 | J4 |
| Dousland Devon | | 5 | L6 |
| Dove Dale Derbys | | 50 | F9 |
| Dove Holes Derbys | | 50 | E5 |
| Dovenby Cumb | | 70 | H8 |
| Dover Kent | | 13 | P2 |
| Dover Castle Kent | | 13 | P2 |
| Dovercourt Essex | | 35 | L9 |
| Doverdale Worcs | | 39 | Q8 |
| Doveridge Derbys | | 40 | F2 |
| Doversgreen Surrey | | 11 | K1 |
| Dowally P & K | | 92 | E6 |
| Dowdeswell Gloucs | | 30 | D9 |
| Dowlais Myr Td | | 27 | M7 |
| Dowland Devon | | 15 | K9 |
| Dowlish Wake Somset | | 7 | K1 |
| Down Ampney Gloucs | | 18 | G2 |
| Downderry Cnwll | | 4 | G9 |
| Downe Gt Lon | | 21 | N10 |
| Downend Gloucs | | 29 | L8 |
| Downend S Glos | | 28 | H12 |
| Downfield C Dund | | 93 | L8 |
| Downgate Cnwll | | 4 | H5 |
| Downham Essex | | 22 | E4 |
| Downham Gt Lon | | 21 | M8 |
| Downham Lancs | | 63 | P12 |
| Downham Market Norfk | | 43 | P9 |
| Down Hatherley Gloucs | | 29 | M4 |
| Downhead Somset | | 17 | N10 |
| Downhead Somset | | 17 | Q7 |
| Downhill P & K | | 92 | G9 |
| Downholme N York | | 65 | K7 |
| Downies Abers | | 95 | Q3 |
| Downley Bucks | | 20 | D4 |
| Down St Mary Devon | | 15 | M10 |
| Downs Crematorium Br & H | | 11 | M8 |
| Downside Surrey | | 20 | H10 |
| Down Thomas Devon | | 5 | K9 |
| Downton Wilts | | 8 | H3 |
| Dowsby Lincs | | 42 | G4 |
| Doynton S Glos | | 17 | Q2 |
| Draethen Caerph | | 27 | P10 |
| Draffan S Lans | | 77 | N3 |
| Drakeholes Notts | | 51 | P3 |
| Drakemyre N Ayrs | | 76 | E2 |
| Drakes Broughton Worcs | | 30 | B4 |
| Draughton N York | | 58 | D4 |
| Draughton Nhants | | 41 | Q11 |
| Drax N York | | 59 | P8 |
| Draycote Warwks | | 41 | K12 |
| Draycott Gloucs | | 30 | F7 |
| Draycott Somset | | 17 | L6 |
| Draycott in the Clay Staffs | | 40 | F2 |
| Draycott in the Moors Staffs | | 50 | C11 |
| Drayton C Port | | 9 | R6 |
| Drayton Leics | | 42 | B10 |
| Drayton Norfk | | 45 | K7 |
| Drayton Oxon | | 19 | N2 |
| Drayton Oxon | | 31 | K6 |
| Drayton Somset | | 17 | K10 |
| Drayton Worcs | | 40 | B11 |
| Drayton Bassett Staffs | | 40 | F6 |
| Drayton Beauchamp Bucks | | 20 | E2 |
| Drayton Manor Park Staffs | | 40 | G7 |
| Drayton Parslow Bucks | | 32 | B10 |
| Drayton St Leonard Oxon | | 19 | P2 |
| Dreen Hill Pembks | | 24 | G6 |
| Drefach Carmth | | 25 | N2 |
| Drefach Carmth | | 26 | D6 |
| Drefach Cerdgn | | 36 | H10 |
| Dreghorn N Ayrs | | 76 | F4 |
| Drellingore Kent | | 13 | N2 |
| Drem E Loth | | 87 | K6 |
| Dresden C Stke | | 50 | B11 |
| Drewsteignton Devon | | 5 | P3 |
| Driffield E R Yk | | 60 | H3 |
| Driffield Gloucs | | 18 | F2 |
| Drift Cnwll | | 2 | C9 |
| Drigg Cumb | | 62 | C3 |
| Drighlington Leeds | | 58 | G8 |
| Drimnin Highld | | 89 | L5 |
| Drimpton Dorset | | 7 | K2 |
| Drimsallie Highld | | 90 | C1 |
| Dringhouses C York | | 59 | N4 |
| Drinkstone Suffk | | 34 | F5 |
| Drinkstone Green Suffk | | 34 | F5 |
| Droitwich Spa Worcs | | 30 | B2 |
| Dron P & K | | 92 | H11 |
| Dronfield Derbys | | 51 | J5 |
| Drongan E Ayrs | | 76 | H7 |
| Dronley Angus | | 93 | L8 |
| Droop Dorset | | 7 | Q2 |
| Droxford Hants | | 9 | Q4 |
| Droylsden Tamesd | | 50 | B2 |
| Druid Denbgs | | 48 | B6 |
| Druidston Pembks | | 24 | F5 |
| Druimarbin Highld | | 90 | E3 |
| Druimavuic Ag & B | | 90 | D7 |
| Druimdrishaig Ag & B | | 83 | L8 |
| Druimindarroch Highld | | 97 | J3 |
| Drum Ag & B | | 83 | P7 |
| Drum P & K | | 86 | C2 |
| Drumalbin S Lans | | 78 | E2 |
| Drumbeg Highld | | 108 | C8 |
| Drumblade Abers | | 102 | D7 |
| Drumbreddon D & G | | 68 | E9 |
| Drumbuie Highld | | 97 | K4 |
| Drumburgh Cumb | | 71 | L4 |
| Drumburn D & G | | 70 | E5 |
| Drumchapel C Glas | | 85 | J8 |
| Drumchastle P & K | | 91 | Q5 |
| Drumclog S Lans | | 77 | L4 |
| Drumeldrie Fife | | 87 | J2 |
| Drumelzier Border | | 79 | J3 |
| Drumfearn Highld | | 97 | J6 |
| Drumfrennie Abers | | 95 | M3 |
| Drumgley Angus | | 93 | M5 |
| Drumguish Highld | | 99 | L8 |
| Drumin Moray | | 101 | J8 |
| Drumjohn D & G | | 77 | J10 |
| Drumlamford S Ayrs | | 68 | H4 |
| Drumlasie Abers | | 95 | K2 |
| Drumleaning Cumb | | 71 | L5 |
| Drumlemble Ag & B | | 75 | K8 |
| Drumlithie Abers | | 95 | N6 |
| Drummoddie D & G | | 69 | K8 |
| Drummore D & G | | 68 | F10 |
| Drummuir Moray | | 101 | M6 |
| Drumnadrochit Highld | | 98 | G3 |
| Drumnagorrach Moray | | 102 | C5 |
| Drumpark D & G | | 78 | E11 |
| Drumrunie Lodge Highld | | 106 | C2 |
| Drumshang S Ayrs | | 76 | E8 |
| Drumuie Highld | | 104 | F11 |
| Drumuillie Highld | | 99 | P5 |
| Drumvaich Stirlg | | 85 | L3 |
| Drunzie P & K | | 86 | D1 |
| Drybeck Cumb | | 64 | C5 |
| Drybridge Moray | | 101 | N3 |
| Drybridge N Ayrs | | 76 | F4 |
| Drybrook Gloucs | | 28 | H5 |
| Dryburgh Border | | 80 | D7 |
| Dry Doddington Lincs | | 42 | C2 |
| Dry Drayton Cambs | | 33 | L4 |
| Drymen Stirlg | | 84 | H5 |
| Drymuir Abers | | 103 | J6 |
| Drynoch Highld | | 96 | E4 |
| Dubford Abers | | 102 | G3 |
| Duchally Highld | | 108 | G11 |
| Ducklington Oxon | | 31 | J11 |
| Duddenhoe End Essex | | 33 | M9 |
| Duddingston C Edin | | 86 | F7 |
| Duddington Nhants | | 42 | E9 |
| Duddlestone Somset | | 16 | H11 |
| Duddo Nthumb | | 81 | K6 |
| Duddon Ches W | | 49 | K3 |
| Dudleston Shrops | | 48 | G7 |
| Dudleston Heath Shrops | | 48 | G7 |
| Dudley Dudley | | 40 | C9 |
| Dudley N Tyne | | 73 | M6 |
| Dudley Port Sandw | | 40 | C8 |
| Dudsbury Dorset | | 8 | F7 |
| Duffield Derbys | | 51 | J11 |
| Duffryn Neath | | 26 | H9 |
| Dufftown Moray | | 101 | L7 |
| Duffus Moray | | 101 | J2 |
| Dufton Cumb | | 64 | C3 |
| Duggleby N York | | 60 | F2 |
| Duirinish Highld | | 97 | L4 |
| Duisdalemore Highld | | 97 | J7 |
| Duisky Highld | | 90 | D2 |
| Duke Street Suffk | | 34 | H8 |
| Dukinfield Tamesd | | 50 | C2 |
| Dukinfield Crematorium Tamesd | | 50 | C2 |
| Dulcote Somset | | 17 | N7 |
| Dulford Devon | | 6 | E2 |
| Dull P & K | | 92 | B6 |
| Dullatur N Lans | | 85 | M7 |
| Dullingham Cambs | | 33 | Q5 |
| Dulnain Bridge Highld | | 99 | P4 |
| Duloe Bed | | 32 | G5 |
| Duloe Cnwll | | 4 | F8 |
| Dulverton Somset | | 16 | C9 |
| Dulwich Gt Lon | | 21 | M8 |
| Dumbarton W Duns | | 84 | G7 |
| Dumbleton Gloucs | | 30 | D7 |
| Dumfries D & G | | 70 | F1 |
| Dumgoyne Stirlg | | 85 | J6 |
| Dummer Hants | | 19 | P10 |
| Dumpton Kent | | 23 | Q9 |
| Dun Angus | | 95 | L9 |
| Dunalastair P & K | | 91 | Q5 |
| Dunan Ag & B | | 84 | C8 |
| Dunan Highld | | 96 | G4 |
| Dunan P & K | | 91 | L5 |
| Dunaverty Ag & B | | 75 | K10 |
| Dunball Somset | | 17 | J7 |
| Dunbar E Loth | | 87 | M6 |
| Dunbeath Highld | | 110 | D9 |
| Dunbeg Ag & B | | 90 | B9 |
| Dunblane Stirlg | | 85 | N3 |
| Dunbog Fife | | 93 | K11 |
| Duncanston Highld | | 107 | J10 |
| Duncanstone Abers | | 102 | D9 |
| Dunchideock Devon | | 6 | B5 |
| Dunchurch Warwks | | 41 | L12 |
| Duncow D & G | | 78 | F11 |
| Duncrievie P & K | | 86 | D1 |
| Duncton W Susx | | 10 | F6 |
| Dundee C Dund | | 93 | M9 |
| Dundee Airport C Dund | | 93 | L9 |
| Dundee Crematorium C Dund | | 93 | L8 |
| Dundon Somset | | 17 | L9 |
| Dundonald S Ayrs | | 76 | F5 |
| Dundonnell Highld | | 106 | B5 |
| Dundraw Cumb | | 71 | K5 |
| Dundreggan Highld | | 98 | D6 |
| Dundrennan D & G | | 70 | C6 |
| Dundry N Som | | 17 | N3 |
| Dunecht Abers | | 95 | G12 |
| Dunfermline Crematorium Fife | | 86 | D5 |
| Dunfield Gloucs | | 18 | G2 |
| Dungavel S Lans | | 77 | L4 |
| Dungeness Kent | | 13 | L6 |
| Dunham-on-the-Hill Ches W | | 49 | J2 |
| Dunham-on-Trent Notts | | 52 | B8 |
| Dunhampton Worcs | | 39 | Q8 |
| Dunham Town Traffd | | 57 | N10 |
| Dunham Woodhouses Traffd | | 57 | N10 |
| Dunholme Lincs | | 52 | E7 |
| Dunino Fife | | 93 | P12 |
| Dunipace Falk | | 85 | N6 |
| Dunkeld P & K | | 92 | F7 |
| Dunkerton BaNES | | 17 | Q4 |
| Dunkeswell Devon | | 6 | F2 |
| Dunkeswick N York | | 58 | H5 |
| Dunkirk Kent | | 23 | L10 |
| Dunkirk S Glos | | 18 | B4 |

Dunk's Green Kent 22 C11
Dunlappie Angus 95 K8
Dunley Worcs 39 P8
Dunlop E Ayrs 76 G2
Dunmaglass Highld 98 H5
Dunmore Falk 85 P5
Dunnet Highld 110 E2
Dunnichen Angus 93 N6
Dunning P & K 92 F11
Dunnington C York 59 P4
Dunnington E R Yk 61 K4
Dunnington Warwks 30 E4
Dunoon Ag & B 84 C7
Dunphail Moray 100 F5
Dunragit D & G 68 F7
Duns Border 80 G4
Dunsby Lincs 42 F5
Dunscore D & G 78 E11
Dunscroft Donc 59 P11
Dunsdale R & Cl 66 E4
Dunsden Green Oxon 20 B7
Dunsdon Devon 14 F9
Dunsfold Surrey 10 G3
Dunsford Devon 5 Q3
Dunshalt Fife 93 J12
Dunshillock Abers 103 K5
Dunsill Notts 51 L8
Dunsley N York 67 J5
Dunsley Staffs 39 Q5
Dunsmore Bucks 20 D3
Dunsop Bridge Lancs 63 M11
Dunstable C Beds 32 E11
Dunstall Staffs 40 F4
Dunstan Nthumb 81 Q9
Dunster Somset 16 D7
Duns Tew Oxon 31 L8
Dunston Gatesd 73 M8
Dunston Lincs 52 F10
Dunston Norfk 45 K9
Dunston Staffs 40 B4
Dunstone Devon 5 M9
Dunstone Devon 5 P5
Dunsville Donc 59 N11
Dunswell E R Yk 61 J7
Dunsyre S Lans 86 C11
Dunterton Devon 4 H4
Duntisbourne Abbots Gloucs 29 N7
Duntisbourne Rouse Gloucs 29 P7
Duntish Dorset 7 Q2
Duntocher W Duns 84 H8
Dunton Bucks 32 B11
Dunton C Beds 33 J7
Dunton Norfk 44 E4
Dunton Bassett Leics 41 M8
Dunton Green Kent 21 P11
Duntulm Highld 104 F7
Dunure S Ayrs 76 E8
Dunvant Swans 26 D9
Dunvegan Highld 104 C11
Dunwich Suffk 35 P3
Durgan Cnwll 2 H9
Durham Dur 73 M11
Durham Cathedral Dur 73 M11
Durham Crematorium Dur 73 M11
Durham Services Dur 73 N12
Durham Tees Valley Airport S on T 65 P5
Durisdeer D & G 78 E8
Durisdeermill D & G 78 E7
Durleigh Somset 16 H8
Durley Hants 9 N4
Durley Wilts 19 J7
Durley Street Hants 9 N4
Durlock Kent 23 P10
Durlock Kent 23 P9
Durness Highld 108 G3
Durno Abers 102 F9
Duror Highld 90 D5
Durran Ag & B 83 P2
Durrington W Susx 10 H8
Durrington Wilts 18 H10
Durris Abers 95 M3
Dursley Gloucs 29 K8
Dursley Cross Gloucs 29 J5
Durston Somset 16 H9
Durweston Dorset 8 C6
Duston Nhants 31 Q2
Duthil Highld 99 P4
Dutton Ches W 57 L11
Duxford Cambs 33 M7
Duxford Oxon 19 L2
Duxford IWM Cambs 33 M7
Dwygyfylchi Conwy 55 K6
Dwyran IoA 54 F8
Dyce C Aber 103 J11
Dyffryn Ardudwy Gwynd 47 J6
Dyffryn Cellwen Neath 27 J6
Dyke Lincs 42 F5
Dyke Moray 100 F4
Dykehead Angus 93 J4
Dykehead Angus 94 F9
Dykehead N Lans 85 P10
Dykehead Stirlg 85 K4
Dykelands Abers 95 M3
Dykends Angus 93 J4
Dykeside Abers 102 F6
Dymchurch Kent 13 L4
Dymock Gloucs 29 J3
Dyrham S Glos 17 Q2
Dysart Fife 86 G4
Dyserth Denbgs 56 C11

E

Eagland Hill Lancs 62 H12
Eagle Lincs 52 C9
Eaglesfield Cumb 70 H9
Eaglesfield D & G 71 K1
Eaglesham E Rens 85 J11
Eagley Bolton 57 N6
Eakring Notts 51 P8
Ealand N Linc 60 D10
Ealing Gt Lon 21 J7
Eals Nthumb 72 C9
Eamont Bridge Cumb 71 Q9
Earby Lancs 58 B5
Eardington Shrops 39 N4
Eardisland Herefs 38 H9
Eardisley Herefs 38 F11
Eardiston Shrops 48 G9
Eardiston Worcs 39 M8
Earith Cambs 33 L2
Earlestown St Hel 57 L9

Earley Wokham 20 C8
Earlham Norfk 45 K8
Earlham Crematorium Norfk 45 K8
Earlish Highld 104 E9
Earls Barton Nhants 32 C4
Earls Colne Essex 34 E10
Earls Common Worcs 30 C3
Earl's Croome Worcs 29 M1
Earlsdon Covtry 40 H10
Earlsferry Fife 87 J3
Earlsfield Gt Lon 21 K8
Earlsford Abers 102 H8
Earlsheaton Kirk 58 H9
Earl Shilton Leics 41 L7
Earl Soham Suffk 35 K4
Earl Sterndale Derbys 50 E7
Earlston Border 80 D6
Earlston E Ayrs 76 G4
Earlswood Surrey 21 L12
Earlswood Warwks 40 E11
Earnley W Susx 10 D10
Earsdon N Tyne 73 N6
Earsham Norfk 45 M11
Eartham W Susx 10 F8
Easby N York 66 E6
Easdale Ag & B 89 P11
Easebourne W Susx 10 E5
Easenhall Warwks 41 L10
Eashing Surrey 10 F2
Easington Bucks 31 P11
Easington Dur 73 P11
Easington E R Yk 61 P9
Easington R & Cl 66 G4
Easington Colliery Dur 73 Q11
Easington Lane Sundld 73 P10
Easingwold N York 66 D12
Eassie and Nevay Angus 93 L6
East Aberthaw V Glam 16 D3
East Allington Devon 5 P9
East Anstey Devon 15 P6
East Ashey IoW 9 P9
East Ashling W Susx 10 D8
East Ayton N York 67 L9
East Barkwith Lincs 52 G7
East Barming Kent 22 E11
East Barnby N York 66 H5
East Barnet Gt Lon 21 L4
East Barns E Loth 87 N7
East Barsham Norfk 44 F4
East Beckham Norfk 45 J3
East Bedfont Gt Lon 20 H8
East Bergholt Suffk 34 H9
East Bilney Norfk 44 F6
East Blatchington E Susx 11 P9
East Boldre Hants 9 L7
Eastbourne Darltn 65 N5
Eastbourne E Susx 12 C9
Eastbourne Crematorium E Susx 12 D9
East Bradenham Norfk 44 F8
East Brent Somset 17 J6
Eastbridge Suffk 35 P4
East Bridgford Notts 51 P11
East Buckland Devon 15 L6
East Budleigh Devon 6 E6
Eastburn C Brad 58 D5
Eastbury Herts 20 H5
Eastbury W Berk 19 K5
East Butterwick N Linc 52 B3
Eastby N York 58 D4
East Calder W Loth 86 C8
East Carleton Norfk 45 K9
East Carlton Leeds 58 G5
East Carlton Nhants 42 B11
East Chaldon (Chaldon Herring) Dorset 8 B10
East Challow Oxon 19 L3
East Charleton Devon 5 P10
East Chelborough Dorset 7 M2
East Chiltington E Susx 11 M7
East Chinnock Somset 17 L12
East Chisenbury Wilts 18 G9
Eastchurch Kent 23 J8
East Clandon Surrey 20 G11
East Claydon Bucks 31 Q8
East Coker Somset 7 M1
Eastcombe Gloucs 29 M7
East Compton Somset 17 N7
East Cornworthy Devon 6 B10
Eastcote Gt Lon 20 H6
Eastcote Nhants 31 P4
Eastcote Solhll 40 G10
Eastcott Wilts 18 F9
Eastcott Cnwll 14 E9
East Cottingwith E R Yk 60 C6
Eastcourt Wilts 19 J8
East Cowes IoW 9 N8
East Cowick E R Yk 59 N9
East Cowton N York 65 N6
East Cranmore Somset 17 P7
East Dean E Susx 12 C9
East Dean Gloucs 28 H5
East Dean Hants 9 J3
East Dean W Susx 10 E7
East Devon Crematorium Devon 6 E4
East Drayton Notts 51 Q6
East Dulwich Gt Lon 21 M8
East Dundry N Som 17 N3
East Ella C KuH 60 H8
Eastend Essex 22 H5
East End Hants 9 L7
East End Hants 19 M8
East End Kent 12 G3
East End Oxon 31 K10
East End Somset 17 P6
Easter Balmoral Abers 94 E3
Easter Compton S Glos 28 G11
Easter Dalziel Highld 107 M11
Eastergate W Susx 10 F8
Easterhouse C Glas 85 L9
Easter Howgate Mdloth 86 F9
Easter Kinkell Highld 107 J10
Easter Moniack Highld 98 H1
Easter Ord Abers 95 N2
Easter Pitkierie Fife 87 L2
Easter Skeld Shet 111 k4
Easter Softlaw Border 80 G7
Easterton Wilts 18 F9
East Everleigh Wilts 18 H9
East Farleigh Kent 22 E11
East Farndon Nhants 41 Q9
East Ferry Lincs 52 B4
Eastfield N Lans 85 P9
Eastfield N York 67 M10

East Fortune E Loth 87 K6
East Garston W Berk 19 L6
Eastgate Dur 72 G12
Eastgate Norfk 45 J5
East Goscote Leics 41 N5
East Grafton Wilts 19 J8
East Grimstead Wilts 9 J2
East Grinstead W Susx 11 N3
East Guldeford E Susx 12 H4
East Haddon Nhants 31 P1
East Hagbourne Oxon 19 N3
East Halton N Linc 61 K9
East Ham Gt Lon 21 N6
Easthampstead Park Crematorium Br For 20 D9
Easthampton Herefs 38 H9
East Hanney Oxon 19 M3
East Hanningfield Essex 22 F3
East Hardwick Wakefd 59 L9
East Harling Norfk 44 G11
East Harlsey N York 65 Q7
East Harnham Wilts 8 G2
East Harptree BaNES 17 N5
East Harting W Susx 10 C6
East Hatch Wilts 8 D2
East Hatley Cambs 33 J6
East Hauxwell N York 65 K7
East Haven Angus 93 P8
East Heckington Lincs 42 H2
East Hedleyhope Dur 73 K11
East Helmsdale Highld 110 B10
East Hendred Oxon 19 M3
East Heslerton N York 67 K11
East Hoathly E Susx 11 Q6
East Holme Dorset 8 C10
Easthope Shrops 39 K3
Easthorpe Essex 34 F11
East Horrington Somset 17 N6
East Horsley Surrey 20 H11
East Howe Bmouth 8 F8
East Huntington C York 59 N3
East Huntspill Somset 17 J7
East Ilsley W Berk 19 N5
Eastington Devon 15 M9
Eastington Gloucs 29 K7
Eastington Gloucs 30 F10
East Keal Lincs 53 L10
East Kennett Wilts 18 G7
East Keswick Leeds 59 J5
East Kilbride S Lans 85 K11
East Kirkby Lincs 53 K10
East Knighton Dorset 8 B9
East Knoyle Wilts 8 C2
East Lambrook Somset 17 L11
East Lancashire Crematorium Bury 57 P7
Eastlands D & G 70 D2
East Langdon Kent 13 P2
East Langton Leics 41 Q8
East Lavant W Susx 10 D8
East Lavington W Susx 10 F6
East Layton N York 65 L5
East Leake Notts 41 M3
Eastleigh Devon 14 H6
Eastleigh Hants 9 M4
East Lexham Norfk 44 E6
Eastling Kent 23 J11
East Linton E Loth 87 L6
East Lockinge Oxon 19 M4
East London Crematorium Gt Lon 21 N6
East Lound N Linc 52 B4
East Lulworth Dorset 8 C10
East Lutton N York 60 G1
East Lydford Somset 17 N9
East Malling Kent 22 E11
East Marden W Susx 10 D7
East Markham Notts 51 Q6
East Martin Hants 8 F4
East Marton N York 58 B4
East Meon Hants 10 B5
East Mersea Essex 23 K1
East Midlands Airport Leics 41 K3
East Molesey Surrey 21 J9
East Morden Dorset 8 D8
East Morton C Brad 58 E6
East Morton D & G 78 E8
East Ness N York 66 F10
Eastney C Port 9 Q7
Eastnor Herefs 29 K2
East Norton Leics 42 B9
Eastoft N Linc 60 D10
East Ogwell Devon 5 Q6
Easton Cambs 32 G3
Easton Devon 5 P3
Easton Dorset 7 Q8
Easton Hants 9 N2
Easton Lincs 42 D5
Easton Norfk 45 J7
Easton Somset 17 M6
Easton Suffk 35 L5
Easton Wilts 18 D6
Easton Grey Wilts 18 C4
Easton-in-Gordano N Som 17 M2
Easton Maudit Nhants 32 C5
Easton-on-the-Hill Nhants 42 E8
Easton Royal Wilts 18 H8
East Orchard Dorset 8 C4
East Peckham Kent 12 D2
East Pennar Pembks 24 G8
East Pennard Somset 17 N8
East Perry Cambs 32 G4
East Portlemouth Devon 5 P11
East Prawle Devon 5 Q11
East Preston W Susx 10 H9
East Putford Devon 14 G8
East Quantoxhead Somset 16 F7
East Rainton Sundld 73 N10
East Ravendale NE Lin 52 H4
East Raynham Norfk 44 E5
Eastrea Cambs 43 J10
East Riding Crematorium E R Yk 60 H1
Eastriggs D & G 71 L3
East Rigton Leeds 59 J5
Eastrington E R Yk 60 D8
Eastrop Swindn 18 H3
East Rounton N York 65 Q6
East Rudham Norfk 44 D5
East Runton Norfk 45 K2
East Ruston Norfk 45 M5
Eastry Kent 23 P11
East Saltoun E Loth 87 J8

East Sheen Gt Lon 21 K8
East Shefford W Berk 19 L6
East Stockwith Lincs 52 B5
East Stoke Dorset 8 C9
East Stoke Notts 51 Q10
East Stour Dorset 8 B3
East Stourmouth Kent 23 N10
East Stowford Devon 15 L6
East Stratton Hants 19 P11
East Studdal Kent 23 P12
East Taphouse Cnwll 4 E7
East-the-Water Devon 14 H6
East Thirston Nthumb 73 L2
East Tilbury Thurr 22 D7
East Tisted Hants 10 B4
East Torrington Lincs 52 G6
East Tuddenham Norfk 44 H6
East Tytherley Hants 9 K2
East Tytherton Wilts 18 E6
East Village Devon 15 P10
East Wall Shrops 39 K3
East Walton Norfk 44 C6
East Week Devon 5 N2
Eastwell Leics 41 Q2
East Wellow Hants 9 K4
East Wemyss Fife 86 G3
East Whitburn W Loth 85 Q9
Eastwick Herts 21 N2
East Wickham Gt Lon 21 P7
East Williamston Pembks 25 J7
East Winch Norfk 44 B6
East Winterslow Wilts 9 J1
East Wittering W Susx 10 C9
East Witton N York 65 K9
Eastwood Notts 51 L10
Eastwood Sthend 22 G6
East Woodburn Nthumb 72 G4
East Woodhay Hants 19 L8
East Worldham Hants 10 C3
East Wretham Norfk 44 F11
East Youlstone Devon 14 E8
Eathorpe Warwks 31 K1
Eaton Ches E 49 Q3
Eaton Ches W 49 L3
Eaton Leics 41 B4
Eaton Norfk 45 K8
Eaton Notts 51 P5
Eaton Oxon 31 K12
Eaton Shrops 39 J4
Eaton Bray C Beds 32 D11
Eaton Constantine Shrops 39 L2
Eaton Green C Beds 32 D11
Eaton Hastings Oxon 19 J2
Eaton Mascott Shrops 39 K2
Eaton Socon Cambs 32 G5
Eaton upon Tern Shrops 49 M10
Ebberston N York 67 K10
Ebbesborne Wake Wilts 8 E3
Ebbw Vale Blae G 27 N6
Ebchester Dur 73 K9
Ebford Devon 6 D5
Ebley Gloucs 29 L7
Ebnal Ches W 49 J6
Ebrington Gloucs 30 F6
Ecchinswell Hants 19 N8
Ecclaw Border 87 P8
Ecclefechan D & G 71 K1
Eccles Border 80 G6
Eccles Kent 22 E10
Eccles Salfd 57 P8
Ecclesall Sheff 50 H4
Ecclesfield Sheff 51 J3
Eccleshall Staffs 49 P9
Eccleshill C Brad 58 F6
Ecclesmachan W Loth 86 C7
Eccles Road Norfk 44 G11
Eccleston Ches W 48 H3
Eccleston Lancs 57 K5
Eccleston St Hel 57 J9
Echt Abers 95 M2
Eckford Border 80 F8
Eckington Derbys 51 K5
Eckington Worcs 29 N1
Ecton Nhants 32 B4
Edale Derbys 50 E4
Eday Ork 111 h1
Eday Airport Ork 111 h1
Edburton W Susx 11 K7
Edderton Highld 107 L5
Eddleston Border 86 F11
Eddlewood S Lans 85 M11
Edenbridge Kent 11 N2
Edenfield Lancs 57 P5
Edenhall Cumb 71 Q8
Edenham Lincs 42 F6
Eden Park Gt Lon 21 M9
Eden Project Cnwll 3 M5
Edensor Derbys 50 G6
Edentaggart Ag & B 84 F4
Edenthorpe Donc 59 N11
Edern Gwynd 46 E4
Edgbaston Birm 40 D9
Edgcott Bucks 31 P9
Edgcott Somset 15 P4
Edge Gloucs 29 L6
Edgefield Norfk 44 H4
Edgefield Green Norfk 44 H4
Edgerton Kirk 58 F10
Edgeworth Gloucs 29 N7
Edgmond Wrekin 49 N10
Edgton Shrops 38 H5
Edgware Gt Lon 21 J5
Edgworth Bl w D 57 N5
Edinbane Highld 104 D11
Edinburgh C Edin 86 F7
Edinburgh Airport C Edin 86 D7
Edinburgh Castle C Edin 86 F7
Edinburgh Old & New Town C Edin 86 F7
Edinburgh Royal Botanic Gardens C Edin 86 E7
Edinburgh Zoo C Edin 86 E7
Edingale Staffs 40 G5
Edingham D & G 70 D3
Edingley Notts 51 P9
Edingthorpe Norfk 45 M4
Edingthorpe Green Norfk 45 M4
Edington Nthumb 73 K4
Edington Somset 17 K8
Edington Wilts 18 D9
Edington Burtle Somset 17 K7
Edingworth Somset 17 J5
Edithmead Somset 17 J6
Edith Weston Rutlnd 42 D8

Edlesborough Bucks 32 D11
Edlingham Nthumb 81 M11
Edlington Lincs 52 H8
Edmondsham Dorset 8 F5
Edmondsley Dur 73 M10
Edmondthorpe Leics 42 C6
Edmonton Gt Lon 21 M5
Edmundbyers Dur 72 H10
Ednam Border 80 G6
Ednaston Derbys 40 H2
Edradynate P & K 92 D5
Edrom Border 80 H3
Edstaston Shrops 49 K8
Edstone Warwks 30 F2
Edvin Loach Herefs 39 M9
Edwalton Notts 41 N1
Edwinstowe Notts 51 N7
Edworth C Beds 32 H8
Edwyn Ralph Herefs 39 M9
Edzell Angus 95 K7
Edzell Woods Abers 95 K7
Efail-fach Neath 26 G9
Efail Isaf Rhondd 27 M11
Efailnewydd Gwynd 46 F4
Efailwen Carmth 25 K4
Efenechtyd Denbgs 48 C4
Effgill D & G 79 L9
Effingham Surrey 20 H11
Efford Crematorium C Plym 5 K8
Egerton Bolton 57 N6
Egerton Kent 12 H1
Eggborough N York 59 M9
Eggbuckland C Plym 5 K8
Eggesford Devon 15 M9
Eggington C Beds 32 D10
Egginton Derbys 40 H2
Eggleston Dur 64 H3
Egham Surrey 20 G8
Egleton Rutlnd 42 C8
Eglingham Nthumb 81 M9
Egloshayle Cnwll 3 M3
Egloskerry Cnwll 4 G3
Eglwysbach Conwy 55 L7
Eglwys Cross Wrexhm 49 J7
Eglwyswrw Pembks 25 K2
Egmanton Notts 51 Q7
Egremont Cumb 70 G12
Egremont Wirral 56 G9
Egton N York 66 H6
Egton Bridge N York 66 H6
Egypt Bucks 20 F6
Eigg Highld 96 F11
Eight Ash Green Essex 34 F10
Eilanreach Highld 97 L6
Eilean Donan Castle Highld 97 M5
Elan Valley Powys 37 P7
Elan Village Powys 37 Q7
Elberton S Glos 28 H10
Elburton C Plym 5 L9
Elcombe Swindn 18 G5
Eldersfield Worcs 29 L3
Elderslie Rens 84 H9
Eldon Dur 65 M2
Elerch Cerdgn 37 L4
Elfhill Abers 95 N5
Elford Staffs 40 F5
Elgin Moray 101 J3
Elgol Highld 96 G6
Elham Kent 13 M2
Elie Fife 87 K3
Elim IoA 54 E3
Eling Hants 9 L5
Elkesley Notts 51 P6
Elkstone Gloucs 29 N6
Ella Abers 102 E4
Ellacombe Torbay 6 C9
Elland Calder 58 E9
Ellary Ag & B 83 L7
Ellastone Staffs 50 E11
Ellel Lancs 63 J10
Ellemford Border 87 N9
Ellenabeich Ag & B 89 P11
Ellenhall Staffs 49 Q9
Ellen's Green Surrey 10 H3
Ellerbeck N York 66 B8
Ellerby N York 66 H5
Ellerdine Heath Wrekin 49 L10
Elleric Ag & B 90 E6
Ellerker E R Yk 60 F8
Ellerton E R Yk 60 C6
Ellerton N York 65 M7
Ellesborough Bucks 20 D3
Ellesmere Shrops 48 H8
Ellesmere Port Ches W 56 H12
Ellingham Norfk 45 N10
Ellingham Nthumb 81 N8
Ellingstring N York 65 L10
Ellington Cambs 32 G3
Ellington Nthumb 73 M3
Elliots Green Somset 18 B10
Ellisfield Hants 19 Q10
Ellishader Highld 104 G8
Ellistown Leics 41 K5
Ellon Abers 103 K8
Ellonby Cumb 71 N8
Elloughton E R Yk 60 F8
Ellwood Gloucs 28 G7
Elm Cambs 43 M8
Elmbridge Worcs 30 B1
Elmdon Essex 33 M8
Elmdon Solhll 40 F10
Elmers End Gt Lon 21 M9
Elmer's Green Lancs 57 J7
Elmesthorpe Leics 41 L8
Elmhurst Staffs 40 E5
Elmley Castle Worcs 29 N1
Elmley Lovett Worcs 39 Q8
Elmore Gloucs 29 K6
Elmore Back Gloucs 29 K5
Elm Park Gt Lon 21 Q6
Elmsett Suffk 34 H7
Elmstead Market Essex 34 H10
Elmsted Kent 13 L2
Elmstone Kent 23 N10
Elmstone Hardwicke Gloucs 29 M4
Elmswell E R Yk 60 G3
Elmswell Suffk 34 G4
Elmton Derbys 51 L6
Elphin Highld 108 E12
Elphinstone E Loth 86 H8
Elrick Abers 95 N1
Elrig D & G 69 J9
Elrington Nthumb 72 F8
Elsdon Nthumb 72 H3
Elsenham Essex 33 N10
Elsfield Oxon 31 M11

Elsham N Linc 60 H10
Elsing Norfk 44 H6
Elslack N York 58 B4
Elson Hants 9 P7
Elsrickle S Lans 86 C12
Elstead Surrey 10 E2
Elsted W Susx 10 D6
Elsthorpe Lincs 42 F5
Elston Notts 51 Q10
Elstow Bed 32 F7
Elstree Herts 21 J4
Elstronwick E R Yk 61 L7
Elswick Lancs 56 H2
Elswick N u Ty 73 M7
Elsworth Cambs 33 K4
Elterwater Cumb 62 G2
Eltham Gt Lon 21 N8
Eltham Crematorium Gt Lon 21 N8
Eltisley Cambs 33 J5
Elton Cambs 42 F10
Elton Ches W 49 J1
Elton Derbys 50 G8
Elton Herefs 39 J7
Elton Notts 51 Q11
Elton S on T 65 P4
Eltringham Nthumb 73 J8
Elvanfoot S Lans 78 F5
Elvaston Derbys 41 K2
Elveden Suffk 34 D2
Elvetham Heath Hants 20 C11
Elvingston E Loth 87 J7
Elvington C York 60 C5
Elvington Kent 23 P12
Elwick Hartpl 66 C2
Elworth Ches E 49 N3
Elworthy Somset 16 E8
Ely Cambs 33 N11
Ely Cardif 16 F2
Emberton M Keyn 32 C6
Embleton Cumb 71 J9
Embleton Nthumb 81 P9
Embo Highld 107 N4
Emborough Somset 17 N6
Embo Street Highld 107 N4
Embsay N York 58 D4
Emery Down Hants 9 K6
Emley Kirk 58 G10
Emmington Oxon 20 C3
Emneth Norfk 43 M8
Emneth Hungate Norfk 43 N8
Empingham Rutlnd 42 D8
Empshott Hants 10 C4
Emstrey Crematorium Shrops 49 K12
Emsworth Hants 10 C8
Enborne W Berk 19 M7
Enborne Row W Berk 19 M7
Enderby Leics 41 M7
Endmoor Cumb 63 K5
Endon Staffs 50 B9
Endon Bank Staffs 50 B9
Enfield Gt Lon 21 M4
Enfield Crematorium Gt Lon 21 M4
Enfield Lock Gt Lon 21 M4
Enfield Wash Gt Lon 21 M4
Enford Wilts 18 G9
Engine Common S Glos 29 J11
Englefield W Berk 19 Q6
Englefield Green Surrey 20 F8
English Bicknor Gloucs 28 G5
Englishcombe BaNES 17 Q4
English Frankton Shrops 49 J9
Enham-Alamein Hants 19 L10
Enmore Somset 16 H8
Enmore Green Dorset 8 C3
Ennerdale Bridge Cumb 70 H11
Enochdhu P & K 92 F3
Ensay Ag & B 88 H6
Ensbury Bmouth 8 F8
Ensdon Shrops 48 H11
Enstone Oxon 31 J8
Enterkinfoot D & G 78 E7
Enville Staffs 39 P5
Eolaigearraidh W Isls 111 a6
Epney Gloucs 29 K6
Epperstone Notts 51 P10
Epping Essex 21 P3
Epping Green Essex 21 N3
Epping Upland Essex 21 N3
Eppleby N York 65 L9
Epsom Surrey 21 K10
Epwell Oxon 31 J6
Epworth N Linc 52 A3
Erbistock Wrexhm 48 G7
Erdington Birm 40 E8
Eridge Green E Susx 12 B3
Erines Ag & B 83 N7
Eriska Ag & B 90 C7
Eriskay W Isls 111 b6
Eriswell Suffk 34 C2
Erith Gt Lon 21 P7
Erlestoke Wilts 18 E9
Ermington Devon 5 M9
Erpingham Norfk 45 J4
Errogie Highld 98 H5
Errol P & K 93 J10
Erskine Rens 84 H8
Erskine Bridge Rens 84 H8
Ervie D & G 68 D5
Erwarton Suffk 35 K9
Erwood Powys 38 C12
Eryholme N York 65 N6
Eryrys Denbgs 48 E4
Escomb Dur 65 L2
Escrick N York 59 N5
Esgairgeiliog Powys 47 M9
Esh Dur 73 L11
Esher Surrey 21 J9
Eshott Nthumb 73 L2
Esh Winning Dur 73 L11
Eskadale Highld 98 F2
Eskbank Mdloth 86 G8
Eskdale Green Cumb 62 D3
Eskdalemuir D & G 79 L8
Esprick Lancs 56 H2
Essendine Rutlnd 42 F7
Essendon Herts 21 L2
Essich Highld 99 J3
Essington Staffs 40 C6
Esslemont Abers 103 J8
Eston R & Cl 66 D4
Etal Nthumb 81 K6
Etchilhampton Wilts 18 F8
Etchingham E Susx 12 E5
Etchinghill Kent 13 M3

Etchinghill Staffs 40 D4
Eton W & M 20 F7
Eton Wick W & M 20 F7
Etruria C Stke 49 Q6
Etteridge Highld 99 K9
Ettersgill Dur 64 F2
Ettiley Heath Ches E 49 N4
Ettingshall Wolves 40 B8
Ettington Warwks 30 H4
Etton C Pete 42 G8
Etton E R Yk 60 G5
Ettrick Border 79 L6
Ettrickbridge Border 79 N4
Ettrickhill Border 79 L6
Etwall Derbys 40 H2
Euston Suffk 34 E2
Euxton Lancs 57 K5
Evanton Highld 107 K8
Evedon Lincs 42 F1
Evelix Highld 107 N4
Evenjobb Powys 38 F9
Evenley Nhants 31 N4
Evenlode Gloucs 30 G8
Evenwood Dur 65 K3
Evercreech Somset 17 P8
Everingham E R Yk 60 D6
Everleigh Wilts 18 H9
Eversholt C Beds 32 E9
Evershot Dorset 7 N2
Eversley Hants 20 C10
Eversley Cross Hants 20 C10
Everthorpe E R Yk 60 F7
Everton C Beds 32 H6
Everton Hants 9 K8
Everton Lpool 56 G9
Everton Notts 51 P3
Evertown D & G 71 M1
Evesbatch Herefs 39 M11
Evesham Worcs 30 D5
Evington C Leic 41 N6
Ewden Village Sheff 50 H2
Ewell Surrey 21 K10
Ewell Minnis Kent 13 N2
Ewelme Oxon 19 Q3
Ewen Gloucs 18 E2
Ewenny V Glam 27 J12
Ewerby Lincs 42 G1
Ewhurst Surrey 10 H3
Ewhurst Green E Susx 12 F5
Ewhurst Green Surrey 10 H3
Ewloe Flints 48 F3
Eworthy Devon 5 J2
Ewshot Hants 20 D11
Ewyas Harold Herefs 28 D3
Exbourne Devon 15 K10
Exbury Hants 9 M7
Exebridge Somset 16 C10
Exelby N York 65 N9
Exeter Devon 6 C4
*Exeter Airport Devon 6 D4*
Exeter & Devon Crematorium Devon 6 C5
*Exeter Services Devon 6 C4*
Exford Somset 15 P5
Exfordsgreen Shrops 39 J2
Exhall Warwks 30 E3
Exhall Warwks 41 J9
Exlade Street Oxon 19 Q4
Exminster Devon 6 C5
*Exmoor National Park 15 P4*
Exmouth Devon 6 D6
Exning Suffk 33 P4
Exton Devon 6 D5
Exton Hants 9 Q4
Exton Rutlnd 42 D7
Exton Somset 16 C9
Exwick Devon 6 B4
Eyam Derbys 50 G5
Eydon Nhants 31 M4
Eye C Pete 42 H9
Eye Herefs 39 J8
Eye Suffk 35 J3
Eyemouth Border 81 K2
Eyeworth C Beds 33 J7
Eyhorne Street Kent 22 G11
Eyke Suffk 35 M6
Eynesbury Cambs 32 H5
Eynsford Kent 22 B9
Eynsham Oxon 31 K11
Eype Dorset 7 L5
Eyre Highld 104 F10
Eythorne Kent 23 P12
Eyton Herefs 39 J9
Eyton Shrops 48 H10
Eyton on Severn Shrops 39 L2
Eyton upon the Weald Moors Wrekin 49 M11

## F

Faccombe Hants 19 L8
Faceby N York 66 C7
Fachwen Powys 48 B11
Faddiley Ches E 49 L5
Fadmoor N York 66 F9
Faerdre Swans 26 F8
Faifley W Duns 84 H8
Failand N Som 17 M2
Failford S Ayrs 76 H6
Failsworth Oldham 50 B1
Fairbourne Gwynd 47 K8
Fairburn N York 59 L8
Fairfield Derbys 50 E6
Fairfield Worcs 40 C11
Fairford Gloucs 18 H1
Fairgirth D & G 70 E4
Fairhaven Lancs 56 G4
Fair Isle Shet 111 m5
*Fair Isle Airport Shet 111 m5*
Fairlands Surrey 20 F11
Fairlie N Ayrs 84 D11
Fairlight E Susx 12 G7
Fairmile Devon 6 E4
Fairmile Surrey 20 H10
Fairnilee Border 79 P3
Fair Oak Hants 9 N4
Fairoak Staffs 49 N8
Fair Oak Green Hants 19 Q8
Fairseat Kent 22 D10
Fairstead Essex 34 C12
Fairstead Norfk 43 Q6
Fairwarp E Susx 11 P5
Fairwater Cardif 27 N12
Fairy Cross Devon 14 G7

Fakenham Norfk 44 F4
Fakenham Magna Suffk 34 E2
Fala Mdloth 87 J9
Fala Dam Mdloth 87 J9
Faldingworth Lincs 52 F6
Faldouët Jersey 7 c2
Falfield S Glos 29 J9
Falkenham Suffk 35 L8
Falkirk Falk 85 P7
Falkirk Crematorium Falk 85 P6
*Falkirk Wheel Falk 85 P7*
Falkland Fife 86 F2
Fallburn S Lans 78 F2
Fallin Stirlg 85 N5
Fallodon Nthumb 81 P9
Fallowfield Manch 57 Q9
Fallowfield Nthumb 72 G7
Falls of Blarghour Ag & B 83 Q1
Falmer E Susx 11 M8
Falmouth Cnwll 3 J8
Falnash Border 79 N7
Falsgrave N York 67 M9
Falstone Nthumb 72 D4
Fanagmore Highld 108 D6
Fancott C Beds 32 E10
Fanellan Highld 98 G1
Fangdale Beck N York 66 D8
Fangfoss E R Yk 60 D4
Fanmore Ag & B 89 J7
Fannich Lodge Highld 106 D8
Fans Border 80 E6
Far Bletchley M Keyn 32 C9
Farcet Cambs 42 H10
Far Cotton Nhants 31 Q3
Fareham Hants 9 P6
Far End Cumb 62 F3
Farewell Staffs 40 E5
Faringdon Oxon 19 K2
Farington Lancs 57 K4
Farlam Cumb 71 Q4
Farleigh N Som 17 M3
Farleigh Surrey 21 M10
Farleigh Hungerford Somset 18 B8
Farleigh Wallop Hants 19 Q10
Farlesthorpe Lincs 53 M8
Farleton Cumb 63 K6
Farleton Lancs 63 L8
Farley Staffs 50 E11
Farley Wilts 9 J2
Farley Green Surrey 10 G2
Farley Hill Wokam 20 C9
Farleys End Gloucs 29 K6
Farlington C Port 9 B8
Farlington N York 59 N1
Farlow Shrops 39 L6
Farmborough BaNES 17 P4
Farmcote Gloucs 30 D8
Farmers Carmth 37 K10
Farmington Gloucs 30 F10
Farmoor Oxon 31 L11
Far Moor Wigan 57 K7
Farmtown Moray 101 P5
Farnborough Gt Lon 21 N9
Farnborough Hants 20 E11
Farnborough W Berk 19 M4
Farnborough Warwks 31 K4
Farnborough Park Hants 20 E11
Farnborough Street Hants 20 E11
Farncombe Surrey 10 F2
Farndish Bed 32 D4
Farndon Ches W 48 H5
Farndon Notts 51 Q9
Farne Islands Nthumb 81 P6
Farnell Angus 93 Q5
Farnham Dorset 8 E4
Farnham Essex 33 M10
Farnham N York 59 J3
Farnham Suffk 35 M5
Farnham Surrey 10 D1
Farnham Common Bucks 20 F6
Farnham Royal Bucks 20 F6
Farningham Kent 22 B9
Farnley Leeds 58 G7
Farnley N York 58 G5
Farnley Tyas Kirk 58 F10
Farnsfield Notts 51 P9
Farnworth Bolton 57 N7
Farnworth Halton 57 K10
Far Oakridge Gloucs 29 N7
Farr Highld 99 K3
Farr Highld 99 M8
Farr Highld 109 M3
Farraline Highld 98 H5
Farringdon Devon 6 D5
Farrington Gurney BaNES 17 P5
Far Sawrey Cumb 62 H3
Farthinghoe Nhants 31 M6
Farthingstone Nhants 31 N3
Fartown Leeds 58 F9
Fartown Leeds 58 G7
Fasnacloich Ag & B 90 D6
Fasnakyle Highld 98 D4
Fassfern Highld 90 D1
Fatfield Sundld 73 N9
Fauldhouse W Loth 85 Q10
Faulkbourne Essex 34 D12
Faulkland Somset 17 Q5
Fauls Shrops 49 L8
Faversham Kent 23 K10
Fawdington N York 66 B11
Fawdon N u Ty 73 M7
Fawkham Green Kent 22 C9
Fawler Oxon 31 J10
Fawley Bucks 20 C6
Fawley Hants 9 M6
Fawley W Berk 19 L5
Faxfleet E R Yk 60 E8
Faygate W Susx 11 K4
Fazakerley Lpool 56 G9
Fazeley Staffs 40 G7
Fearby N York 65 L10
Fearn Highld 107 N7
Fearnan P & K 91 Q7
Fearnbeg Highld 105 L9
Fearnmore Highld 105 K9
Fearnoch Ag & B 83 P7
Featherstone Staffs 40 C6
Featherstone Wakefd 59 K9
Feckenham Worcs 30 D2
Feering Essex 34 E11
Feetham N York 64 H7
Felbridge Surrey 11 M3
Felbrigg Norfk 45 K3
Felcourt Surrey 11 M2
Felindre Carmth 25 Q6

Felindre Carmth 26 D5
Felindre Powys 38 D6
Felindre Swans 26 E8
Felindre Farchog Pembks 36 B11
Felingwm Isaf Carmth 26 C4
Felingwm Uchaf Carmth 26 C4
Felixkirk N York 66 C9
Felixstowe Suffk 35 L9
Felling Gatesd 73 M8
Felmersham Bed 32 E5
Felmingham Norfk 45 L4
Felpham W Susx 10 F9
Felsham Suffk 34 F5
Felsted Essex 34 B11
Feltham Gt Lon 20 H8
Felthamhill Surrey 20 H8
Felthorpe Norfk 45 J6
Felton Herefs 39 L11
Felton N Som 17 M3
Felton Nthumb 73 L2
Felton Butler Shrops 48 H11
Feltwell Norfk 44 B11
Fence Lancs 57 P2
Fence Rothm 51 K4
Fencott Oxon 31 M10
Fendike Corner Lincs 53 M10
Fen Ditton Cambs 33 M5
Fen Drayton Cambs 33 K3
Fen Street Norfk 44 G10
Fenham Nthumb 81 N4
Fenn Green Shrops 39 P5
Fenn Street Medway 22 F8
Fenny Bentley Derbys 50 F10
Fenny Bridges Devon 6 F3
Fenny Compton Warwks 31 K4
Fenny Drayton Leics 41 J7
Fenstanton Cambs 33 K3
Fenton Cambs 33 K2
Fenton Cumb 71 Q4
Fenton Lincs 52 B8
Fenton Lincs 52 C12
Fenton Notts 52 B6
Fenton Nthumb 81 K7
Fenton Barns E Loth 87 K6
Fenwick Donc 59 N10
Fenwick E Ayrs 76 H3
Fenwick Nthumb 73 J6
Fenwick Nthumb 81 M6
Feock Cnwll 3 J7
Feolin Ferry Ag & B 82 F8
Fergushill N Ayrs 76 F3
Feriniquarrie Highld 104 B11
Fern Angus 94 H9
Ferndale Rhondd 27 L9
Ferndown Dorset 8 F7
Ferness Highld 100 E6
Fernham Oxon 19 K3
Fernhill Heath Worcs 39 Q9
Fernhurst W Susx 10 E4
Fernie Fife 93 K11
Ferniegair S Lans 85 M11
Fernilea Highld 96 D3
Fernilee Derbys 50 D5
Fernwood Notts 52 B12
Ferrensby N York 59 J3
Ferrindonald Highld 97 J7
Ferring W Susx 10 H9
*Ferrybridge Services Wakefd 59 L9*
Ferryden Angus 95 M9
Ferryhill Dur 65 M2
Ferryhill Station Dur 65 N2
Ferry Point Highld 107 M5
Ferryside Carmth 25 N6
Ferrytown Highld 107 M5
Fersfield Norfk 44 H12
Fersit Highld 91 K2
Feshiebridge Highld 99 M8
Fetcham Surrey 21 J11
Fetlar Shet 111 m2
Fetterangus Abers 103 K5
Fettercairn Abers 95 K7
Fewston N York 58 G4
Ffairfach Carmth 26 E5
Ffair Rhos Cerdgn 37 M7
Ffestiniog Gwynd 47 L3
*Ffestiniog Railway Gwynd 47 K3*
Fforest Carmth 26 D7
Fforest Fach Swans 26 E9
Ffostrasol Cerdgn 36 F10
Ffrith Flints 48 F4
Ffynnongroyw Flints 56 D11
Fiag Lodge Highld 108 H9
Fickleshole Surrey 21 M10
Fiddington Somset 16 G7
Fiddleford Dorset 8 B5
Fiddlers Green Cnwll 3 J5
Field Staffs 40 D2
Field Dalling Norfk 44 G3
Field Head Leics 41 L5
Fifehead Magdalen Dorset 8 B3
Fifehead Neville Dorset 8 B5
Fifehead St Quintin Dorset 8 B5
Fife Keith Moray 101 M5
Fifield Oxon 30 G9
Fifield W & M 20 E7
Figheldean Wilts 18 H10
Filby Norfk 45 P7
Filey N York 67 N10
Filgrave M Keyn 32 C7
Filkins Oxon 30 G12
Filleigh Devon 15 L6
Fillingham Lincs 52 D6
Fillongley Warwks 40 H9
Filton S Glos 28 H11
Fimber E R Yk 60 F3
Finavon Angus 93 N4
Fincham Norfk 44 B8
Finchampstead Wokam 20 C10
Fincharn Ag & B 83 N3
Finchdean Hants 10 B7
Finchingfield Essex 34 B9
Finchley Gt Lon 21 L5
Findern Derbys 40 H2
Findhorn Moray 100 G3
Findhorn Bridge Highld 99 M4
Findochty Moray 101 N2
Findo Gask P & K 92 G10
Findon Abers 95 Q3
Findon W Susx 10 H8
Findon Mains Highld 107 K9
Findrack House Abers 95 K2
Finedon Nhants 32 D3

Fingask P & K 92 H10
Fingest Bucks 20 C5
Finghall N York 65 L9
Fingland D & G 77 M7
Finglesham Kent 23 P11
Fingringhoe Essex 34 G11
Finlarig Stirlg 91 N9
Finmere Oxon 31 N7
Finnart P & K 91 M5
Finningham Suffk 34 H3
Finningley Donc 51 P2
Finsbay W Isls 111 c4
Finstall Worcs 40 C12
Finsthwaite Cumb 62 G5
Finstock Oxon 31 J10
Finstown Ork 111 h2
Fintry Abers 102 G4
Fintry Stirlg 85 K5
Finzean Abers 95 K4
Fionnphort Ag & B 88 G10
Fionnsbhagh W Isls 111 c4
Firbank Cumb 63 L4
Firbeck Rothm 51 M3
Firby N York 60 C2
Firby N York 65 M9
Firle E Susx 11 P8
Firsby Lincs 53 M10
Fir Tree Dur 65 K1
Fishbourne IoW 9 P8
Fishbourne W Susx 10 D8
Fishburn Dur 65 P2
Fishcross Clacks 85 P4
Fisherford Abers 102 E8
Fisherrow E Loth 86 G7
Fisher's Pond Hants 9 N4
Fisherton Highld 107 M11
Fisherton S Ayrs 76 E7
Fisherton de la Mere Wilts 18 E11
Fishguard Pembks 24 G2
Fishlake Donc 59 P10
Fishnish Pier Ag & B 89 N7
Fishponds Bristl 17 P2
Fishtoft Lincs 43 K2
Fishtoft Drove Lincs 43 K1
Fiskavaig Highld 96 D3
Fiskerton Lincs 52 F8
Fiskerton Notts 51 Q9
Fittleton Wilts 18 G10
Fittleworth W Susx 10 G6
Fitz Shrops 49 J11
Fitzhead Somset 16 F9
Fitzwilliam Wakefd 59 K10
Five Ash Down E Susx 11 P5
Five Ashes E Susx 12 B5
Fivehead Somset 17 J10
Fivelanes Cnwll 4 F4
Five Oak Green Kent 12 D2
Five Oaks Jersey 7 c2
Five Oaks W Susx 10 H4
Five Roads Carmth 26 C7
Flackwell Heath Bucks 20 E5
Fladbury Worcs 30 C5
Fladdabister Shet 111 k4
Flagg Derbys 50 F7
Flamborough E R Yk 67 Q12
Flamborough Head E R Yk 67 Q12
*Flamingo Land Theme Park N York 66 H10*
Flamstead Herts 20 H1
Flansham W Susx 10 F9
Flanshaw Wakefd 58 H9
Flasby N York 58 C3
Flash Staffs 50 D7
Flashader Highld 104 D10
Flaunden Herts 20 G4
Flawborough Notts 42 B2
Flawith N York 59 L2
Flax Bourton N Som 17 M3
Flaxby N York 59 K3
Flaxley Gloucs 29 J6
Flaxpool Somset 16 F8
Flaxton N York 59 P2
Fleckney Leics 41 P8
Flecknoe Warwks 31 L2
Fledborough Notts 52 B8
Fleet Dorset 7 P6
Fleet Hants 20 D11
Fleet Lincs 43 L5
Fleet Hargate Lincs 43 L5
*Fleet Services Hants 20 C11*
Fleetwood Lancs 62 G11
Flemingston V Glam 16 D3
Flemington S Lans 85 L10
Flempton Suffk 34 D3
Fletchertown Cumb 71 K7
Fletching E Susx 11 N5
Flexbury Cnwll 14 D10
Flexford Surrey 20 E12
Flimby Cumb 70 G8
Flimwell E Susx 12 E4
Flint Flints 48 E2
Flintham Notts 51 Q10
Flinton E R Yk 61 L7
Flitcham Norfk 44 C5
Flitton C Beds 32 F9
Flitwick C Beds 32 F9
Flixborough N Linc 60 E10
Flixborough Stather N Linc 60 E10
Flixton N York 67 M10
Flixton Suffk 45 M11
Flixton Traffd 57 N9
Flockton Kirk 58 G10
Flockton Green Kirk 58 G10
Flodigarry Highld 104 F7
Flookburgh Cumb 62 G7
Flordon Norfk 45 K10
Flore Nhants 31 N3
Flowton Suffk 34 H7
Flushing Cnwll 3 J8
Fluxton Devon 6 E4
Flyford Flavell Worcs 30 C3
Fobbing Thurr 22 E6
Fochabers Moray 101 L4
Fochriw Caerph 27 M7
Fockerby N Linc 60 E9
Foddington Somset 17 N9
Foel Powys 48 B12
Foggathorpe E R Yk 60 D6
Fogo Border 80 G4
Fogwatt Moray 101 K4
Foindle Highld 108 D6
Folda Angus 94 C8
Fole Staffs 50 D12
Foleshill Covtry 41 J10
Folke Dorset 17 P12
Folkestone Kent 13 N3

Folkingham Lincs....42 F4
Folkington E Susx....12 C8
Folksworth Cambs....42 G11
Folkton N York....67 M10
Folla Rule Abers....102 F8
Follifoot N York....59 J4
Folly Gate Devon....15 K11
Fonthill Bishop Wilts....8 D2
Fonthill Gifford Wilts....8 D2
Fontmell Magna Dorset....8 C4
Fontmell Parva Dorset....8 C5
Fontwell W Susx....10 F8
Foolow Derbys....50 F5
Forbestown Abers....101 M11
Forcett N York....65 L5
Ford Ag & B....83 N3
Ford Bucks....31 Q11
Ford Derbys....51 K5
Ford Devon....14 G7
Ford Gloucs....30 E8
Ford Nthumb....81 K6
Ford Somset....16 E9
Ford Staffs....50 E9
Ford W Susx....10 F8
Ford Wilts....18 C6
Fordcombe Kent....11 Q3
Fordell Fife....86 D5
Forden Powys....38 E2
Ford End Essex....34 B12
Forder Green Devon....5 Q6
Fordham Cambs....33 Q3
Fordham Essex....34 F10
Fordham Norfk....43 P9
Fordingbridge Hants....8 G5
Fordon E R Yk....67 M11
Fordoun Abers....95 M6
Fordstreet Essex....34 F10
Ford Street Somset....16 F11
Fordwich Kent....23 M10
Fordyce Abers....102 D3
Forebridge Staffs....40 B3
Forest Guern....6 b2
Forest Chapel Ches E....50 C6
Forest Gate Gt Lon....21 N6
Forest Green Surrey....10 H2
Forest Hall N Tyne....73 M6
Forest Hill Gt Lon....21 M8
Forest Hill Oxon....31 N11
Forest Lane Head N York....59 J3
Forest Mill Clacks....85 Q4
Forest of Bowland Lancs....63 L10
Forest of Dean Gloucs....28 H6
Forest of Dean
Crematorium Gloucs....28 H6
Forest Park
Crematorium Gt Lon....21 P5
Forest Row E Susx....11 N3
Forestside W Susx....10 C7
Forfar Angus....93 M5
Forgandenny P & K....92 G11
Forge Hammer Torfn....28 C9
Forgie Moray....101 M4
Forgieside Moray....101 M5
Forgue Abers....102 D6
Formby Sefton....56 F7
Forncett End Norfk....45 J10
Forncett St Mary Norfk....45 J10
Forncett St Peter Norfk....45 J10
Fornham All Saints Suffk....34 D4
Fornham St Martin Suffk....34 E4
Fornighty Highld....100 E5
Forres Moray....100 F4
Forsbrook Staffs....50 C11
Forse Highld....110 E8
Forsinard Highld....109 Q7
Fort Augustus Highld....98 E7
Forteviot P & K....92 F11
Forth S Lans....85 Q11
Forthampton Gloucs....29 M3
Forth Rail Bridge C Edin....86 D6
Forth Road Bridge Fife....86 D6
Fortingall P & K....91 Q6
Forton Hants....19 M11
Forton Lancs....63 J11
Forton Shrops....48 H11
Forton Somset....7 J2
Forton Staffs....49 N10
Fortrie Abers....102 E6
Fortrose Highld....107 M10
Fortuneswell Dorset....7 P7
Fort William Highld....90 F2
Forty Hill Gt Lon....21 M4
Fosbury Wilts....19 K8
Foscot Oxon....30 G9
Fosdyke Lincs....43 K4
Foss P & K....92 B4
Fossebridge Gloucs....30 E11
Foster Street Essex....21 P2
Foston Derbys....40 F2
Foston Leics....41 N8
Foston Lincs....42 C2
Foston N York....59 P2
Foston on the Wolds
E R Yk....61 J3
Fotherby Lincs....53 K5
Fotheringhay Nhants....42 F10
Foula Airport Shet....111 J5
Foulden Border....81 K3
Foulden Norfk....44 C9
Foul End Warwks....40 G8
Foulness Island Essex....23 J5
Foulon Vale
Crematorium Guern....6 b2
Foulridge Lancs....58 B6
Foulsham Norfk....44 G5
Fountainhall Border....87 J11
Four Ashes Suffk....34 G3
Four Crosses Powys....48 F10
Four Elms Kent....11 P1
Four Forks Somset....16 G8
Four Gotes Cambs....43 M6
Four Lanes Cnwll....2 G7
Four Marks Hants....9 R1
Four Mile Bridge IoA....54 C6
Four Oaks Birm....40 E7
Four Oaks Solhll....40 G10
Fourpenny Highld....107 N4
Four Roads Carmth....25 Q7
Fourstones Nthumb....72 F7
Four Throws Kent....12 F4
Fovant Wilts....8 E3
Foveran Abers....103 K9
Fowey Cnwll....4 D9
Fowlhall Kent....12 E2
Fowlis Angus....93 K8
Fowlis Wester P & K....92 D10
Fowlmere Cambs....33 L7

Fownhope Herefs....28 G3
Foxbar Rens....84 H10
Foxcote Somset....17 Q5
Foxdale IoM....56 b5
Foxearth Essex....34 D7
Foxfield Cumb....62 E5
Foxhole Cnwll....3 L5
Foxholes N York....67 L11
Foxley Norfk....44 H6
Foxt Staffs....50 D10
Foxton Cambs....33 L7
Foxton Leics....41 P9
Foxton N York....65 Q8
Foxwood Shrops....39 L6
Foy Herefs....28 H3
Foyers Highld....98 G5
Foynesfield Highld....100 D5
Fraddon Cnwll....3 K4
Fradley Staffs....40 F5
Fradswell Staffs....40 C2
Fraisthorpe E R Yk....61 K2
Framfield E Susx....11 P6
Framingham Earl Norfk....45 L9
Framingham Pigot Norfk....45 L9
Framlingham Suffk....35 L4
Frampton Dorset....7 P4
Frampton Lincs....43 K3
Frampton Cotterell S Glos....29 J11
Frampton Mansell Gloucs....29 N8
Frampton-on-Severn
Gloucs....29 K7
Framsden Suffk....35 K5
Framwellgate Moor Dur....73 M11
Franche Worcs....39 P6
Frankby Wirral....56 E10
Frankley Worcs....40 C10
Frankley Services Worcs....40 C10
Frankton Warwks....41 K12
Frant E Susx....12 C3
Fraserburgh Abers....103 K2
Frating Essex....34 H11
Frating Green Essex....34 H11
Fratton C Port....9 Q7
Freathy Cnwll....5 J9
Freckenham Suffk....33 Q3
Freckleton Lancs....56 H3
Freeby Leics....42 B6
Freefolk Hants....19 N10
Freeland Oxon....31 K10
Freethorpe Norfk....45 N9
Freethorpe Common
Norfk....45 N8
Freiston Lincs....43 L2
Fremington Devon....15 J6
Fremington N York....65 J7
Frenchay S Glos....28 H12
Frenich P & K....92 C4
Frensham Surrey....10 D2
Freshfield Sefton....56 F7
Freshford Wilts....18 B8
Freshwater IoW....9 K9
Fressingfield Suffk....35 L2
Freston Suffk....35 J8
Freswick Highld....110 G3
Fretherne Gloucs....29 K6
Frettenham Norfk....45 L6
Freuchie Fife....86 F2
Freystrop Pembks....24 G6
Friar Park Sandw....40 D8
Friday Bridge Cambs....43 M8
Friday Street Suffk....35 N5
Fridaythorpe E R Yk....60 E3
Friern Barnet Gt Lon....21 L5
Friesthorpe Lincs....52 F6
Frieston Lincs....42 D1
Frieth Bucks....20 C5
Friford Oxon....19 M2
Frilsham W Berk....19 P6
Frimley Surrey....20 E10
Frindsbury Medway....22 E9
Fring Norfk....44 C3
Fringford Oxon....31 N8
Frinsted Kent....22 H11
Frinton-on-Sea Essex....35 K11
Friockheim Angus....93 Q6
Frisby on the Wreake
Leics....41 P4
Friskney Lincs....53 M11
Friston E Susx....12 B9
Friston Suffk....35 N5
Fritchley Derbys....51 J9
Fritham Hants....9 J5
Frithelstock Devon....14 H8
Frithelstock Stone Devon....14 H8
Frithville Lincs....53 K12
Frittenden Kent....12 F2
Frittiscombe Devon....5 Q10
Fritton Norfk....45 K10
Fritton Norfk....45 P9
Fritwell Oxon....31 M8
Frizinghall C Brad....58 F7
Frizington Cumb....70 G11
Frocester Gloucs....29 K8
Frodesley Shrops....39 K2
Frodsham Ches W....57 K12
Frogden Border....80 G8
Frogden Border....80 G8
Frogmore Devon....5 P10
Frognall Lincs....42 G7
Frog Pool Worcs....39 P8
Frogwell Cnwll....4 H6
Frolesworth Leics....41 L8
Frome Somset....18 B10
Frome St Quintin Dorset....7 N3
Fromes Hill Herefs....39 M11
Froncysyllte Denbgs....48 F7
Fron-goch Gwynd....47 P4
Fron Isaf Wrexhm....48 F7
Frosterley Dur....72 H12
Froxfield Wilts....19 K7
Froxfield Green Hants....10 B5
Fryern Hill Hants....9 M4
Fryerning Essex....22 D4
Fuinary Highld....89 M7
Fulbeck Lincs....52 D12
Fulbourn Cambs....33 N5
Fulbrook Oxon....30 H10
Fulflood Hants....9 M2
Fulford C York....59 N4
Fulford Somset....16 G9
Fulford Staffs....50 C12
Fulham Gt Lon....21 L7
Fulking W Susx....11 K7
Fullarton N Ayrs....76 F4
Fuller Street Essex....34 C12

Fullerton Hants....19 L11
Fulletby Lincs....53 J8
Fullready Warwks....30 H5
Full Sutton E R Yk....60 D3
Fullwood E Ayrs....76 G2
Fulmer Bucks....20 F6
Fulmodeston Norfk....44 G4
Fulnetby Lincs....52 F7
Fulney Lincs....43 J5
Fulstow Lincs....53 K4
Fulwell Sundld....73 P8
Fulwood Lancs....57 K3
Fulwood Sheff....50 H4
Fundenhall Norfk....45 J10
Funtington W Susx....10 C8
Funtullich P & K....92 B9
Furley Devon....6 H2
Furnace Ag & B....83 Q3
Furnace Carmth....26 E3
Furnace Vale Derbys....50 D4
Furneux Pelham Herts....33 L10
Furzley Hants....9 K4
Fyfield Essex....22 C3
Fyfield Hants....19 K10
Fyfield Oxon....19 M2
Fyfield Wilts....18 G7
Fyfield Wilts....18 H8
Fylingthorpe N York....67 K6
Fyning W Susx....10 D5
Fyvie Abers....102 G7

**G**

Gabroc Hill E Ayrs....76 H2
Gaddesby Leics....41 P5
Gaddesden Row Herts....20 G2
Gadgirth S Ayrs....76 G6
Gaerllwyd Mons....28 E9
Gaerwen IoA....54 F7
Gailes N Ayrs....76 F4
Gailey Staffs....40 B5
Gainford Dur....65 L4
Gainsborough Lincs....52 B5
Gainsford End Essex....34 C9
Gairloch Highld....105 M7
Gairlochy Highld....98 B11
Gairneybridge P & K....86 D3
Gaitsgill Cumb....71 N6
Galashiels Border....80 C7
Galgate Lancs....63 J10
Galhampton Somset....17 P9
Gallanachbeg Ag & B....90 B10
Gallanachmore Ag & B....89 R10
Gallatown Fife....86 G4
Galleywood Essex....22 E3
Gallovie Highld....98 H10
Galloway Forest Park....69 L3
Gallowfauld Angus....93 M7
Gallowhill P & K....92 H7
Galltair Highld....97 L5
Galmpton Devon....5 N11
Galmpton Torbay....6 B10
Galphay N York....65 M11
Galston E Ayrs....76 H4
Gamblesby Cumb....72 B11
Gamlingay Cambs....33 J6
Gamlingay Great Heath
Cambs....32 H6
Gamrie Abers....102 G3
Gamston Notts....51 N12
Gamston Notts....51 P5
Ganavan Bay Ag & B....90 B9
Ganllwyd Gwynd....47 M6
Gannachy Angus....95 K7
Ganstead E R Yk....61 K7
Ganthorpe N York....66 F12
Ganton N York....67 L11
Garbity Moray....101 L5
Garboldisham Norfk....34 G1
Garbole Highld....99 L4
Garchory Abers....101 L12
Gardeners Green Wokham....20 D9
Gardenstown Abers....102 G3
Garden Village Sheff....50 H2
Garderhouse Shet....111 k4
Gare Hill Somset....18 B11
Garelochhead Ag & B....84 D5
Garford Oxon....19 M2
Garforth Leeds....59 K7
Gargrave N York....58 B4
Gargunnock Stirlg....85 M4
Garlic Street Norfk....45 K12
Garlieston D & G....69 L9
Garlinge Kent....23 P9
Garlinge Green Kent....23 L11
Garlogie Abers....95 M2
Garmond Abers....102 G5
Garmouth Moray....101 L3
Garmston Shrops....39 L2
Garn-Dolbenmaen Gwynd....46 H3
Garnkirk N Lans....85 L8
Garrabost W Isls....111 e2
Garrallan E Ayrs....77 J7
Garras Cnwll....2 G10
Garreg Gwynd....47 K3
Garrigill Cumb....72 D11
Garroch D & G....69 N3
Garrochtrie D & G....68 F10
Garrochty Ag & B....84 B11
Garros Highld....104 G9
Garsdale Head Cumb....64 E8
Garsdon Wilts....18 E4
Garshall Green Staffs....40 C1
Garsington Oxon....31 M12
Garstang Lancs....63 J12
Garston Herts....20 H4
Garston Lpool....56 H11
Gartachossan Ag & B....82 E10
Gartcosh N Lans....85 L9
Garth Powys....37 Q10
Garth Wrexhm....48 F7
Garthamlock C Glas....85 L9
Garthmyl Powys....38 E3
Garthorpe Leics....42 B6
Garthorpe N Linc....60 E9
Garth Row Cumb....63 K3
Gartly Abers....102 C8
Gartmore Stirlg....85 J4
Gartness N Lans....85 N9
Gartness Stirlg....84 H5
Gartocharn W Duns....84 G5
Garton-on-the-Wolds
E R Yk....60 G3
Garvald E Loth....87 L7

Garvan Highld....90 D2
Garvard Ag & B....82 E5
Garve Highld....106 G9
Garvellachs Ag & B....83 K2
Garvestone Norfk....44 G8
Garvock Inver....84 D8
Garway Herefs....28 E4
Garyvard W Isls....111 d2
Gasper Wilts....8 B2
Gastard Wilts....18 C7
Gasthorpe Norfk....34 F1
Gaston Green Essex....33 N12
Gatcombe IoW....9 N9
Gate Burton Lincs....52 B7
Gateforth N York....59 M8
Gatehead E Ayrs....76 G4
Gate Helmsley N York....59 P3
Gatehouse Nthumb....72 E3
Gatehouse of Fleet D & G....69 N7
Gateley Norfk....44 F5
Gatenby N York....65 N9
Gateshaw Border....80 G9
Gateshead Gatesd....73 M8
Gateside Angus....93 M6
Gateside E Rens....84 H10
Gateside Fife....86 E1
Gateside N Ayrs....84 F11
Gateslack D & G....78 E8
Gatley Stockp....57 Q10
Gattonside Border....80 D7
Gatwick Airport W Susx....11 L2
Gaulby Leics....41 P7
Gauldry Fife....93 L10
Gauldswell P & K....93 J5
Gautby Lincs....52 H8
Gavinton Border....80 G4
Gawcott Bucks....31 P7
Gawsworth Ches E....50 B6
Gawthrop Cumb....63 M5
Gawthwaite Cumb....62 F5
Gaydon Warwks....31 J4
Gayhurst M Keyn....32 C7
Gayle N York....64 F9
Gayles N York....65 K6
Gayton Nhants....31 P4
Gayton Norfk....44 C6
Gayton Staffs....40 C2
Gayton le Marsh Lincs....53 L6
Gayton Thorpe Norfk....44 C6
Gaywood Norfk....43 Q6
Gazeley Suffk....34 C4
Gearraidh Bhaird W Isls....111 d2
Geary Highld....104 C9
Gedding Suffk....34 F5
Geddington Nhants....42 C12
Gedling Notts....51 N11
Gedney Lincs....43 L5
Gedney Broadgate Lincs....43 L5
Gedney Drove End Lincs....43 M4
Gedney Dyke Lincs....43 L5
Gedney Hill Lincs....43 K7
Geeston Rutlnd....42 E8
Geldeston Norfk....45 N10
Gellifor Denbgs....48 D3
Gelligaer Caerph....27 N9
Gellilydan Gwynd....47 L4
Gellinudd Neath....26 G7
Gellyburn P & K....92 G7
Gellywen Carmth....25 M4
Gelston D & G....70 C4
Gelston Lincs....42 C2
Gembling E R Yk....61 J3
Gentleshaw Staffs....40 D5
Georgefield D & G....79 L9
George Green Bucks....20 F7
Georgeham Devon....14 H4
Georgemas Junction
Station Highld....110 D4
George Nympton Devon....15 M7
Georth Ork....111 h2
Germansweek Devon....5 J4
Gerrans Cnwll....3 K8
Gerrards Cross Bucks....20 G6
Gerrick R & Cl....66 G5
Gestingthorpe Essex....34 D8
Geuffordd Powys....48 E11
Gidea Park Gt Lon....21 Q5
Giffnock E Rens....85 J10
Gifford E Loth....87 K8
Giffordtown Fife....93 K12
Giggleswick N York....63 P9
Gigha Ag & B....75 J3
Gilberdyke E R Yk....60 E8
Gilchriston E Loth....87 J8
Gilcrux Cumb....70 H7
Gildersome Leeds....58 G8
Gildingwells Rothm....51 M4
Gilesgate Moor Dur....73 N11
Gileston V Glam....16 D3
Gilfach Caerph....27 N8
Gilfach Goch Brdgnd....27 K10
Gilfachrheda Cerdgn....36 G8
Gilgarran Cumb....70 G10
Gillamoor N York....66 F9
Gillen Highld....104 C9
Gillesbie D & G....79 J9
Gilling East N York....66 E11
Gillingham Dorset....8 B3
Gillingham Medway....22 F9
Gillingham Norfk....45 N10
Gilling West N York....65 L6
Gillock Highld....110 E4
Gills Highld....110 G2
Gilmanscleuch Border....79 M5
Gilmerton C Edin....86 F8
Gilmerton P & K....92 D10
Gilmonby Dur....64 H5
Gilmorton Leics....41 M9
Gilroes Crematorium
C Leic....41 M6
Gilsland Nthumb....72 B7
Gilstcosh N Lans....85 L9
Gilston Border....87 J10
Gilston Herts....21 N2
Gilwern Mons....27 Q6
Gimingham Norfk....45 L3
Gipping Suffk....34 H4
Gipsey Bridge Lincs....53 J12
Girdle Toll N Ayrs....76 F3
Girlsta Shet....111 k4
Girsby N York....65 N6
Girthon D & G....69 N8
Girton Cambs....33 L4
Girton Notts....52 B9
Girvan S Ayrs....76 D10
Gisburn Lancs....63 P11
Gisleham Suffk....45 Q11
Gislingham Suffk....34 H3

Gissing Norfk....45 J11
Gittisham Devon....6 F3
Gladestry Powys....38 E10
Gladsmuir E Loth....87 J7
Glais Swans....26 F8
Glaisdale N York....66 H6
Glamis Angus....93 L6
Glanaman Carmth....26 F6
Glandford Norfk....44 H2
Glandwr Pembks....25 L3
Glandyfi Cerdgn....47 L11
Glanllynfi Brdgnd....27 J10
Glan-rhyd Powys....26 G7
Glanton Nthumb....81 M10
Glanvilles Wootton Dorset....7 P2
Glan-y-don Flints....56 D11
Glapthorn Nhants....42 E11
Glapwell Derbys....51 L7
Glasbury Powys....27 P2
Glascwm Powys....38 D10
Glasfryn Conwy....55 N10
Glasgow C Glas....85 K9
Glasgow Airport Rens....84 H9
Glasgow Science Centre
C Glas....85 J9
Glasinfryn Gwynd....54 H7
Glasnacardoch Bay Highld....97 J9
Glasnakille Highld....96 G7
Glassford S Lans....77 M3
Glasshouse Gloucs....29 J5
Glasshouses N York....58 F2
Glasson Cumb....71 L4
Glasson Lancs....63 J10
Glassonby Cumb....72 B12
Glasterlaw Angus....93 Q5
Glaston Rutlnd....42 C9
Glastonbury Somset....17 M8
Glatton Cambs....42 G11
Glazebrook Warrtn....57 M9
Glazebury Warrtn....57 M9
Glazeley Shrops....39 N5
Gleaston Cumb....62 F7
Glebe Highld....98 G5
Gledhow Leeds....58 H6
Gledpark D & G....69 P8
Gledrid Shrops....48 F7
Glemsford Suffk....34 D7
Glenallachie Moray....101 K7
Glenancross Highld....97 J10
Glenaros House Ag & B....89 L7
Glenbarr Ag & B....75 K5
Glenbarry Abers....102 D4
Glenbeg Highld....89 M4
Glenbervie Abers....95 M6
Glenboig N Lans....85 M8
Glenborrodale Highld....89 M4
Glenbranter Ag & B....84 B4
Glenbreck Border....78 H5
Glenbrittle House Highld....96 E5
Glenbuck E Ayrs....77 M5
Glencally Angus....94 F8
Glencaple D & G....70 G2
Glencarron Lodge Highld....105 R11
Glencarse P & K....92 H10
Glen Clunie Lodge Abers....94 C5
Glencoe Highld....90 F5
Glencothe Border....78 H3
Glencraig Fife....86 E4
Glencrosh D & G....78 C10
Glendale Highld....104 B11
Glendaruel Ag & B....83 Q6
Glendevon P & K....86 B2
Glendoe Lodge Highld....98 E7
Glendoick P & K....93 J10
Glenduckie Fife....93 K11
Glenegedale Ag & B....74 D3
Glenelg Highld....97 L6
Glenernev Moray....100 F6
Glenfarg P & K....92 G12
Glenfield Leics....41 M6
Glenfinnan Highld....97 M12
Glenfintaig Lodge Highld....98 C10
Glenfoot P & K....92 H11
Glenfyne Lodge Ag & B....90 H12
Glengarnock N Ayrs....84 F11
Glengolly Highld....110 C3
Glengorm Castle Ag & B....89 K5
Glengrasco Highld....96 E1
Glenholm Border....78 H3
Glenhoul D & G....69 N2
Glenisla Angus....94 D9
Glenkin Ag & B....84 C7
Glenkindie Abers....101 N11
Glenlivet Moray....101 J9
Glenlochar D & G....70 C3
Glenlomond P & K....86 E2
Glenluce D & G....68 G7
Glenmassen Ag & B....84 B5
Glenmavis N Lans....85 M9
Glen Maye IoM....56 b5
Glenmore Highld....96 E2
Glenmore Lodge Highld....99 P7
Glen Nevis House Highld....90 F2
Glenochil Clacks....85 P4
Glen Parva Leics....41 M7
Glenquiech Angus....94 G9
Glenralloch Ag & B....83 M8
Glenridding Cumb....71 N11
Glenrothes Fife....86 F3
Glenshero Lodge Highld....98 H9
Glenstriven Ag & B....84 B7
Glentham Lincs....52 E5
Glentrool D & G....69 J4
Glen Trool Lodge D & G....69 K3
Glentruim House Highld....99 K9
Glentworth Lincs....52 D6
Glenuig Highld....89 N2
Glenvarragill Highld....96 F2
Glen Vine IoM....56 c5
Glenwhilly D & G....68 G5
Glespin S Lans....78 D4
Glewstone Herefs....28 G4
Glinton C Pete....42 G8
Glooston Leics....41 Q8
Glossop Derbys....50 D3
Gloster Hill Nthumb....81 Q12
Gloucester Gloucs....29 L5
Gloucester
Crematorium Gloucs....29 L5
Gloucester Services
Gloucs....29 L6
Gloucestershire Airport
Gloucs....29 M5
Glusburn N York....58 D5
Glutt Lodge Highld....110 B8
Glympton Oxon....31 K9

Glynarthen Cerdgn 36 E10
Glyn Ceiriog Wrexhm 48 E7
Glyncorrwg Neath 27 J8
Glynde E Susx 11 P8
Glyndyfrdwy Denbgs 48 D7
Glynneath Neath 27 J7
Glynn Valley
  Crematorium Cnwll 3 N3
Glyntaff Crematorium
  Rhondd 27 M10
Glyntawe Powys 26 H5
Glynteg Carmth 25 N2
Gnosall Staffs 49 P10
Gnosall Heath Staffs 49 P10
Goadby Leics 41 Q7
Goadby Marwood Leics 41 R3
Goatacre Wilts 18 F5
Goathill Dorset 17 P11
Goathland N York 67 J7
Goathurst Somset 16 H8
Gobowen Shrops 48 F8
Godalming Surrey 10 F2
Goddard's Green Kent 12 G3
Godmanchester Cambs 33 J3
Godmanstone Dorset 7 P4
Godmersham Kent 23 K12
Godney Somset 17 L7
Godolphin Cross Cnwll 2 F9
Godre'r-graig Neath 26 G7
Godshill IoW 9 N10
Godstone Surrey 21 M11
Goetre Mons 28 C7
Goff's Oak Herts 21 M3
Gogar C Edin 86 E7
Goginan Cerdgn 37 L4
Golan Gwynd 46 H3
Golant Cnwll 4 D8
Golberdon Cnwll 4 H6
Golborne Wigan 57 L8
Golcar Kirk 58 E10
Goldcliff Newpt 28 D11
Golden Green Kent 12 D1
Goldenhill C Stke 49 Q5
Golden Pot Hants 10 B2
Golders Green Gt Lon 21 K6
Golders Green
  Crematorium Gt Lon 21 K6
Goldhanger Essex 22 H2
Goldington Bed 32 F6
Goldsborough N York 59 J3
Goldsborough N York 67 J5
Golds Green Sandw 40 C8
Goldsithney Cnwll 2 E9
Goldsworth Park Surrey 20 F10
Goldthorpe Barns 59 L12
Goldworthy Devon 14 G7
Gollanfield Highld 107 N10
Golspie Highld 107 L5
Gomeldon Wilts 8 H1
Gomshall Surrey 10 H1
Gonalston Notts 51 P10
Gonerby Hill Foot Lincs 42 C3
Gonfirth Shet 111 k3
Good Easter Essex 22 D2
Gooderstone Norfk 44 C9
Goodleigh Devon 15 K5
Goodmanham E R Yk 60 F5
Goodmayes Gt Lon 21 P6
Goodnestone Kent 23 K10
Goodnestone Kent 23 N11
Goodrich Herefs 28 G5
Goodrington Torbay 6 B10
Goodshaw Lancs 57 P4
Goodwick Pembks 24 G2
Goodworth Clatford
  Hants 19 L11
Goole E R Yk 60 C9
Goom's Hill Worcs 30 D3
Goonbell Cnwll 2 G6
Goonhavern Cnwll 2 H5
Goonvrea Cnwll 2 G6
Goosecruives Abers 95 M5
Gooseford Devon 5 N2
Goose Green Essex 35 J10
Goose Green S Glos 17 P2
Gooseham Cnwll 14 E8
Goosey Oxon 19 L3
Goosnargh Lancs 57 K2
Goostrey Ches E 49 P2
Gordano Services N Som 17 N2
Gordon Border 80 E5
Gordon Arms Hotel
  Border 79 L4
Gordonstown Abers 102 D4
Gordonstown Abers 102 F7
Gorebridge Mdloth 86 G9
Gorefield Cambs 43 L7
Gores Wilts 18 G8
Gorey Jersey 7 c2
Goring Oxon 19 P5
Goring-by-Sea W Susx 10 H9
Gorleston on Sea Norfk 45 Q8
Gornal Wood
  Crematorium Dudley 40 B8
Gorrachie Abers 102 F4
Gorran Churchtown Cnwll 3 M7
Gorran Haven Cnwll 3 M7
Gorsedd Flints 56 D12
Gorse Hill Swindn 18 H4
Gorseinon Swans 26 D4
Gorsgoch Cerdgn 36 H9
Gorslas Carmth 26 D6
Gorsley Gloucs 29 J4
Gorsley Common Herefs 29 J4
Gorstan Highld 106 H9
Gorsty Hill Staffs 40 E2
Gorten Ag & B 89 P9
Gorthleck Highld 98 G5
Gorton Manch 50 B2
Gosbeck Suffk 35 J5
Gosberton Lincs 43 J4
Gosfield Essex 34 D10
Gosforth Cumb 62 C2
Gosforth N u Ty 73 M7
Gospel End Staffs 40 B8
Gosport Hants 9 Q8
Gossington Gloucs 29 K8
Gotham Notts 41 M2
Gotherington Gloucs 29 N3
Gotton Somset 16 H9
Goudhurst Kent 12 E3
Goulceby Lincs 53 J7
Gourdas Abers 102 G7
Gourdie C Dund 93 L8
Gourdon Abers 95 N7
Gourock Inver 84 D7
Govan C Glas 85 J9

Goveton Devon 5 P10
Govilon Mons 28 B6
Gowdall E R Yk 59 N9
Gower Highld 106 H10
Gower Swans 26 C10
Gowerton Swans 26 D9
Gowkhall Fife 86 C5
Goxhill E R Yk 61 K5
Goxhill N Linc 61 J9
Grabhair W Isls 111 d3
Graffham W Susx 10 E6
Grafham Cambs 32 G3
Grafham Surrey 10 G2
Grafton N York 59 K2
Grafton Oxon 19 J1
Grafton Shrops 48 H10
Grafton Worcs 29 N2
Grafton Flyford Worcs 30 C3
Grafton Regis Nhants 31 Q5
Grafton Underwood
  Nhants 32 D2
Grafty Green Kent 12 G1
Graig Conwy 55 L7
Graig-fechan Denbgs 48 D5
Grain Medway 22 H7
Grainsby Lincs 53 J4
Grainthorpe Lincs 53 L4
Grampound Cnwll 3 L6
Grampound Road Cnwll 3 K5
Gramsdal W Isls 111 b5
Gramsdale W Isls 111 b5
Granborough Bucks 31 Q8
Granby Notts 41 Q1
Grandborough Warwks 31 L2
Grand Chemins Jersey 7 c2
Grandes Rocques Guern 6 b1
Grandtully P & K 92 D5
Grange Cumb 71 L11
Grange Medway 22 F9
Grange P & K 93 K10
Grange Crossroads Moray 101 N4
Grange Hall Moray 100 G3
Grangehall S Lans 78 F1
Grange Hill Essex 21 N5
Grangemill Derbys 50 G8
Grange Moor Kirk 58 G10
Grangemouth Falk 85 Q6
Grange of Lindores Fife 93 J11
Grange-over-Sands Cumb 62 H6
Grangepans Falk 86 B6
Grangetown R & Cl 66 D4
Grangetown Sundld 73 P9
Grange Villa Dur 73 M9
Gransmoor E R Yk 61 J3
Granston Pembks 24 F2
Grantchester Cambs 33 M6
Grantham Lincs 42 D3
Grantham Crematorium
  Lincs 42 D3
Granton C Edin 86 F6
Grantown-on-Spey Highld 100 H8
Grantshouse Border 87 P8
Grasby Lincs 52 F3
Grasmere Cumb 62 G1
Grasscroft Oldham 58 C12
Grassendale Lpool 56 H10
Grassington N York 58 D2
Grassmoor Derbys 51 K7
Grassthorpe Notts 52 B9
Grateley Hants 19 J11
Graveley Cambs 33 J4
Graveley Herts 32 H10
Gravelly Hill Birm 40 E9
Graveney Kent 23 K10
Gravesend Kent 22 D8
Gravir W Isls 111 d3
Grayingham Lincs 52 D4
Grayrigg Cumb 63 L3
Grays Thurr 22 C7
Grayshott Hants 10 E3
Grayswood Surrey 10 E3
Greasbrough Rothm 51 K2
Greasby Wirral 56 F10
Great Abington Cambs 33 N7
Great Addington Nhants 32 D2
Great Alne Warwks 30 E3
Great Altcar Lancs 56 G7
Great Amwell Herts 21 M2
Great Asby Cumb 64 C5
Great Ashfield Suffk 34 G4
Great Ayton N York 66 D5
Great Baddow Essex 22 E3
Great Badminton S Glos 18 B4
Great Bardfield Essex 34 B10
Great Barford Bed 32 G6
Great Barr Sandw 40 D8
Great Barrington Gloucs 30 G10
Great Barrow Ches W 49 J2
Great Barton Suffk 34 E4
Great Barugh N York 66 G10
Great Bavington Nthumb 72 H5
Great Bealings Suffk 35 K7
Great Bedwyn Wilts 19 J7
Great Bentley Essex 35 J11
Great Billing Nhants 32 B4
Great Bircham Norfk 44 C4
Great Blakenham Suffk 35 J6
Great Blencow Cumb 71 P8
Great Bolas Wrekin 49 M10
Great Bookham Surrey 21 J11
Great Bourton Oxon 31 L5
Great Bowden Leics 41 Q9
Great Bradley Suffk 34 B6
Great Braxted Essex 22 G1
Great Bricett Suffk 34 G6
Great Brickhill Bucks 32 C10
Great Brington Nhants 31 P2
Great Bromley Essex 34 H10
Great Broughton Cumb 70 H8
Great Broughton N York 66 D6
Great Budworth Ches W 57 M12
Great Burdon Darltn 65 N4
Great Burstead Essex 22 D5
Great Busby N York 66 D6
Great Carlton Lincs 53 L6
Great Casterton Rutlnd 42 E8
Great Chalfield Wilts 18 C7
Great Chart Kent 13 J2
Great Chatwell Staffs 49 P11
Great Chell C Stke 49 Q5
Great Chesterford Essex 33 N8
Great Cheverell Wilts 18 E8
Great Chishill Cambs 33 L8
Great Clacton Essex 35 K12
Great Clifton Cumb 70 G9
Great Coates NE Lin 61 L11

Great Comberton Worcs 29 N1
Great Corby Cumb 71 P5
Great Cornard Suffk 34 E8
Great Cowden E R Yk 61 L6
Great Coxwell Oxon 19 J3
Great Cransley Nhants 32 B2
Great Cressingham Norfk 44 E9
Great Crosthwaite Cumb 71 L10
Great Cubley Derbys 50 F12
Great Cumbrae Island
  N Ayrs 84 C10
Great Dalby Leics 41 Q5
Great Doddington Nhants 32 C4
Great Dunham Norfk 44 E7
Great Dunmow Essex 33 Q11
Great Durnford Wilts 18 G12
Great Easton Essex 33 P10
Great Easton Leics 42 C10
Great Eccleston Lancs 56 H2
Great Ellingham Norfk 44 G10
Great Elm Somset 17 Q6
Great Everdon Nhants 31 N3
Great Eversden Cambs 33 K6
Great Fencote N York 65 M8
Great Finborough Suffk 34 G5
Greatford Lincs 42 F7
Great Fransham Norfk 44 E7
Great Gaddesden Herts 20 G2
Greatgate Staffs 50 D11
Great Gidding Cambs 42 G12
Great Givendale E R Yk 60 E4
Great Glemham Suffk 35 M4
Great Glen Leics 41 P7
Great Gonerby Lincs 42 C3
Great Gransden Cambs 33 J5
Great Green Cambs 33 J7
Great Green Suffk 34 F5
Great Habton N York 66 G11
Great Hale Lincs 42 G2
Great Hallingbury Essex 33 N11
Greatham Hants 10 C4
Greatham Hartpl 66 C3
Greatham W Susx 10 G6
Great Hampden Bucks 20 D3
Great Harrowden Nhants 32 C3
Great Harwood Lancs 57 N3
Great Haseley Oxon 19 Q1
Great Hatfield E R Yk 61 K5
Great Haywood Staffs 40 D3
Great Heck N York 59 N9
Great Henny Essex 34 E8
Great Hinton Wilts 18 D8
Great Hockham Norfk 44 F10
Great Holland Essex 35 K11
Great Hollands Br For 20 D9
Great Horkesley Essex 34 F9
Great Hormead Herts 33 L10
Great Horton C Brad 58 F7
Great Horwood Bucks 31 Q7
Great Houghton Barns 59 K11
Great Houghton Nhants 32 B5
Great Hucklow Derbys 50 F5
Great Kelk E R Yk 61 J3
Great Kimble Bucks 20 D3
Great Kingshill Bucks 20 E4
Great Langdale Cumb 62 F2
Great Langton N York 65 N8
Great Leighs Essex 34 C12
Great Limber Lincs 52 G2
Great Linford M Keyn 32 C8
Great Livermere Suffk 34 E3
Great Longstone Derbys 50 G6
Great Lumley Dur 73 N10
Great Malvern Worcs 39 P11
Great Maplestead Essex 34 D9
Great Marton Bpool 56 G2
Great Massingham Norfk 44 D5
Great Milton Oxon 19 Q1
Great Missenden Bucks 20 E3
Great Mitton Lancs 57 N2
Great Mongeham Kent 23 Q12
Great Moulton Norfk 45 J11
Great Musgrave Cumb 64 D5
Great Ness Shrops 48 H10
Great Notley Essex 34 C11
Great Oak Mons 28 D6
Great Oakley Essex 35 K10
Great Oakley Nhants 42 C11
Great Offley Herts 32 G10
Great Ormside Cumb 64 C4
Great Orton Cumb 71 M5
Great Ouseburn N York 59 K2
Great Oxendon Nhants 41 Q10
Great Paxton Cambs 33 J4
Great Plumpton Lancs 56 H3
Great Plumstead Norfk 45 L7
Great Ponton Lincs 42 D4
Great Preston Leeds 59 K8
Great Raveley Cambs 33 J1
Great Rissington Gloucs 30 G10
Great Rollright Oxon 31 J7
Great Ryburgh Norfk 44 F5
Great Ryton Shrops 39 J2
Great Saling Essex 34 B10
Great Salkeld Cumb 71 Q8
Great Sampford Essex 33 Q9
Great Saughall Ches W 48 G2
Great Shefford W Berk 19 L6
Great Shelford Cambs 33 M6
Great Smeaton N York 65 N6
Great Snoring Norfk 44 F4
Great Somerford Wilts 18 E4
Great Soudley Shrops 49 N9
Great Stainton Darltn 65 N3
Great Stambridge Essex 22 G4
Great Staughton Cambs 32 G4
Great Steeping Lincs 53 M9
Greatstone-on-Sea Kent 13 L5
Great Strickland Cumb 71 Q10
Great Stukeley Cambs 32 H2
Great Sturton Lincs 52 H7
Great Swinburne Nthumb 72 G6
Great Tew Oxon 31 K8
Great Tey Essex 34 E10
Great Thurlow Suffk 34 B6
Great Torrington Devon 15 J8
Great Tosson Nthumb 72 H2
Great Totham Essex 22 G2
Great Totham Essex 22 G2
Great Urswick Cumb 62 F7
Great Wakering Essex 22 H6
Great Waldingfield Suffk 34 E7
Great Walsingham Norfk 44 F3
Great Waltham Essex 22 C2
Great Warley Essex 22 C5
Great Washbourne Gloucs 29 N2

Great Weeke Devon 5 P3
Great Wenham Suffk 34 H8
Great Whittington
  Nthumb 72 H6
Great Wigborough Essex 23 J1
Great Wilbraham Cambs 33 N5
Great Wishford Wilts 8 F1
Great Witcombe Gloucs 29 M6
Great Witley Worcs 39 N8
Great Wolford Warwks 30 G7
Greatworth Nhants 31 M6
Great Wratting Suffk 34 B7
Great Wymondley Herts 32 H10
Great Wyrley Staffs 40 C6
Great Yarmouth Norfk 45 Q8
Great Yarmouth
  Crematorium Norfk 45 Q9
Great Yeldham Essex 34 C8
Greenburn W Loth 85 Q10
Green End Herts 33 K11
Green End Herts 33 K9
Greenfield Ag & B 84 D5
Greenfield C Beds 32 F9
Greenfield Flints 56 E12
Greenfield Highld 98 B8
Greenfield Oldham 58 C12
Greenford Gt Lon 21 J7
Greengairs N Lans 85 N8
Greengates C Brad 58 G6
Greenham Somset 16 E11
Green Hammerton N York 59 L3
Greenhaugh Nthumb 72 E4
Greenhead Nthumb 72 C7
Green Heath Staffs 40 C5
Greenhill D & G 78 H11
Greenhill Falk 85 N7
Greenhill Kent 23 M9
Greenhill S Lans 78 F3
Greenhithe Kent 22 C8
Greenholm E Ayrs 77 J4
Greenhouse Border 80 D9
Greenhow Hill N York 58 E2
Greenland Highld 110 E3
Greenland Sheff 51 K3
Greenlaw Border 80 F5
Greenlea D & G 70 G1
Greenloaning P & K 85 N2
Greenmount Bury 57 P6
Greenock Inver 84 E7
Greenodd Cumb 62 G6
Green Ore Somset 17 N6
Green Quarter Cumb 63 J2
Greenshields S Lans 86 B12
Greenside Gatesd 73 K8
Greenside Kirk 58 F10
Greens Norton Nhants 31 P4
Greenstead Green Essex 34 D10
Green Street Herts 21 J4
Green Street Herts 33 M11
Green Street Green Kent 22 C8
Green Tye Herts 33 M11
Greenway Somset 17 J10
Greenwich Gt Lon 21 M7
Greenwich Maritime
  Gt Lon 21 M7
Greet Gloucs 30 D7
Greete Shrops 39 L7
Greetham Lincs 53 K8
Greetham Rutlnd 42 D7
Greetland Calder 58 E9
Greinton Somset 17 K8
Greosabhagh W Isls 111 c3
Gresford Wrexhm 48 G5
Gresham Norfk 45 J3
Greshornish House
  Hotel Highld 104 D10
Gressenhall Norfk 44 F7
Gressenhall Green Norfk 44 F6
Gressingham Lancs 63 K8
Greta Bridge Dur 65 J5
Gretna D & G 71 M3
Gretna Green D & G 71 M2
Gretna Services D & G 71 L2
Gretton Gloucs 30 D7
Gretton Nhants 42 C10
Gretton Shrops 39 K3
Grewelthorpe N York 65 M11
Greygarth N York 65 L12
Greys Green Oxon 20 B6
Greysouthen Cumb 70 H9
Greystoke Cumb 71 P8
Greystone Angus 93 P7
Greywell Hants 20 B12
Griff Warwks 41 J9
Griffithstown Torfn 28 C8
Grimeford Village Lancs 57 L6
Grimesthorpe Sheff 51 J3
Grimethorpe Barns 59 K11
Grimley Worcs 39 Q9
Grimmet S Ayrs 76 F8
Grimoldby Lincs 53 L6
Grimpo Shrops 48 G9
Grimsargh Lancs 57 L3
Grimsby NE Lin 61 M11
Grimsby Crematorium
  NE Lin 53 J3
Grimscote Nhants 31 P4
Grimscott Cnwll 14 E10
Grimshaw Bl w D 57 N4
Grimshader W Isls 111 d2
Grimsthorpe Lincs 42 F5
Grimston Leics 41 P3
Grimston Norfk 44 C5
Grimstone Dorset 7 P4
Grimstone End Suffk 34 F3
Grindale E R Yk 67 N12
Grindleford Derbys 50 G5
Grindleton Lancs 63 N11
Grindley Brook Shrops 49 K7
Grindlow Derbys 50 F5
Grindon Staffs 50 E9
Gringley on the Hill Notts 51 Q3
Grinsdale Cumb 71 M4
Grinshill Shrops 49 K10
Grinton N York 65 J7
Griomaisiadar W Isls 111 d2
Griomsaigh W Isls 111 b5
Grishipoll Ag & B 88 F5
Gristhorpe N York 67 M10
Griston Norfk 44 F9

Gritley Ork 111 h2
Grittenham Wilts 18 F4
Grittleton Wilts 18 C5
Grizebeck Cumb 62 E5
Grizedale Cumb 62 G4
Groby Leics 41 M6
Groes Conwy 55 Q8
Groes-faen Rhondd 27 M11
Groeslon Gwynd 54 F9
Groes-Wen Caerph 27 N10
Grogarry W Isls 111 a5
Grogport Ag & B 75 M4
Groigearraidh W Isls 111 a5
Gronant Flints 56 C11
Groombridge E Susx 11 Q3
Grosebay W Isls 111 c3
Grosmont Mons 28 E4
Grosmont N York 67 J6
Groton Suffk 34 F8
Grouville Jersey 7 c2
Grove Notts 51 Q5
Grove Oxon 19 L3
Grove Green Kent 22 F11
Grove Park Gt Lon 21 N8
Grovesend Swans 26 D6
Gruinard Highld 105 P4
Gruinart Ag & B 82 D9
Grula Highld 96 D4
Gruline Ag & B 89 L8
Grundisburgh Suffk 35 K6
Gruting Shet 111 j4
Grutness Shet 111 k5
Gualachulain Highld 90 F7
Guardbridge Fife 93 M11
Guarlford Worcs 39 P11
Guay P & K 92 E6
Guernsey Guern 6 b2
Guernsey Airport Guern 6 b2
Guestling Green E Susx 12 G7
Guestling Thorn E Susx 12 G6
Guestwick Norfk 44 H5
Guide Bridge Tamesd 50 B2
Guilden Morden Cambs 33 J7
Guilden Sutton Ches W 49 J2
Guildford Surrey 20 F12
Guildford Crematorium
  Surrey 10 F2
Guildtown P & K 92 G8
Guilsborough Nhants 41 P11
Guilsfield Powys 48 E12
Guiltreehill S Ayrs 76 F8
Guineaford Devon 15 J5
Guisborough R & Cl 66 E4
Guiseley Leeds 58 G6
Guist Norfk 44 G5
Guiting Power Gloucs 30 E8
Gullane E Loth 87 J5
Gulval Cnwll 2 D9
Gulworthy Devon 5 K5
Gumfreston Pembks 25 J8
Gumley Leics 41 P9
Gunby Lincs 42 D6
Gunby Lincs 53 M9
Gundleton Hants 9 Q2
Gun Hill E Susx 12 C7
Gunn Devon 15 K5
Gunnerside N York 64 G7
Gunnerton Nthumb 72 G6
Gunness N Linc 60 E11
Gunnislake Cnwll 5 J6
Gunnista Shet 111 k4
Gunthorpe N Linc 52 B4
Gunthorpe Norfk 44 G3
Gunthorpe Notts 51 P11
Gunwalloe Cnwll 2 F10
Gurnard IoW 9 N8
Gurney Slade Somset 17 N6
Gurnos Powys 26 G7
Gussage All Saints Dorset 8 E5
Gussage St Andrew
  Dorset 8 E5
Gussage St Michael
  Dorset 8 E5
Guston Kent 13 P2
Gutcher Shet 111 k2
Guthrie Angus 93 P5
Guyhirn Cambs 43 L8
Guyzance Nthumb 81 P12
Gwaenysgor Flints 56 C11
Gwalchmai IoA 54 E6
Gwaun-Cae-Gurwen
  Carmth 26 F6
Gweek Cnwll 2 G9
Gwenddwr Powys 38 C12
Gwennap Cnwll 2 H7
Gwennap Mining
  District Cnwll 2 H7
Gwent Crematorium
  Mons 28 C8
Gwernaffield Flints 48 E3
Gwernesney Mons 28 E8
Gwernogle Carmth 26 D3
Gwernymynydd Flints 48 E3
Gwespyr Flints 56 C11
Gwinear Cnwll 2 E8
Gwithian Cnwll 2 E7
Gwyddelwern Denbgs 48 C6
Gwyddgrug Carmth 26 C2
Gwytherin Conwy 55 N8

## H

Habberley Shrops 38 H2
Habberley Worcs 39 P6
Habergham Lancs 57 P3
Habertoft Lincs 53 N9
Habrough NE Lin 61 K10
Hacconby Lincs 42 F5
Haceby Lincs 42 E3
Hacheston Suffk 35 M5
Hackbridge Gt Lon 21 L9
Hackenthorpe Sheff 51 K4
Hackford Norfk 44 H9
Hackforth N York 65 M8
Hackland Ork 111 h2
Hackleton Nhants 32 B6
Hacklinge Kent 23 Q11
Hackness N York 67 L9
Hackney Gt Lon 21 M6
Hackthorn Lincs 52 E7
Hackthorpe Cumb 71 Q10
Hadden Border 80 G7
Haddenham Bucks 20 B2
Haddenham Cambs 33 M2
Haddington E Loth 87 K7

Haddington Lincs....52 D10
Haddiscoe Norfk....45 P10
Haddo Abers....102 H7
Haddon Cambs....42 G10
Hadfield Derbys....50 D2
Hadham Ford Herts....33 M11
Hadleigh Essex....22 F6
Hadleigh Suffk....34 G8
Hadley Worcs....39 Q8
Hadley Wrekin....49 M12
Hadley End Staffs....40 F4
Hadley Wood Gt Lon....21 L4
Hadlow Kent....22 D12
Hadlow Down E Susx....11 Q5
Hadnall Shrops....49 K10
Hadrian's Wall Nthumb....72 G6
Hadstock Essex....33 N7
Hadzor Worcs....30 B2
Haggersta Shet....111 k4
Haggerston Nthumb....81 L5
Haggs Falk....85 N7
Hagley Herefs....28 G1
Hagley Worcs....40 B10
Hagworthingham Lincs....53 K9
Haile Cumb....62 B1
Hailey Oxon....31 J10
Hailsham E Susx....12 C8
Hainault Gt Lon....21 P5
Hainford Norfk....45 K6
Hainton Lincs....52 H6
Haisthorpe E R Yk....61 J2
Hakin Pembks....24 F7
Halam Notts....51 P9
Halbeath Fife....86 D5
Halberton Devon....6 D1
Halcro Highld....110 E4
Hale Cumb....63 J4
Hale Halton....57 J11
Hale Hants....8 H4
Hale Surrey....10 D1
Hale Traffd....57 P10
Halebarns Traffd....57 P10
Hales Norfk....45 N10
Hales Staffs....49 N8
Halesowen Dudley....40 C10
Hales Place Kent....23 M10
Hale Street Kent....22 D12
Halesworth Suffk....35 N2
Halewood Knows....57 J10
Halford Devon....5 Q5
Halford Warwks....30 H5
Halfpenny Green Staffs....39 P4
Halfway House Shrops....48 G12
Halfway Houses Kent....22 H8
Halifax Calder....58 E8
Halket E Ayrs....84 G11
Halkirk Highld....110 D4
Halkyn Flints....48 E2
Hall E Rens....84 G11
Halland E Susx....11 P6
Hallaton Leics....42 B10
Hallatrow BaNES....17 P5
Hallbankgate Cumb....72 B8
Hall Dunnerdale Cumb....62 E3
Hallen S Glos....28 G11
Hallgarth Dur....73 N11
Hall Glen Falk....85 P7
Hall Green Birm....40 E10
Hallin Highld....104 C9
Halling Medway....22 E10
Hallington Lincs....53 K6
Hallington Nthumb....72 H6
Halliwell Bolton....57 M6
Halloughton Notts....51 P9
Hallow Worcs....39 P9
Hall's Green Herts....33 J10
Hallyne Border....79 K2
Halmore Gloucs....29 J8
Halnaker W Susx....10 E8
Halsall Lancs....56 G6
Halse Nhants....31 M6
Halse Somset....16 F9
Halsetown Cnwll....2 D7
Halsham E R Yk....61 M8
Halstead Essex....34 D10
Halstead Kent....21 P10
Halstead Leics....41 Q6
Halstock Dorset....7 M2
Haltemprice Crematorium E R Yk....60 H7
Haltham Lincs....53 J10
Halton Bucks....20 E2
Halton Halton....57 K11
Halton Lancs....63 J8
Halton Leeds....59 J7
Halton Nthumb....72 H7
Halton Wrexhm....48 F7
Halton East N York....58 D4
Halton Gill N York....64 F11
Halton Holegate Lincs....53 L9
Halton Lea Gate Nthumb....72 C8
Halton Shields Nthumb....72 H7
Halton West N York....63 Q10
Haltwhistle Nthumb....72 D7
Halvergate Norfk....45 N8
Halwell Devon....5 Q9
Halwill Devon....14 H11
Halwill Junction Devon....14 H11
Ham Devon....6 H3
Ham Gloucs....29 J8
Ham Gt Lon....21 J8
Ham Kent....23 P11
Ham Somset....16 H10
Ham Wilts....19 K8
Hambleden Bucks....20 C6
Hambledon Hants....9 Q4
Hambledon Surrey....10 F3
Hamble-le-Rice Hants....9 N6
Hambleton Lancs....56 G1
Hambleton N York....59 M7
Hambridge Somset....17 K10
Hambrook W Susx....10 C8
Hameringham Lincs....53 K9
Hamerton Cambs....32 G2
Ham Green Worcs....30 D2
Hamilton S Lans....85 M11
Hamilton Services S Lans....85 M10
Hamlet Dorset....7 N2
Hammersmith Gt Lon....21 K7
Hammerwich Staffs....40 E6
Hammoon Dorset....8 B5
Hamnavoe Shet....111 k4
Hampden Park E Susx....12 C9
Hampnett Gloucs....30 E10
Hampole Donc....59 L11
Hampreston Dorset....8 F7

Hampstead Gt Lon....21 L6
Hampstead Norreys W Berk....19 N5
Hampsthwaite N York....58 H3
Hampton C Pete....42 G10
Hampton Gt Lon....21 J9
Hampton Kent....23 M9
Hampton Shrops....39 N5
Hampton Swindn....18 H3
Hampton Worcs....30 D5
Hampton Bishop Herefs....28 G2
Hampton Court Palace Gt Lon....21 J9
Hampton Heath Ches W....49 J5
Hampton-in-Arden Solhll....40 G10
Hampton Lovett Worcs....30 B2
Hampton Lucy Warwks....30 G3
Hampton Magna Warwks....30 H2
Hampton Poyle Oxon....31 L10
Hampton Wick Gt Lon....21 J9
Hamptworth Wilts....9 J4
Hamsey E Susx....11 N7
Hamstall Ridware Staffs....40 E4
Hamstead Birm....40 D8
Hamstead Marshall W Berk....19 M7
Hamsterley Dur....65 K2
Hamsterley Dur....73 K9
Hamstreet Kent....13 L4
Ham Street Somset....17 M8
Hamworthy Poole....8 E8
Hanbury Staffs....40 F2
Hanbury Worcs....30 C2
Hanchurch Staffs....49 Q7
Handa Island Highld....108 C6
Hand and Pen Devon....6 E4
Handbridge Ches W....48 H3
Handcross W Susx....11 L4
Handforth Ches E....57 Q11
Handley Ches W....49 J4
Handley Derbys....51 J8
Handsworth Birm....40 D9
Handsworth Sheff....51 K4
Hanford C Stke....49 Q7
Hanging Heaton Kirk....58 G9
Hanging Houghton Nhants....41 Q11
Hanging Langford Wilts....18 F12
Hangleton Br & H....11 L8
Hanham S Glos....17 P2
Hankelow Ches E....49 M6
Hankerton Wilts....29 N9
Hanley C Stke....50 B10
Hanley Castle Worcs....39 Q12
Hanley Child Worcs....39 M8
Hanley Swan Worcs....39 P12
Hanley William Worcs....39 M8
Hanlith N York....58 B2
Hanmer Wrexhm....49 J7
Hannaford Devon....15 K6
Hannington Hants....19 N9
Hannington Nhants....32 B3
Hannington Swindn....18 H3
Hannington Wick Swindn....18 H2
Hanslope M Keyn....32 B7
Hanthorpe Lincs....42 F5
Hanwell Gt Lon....21 J7
Hanwell Oxon....31 K5
Hanwood Shrops....49 J12
Hanworth Gt Lon....20 H8
Hanworth Norfk....45 K3
Happendon S Lans....78 E3
Happendon Services S Lans....78 D3
Happisburgh Norfk....45 N4
Happisburgh Common Norfk....45 N4
Hapsford Ches W....49 J1
Hapton Lancs....57 P3
Hapton Norfk....45 K10
Harberton Devon....5 Q8
Harbertonford Devon....5 Q8
Harbledown Kent....23 L10
Harborne Birm....40 D10
Harborough Magna Warwks....41 L10
Harbottle Nthumb....81 K12
Harbourneford Devon....5 P7
Harbury Warwks....31 J3
Harby Leics....41 Q2
Harby Notts....52 C8
Harcombe Devon....6 B6
Harcombe Devon....6 F5
Harcombe Bottom Devon....7 J4
Harden C Brad....58 E6
Harden Wsall....40 D7
Hardenhuish Wilts....18 D6
Hardgate Abers....95 N2
Hardgate D & G....70 D3
Hardgate W Duns....84 H8
Hardham W Susx....10 G6
Hardingham Norfk....44 H8
Hardingstone Nhants....31 Q3
Hardington Somset....17 Q5
Hardington Mandeville Somset....7 M1
Hardington Marsh Somset....7 M2
Hardington Moor Somset....7 M1
Hardisworthy Devon....14 E7
Hardley Hants....9 M6
Hardley Street Norfk....45 N9
Hardraw N York....64 F8
Hardstoft Derbys....51 K8
Hardway Hants....9 Q7
Hardway Somset....17 Q8
Hardwick Bucks....32 B11
Hardwick Cambs....33 L5
Hardwick Nhants....32 C3
Hardwick Norfk....45 K11
Hardwick Oxon....31 J11
Hardwick Oxon....31 M7
Hardwick Wsall....40 E7
Hardwicke Gloucs....29 L6
Hardwicke Gloucs....29 M4
Hardwick Hall Dur....65 N2
Hardy's Green Essex....34 F11
Hare Croft C Brad....58 E7
Harefield Gt Lon....20 G5
Hare Green Essex....34 H10
Hare Hatch Wokham....20 C7
Harehill Derbys....40 F1
Harehills Leeds....59 J7
Harelaw Border....80 G5
Harelaw D & G....79 N12
Harescombe Gloucs....29 L6
Haresfield Gloucs....29 L6
Harestock Hants....9 M2

Hare Street Essex....21 N2
Hare Street Herts....33 L10
Harewood Leeds....58 H5
Harewood End Herefs....28 F4
Harford Devon....5 M8
Hargrave Ches W....49 J3
Hargrave Nhants....32 E3
Hargrave Suffk....34 C5
Harkstead Suffk....35 K9
Harlaston Staffs....40 G5
Harlaxton Lincs....42 C4
Harlech Gwynd....47 J5
Harlech Castle Gwynd....47 J5
Harlescott Shrops....49 J11
Harlesden Gt Lon....21 K6
Harlesthorpe Derbys....51 L5
Harleston Devon....5 Q10
Harleston Norfk....45 L12
Harleston Suffk....34 G5
Harlestone Nhants....31 P2
Harle Syke Lancs....57 Q2
Harley Rothm....51 J2
Harley Shrops....39 L2
Harlington C Beds....32 E10
Harlington Donc....51 L1
Harlington Gt Lon....20 H7
Harlosh Highld....96 C2
Harlow Essex....21 N2
Harlow Carr RHS N York....58 H4
Harlow Hill Nthumb....73 J7
Harlthorpe E R Yk....60 C6
Harlton Cambs....33 L6
Harlyn Cnwll....3 K1
Harman's Cross Dorset....8 E10
Harmby N York....65 K9
Harmer Green Herts....33 J12
Harmer Hill Shrops....49 J10
Harmston Lincs....52 D10
Harnage Shrops....39 K2
Harnhill Gloucs....18 F1
Harold Hill Gt Lon....21 Q5
Haroldston West Pembks....24 F6
Haroldswick Shet....111 m2
Harold Wood Gt Lon....22 B5
Harome N York....66 F10
Harpenden Herts....21 J1
Harpford Devon....6 E5
Harpham E R Yk....61 J2
Harpley Norfk....44 D5
Harpley Worcs....39 M9
Harpole Nhants....31 P2
Harpsdale Highld....110 D5
Harpswell Lincs....52 D5
Harpurhey Manch....57 Q8
Harraby Cumb....71 N5
Harracott Devon....15 K6
Harrapool Highld....97 J5
Harrietfield P & K....92 E9
Harrietsham Kent....22 G11
Harringay Gt Lon....21 L6
Harrington Cumb....70 G9
Harrington Lincs....53 L8
Harrington Nhants....41 Q10
Harringworth Nhants....42 D10
Harris W Isls....111 c3
Harrogate N York....58 H3
Harrogate Crematorium N York....59 J4
Harrold Bed....32 D5
Harrow Gt Lon....21 J6
Harrowbarrow Cnwll....5 J6
Harrowgate Village Darltn....65 N4
Harrow Green Suffk....34 E6
Harrow on the Hill Gt Lon....21 J6
Harrow Weald Gt Lon....21 J5
Harston Cambs....33 L6
Harston Leics....42 B4
Harswell E R Yk....60 E6
Hart Hartpl....66 C1
Hartburn Nthumb....73 J4
Hartburn S on T....65 Q4
Hartest Suffk....34 D6
Hartfield E Susx....11 P3
Hartford Cambs....33 J3
Hartford Ches W....49 L2
Hartfordbridge Hants....20 C10
Hartford End Essex....34 B12
Hartforth N York....65 L6
Hartgrove Dorset....8 C4
Harthill Ches W....49 J4
Harthill N Lans....85 Q9
Harthill Rothm....51 L5
Hartington Derbys....50 F7
Hartland Devon....14 E7
Hartland Quay Devon....14 D7
Hartlebury Worcs....39 Q7
Hartlepool Hartpl....66 C2
Hartlepool Crematorium Hartpl....66 C2
Hartley Cumb....64 E6
Hartley Kent....12 F3
Hartley Kent....22 C9
Hartley Wespall Hants....20 B10
Hartley Wintney Hants....20 C11
Hartlip Kent....22 G9
Harton N York....60 C2
Harton S Tyne....73 P7
Hartpury Gloucs....29 L4
Hartshead Kirk....58 F9
Hartshead Moor Services Calder....58 F8
Hartshill C Stke....49 Q6
Hartshill Warwks....41 J8
Hartshorne Derbys....41 J4
Hartwell Nhants....32 B6
Hartwith N York....58 G2
Hartwood N Lans....85 P10
Hartwoodmyres Border....79 N4
Harvel Kent....22 D10
Harvington Worcs....30 D4
Harvington Worcs....39 Q7
Harwell Notts....51 P3
Harwell Oxon....19 N3
Harwich Essex....35 L9
Harwood Dale N York....67 L8
Harwood Park Crematorium Herts....33 J11
Harworth Notts....51 N3
Hasbury Dudley....40 C10
Hascombe Surrey....10 G3
Haselbech Nhants....41 P11
Haselbury Plucknett Somset....7 L1
Haseley Warwks....30 G1
Haselor Warwks....30 E3
Hasfield Gloucs....29 L4
Haskayne Lancs....56 G7

Hasketon Suffk....35 L6
Haslemere Surrey....10 E4
Haslingden Lancs....57 P4
Haslingfield Cambs....33 L6
Haslington Ches E....49 N4
Hassingham Norfk....45 N8
Hassocks W Susx....11 L7
Hassop Derbys....50 G6
Haster Highld....110 G5
Hastingleigh Kent....13 L2
Hastings E Susx....12 G7
Hastings Crematorium E Susx....12 G7
Hastingwood Essex....21 Q1
Hastoe Herts....20 E2
Haswell Dur....73 P11
Haswell Plough Dur....73 P11
Hatch Beauchamp Somset....17 J11
Hatch End Gt Lon....21 J5
Hatchmere Ches W....49 K2
Hatcliffe NE Lin....52 H4
Hatfield Donc....59 P11
Hatfield Herefs....39 L9
Hatfield Herts....21 K2
Hatfield Broad Oak Essex....33 N12
Hatfield Heath Essex....21 Q1
Hatfield Peverel Essex....22 F2
Hatfield Woodhouse Donc....59 P11
Hatford Oxon....19 K2
Hatherden Hants....19 K10
Hatherleigh Devon....15 J10
Hathern Leics....41 L3
Hatherop Gloucs....30 F11
Hathersage Derbys....50 G5
Hathersage Booths Derbys....50 G5
Hatherton Ches E....49 M6
Hatherton Staffs....40 C5
Hatley St George Cambs....33 J6
Hatt Cnwll....5 J7
Hattersley Tamesd....50 C2
Hatton Abers....103 L7
Hatton Angus....93 N7
Hatton Derbys....40 G2
Hatton Gt Lon....20 H8
Hatton Lincs....52 H7
Hatton Shrops....39 J4
Hatton Warrtn....57 L11
Hatton Warwks....30 G1
Hatton of Fintray Abers....102 H11
Haugh E Ayrs....76 H6
Haugham Lincs....53 K7
Haughhead E Duns....85 K7
Haughley Suffk....34 G4
Haughley Green Suffk....34 G4
Haugh of Glass Moray....101 M7
Haugh of Urr D & G....70 D3
Haughs of Kinnaird Angus....93 Q4
Haughton Ches E....49 L4
Haughton Shrops....48 H9
Haughton Staffs....49 Q10
Haughton le Skerne Darltn....65 N4
Haultwick Herts....33 K11
Haunton Staffs....40 G5
Hauxton Cambs....33 M6
Havant Hants....10 B8
Havant Crematorium Hants....10 B8
Havenstreet IoW....9 P8
Havercroft Wakefd....59 K10
Haverfordwest Pembks....24 G6
Haverhill Suffk....33 Q7
Haverigg Cumb....62 D6
Havering-atte-Bower Gt Lon....21 P5
Haversham M Keyn....32 B8
Haverthwaite Cumb....62 G5
Havyat N Som....17 L4
Hawarden Flints....48 G3
Hawbush Green Essex....34 D11
Hawen Cerdgn....36 F10
Hawes N York....64 F9
Hawe's Green Norfk....45 L9
Hawford Worcs....39 Q9
Hawick Border....80 C10
Hawkchurch Devon....7 J3
Hawkedon Suffk....34 D6
Hawkeridge Wilts....18 C9
Hawkesbury S Glos....18 B4
Hawkesbury Upton S Glos....18 B4
Hawkhurst Kent....12 F4
Hawkinge Kent....13 N3
Hawkinge Crematorium Kent....13 M3
Hawkley Hants....10 C4
Hawkridge Somset....15 P6
Hawkshead Cumb....62 G3
Hawkshead Hill Cumb....62 G3
Hawksland S Lans....78 D2
Hawkstone Shrops....49 L9
Hawkswick N York....64 G12
Hawksworth Leeds....58 F6
Hawksworth Notts....51 Q11
Hawkwell Essex....22 G5
Hawley Hants....20 D10
Hawling Gloucs....30 E9
Hawnby N York....66 C9
Haworth C Brad....58 D6
Hawstead Suffk....34 E5
Hawthorn Dur....73 P10
Hawthorn Hill Lincs....52 H11
Hawton Notts....52 B12
Haxby C York....59 N3
Haxey N Linc....51 Q2
Haycombe Crematorium BaNES....17 Q3
Haydock St Hel....57 K9
Haydon Bridge Nthumb....72 F7
Haydon Wick Swindn....18 G4
Hayes Gt Lon....20 H7
Hayes Gt Lon....21 N9
Hayes End Gt Lon....20 H7
Hayfield Ag & B....90 E10
Hayfield Derbys....50 D4
Hayhillock Angus....93 N7
Hayle Cnwll....2 E8
Hayle Port Cnwll....2 E8
Hayley Green Dudley....40 C10
Hayling Island Hants....10 B9
Haynes (Church End) C Beds....32 F8
Haynes (Northwood End) C Beds....32 F8

Haynes (Silver End) C Beds....32 F8
Haynes (West End) C Beds....32 F8
Hay-on-Wye Powys....27 P1
Hayscastle Pembks....24 F4
Hayscastle Cross Pembks....24 F4
Hay Street Herts....33 L10
Hayton Cumb....70 H7
Hayton Cumb....71 Q4
Hayton E R Yk....60 E5
Hayton Notts....51 Q4
Haytor Vale Devon....5 P5
Haytown Devon....14 G8
Haywards Heath W Susx....11 M5
Haywood Donc....59 N10
Hazelbank S Lans....77 P3
Hazelbury Bryan Dorset....7 Q2
Hazeleigh Essex....22 G3
Hazel Grove Stockp....50 B4
Hazelton Walls Fife....93 L10
Hazelwood Derbys....51 J10
Hazlemere Bucks....20 E4
Hazlerigg N u Ty....73 M6
Hazleton Gloucs....30 E9
Heacham Norfk....44 B3
Headbourne Worthy Hants....9 N2
Headcorn Kent....12 G2
Headingley Leeds....58 H7
Headington Oxon....31 M11
Headlam Dur....65 L4
Headlesscross N Lans....85 Q10
Headless Cross Worcs....30 D2
Headley Hants....10 D3
Headley Hants....19 N8
Headley Surrey....21 K11
Headley Down Hants....10 D3
Headon Notts....51 Q5
Heads Nook Cumb....71 P5
Heage Derbys....51 J10
Healaugh N York....59 L5
Healaugh N York....64 H7
Heald Green Stockp....57 Q10
Heale Somset....16 H11
Heale Somset....17 K10
Healey N York....65 L10
Healeyfield Dur....73 J10
Healing NE Lin....61 L11
Heamoor Cnwll....2 C9
Heanor Derbys....51 K10
Heanton Punchardon Devon....15 J5
Heapham Lincs....52 C6
Heart of England Crematorium Warwks....41 J8
Heart of Scotland Services N Lans....85 Q9
Heasley Mill Devon....15 M6
Heast Highld....96 H6
Heath Derbys....51 K7
Heath Wakefd....59 J9
Heath and Reach C Beds....32 D10
Heathcote Derbys....50 F8
Heather Leics....41 K5
Heathfield E Susx....12 C6
Heathfield Somset....16 F10
Heath Green Worcs....40 E12
Heath Hall D & G....78 G11
Heath Hayes & Wimblebury Staffs....40 D5
Heath Hill Shrops....49 N11
Heathrow Airport Gt Lon....20 H8
Heathton Shrops....39 P4
Heath Town Wolves....40 B7
Heatley Warrtn....57 N10
Heaton C Brad....58 F7
Heaton N u Ty....73 M7
Heaton Staffs....50 C8
Heaton Chapel Stockp....57 Q9
Heaton Mersey Stockp....57 Q10
Heaton Norris Stockp....50 B3
Heaton's Bridge Lancs....56 H6
Heaverham Kent....22 C10
Heavitree Devon....6 C4
Hebburn S Tyne....73 N7
Hebden N York....58 D2
Hebden Bridge Calder....58 C8
Hebing End Herts....33 K11
Hebron Carmth....25 L4
Hebron Nthumb....73 L3
Heckfield Hants....20 B10
Heckfield Green Suffk....35 K2
Heckfordbridge Essex....34 F11
Heckington Lincs....42 G2
Heckmondwike Kirk....58 G9
Heddington Wilts....18 E7
Heddon-on-the-Wall Nthumb....73 K7
Hedenham Norfk....45 M10
Hedge End Hants....9 N5
Hedgerley Bucks....20 F6
Hedging Somset....17 J9
Hedley on the Hill Nthumb....73 J8
Hednesford Staffs....40 D5
Hedon E R Yk....61 K8
Hedsor Bucks....20 E6
Heglibister Shet....111 k4
Heighington Darltn....65 M3
Heighington Lincs....52 E8
Heightington Worcs....39 N7
Heiton Border....80 F7
Hele Devon....6 D3
Hele Devon....15 J3
Helensburgh Ag & B....84 E6
Helenton S Ayrs....76 G5
Helford Cnwll....2 H9
Helford Passage Cnwll....2 H9
Helhoughton Norfk....44 E5
Helions Bumpstead Essex....33 Q8
Helland Cnwll....3 N2
Hellescott Cnwll....4 G3
Hellesdon Norfk....45 K7
Hellidon Nhants....31 M3
Hellifield N York....63 Q10
Hellingly E Susx....12 C7
Helmdon Nhants....31 N5
Helme Kirk....58 E10
Helmingham Suffk....35 K5
Helmsdale Highld....110 B11
Helmshore Lancs....57 P5
Helmsley N York....66 E10
Helperby N York....59 K1
Helperthorpe N York....67 K12
Helpringham Lincs....42 G3
Helpston C Pete....42 G8
Helsby Ches W....49 J1

Helston Cnwll 2 F9
Helstone Cnwll 4 D4
Helton Cumb 71 Q10
Hemel Hempstead Herts 20 C2
Hemerdon Devon 5 L8
Hemingbrough N York 59 P7
Hemingby Lincs 53 J8
Hemingford Abbots Cambs 33 J3
Hemingford Grey Cambs 33 J3
Hemingstone Suffk 35 J6
Hemington Leics 41 L2
Hemington Nhants 42 F12
Hemington Somset 17 Q5
Hemley Suffk 35 L8
Hemlington Middsb 66 C5
Hempnall Norfk 45 L10
Hempnall Green Norfk 45 L10
Hempriggs Moray 100 H3
Hempstead Essex 33 Q8
Hempstead Norfk 44 H3
Hempstead Norfk 45 N5
Hempton Norfk 44 E4
Hempton Oxon 31 K7
Hemsby Norfk 45 P6
Hemswell Lincs 52 D5
Hemswell Cliff Lincs 52 D5
Hemsworth Wakefd 59 K10
Hemyock Devon 16 F12
Hendon Gt Lon 21 K5
Hendon Sundld 73 P9
Hendon Crematorium Gt Lon 21 K5
Hendy Carmth 26 D7
Henfield W Susx 11 K6
Hengoed Caerph 27 N9
Hengoed Powys 38 E10
Hengrave Suffk 34 D3
Henham Essex 33 N10
Heniarth Powys 38 D1
Henlade Somset 16 H10
Henley Dorset 7 Q2
Henley Somset 17 L9
Henley Suffk 35 J6
Henley W Susx 10 E5
Henley-in-Arden Warwks 30 F2
Henley-on-Thames Oxon 20 C6
Henley's Down E Susx 12 E7
Henllan Cerdgn 36 F11
Henllan Denbgs 55 Q7
Henllys Torfn 28 B9
Henlow C Beds 32 H8
Hennock Devon 5 Q4
Henny Street Essex 34 E8
Henryd Conwy 55 L6
Henry's Moat (Castell Hendre) Pembks 24 H4
Hensall N York 59 N9
Henshaw Nthumb 72 D7
Hensingham Cumb 70 G11
Henstead Suffk 45 P11
Hensting Hants 9 N3
Henstridge Somset 17 Q11
Henstridge Ash Somset 17 Q11
Henton Oxon 20 C3
Henton Somset 17 L7
Henwick Worcs 39 Q10
Henwood Cnwll 4 G5
Heol-y-Cyw Brdgnd 27 K11
Hepple Nthumb 72 H1
Hepscott Nthumb 73 L4
Heptonstall Calder 58 C8
Hepworth Kirk 58 F11
Hepworth Suffk 34 G2
Herbrandston Pembks 24 F7
Hereford Herefs 28 F2
Hereford Crematorium Herefs 28 F2
Hereson Kent 23 Q9
Heribusta Highld 104 E8
Heriot C Edin 86 E8
Hermiston C Edin 86 E8
Hermitage Border 79 P9
Hermitage Dorset 7 P2
Hermitage W Berk 19 N6
Hermon Carmth 25 N3
Hermon Pembks 25 L3
Herne Kent 23 M9
Herne Bay Kent 23 M9
Herne Hill Gt Lon 21 L8
Herne Pound Kent 22 D11
Hernhill Kent 23 K10
Herodsfoot Cnwll 4 F7
Heronsford S Ayrs 68 F3
Herriard Hants 19 Q10
Herringfleet Suffk 45 P9
Herringswell Suffk 34 C3
Herringthorpe Rothm 51 K3
Herrington Sundld 73 P9
Hersden Kent 23 M10
Hersham Surrey 20 H9
Herstmonceux E Susx 12 D7
Herston Ork 111 h3
Hertford Herts 21 M2
Hertford Heath Herts 21 M2
Hertingfordbury Herts 21 L2
Hesketh Bank Lancs 57 J4
Hesketh Lane Lancs 57 L1
Hesket Newmarket Cumb 71 M7
Hesleden Dur 73 Q2
Heslington C York 59 N4
Hessay C York 59 M4
Hessenford Cnwll 4 G8
Hessett Suffk 34 F4
Hessle E R Yk 60 H8
Hessle Wakefd 59 K10
Hest Bank Lancs 63 J8
Heston Gt Lon 20 H7
Heston Services Gt Lon 20 H7
Hestwall Ork 111 g2
Heswall Wirral 56 F11
Hethe Oxon 31 N8
Hethersett Norfk 45 J8
Hethersgill Cumb 71 P3
Hett Dur 73 M12
Hetton N York 58 C3
Hetton-le-Hole Sundld 73 N10
Heugh Nthumb 73 J6
Heughhead Abers 101 M11
Heugh Head Border 87 Q3
Heveningham Suffk 35 M3
Hever Kent 11 P2
Heversham Cumb 63 J5
Hevingham Norfk 45 K6
Hewas Water Cnwll 3 L6
Hewelsfield Gloucs 28 G8
Hewish Somset 7 K2

Hewood Dorset 7 J3
Hexham Nthumb 72 G7
Hextable Kent 21 P8
Hexthorpe Donc 51 M1
Hexton Herts 32 F10
Hexworthy Cnwll 4 H4
Hexworthy Devon 5 N6
Heybridge Essex 22 D4
Heybridge Essex 22 G2
Heybrook Bay Devon 5 K9
Heydon Cambs 33 M8
Heydon Norfk 45 J5
Heydour Lincs 42 E3
Heylipoll Ag & B 88 B7
Heylor Shet 111 j3
Heysham Lancs 62 H9
Heyshott W Susx 10 E6
Heytesbury Wilts 18 D11
Heythrop Oxon 31 J8
Heywood Rochdl 57 Q6
Heywood Wilts 18 C9
Hibaldstow N Linc 52 D3
Hickleton Donc 59 L12
Hickling Norfk 45 N5
Hickling Notts 41 P2
Hickling Green Norfk 45 N5
Hickstead W Susx 11 L6
Hidcote Bartrim Gloucs 30 F5
Hidcote Boyce Gloucs 30 F6
High Ackworth Wakefd 59 K9
Higham Barns 58 H11
Higham Derbys 51 K8
Higham Kent 12 C1
Higham Kent 22 E8
Higham Lancs 57 P2
Higham Suffk 34 C4
Higham Suffk 34 G9
Higham Ferrers Nhants 32 D3
Higham Gobion C Beds 32 F9
Higham Hill Gt Lon 21 M5
Higham on the Hill Leics 41 J8
Highampton Devon 14 H10
Highams Park Gt Lon 21 M5
High Ardwell D & G 68 E9
High Auldgirth D & G 78 E10
High Bankhill Cumb 71 Q7
High Beach Essex 21 N4
High Bentham N York 63 M8
High Bickington Devon 15 K7
High Biggins Cumb 63 L6
High Blantyre S Lans 85 L10
High Bonnybridge Falk 85 N7
High Bray Devon 15 M5
Highbridge Somset 17 J6
Highbrook W Susx 11 M4
High Brooms Kent 12 C2
Highburton Kirk 58 F10
Highbury Gt Lon 21 L6
Highbury Somset 17 Q6
High Casterton Cumb 63 L6
High Catton E R Yk 60 C4
Highclere Hants 19 M8
Highcliffe Dorset 8 H8
High Coniscliffe Darltn 65 M5
High Crosby Cumb 71 P4
High Cross E Ayrs 76 G3
High Cross Hants 10 B5
High Cross Herts 33 K11
High Cross Warwks 30 G1
High Drummore D & G 68 F11
High Easter Essex 22 C1
High Ellington N York 65 L10
Higher Ansty Dorset 8 B6
Higher Bartle Lancs 57 J3
Higher Bockhampton Dorset 7 Q4
High Brixham Torbay 6 C10
High Ercall Wrekin 49 L11
Higher Chillington Somset 7 K2
Higher Folds Wigan 57 M8
Higher Gabwell Devon 6 C8
Higher Heysham Lancs 62 H9
Higher Irlam Salfd 57 N9
Higher Kinnerton Flints 48 G4
Higher Muddiford Devon 15 K5
Higher Penwortham Lancs 57 K3
Higher Prestacott Devon 14 G11
Higher Town Cnwll 3 J6
Higher Town Cnwll 3 M4
Higher Town IoS 2 C1
Higher Walton Lancs 57 L4
Higher Walton Warrtn 57 L10
Higher Wambrook Somset 6 H2
Higher Waterston Dorset 7 Q4
Higher Wheelton Lancs 57 L4
Higher Whitley Ches W 57 L11
Higher Wincham Ches W 57 M12
Higher Wraxall Dorset 7 N3
Higher Wych Ches W 49 J6
High Etherley Dur 65 L2
Highfield Gatesd 73 K8
Highfield N Ayrs 76 E2
High Garrett Essex 34 C10
Highgate Gt Lon 21 L6
High Grantley N York 65 M12
High Green Norfk 45 J11
High Green Norfk 45 J8
High Green Sheff 51 J2
High Halden Kent 12 H3
High Halstow Medway 22 F7
High Ham Somset 17 K9
High Harrogate N York 58 H3
High Hatton Shrops 49 L9
High Hauxley Nthumb 73 M1
High Hawsker N York 67 K6
High Hesket Cumb 71 P6
High Hoyland Barns 58 H11
High Hurstwood E Susx 11 P5
High Hutton N York 60 D1
High Ireby Cumb 71 K7
High Kilburn N York 66 D10
High Lands Dur 65 K3
Highlane Derbys 51 K4
High Lane Stockp 50 C4
High Lanes Cnwll 2 E8
Highleadon Gloucs 29 K4
High Legh Ches E 57 M11
Highleigh W Susx 10 D9
High Leven S on T 66 C5
Highley Shrops 39 N5
High Littleton BaNES 17 J5
High Lorton Cumb 71 J9
High Marnham Notts 52 B9
High Melton Donc 51 L1
High Mickley Nthumb 73 J8

Highmoor Oxon 20 B6
Highmoor Cross Oxon 20 B6
Highnam Gloucs 29 K5
High Newport Sundld 73 P9
High Newton Cumb 62 H5
High Nibthwaite Cumb 62 F4
High Offley Staffs 49 N9
High Ongar Essex 22 C3
High Onn Staffs 49 P11
High Park Corner Essex 34 G11
High Pennyvenie E Ayrs 76 H9
High Roding Essex 33 P12
High Salvington W Susx 10 H8
High Spen Gatesd 73 K8
Highsted Kent 22 H10
High Street Cnwll 3 J5
Highstreet Kent 23 L10
Highstreet Green Surrey 10 F3
Hightae D & G 78 H11
Highter's Heath Birm 40 E10
Hightown Sefton 56 F7
Hightown Green Suffk 34 F5
High Toynton Lincs 53 J9
High Valleyfield Fife 86 B5
Highweek Devon 6 B8
Highwood Hill Gt Lon 21 K5
Highworth Swindn 18 H3
High Wray Cumb 62 G3
High Wych Herts 21 P1
High Wycombe Bucks 20 D5
Hilborough Norfk 44 D9
Hilcott Wilts 18 G8
Hildenborough Kent 12 C1
Hilden Park Kent 12 C1
Hildersham Cambs 33 N7
Hilderstone Staffs 40 C1
Hilderthorpe E R Yk 61 K2
Hilgay Norfk 43 P9
Hill S Glos 28 H3
Hill Warwks 31 L2
Hillam N York 59 L8
Hill Brow Hants 10 C5
Hillbutts Dorset 8 E7
Hill Chorlton Staffs 49 P7
Hillclifflane Derbys 50 H10
Hill Common Somset 16 F10
Hilldyke Lincs 43 K1
Hill End Fife 86 C3
Hillend Fife 86 D5
Hill End Gloucs 29 M2
Hillend Mdloth 86 F8
Hillend N Lans 85 N9
Hillesden Bucks 31 P8
Hillesley Gloucs 29 K10
Hillfarrance Somset 16 F10
Hill Green Kent 22 G10
Hillhead Abers 102 D8
Hill Head Hants 9 P6
Hillhead S Lans 78 F2
Hillhead of Cocklaw Abers 103 M6
Hilliclay Highld 110 D3
Hillingdon Gt Lon 20 H6
Hillington C Glas 85 J9
Hillington Norfk 44 C5
Hillmorton Warwks 41 M11
Hill of Beath Fife 86 D4
Hill of Fearn Highld 107 N6
Hillowton D & G 70 C3
Hill Ridware Staffs 40 E4
Hillside Abers 95 Q3
Hillside Angus 95 L9
Hill Side Kirk 58 F10
Hills Town Derbys 51 L6
Hillstreet Hants 9 K4
Hillswick Shet 111 j3
Hill Top Sandw 40 C8
Hill Top Wakefd 59 J10
Hillwell Shet 111 k5
Hilmarton Wilts 18 E6
Hilperton Wilts 18 C8
Hilsea C Port 9 Q6
Hilston E R Yk 61 M7
Hilton Border 81 J4
Hilton Cambs 33 J4
Hilton Cumb 64 D4
Hilton Derbys 40 G2
Hilton Dorset 8 B6
Hilton Dur 65 L3
Hilton Highld 107 P7
Hilton S on T 66 C5
Hilton Shrops 39 P3
Hilton Park Services Staffs 40 C6
Himbleton Worcs 30 C3
Himley Staffs 39 Q4
Hincaster Cumb 63 K5
Hinchley Wood Surrey 21 J9
Hinckley Leics 41 K8
Hinderclay Suffk 34 G2
Hinderwell N York 66 H4
Hindhead Surrey 10 E3
Hindley Wigan 57 L7
Hindlip Worcs 39 Q9
Hindolveston Norfk 44 G4
Hindon Wilts 8 D2
Hindringham Norfk 44 G3
Hingham Norfk 44 G9
Hinstock Shrops 49 M9
Hintlesham Suffk 34 H7
Hinton Herefs 28 D2
Hinton S Glos 17 Q2
Hinton Shrops 38 H1
Hinton Ampner Hants 9 P2
Hinton Blewett BaNES 17 N5
Hinton Charterhouse BaNES 18 B8
Hinton-in-the-Hedges Nhants 31 M6
Hinton Martell Dorset 8 E6
Hinton on the Green Worcs 30 D6
Hinton Parva Swindn 19 J4
Hinton St George Somset 7 K1
Hinton St Mary Dorset 8 B4
Hinton Waldrist Oxon 19 L2
Hints Staffs 40 F6
Hinwick Bed 32 D5
Hinxhill Kent 13 K2
Hinxton Cambs 33 M7
Hinxworth Herts 32 H8
Hipperholme Calder 58 E8
Hipswell N York 65 L7
Hirn Abers 95 M2
Hirnant Powys 48 B10
Hirst Nthumb 73 M4
Hirst Courtney N York 59 N8
Hirwaun Rhondd 27 K7
Hiscott Devon 15 J7

Histon Cambs 33 M4
Hitcham Suffk 34 G6
Hitcham Causeway Suffk 34 G6
Hitcham Street Suffk 34 G6
Hitchin Herts 32 H10
Hither Green Gt Lon 21 M8
Hittisleigh Devon 5 P2
Hive E R Yk 60 E7
Hixon Staffs 40 D3
Hoaden Kent 23 N10
Hoar Cross Staffs 40 F3
Hoarwithy Herefs 28 G3
Hoath Kent 23 M9
Hobarris Shrops 38 F6
Hobkirk Border 80 D11
Hobson Dur 73 L9
Hoby Leics 41 P4
Hockering Norfk 44 H7
Hockerton Notts 51 Q9
Hockley Essex 22 G5
Hockley Heath Solhll 40 F11
Hockliffe C Beds 32 D10
Hockwold cum Wilton Norfk 44 C11
Hockworthy Devon 16 D11
Hoddesdon Herts 21 M2
Hoddlesden Bl w D 57 N4
Hoddom Cross D & G 71 J2
Hoddom Mains D & G 71 J2
Hodgeston Pembks 24 H8
Hodnet Shrops 49 L9
Hodsock Notts 51 N4
Hodsoll Street Kent 22 D10
Hodthorpe Derbys 51 M5
Hoe Norfk 44 G6
Hogben's Hill Kent 23 K11
Hoggeston Bucks 32 B10
Hoggrill's End Warwks 40 G8
Hoghton Lancs 57 L4
Hognaston Derbys 50 G10
Hogsthorpe Lincs 53 N8
Holbeach Lincs 43 K5
Holbeach Bank Lincs 43 K5
Holbeach Clough Lincs 43 K5
Holbeach Drove Lincs 43 K7
Holbeach Hurn Lincs 43 L4
Holbeach St Johns Lincs 43 K6
Holbeach St Mark's Lincs 43 L4
Holbeach St Matthew Lincs 43 L4
Holbeck Notts 51 M6
Holberrow Green Worcs 30 D3
Holbeton Devon 5 M9
Holborn Gt Lon 21 L7
Holbrook Derbys 51 J11
Holbrook Suffk 35 J9
Holbrooks Covtry 41 J10
Holbury Hants 9 M6
Holcombe Devon 6 C7
Holcombe Somset 17 P6
Holcombe Rogus Devon 16 E11
Holcot Nhants 32 B3
Holden Lancs 63 P11
Holdenby Nhants 31 P1
Holder's Green Essex 33 Q10
Holdgate Shrops 39 K4
Holdingham Lincs 42 F1
Holditch Dorset 7 J3
Holemoor Devon 14 H10
Holford Somset 16 F7
Holgate C York 59 N4
Holker Cumb 62 G6
Holkham Norfk 44 E2
Hollacombe Devon 14 G10
Holland Fen Lincs 52 H12
Holland-on-Sea Essex 35 K12
Hollandstoun Ork 111 i1
Hollee D & G 71 L2
Hollesley Suffk 35 M7
Hollicombe Torbay 6 B9
Hollingbourne Kent 22 G11
Hollingbury Br & H 11 L8
Hollingdon Bucks 32 C10
Hollington Derbys 50 G11
Hollington Staffs 50 D11
Hollingworth Tamesd 50 D2
Hollinsclough Staffs 50 E7
Hollins End Sheff 51 J4
Hollins Green Warrtn 57 M10
Hollinswood Wrekin 39 N1
Hollocombe Devon 15 L9
Holloway Derbys 51 J9
Holloway Gt Lon 21 L6
Hollowell Nhants 41 P11
Hollowmoor Heath Ches W 49 J2
Hollows D & G 79 N12
Hollybush Caerph 27 N7
Hollybush E Ayrs 76 G8
Hollybush Herefs 29 K2
Hollym E R Yk 61 N8
Holmbridge Kirk 58 E11
Holmbury St Mary Surrey 10 H2
Holmbush Cnwll 3 M5
Holmcroft Staffs 40 B3
Holme Cambs 42 H11
Holme Cumb 63 K6
Holme Kirk 58 E11
Holme N York 65 P10
Holme Notts 52 B10
Holme Chapel Lancs 57 Q3
Holme Hale Norfk 44 E8
Holme Lacy Herefs 28 G2
Holme Marsh Herefs 38 G10
Holme next the Sea Norfk 44 B2
Holme on the Wolds E R Yk 60 G5
Holme Pierrepont Notts 51 N11
Holmer Herefs 28 F1
Holmer Green Bucks 20 E4
Holme St Cuthbert Cumb 70 H6
Holmes Chapel Ches E 49 N3
Holmesfield Derbys 50 H5
Holmeswood Lancs 56 H5
Holmethorpe Surrey 21 L12
Holme upon Spalding Moor E R Yk 60 D6
Holmewood Derbys 51 K7
Holmfirth Kirk 58 F11
Holmhead E Ayrs 77 J7
Holmpton E R Yk 61 N9
Holmrook Cumb 62 C3
Holmsford Bridge Crematorium N Ayrs 76 F4
Holmside Dur 73 L10
Holne Devon 5 N6

Holnicote Somset 16 C6
Holsworthy Devon 14 F10
Holsworthy Beacon Devon 14 G9
Holt Dorset 8 F6
Holt Norfk 44 H3
Holt Wilts 18 C8
Holt Worcs 39 P9
Holt Wrexhm 48 H5
Holtby C York 59 P4
Holt End Worcs 40 E12
Holt Heath Worcs 39 P9
Holton Oxon 31 N11
Holton Somset 17 P10
Holton cum Beckering Lincs 52 G7
Holton le Clay Lincs 53 J3
Holton le Moor Lincs 52 F4
Holton St Mary Suffk 34 H8
Holwell Dorset 7 Q1
Holwell Herts 32 G9
Holwell Leics 41 Q3
Holwell Oxon 30 G11
Holwick Dur 64 G3
Holybourne Hants 10 B2
Holyhead IoA 54 C5
Holy Island IoA 54 C5
Holy Island Nthumb 81 N5
Holy Island Nthumb 81 N6
Holymoorside Derbys 51 J7
Holyport W & M 20 E7
Holystone Nthumb 72 G1
Holytown N Lans 85 M10
Holytown Crematorium N Lans 85 N10
Holywell C Beds 32 E12
Holywell Cambs 33 K3
Holywell Cnwll 2 H4
Holywell Dorset 7 N2
Holywell Flints 48 E1
Holywell Green Calder 58 E9
Holywell Lake Somset 16 F11
Holywell Row Suffk 34 B2
Holywood D & G 78 F11
Holywood Village D & G 78 F11
Homer Shrops 39 L2
Homer Green Sefton 56 G8
Homersfield Suffk 45 L11
Homington Wilts 8 G3
Honeybourne Worcs 30 E5
Honeychurch Devon 15 L10
Honeystreet Wilts 18 G8
Honey Tye Suffk 34 F9
Honiley Warwks 40 G11
Honing Norfk 45 M5
Honingham Norfk 44 H7
Honington Lincs 42 D2
Honington Suffk 34 E2
Honington Warwks 30 H5
Honiton Devon 6 F3
Honley Kirk 58 F10
Honor Oak Crematorium Gt Lon 21 M8
Hooe C Plym 5 K9
Hooe E Susx 12 E7
Hoo Green Ches E 57 N11
Hoohill Bpool 56 G2
Hook Gt Lon 21 J9
Hook Hants 20 B11
Hook Pembks 24 G6
Hook Wilts 18 F4
Hooke Dorset 7 M3
Hook Green Kent 12 D3
Hook Green Kent 22 C8
Hook Norton Oxon 31 J7
Hookway Devon 15 P11
Hooley Surrey 21 L11
Hoo St Werburgh Medway 22 F8
Hooton Levitt Rothm 51 M3
Hooton Pagnell Donc 59 L11
Hooton Roberts Rothm 51 L2
Hope Derbys 50 F5
Hope Devon 5 N11
Hope Flints 48 F4
Hope Staffs 50 E9
Hope Bagot Shrops 39 L7
Hope Bowdler Shrops 39 J4
Hopehouse Border 79 L5
Hopeman Moray 100 H2
Hope Mansell Herefs 28 H5
Hopesay Shrops 38 H5
Hope under Dinmore Herefs 39 K10
Hopgrove C York 59 N3
Hopperton N York 59 K3
Hopstone Shrops 39 P4
Hopton Derbys 50 H9
Hopton Staffs 40 C3
Hopton Suffk 34 G2
Hopton Cangeford Shrops 39 K6
Hopton Castle Shrops 38 G6
Hoptonheath Shrops 38 H6
Hopton on Sea Norfk 45 Q9
Hopton Wafers Shrops 39 M6
Hopwas Staffs 40 F6
Hopwood Worcs 40 D11
Hopwood Park Services Worcs 40 D11
Horam E Susx 12 C5
Horbling Lincs 42 G3
Horbury Wakefd 58 H9
Horden Dur 73 Q11
Hordle Hants 9 J8
Hordley Shrops 48 H8
Horfield Bristl 17 N2
Horham Suffk 35 K3
Horkesley Heath Essex 34 G10
Horkstow N Linc 60 G9
Horley Oxon 31 K5
Horley Surrey 11 L2
Hornblotton Green Somset 17 N9
Hornby Lancs 63 L8
Hornby N York 65 L8
Hornby N York 65 P6
Horncastle Lincs 53 J9
Hornchurch Gt Lon 21 Q6
Horncliffe Nthumb 81 K4
Horndean Border 81 J4
Horndean Hants 10 B7
Horndon Devon 5 L4
Horndon on the Hill Thurr 22 D6
Horne Surrey 11 M2
Horner Somset 16 B7
Horning Norfk 45 M6

Horninghold - Kelfield 181


**Horninghold** Leics 42 B10
**Horninglow** Staffs 40 G3
**Horningsea** Cambs 33 M4
**Horningsham** Wilts 18 B11
**Horningtoft** Norfk 44 F5
**Horns Cross** Devon 14 G7
**Hornsea** E R Yk 61 K5
**Hornsey** Gt Lon 21 L5
**Hornton** Oxon 31 K5
**Horra** Shet 111 k2
**Horrabridge** Devon 5 K6
**Horringer** Suffk 34 D4
**Horrocksford** Lancs 63 N12
**Horsebridge** Devon 5 J5
**Horsebridge** E Susx 12 C7
**Horsebridge** Hants 9 L2
**Horsehay** Wrekin 39 M1
**Horseheath** Cambs 33 P7
**Horsehouse** N York 65 J10
**Horsell** Surrey 20 F10
**Horseman's Green** Wrexhm 49 J7
**Horsey** Norfk 45 P5
**Horsey** Somset 17 J8
**Horsford** Norfk 45 K6
**Horsforth** Leeds 58 G6
**Horsham** W Susx 11 J4
**Horsham** Worcs 39 N9
**Horsham St Faith** Norfk 45 K7
**Horsington** Lincs 52 H9
**Horsington** Somset 17 Q10
**Horsley** Derbys 51 J11
**Horsley** Gloucs 29 L8
**Horsley** Nthumb 72 F2
**Horsley** Nthumb 73 J7
**Horsleycross Street** Essex 35 J10
**Horsleyhill** Border 80 C9
**Horsley Woodhouse** Derbys 51 K11
**Horsmonden** Kent 12 E2
**Horspath** Oxon 31 M12
**Horstead** Norfk 45 L6
**Horsted Keynes** W Susx 11 M5
**Horton** Bucks 32 D11
**Horton** Dorset 8 F6
**Horton** Lancs 63 Q11
**Horton** Nhants 32 B6
**Horton** S Glos 18 A4
**Horton** Somset 17 J12
**Horton** Staffs 50 C8
**Horton** Swans 26 C10
**Horton** W & M 20 G8
**Horton** Wilts 18 F7
**Horton** Wrekin 49 M11
**Horton-cum-Studley** Oxon 31 N10
**Horton Green** Ches W 49 J5
**Horton-in-Ribblesdale** N York 64 E12
**Horton Kirby** Kent 22 C9
**Horwich** Bolton 57 M6
**Horwood** Devon 15 J6
**Hoscote** Border 79 N6
**Hose** Leics 41 Q2
**Hosh** P & K 92 C10
**Hoswick** Shet 111 k5
**Hotham** E R Yk 60 F7
**Hothfield** Kent 13 J2
**Hoton** Leics 41 M3
**Hough** Ches E 49 N5
**Hougham** Lincs 42 C2
**Hough Green** Halton 57 J10
**Hough-on-the-Hill** Lincs 42 D2
**Houghton** Cambs 33 J3
**Houghton** Hants 9 K2
**Houghton** Pembks 24 H7
**Houghton** W Susx 10 G7
**Houghton Conquest** C Beds 32 F8
**Houghton Green** E Susx 12 H5
**Houghton-le-Spring** Sundld 73 N10
**Houghton on the Hill** Leics 41 P6
**Houghton Regis** C Beds 32 E11
**Houghton St Giles** Norfk 44 F3
**Hound Green** Hants 20 B10
**Houndslow** Border 80 E5
**Houndwood** Border 87 Q9
**Hounslow** Gt Lon 21 J8
**Househill** Highld 100 D4
**Houses Hill** Kirk 58 G10
**Housieside** Abers 103 J9
**Houston** Rens 84 G9
**Houstry** Highld 110 D8
**Houton** Ork 111 g2
**Hove** Br & H 11 L8
**Hoveringham** Notts 51 P10
**Hoveton** Norfk 45 M6
**Hovingham** N York 66 F11
**How Caple** Herefs 28 H3
**Howden** E R Yk 60 D8
**Howden-le-Wear** Dur 65 L2
**Howe** Highld 110 F4
**Howe** N York 65 P10
**Howe** Norfk 45 L9
**Howe Bridge Crematorium** Wigan 57 M8
**Howe Green** Essex 22 E3
**Howegreen** Essex 22 G3
**Howell** Lincs 42 G2
**Howe of Teuchar** Abers 102 G6
**Howes** D & G 71 K3
**Howe Street** Essex 22 E1
**Howe Street** Essex 34 B9
**Howey** Powys 38 C9
**Howgate** Cumb 70 G10
**Howgate** Mdloth 86 F10
**Howick** Nthumb 81 Q10
**Howlett End** Essex 33 P9
**Howley** Somset 6 H2
**How Mill** Cumb 71 Q4
**Howmore** W Isls 111 a5
**Hownam** Border 80 G9
**Howsham** N Linc 52 E3
**Howsham** N York 60 C2
**Howtel** Nthumb 81 J7
**How Wood** Herts 21 J3
**Howwood** Rens 84 G10
**Hoxa** Ork 111 h3
**Hoxne** Suffk 35 K2
**Hoy** Ork 111 g3
**Hoylake** Wirral 56 E10
**Hoyland Nether** Barns 51 J1
**Hoyland Swaine** Barns 58 H12
**Hubberston** Pembks 24 F7
**Huby** N York 58 H5
**Huby** N York 59 M2
**Hucclecote** Gloucs 29 M5
**Hucking** Kent 22 G10
**Hucknall** Notts 51 M10
**Huddersfield** Kirk 58 F10
**Huddersfield Crematorium** Kirk 58 F9
**Huddington** Worcs 30 C3
**Hudswell** N York 65 K7
**Huggate** E R Yk 60 F3
**Hughenden Valley** Bucks 20 D4
**Hughley** Shrops 39 K3
**Hugh Town** IoS 2 c2
**Huish** Devon 15 J9
**Huish** Wilts 18 G7
**Huish Champflower** Somset 16 E9
**Huish Episcopi** Somset 17 L10
**Hulcott** Bucks 32 C12
**Hulham** Devon 6 D6
**Hulland** Derbys 50 G10
**Hulland Ward** Derbys 50 G10
**Hullavington** Wilts 18 D4
**Hullbridge** Essex 22 F4
**Hull, Kingston upon** C KuH 61 J8
**Hulme** Manch 57 Q9
**Hulme** Staffs 50 C10
**Hulme** Warrtn 57 L9
**Hulme End** Staffs 50 E8
**Hulme Walfield** Ches E 49 Q3
**Hulverstone** IoW 9 L9
**Hulver Street** Suffk 45 P11
**Humber Bridge** N Linc 60 H8
*Humberside Airport* N Linc 61 J11
**Humberston** NE Lin 53 K3
**Humberstone** C Leic 41 N6
**Humbie** E Loth 87 J9
**Humbleton** E R Yk 61 L7
**Humby** Lincs 42 E4
**Hume** Border 80 F6
**Humshaugh** Nthumb 72 G6
**Huna** Highld 110 G2
**Huncote** Leics 41 M7
**Hundalee** Border 80 E9
**Hunderthwaite** Dur 64 H4
**Hundleby** Lincs 53 L9
**Hundleton** Pembks 24 G8
**Hundon** Suffk 34 C7
**Hundred House** Powys 38 C10
**Hungarton** Leics 41 P6
**Hungerford** Somset 16 E7
**Hungerford** W Berk 19 K7
**Hungerford Newtown** W Berk 19 L6
**Hungerstone** Herefs 28 E2
**Hunmanby** N York 67 N11
**Hunningham** Warwks 31 J1
**Hunsbury Hill** Nhants 31 Q3
**Hunsdon** Herts 21 N1
**Hunsingore** N York 59 K4
**Hunslet** Leeds 58 H7
**Hunsonby** Cumb 64 B1
**Hunstanton** Norfk 43 Q3
**Hunstanworth** Dur 72 G10
**Hunsterson** Ches E 49 M6
**Hunston** Suffk 34 F3
**Hunston** W Susx 10 D9
**Hunstrete** BaNES 17 P4
**Hunsworth** Kirk 58 F8
**Hunter's Quay** Ag & B 84 C7
**Huntham** Somset 17 J10
**Hunthill Lodge** Angus 94 H7
**Huntingdon** Cambs 33 J3
**Huntingfield** Suffk 35 M2
**Huntington** C York 59 N3
**Huntington** Ches W 48 H3
**Huntington** E Loth 87 J7
**Huntington** Herefs 38 F10
**Huntington** Staffs 40 C5
**Huntley** Gloucs 29 J5
**Huntly** Abers 102 C7
**Hunton** Kent 22 E12
**Hunton** N York 65 L8
**Huntscott** Somset 16 C7
**Huntsham** Devon 16 D11
**Huntshaw** Devon 15 J7
**Huntspill** Somset 17 J7
**Huntstile** Somset 16 H9
**Huntworth** Somset 17 J8
**Hunwick** Dur 65 L2
**Hunworth** Norfk 44 H3
**Hurdcott** Wilts 8 H1
**Hurdsfield** Ches E 50 B6
**Hurley** W & M 20 D6
**Hurley** Warwks 40 G8
**Hurley Common** Warwks 40 G7
**Hurlford** E Ayrs 76 H4
**Hurn** Dorset 8 G7
**Hursley** Hants 9 M3
**Hurst** Wokham 20 C8
**Hurstbourne Priors** Hants 19 M10
**Hurstbourne Tarrant** Hants 19 L9
**Hurst Green** E Susx 12 E5
**Hurst Green** Essex 34 H12
**Hurst Green** Lancs 57 M2
**Hurst Green** Surrey 21 N12
**Hurst Hill** Dudley 40 B8
**Hurstpierpoint** W Susx 11 L6
**Hurstwood** Lancs 57 Q3
**Hurtiso** Ork 111 h2
**Hurworth-on-Tees** Darltn 65 N5
**Hurworth Place** Darltn 65 N5
**Husbands Bosworth** Leics 41 N10
**Husborne Crawley** C Beds 32 D9
**Husthwaite** N York 66 D11
**Hutcliffe Wood Crematorium** Sheff 51 J4
**Huthwaite** Notts 51 L8
**Huttoft** Lincs 53 N8
**Hutton** Border 81 J4
**Hutton** E R Yk 60 H4
**Hutton** Essex 22 D4
**Hutton** Lancs 57 J4
**Hutton** N Som 17 J4
**Hutton Buscel** N York 67 L10
**Hutton Conyers** N York 65 N11
**Hutton Cranswick** E R Yk 60 H4
**Hutton End** Cumb 71 P7
**Hutton Henry** Dur 65 Q1
**Hutton-le-Hole** N York 66 G9
**Hutton Lowcross** R & Cl 66 E5
**Hutton Magna** Dur 65 K5
**Hutton Roof** Cumb 63 K6
**Hutton Roof** Cumb 71 M8
**Hutton Rudby** N York 66 C6
**Hutton Sessay** N York 66 C11
**Hutton Wandesley** N York 59 L4
**Huxham** Devon 6 C4
**Huxley** Ches W 49 K3
**Huyton** Knows 57 J10
**Hycemoor** Cumb 62 C4
**Hyde** Tamesd 50 C2
**Hyde Heath** Bucks 20 E4
**Hyde Lea** Staffs 40 B4
Hylands House & Park Essex 22 D3
**Hyndford Bridge** S Lans 78 E1
**Hynish** Ag & B 88 C8
**Hyssington** Powys 38 F4
**Hythe** Essex 34 G10
**Hythe** Hants 9 M6
**Hythe** Kent 13 M3
**Hythe End** W & M 20 G8

## I

**Ibberton** Dorset 8 B6
**Ible** Derbys 50 G9
**Ibsley** Hants 8 H5
**Ibstock** Leics 41 K5
**Ibstone** Bucks 20 C5
**Ibthorpe** Hants 19 L9
**Iburndale** N York 67 J6
**Ibworth** Hants 19 P9
**Ichrachan** Ag & B 90 D9
**Ickburgh** Norfk 44 D10
**Ickenham** Gt Lon 20 H6
**Ickford** Bucks 31 N11
**Ickham** Kent 23 N10
**Ickleford** Herts 32 H9
**Icklesham** E Susx 12 G6
**Ickleton** Cambs 33 M7
**Icklingham** Suffk 34 C3
**Ickornshaw** N York 58 C5
**Ickwell Green** C Beds 32 G7
**Icomb** Gloucs 30 G9
**Idbury** Oxon 30 G9
**Iddesleigh** Devon 15 K9
**Ide** Devon 6 B5
**Ideford** Devon 6 B7
**Ide Hill** Kent 21 P11
**Iden** E Susx 12 H5
**Iden Green** Kent 12 E3
**Iden Green** Kent 12 F4
**Idle** C Brad 58 F6
**Idless** Cnwll 3 J6
**Idlicote** Warwks 30 H5
**Idmiston** Wilts 18 H12
**Idole** Carmth 25 P6
**Idridgehay** Derbys 50 H10
**Idrigill** Highld 104 E9
**Idstone** Oxon 19 J4
**Iffley** Oxon 31 M12
**Ifield** W Susx 11 K3
**Ifold** W Susx 10 G4
**Iford** Bmouth 8 G8
**Iford** E Susx 11 N8
**Ifton** Mons 28 F10
**Ightfield** Shrops 49 L7
**Ightham** Kent 22 C11
**Ilam** Staffs 50 F10
**Ilchester** Somset 17 M10
**Ilderton** Nthumb 81 L9
**Ilford** Gt Lon 21 N6
**Ilford** Somset 17 K11
**Ilfracombe** Devon 15 J3
**Ilkeston** Derbys 51 L11
**Ilketshall St Andrew** Suffk 45 N11
**Ilketshall St Margaret** Suffk 45 M11
**Ilkley** C Brad 58 E5
**Illand** Cnwll 4 G5
**Illey** Dudley 40 C10
**Illogan** Cnwll 2 G7
**Illston on the Hill** Leics 41 P7
**Ilmer** Bucks 20 C3
**Ilmington** Warwks 30 G5
**Ilminster** Somset 17 J12
**Ilsington** Devon 5 Q5
**Ilston** Swans 26 D10
**Ilton** N York 65 L11
**Ilton** Somset 17 J11
**Imachar** N Ayrs 75 N4
**Immingham** NE Lin 61 K10
**Immingham Dock** NE Lin 61 K10
**Impington** Cambs 33 M4
**Ince** Ches W 57 J12
**Ince Blundell** Sefton 56 G8
**Ince-in-Makerfield** Wigan 57 L7
**Inchbae Lodge Hotel** Highld 106 G8
**Inchbare** Angus 95 K8
**Inchberry** Moray 101 L4
**Incheril** Highld 105 Q9
**Inchinnan** Rens 84 H8
**Inchlaggan** Highld 98 B8
**Inchmichael** P & K 93 J9
**Inchnacardoch Hotel** Highld 98 E6
**Inchnadamph** Highld 108 E10
**Inchture** P & K 93 K9
**Inchvuilt** Highld 98 C2
**Inchyra** P & K 92 H10
**Indian Queens** Cnwll 3 K4
**Ingatestone** Essex 22 D4
**Ingbirchworth** Barns 58 G11
**Ingestre** Staffs 40 C3
**Ingham** Lincs 52 D6
**Ingham** Norfk 45 N5
**Ingham** Suffk 34 E3
**Ingham Corner** Norfk 45 N5
**Ingleby** Derbys 41 J3
**Ingleby Arncliffe** N York 66 C7
**Ingleby Barwick** S on T 66 C5
**Ingleby Greenhow** N York 66 E6
**Ingleigh Green** Devon 15 K10
**Inglesbatch** BaNES 17 Q4
**Inglesham** Swindn 18 H2
**Ingleston** D & G 70 F3
**Ingleton** Dur 65 L4
**Ingleton** N York 63 M7
**Inglewhite** Lancs 57 K2
**Ingoe** Nthumb 73 J6
**Ingol** Lancs 57 K3
**Ingoldisthorpe** Norfk 44 B4
**Ingoldmells** Lincs 53 N9
**Ingoldsby** Lincs 42 E4
**Ingram** Nthumb 81 L10
**Ingrave** Essex 22 D5
**Ingrow** C Brad 58 D6
**Ings** Cumb 63 J3
**Ingst** S Glos 28 G10
**Ingthorpe** Rutlnd 42 E8
**Ingworth** Norfk 45 K4
**Inkberrow** Worcs 30 D3
**Inkhorn** Abers 103 J7
**Inkpen** W Berk 19 L7
**Inkstack** Highld 110 F2
**Innellan** Ag & B 84 C8
**Innerleithen** Border 79 M2
**Innerleven** Fife 86 H3
**Innermessan** D & G 68 E6
**Innerwick** E Loth 87 N7
**Innesmill** Moray 101 K3
**Insch** Abers 102 E9
**Insh** Highld 99 M8
**Inskip** Lancs 57 J2
**Instow** Devon 14 H6
**Intake** Sheff 51 K4
**Inver** Abers 94 D4
**Inver** Highld 107 P6
**Inver** P & K 92 F7
**Inverailort** Highld 97 K12
**Inveralligin** Highld 105 M10
**Inverallochy** Abers 103 L3
**Inveran** Highld 107 J3
**Inveraray** Ag & B 84 B2
**Inverarish** Highld 96 G3
**Inverarity** Angus 93 M6
**Inverarnan** Stirlg 91 J11
**Inverasdale** Highld 105 M5
**Inverbeg** Ag & B 84 F4
**Inverbervie** Abers 95 N7
**Inver-boyndie** Abers 102 E3
**Invercreran House Hotel** Ag & B 90 D7
**Inverdruie** Highld 99 N6
**Inveresk** E Loth 86 G7
**Inveresragan** Ag & B 90 D8
**Inverey** Abers 94 B4
**Inverfarigaig** Highld 98 G4
**Inverfolla** Ag & B 90 C7
**Invergarry** Highld 98 D8
**Invergeldie** P & K 91 Q10
**Invergloy** Highld 98 C10
**Invergordon** Highld 107 L8
**Invergowrie** P & K 93 L9
**Inverguseran** Highld 97 K8
**Inverhadden** P & K 91 P5
**Inverherive Hotel** Stirlg 91 K10
**Inverie** Highld 97 K9
**Inverinan** Ag & B 90 D11
**Inverinate** Highld 97 N5
**Inverkeilor** Angus 93 R6
**Inverkeithing** Fife 86 D5
**Inverkeithny** Abers 102 E6
**Inverkip** Inver 84 D8
**Inverkirkaig** Highld 108 B10
**Inverlael** Highld 106 C5
**Inverlair** Highld 98 D11
**Inverliever Lodge** Ag & B 83 N2
**Inverlochy** Ag & B 90 G10
**Invermark** Angus 94 G6
**Invermoriston** Highld 98 F5
**Invernaver** Highld 109 M4
**Inverness** Highld 107 L12
*Inverness Airport* Highld 107 M11
**Inverness Crematorium** Highld 99 J1
**Invernoaden** Ag & B 84 C4
**Inveroran Hotel** Ag & B 90 H7
**Inverquharity** Angus 93 M4
**Inverquhomery** Abers 103 L6
**Inverroy** Highld 98 C11
**Inversanda** Highld 90 C4
**Invershiel** Highld 97 N6
**Invershin** Highld 107 J3
**Invershore** Highld 110 F8
**Inversnaid Hotel** Stirlg 84 F2
**Inverugie** Abers 103 M6
**Inveruglas** Ag & B 84 F2
**Inveruglass** Highld 99 M8
**Inverurie** Abers 102 G10
**Inwardleigh** Devon 15 K11
**Inworth** Essex 34 E12
**Iona** Ag & B 88 G10
**Iping** W Susx 10 D5
**Ipplepen** Devon 5 Q7
**Ipsden** Oxon 19 Q4
**Ipstones** Staffs 50 D10
**Ipswich** Suffk 35 J7
**Ipswich Crematorium** Suffk 35 K7
**Irby** Wirral 56 F11
**Irby in the Marsh** Lincs 53 M10
**Irby upon Humber** NE Lin 52 H3
**Irchester** Nhants 32 D4
**Ireby** Cumb 71 K7
**Ireby** Lancs 63 M7
**Ireleth** Cumb 62 E6
**Ireshopeburn** Dur 72 F12
**Irlam** Salfd 57 N9
**Irnham** Lincs 42 E5
**Iron Acton** S Glos 29 J11
**Ironbridge** Wrekin 39 M2
Ironbridge Gorge Wrekin 39 M2
**Ironmacannie** D & G 69 P4
**Ironville** Derbys 51 K9
**Irstead** Norfk 45 M6
**Irthington** Cumb 71 P4
**Irthlingborough** Nhants 32 D3
**Irton** N York 67 L10
**Irvine** N Ayrs 76 F4
**Isauld** Highld 110 A3
**Isbister** Shet 111 k2
**Isbister** Shet 111 m3
**Isfield** E Susx 11 N6
**Isham** Nhants 32 C3
**Isington** Hants 10 C2
**Islay** Ag & B 82 E7
*Islay Airport* Ag & B 74 D3
**Isle Abbotts** Somset 17 J11
**Isle Brewers** Somset 17 K11
**Isleham** Cambs 33 Q2
**Isle of Dogs** Gt Lon 21 M7
**Isle of Grain** Medway 22 G7
**Isle of Lewis** W Isls 111 d2
**Isle of Man** IoM 56 c4
*Isle of Man Ronaldsway Airport* IoM 56 b7
**Isle of Mull** Ag & B 89 M8
**Isle of Purbeck** Dorset 8 E10
**Isle of Sheppey** Kent 23 J9
**Isle of Skye** Highld 96 E3
**Isle of Thanet** Kent 23 P9
**Isle of Walney** Cumb 62 E8
**Isle of Whithorn** D & G 69 L10
**Isle of Wight** IoW 9 N9
**Isle of Wight Crematorium** IoW 9 N8
**Isleornsay** Highld 97 J7
**Isles of Scilly** IoS 2 c2
*Isles of Scilly St Mary's Airport* IoS 2 c2
**Islesteps** D & G 70 F2
**Isleworth** Gt Lon 21 J8
**Isley Walton** Leics 41 K3
**Islibhig** W Isls 111 b2
**Islington** Gt Lon 21 L6
**Islington Crematorium** Gt Lon 21 L5
**Islip** Nhants 32 E2
**Islip** Oxon 31 M10
**Islivig** W Isls 111 b2
**Isombridge** Wrekin 49 L11
**Itchen Abbas** Hants 9 N2
**Itchen Stoke** Hants 9 P2
**Itchingfield** W Susx 11 J4
**Itteringham** Norfk 45 J4
**Itton** Mons 28 F9
**Itton Common** Mons 28 F9
**Ivegill** Cumb 71 N6
**Iver** Bucks 20 G7
**Iver Heath** Bucks 20 G6
**Iveston** Dur 73 K10
**Ivinghoe** Bucks 32 D12
**Ivinghoe Aston** Bucks 32 D12
**Ivington** Herefs 39 J10
**Ivybridge** Devon 5 M8
**Ivychurch** Kent 13 K5
**Ivy Hatch** Kent 22 C11
**Iwade** Kent 22 H9
**Iwerne Courtney or Shroton** Dorset 8 C5
**Iwerne Minster** Dorset 8 C5
**Ixworth** Suffk 34 F3
**Ixworth Thorpe** Suffk 34 F3

## J

**Jack-in-the-Green** Devon 6 D4
**Jackton** S Lans 85 K11
**Jacobstow** Cnwll 4 F2
**Jacobstowe** Devon 15 K10
**Jameston** Pembks 25 J8
**Jamestown** Highld 106 H10
**Jamestown** W Duns 84 G6
**Janetstown** Highld 110 E8
**Janetstown** Highld 110 G5
**Jardine Hall** D & G 78 H10
**Jarrow** S Tyne 73 N7
**Jasper's Green** Essex 34 C10
**Jawcraig** Falk 85 P7
**Jaywick** Essex 23 M1
**Jedburgh** Border 80 E9
**Jeffreyston** Pembks 25 J7
**Jemimaville** Highld 107 M8
**Jerbourg** Guern 6 c2
**Jersey** Jersey 7 b1
*Jersey Airport* Jersey 7 a2
**Jersey Crematorium** Jersey 7 b2
**Jesmond** N u Ty 73 M7
**Jevington** E Susx 12 C9
**Jockey End** Herts 20 G1
**Johnby** Cumb 71 N8
*John Lennon Airport* Lpool 56 H11
**John o' Groats** Highld 110 H2
**Johnshaven** Abers 95 N8
**Johnston** Pembks 24 G6
**Johnstone** D & G 79 L8
**Johnstone** Rens 84 G9
**Johnstonebridge** D & G 78 H9
**Johnstown** Carmth 25 P5
**Johnstown** Wrexhm 48 F6
**Joppa** C Edin 86 G7
**Joppa** Cerdgn 37 J7
**Joppa** S Ayrs 76 G7
**Jordanston** Pembks 24 G3
**Joyden's Wood** Kent 21 P8
**Juniper** Nthumb 72 G8
**Juniper Green** C Edin 86 E8
**Jura** Ag & B 82 G6
Jurassic Coast Devon 7 J5
**Jurby** IoM 56 c2

## K

**Kaber** Cumb 64 E5
**Kaimend** S Lans 86 B11
**Kames** Ag & B 83 P8
**Kames** E Ayrs 77 L6
**Kea** Cnwll 3 J7
**Keadby** N Linc 60 E10
**Keal Cotes** Lincs 53 K10
**Kearsley** Bolton 57 N7
**Kearsney** Kent 13 P2
**Kearstwick** Cumb 63 L6
**Kedington** Suffk 34 B7
**Kedleston** Derbys 50 H11
**Keelby** Lincs 61 K11
**Keele** Staffs 49 P6
Keele Services Staffs 49 P6
**Keelham** C Brad 58 E7
**Keeston** Pembks 24 F5
**Keevil** Wilts 18 D8
**Kegworth** Leics 41 L3
**Kehelland** Cnwll 2 F7
**Keig** Abers 102 D10
**Keighley** C Brad 58 D6
**Keighley Crematorium** C Brad 58 D6
**Keilarsbrae** Clacks 85 P4
**Keillour** P & K 92 E9
**Keiloch** Abers 94 C4
**Keils** Ag & B 82 G8
**Keinton Mandeville** Somset 17 M9
**Keir Mill** D & G 78 E9
**Keisley** Cumb 64 D3
**Keiss** Highld 110 G4
**Keith** Moray 101 N5
**Keithick** P & K 93 J7
**Keithock** Angus 95 K8
**Keithtown** Highld 106 H10
**Kelbrook** Lancs 58 B5
**Kelby** Lincs 42 E2
**Keld** N York 64 F7
**Kelfield** N York 59 N6

Kelham Notts 51 Q9
Kelhead D & G 71 J2
Kellamergh Lancs 56 H3
Kellas Angus 93 M8
Kellas Moray 101 J5
Kellaton Devon 5 Q11
Kelling Norfk 44 H2
Kellington N York 59 M8
Kelloe Dur 73 N12
Kelloholm D & G 77 M8
Kelly Devon 5 J4
Kelmarsh Nhants 41 Q10
Kelmscott Oxon 19 J2
Kelsale Suffk 35 N4
Kelsall Ches W 49 K2
Kelshall Herts 33 K9
Kelsick Cumb 71 K5
Kelso Border 80 G7
Kelstedge Derbys 51 J7
Kelstern Lincs 53 J3
Kelston BaNES 17 Q3
Keltneyburn P & K 92 B6
Kelton D & G 70 G2
Kelty Fife 86 D4
Kelvedon Essex 34 E11
Kelvedon Hatch Essex 22 C4
Kelynack Cnwll 2 B9
Kemback Fife 93 M11
Kemberton Shrops 39 N2
Kemble Gloucs 29 P8
Kemerton Worcs 29 N2
Kemeys Commander Mons 28 D7
Kemnay Abers 102 F11
Kempley Gloucs 29 J3
Kempley Green Gloucs 29 J3
Kempsey Worcs 39 Q11
Kempsford Gloucs 18 H2
Kempshott Hants 19 P10
Kempston Bed 32 E7
Kempton Shrops 38 G5
Kemp Town Br & H 11 M8
Kemsing Kent 22 B10
Kenardington Kent 13 J4
Kenchester Herefs 38 H12
Kencot Oxon 30 G12
Kendal Cumb 63 K4
Kenfig Brdgnd 26 H11
Kenilworth Warwks 40 H12
Kenley Gt Lon 21 L10
Kenley Shrops 39 K3
Kenmore P & K 92 B6
Kenmore Highld 105 L10
Kenn Devon 6 C6
Kenn N Som 17 K3
Kennacraig Ag & B 83 M9
Kennall Vale Cnwll 2 H8
Kennerleigh Devon 15 P10
Kennessee Green Sefton 56 H8
Kennet Clacks 85 Q5
Kennethmont Abers 102 C9
Kennett Cambs 34 B3
Kennford Devon 6 C5
Kenninghall Norfk 44 G11
Kennington Kent 13 K2
Kennington Oxon 19 N1
Kennoway Fife 86 G2
Kenny Somset 17 J11
Kennyhill Suffk 33 Q2
Kennythorpe N York 60 D2
Kenovay Ag & B 88 C7
Kensaleyre Highld 104 F11
Kensington Gt Lon 21 K7
Kensington Palace Gt Lon 21 K7
Kensworth Common C Beds 32 E12
Kentallen Highld 90 D5
Kent and Sussex Crematorium Kent 12 C3
Kentchurch Herefs 28 E4
Kentford Suffk 34 B4
Kentisbeare Devon 6 E2
Kentisbury Devon 15 L4
Kentish Town Gt Lon 21 L6
Kentmere Cumb 63 J2
Kenton Devon 6 C6
Kenton Gt Lon 21 J6
Kenton N u Ty 73 L7
Kenton Suffk 35 K4
Kenton Bankfoot N u Ty 73 L7
Kentra Highld 89 N3
Kent's Green Gloucs 29 K4
Kent's Oak Hants 9 K3
Kenwyn Cnwll 3 J6
Keoldale Highld 108 G3
Keppoch Highld 97 M5
Kepwick N York 66 C8
Keresley Covtry 40 H10
Kerrera Ag & B 89 Q10
Kerris Cnwll 2 C9
Kerry Powys 38 D4
Kerrycroy Ag & B 84 B10
Kersall Notts 51 Q8
Kersbrook Devon 6 E6
Kersey Suffk 34 G7
Kershader W Isls 111 d2
Kerswell Devon 6 E2
Kerswell Green Worcs 39 Q11
Kesgrave Suffk 35 K7
Kessingland Suffk 45 Q10
Kestle Cnwll 3 L6
Kestle Mill Cnwll 3 J4
Keston Gt Lon 21 N9
Keswick Cumb 71 L10
Keswick Norfk 45 K8
Kettering Nhants 32 C2
Kettering Crematorium Nhants 32 C2
Ketteringham Norfk 45 J9
Kettins P & K 93 J7
Kettlebaston Suffk 34 F6
Kettlebridge Fife 86 G2
Kettlebrook Staffs 40 G6
Kettleburgh Suffk 35 L5
Kettleholm D & G 79 J12
Kettleshulme Ches E 50 C5
Kettlesing N York 58 G3
Kettlesing Bottom N York 58 G3
Kettlestone Norfk 44 F4
Kettlethorpe Lincs 52 C8
Kettletoft Ork 111 i1
Kettlewell N York 64 H11
Ketton Rutlnd 42 E8
Kew Gt Lon 21 J7
Kew Royal Botanic Gardens Gt Lon 21 J7
Kewstoke N Som 17 J4

Kexby C York 60 C4
Kexby Lincs 52 C6
Key Green Ches E 50 B7
Keyham Leics 41 P6
Keyhaven Hants 9 K8
Keyingham E R Yk 61 L8
Keymer W Susx 11 L7
Keynsham BaNES 17 P3
Keysoe Bed 32 F4
Keysoe Row Bed 32 F5
Keyston Cambs 32 F2
Keyworth Notts 41 N2
Kibblesworth Gatesd 73 M9
Kibworth Beauchamp Leics 41 P8
Kibworth Harcourt Leics 41 P8
Kidbrooke Gt Lon 21 N7
Kidderminster Worcs 39 Q6
Kiddington Oxon 31 L10
Kidmore End Oxon 20 B7
Kidsdale D & G 69 L10
Kidsgrove Staffs 49 Q5
Kidwelly Carmth 25 P7
Kiel Crofts Ag & B 90 C8
Kielder Nthumb 72 B3
Kielder Forest 72 B4
Kiells Ag & B 83 J8
Kilbarchan Rens 84 G9
Kilberg Highld 97 J8
Kilberry Ag & B 83 K9
Kilbirnie N Ayrs 84 E11
Kilbride Ag & B 83 L7
Kilbride Ag & B 83 Q9
Kilbuiack Moray 100 G4
Kilburn Derbys 51 J10
Kilburn Gt Lon 21 K6
Kilburn N York 66 D10
Kilby Leics 41 N8
Kilchamaig Ag & B 83 M10
Kilchattan Ag & B 82 E4
Kilchattan Ag & B 84 B11
Kilcheran Ag & B 89 Q8
Kilchoan Highld 89 K4
Kilchoman Ag & B 82 C9
Kilchrenan Ag & B 90 E10
Kilconquhar Fife 87 J2
Kilcot Gloucs 29 J4
Kilcoy Highld 107 J11
Kilcreggan Ag & B 84 D6
Kildale N York 66 G5
Kildalloig Ag & B 75 L8
Kildary Highld 107 M7
Kildavaig Ag & B 83 Q9
Kildavanan Ag & B 83 Q9
Kildonan Highld 109 Q10
Kildonan N Ayrs 75 Q8
Kildonan Lodge Highld 109 Q10
Kildonnan Highld 96 F11
Kildrochet House D & G 68 E7
Kildrummy Abers 101 N10
Kildwick N York 58 D5
Kilfinan Ag & B 83 P7
Kilfinnan Highld 98 C9
Kilgetty Pembks 25 K7
Kilgrammie S Ayrs 76 E10
Kilham E R Yk 60 H2
Kilkenneth Ag & B 88 B7
Kilkenzie Ag & B 75 K7
Kilkerran Ag & B 75 L8
Kilkhampton Cnwll 14 E9
Killamarsh Derbys 51 L5
Killay Swans 26 E9
Killearn Stirlg 85 J6
Killen Highld 107 L10
Killerby Darltn 65 L4
Killerton Devon 6 D3
Killichonan Highld 91 M5
Killiechonate Highld 98 C11
Killiechronan Ag & B 89 L7
Killiecrankie P & K 92 D3
Killilan Highld 97 N4
Killimster Highld 110 G4
Killin Stirlg 91 N9
Killinghall N York 58 H3
Killington Cumb 63 L5
Killingworth N Tyne 73 M6
Killochyett Border 87 J12
Kilmacolm Inver 84 F8
Kilmahog Stirlg 85 K2
Kilmahumaig Ag & B 83 L4
Kilmaluag Highld 104 F7
Kilmany Fife 93 L10
Kilmarnock E Ayrs 76 G4
Kilmartin Ag & B 83 M3
Kilmaurs E Ayrs 76 G3
Kilmelford Ag & B 83 M1
Kilmersdon Somset 17 Q6
Kilmeston Hants 9 P3
Kilmichael Ag & B 75 K7
Kilmichael Glassary Ag & B 83 N4
Kilmichael of Inverlussa Ag & B 83 L6
Kilmington Devon 6 H4
Kilmington Wilts 18 B12
Kilmington Common Wilts 8 B1
Kilmington Street Wilts 8 B1
Kilmorack Highld 106 H12
Kilmore Ag & B 90 B10
Kilmore Highld 97 J8
Kilmory Ag & B 83 J8
Kilmory Highld 89 L3
Kilmory N Ayrs 75 P7
Kilmuir Highld 104 C11
Kilmuir Highld 104 E8
Kilmuir Highld 107 L11
Kilmuir Highld 107 M7
Kilmun Ag & B 84 C6
Kilnave Ag & B 82 D8
Kilncadzow S Lans 77 P2
Kilndown Kent 12 E3
Kilninver Ag & B 89 Q11
Kilnsea E R Yk 61 P10
Kilnsey N York 58 C1
Kilnwick E R Yk 60 G4
Kiloran Ag & B 82 E4
Kilpatrick N Ayrs 75 N7
Kilpeck Herefs 28 E3
Kilpin E R Yk 60 D8
Kilrenny Fife 87 L2
Kilsby Nhants 41 M2
Kilspindie P & K 93 J9
Kilstay D & G 68 F10

Kilsyth N Lans 85 M7
Kiltarlity Highld 98 G2
Kilton R & Cl 66 F4
Kilton Thorpe R & Cl 66 F4
Kilvaxter Highld 104 E8
Kilve Somset 16 F7
Kilvington Notts 42 B2
Kilwinning N Ayrs 76 E3
Kimberley Norfk 44 H9
Kimberley Notts 51 L11
Kimberworth Rothm 51 K3
Kimblesworth Dur 73 M10
Kimbolton Cambs 32 F4
Kimbolton Herefs 39 K9
Kimcote Leics 41 N9
Kimmeridge Dorset 8 D10
Kimpton Hants 19 J10
Kimpton Herts 32 H11
Kinbrace Highld 109 Q8
Kinbuck Stirlg 85 N3
Kincaple Fife 93 N11
Kincardine Fife 85 Q5
Kincardine Highld 107 K5
Kincardine Bridge Fife 85 Q5
Kincardine O'Neil Abers 95 K3
Kinclaven P & K 92 H7
Kincorth C Aber 95 Q2
Kincorth House Moray 100 F3
Kincraig Highld 99 M7
Kincraigie P & K 92 E6
Kindallachan P & K 92 E6
Kinerarach Ag & B 75 J2
Kineton Gloucs 30 E8
Kineton Warwks 31 J4
Kinfauns P & K 92 H10
Kingarth Ag & B 84 B10
Kingcausie Abers 95 P3
Kingcood Mons 28 E7
Kingerby Lincs 52 F5
Kingham Oxon 30 H8
Kingholm Quay D & G 70 F2
Kinghorn Fife 86 F5
Kinglassie Fife 86 E3
Kingoldrum Angus 93 L5
Kingoodie P & K 93 L9
Kingsand Cnwll 5 J9
Kingsbarns Fife 93 Q12
Kingsbridge Devon 5 P10
Kingsbridge Somset 16 D8
King's Bromley Staffs 40 E4
Kingsburgh Highld 104 E10
Kingsbury Gt Lon 21 J5
Kingsbury Warwks 40 G8
Kingsbury Episcopi Somset 17 L11
King's Caple Herefs 28 G3
Kingsclere Hants 19 N8
King's Cliffe Nhants 42 E10
Kings Clipstone Notts 51 N7
Kingscote Gloucs 29 L9
Kingscott Devon 15 J8
King's Coughton Warwks 30 E3
Kingscross N Ayrs 75 Q6
Kingsdon Somset 17 M10
Kingsdown Kent 13 Q1
Kingsdown Swindn 18 H3
Kingsdown Wilts 18 B7
Kingsdown Crematorium Swindn 18 H3
Kingseat Fife 86 D4
Kingsey Bucks 20 C3
Kingsfold W Susx 11 J3
Kingsford C Aber 95 P1
Kingsford E Ayrs 76 H2
Kingsgate Kent 23 Q8
Kingshall Street Suffk 34 F4
King's Heath Birm 40 E10
Kings Hill Kent 22 D11
King's Hill Wsall 40 C8
Kings House Hotel Highld 90 H5
Kingshouse Hotel Stirlg 91 N11
Kingshurst Solhll 40 F9
Kingskerswell Devon 6 B8
Kingskettle Fife 86 G1
Kingsland Herefs 39 J9
Kingsland IoA 54 C5
Kings Langley Herts 20 H3
Kingsley Ches W 49 K1
Kingsley Hants 10 C3
Kingsley Staffs 50 D10
Kingsley Green W Susx 10 E4
Kingsley Park Nhants 31 Q2
King's Lynn Norfk 43 P6
Kings Meaburn Cumb 64 B4
King's Mills Guern 6 b2
Kingsmuir Angus 93 N6
Kings Muir Border 79 L2
Kingsmuir Fife 87 K1
Kingsnorth Kent 13 J3
King's Norton Birm 40 D10
King's Norton Leics 41 P7
Kings Nympton Devon 15 M8
King's Pyon Herefs 38 H11
Kings Ripton Cambs 33 J2
King's Somborne Hants 9 L2
King's Stag Dorset 7 Q1
King's Stanley Gloucs 29 L7
King's Sutton Nhants 31 L6
Kingstanding Birm 40 E8
Kingsteignton Devon 6 B8
Kingsthorne Herefs 28 F3
Kingsthorpe Nhants 31 Q2
Kingston Cambs 33 K6
Kingston Cnwll 4 H5
Kingston Devon 5 M10
Kingston Devon 7 Q2
Kingston Dorset 7 P2
Kingston Dorset 8 E10
Kingston E Loth 87 K6
Kingston IoW 9 M10
Kingston Kent 23 M12
Kingston Bagpuize Oxon 19 L2
Kingston Blount Oxon 20 B4
Kingston Deverill Wilts 18 C12
Kingstone Herefs 28 E2
Kingstone Somset 17 K12
Kingstone Staffs 40 D2
Kingston Lacy House & Gardens Dorset 8 E7
Kingston Lisle Oxon 19 K4
Kingston near Lewes E Susx 11 N8
Kingston on Soar Notts 41 M2
Kingston on Spey Moray 101 L3
Kingston Russell Dorset 7 N5
Kingston St Mary Somset 16 G9
Kingston Seymour N Som 17 K3
Kingston upon Hull C KuH 61 J8

Kingston upon Thames Gt Lon 21 J9
Kingston upon Thames Crematorium Gt Lon 21 J9
King's Walden Herts 32 G11
Kingswear Devon 6 B11
Kingswells C Aber 95 P1
Kings Weston Bristl 28 G12
Kingswinford Dudley 40 B9
Kingswood Bucks 31 P9
Kingswood Gloucs 29 K9
Kingswood S Glos 17 P2
Kingswood Somset 16 F8
Kingswood Surrey 21 K11
Kingswood Warwks 40 F12
Kingswood Common Staffs 39 Q2
Kings Worthy Hants 9 N2
Kingthorpe Lincs 52 G8
Kington Herefs 38 F10
Kington S Glos 28 H10
Kington Worcs 30 C3
Kington Langley Wilts 18 D5
Kington Magna Dorset 8 B3
Kington St Michael Wilts 18 D5
Kingussie Highld 99 L3
Kingweston Somset 17 M9
Kinharrachie Abers 103 J8
Kinharvie D & G 70 F3
Kinkell Bridge P & K 92 D11
Kinknockie Abers 103 L7
Kinleith C Edin 86 E8
Kinlet Shrops 39 N6
Kinloch Highld 96 E9
Kinloch Highld 108 D8
Kinloch Highld 109 K5
Kinloch P & K 92 H6
Kinlochard Stirlg 84 H3
Kinlochbervie Highld 108 E4
Kinlocheil Highld 90 D1
Kinlochewe Highld 105 Q9
Kinloch Hourn Highld 97 N8
Kinlochlaggan Highld 98 G10
Kinlochleven Highld 90 G4
Kinlochmoidart Highld 89 P2
Kinlochnanuagh Highld 97 K11
Kinloch Rannoch P & K 91 P5
Kinloss Moray 100 G3
Kinmel Bay Conwy 55 P5
Kinmuck Abers 102 H10
Kinmundy Abers 103 J10
Kinnabus Ag & B 74 D7
Kinnadie Abers 103 K6
Kinnaird P & K 92 E4
Kinneff Abers 95 N6
Kinnelhead D & G 78 G8
Kinnell Angus 93 Q5
Kinnerley Shrops 48 G10
Kinnersley Herefs 38 G11
Kinnersley Worcs 39 Q12
Kinnerton Powys 38 E9
Kinnesswood P & K 86 E2
Kinnordy Angus 93 L5
Kinoulton Notts 41 P2
Kinross P & K 86 D2
Kinrossie P & K 92 H8
Kinross Services P & K 86 D2
Kinsham Herefs 38 G8
Kinsham Worcs 29 N2
Kinsley Wakefd 59 K10
Kinson Bmouth 8 F7
Kintail Highld 97 P6
Kintbury W Berk 19 L7
Kintessack Moray 100 F4
Kintillo P & K 92 G11
Kinton Herefs 38 H7
Kinton Shrops 48 G10
Kintore Abers 102 G11
Kintour Ag & B 74 F3
Kintra Ag & B 74 D3
Kintra Ag & B 88 H10
Kintraw Ag & B 83 M3
Kintyre Ag & B 75 L5
Kinveachy Highld 99 N5
Kinver Staffs 39 Q5
Kippax Leeds 59 K7
Kippen Stirlg 85 L4
Kippford or Scaur D & G 70 D5
Kipping's Cross Kent 12 D3
Kirbister Ork 111 h2
Kirby Bedon Norfk 45 L8
Kirby Bellars Leics 41 Q4
Kirby Cane Norfk 45 N10
Kirby Cross Essex 35 K11
Kirby Grindalythe N York 60 F1
Kirby Hill N York 59 K1
Kirby Hill N York 65 K6
Kirby Knowle N York 66 C9
Kirby-le-Soken Essex 35 K11
Kirby Misperton N York 66 H10
Kirby Muxloe Leics 41 M6
Kirby Underdale E R Yk 60 D3
Kirby Wiske N York 65 P9
Kirdford W Susx 10 G5
Kirk Highld 110 F4
Kirkabister Shet 111 k4
Kirkandrews D & G 69 N9
Kirkandrews upon Eden Cumb 71 M4
Kirkbampton Cumb 71 L4
Kirkbean D & G 70 F4
Kirk Bramwith Donc 59 N10
Kirkbride Cumb 71 K4
Kirkbuddo Angus 93 N7
Kirkburn Border 79 L2
Kirkburn E R Yk 60 G3
Kirkburton Kirk 58 G10
Kirkby Knows 56 H8
Kirkby Lincs 52 F5
Kirkby N York 66 D6
Kirkby Fleetham N York 65 M8
Kirkby Green Lincs 52 F11
Kirkby-in-Ashfield Notts 51 L9
Kirkby-in-Furness Cumb 62 E6
Kirkby la Thorpe Lincs 42 F2
Kirkby Lonsdale Cumb 63 L6
Kirkby Malham N York 58 B3
Kirkby Mallory Leics 41 L6
Kirkby Malzeard N York 65 M11
Kirkbymoorside N York 66 F9
Kirkby on Bain Lincs 53 J10
Kirkby Overblow N York 59 J4
Kirkby Stephen Cumb 64 E6
Kirkby Thore Cumb 64 B3
Kirkby Underwood Lincs 42 F5
Kirkby Wharf N York 59 K5
Kirkcaldy Fife 86 F4

Kirkcaldy Crematorium Fife 86 F4
Kirkcambeck Cumb 71 Q2
Kirkchrist D & G 69 P8
Kirkcolm D & G 68 D5
Kirkconnel D & G 77 M8
Kirkconnell D & G 70 F2
Kirkcowan D & G 69 J7
Kirkcudbright D & G 69 P8
Kirkdale Lpool 56 G9
Kirk Deighton N York 59 K4
Kirk Ella E R Yk 60 H8
Kirkfieldbank S Lans 77 P3
Kirkgunzeon D & G 70 E3
Kirk Hallam Derbys 51 L11
Kirkham Lancs 56 H3
Kirkham N York 60 C2
Kirkhamgate Wakefd 58 H9
Kirk Hammerton N York 59 L3
Kirkhaugh Nthumb 72 C10
Kirkheaton Kirk 58 F9
Kirkheaton Nthumb 72 H5
Kirkhill Highld 107 J12
Kirkhope S Lans 78 F7
Kirkibost Highld 96 G6
Kirkinch P & K 93 K6
Kirkinner D & G 69 K8
Kirkintilloch E Duns 85 L8
Kirk Ireton Derbys 50 H10
Kirkland Cumb 70 H11
Kirkland D & G 77 M8
Kirkland D & G 78 D10
Kirkland D & G 78 G10
Kirk Langley Derbys 50 H11
Kirkleatham R & Cl 66 E3
Kirkleatham Crematorium R & Cl 66 E3
Kirklevington S on T 66 B5
Kirkley Suffk 45 Q10
Kirklington N York 65 N10
Kirklington Notts 51 P8
Kirklinton Cumb 71 N3
Kirkliston C Edin 86 D7
Kirkmabreck D & G 69 L7
Kirkmaiden D & G 68 F10
Kirk Merrington Dur 65 M2
Kirk Michael IoM 56 c4
Kirkmichael P & K 94 B9
Kirkmichael S Ayrs 76 F9
Kirkmuirhill S Lans 77 N3
Kirknewton Nthumb 81 J8
Kirknewton W Loth 86 D8
Kirkney Abers 101 P8
Kirk of Shotts N Lans 85 P9
Kirkoswald Cumb 71 Q7
Kirkoswald S Ayrs 76 D9
Kirkpatrick D & G 78 E10
Kirkpatrick Durham D & G 70 C2
Kirkpatrick-Fleming D & G 71 L2
Kirk Sandall Donc 59 N11
Kirksanton Cumb 62 D6
Kirk Smeaton N York 59 M10
Kirkstall Leeds 58 H7
Kirkstead Lincs 52 H10
Kirkstile Abers 102 C8
Kirkstile D & G 79 M10
Kirkstyle Highld 110 G2
Kirkthorpe Wakefd 59 J9
Kirkton Abers 102 E9
Kirkton D & G 78 F11
Kirkton Fife 93 L10
Kirkton Highld 97 L4
Kirkton Highld 97 N2
Kirkton Highld 92 E11
Kirkton Manor Border 79 L2
Kirkton of Airlie Angus 93 K5
Kirkton of Auchterhouse Angus 93 L7
Kirkton of Barevan Highld 107 N11
Kirkton of Collace P & K 92 H8
Kirkton of Glenbuchat Abers 101 M11
Kirkton of Logie Buchan Abers 103 K8
Kirkton of Maryculter Abers 95 P3
Kirkton of Menmuir Angus 95 J8
Kirkton of Monikie Angus 93 N7
Kirkton of Rayne Abers 102 F8
Kirkton of Skene Abers 95 N1
Kirkton of Strathmartine Angus 93 L8
Kirkton of Tealing Angus 93 M7
Kirkton of Tough Abers 102 D11
Kirktown Abers 103 K3
Kirktown Abers 103 M5
Kirktown of Alvah Abers 102 E4
Kirktown of Bourtie Abers 102 G9
Kirktown of Fetteresso Abers 95 P5
Kirktown of Mortlach Moray 101 L7
Kirktown of Slains Abers 103 L9
Kirkurd Border 86 D12
Kirkwall Ork 111 h2
Kirkwall Airport Ork 111 h2
Kirkwhelpington Nthumb 72 H4
Kirk Yetholm Border 80 H8
Kirmington N Linc 61 J11
Kirmond le Mire Lincs 52 H5
Kirn Ag & B 84 C7
Kirriemuir Angus 93 L5
Kirstead Green Norfk 45 L10
Kirtlebridge D & G 71 K2
Kirtling Cambs 34 B5
Kirtling Green Cambs 34 B5
Kirtlington Oxon 31 L9
Kirtomy Highld 109 N3
Kirton Lincs 43 K3
Kirton Notts 51 P7
Kirton Suffk 35 L4
Kirtonhill W Duns 84 G7
Kirton in Lindsey N Linc 52 D4
Kirwaugh D & G 69 K8
Kishorn Highld 97 L2
Kislingbury Nhants 31 P3
Kittisford Somset 16 E10
Kitt's Green Birm 40 F9
Kittybrewster C Aber 95 Q1
Kivernoll Herefs 28 F3
Kiveton Park Rothm 51 L4
Knaith Lincs 52 B6
Knap Corner Dorset 8 B3
Knaphill Surrey 20 F10
Knapp Somset 17 J10

Knapton C York 59 M4
Knapton N York 67 J11
Knapton Norfk 45 M4
Knapwell Cambs 33 K4
Knaresborough N York 59 J3
Knaven Abers 103 J6
Knayton N York 66 B9
Knebworth Herts 33 J11
Knedlington E R Yk 60 C8
Kneesall Notts 51 P7
Kneeton Notts 51 P10
Knelston Swans 26 C10
Knenhall Staffs 50 B12
Knightcote Warwks 31 K4
Knightley Staffs 49 P9
Knighton C Leic 41 N7
Knighton Dorset 7 N1
Knighton Kent 12 D3
Knighton Powys 38 F7
Knighton Somset 16 G7
Knighton Staffs 49 N7
Knighton Staffs 49 N9
Knighton on Teme Worcs 39 L7
Knightwick Worcs 39 N10
Knill Herefs 38 F9
Knipton Leics 42 B4
Kniveton Derbys 50 G10
Knock Cumb 64 C3
Knock Highld 97 J7
Knock Moray 102 C5
Knock W Isls 111 d2
Knockally Highld 110 D9
Knockan Highld 106 D1
Knockando Moray 101 J7
Knockbain Highld 98 H1
Knockbain Highld 107 K10
Knock Castle N Ayrs 84 D9
Knockdee Highld 110 D4
Knockdow Ag & B 84 B8
Knockdown Wilts 18 C3
Knockeen S Ayrs 76 E11
Knockenkelly N Ayrs 75 Q7
Knockentiber E Ayrs 76 G4
Knockholt Kent 21 P10
Knockholt Pound Kent 21 P10
Knockin Shrops 48 G10
Knockinlaw E Ayrs 76 G4
Knocknain D & G 68 C6
Knockrome Ag & B 82 H8
Knocksharry IoM 56 b4
Knocksheen D & G 69 N3
Knockvennie Smithy D & G 70 C2
Knodishall Suffk 35 N4
Knodishall Common Suffk 35 P5
Knole Somset 17 L10
Knolls Green Ches E 57 P11
Knolton Wrexhm 48 H7
Knook Wilts 18 D11
Knossington Leics 42 B8
Knott End-on-Sea Lancs 62 G11
Knotting Bed 32 E4
Knotting Green Bed 32 E4
Knottingley Wakefd 59 L9
Knotty Ash Lpool 56 H9
Knowbury Shrops 39 L7
Knowe D & G 69 J5
Knowehead D & G 69 N2
Knoweside S Ayrs 76 E8
Knowl Bristl 17 N3
Knowle Devon 6 D2
Knowle Devon 6 E6
Knowle Devon 15 J5
Knowle Devon 15 N10
Knowle Shrops 39 L7
Knowle Solhll 40 F11
Knowle Somset 16 C7
Knowlefield Cumb 71 N4
Knowle Green Lancs 57 L2
Knowle St Giles Somset 7 J1
Knowl Hill W & M 20 D7
Knowsley Knows 56 H9
Knowsley Safari Park Knows 57 J9
Knowstone Devon 15 P7
Knox Bridge Kent 12 F2
Knoydart Highld 97 L8
Knucklas Powys 38 F7
Knuston Nhants 32 D4
Knutsford Ches E 57 N12
Knutsford Services Ches E 57 N12
Krumlin Calder 58 D9
Kuggar Cnwll 2 G11
Kyleakin Highld 97 K4
Kyle of Lochalsh Highld 97 K4
Kylerhea Highld 97 L5
Kylesku Highld 108 G10
Kylesmorar Highld 97 L10
Kyles Scalpay W Isls 111 c3
Kylestrome Highld 108 G10
Kynnersley Wrekin 49 M11
Kyrewood Worcs 39 L8

**L**

Lacasaigh W Isls 111 d2
Lacasdal W Isls 111 d2
Laceby NE Lin 52 H3
Lacey Green Bucks 20 D4
Lach Dennis Ches W 49 N2
Lackford Suffk 34 D3
Lackford Green Suffk 34 D3
Lacock Wilts 18 D7
Ladbroke Warwks 31 K3
Laddingford Kent 12 E1
Ladock Cnwll 3 K5
Lady Ork 111 i1
Ladybank Fife 93 K12
Ladygill S Lans 78 F4
Lady Hall Cumb 62 E5
Ladykirk Border 81 J5
Ladywood Birm 40 D9
Ladywood Worcs 39 Q9
La Fontenelle Guern 6 c1
Lag D & G 78 E10
Laga Highld 89 N4
Lagavulin Ag & B 74 F4
Lagg N Ayrs 75 P7
Laggan Highld 98 D9
Laggan Highld 99 J9
Lagganlia Highld 99 M8
La Grève de Lecq Jersey 7 a1
Laid Highld 108 H4
Laide Highld 105 N4
Laig Highld 96 F11

Laigh Clunch E Ayrs 76 H2
Laigh Fenwick E Ayrs 76 H3
Laigh Glenmuir E Ayrs 77 K7
Laighstonehall S Lans 85 M11
Laindon Essex 22 D5
Lairg Highld 107 J2
Laisterdyke C Brad 58 F7
Lake IoW 9 P10
Lake Wilts 18 G11
Lake District National Park Cumb 62 L1
Lakenheath Suffk 44 B12
Lakesend Norfk 43 N10
Laleston Brdgnd 27 J11
Lamarsh Essex 34 E3
Lamas Norfk 45 L5
Lambden Border 80 G5
Lamberhurst Kent 12 D3
Lamberhurst Down Kent 12 D3
Lamberton Border 81 K3
Lambeth Gt Lon 21 L7
Lambeth Crematorium Gt Lon 21 L8
Lambfair Green Suffk 34 B6
Lambley Notts 51 N10
Lambley Nthumb 72 C8
Lambourn W Berk 19 K5
Lambourne End Essex 21 P5
Lambs Green W Susx 11 K3
Lamerton Devon 5 K5
Lamesley Gatesd 73 M8
Lamington S Lans 78 F3
Lamlash N Ayrs 75 Q6
Lamonby Cumb 71 N8
Lamorna Cnwll 2 C10
Lamorran Cnwll 3 K7
Lampeter Cerdgn 37 J10
Lampeter Velfrey Pembks 25 K6
Lamphey Pembks 24 H7
Lamplugh Cumb 70 H10
Lamport Nhants 41 Q11
Lamyatt Somset 17 P8
Lanark S Lans 77 P3
Lancaster Lancs 63 J9
Lancaster & Morecambe Crematorium Lancs 63 J9
Lancaster Services Lancs 63 J10
Lanchester Dur 73 L10
Lancing W Susx 11 J8
L'Ancresse Guern 6 c1
Landbeach Cambs 33 M4
Landcross Devon 14 H7
Landerberry Abers 95 M2
Landford Wilts 9 J4
Land-hallow Highld 110 E8
Landican Crematorium Wirral 56 F10
Landimore Swans 26 C9
Landkey Devon 15 K6
Landore Swans 26 F9
Landrake Cnwll 4 J4
Land's End Airport Cnwll 2 B9
Landulph Cnwll 5 J7
Lane Cnwll 3 J4
Laneast Cnwll 4 F4
Lane End Bucks 20 D5
Lane End Wilts 18 B10
Lane Ends Derbys 40 G1
Laneham Notts 52 B8
Lane Head Dur 65 K5
Lane Head Dur 72 F11
Lane Head Wsall 40 C7
Langaller Somset 16 H10
Langar Notts 41 Q1
Langbank Rens 84 F8
Langbar N York 58 E4
Langcliffe N York 63 P8
Langdale End N York 67 K8
Langdown Hants 9 M6
Langdyke Fife 86 G2
Langenhoe Essex 34 G11
Langford C Beds 32 H8
Langford Devon 6 D3
Langford Essex 22 G2
Langford Notts 52 B10
Langford Oxon 30 G12
Langford Budville Somset 16 F10
Langham Essex 34 G9
Langham Norfk 44 G2
Langham Rutlnd 42 B7
Langham Suffk 34 F3
Langho Lancs 57 N3
Langholm D & G 79 M11
Langlee Border 80 C7
Langley Hants 9 M7
Langley Herts 32 H11
Langley Kent 22 F11
Langley Nthumb 72 E8
Langley Slough 20 G7
Langley Somset 16 E9
Langley W Susx 10 D5
Langley Warwks 30 F2
Langley Burrell Wilts 18 D6
Langley Green Essex 34 E11
Langley Marsh Somset 16 E9
Langley Park Dur 73 L11
Langley Street Norfk 45 N9
Langley Upper Green Essex 33 M9
Langney E Susx 12 D9
Langold Notts 51 N4
Langore Cnwll 4 G3
Langport Somset 17 K10
Langrick Lincs 43 J1
Langridge BaNES 17 Q3
Langrigg Cumb 71 J6
Langrish Hants 10 B5
Langsett Barns 50 G2
Langside P & K 92 B11
Langstone Hants 10 B8
Langthorne N York 65 M8
Langthorpe N York 59 K1
Langthwaite N York 64 H7
Langtoft E R Yk 60 H2
Langtoft Lincs 42 G7
Langton Dur 65 L4
Langton Lincs 52 H9
Langton Lincs 53 L9
Langton N York 60 E12
Langton by Wragby Lincs 52 G7
Langton Green Kent 12 B3
Langton Herring Dorset 7 N6
Langton Matravers Dorset 8 E10
Langtree Devon 14 H8
Langwathby Cumb 71 R8
Langwell House Highld 110 D10

Langwith Derbys 51 M6
Langwith Junction Derbys 51 L12
Langworth Lincs 52 F8
Lanhydrock House & Gardens Cnwll 3 N3
Lanivet Cnwll 3 M3
Lanlivery Cnwll 3 N4
Lanner Cnwll 2 G7
Lanreath Cnwll 4 E9
Lansallos Cnwll 4 E9
Lanteglos Cnwll 3 D4
Lanteglos Highway Cnwll 4 E9
Lanton Border 80 E9
Lanton Nthumb 81 K7
Lapford Devon 15 M9
Laphroaig Ag & B 74 E4
Lapley Staffs 49 Q11
Lapworth Warwks 40 F12
Larachbeg Highld 89 N6
Larbert Falk 85 P6
Largie Abers 102 D8
Largiemore Ag & B 83 P6
Largoward Fife 87 J1
Largs N Ayrs 84 D10
Largybeg N Ayrs 75 Q7
Largymore N Ayrs 75 Q7
Larkfield Inver 84 D7
Larkfield Kent 22 E10
Larkhall S Lans 77 M2
Larkhill Wilts 18 G11
Larling Norfk 44 G11
La Rocque Jersey 7 c2
Lartington Dur 64 H4
Lasham Hants 10 A2
Lasswade Mdloth 86 G8
Lastingham N York 66 G9
Latchingdon Essex 22 G4
Latchley Cnwll 5 J5
Lathbury M Keyn 32 C7
Latheron Highld 110 E8
Latheronwheel Highld 110 E8
Lathones Fife 87 J1
Latimer Bucks 20 G4
Latteridge S Glos 29 J10
Lattiford Somset 17 Q10
Latton Wilts 18 G2
Lauder Border 80 C5
Laugharne Carmth 25 M6
Laughterton Lincs 52 B8
Laughton E Susx 11 P7
Laughton Leics 41 P9
Laughton Lincs 42 F4
Laughton Lincs 52 B4
Laughton-en-le-Morthen Rothm 51 M4
Launcells Cnwll 14 E10
Launceston Cnwll 4 H4
Launton Oxon 31 N9
Laurencekirk Abers 95 L1
Laurieston D & G 69 P6
Laurieston Falk 85 Q7
Lavendon M Keyn 32 D6
Lavenham Suffk 34 F7
Lavernock V Glam 16 G3
Laversdale Cumb 71 P3
Laverstock Wilts 8 H2
Laverstoke Hants 19 N10
Laverton Gloucs 30 E7
Laverton N York 65 M11
Laverton Somset 18 B9
La Villette Guern 6 b2
Lavister Wrexhm 48 G4
Law S Lans 85 N11
Lawers P & K 91 Q8
Lawford Essex 34 H9
Lawford Somset 16 F8
Law Hill S Lans 85 N11
Lawhitton Cnwll 4 H4
Lawkland N York 63 P8
Lawns Wood Crematorium Leeds 58 H6
Lawrenny Pembks 24 H7
Lawshall Suffk 34 E6
Laxay W Isls 111 d2
Laxdale W Isls 111 d2
Laxey IoM 56 d4
Laxfield Suffk 35 L3
Laxford Bridge Highld 108 G6
Laxo Shet 111 k3
Laxton E R Yk 60 D8
Laxton Nhants 42 D10
Laxton Notts 51 Q7
Laycock C Brad 58 D6
Layer Breton Essex 34 F12
Layer-de-la-Haye Essex 34 F11
Layer Marney Essex 34 F12
Layham Suffk 34 G8
Laymore Dorset 7 K2
Laytham E R Yk 60 D6
Lazonby Cumb 71 Q7
Lea Derbys 51 J8
Lea Herefs 28 H4
Lea Lincs 52 B6
Lea Shrops 38 G4
Lea Wilts 18 E4
Leachkin Highld 107 K12
Leadburn Border 86 F10
Leadenham Lincs 52 D11
Leaden Roding Essex 22 C1
Leadgate Dur 73 K9
Leadhills S Lans 78 E6
Leafield Oxon 30 H10
Leagrave Luton 32 F11
Leake Common Side Lincs 53 L11
Lealholm N York 66 G6
Lealt Highld 104 G9
Lea Marston Warwks 40 G8
Leamington Hastings Warwks 31 L2
Leamington Spa Warwks 30 H2
Leap Cross E Susx 12 C7
Leasgill Cumb 63 J5
Leasingham Lincs 42 F1
Leasingthorne Dur 65 M2
Leatherhead Surrey 21 J11
Leathley N York 58 G5
Leaton Shrops 49 J10
Leaveland Kent 23 J11
Leavenheath Suffk 34 F8
Leavening N York 60 D2
Leaves Green Gt Lon 21 N10
Lebberston N York 67 M10
Le Bourg Guern 6 b2
Lechlade on Thames Gloucs 18 H2
Lecht Gruinart Ag & B 82 D8
Leck Lancs 63 M6

Leckbuie P & K 91 Q8
Leckford Hants 19 L12
Leckhampstead Bucks 31 Q6
Leckhampstead W Berk 19 M5
Leckhampstead Thicket W Berk 19 M5
Leckhampton Gloucs 29 N5
Leckmelm Highld 106 C4
Leconfield E R Yk 60 H5
Ledaig Ag & B 90 C8
Ledburn Bucks 32 C11
Ledbury Herefs 29 J2
Ledgemoor Herefs 38 H11
Ledmore Junction Highld 108 E12
Ledsham Leeds 59 L8
Ledston Leeds 59 L8
Ledwell Oxon 31 K8
Lee Devon 14 H3
Lee Gt Lon 21 M8
Leebotwood Shrops 39 J4
Lee Brockhurst Shrops 49 K9
Leece Cumb 62 E8
Lee Chapel Essex 22 E6
Lee Clump Bucks 20 E3
Leeds Kent 22 G11
Leeds Leeds 58 H7
Leeds Bradford Airport Leeds 58 G6
Leeds Castle Kent 22 G11
Leedstown Cnwll 2 E8
Leek Staffs 50 C9
Leek Wootton Warwks 30 H1
Lee Mill Devon 5 M8
Leeming N York 65 N9
Leeming Bar N York 65 M9
Lee-on-the-Solent Hants 9 P7
Lees Derbys 50 H12
Lees Oldham 58 C12
Lees Green Derbys 50 H12
Leesthorpe Leics 42 B7
Leeswood Flints 48 F4
Leetown P & K 93 J10
Leftwich Ches W 49 M2
Legbourne Lincs 53 L6
Legerwood Border 80 D5
Legoland W & M 20 F8
Legsby Lincs 52 G6
Leicester C Leic 41 N6
Leicester Forest East Services Leics 41 M7
Leigh Dorset 7 N2
Leigh Gloucs 29 M4
Leigh Kent 12 B2
Leigh Surrey 11 K1
Leigh Wigan 57 M8
Leigh Wilts 18 F3
Leigh Worcs 39 P10
Leigh Beck Essex 22 F6
Leigh Delamere Wilts 18 C5
Leigh Delamere Services Wilts 18 D5
Leigh Green Kent 12 H4
Leigh Knoweglass S Lans 77 K2
Leigh-on-Sea Sthend 22 G6
Leigh Park Dorset 8 F7
Leigh Sinton Worcs 39 P11
Leighswood Wsall 40 D7
Leighterton Gloucs 29 L9
Leighton Powys 38 E2
Leighton Shrops 39 L2
Leighton Bromswold Cambs 32 G2
Leighton Buzzard C Beds 32 D10
Leigh upon Mendip Somset 17 Q6
Leigh Woods N Som 17 N2
Leinthall Earls Herefs 39 J8
Leinthall Starkes Herefs 38 H8
Leintwardine Herefs 38 H7
Leire Leics 41 M9
Leiston Suffk 35 P4
Leith C Edin 86 F7
Leitholm Border 80 G5
Lelant Cnwll 2 E8
Lelley E R Yk 61 L7
Lempitlaw Border 80 G7
Lemreway W Isls 111 d3
Lemsford Herts 21 K2
Lenchwick Worcs 30 D5
Lendalfoot S Ayrs 68 F7
Lendrick Stirlg 85 J2
Lendrum Terrace Abers 103 M7
Lenham Kent 22 H11
Lenham Heath Kent 22 H12
Lenie Highld 98 G4
Lennel Border 80 H6
Lennox Plunton D & G 69 N8
Lennoxtown E Duns 85 K7
Lenton C Nott 51 M11
Lenton Lincs 42 E4
Lenwade Norfk 44 H6
Lenzie E Duns 85 L8
Leochel-Cushnie Abers 102 C12
Leominster Herefs 39 J9
Leonard Stanley Gloucs 29 L7
Lephin Highld 104 B11
Leppington N York 60 D2
Lepton Kirk 58 G10
Lerags Ag & B 90 B10
L'Erée Guern 6 a2
Lerryn Cnwll 4 E8
Lerwick Shet 111 k4
Lesbury Nthumb 81 P10
Leslie Abers 102 D9
Leslie Fife 86 F2
Lesmahagow S Lans 78 D2
Lesnewth Cnwll 4 D3
Les Quartiers Guern 6 c1
Les Quennevais Jersey 7 a2
Lessingham Norfk 45 N5
Lessonhall Cumb 71 K5
Leswalt D & G 68 D6
L'Etacq Jersey 7 a1
Letchmore Heath Herts 21 J4
Letchworth Garden City Herts 32 H9
Letcombe Bassett Oxon 19 L4
Letcombe Regis Oxon 19 L4
Letham Angus 93 P6
Letham Border 80 F11
Letham Falk 85 P6
Letham Fife 93 K11
Letham Grange Angus 93 Q6
Lethendy P & K 92 G7
Lethenty Abers 102 D10
Lethenty Abers 102 H7
Letheringham Suffk 35 L5

Letheringsett Norfk 44 H3
Letterewe Highld 105 P7
Letterfearn Highld 97 M5
Letterfinlay Lodge Hotel Highld 98 C10
Lettermorar Highld 97 K10
Letters Highld 106 C5
Lettershaw S Lans 78 E5
Letterston Pembks 24 G3
Lettoch Highld 99 Q5
Lettoch Highld 100 H8
Letton Herefs 38 G11
Letty Green Herts 21 L2
Letwell Rothm 51 M4
Leuchars Fife 93 M10
Leumrabhagh W Isls 111 d3
Leurbost W Isls 111 d2
Levedale Staffs 40 B4
Leven E R Yk 61 J5
Leven Fife 86 H3
Levens Cumb 63 J5
Levens Green Herts 33 K11
Levenshulme Manch 57 Q9
Levenwick Shet 111 k5
Leverburgh W Isls 111 c4
Leverington Cambs 43 M7
Leverstock Green Herts 20 H3
Leverton Lincs 43 L1
Le Villocq Guern 6 b1
Levington Suffk 35 K8
Levisham N York 67 J8
Lew Oxon 31 J11
Lewannick Cnwll 4 G4
Lewdown Devon 5 K3
Lewes E Susx 11 N7
Leweston Pembks 24 G4
Lewisham Gt Lon 21 M8
Lewisham Crematorium Gt Lon 21 N8
Lewiston Highld 98 G4
Lewistown Brdgnd 27 K10
Lewknor Oxon 20 B4
Lewson Street Kent 23 J10
Lewtrenchard Devon 5 K3
Lexden Essex 34 F10
Lexworthy Somset 16 H8
Leybourne Kent 22 D10
Leyburn N York 65 K9
Leygreen Herts 32 G10
Ley Hill Bucks 20 F3
Leyland Lancs 57 K4
Leylodge Abers 102 G11
Leys Abers 103 K5
Leys P & K 93 J7
Leysdown-on-Sea Kent 23 K8
Leysmill Angus 93 Q6
Leys of Cossans Angus 93 L6
Leysters Herefs 39 K8
Leyton Gt Lon 21 M6
Leytonstone Gt Lon 21 N6
Lezant Cnwll 4 H4
Lhanbryde Moray 101 K3
Libanus Powys 27 L4
Libberton S Lans 78 G1
Liberton C Edin 86 F8
Lichfield Staffs 40 E5
Lichfield & District Crematorium Staffs 40 F5
Lickey Worcs 40 C11
Lickey End Worcs 40 C11
Lickfold W Susx 10 E5
Liddesdale Highld 89 Q4
Liddington Swindn 18 H5
Lidgate Suffk 34 C5
Lidlington C Beds 32 E8
Liff Angus 93 L8
Lifford Birm 40 D10
Lifton Devon 5 J3
Liftondown Devon 4 H3
Lighthorne Warwks 31 J3
Lighthorne Heath Warwks 31 J3
Lightwater Surrey 20 E10
Lightwater Valley Theme Park N York 65 M11
Lightwood C Stke 50 B11
Lilbourne Nhants 41 M11
Lilleshall Wrekin 49 N11
Lilley Herts 32 G10
Lilliesleaf Border 80 C8
Lillingstone Dayrell Bucks 31 P6
Lillingstone Lovell Bucks 31 P6
Lillington Dorset 7 P1
Lilliput Poole 8 F9
Lilstock Somset 16 F7
Limbury Luton 32 F11
Limekilnburn S Lans 77 M2
Limekilns Fife 86 C5
Limerigg Falk 85 P8
Limerstone IoW 9 M10
Lime Street Worcs 29 L3
Limington Somset 17 M10
Limpenhoe Norfk 45 N8
Limpley Stoke Wilts 18 B8
Limpsfield Surrey 21 N11
Limpsfield Chart Surrey 21 N11
Linby Notts 51 M9
Linchmere W Susx 10 D4
Lincluden D & G 78 F12
Lincoln Lincs 52 D8
Lincoln Crematorium Lincs 52 E9
Lincomb Worcs 39 P8
Lindale Cumb 62 H6
Lindal in Furness Cumb 62 F7
Lindfield W Susx 11 M5
Lindford Hants 10 D3
Lindley Kirk 58 F9
Lindores Fife 93 K11
Lindridge Worcs 39 M8
Lindsell Essex 33 Q10
Lindsey Suffk 34 G7
Lindsey Tye Suffk 34 G7
Lingdale R & Cl 66 F4
Lingen Herefs 38 G8
Lingfield Surrey 11 M2
Lingwood Norfk 45 N8
Linicro Highld 104 E8
Linkend Worcs 29 L3
Linkenholt Hants 19 L8
Linkinhorne Cnwll 4 G5
Linktown Fife 86 F4
Linkwood Moray 101 K3
Linley Shrops 38 G4
Linley Green Herefs 39 M10
Linlithgow W Loth 86 B6
Linn Crematorium E Rens 85 K10
Linsidemore Highld 107 J3

Linslade C Beds 32 C10
Linstead Parva Suffk 35 M2
Linstock Cumb 71 N4
Linthurst Worcs 40 D11
Linthwaite Kirk 58 E10
Lintlaw Border 87 Q9
Lintmill Moray 101 P3
Linton Border 80 G8
Linton Cambs 33 P7
Linton Derbys 40 H4
Linton Herefs 28 H4
Linton Kent 22 F12
Linton Leeds 59 K5
Linton N York 58 C2
Linton Hill Herefs 29 J4
Linton-on-Ouse N York 59 L3
Linwood Lincs 52 G6
Linwood Rens 84 G9
Lionacleit W Isls 111 b5
Lional W Isls 111 e1
Liphook Hants 10 D4
Liscard Wirral 56 F9
Liscombe Somset 15 P5
Liskeard Cnwll 4 F7
Lismore Ag & B 90 B7
Liss Hants 10 C5
Lissett E R Yk 61 K3
Lissington Lincs 52 G6
Lisvane Cardif 27 P11
Liswerry Newpt 28 D10
Litcham Norfk 44 E6
Litchborough Nhants 31 N4
Litchfield Hants 19 M9
Litherland Sefton 56 G8
Litlington Cambs 33 K8
Litlington E Susx 11 Q9
Little Abington Cambs 33 N7
Little Addington Nhants 32 D3
Little Airies D & G 69 K9
Little Alne Warwks 30 F2
Little Altcar Sefton 56 F7
Little Amwell Herts 21 M2
Little Aston Staffs 40 E7
Little Ayton N York 66 D5
Little Baddow Essex 22 F2
Little Badminton S Glos 18 B4
Little Bampton Cumb 71 L5
Little Bardfield Essex 33 Q9
Little Barford Bed 32 H5
Little Barningham Norfk 45 J4
Little Barrington Gloucs 30 G10
Little Barrow Ches W 49 J2
Little Bavington Nthumb 72 H5
Little Bedwyn Wilts 19 K7
Little Bentley Essex 35 J10
Little Berkhamsted Herts 21 L2
Little Billing Nhants 32 B4
Little Billington C Beds 32 D11
Little Birch Herefs 28 F3
Little Blakenham Suffk 34 H7
Little Blencow Cumb 71 P8
Little Bognor W Susx 10 G6
Little Bollington Ches E 57 N10
Little Bookham Surrey 20 H11
Littleborough Notts 52 B7
Littleborough Rochdl 58 C10
Littlebourne Kent 23 N11
Little Bourton Oxon 31 L5
Little Braxted Essex 22 G1
Little Brechin Angus 95 J9
Littlebredy Dorset 7 N5
Little Brickhill M Keyn 32 C9
Little Brington Nhants 31 P2
Little Bromley Essex 34 H10
Little Budworth Ches W 49 L3
Littleburn Highld 107 K10
Little Burstead Essex 22 D5
Littlebury Essex 33 N8
Littlebury Green Essex 33 M8
Little Bytham Lincs 42 E6
Little Carlton Lincs 53 L6
Little Casterton Rutlnd 42 E8
Little Cawthorpe Lincs 53 K6
Little Chalfont Bucks 20 F4
Little Chart Kent 12 H2
Little Chesterford Essex 33 N8
Little Cheverell Wilts 18 E9
Little Chishill Cambs 33 L8
Little Clacton Essex 35 J11
Little Clifton Cumb 70 H9
Little Coates NE Lin 53 J2
Little Comberton Worcs 30 C5
Little Common E Susx 12 E8
Little Compton Warwks 30 H7
Little Cornard Suffk 34 E8
Little Cowarne Herefs 39 L11
Little Coxwell Oxon 19 K3
Little Crakehall N York 65 M9
Little Cressingham Norfk 44 E9
Little Crosby Sefton 56 G8
Little Cubley Derbys 50 F12
Little Dalby Leics 41 Q5
Littledean Gloucs 29 J6
Little Dewchurch Herefs 28 F3
Little Ditton Cambs 33 Q5
Little Downham Cambs 43 N12
Little Driffield E R Yk 60 H3
Little Dunham Norfk 44 E7
Little Dunkeld P & K 92 F7
Little Dunmow Essex 33 Q11
Little Durnford Wilts 8 G1
Little Easton Essex 33 P11
Little Eaton Derbys 51 J4
Little Ellingham Norfk 44 G9
Little Everdon Nhants 31 N3
Little Eversden Cambs 33 L6
Little Faringdon Oxon 19 J1
Little Fencote N York 65 M8
Little Fenton N York 59 M7
Little Fransham Norfk 44 E7
Little Gaddesden Herts 20 F2
Little Glemham Suffk 35 M5
Little Gorsley Herefs 29 J4
Little Gransden Cambs 33 J6
Little Green Somset 17 Q6
Little Hadham Herts 33 M11
Little Hale Lincs 42 G2
Little Hallam Derbys 51 L11
Little Hallingbury Essex 33 N12
Littleham Devon 6 D6
Littleham Devon 14 E7
Littlehampton W Susx 10 G9
Little Harrowden Nhants 32 C3
Little Haseley Oxon 19 Q1
Little Haven Pembks 24 F6
Little Haven W Susx 11 J4
Little Hay Staffs 40 E7

Little Haywood Staffs 40 D3
Littlehempston Devon 5 Q7
Little Hereford Herefs 39 K8
Little Horkesley Essex 34 F9
Little Hormead Herts 33 L10
Little Horsted E Susx 11 P6
Little Horton C Brad 58 F7
Little Horwood Bucks 32 B10
Little Houghton Barns 59 K11
Little Houghton Nhants 32 B5
Little Hucklow Derbys 50 F5
Little Hutton N York 66 C11
Little Irchester Nhants 32 C4
Little Keyford Somset 17 B10
Little Kimble Bucks 20 D3
Little Kineton Warwks 31 J4
Little Kingshill Bucks 20 E4
Little Knox D & G 70 D4
Little Langdale Cumb 62 G2
Little Langford Wilts 18 F12
Little Leigh Ches W 49 L1
Little Leighs Essex 34 C12
Little Lever Bolton 57 N7
Little Linford M Keyn 32 B7
Little Load Somset 17 L10
Little London E Susx 12 C6
Little London Hants 19 L10
Little London Hants 19 Q8
Little Longstone Derbys 50 F6
Little Maplestead Essex 34 D9
Little Marcle Herefs 29 J2
Little Marlow Bucks 20 E6
Little Massingham Norfk 44 D5
Little Melton Norfk 45 J8
Littlemill Abers 94 E3
Littlemill Highld 100 E5
Little Mill Mons 28 C8
Little Milton Oxon 19 Q1
Little Missenden Bucks 20 E4
Littlemoor Oxon 31 M12
Little Musgrave Cumb 64 D5
Little Ness Shrops 48 H10
Little Newcastle Pembks 24 G3
Little Newsham Dur 65 K4
Little Norton Somset 17 L11
Little Oakley Essex 35 K10
Little Oakley Nhants 42 C11
Little Orton Cumb 71 M5
Littleover C Derb 41 J1
Little Packington Warwks 40 G9
Little Paxton Cambs 32 H4
Little Petherick Cnwll 3 K2
Little Plumstead Norfk 45 M7
Little Ponton Lincs 42 D4
Littleport Cambs 43 P11
Little Preston Nhants 31 N4
Little Raveley Cambs 33 J2
Little Reedness E R Yk 60 D9
Little Ribston N York 59 J4
Little Rissington Gloucs 30 F9
Little Rollright Oxon 30 H7
Little Ryburgh Norfk 44 F5
Little Salkeld Cumb 71 Q8
Little Sampford Essex 33 Q9
Little Saughall Ches W 48 G2
Little Saxham Suffk 34 D4
Little Scatwell Highld 106 F10
Little Shelford Cambs 33 M6
Little Singleton Lancs 56 G2
Little Skipwith N York 59 P6
Little Smeaton N York 59 M10
Little Snoring Norfk 44 F4
Little Sodbury S Glos 18 A4
Little Somborne Hants 9 L2
Little Somerford Wilts 18 E4
Little Soudley Shrops 49 N9
Little Stainton Darltn 65 N4
Little Stanney Ches W 48 H1
Little Staughton Bed 32 F4
Little Steeping Lincs 53 M10
Little Stoke Staffs 40 B2
Littlestone-on-Sea Kent 13 L5
Little Stonham Suffk 35 J5
Little Stretton Leics 41 P7
Little Stretton Shrops 39 J4
Little Strickland Cumb 71 Q10
Little Stukeley Cambs 32 H2
Little Sugnall Staffs 49 P8
Little Swinburne Nthumb 72 G5
Little Sypland D & G 70 B5
Little Tew Oxon 31 J8
Little Tey Essex 34 E11
Little Thetford Cambs 33 N2
Little Thorpe Dur 73 Q11
Littlethorpe Leics 41 M7
Littlethorpe N York 59 J1
Little Thurlow Suffk 34 B6
Little Thurrock Thurr 22 D7
Littleton Ches W 48 H3
Littleton D & G 69 Q7
Littleton Hants 9 M2
Littleton Somset 17 L9
Littleton Surrey 20 H9
Littleton Drew Wilts 18 C5
Littleton-on-Severn S Glos 28 H10
Littleton Pannell Wilts 18 E9
Little Torrington Devon 15 J8
Littletown Dur 73 N11
Little Town Lancs 57 M2
Little Urswick Cumb 62 F7
Little Wakering Essex 22 H6
Little Walden Essex 33 N8
Little Waldingfield Suffk 34 F7
Little Walsingham Norfk 44 F3
Little Waltham Essex 22 E2
Little Weighton E R Yk 60 G7
Little Wenlock Wrekin 39 M2
Little Weston Somset 17 N10
Little Whitefield IoW 9 P9
Littlewick Green W & M 20 D7
Little Wilbraham Cambs 33 N5
Little Witcombe Gloucs 29 M6
Little Witley Worcs 39 P8
Little Wittenham Oxon 19 P3
Little Wolford Warwks 30 H7
Littleworth Oxon 19 K2
Littleworth Staffs 40 C3
Littleworth Worcs 30 B4
Little Wymington Bed 32 D4
Little Wymondley Herts 33 H10
Little Wyrley Staffs 40 D6
Little Yeldham Essex 34 C8
Litton Derbys 50 F6
Litton N York 64 G11

Litton Somset 17 N5
Litton Cheney Dorset 7 M5
Liurbost W Isls 111 d2
Liverpool Lpool 56 G10
Liverpool Maritime Mercantile City Lpool 56 G10
Liversedge Kirk 58 G9
Liverton Devon 5 Q5
Liverton R & Cl 66 G4
Livingston W Loth 86 C8
Livingston Village W Loth 86 C8
Lixwm Flints 48 D2
Lizard Cnwll 2 G12
Llanaelhaearn Gwynd 46 F3
Llanafan Cerdgn 37 L6
Llanafan-Fawr Powys 37 Q9
Llanallgo IoA 54 G5
Llanarmon Dyffryn Ceiriog Wrexhm 48 D8
Llanarmon-yn-Ial Denbgs 48 E4
Llanarth Cerdgn 36 G8
Llanarth Mons 28 D6
Llanarthne Carmth 26 D5
Llanasa Flints 56 C11
Llanbadarn Fawr Cerdgn 37 K4
Llanbadarn Fynydd Powys 38 C6
Llanbadoc Mons 28 D8
Llanbeder Mons 28 D10
Llanbedr Gwynd 47 J6
Llanbedr Powys 27 P5
Llanbedr-Dyffryn-Clwyd Denbgs 48 D4
Llanbedrgoch IoA 54 G5
Llanbedrog Gwynd 46 E5
Llanbedr-y-Cennin Conwy 55 L7
Llanberis Gwynd 54 H9
Llanbethery V Glam 16 D3
Llanbister Powys 38 C7
Llanblethian V Glam 16 D2
Llanboidy Carmth 25 L4
Llanbradach Caerph 27 N10
Llanbrynmair Powys 47 P10
Llancadle V Glam 16 D3
Llancarfan V Glam 16 E3
Llancloudy Herefs 28 F5
Llandaff Cardif 27 N12
Llandanwg Gwynd 47 J5
Llanddaniel Fab IoA 54 G7
Llanddarog Carmth 26 C5
Llanddeiniol Cerdgn 37 J6
Llanddeiniolen Gwynd 54 G8
Llandderfel Gwynd 47 R4
Llanddeusant Carmth 26 H5
Llanddeusant IoA 54 D5
Llanddew Powys 27 M3
Llanddewi Swans 26 B10
Llanddewi Brefi Cerdgn 37 L9
Llanddewi Rhydderch Mons 28 D6
Llanddewi Velfrey Pembks 25 K5
Llanddewi Ystradenni Powys 38 C8
Llanddoget Conwy 55 L8
Llanddona IoA 54 H5
Llanddowror Carmth 25 M6
Llanddulas Conwy 55 N6
Llanddwywe Gwynd 47 J6
Llanddyfnan IoA 54 G6
Llandefaelog-Tre'r-Graig Powys 27 N3
Llandefalle Powys 27 M2
Llandegfan IoA 54 H6
Llandegla Denbgs 48 E5
Llandegley Powys 38 D9
Llandegveth Mons 28 D9
Llandeilo Carmth 26 E4
Llandeilo Graban Powys 38 C12
Llandeloy Pembks 24 F4
Llandenny Mons 28 E7
Llandevaud Newpt 28 E10
Llandevenny Mons 28 E10
Llandinam Powys 38 B5
Llandissilio Pembks 25 K5
Llandogo Mons 28 F7
Llandough V Glam 16 D2
Llandough V Glam 16 F2
Llandovery Carmth 26 G2
Llandow V Glam 16 C2
Llandre Carmth 37 L11
Llandre Cerdgn 37 K4
Llandre Isaf Pembks 25 K3
Llandrillo Denbgs 48 B7
Llandrillo-yn-Rhos Conwy 55 M5
Llandrindod Wells Powys 38 C9
Llandrinio Powys 48 F11
Llandudno Conwy 55 L5
Llandudno Junction Conwy 55 L6
Llandulas Powys 37 P11
Llandwrog Gwynd 54 F9
Llandybie Carmth 26 E6
Llandyfaelog Carmth 25 P6
Llandyfriog Cerdgn 36 F11
Llandygai Gwynd 54 H7
Llandygwydd Cerdgn 36 D11
Llandynog Denbgs 48 C3
Llandyssil Powys 38 E3
Llandysul Cerdgn 36 G11
Llanedeyrn Cardif 27 P11
Llaneglwys Powys 27 M2
Llanegryn Gwynd 47 K9
Llanegwad Carmth 26 C5
Llaneilian IoA 54 F3
Llanelian-yn-Rhôs Conwy 55 M6
Llanelidan Denbgs 48 C5
Llanellen Mons 28 C6
Llanelli Carmth 26 C7
Llanelli Crematorium Carmth 26 D8
Llanelltyd Gwynd 47 L7
Llanelwedd Powys 38 B10
Llanenddwyn Gwynd 47 J6
Llanengan Gwynd 46 E6
Llanerchymedd IoA 54 F5
Llanerfyl Powys 48 B12
Llanfachraeth IoA 54 D5
Llanfachreth Gwynd 47 M6
Llanfaelog IoA 54 D7
Llanfaelrhys Gwynd 46 D6
Llanfaethlu IoA 54 D4
Llanfair Gwynd 47 J5
Llanfair Caereinion Powys 38 C2
Llanfair Clydogau Cerdgn 37 K9
Llanfair Dyffryn Clwyd Denbgs 48 D4

Llanfairfechan Conwy 55 K6
Llanfairpwllgwyngyll IoA 54 G7
Llanfair Talhaiarn Conwy 55 N7
Llanfair Waterdine Shrops 38 E6
Llanfair-yn-Neubwll IoA 54 D6
Llanfallteg Carmth 25 K5
Llanfallteg West Carmth 25 K5
Llanfarian Cerdgn 37 J5
Llanfechain Powys 48 E10
Llanfechell IoA 54 E4
Llanferres Denbgs 48 E4
Llanfihangel-ar-arth Carmth 36 G11
Llanfihangel Glyn Myfyr Conwy 55 P10
Llanfihangel Nant Bran Powys 27 K2
Llanfihangel Rhydithon Powys 38 D8
Llanfihangel Rogiet Mons 28 E10
Llanfihangel-y-Creuddyn Cerdgn 37 L5
Llanfihangel-yng-Ngwynfa Powys 48 C11
Llanfihangel yn Nhowyn IoA 54 D6
Llanfihangel-y-traethau Gwynd 47 K4
Llanfilo Powys 27 N3
Llanfoist Powys 28 C6
Llanfor Gwynd 47 Q4
Llanfrechfa Torfn 28 C9
Llanfrynach Powys 27 M4
Llanfwrog Denbgs 48 D4
Llanfwrog IoA 54 D5
Llanfyllin Powys 48 D10
Llanfynydd Carmth 26 D4
Llanfynydd Flints 48 F4
Llanfyrnach Pembks 25 L3
Llangadfan Powys 48 B12
Llangadog Carmth 26 F3
Llangadwaladr IoA 54 E7
Llangaffo IoA 54 F7
Llangammarch Wells Powys 37 Q10
Llangan V Glam 16 K12
Llangarron Herefs 28 F5
Llangathen Carmth 26 D4
Llangattock Powys 27 P5
Llangattock Lingoed Mons 28 D5
Llangedwyn Powys 48 E10
Llangefni Gwynd 54 F6
Llangeinor Brdgnd 27 J10
Llangeitho Cerdgn 37 K8
Llangeler Carmth 36 F11
Llangelynin Gwynd 47 J9
Llangendeirne Carmth 26 B6
Llangennech Carmth 26 D8
Llangennith Swans 25 P9
Llangernyw Conwy 55 N7
Llangian Gwynd 46 E5
Llangloffan Pembks 24 F3
Llanglydwen Carmth 25 L4
Llangoed IoA 54 H6
Llangollen Denbgs 48 E8
Llangolman Pembks 25 K4
Llangors Powys 27 N4
Llangower Gwynd 47 P5
Llangrannog Cerdgn 36 E9
Llangristiolus IoA 54 F6
Llangrove Herefs 28 F5
Llangunllo Powys 38 E7
Llangunnor Carmth 25 P5
Llangurig Powys 37 P5
Llangwm Conwy 47 Q3
Llangwm Mons 28 E8
Llangwm Pembks 24 H6
Llangwnnadl Gwynd 46 D5
Llangwyryfon Cerdgn 37 K6
Llangybi Cerdgn 37 K9
Llangybi Gwynd 46 G3
Llangybi Mons 28 D9
Llangynhafal Denbgs 48 D3
Llangynidr Powys 27 N5
Llangynin Carmth 25 M5
Llangynog Carmth 25 N6
Llangynog Powys 48 B9
Llangynwyd Brdgnd 27 J10
Llanhamlach Powys 27 M4
Llanharan Rhondd 27 L11
Llanharry Rhondd 27 L11
Llanhennock Mons 28 D9
Llanhilleth Blae G 27 P8
Llanidloes Powys 37 Q4
Llaniestyn Gwynd 46 E5
Llanigon Powys 27 P2
Llanilar Cerdgn 37 K5
Llanilid Rhondd 27 K11
Llanina Cerdgn 36 G8
Llanishen Cardif 27 N11
Llanishen Mons 28 F7
Llanllechid Conwy 55 J7
Llanllowell Mons 28 D8
Llanllugan Powys 38 C2
Llanllwch Carmth 25 P5
Llanllwchaiarn Powys 38 D4
Llanllwni Carmth 36 H11
Llanllyfni Gwynd 54 F10
Llanmadoc Swans 25 Q9
Llanmaes V Glam 16 D3
Llanmartin Newpt 28 D10
Llanmiloe Carmth 25 M7
Llannefydd Conwy 55 P7
Llannon Carmth 26 D7
Llannor Gwynd 46 F4
Llanon Cerdgn 36 H7
Llanover Mons 28 C7
Llanpumsaint Carmth 25 P3
Llanrhaeadr-ym-Mochnant Powys 48 D9
Llanrhian Pembks 24 E3
Llanrhidian Swans 26 C9
Llanrhychwyn Conwy 55 L8
Llanrhyddlad IoA 54 D4
Llanrhystud Cerdgn 37 J7
Llanrug Gwynd 54 G8
Llanrumney Cardif 27 P11
Llanrwst Conwy 55 L8
Llansadurnen Carmth 25 M6
Llansadwrn Carmth 26 F3
Llansadwrn IoA 54 H6
Llansaint Carmth 25 P7
Llansamlet Swans 26 F8
Llansanffraid Glan Conwy Conwy 55 L6

Llansannan Conwy 55 N8
Llansantffraed Powys 27 N4
Llansantffraed-Cwmdeuddwr Powys 37 Q7
Llansantffraed-in-Elvel Powys 38 C10
Llansantffraid Cerdgn 36 H7
Llansantffraid-ym-Mechain Powys 48 E10
Llansawel Carmth 26 E2
Llansilin Powys 48 E9
Llansoy Mons 28 E8
Llanspyddid Powys 27 L3
Llanstadwell Pembks 24 G7
Llansteffan Carmth 25 N6
Llantarnam Torfn 28 C9
Llanteg Pembks 25 L6
Llanthewy Skirrid Mons 28 D5
Llanthony Mons 28 C4
Llantilio-Crossenny Mons 28 D6
Llantilio Pertholey Mons 28 C5
Llantrisant Mons 28 D9
Llantrisant Rhondd 27 L11
Llantrithyd V Glam 16 E2
Llantwit Fardre Rhondd 27 M10
Llantwit Major V Glam 16 C3
Llanuwchllyn Gwynd 47 P5
Llanvaches Newpt 28 E9
Llanvair Discoed Mons 28 E9
Llanvapley Mons 28 D6
Llanvetherine Mons 28 D5
Llanvihangel Crucorney Mons 28 C5
Llanwddyn Powys 48 B10
Llanwenog Cerdgn 36 H10
Llanwern Newpt 28 D10
Llanwinio Carmth 25 M4
Llanwnda Gwynd 54 F9
Llanwnda Pembks 24 G2
Llanwnnen Cerdgn 37 J10
Llanwnog Powys 38 B4
Llanwrda Carmth 26 F3
Llanwrin Powys 47 M9
Llanwrthwl Powys 37 Q7
Llanwrtyd Wells Powys 37 P10
Llanwyddelan Powys 38 C2
Llanyblodwel Shrops 48 E10
Llanybri Carmth 25 N6
Llanybydder Carmth 36 H10
Llanycefn Pembks 25 J4
Llanychaer Pembks 24 H2
Llanymawddwy Gwynd 47 P7
Llanymynech Powys 48 F10
Llanynghenedl IoA 54 D5
Llanynys Denbgs 48 C3
Llanyre Powys 38 B9
Llanystumdwy Gwynd 46 H4
Llanywern Powys 27 M3
Llawhaden Pembks 25 J5
Llawryglyn Powys 37 Q3
Llay Wrexhm 48 G4
Llechrhyd Caerph 27 M7
Llechryd Cerdgn 36 D11
Lledrod Cerdgn 37 K6
Lleyn Peninsula Gwynd 46 E4
Llithfaen Gwynd 46 F3
Lloc Flints 56 D12

Llwydcoed Rhondd 27 L7
Llwydcoed Crematorium Rhondd 27 L7
Llwydiarth Powys 48 B11
Llwyncelyn Cerdgn 36 G8
Llwyndafydd Cerdgn 36 F9
Llwyngwril Gwynd 47 J9
Llwynmawr Wrexhm 48 E7
Llwynypia Rhondd 27 L9
Llynclys Shrops 48 F10
Llynfaes IoA 54 E6
Llysfaen Conwy 55 N6
Llyswen Powys 27 N2
Llysworney V Glam 16 C2
Llys-y-frân Pembks 24 H4
Llywel Powys 27 J3
Loan Falk 85 Q7
Loanhead Mdloth 86 F8
Loaningfoot D & G 70 F4
Loans S Ayrs 76 F5
Lobhillcross Devon 5 K3
Lochailort Highld 97 K12
Lochaline Highld 89 N7
Lochans D & G 68 E7
Locharbriggs D & G 78 G11
Lochavich Ag & B 90 C12
Lochawe Ag & B 90 F10
Loch Baghasdail W Isls 111 b6
Lochboisdale W Isls 111 b6
Lochbuie Ag & B 89 M10
Lochcarron Highld 97 M2
Lochdar W Isls 111 a5
Lochdon Ag & B 89 P9
Lochdonhead Ag & B 89 P9
Lochead Ag & B 83 L7
Lochearnhead Stirlg 91 N10
Lochee C Dund 93 L8
Locheilside Station Highld 90 D1
Lochend Highld 98 H2
Locheport W Isls 111 b4
Loch Euphoirt W Isls 111 b4
Lochfoot D & G 70 E2
Lochgair Ag & B 83 P5
Lochgelly Fife 86 E4
Lochgilphead Ag & B 83 N5
Lochgoilhead Ag & B 84 D3
Lochieheads Fife 93 J11
Lochill Moray 101 K3
Lochindorb Lodge Highld 100 E8
Lochinver Highld 108 C10
Loch Lomond and The Trossachs National Park 84 H1
Lochluichart Highld 106 F9
Lochmaben D & G 78 H11
Lochmaddy W Isls 111 b4
Loch Maree Hotel Highld 105 N8
Loch nam Madadh W Isls 111 b4
Loch Ness Highld 98 G4
Lochore Fife 86 E3
Lochranza N Ayrs 75 P3
Lochside Abers 95 M8
Lochside D & G 78 F12
Lochside Highld 107 N11
Lochslin Highld 107 N6
Lochton S Ayrs 68 H3
Lochty Angus 93 J9
Lochty Fife 87 K1
Lochuisge Highld 89 Q5

Lochwinnoch Rens ... 84 F10
Lochwood D & G ... 78 H9
Lockengate Cnwll ... 3 M4
Lockerbie D & G ... 79 J11
Lockeridge Wilts ... 18 G7
Lockerley Hants ... 9 K3
Locking N Som ... 17 J4
Locking Stumps Warrtn ... 57 M9
Lockington E R Yk ... 60 G5
Lockleywood Shrops ... 49 M9
Locksbottom Gt Lon ... 21 N9
Locks Heath Hants ... 9 N6
Lockton N York ... 67 J9
Loddington Leics ... 42 B9
Loddington Nhants ... 32 B2
Loddiswell Devon ... 5 P9
Loddon Norfk ... 45 M9
Lode Cambs ... 33 N4
Lode Heath Solhll ... 40 F10
Loders Dorset ... 7 L4
Lodge Hill Crematorium
Birm ... 40 D10
Lodsworth W Susx ... 10 E5
Lofthouse Leeds ... 59 J8
Lofthouse N York ... 65 K11
Lofthouse Gate Wakefd ... 59 J8
Loftus R & Cl ... 66 G4
Logan E Ayrs ... 77 K7
Loganlea W Loth ... 86 B9
Loggerheads Staffs ... 49 N8
Logie Angus ... 95 L8
Logie Fife ... 93 M10
Logie Moray ... 100 F5
Logie Coldstone Abers ... 94 G2
Logie Newton Abers ... 102 E7
Logie Pert Angus ... 95 L8
Logierait P & K ... 92 E5
Logierieve Abers ... 103 J9
Login Carmth ... 25 K4
Lolworth Cambs ... 33 L4
Lonbain Highld ... 105 K10
Londesborough E R Yk ... 60 E5
London Gt Lon ... 21 L7
London Apprentice Cnwll ... 3 M6
London Colney Herts ... 21 J3
Londonderry N York ... 65 N9
London Gateway
Services Gt Lon ... 21 K5
Londonthorpe Lincs ... 42 D3
London Zoo ZSL Gt Lon ... 21 L6
Londubh Highld ... 105 M6
Lonemore Highld ... 105 L6
Long Ashton N Som ... 17 M3
Long Bank Worcs ... 39 N7
Long Bennington Lincs ... 42 B2
Longbenton N Tyne ... 73 M7
Longborough Gloucs ... 30 F8
Long Bredy Dorset ... 7 L4
Longbridge Birm ... 40 D11
Longbridge Deverill Wilts ... 18 C11
Long Buckby Nhants ... 31 N1
Longburton Dorset ... 7 P1
Long Clawson Leics ... 41 Q3
Longcliffe Derbys ... 50 G9
Longcombe Devon ... 5 Q8
Long Compton Staffs ... 49 Q10
Long Compton Warwks ... 30 H7
Longcot Oxon ... 19 J3
Long Crendon Bucks ... 20 B2
Long Crichel Dorset ... 8 E5
Longden Shrops ... 38 H2
Long Ditton Surrey ... 21 J9
Longdon Staffs ... 40 E5
Longdon Worcs ... 29 L2
Longdon Green Staffs ... 40 E5
Longdon upon Tern
Wrekin ... 49 L11
Longdown Devon ... 6 B5
Longdowns Cnwll ... 2 H8
Long Duckmanton Derbys ... 51 K6
Long Eaton Derbys ... 41 L2
Longfield Kent ... 22 C9
Longford Covtry ... 41 J10
Longford Derbys ... 50 G12
Longford Gloucs ... 29 L5
Longford Shrops ... 49 M8
Longford Wrekin ... 49 N10
Longforgan P & K ... 93 K9
Longformacus Border ... 87 N10
Longframlington Nthumb ... 73 K1
Long Green Ches W ... 49 J2
Longham Dorset ... 8 F7
Longham Norfk ... 44 F7
Long Hanborough Oxon ... 31 K10
Longhaven Abers ... 103 M7
Longhirst Nthumb ... 73 M3
Longhope Gloucs ... 29 J5
Longhope Ork ... 111 g3
Longhorsley Nthumb ... 73 K2
Longhoughton Nthumb ... 81 P10
Long Itchington Warwks ... 31 K2
Longlane Derbys ... 50 G12
Long Lawford Warwks ... 41 L11
Longleat Safari &
Adventure Park Wilts ... 18 B11
Longlevens Gloucs ... 29 L5
Longleys P & K ... 93 K7
Long Load Somset ... 17 L10
Longmanhill Abers ... 102 F3
Long Marston Herts ... 20 E1
Long Marston N York ... 59 L4
Long Marston Warwks ... 30 F4
Long Marton Cumb ... 64 C3
Long Melford Suffk ... 34 E7
Longmoor Camp Hants ... 10 C4
Longmoss Ches E ... 50 B6
Long Newnton Gloucs ... 29 M9
Longnewton Border ... 80 D8
Long Newton E Loth ... 87 K8
Longnewton S on T ... 65 P4
Longney Gloucs ... 29 K6
Longniddry E Loth ... 87 J7
Longnor Shrops ... 39 J3
Longnor Staffs ... 50 E7
Longparish Hants ... 19 M10
Long Preston N York ... 63 Q9
Longridge Lancs ... 57 L2
Longridge W Loth ... 85 Q9
Longriggend N Lans ... 85 N8
Long Riston E R Yk ... 61 J6
Longrock Cnwll ... 2 D9
Longsdon Staffs ... 50 C9
Longside Abers ... 103 L6
Longstanton Cambs ... 33 L4
Longstock Hants ... 19 L12
Longstowe Cambs ... 33 K6

Long Stratton Norfk ... 45 K10
Long Street M Keyn ... 32 B7
Longstreet Wilts ... 18 G9
Long Sutton Hants ... 10 B1
Long Sutton Lincs ... 43 L5
Long Sutton Somset ... 17 L10
Longthorpe C Pete ... 42 G9
Long Thurlow Suffk ... 34 G3
Longthwaite Cumb ... 71 N10
Longton Lancs ... 57 J4
Longtown Cumb ... 71 N2
Longtown Herefs ... 28 C3
Longueville Jersey ... 7 c2
Longville in the Dale
Shrops ... 39 K4
Long Waste Wrekin ... 49 L11
Long Whatton Leics ... 41 L3
Longwick Bucks ... 20 C3
Long Wittenham Oxon ... 19 P3
Longwitton Nthumb ... 73 J3
Longwood D & G ... 70 B4
Longworth Oxon ... 19 L2
Longyester E Loth ... 87 K8
Lonmay Abers ... 103 L4
Lonmore Highld ... 104 C12
Looe Cnwll ... 4 F9
Loose Kent ... 22 F11
Loosley Row Bucks ... 20 D4
Lootcherbrae Abers ... 102 D5
Lopen Somset ... 17 K12
Loppington Shrops ... 49 J9
Lordshill C Sotn ... 9 L4
Lords Wood Medway ... 22 F10
Lornty P & K ... 92 H6
Loscoe Derbys ... 51 K10
Lossiemouth Moray ... 101 K2
Lostock Gralam Ches W ... 49 M1
Lostock Green Ches W ... 49 M2
Lostwithiel Cnwll ... 4 D8
Lothbeg Highld ... 107 Q1
Lothersdale N York ... 58 C5
Lothmore Highld ... 110 A12
Loudwater Bucks ... 20 E5
Loughborough Leics ... 41 M4
Loughborough
Crematorium Leics ... 41 M4
Loughor Swans ... 26 D8
Loughton Essex ... 21 N4
Loughton M Keyn ... 32 B8
Lound Lincs ... 42 F6
Lound Notts ... 51 P4
Lound Suffk ... 45 Q9
Lount Leics ... 41 K4
Louth Lincs ... 53 K6
Lovedean Hants ... 10 B7
Lover Wilts ... 8 H4
Loversall Donc ... 51 M2
Loves Green Essex ... 22 D3
Loveston Pembks ... 25 J7
Lovington Somset ... 17 N9
Low Ackworth Wakefd ... 59 K10
Low Barbeth D & G ... 68 D6
Low Bentham N York ... 63 M8
Low Biggins Cumb ... 63 L6
Low Borrowbridge Cumb ... 63 L3
Low Bradfield Sheff ... 50 H3
Low Bradley N York ... 58 D5
Low Burnham N Linc ... 52 A3
Lowca Cumb ... 70 F10
Low Catton E R Yk ... 60 C4
Low Crosby Cumb ... 71 P4
Lowdham Notts ... 51 P10
Lower Aisholt Somset ... 16 G8
Lower Ansty Dorset ... 8 B6
Lower Apperley Gloucs ... 29 M4
Lower Ashton Devon ... 6 A6
Lower Assendon Oxon ... 20 C6
Lower Bartle Lancs ... 57 J3
Lower Basildon W Berk ... 19 Q5
Lower Beeding W Susx ... 11 K5
Lower Benefield Nhants ... 42 E11
Lower Bentley Worcs ... 30 C2
Lower Boddington
Nhants ... 31 L2
Lower Bourne Surrey ... 10 D2
Lower Brailes Warwks ... 30 H6
Lower Breakish Highld ... 97 J5
Lower Broadheath Worcs ... 39 P10
Lower Broxwood Herefs ... 38 G10
Lower Bullingham Herefs ... 28 F2
Lower Burgate Hants ... 8 H4
Lower Caldecote C Beds ... 32 H7
Lower Chapel Powys ... 27 L2
Lower Chicksgrove Wilts ... 8 E2
Lower Chute Wilts ... 19 K9
Lower Clapton Gt Lon ... 21 M6
Lower Clent Worcs ... 40 B10
Lower Cumberworth Kirk ... 58 G11
Lower Dean Bed ... 32 F3
Lower Diabaig Highld ... 105 L9
Lower Dicker E Susx ... 12 B7
Lower Down Shrops ... 38 G5
Lower Dunsforth N York ... 59 K2
Lower Egleton Herefs ... 39 L11
Lower End M Keyn ... 32 D8
Lower Eythorne Kent ... 23 P12
Lower Failand N Som ... 17 M2
Lower Farringdon Hants ... 10 B3
Lower Feltham Gt Lon ... 20 H8
Lower Froyle Hants ... 10 C2
Lower Gabwell Devon ... 6 C8
Lower Gledfield Highld ... 107 K4
Lower Godney Somset ... 17 L7
Lower Gornal Dudley ... 40 B8
Lower Gravenhurst
C Beds ... 32 G9
Lower Green Kent ... 12 C3
Lower Green Kent ... 12 C3
Lower Halliford Surrey ... 20 H9
Lower Halstow Kent ... 22 G9
Lower Hamworthy Poole ... 8 E8
Lower Hardres Kent ... 23 M11
Lower Hartwell Bucks ... 20 C2
Lower Hergest Herefs ... 38 F10
Lower Heyford Oxon ... 31 L8
Lower Heysham Lancs ... 62 H9
Lower Houses Kirk ... 58 F10
Lower Irlam Salfd ... 57 N9
Lower Killeyan Ag & B ... 74 D4
Lower Langford N Som ... 17 L4
Lower Largo Fife ... 86 H2
Lower Leigh Staffs ... 40 D1
Lower Loxhore Devon ... 15 K5
Lower Lydbrook Gloucs ... 28 G5
Lower Lye Herefs ... 38 H8
Lower Machen Newpt ... 27 P10

Lower Merridge Somset ... 16 G8
Lower Middleton
Cheney Nhants ... 31 L6
Lower Moor Worcs ... 30 C5
Lower Morton S Glos ... 28 H9
Lower Nazeing Essex ... 21 N3
Lower Penarth V Glam ... 16 F3
Lower Penn Staffs ... 39 Q3
Lower Peover Ches E ... 49 N1
Lower Quinton Warwks ... 30 F5
Lower Raydon Suffk ... 34 G8
Lower Roadwater Somset ... 16 D8
Lower Seagry Wilts ... 18 E5
Lower Shelton C Beds ... 32 E8
Lower Shiplake Oxon ... 20 C7
Lower Shuckburgh
Warwks ... 31 L2
Lower Slaughter Gloucs ... 30 F9
Lower Standen Kent ... 13 N3
Lower Stanton St
Quintin Wilts ... 18 D5
Lower Stoke Medway ... 22 G8
Lower Stone Gloucs ... 29 J9
Lower Stow Bedon Norfk ... 44 F10
Lower Street Norfk ... 45 L3
Lower Street Suffk ... 35 J6
Lower Swanwick Hants ... 9 M5
Lower Swell Gloucs ... 30 F8
Lower Tean Staffs ... 50 D12
Lower Town Devon ... 5 P5
Lower Town Pembks ... 24 G2
Lower Upcott Devon ... 6 B6
Lower Upham Hants ... 9 N4
Lower Weare Somset ... 17 K5
Lower Welson Herefs ... 38 F11
Lower Westmancote
Worcs ... 29 N2
Lower Whatley Somset ... 17 Q6
Lower Whitley Ches W ... 57 L11
Lower Wield Hants ... 19 Q11
Lower Willingdon E Susx ... 12 C9
Lower Withington Ches E ... 49 P2
Lower Woodford Wilts ... 8 G1
Lower Wraxhall Dorset ... 7 N3
Lowesby Leics ... 41 Q6
Lowestoft Suffk ... 45 Q10
Loweswater Cumb ... 71 J10
Low Fell Gatesd ... 73 M8
Lowfield Heath W Susx ... 11 L3
Low Gartachorrans Stirlg ... 84 H6
Low Grantley N York ... 65 M12
Low Ham Somset ... 17 L9
Low Harrogate N York ... 58 H3
Low Hesket Cumb ... 71 P6
Low Hutton N York ... 60 D1
Lowick Nhants ... 32 E1
Lowick Nthumb ... 81 L6
Lowick Green Cumb ... 62 F5
Low Lorton Cumb ... 71 J9
Low Marnham Notts ... 52 B9
Low Mill N York ... 66 F8
Low Moorsley Sundld ... 73 N10
Low Moresby Cumb ... 70 G10
Low Newton Cumb ... 62 H6
Low Row Cumb ... 72 B8
Low Row N York ... 64 H7
Low Salchrie D & G ... 68 D6
Low Santon N Linc ... 52 D10
Lowsonford Warwks ... 30 F1
Low Tharston Norfk ... 45 K10
Lowther Cumb ... 71 Q10
Lowthorpe E R Yk ... 61 J3
Lowton Somset ... 16 G11
Low Torry Fife ... 86 B5
Low Worsall N York ... 65 P5
Low Wray Cumb ... 62 G2
Loxbeare Devon ... 16 C11
Loxhill Surrey ... 10 G3
Loxhore Devon ... 15 K4
Loxley Warwks ... 30 H4
Loxton N Som ... 17 K5
Loxwood W Susx ... 10 G4
Loyal Lodge Highld ... 109 L6
Lubenham Leics ... 41 P9
Luccombe Somset ... 16 C7
Luccombe Village IoW ... 9 P10
Lucker Nthumb ... 81 N9
Luckett Cnwll ... 5 J5
Lucking Street Essex ... 34 D9
Luckington Wilts ... 18 C4
Lucklawhill Fife ... 93 M10
Luckwell Bridge Somset ... 16 B8
Lucton Herefs ... 38 H8
Ludag W Isls ... 111 b6
Ludborough Lincs ... 53 J4
Ludbrook Devon ... 5 N8
Ludchurch Pembks ... 25 K6
Luddenden Calder ... 58 D8
Luddenden Foot Calder ... 58 D8
Luddesdown Kent ... 22 D9
Luddington N Linc ... 60 E10
Luddington Warwks ... 30 F4
Luddington in the
Brook Nhants ... 42 F12
Ludford Lincs ... 52 H5
Ludford Shrops ... 39 K7
Ludgershall Bucks ... 31 P10
Ludgershall Wilts ... 19 J9
Ludgvan Cnwll ... 2 D8
Ludham Norfk ... 45 N6
Ludlow Shrops ... 39 K7
Ludney Somset ... 7 K1
Ludwell Wilts ... 8 D3
Ludworth Dur ... 73 P11
Luffincott Devon ... 5 J2
Luffness E Loth ... 87 J6
Lugar E Ayrs ... 77 K7
Luggate Burn E Loth ... 87 L7
Luggiebank N Lans ... 85 M8
Lugton E Ayrs ... 84 G11
Lugwardine Herefs ... 28 G1
Luib Highld ... 96 H4
Luing Ag & B ... 83 L2
Lulham Herefs ... 28 E1
Lullington Derbys ... 40 G5
Lullington Somset ... 18 B9
Lulsgate Bottom N Som ... 17 M3
Lulsley Worcs ... 39 N10
Lumb Calder ... 58 D9
Lumby N York ... 59 L7
Lumloch E Duns ... 85 K8
Lumphanan Abers ... 95 J2
Lumphinnans Fife ... 86 E4
Lumsden Abers ... 101 N10
Lunan Angus ... 95 L10
Lunanhead Angus ... 93 N5
Luncarty P & K ... 92 G9
Lund E R Yk ... 60 G5

Lund N York ... 59 P7
Lundie Angus ... 93 K8
Lundin Links Fife ... 86 H2
Lundin Mill Fife ... 86 H2
Lundy Devon ... 14 C3
Lunga Ag & B ... 83 K2
Lunna Shet ... 111 k3
Lunsford Kent ... 22 E10
Lunsford's Cross E Susx ... 12 E7
Lunt Sefton ... 56 G8
Luppitt Devon ... 6 F2
Lupset Wakefd ... 58 H9
Lupton Cumb ... 63 K6
Lurgashall W Susx ... 10 F5
Lurley Devon ... 16 C12
Luscombe Devon ... 5 Q8
Luss Ag & B ... 84 F4
Lussagiven Ag & B ... 83 J6
Lusta Highld ... 104 C10
Lustleigh Devon ... 5 Q4
Luston Herefs ... 39 J9
Luthermuir Abers ... 95 L8
Luthrie Fife ... 93 K10
Luton Devon ... 6 B7
Luton Devon ... 6 E3
Luton Luton ... 32 F11
Luton Medway ... 22 F9
Luton Airport Luton ... 32 G11
Lutterworth Leics ... 41 M9
Lutton Devon ... 5 M8
Lutton Devon ... 5 N7
Lutton Lincs ... 43 M5
Lutton Nhants ... 42 G11
Luxborough Somset ... 16 D8
Luxulyan Cnwll ... 3 M4
Luxulyan Valley Cnwll ... 3 N4
Lybster Highld ... 110 F8
Lydbury North Shrops ... 38 G5
Lydd Kent ... 13 K6
Lydd Airport Kent ... 13 K6
Lydden Kent ... 13 N2
Lydden Kent ... 23 Q9
Lyddington Rutlnd ... 42 C10
Lydeard St Lawrence
Somset ... 16 F9
Lydford Devon ... 5 K3
Lydford on Fosse Somset ... 17 N9
Lydgate Calder ... 58 B8
Lydham Shrops ... 38 G4
Lydiard Millicent Wilts ... 18 G4
Lydiard Tregoze Swindn ... 18 G4
Lydiate Sefton ... 56 G7
Lydiate Ash Worcs ... 40 C11
Lydlinch Dorset ... 17 Q12
Lydney Gloucs ... 28 H7
Lydstep Pembks ... 25 J8
Lye Dudley ... 40 B10
Lye Green E Susx ... 11 P4
Lye Green Warwks ... 30 G2
Lye's Green Wilts ... 18 B10
Lyford Oxon ... 19 L2
Lymbridge Green Kent ... 13 L2
Lyme Regis Dorset ... 7 J4
Lyminge Kent ... 13 M2
Lymington Hants ... 9 K8
Lyminster W Susx ... 10 G8
Lymm Warrtn ... 57 M10
Lymm Services Warrtn ... 57 M11
Lympne Kent ... 13 L3
Lympsham Somset ... 17 J5
Lympstone Devon ... 6 D6
Lynch Highld ... 99 L8
Lynch Green Norfk ... 45 J8
Lyndhurst Hants ... 9 K6
Lyndon Rutlnd ... 42 C8
Lyndon Green Birm ... 40 F9
Lyne Border ... 79 K1
Lyne Surrey ... 20 G9
Lyneal Shrops ... 49 J8
Lyneham Oxon ... 30 H9
Lyneham Wilts ... 18 F5
Lynemouth Nthumb ... 73 N3
Lyne of Skene Abers ... 102 G12
Lyness Ork ... 111 g3
Lyng Norfk ... 44 H6
Lyng Somset ... 17 J9
Lynmouth Devon ... 15 M3
Lynsted Kent ... 22 H10
Lynton Devon ... 15 M3
Lyon's Gate Dorset ... 7 P2
Lyonshall Herefs ... 38 G10
Lytchett Matravers
Dorset ... 8 D8
Lytchett Minster Dorset ... 8 E8
Lyth Highld ... 110 F3
Lytham Lancs ... 56 G4
Lytham St Anne's Lancs ... 56 G4
Lythe N York ... 67 J5
Lythmore Highld ... 110 D3

M

Mabe Burnthouse Cnwll ... 2 H8
Mablethorpe Lincs ... 53 N6
Macclesfield Ches E ... 50 B6
Macclesfield
Crematorium Ches E ... 50 B6
Macduff Abers ... 102 F3
Macharioch Ag & B ... 75 L9
Machen Caerph ... 27 P10
Machrie N Ayrs ... 75 N5
Machrihanish Ag & B ... 75 J8
Machrins Ag & B ... 82 E5
Machynlleth Powys ... 47 M10
Machynys Carmth ... 26 C9
Mackworth Derbys ... 50 H12
Macmerry E Loth ... 87 J7
Madderty P & K ... 92 E10
Maddiston Falk ... 85 Q7
Madeley Staffs ... 49 P6
Madeley Wrekin ... 39 M2
Madingley Cambs ... 33 L5
Madley Herefs ... 28 E2
Madresfield Worcs ... 39 P11
Madron Cnwll ... 2 D9
Maenclochog Pembks ... 25 J4
Maendy V Glam ... 16 D2
Maentwrog Gwynd ... 47 L3
Maen-y-groes Cerdgn ... 36 F8
Maer Staffs ... 49 P7
Maerdy Rhondd ... 27 K8
Maesbrook Shrops ... 48 G9
Maesbury Shrops ... 48 G9
Maesbury Marsh Shrops ... 48 G9
Maesllyn Cerdgn ... 36 F10

Maesteg Brdgnd ... 27 J10
Maesybont Carmth ... 26 D5
Maesycwmmer Caerph ... 27 N9
Maggieknockater Moray ... 101 L6
Magham Down E Susx ... 12 C7
Maghull Sefton ... 56 G8
Magna Park Leics ... 41 L9
Magor Mons ... 28 E10
Magor Services Mons ... 28 E10
Maidenbower W Susx ... 11 L3
Maiden Bradley Wilts ... 18 B11
Maidencombe Torbay ... 6 C8
Maidenhayne Devon ... 6 H4
Maiden Head N Som ... 17 M3
Maidenhead W & M ... 20 E7
Maiden Newton Dorset ... 7 N4
Maidens S Ayrs ... 76 D9
Maiden's Green Br For ... 20 E8
Maiden Wells Pembks ... 24 G8
Maidford Nhants ... 31 N4
Maids Moreton Bucks ... 31 P7
Maidstone Kent ... 22 E10
Maidstone Services Kent ... 22 G11
Maidwell Nhants ... 41 Q11
Mail Shet ... 111 k4
Maindee Newpt ... 28 C10
Mainland Ork ... 111 h2
Mainland Shet ... 111 k4
Mainsforth Dur ... 65 N2
Mains of Balhall Angus ... 94 H8
Mains of Balnakettle
Abers ... 95 K7
Mains of Dalvey Highld ... 100 H8
Mains of Haulkerton
Abers ... 95 L7
Mains of Lesmoir Abers ... 101 N9
Mains of Melgunds Angus ... 93 P5
Mainsriddle D & G ... 70 F4
Mainstone Shrops ... 38 F5
Maisemore Gloucs ... 29 L5
Major's Green Worcs ... 40 E11
Malborough Devon ... 5 P11
Maldon Essex ... 22 G3
Malham N York ... 58 B2
Maligar Highld ... 104 G9
Mallaig Highld ... 97 J9
Mallaigvaig Highld ... 97 J9
Malleny Mills C Edin ... 86 E8
Malltraeth IoA ... 54 E7
Mallwyd Gwynd ... 47 P8
Malmesbury Wilts ... 18 D4
Malmsmead Devon ... 15 N3
Malpas Ches W ... 49 J6
Malpas Cnwll ... 3 J7
Malpas Newpt ... 28 C10
Maltby Rothm ... 51 M3
Maltby S on T ... 66 C5
Maltby le Marsh Lincs ... 53 M7
Maltman's Hill Kent ... 12 H2
Malton N York ... 66 H12
Malvern Hills ... 39 P12
Malvern Link Worcs ... 39 P11
Malvern Wells Worcs ... 29 K1
Mamble Worcs ... 39 M7
Mamhilad Mons ... 28 C7
Manaccan Cnwll ... 2 H10
Manafon Powys ... 38 C2
Manais W Isls ... 111 c3
Manaton Devon ... 5 P4
Manby Lincs ... 53 L6
Mancetter Warwks ... 40 H7
Manchester Manch ... 57 J8
Manchester Airport Manch ... 57 P11
Manchester Cathedral
Salfd ... 57 P8
Manchester
Crematorium Manch ... 57 P9
Mancot Flints ... 48 G3
Mandally Highld ... 98 D8
Manea Cambs ... 43 M11
Maney Birm ... 40 E8
Manfield N York ... 65 L5
Mangotsfield S Glos ... 17 P2
Manish W Isls ... 111 c3
Manley Ches W ... 49 J2
Manmoel Caerph ... 27 P7
Mannel Ag & B ... 88 C8
Manningford Bohune
Wilts ... 18 G8
Manningford Bruce Wilts ... 18 G8
Manningham C Brad ... 58 F7
Manning's Heath W Susx ... 11 K4
Mannington Dorset ... 8 F6
Manningtree Essex ... 34 H9
Mannofield C Aber ... 95 Q2
Manorbier Pembks ... 25 J8
Manorbier Newton
Pembks ... 24 H8
Manorhill Border ... 80 F7
Manorowen Pembks ... 24 G2
Manor Park Gt Lon ... 21 N6
Manor Park
Crematorium Gt Lon ... 21 N6
Mansell Gamage Herefs ... 38 H12
Mansell Lacy Herefs ... 38 H11
Mansfield E Ayrs ... 77 K8
Mansfield Notts ... 51 M8
Mansfield & District
Crematorium Notts ... 51 M8
Mansfield Woodhouse
Notts ... 51 M8
Manston Dorset ... 8 B4
Manston Kent ... 23 Q9
Manston Leeds ... 59 J7
Manswood Dorset ... 8 E6
Manthorpe Lincs ... 42 F7
Manton N Linc ... 52 E4
Manton Rutlnd ... 42 C8
Manton Wilts ... 18 H7
Manuden Essex ... 33 M10
Maperton Somset ... 17 P10
Maplebeck Notts ... 51 P8
Mapledurham Oxon ... 19 R5
Mapledurwell Hants ... 20 B12
Maplehurst W Susx ... 11 J5
Maplescombe Kent ... 22 C10
Mapleton Derbys ... 50 F10
Mapperley Derbys ... 51 K11
Mapperley Park C Nott ... 51 M11
Mapperton Dorset ... 7 M3
Mappleborough Green
Warwks ... 30 E2
Mappleton E R Yk ... 61 L5
Mapplewell Barns ... 59 J11
Mappowder Dorset ... 7 Q2
Marazanvose Cnwll ... 2 H6
Marazion Cnwll ... 2 D9

| Place | County | Page | Grid |
|---|---|---|---|
| Marbury | Ches E | 49 | K6 |
| March | Cambs | 43 | L10 |
| March | S Lans | 78 | G6 |
| Marcham | Oxon | 19 | M2 |
| Marchamley | Shrops | 49 | L9 |
| Marchington | Staffs | 40 | F2 |
| Marchros | Gwynd | 46 | E6 |
| Marchwiel | Wrexhm | 48 | G6 |
| Marchwood | Hants | 9 | L5 |
| Marcross | V Glam | 16 | C3 |
| Marden | Herefs | 39 | K11 |
| Marden | Kent | 12 | E2 |
| Marden | Wilts | 18 | G8 |
| Marden Thorn | Kent | 12 | F2 |
| Mardy | Mons | 28 | C5 |
| Mareham le Fen | Lincs | 53 | J10 |
| Mareham on the Hill | Lincs | 53 | J9 |
| Marehill | W Susx | 10 | G6 |
| Maresfield | E Susx | 11 | P5 |
| Marfleet | C KuH | 61 | K8 |
| Marford | Wrexhm | 48 | G4 |
| Margam | Neath | 26 | G10 |
| Margam Crematorium | Neath | 26 | H10 |
| Margaret Marsh | Dorset | 8 | B4 |
| Margaretting | Essex | 22 | D3 |
| Margaretting Tye | Essex | 22 | D3 |
| Margate | Kent | 23 | Q8 |
| Margnaheglish | N Ayrs | 75 | Q6 |
| Margrie | D & G | 69 | N8 |
| Margrove Park | R & Cl | 66 | F4 |
| Marham | Norfk | 44 | B7 |
| Marhamchurch | Cnwll | 14 | D10 |
| Marholm | C Pete | 42 | G9 |
| Mariansleigh | Devon | 15 | M7 |
| Marine Town | Kent | 22 | H8 |
| Marionburgh | Abers | 95 | L1 |
| Marishader | Highld | 104 | G9 |
| Maristow | Devon | 5 | K7 |
| Marjoriebanks | D & G | 78 | H11 |
| Mark | Somset | 17 | K6 |
| Markbeech | Kent | 11 | P2 |
| Markby | Lincs | 53 | M7 |
| Mark Cross | E Susx | 12 | C4 |
| Markeaton Crematorium | C Derb | 51 | J12 |
| Market Bosworth | Leics | 41 | K6 |
| Market Deeping | Lincs | 42 | G7 |
| Market Drayton | Shrops | 49 | M8 |
| Market Harborough | Leics | 41 | Q9 |
| Market Lavington | Wilts | 18 | E9 |
| Market Overton | Rutlnd | 42 | C6 |
| Market Rasen | Lincs | 52 | G5 |
| Market Stainton | Lincs | 52 | H6 |
| Market Warsop | Notts | 51 | M7 |
| Market Weighton | E R Yk | 60 | F6 |
| Market Weston | Suffk | 34 | G2 |
| Markfield | Leics | 41 | L5 |
| Markham | Caerph | 27 | N8 |
| Markham Moor | Notts | 51 | Q6 |
| Markinch | Fife | 86 | G2 |
| Markington | N York | 58 | H2 |
| Markle | E Loth | 87 | L6 |
| Marksbury | BaNES | 17 | P4 |
| Marks Tey | Essex | 34 | E11 |
| Markyate | Herts | 32 | F12 |
| Marlborough | Wilts | 18 | H7 |
| Marlcliff | Warwks | 30 | E4 |
| Marldon | Devon | 6 | B9 |
| Marlesford | Suffk | 35 | M5 |
| Marlingford | Norfk | 45 | J8 |
| Marloes | Pembks | 24 | E7 |
| Marlow | Bucks | 20 | D6 |
| Marlow Bottom | Bucks | 20 | D6 |
| Marlpit Hill | Kent | 11 | N1 |
| Marnhull | Dorset | 8 | B4 |
| Marple | Stockp | 50 | C3 |
| Marr | Donc | 59 | L12 |
| Marrick | N York | 65 | J7 |
| Marsden | Kirk | 58 | D10 |
| Marsden | S Tyne | 73 | P7 |
| Marshalswick | Herts | 21 | J2 |
| Marsham | Norfk | 45 | K5 |
| Marsh Baldon | Oxon | 19 | P2 |
| Marshborough | Kent | 23 | P11 |
| Marshbrook | Shrops | 38 | H4 |
| Marshchapel | Lincs | 53 | K4 |
| Marsh Farm | Luton | 32 | F10 |
| Marshfield | Newpt | 28 | B11 |
| Marshfield | S Glos | 18 | B6 |
| Marshgate | Cnwll | 4 | E2 |
| Marsh Gibbon | Bucks | 31 | N9 |
| Marsh Green | Devon | 6 | E4 |
| Marsh Green | Kent | 11 | N2 |
| Marshland St James | Norfk | 43 | N8 |
| Marsh Lane | Derbys | 51 | K5 |
| Marsh Street | Somset | 16 | D7 |
| Marshwood | Dorset | 7 | K3 |
| Marske | N York | 65 | K7 |
| Marske-by-the-Sea | R & Cl | 66 | E3 |
| Marston | Herefs | 38 | G10 |
| Marston | Lincs | 42 | C2 |
| Marston | Oxon | 31 | M11 |
| Marston | Staffs | 40 | B3 |
| Marston | Wilts | 18 | E9 |
| Marston Green | Solhll | 40 | F9 |
| Marston Magna | Somset | 17 | N10 |
| Marston Meysey | Wilts | 18 | G2 |
| Marston Montgomery | Derbys | 50 | F12 |
| Marston Moretaine | C Beds | 32 | E8 |
| Marston on Dove | Derbys | 40 | G2 |
| Marston St Lawrence | Nhants | 31 | M6 |
| Marston Trussell | Nhants | 41 | P9 |
| Marstow | Herefs | 28 | G5 |
| Marsworth | Bucks | 20 | E1 |
| Marten | Wilts | 19 | K8 |
| Martham | Norfk | 45 | P6 |
| Martin | Hants | 8 | F4 |
| Martin | Kent | 13 | Q1 |
| Martin | Lincs | 52 | G10 |
| Martinhoe | Devon | 15 | L3 |
| Martin Hussingtree | Worcs | 39 | Q9 |
| Martinstown | Dorset | 7 | P5 |
| Martlesham | Suffk | 35 | L7 |
| Martlesham Heath | Suffk | 35 | L7 |
| Martletwy | Pembks | 24 | H6 |
| Martley | Worcs | 39 | N9 |
| Martock | Somset | 17 | L11 |
| Marton | Ches E | 49 | Q2 |
| Marton | E R Yk | 61 | K6 |
| Marton | Lincs | 52 | B7 |
| Marton | Middsb | 66 | D4 |
| Marton | N York | 59 | K2 |
| Marton | N York | 66 | G10 |
| Marton | Shrops | 38 | F2 |
| Marton | Warwks | 31 | K1 |
| Marton-le-Moor | N York | 65 | P12 |
| Martyr Worthy | Hants | 9 | N2 |
| Marwell Wildlife | Hants | 9 | N3 |
| Marwick | Ork | 111 | J2 |
| Marwood | Devon | 15 | J5 |
| Marybank | Highld | 106 | H10 |
| Maryburgh | Highld | 107 | J10 |
| Marygold | Border | 87 | P9 |
| Maryhill | C Glas | 85 | J8 |
| Maryhill Crematorium | C Glas | 85 | J8 |
| Marykirk | Abers | 95 | L8 |
| Marylebone | Gt Lon | 21 | L7 |
| Marylebone | Wigan | 57 | L7 |
| Marypark | Moray | 101 | J7 |
| Maryport | Cumb | 70 | G8 |
| Maryport | D & G | 68 | F11 |
| Marystow | Devon | 5 | J4 |
| Mary Tavy | Devon | 5 | K4 |
| Maryton | Angus | 95 | L10 |
| Marywell | Abers | 95 | J3 |
| Marywell | Abers | 95 | Q3 |
| Marywell | Angus | 93 | Q6 |
| Masham | N York | 65 | L10 |
| Masongill | N York | 63 | M7 |
| Masonhill Crematorium | S Ayrs | 76 | F7 |
| Mastin Moor | Derbys | 51 | L5 |
| Matching Green | Essex | 21 | Q2 |
| Matching Tye | Essex | 21 | P2 |
| Matfen | Nthumb | 73 | J6 |
| Matfield | Kent | 12 | D2 |
| Mathern | Mons | 28 | F9 |
| Mathon | Herefs | 39 | N11 |
| Mathry | Pembks | 24 | F3 |
| Matlask | Norfk | 45 | J3 |
| Matlock | Derbys | 50 | H8 |
| Matlock Bath | Derbys | 50 | H8 |
| Matson | Gloucs | 29 | L5 |
| Mattersey | Notts | 51 | P3 |
| Mattingley | Hants | 20 | B10 |
| Mattishall | Norfk | 44 | H7 |
| Mattishall Burgh | Norfk | 44 | H7 |
| Mauchline | E Ayrs | 76 | H6 |
| Maud | Abers | 103 | J6 |
| Maufant | Jersey | 7 | c1 |
| Maugersbury | Gloucs | 30 | G8 |
| Maughold | IoM | 56 | e3 |
| Mauld | Highld | 98 | E2 |
| Maulden | C Beds | 32 | F8 |
| Maulds Meaburn | Cumb | 64 | B4 |
| Maunby | N York | 65 | N9 |
| Maundown | Somset | 16 | E9 |
| Mautby | Norfk | 45 | P7 |
| Mavesyn Ridware | Staffs | 40 | E4 |
| Mavis Enderby | Lincs | 53 | K9 |
| Mawbray | Cumb | 70 | H6 |
| Mawdesley | Lancs | 57 | J6 |
| Mawdlam | Brdgnd | 26 | H11 |
| Mawgan | Cnwll | 2 | G10 |
| Mawgan Porth | Cnwll | 3 | J3 |
| Mawla | Cnwll | 2 | G6 |
| Mawnan | Cnwll | 2 | H9 |
| Mawnan Smith | Cnwll | 2 | H9 |
| Mawsley | Nhants | 32 | B2 |
| Maxey | C Pete | 42 | G8 |
| Maxstoke | Warwks | 40 | G9 |
| Maxton | Border | 80 | E7 |
| Maxton | Kent | 13 | P2 |
| Maxwell Town | D & G | 70 | F1 |
| Maxworthy | Cnwll | 4 | G2 |
| May Bank | Staffs | 49 | Q6 |
| Maybole | S Ayrs | 76 | E8 |
| Maybury | Surrey | 20 | G10 |
| Mayfield | E Susx | 12 | C5 |
| Mayfield | Mdloth | 86 | G8 |
| Mayfield | Staffs | 50 | F10 |
| Mayford | Surrey | 20 | F11 |
| May Hill | Gloucs | 29 | J5 |
| Mayland | Essex | 22 | H3 |
| Maylandsea | Essex | 22 | H3 |
| Maynard's Green | E Susx | 12 | C6 |
| Maypole | Birm | 40 | E10 |
| Maypole Green | Norfk | 45 | N10 |
| Maypole Green | Suffk | 34 | F5 |
| Meadgate | BaNES | 17 | P5 |
| Meadle | Bucks | 20 | C3 |
| Meadowfield | Dur | 73 | M11 |
| Meadwell | Devon | 5 | J4 |
| Meanwood | Leeds | 58 | H6 |
| Meare | Somset | 17 | L7 |
| Meare Green | Somset | 16 | H10 |
| Meare Green | Somset | 17 | J10 |
| Mearns | E Rens | 85 | J11 |
| Mears Ashby | Nhants | 32 | B4 |
| Measham | Leics | 41 | J5 |
| Meathop | Cumb | 62 | H6 |
| Meavy | Devon | 5 | L6 |
| Medbourne | Leics | 42 | B10 |
| Meddon | Devon | 14 | E8 |
| Meden Vale | Notts | 51 | M6 |
| Medmenham | Bucks | 20 | D6 |
| Medomsley | Dur | 73 | K9 |
| Medstead | Hants | 19 | Q12 |
| Medway Crematorium | Kent | 22 | E10 |
| Medway Services | Medway | 22 | G10 |
| Meerbrook | Staffs | 50 | C8 |
| Meesden | Herts | 33 | M9 |
| Meeth | Devon | 15 | J9 |
| Meeting House Hill | Norfk | 45 | M5 |
| Meidrim | Carmth | 25 | M5 |
| Meifod | Powys | 48 | D11 |
| Meigle | P & K | 93 | K6 |
| Meikle Carco | D & G | 77 | M3 |
| Meikle Earnock | S Lans | 85 | M11 |
| Meikle Kilmory | Ag & B | 83 | R10 |
| Meikle Obney | P & K | 92 | G7 |
| Meikleour | P & K | 92 | H7 |
| Meikle Wartle | Abers | 102 | F8 |
| Meinciau | Carmth | 26 | B6 |
| Meir | C Stke | 50 | C11 |
| Melbourn | Cambs | 33 | L7 |
| Melbourne | Derbys | 41 | J3 |
| Melbourne | E R Yk | 60 | D5 |
| Melbury Abbas | Dorset | 8 | C4 |
| Melbury Bubb | Dorset | 7 | N2 |
| Melbury Osmond | Dorset | 7 | N2 |
| Melchbourne | Bed | 32 | E4 |
| Melcombe Bingham | Dorset | 8 | B6 |
| Meldon | Devon | 5 | L2 |
| Meldon | Nthumb | 73 | K4 |
| Meldreth | Cambs | 33 | L7 |
| Meldrum | Stirlg | 85 | M3 |
| Melfort | Ag & B | 90 | B12 |
| Meliden | Denbgs | 56 | C11 |
| Melin-y-wig | Denbgs | 48 | B6 |
| Melkinthorpe | Cumb | 71 | Q9 |
| Melkridge | Nthumb | 72 | D7 |
| Melksham | Wilts | 18 | D7 |
| Melling | Lancs | 63 | L7 |
| Melling | Sefton | 56 | H8 |
| Mellis | Suffk | 34 | H2 |
| Mellon Charles | Highld | 105 | M4 |
| Mellon Udrigle | Highld | 105 | N3 |
| Mellor | Lancs | 57 | M3 |
| Mellor | Stockp | 50 | C3 |
| Mellor Brook | Lancs | 57 | M3 |
| Mells | Somset | 17 | Q6 |
| Melmerby | Cumb | 72 | B12 |
| Melmerby | N York | 65 | J9 |
| Melmerby | N York | 65 | N11 |
| Melness | Highld | 109 | K4 |
| Melplash | Dorset | 7 | L3 |
| Melrose | Border | 80 | D7 |
| Melsetter | Ork | 111 | g3 |
| Melsonby | N York | 65 | L6 |
| Meltham | Kirk | 58 | E11 |
| Melton | E R Yk | 60 | G8 |
| Melton | Suffk | 35 | L6 |
| Melton Constable | Norfk | 44 | H4 |
| Melton Mowbray | Leics | 41 | Q4 |
| Melton Ross | N Linc | 60 | H11 |
| Melvaig | Highld | 105 | L5 |
| Melverley | Shrops | 48 | G11 |
| Melvich | Highld | 109 | Q3 |
| Membury | Devon | 6 | H3 |
| Membury Services | W Berk | 19 | K5 |
| Memsie | Abers | 103 | K3 |
| Memus | Angus | 93 | M4 |
| Menai Bridge | IoA | 54 | H7 |
| Mendham | Suffk | 35 | L2 |
| Mendip Crematorium | Somset | 17 | N7 |
| Mendip Hills | | 17 | M5 |
| Mendlesham | Suffk | 34 | H4 |
| Mendlesham Green | Suffk | 34 | H4 |
| Menheniot | Cnwll | 4 | G7 |
| Mennock | D & G | 77 | N9 |
| Menston | C Brad | 58 | F5 |
| Menstrie | Clacks | 85 | P4 |
| Mentmore | Bucks | 32 | C11 |
| Meoble | Highld | 97 | L11 |
| Meole Brace | Shrops | 49 | J12 |
| Meonstoke | Hants | 9 | Q4 |
| Meopham | Kent | 22 | D9 |
| Mepal | Cambs | 33 | M1 |
| Meppershall | C Beds | 32 | G9 |
| Mere | Ches E | 57 | N11 |
| Mere | Wilts | 8 | C2 |
| Mere Brow | Lancs | 56 | H5 |
| Mereclough | Lancs | 57 | Q3 |
| Mere Green | Birm | 40 | E7 |
| Mereworth | Kent | 22 | D11 |
| Meriden | Solhll | 40 | G10 |
| Merkadale | Highld | 96 | D4 |
| Merley | Poole | 8 | F7 |
| Merrion | Pembks | 24 | G8 |
| Merriott | Somset | 7 | L1 |
| Merrow | Surrey | 20 | G12 |
| Merry Hill | Herts | 21 | J5 |
| Merryhill | Wolves | 40 | B7 |
| Merrymeet | Cnwll | 4 | G7 |
| Mersea Island | Essex | 23 | K1 |
| Mersham | Kent | 13 | K3 |
| Merstham | Surrey | 21 | L11 |
| Merston | W Susx | 10 | E9 |
| Merstone | IoW | 9 | N9 |
| Merther | Cnwll | 3 | L5 |
| Merthyr Cynog | Powys | 27 | L2 |
| Merthyr Mawr | Brdgnd | 27 | J12 |
| Merthyr Tydfil | Myr Td | 27 | M7 |
| Merthyr Vale | Myr Td | 27 | M8 |
| Merton | Devon | 15 | J9 |
| Merton | Gt Lon | 21 | K9 |
| Merton | Norfk | 44 | F9 |
| Merton | Oxon | 31 | M9 |
| Meshaw | Devon | 15 | M8 |
| Messing | Essex | 34 | E11 |
| Messingham | N Linc | 52 | C3 |
| Metfield | Suffk | 35 | L1 |
| Metherell | Cnwll | 5 | J6 |
| Metheringham | Lincs | 52 | F10 |
| Methil | Fife | 86 | H3 |
| Methilhill | Fife | 86 | G3 |
| Methlick | Abers | 102 | H7 |
| Methven | P & K | 92 | F9 |
| Methwold | Norfk | 44 | C10 |
| Methwold Hythe | Norfk | 44 | B10 |
| Mettingham | Suffk | 45 | M11 |
| Metton | Norfk | 45 | K3 |
| Mevagissey | Cnwll | 3 | M6 |
| Mexborough | Donc | 51 | L2 |
| Mey | Highld | 110 | F2 |
| Meyllteyrn | Gwynd | 46 | D5 |
| Meysey Hampton | Gloucs | 18 | G3 |
| Miabhig | W Isls | 111 | c2 |
| Miavaig | W Isls | 111 | c2 |
| Michaelchurch | Herefs | 28 | F4 |
| Michaelchurch Escley | Herefs | 28 | C3 |
| Michaelstone-y-Fedw | Newpt | 27 | P11 |
| Michaelston-le-Pit | V Glam | 16 | F2 |
| Michaelstow | Cnwll | 4 | D4 |
| Michaelwood Services | Gloucs | 29 | J9 |
| Micheldever | Hants | 19 | N11 |
| Micheldever Station | Hants | 19 | N11 |
| Michelmersh | Hants | 9 | L3 |
| Mickfield | Suffk | 35 | J4 |
| Micklebring | Donc | 51 | L2 |
| Mickleby | N York | 66 | H5 |
| Micklefield | Leeds | 59 | K7 |
| Mickleham | Surrey | 21 | J11 |
| Mickleover | C Derb | 40 | H1 |
| Mickleton | Dur | 64 | H3 |
| Mickleton | Gloucs | 30 | F5 |
| Mickletown | Leeds | 59 | K8 |
| Mickle Trafford | Ches W | 49 | J2 |
| Mickley | N York | 65 | M11 |
| Mickley Square | Nthumb | 73 | J8 |
| Mid Ardlaw | Abers | 103 | K3 |
| Midbea | Ork | 111 | h1 |
| Mid Beltie | Abers | 95 | K2 |
| Mid Calder | W Loth | 86 | C8 |
| Mid Clyth | Highld | 110 | F8 |
| Mid Culbeuchly | Abers | 102 | E3 |
| Middle Aston | Oxon | 31 | L8 |
| Middle Barton | Oxon | 31 | K8 |
| Middlebie | D & G | 71 | K1 |
| Middlebridge | P & K | 92 | D3 |
| Middle Chinnock | Somset | 17 | L12 |
| Middle Claydon | Bucks | 31 | Q8 |
| Middleham | N York | 65 | K9 |
| Middlehill | Wilts | 18 | B7 |
| Middlehope | Shrops | 39 | J4 |
| Middle Kames | Ag & B | 83 | N5 |
| Middle Littleton | Worcs | 30 | E5 |
| Middlemarsh | Dorset | 7 | P2 |
| Middle Mayfield | Staffs | 50 | F10 |
| Middle Rasen | Lincs | 52 | F5 |
| Middle Rocombe | Devon | 6 | B8 |
| Middlesbrough | Middsb | 66 | C4 |
| Middleshaw | Cumb | 63 | K4 |
| Middlesmoor | N York | 65 | J11 |
| Middlestone | Dur | 65 | M2 |
| Middlestown | Wakefd | 58 | H10 |
| Middlethird | Border | 80 | F5 |
| Middleton | Ag & B | 88 | B7 |
| Middleton | Derbys | 50 | G8 |
| Middleton | Derbys | 50 | H9 |
| Middleton | Essex | 34 | E8 |
| Middleton | Hants | 19 | M11 |
| Middleton | Herefs | 39 | K8 |
| Middleton | Leeds | 58 | H8 |
| Middleton | N York | 58 | E4 |
| Middleton | N York | 66 | H9 |
| Middleton | Nhants | 42 | B11 |
| Middleton | Norfk | 43 | Q6 |
| Middleton | Nthumb | 73 | J4 |
| Middleton | P & K | 86 | D2 |
| Middleton | Rochdl | 57 | Q7 |
| Middleton | Shrops | 39 | K6 |
| Middleton | Suffk | 35 | N3 |
| Middleton | Swans | 25 | P10 |
| Middleton | Warwks | 40 | F7 |
| Middleton Cheney | Nhants | 31 | L6 |
| Middleton Crematorium | Rochdl | 58 | B11 |
| Middleton-in-Teesdale | Dur | 64 | G3 |
| Middleton Moor | Suffk | 35 | N4 |
| Middleton One Row | Darltn | 65 | P5 |
| Middleton-on-Sea | W Susx | 10 | F9 |
| Middleton on the Hill | Herefs | 39 | K8 |
| Middleton on the Wolds | E R Yk | 60 | G4 |
| Middleton Park | C Aber | 103 | J11 |
| Middleton Quernhow | N York | 65 | N10 |
| Middleton St George | Darltn | 65 | N5 |
| Middleton Scriven | Shrops | 39 | M5 |
| Middleton Stoney | Oxon | 31 | M9 |
| Middleton Tyas | N York | 65 | M6 |
| Middle Town | IoS | 2 | b3 |
| Middletown | Powys | 48 | F11 |
| Middle Tysoe | Warwks | 31 | J5 |
| Middle Wallop | Hants | 19 | K12 |
| Middlewich | Ches E | 49 | N3 |
| Middle Winterslow | Wilts | 9 | J2 |
| Middlewood | Cnwll | 4 | G5 |
| Middle Woodford | Wilts | 18 | G12 |
| Middlewood Green | Suffk | 34 | H5 |
| Middleyard | E Ayrs | 77 | J5 |
| Middlezoy | Somset | 17 | K9 |
| Midford | BaNES | 18 | B8 |
| Midgham | W Berk | 19 | P7 |
| Midgley | Calder | 58 | D8 |
| Midgley | Wakefd | 58 | H10 |
| Midhopestones | Sheff | 50 | G2 |
| Midhurst | W Susx | 10 | D6 |
| Mid Lavant | W Susx | 10 | D8 |
| Midlem | Border | 80 | C8 |
| Mid Mains | Highld | 98 | F2 |
| Midpark | Ag & B | 83 | Q10 |
| Midsomer Norton | BaNES | 17 | P5 |
| Midtown | Highld | 109 | K4 |
| Mid Warwickshire Crematorium | Warwks | 30 | H3 |
| Mid Yell | Shet | 111 | k2 |
| Migvie | Abers | 94 | G2 |
| Milborne Port | Somset | 17 | P11 |
| Milborne St Andrew | Dorset | 8 | B7 |
| Milborne Wick | Somset | 17 | P11 |
| Milbourne | Nthumb | 73 | K6 |
| Milbourne | Wilts | 18 | D4 |
| Milburn | Cumb | 64 | C2 |
| Milbury Heath | S Glos | 29 | J10 |
| Milby | N York | 59 | K1 |
| Milcombe | Oxon | 31 | K7 |
| Milden | Suffk | 34 | F7 |
| Mildenhall | Suffk | 34 | B2 |
| Mildenhall | Wilts | 18 | H6 |
| Mileham | Norfk | 44 | F6 |
| Mile Oak | Br & H | 11 | K8 |
| Milesmark | Fife | 86 | C5 |
| Miles Platting | Manch | 57 | Q8 |
| Mile Town | Kent | 22 | H8 |
| Milfield | Nthumb | 81 | K7 |
| Milford | Derbys | 51 | J10 |
| Milford | Devon | 14 | E7 |
| Milford | Staffs | 40 | C4 |
| Milford | Surrey | 10 | F2 |
| Milford Haven | Pembks | 24 | F7 |
| Milford on Sea | Hants | 9 | K8 |
| Milkwall | Gloucs | 28 | G7 |
| Milland | W Susx | 10 | D4 |
| Mill Bank | Calder | 58 | D9 |
| Millbreck | Abers | 103 | K6 |
| Millbridge | Surrey | 10 | D2 |
| Millbrook | C Beds | 32 | E8 |
| Millbrook | C Sotn | 9 | L5 |
| Millbrook | Cnwll | 5 | J9 |
| Millbrook | Jersey | 7 | b2 |
| Mill Brow | Stockp | 50 | C3 |
| Millbuie | Abers | 102 | G12 |
| Millbuie | Highld | 107 | J11 |
| Millcorner | E Susx | 12 | F5 |
| Millcraig | Highld | 107 | L7 |
| Milldale | Staffs | 50 | F9 |
| Mill End | Bucks | 20 | C6 |
| Mill End | Herts | 33 | K9 |
| Millerhill | Mdloth | 86 | G8 |
| Miller's Dale | Derbys | 50 | F6 |
| Millerston | C Glas | 85 | L9 |
| Mill Green | Cambs | 33 | P7 |
| Mill Green | Essex | 22 | D3 |
| Mill Green | Lincs | 43 | J5 |
| Mill Green | Suffk | 34 | F8 |
| Mill Green | Suffk | 34 | G5 |
| Mill Green | Suffk | 35 | J5 |
| Millhalf | Herefs | 38 | F11 |
| Millheugh | S Lans | 77 | M2 |
| Mill Hill | Gt Lon | 21 | K5 |
| Millhouse | Ag & B | 83 | P8 |
| Millhousebridge | D & G | 78 | H10 |
| Millhouse Green | Barns | 58 | G12 |
| Millhouses | Sheff | 51 | J4 |
| Miliken Park | Rens | 84 | G9 |
| Millington | E R Yk | 60 | E4 |
| Millmeece | Staffs | 49 | Q8 |
| Mill of Drummond | P & K | 92 | C11 |
| Mill of Haldane | W Duns | 84 | G6 |
| Millom | Cumb | 62 | D6 |
| Millport | N Ayrs | 84 | C11 |
| Mill Street | Suffk | 34 | H3 |
| Millthrop | Cumb | 63 | M4 |
| Milltimber | C Aber | 95 | P2 |
| Milltown | Abers | 101 | K12 |
| Milltown | Abers | 101 | N11 |
| Milltown | D & G | 71 | M1 |
| Milltown | Devon | 15 | K4 |
| Milltown of Campfield | Abers | 95 | L2 |
| Milltown of Edinville | Moray | 101 | K7 |
| Milltown of Learney | Abers | 95 | K2 |
| Milnathort | P & K | 86 | D2 |
| Milngavie | E Duns | 85 | J7 |
| Milnrow | Rochdl | 58 | B10 |
| Milnthorpe | Cumb | 63 | J6 |
| Milovaig | Highld | 104 | B11 |
| Milson | Shrops | 39 | M7 |
| Milstead | Kent | 22 | H10 |
| Milston | Wilts | 18 | H10 |
| Milthorpe | Nhants | 31 | N5 |
| Milton | C Stke | 50 | B10 |
| Milton | Cambs | 33 | M4 |
| Milton | Cumb | 71 | Q4 |
| Milton | D & G | 68 | G8 |
| Milton | D & G | 70 | D2 |
| Milton | Derbys | 40 | H3 |
| Milton | Highld | 97 | J2 |
| Milton | Highld | 98 | G3 |
| Milton | Highld | 107 | J11 |
| Milton | Highld | 107 | M7 |
| Milton | Highld | 110 | G5 |
| Milton | Inver | 84 | F8 |
| Milton | Kent | 22 | D8 |
| Milton | Moray | 101 | J10 |
| Milton | Moray | 101 | P3 |
| Milton | N Som | 17 | J4 |
| Milton | Notts | 51 | P6 |
| Milton | Oxon | 19 | N3 |
| Milton | Oxon | 31 | L7 |
| Milton | P & K | 94 | B9 |
| Milton | Pembks | 24 | H8 |
| Milton | Somset | 17 | L10 |
| Milton | Stirlg | 84 | H3 |
| Milton | W Duns | 84 | G7 |
| Milton Abbas | Dorset | 8 | B7 |
| Milton Abbot | Devon | 5 | J4 |
| Milton Bryan | C Beds | 32 | D10 |
| Milton Clevedon | Somset | 17 | P8 |
| Milton Combe | Devon | 5 | K7 |
| Milton Damerel | Devon | 14 | G9 |
| Milton Ernest | Bed | 32 | E5 |
| Milton Green | Ches W | 49 | J4 |
| Milton Hill | Oxon | 19 | M3 |
| Milton Keynes | M Keyn | 32 | C8 |
| Milton Lilbourne | Wilts | 18 | H8 |
| Milton Malsor | Nhants | 31 | Q3 |
| Milton Morenish | P & K | 91 | P8 |
| Milton of Auchinhove | Abers | 95 | J2 |
| Milton of Balgonie | Fife | 86 | G3 |
| Milton of Buchanan | Stirlg | 84 | G5 |
| Milton of Campsie | E Duns | 85 | L7 |
| Milton of Leys | Highld | 99 | K1 |
| Milton of Murtle | C Aber | 95 | P2 |
| Milton of Tullich | Abers | 94 | F3 |
| Milton on Stour | Dorset | 8 | B2 |
| Milton Regis | Kent | 22 | H9 |
| Milton-under-Wychwood | Oxon | 30 | H9 |
| Milverton | Somset | 16 | F10 |
| Milverton | Warwks | 30 | H2 |
| Milwich | Staffs | 40 | C2 |
| Minard | Ag & B | 83 | P4 |
| Minchinhampton | Gloucs | 29 | M8 |
| Minehead | Somset | 16 | C6 |
| Minera | Wrexhm | 48 | F5 |
| Minety | Wilts | 18 | F3 |
| Minffordd | Gwynd | 47 | J4 |
| Mingarrypark | Highld | 89 | N3 |
| Miningsby | Lincs | 53 | K10 |
| Minions | Cnwll | 4 | G6 |
| Minishant | S Ayrs | 76 | F8 |
| Minllyn | Gwynd | 47 | P8 |
| Minnigaff | D & G | 69 | K6 |
| Minnonie | Abers | 102 | G4 |
| Minskip | N York | 59 | K2 |
| Minstead | Hants | 9 | K5 |
| Minsted | W Susx | 10 | D6 |
| Minster | Kent | 23 | J8 |
| Minster | Kent | 23 | P9 |
| Minsterley | Shrops | 38 | G2 |
| Minster Lovell | Oxon | 30 | H10 |
| Minsterworth | Gloucs | 29 | K5 |
| Minterne Magna | Dorset | 7 | P2 |
| Minting | Lincs | 52 | H8 |
| Mintlaw | Abers | 103 | K6 |
| Mintlyn Crematorium | Norfk | 43 | Q6 |
| Minto | Border | 80 | D9 |
| Minton | Shrops | 38 | H4 |
| Mirehouse | Cumb | 70 | F11 |
| Mireland | Highld | 110 | G4 |
| Mirfield | Kirk | 58 | G9 |
| Miserden | Gloucs | 29 | N7 |
| Miskin | Rhondd | 27 | L11 |
| Misson | Notts | 51 | P2 |
| Misterton | Leics | 41 | M10 |
| Misterton | Notts | 51 | Q2 |
| Misterton | Somset | 7 | L2 |
| Mistley | Essex | 35 | J9 |
| Mitcham | Gt Lon | 21 | L9 |
| Mitcheldean | Gloucs | 29 | J5 |
| Mitchell | Cnwll | 3 | J5 |
| Mitchellslacks | D & G | 78 | F9 |
| Mitchel Troy | Mons | 28 | F6 |
| Mitford | Nthumb | 73 | L4 |
| Mithian | Cnwll | 2 | H5 |
| Mixbury | Oxon | 31 | N7 |
| Mobberley | Ches E | 57 | P11 |
| Mobberley | Staffs | 50 | D11 |

Mochdre Powys 38 C4
Mochrum D & G 69 J9
Mockbeggar Kent 12 E1
Mockerkin Cumb 70 H10
Modbury Devon 5 N9
Moddershall Staffs 50 B12
Moelfre IoA 54 G4
Moelfre Powys 48 E9
Moffat D & G 78 H7
Moggerhanger C Beds 32 G6
Moira Leics 40 H4
Mol-chlach Highld 96 E7
Mold Flints 48 E3
Moldgreen Kirk 58 F10
Molehill Green Essex 33 P10
Molescroft E R Yk 60 H6
Molesworth Cambs 32 F2
Molland Devon 15 N6
Mollington Ches W 48 H2
Mollington Oxon 31 K5
Mollinsburn N Lans 85 M8
Mondynes Abers 95 M6
Monewden Suffk 35 L5
Moneydie P & K 92 F9
Moniaive D & G 78 C10
Monifieth Angus 93 N8
Monikie Angus 93 N7
Monimail Fife 93 K11
Monken Hadley Gt Lon 21 K4
Monk Fryston N York 59 L8
Monkhide Herefs 39 L12
Monkhill Cumb 71 M4
Monkhopton Shrops 39 L4
Monkland Herefs 39 J10
Monkleigh Devon 14 H7
Monknash V Glam 16 C3
Monkokehampton Devon 15 K10
Monkseaton N Tyne 73 N6
Monks Eleigh Suffk 34 F7
Monk's Gate W Susx 11 K5
Monks Heath Ches E 49 Q1
Monk Sherborne Hants 19 Q9
Monksilver Somset 16 E8
Monks Kirby Warwks 41 L10
Monk Soham Suffk 35 K4
Monks Risborough Bucks 20 D3
Monksthorpe Lincs 53 M9
Monk Street Essex 33 P10
Monkswood Mons 28 D8
Monkton Devon 6 G3
Monkton Kent 23 P9
Monkton S Ayrs 76 F6
Monkton S Tyne 73 N8
Monkton Combe BaNES 18 B8
Monkton Deverill Wilts 18 C12
Monkton Farleigh Wilts 18 B7
Monkton Heathfield Somset 16 H10
Monkton Wyld Dorset 7 J4
Monkwearmouth Sundld 73 P8
Monkwood Hants 9 Q2
Monmore Green Wolves 40 B7
Monmouth Mons 28 F6
Monnington on Wye Herefs 38 G12
Monreith D & G 69 J10
Montacute Somset 17 M11
Montford Shrops 48 H11
Montford Bridge Shrops 48 H11
Montgarrie Abers 102 D10
Montgomery Powys 38 E3
Montrose Angus 95 L9
Mont Saint Guern 6 b2
Monxton Hants 19 K11
Monyash Derbys 50 F7
Monymusk Abers 102 F11
Monzie P & K 92 C9
Moodiesburn N Lans 85 L8
Moonzie Fife 93 L11
Moor Allerton Leeds 58 H6
Moorby Lincs 53 J10
Moor Crichel Dorset 8 E6
Moordown Bmouth 8 G8
Moore Halton 57 L11
Moor End Calder 58 D8
Moorends Donc 59 P10
Moorhead C Brad 58 F6
Moorhouse Cumb 71 M4
Moorhouse Notts 51 Q7
Moorhouse Bank Surrey 21 N11
Moorlinch Somset 17 K8
Moor Monkton N York 59 L3
Moorsholm R & Cl 66 F5
Moorside Dorset 8 B4
Moor Street Birm 40 C10
Moorswater Cnwll 4 F7
Moorthorpe Wakefd 59 L11
Moortown Leeds 58 H6
Moortown Lincs 52 F4
Morangie Highld 107 M5
Morar Highld 97 J10
Moray Crematorium Moray 101 M3
Morborne Cambs 42 G10
Morchard Bishop Devon 15 N10
Morcombelake Dorset 7 K4
Morcott Rutlnd 42 D9
Morda Shrops 48 F9
Morden Dorset 8 D8
Morden Gt Lon 21 K9
Mordiford Herefs 28 G2
Mordon Dur 65 N3
More Shrops 38 G4
Morebath Devon 16 C10
Morebattle Border 80 G8
Morecambe Lancs 62 H8
Moredon Swindn 18 G4
Morefield Highld 106 D4
Morehall Kent 13 N3
Moreleigh Devon 5 P9
Morenish P & K 91 N8
Morestead Hants 9 N3
Moreton Dorset 8 B9
Moreton Essex 21 Q3
Moreton Herefs 39 J8
Moreton Oxon 20 B3
Moreton Wirral 56 F10
Moreton Corbet Shrops 49 K10
Moretonhampstead Devon 5 P3
Moreton-in-Marsh Gloucs 30 G7
Moreton Jeffries Herefs 39 L11
Moreton Morrell Warwks 30 H3
Moreton on Lugg Herefs 39 J11
Moreton Pinkney Nhants 31 M4
Moreton Say Shrops 49 L8

Moreton Valence Gloucs 29 K6
Morfa Nefyn Gwynd 46 E4
Morham E Loth 87 K7
Morland Cumb 64 B3
Morley Ches E 57 P11
Morley Derbys 51 K11
Morley Leeds 58 H8
Morley St Botolph Norfk 44 H9
Morley Green Ches E 57 P11
Morningside C Edin 86 F7
Morningside N Lans 85 N11
Morningthorpe Norfk 45 K10
Morpeth Nthumb 73 L4
Morphie Abers 95 L8
Morrey Staffs 40 E4
Morriston Swans 26 F8
Morston Norfk 44 G2
Mortehoe Devon 14 H3
Morthen Rothm 51 L3
Mortimer W Berk 19 Q7
Mortimer West End Hants 19 Q7
Mortlake Gt Lon 21 K8
Mortlake Crematorium Gt Lon 21 K8
Morton Cumb 71 N5
Morton Derbys 51 K8
Morton Lincs 42 F5
Morton Lincs 52 B5
Morton Notts 51 Q9
Morton Shrops 48 F9
Mortonhall Crematorium C Edin 86 F8
Morton-on-Swale N York 65 N8
Morton on the Hill Norfk 45 J6
Morvah Cnwll 2 B8
Morvich Highld 97 N15
Morville Shrops 39 M4
Morwenstow Cnwll 14 D10
Mosborough Sheff 51 K5
Moscow E Ayrs 76 H4
Moseley Birm 40 E10
Moseley Wolves 40 C7
Moseley Worcs 39 P9
Moss Ag & B 88 B7
Moss Donc 59 N10
Mossat Abers 101 N10
Mossbank Shet 111 k3
Moss Bank St Hel 57 K8
Mossbay Cumb 70 G9
Mossblown S Ayrs 76 G6
Mossburnford Border 80 F10
Mossdale D & G 69 P5
Mossdale E Ayrs 76 H9
Moss Edge Lancs 62 H12
Mossend N Lans 85 M10
Mossley Tamesd 50 C1
Mosspaul Hotel Border 79 N8
Moss-side Highld 100 D4
Mosstodloch Moray 101 L4
Mossyard D & G 69 M8
Mossy Lea Lancs 57 K6
Mosterton Dorset 7 L2
Moston Manch 57 Q8
Mostyn Flints 56 D11
Motcombe Dorset 8 C3
Mothecombe Devon 5 M10
Motherby Cumb 71 N9
Motherwell N Lans 85 M10
Motspur Park Gt Lon 21 K9
Mottingham Gt Lon 21 N8
Mottisfont Hants 9 K3
Mottistone IoW 9 L10
Mottram in Longdendale Tamesd 50 C2
Mottram St Andrew Ches E 57 Q12
Mouldsworth Ches W 49 J2
Moulin P & K 92 E4
Moulsecoomb Br & H 11 M8
Moulsford Oxon 19 P4
Moulsoe M Keyn 32 C8
Moultavie Highld 107 K7
Moulton Ches W 49 M2
Moulton Lincs 43 K5
Moulton N York 65 M6
Moulton Nhants 32 B4
Moulton Suffk 34 B4
Moulton V Glam 16 E3
Moulton Chapel Lincs 43 J6
Moulton St Mary Norfk 45 N8
Moulton Seas End Lincs 43 K5
Mount Cnwll 4
Mountain C Brad 58 E7
Mountain Ash Rhondd 27 L8
Mountain Cross Border 86 D11
Mount Ambrose Cnwll 2 G7
Mount Bures Essex 34 E9
Mountfield E Susx 12 E6
Mountgerald House Highld 107 J9
Mount Hawke Cnwll 2 G6
Mountjoy Cnwll 3 K4
Mount Lothian Mdloth 86 F10
Mountnessing Essex 22 D4
Mounton Mons 28 F9
Mount Pleasant Derbys 51 J10
Mount Pleasant Suffk 34 C7
Mountsett Crematorium Dur 73 L9
Mountsorrel Leics 41 N5
Mount Tabor Calder 58 D8
Mousehole Cnwll 2 C9
Mouswald D & G 70 H2
Mow Cop Ches E 49 Q4
Mowhaugh Border 80 H9
Mowmacre Hill C Leic 41 N6
Mowsley Leics 41 N9
Moy Highld 98 F11
Moy Highld 99 L3
Moyle Highld 97 M6
Moylegrove Pembks 36 B10
Muasdale Ag & B 75 K4
Muchalls Abers 95 P4
Much Birch Herefs 28 F3
Much Cowarne Herefs 39 L11
Much Dewchurch Herefs 28 F3
Muchelney Somset 17 K10
Muchelney Ham Somset 17 L10
Much Hadham Herts 33 L11
Much Hoole Lancs 57 J4
Muchlarnick Cnwll 4 F8
Much Marcle Herefs 28 H3
Much Wenlock Shrops 39 L3
Muck Highld 89 J1
Muckleburgh Collection Norfk 44 H2
Mucklestone Staffs 49 N7

Muckton Lincs 53 L7
Muddiford Devon 15 K5
Muddles Green E Susx 12 B7
Mudford Somset 17 N11
Mudford Sock Somset 17 N11
Mugdock Stirlg 85 J7
Mugeary Highld 96 E2
Muggington Derbys 50 H11
Muirden Abers 102 F5
Muirdrum Angus 93 P8
Muiresk Abers 102 F5
Muirhead Angus 93 L8
Muirhead Fife 86 F2
Muirhead N Lans 85 L8
Muirkirk E Ayrs 77 L6
Muirmill Stirlg 85 M6
Muir of Fowlis Abers 102 D11
Muir of Miltonduff Moray 101 J4
Muir of Ord Highld 107 J11
Muirshearlich Highld 98 A11
Muirtack Abers 103 K7
Muirton P & K 85 Q1
Muirton Mains Highld 106 H10
Muirton of Ardblair P & K 92 H7
Muker N York 64 G7
Mulbarton Norfk 45 K9
Mulben Moray 101 L5
Mull Ag & B 89 M8
Mullion Cnwll 2 G11
Mullion Cove Cnwll 2 F11
Mumby Lincs 53 N8
Munderfield Row Herefs 39 M10
Munderfield Stocks Herefs 39 M11
Mundesley Norfk 45 M3
Mundford Norfk 44 D10
Mundham Norfk 45 M9
Mundon Hill Essex 22 G3
Mungrisdale Cumb 71 M9
Munlochy Highld 107 K10
Munnoch N Ayrs 76 E2
Munsley Herefs 29 J1
Munslow Shrops 39 K5
Murchington Devon 5 N3
Murcott Oxon 31 N10
Murkle Highld 110 D3
Murlaggan Highld 97 P10
Murroes Angus 93 N8
Murrow Cambs 43 L8
Mursley Bucks 32 B10
Murthill Angus 93 N4
Murthly P & K 92 G7
Murton C York 59 P4
Murton Cumb 64 D3
Murton Dur 73 P10
Murton Nthumb 81 K5
Musbury Devon 6 H4
Musselburgh E Loth 86 G7
Muston Leics 42 B3
Muston N York 67 N10
Muswell Hill Gt Lon 21 L5
Mutehill D & G 69 P8
Mutford Suffk 45 P11
Muthill P & K 92 C11
Mybster Highld 110 D5
Myddfai Carmth 26 G3
Myddle Shrops 49 J10
Mydroilyn Cerdgn 36 G9
Mylor Cnwll 3 J8
Mylor Bridge Cnwll 3 J8
Mynachlog ddu Pembks 25 K3
Mynydd-bach Mons 28 F9
Mynydd-Bach Swans 26 E8
Mynyddgarreg Carmth 25 P7
Mynydd Isa Flints 48 F3
Myrebird Abers 95 M3
Myredykes Border 72 B2
Mytchett Surrey 20 E11
Mytholm Calder 58 C8
Mytholmroyd Calder 58 D8
Myton-on-Swale N York 59 K2

**N**

Naast Highld 105 M6
Na Buirgh W Isls 111 c3
Naburn C York 59 N5
Nab Wood Crematorium C Brad 58 F6
Nackington Kent 23 M11
Nacton Suffk 35 K8
Nafferton E R Yk 60 H3
Nailbourne Somset 16 G9
Nailsea N Som 17 L3
Nailstone Leics 41 K6
Nailsworth Gloucs 29 L8
Nairn Highld 100 D4
Nannerch Flints 48 D2
Nanpantan Leics 41 L4
Nanpean Cnwll 3 L5
Nanstallon Cnwll 3 M3
Nanternis Cerdgn 36 F8
Nantgaredig Carmth 26 C5
Nantglyn Denbgs 55 Q8
Nantmel Powys 38 B8
Nantmor Gwynd 47 K3
Nant Peris Gwynd 54 H9
Nantwich Ches E 49 M5
Nantyglo Blae G 27 P6
Nant-y-moel Brdgnd 27 K9
Naphill Bucks 20 D4
Napton on the Hill Warwks 31 L2
Narberth Pembks 25 J6
Narborough Leics 41 M7
Narborough Norfk 44 C7
Nasareth Gwynd 54 F10
Naseby Nhants 41 P10
Nash Bucks 32 B9
Nash Newpt 28 D11
Nash Shrops 39 L7
Nassington Nhants 42 F10
Nateby Cumb 64 E6
Nateby Lancs 63 J12
National Memorial Arboretum Staffs 40 F5
National Motor Museum (Beaulieu) Hants 9 L6
National Space Science Centre C Leic 41 N6
Natland Cumb 63 K4
Naughton Suffk 34 G7
Naunton Gloucs 30 E9

Naunton Worcs 29 M2
Naunton Beauchamp Worcs 30 C4
Navenby Lincs 52 E10
Navestock Essex 21 Q4
Navestock Side Essex 22 C4
Navidale House Hotel Highld 110 B11
Navity Highld 107 M9
Nawton N York 66 F9
Nayland Suffk 34 F9
Nazeing Essex 21 N3
Neap Shet 111 k4
Near Cotton Staffs 50 E10
Near Sawrey Cumb 62 G3
Neasden Gt Lon 21 K6
Neasham Darltn 65 N5
Neath Neath 26 G8
Neatham Hants 10 C3
Neatishead Norfk 45 M6
Nebo Cerdgn 37 J7
Nebo Conwy 55 M9
Nebo Gwynd 54 F10
Nebo IoA 54 G4
Necton Norfk 44 E8
Nedd Highld 108 C8
Nedging Suffk 34 G7
Nedging Tye Suffk 34 G6
Needham Norfk 45 K1
Needham Lake & Nature Reserve Suffk 34 H6
Needham Market Suffk 34 H6
Needingworth Cambs 33 K3
Neen Savage Shrops 39 M6
Neen Sollars Shrops 39 M7
Neenton Shrops 39 M5
Nefyn Gwynd 46 E4
Neilston E Rens 84 H10
Nelson Caerph 27 M9
Nelson Lancs 57 Q2
Nemphlar S Lans 77 P3
Nempnett Thrubwell BaNES 17 M4
Nenthead Cumb 72 E11
Nenthorn Border 80 F6
Nercwys Flints 48 E4
Nereabolls Ag & B 82 C11
Nerston S Lans 85 L10
Nesbit Nthumb 81 K7
Nesfield N York 58 E4
Nesscliffe Shrops 48 H10
Neston Ches W 56 F12
Neston Wilts 18 C7
Netchwood Shrops 39 L4
Nether Alderley Ches E 49 Q1
Netheravon Wilts 18 G10
Nether Blainslie Border 80 D5
Netherbrae Abers 102 G4
Nether Broughton Leics 41 P3
Netherburn S Lans 77 N2
Netherbury Dorset 7 L3
Netherby N York 59 J5
Nether Cerne Dorset 7 P3
Nethercleuch D & G 79 J10
Nether Compton Dorset 17 N11
Nether Crimond Abers 102 H10
Nether Dallachy Moray 101 M3
Netherend Gloucs 28 G8
Netherfield E Susx 12 E6
Netherfield Notts 51 N11
Nether Fingland S Lans 78 F6
Netherhampton Wilts 8 G2
Nether Handwick Angus 93 L7
Nether Haugh Rothm 51 K2
Netherhay Dorset 7 K2
Nether Headon Notts 51 Q5
Nether Heage Derbys 51 J10
Nether Heyford Nhants 31 P3
Nether Howcleugh S Lans 78 G6
Nether Kellet Lancs 63 J8
Nether Kinmundy Abers 103 L6
Nether Langwith Notts 51 M6
Netherlaw D & G 70 C6
Netherley Abers 95 P4
Nethermill D & G 78 G10
Nethermuir Abers 103 J6
Netherne-on-the-Hill Surrey 21 L11
Netheroyd Hill Kirk 58 F9
Nether Padley Derbys 50 G5
Netherplace E Rens 85 J11
Nether Poppleton C York 59 M4
Netherseal Derbys 40 H5
Nether Silton N York 66 C8
Nether Stowey Somset 16 G8
Netherthong Kirk 58 F11
Netherthorpe Angus 93 P4
Netherton Devon 6 B8
Netherton Dudley 40 C9
Netherton Kirk 58 F10
Netherton N Lans 85 N11
Netherton Nthumb 81 K11
Netherton P & K 92 H5
Netherton Sefton 56 G8
Netherton Stirlg 85 J7
Netherton Wakefd 58 H10
Nethertown Cumb 62 B1
Nethertown Highld 110 G1
Nethertown Staffs 40 E4
Netherurd Border 86 D12
Nether Wallop Hants 19 K12
Nether Wasdale Cumb 62 D3
Nether Westcote Gloucs 30 G9
Nether Whitacre Warwks 40 G8
Nether Whitecleuch S Lans 78 D5
Nether Winchendon Bucks 31 Q10
Netherwitton Nthumb 73 L3
Nethy Bridge Highld 99 Q5
Netley Hants 9 M6
Netley Marsh Hants 9 K5
Nettlebed Oxon 20 B6
Nettlebridge Somset 17 P6
Nettlecombe Dorset 7 M4
Nettleden Herts 20 G2
Nettleham Lincs 52 E8
Nettlestead Kent 22 D11
Nettlestead Green Kent 22 D12
Nettlestone IoW 9 Q8
Nettlesworth Dur 73 M10
Nettleton Lincs 52 G4
Nettleton Wilts 18 B5
Netton Wilts 18 G12
Nevendon Essex 22 F3
Nevern Pembks 36 B11
Nevill Holt Leics 42 B10
New Abbey D & G 70 F3

New Aberdour Abers 103 J3
New Addington Gt Lon 21 M10
Newall Leeds 58 G5
New Alresford Hants 9 P2
New Alyth P & K 93 J6
Newark Ork 111 i1
Newark-on-Trent Notts 52 B11
Newarthill N Lans 85 N10
New Ash Green Kent 22 C9
New Balderton Notts 52 B11
New Barn Kent 22 C9
New Barnet Gt Lon 21 L4
Newbattle Mdloth 86 G8
New Bewick Nthumb 81 M9
Newbie D & G 71 K3
Newbiggin Cumb 64 B2
Newbiggin Cumb 71 P9
Newbiggin Cumb 71 Q6
Newbiggin Dur 64 G3
Newbiggin Dur 64 H9
Newbiggin-by-the-Sea Nthumb 73 N4
Newbigging Angus 93 K7
Newbigging Angus 93 M8
Newbigging Angus 93 N8
Newbigging S Lans 86 B11
Newbiggin-on-Lune Cumb 63 N2
New Bilton Warwks 41 L11
Newbold Derbys 51 J6
Newbold on Avon Warwks 41 L11
Newbold on Stour Warwks 30 G5
Newbold Pacey Warwks 30 H3
Newbold Verdon Leics 41 K6
New Bolingbroke Lincs 53 K11
Newborough C Pete 42 H8
Newborough IoA 54 F8
Newborough Staffs 40 F3
New Boultham Lincs 52 D8
Newbourne Suffk 35 L8
New Bradwell M Keyn 32 B8
New Brampton Derbys 51 J6
New Brancepeth Dur 73 M11
Newbridge C Edin 86 D7
Newbridge Caerph 27 P8
Newbridge Cnwll 2 C9
Newbridge D & G 78 F11
Newbridge Hants 9 K4
Newbridge IoW 9 M9
Newbridge Green Worcs 29 L2
Newbridge-on-Wye Powys 38 B9
New Brighton Wirral 56 F9
Newbrough Nthumb 72 F7
New Buckenham Norfk 44 H11
Newbuildings Devon 15 N10
Newburgh Abers 103 K4
Newburgh Abers 103 K9
Newburgh Fife 93 J11
Newburgh Lancs 57 J6
Newburgh Priory N York 66 D11
Newburn N u Ty 73 L7
Newbury Somset 17 Q6
Newbury W Berk 19 M7
Newbury Park Gt Lon 21 N6
Newby Cumb 64 B4
Newby Lancs 63 P11
Newby N York 63 N8
Newby N York 66 C5
Newby Bridge Cumb 62 G5
Newby East Cumb 71 P4
New Byth Abers 102 H5
Newby West Cumb 71 M5
Newcastle Mons 28 E5
Newcastle Shrops 38 F5
Newcastle Airport Nthumb 73 L6
Newcastle Emlyn Carmth 36 E11
Newcastleton Border 79 P10
Newcastle-under-Lyme Staffs 49 Q6
Newcastle upon Tyne N u Ty 73 M7
Newchapel Pembks 36 D11
Newchapel Surrey 11 M2
Newchurch IoW 9 P9
Newchurch Kent 13 K4
Newchurch Mons 28 E8
Newchurch Powys 38 E11
Newchurch Staffs 40 F3
New Costessey Norfk 45 K7
Newcraighall C Edin 86 G7
New Crofton Wakefd 59 K10
New Cross Gt Lon 21 M7
New Cross Somset 17 K11
New Cumnock E Ayrs 77 K8
New Deer Abers 103 J6
New Denham Bucks 20 G6
Newdigate Surrey 11 K2
New Duston Nhants 31 Q2
New Earswick C York 59 N3
New Edlington Donc 51 M2
New Elgin Moray 101 J3
New Ellerby E R Yk 61 K6
Newell Green Br For 20 E8
New Eltham Gt Lon 21 N8
New End Worcs 30 D3
Newenden Kent 12 G5
New England C Pete 42 H9
Newent Gloucs 29 J4
Newfield Dur 65 L2
Newfield Highld 107 N7
New Fletton C Pete 42 H9
New Forest National Park 9 K6
Newgale Pembks 24 F4
New Galloway D & G 69 P4
Newgate Street Herts 21 L3
New Gilston Fife 87 J1
New Grimsby IoS 2 b1
Newhall Ches E 49 L6
New Hartley Nthumb 73 N5
Newhaven C Edin 86 F7
Newhaven E Susx 11 N9
New Haw Surrey 20 G10
New Hedges Pembks 25 K8
New Holland N Linc 61 J9
Newholm N York 67 J5
New Houghton Derbys 51 L7
New Houghton Norfk 44 D5
Newhouse N Lans 85 N10
New Hutton Cumb 63 K4
Newick E Susx 11 N6
Newingreen Kent 13 M3
Newington Kent 22 G9
Newington Kent 23 N11
Newington Oxon 19 Q2
New Inn Carmth 26 C2
New Inn Torfn 28 C8

New Invention Shrops .... 38 F6
New Lakenham Norfk .... 45 K8
New Lanark S Lans ....... 78 E1
New Lanark Village S Lans .. 78 E1
Newland C KuH ............ 61 J7
Newland Gloucs ........... 28 G6
Newland N York ........... 59 P8
Newland Somset .......... 15 P5
Newland Worcs ............ 39 P11
Newlandrig Mdloth ........ 86 H9
Newlands Border .......... 79 Q9
Newlands Nthumb ......... 73 J9
Newlands of Dundurcas
  Moray .................. 101 L5
New Langholm D & G ..... 79 M11
New Leake Lincs .......... 53 L11
New Leeds Abers ......... 103 K4
New Lodge Barns .......... 59 J11
New Longton Lancs ....... 57 K4
New Luce D & G ........... 68 G6
Newlyn Cnwll ............... 2 C9
Newmachar Abers ........ 103 J10
Newmains N Lans ......... 85 N10
New Malden Gt Lon ....... 21 K9
Newman's Green Suffk ... 34 E7
Newmarket Suffk .......... 33 Q4
Newmarket W Isls ........ 111 d2
New Marske R & Cl ....... 66 E4
New Marston Oxon ........ 31 M11
New Mill Abers ............ 95 N5
Newmill Border ............ 79 P6
New Mill Cnwll .............. 2 C8
New Mill Kirk .............. 58 F11
Newmill Moray ............ 101 N5
Newmillerdam Wakefd .... 59 J10
Newmill of Inshewan
  Angus ................... 94 G9
Newmills C Edin ........... 86 E8
New Mills Derbys .......... 50 D4
Newmills Fife ............. 86 B5
Newmills Mons ............ 28 F7
New Mills Powys .......... 38 C2
Newmiln P & K ............ 92 G9
Newmilns E Ayrs .......... 77 J4
New Milton Hants .......... 9 J8
New Mistley Essex ........ 35 J9
New Moat Pembks ........ 25 J4
Newney Green Essex ..... 22 D3
Newnham Gloucs .......... 29 J6
Newnham Hants ........... 20 B11
Newnham Herts ........... 33 J8
Newnham Kent ............ 23 J11
Newnham Nhants .......... 31 M3
Newnham Worcs ........... 39 M8
New Ollerton Notts ........ 51 P7
New Oscott Birm .......... 40 E8
New Pitsligo Abers ....... 103 J4
Newport Cnwll .............. 4 H3
Newport E R Yk ........... 60 E7
Newport Essex ............ 33 N9
Newport Gloucs ........... 29 J8
Newport Highld .......... 110 D10
Newport IoW ............... 9 N9
Newport Newpt ........... 28 C10
Newport Pembks .......... 25 J2
Newport Wrekin ........... 49 N10
Newport-on-Tay Fife ...... 93 M9
Newport Pagnell M Keyn .. 32 C7
Newport Pagnell
  Services M Keyn ........ 32 C7
New Prestwick S Ayrs .... 76 F6
New Quay Cerdgn ......... 36 F8
Newquay Cnwll ............. 3 J4
Newquay Airport Cnwll .... 3 K3
New Rackheath Norfk ..... 45 L7
New Radnor Powys ........ 38 E9
New Ridley Nthumb ....... 73 J8
New Romney Kent ......... 13 K5
New Rossington Donc ..... 51 N2
New Sauchie Clacks ...... 85 P4
Newseat Abers ........... 102 H7
Newsham Lancs ........... 57 K2
Newsham N York .......... 65 K5
Newsham N York .......... 65 K5
Newsham Nthumb ......... 73 N5
New Sharlston Wakefd .... 59 J9
Newsholme E R Yk ........ 60 C8
New Silksworth Sundld ... 73 P9
Newsome Kirk ............. 58 F10
New Somerby Lincs ....... 42 D3
New Southgate
  Crematorium Gt Lon .... 21 L5
Newstead Border .......... 80 D7
Newstead Notts .......... 51 L9
Newstead Nthumb ......... 81 N8
New Stevenston N Lans ... 85 M10
Newthorpe Notts .......... 51 L10
Newton Ag & B ........... 83 Q4
Newton Border ............ 80 E9
Newton Brdgnd ........... 26 H12
Newton C Beds ........... 32 H7
Newton Cambs ............ 33 M6
Newton Cambs ............ 43 M7
Newton Ches W ........... 48 H2
Newton Ches W ........... 49 J4
Newton Cumb ............. 62 E7
Newton Derbys ........... 51 K8
Newton Herefs ............ 28 D3
Newton Herefs ............ 39 K10
Newton Highld ........... 107 J11
Newton Highld ........... 107 M11
Newton Highld ........... 107 M8
Newton Highld ........... 110 G6
Newton Lincs ............. 42 F3
Newton Mdloth ............ 86 G8
Newton Moray ............ 100 H3
Newton Moray ............ 101 J3
Newton Nhants ............ 42 C12
Newton Norfk ............. 44 D7
Newton Notts ............. 51 P11
Newton Nthumb ........... 73 J7
Newton Nthumb ........... 73 J3
Newton S Lans ............ 78 F3
Newton S Lans ............ 85 L10
Newton Sandw ............ 40 D8
Newton Staffs ............ 40 D3
Newton Suffk ............. 34 F8
Newton W Loth ........... 86 C6
Newton Warwks ........... 41 M10
Newton Abbot Devon ...... 6 B8
Newton Arlosh Cumb ...... 71 K9
Newton Aycliffe Dur ...... 65 M3
Newton Bewley Hartpl .... 66 C3
Newton Blossomville
  M Keyn ................... 32 D6
Newton Bromswold
  Nhants .................. 32 E4
Newton Burgoland Leics .. 41 J6

Newton-by-the-Sea
  Nthumb .................. 81 P8
Newton by Toft Lincs ..... 52 F6
Newton Ferrers Devon ..... 5 L9
Newton Ferry W Isls ..... 111 b4
Newton Flotman Norfk .... 45 K9
Newtongrange Mdloth ..... 86 G8
Newton Green Mons ...... 28 F9
Newton Harcourt Leics ... 41 N9
Newton Heath Manch ..... 57 Q8
Newtonhill Abers ......... 95 P4
Newton-in-Bowland
  Lancs ................... 63 M11
Newton Kyme N York ..... 59 L5
Newton-le-Willows N York .. 65 L9
Newton-le-Willows St Hel .. 57 L9
Newtonloan Mdloth ....... 86 G9
Newton Longville Bucks ... 32 C9
Newton Mearns E Rens ... 85 J11
Newtonmill Angus ........ 95 M4
Newtonmore Highld ....... 99 K8
Newton Morrell N York ... 65 M5
Newton of Balcanquhal
  P & K .................... 92 H12
Newton of Balcormo Fife .. 87 K2
Newton-on-Ouse N York .. 59 L3
Newton-on-Rawcliffe
  N York ................... 66 H9
Newton-on-the-Moor
  Nthumb .................. 81 N12
Newton on Trent Lincs ... 52 B8
Newton Poppleford
  Devon .................... 6 E5
Newton Purcell Oxon ..... 31 N7
Newton Regis Warwks .... 40 H6
Newton Reigny Cumb ..... 71 P8
Newton St Cyres Devon .. 15 Q11
Newton St Faith Norfk .... 45 K8
Newton St Loe BaNES .... 17 Q3
Newton St Petrock Devon .. 14 G9
Newton Solney Derbys .... 40 H3
Newton Stacey Hants .... 19 M11
Newton Stewart D & G .... 69 K6
Newton Tony Wilts ....... 19 J11
Newton Tracey Devon .... 15 J6
Newton under
  Roseberry R & Cl ....... 66 D5
Newton upon Derwent
  E R Yk .................. 60 C4
Newton Valence Hants ... 10 B4
Newton Wamphray D & G .. 78 H9
Newton with Scales Lancs .. 57 J3
Newtown Cumb ........... 70 H6
Newtown Cumb ........... 71 P3
Newtown D & G ........... 77 N8
Newtown Devon ............ 6 E3
Newtown Devon ........... 15 N7
New Town Dorset .......... 8 D4
New Town Dorset .......... 8 E4
New Town E Susx ......... 11 P6
Newtown Gloucs .......... 29 J8
Newtown Hants ............ 9 Q5
Newtown Herefs .......... 29 J2
Newtown Herefs .......... 39 L12
Newtown Highld .......... 98 E12
Newtown IoW .............. 9 M8
Newtown Nthumb ......... 81 L8
Newtown Poole ............. 8 F8
Newtown Powys .......... 38 C4
Newtown Shrops .......... 48 H10
Newtown Shrops .......... 49 J8
Newtown Somset .......... 5 M8
Newtown Staffs .......... 50 B8
Newtown Wigan .......... 57 K7
Newtown Worcs .......... 39 Q10
Newtown Linford Leics ... 41 M5
Newtown of Beltrees
  Rens .................... 84 F10
Newtown St Boswells
  Border ................... 80 D7
New Tredegar Caerph ..... 27 N7
New Trows S Lans ........ 77 N4
Newtyle Angus ........... 93 K7
New Walsoken Cambs .... 43 M8
New Waltham NE Lin ..... 53 J3
New Winton E Loth ....... 87 J7
Newyork Ag & B ........... 83 P2
New York Lincs ........... 53 J11
Neyland Pembks .......... 24 G7
Nicholashayne Devon ..... 16 E11
Nicholaston Swans ....... 26 C10
Nidd N York ............... 58 H3
Niddrie C Edin ............ 86 G8
Nigg C Aber .............. 95 Q2
Nigg Highld .............. 107 N8
Nigg Ferry Highld ........ 107 N8
Ninebanks Nthumb ....... 72 E9
Nine Elms Swindn ........ 18 G4
Ninfield E Susx ........... 12 E7
Ningwood IoW .............. 9 L9
Nisbet Border ............. 80 F8
Nisbet Hill Border ........ 80 H4
Niton IoW ................... 9 N11
Nitshill C Glas ............ 85 J10
Nocton Lincs ............. 52 F10
Noke Oxon ................. 31 M10
Nolton Pembks ........... 24 F5
Nolton Haven Pembks .... 24 F5
No Man's Heath Ches W .. 49 K6
No Man's Heath Warwks .. 40 H6
Nomansland Devon ....... 15 P9
Nomansland Wilts .......... 9 J4
Noneley Shrops ........... 49 J9
Nonington Kent ........... 23 N11
Nook Cumb ................ 63 K6
Norbiton Gt Lon ........... 21 K9
Norbury Ches E .......... 49 K6
Norbury Derbys ........... 50 F11
Norbury Gt Lon ........... 21 L9
Norbury Shrops .......... 38 G4
Norbury Staffs ............ 49 P10
Norchard Worcs ........... 39 Q8
Nordelph Norfk ........... 43 N9
Nordley Shrops ........... 39 M3
Norfolk Broads Norfk ..... 45 N9
Norham Nthumb ........... 81 J5
Norley Ches W ............ 49 K2
Norleywood Hants ......... 9 L7
Normanby Lincs .......... 52 E6
Normanby N Linc ......... 60 F10
Normanby N York ......... 66 G10
Normanby R & Cl ......... 66 D4
Normanby le Wold Lincs .. 52 G5
Normandy Surrey ......... 20 E11
Norman's Green Devon .... 6 E3
Normanton C Derb ....... 41 J2
Normanton Leics ......... 42 B2
Normanton Notts ......... 51 P9

Normanton Wakefd ....... 59 J9
Normanton le Heath Leics .. 41 J5
Normanton on Cliffe Lincs .. 42 D2
Normanton on Soar Notts .. 41 L3
Normanton on the
  Wolds Notts ............ 41 N2
Normanton on Trent
  Notts .................... 52 B9
Norris Green Lpool ....... 56 H9
Norris Hill Leics .......... 41 J4
Norristhorpe Kirk ......... 58 G9
Northall Bucks ........... 32 D11
Northallerton N York ..... 65 N8
Northam C Sotn ............ 9 M5
Northam Devon ........... 14 H6
Northampton Nhants ..... 31 Q2
Northampton Worcs ...... 39 Q8
Northampton Services
  Nhants .................. 31 Q3
North Anston Rothm ..... 51 M4
North Ascot Br For ...... 20 E9
North Aston Oxon ........ 31 L8
Northaw Herts ............ 21 L3
Northay Somset ........... 6 H1
North Baddesley Hants ... 9 L4
North Ballachulish Highld .. 90 E4
North Barrow Somset .... 17 N9
North Barsham Norfk ..... 44 F3
North Benfleet Essex ..... 22 F5
North Bersted W Susx ... 10 E9
North Berwick E Loth .... 87 K5
North Boarhunt Hants ..... 9 P5
Northborough C Pete ..... 42 G8
Northbourne Kent ........ 23 P11
North Bovey Devon ........ 5 P4
North Bradley Wilts ...... 18 C5
North Brentor Devon ...... 5 K4
North Brewham Somset ... 17 Q8
Northbrook Hants ........ 19 N11
North Buckland Devon ... 14 H4
North Burlingham Norfk .. 45 N7
North Cadbury Somset ... 17 P10
North Carlton Lincs ...... 52 D7
North Carlton Notts ...... 51 N4
North Cave E R Yk ....... 60 F7
North Cerney Gloucs ..... 30 D11
North Chailey E Susx .... 11 N6
Northchapel W Susx ..... 10 F4
North Charford Hants ...... 8 H4
North Charlton Nthumb ... 81 N9
North Cheam Gt Lon ..... 21 K9
North Cheriton Somset ... 17 Q10
North Chideock Dorset .... 7 K4
Northchurch Herts ....... 20 F2
North Cliffe E R Yk ...... 60 E6
North Clifton Notts ...... 52 B8
North Cockerington Lincs .. 53 L5
North Connel Ag & B ..... 90 C9
North Cornelly Brdgnd ... 26 H11
North Cotes Lincs ....... 53 K4
Northcott Devon ........... 4 H2
Northcourt Oxon .......... 19 N2
North Cove Suffk ......... 45 P11
North Cowton N York .... 65 M6
North Crawley M Keyn ... 32 D7
North Creake Norfk ...... 44 E3
North Curry Somset ...... 17 J10
North Dalton E R Yk ..... 60 F4
North Deighton N York ... 59 K4
North Devon
  Crematorium Devon .... 15 J6
Northdown Kent .......... 23 Q8
North Downs ............. 22 H11
North Duffield N York .... 59 P6
North Duntulm Highld ... 104 F7
North East Surrey
  Crematorium Gt Lon ... 21 K9
North Elmham Norfk ..... 44 G6
North Elmsall Wakefd .... 59 L10
North End C Port .......... 9 Q7
North End Essex .......... 33 Q11
North End Hants ........... 8 G4
North End Nhants ........ 32 D3
North End W Susx ....... 10 F8
Northend Warwks ......... 31 K4
Northenden Manch ....... 57 P10
North Erradale Highld ... 105 L6
North Evington C Leic ... 41 N6
North Fambridge Essex .. 22 G4
North Ferriby E R Yk .... 60 G8
Northfield Birm .......... 40 D10
Northfield C Aber ....... 103 J12
Northfield E R Yk ........ 60 H8
Northfields Lincs ......... 42 E8
Northfleet Kent .......... 22 D8
North Frodingham E R Yk .. 61 J4
North Gorley Hants ........ 8 H5
North Green Suffk ........ 35 M4
North Greetwell Lincs .... 52 E8
North Grimston N York ... 60 E1
North Haven Shet ....... 111 m5
North Hayling Hants ..... 10 B9
North Hill Cnwll ............ 4 G5
North Hillingdon Gt Lon .. 20 H6
North Hinksey Village
  Oxon .................... 31 L11
North Holmwood Surrey .. 11 J1
North Huish Devon ........ 5 P8
North Hykeham Lincs .... 52 D9
Northiam E Susx ......... 12 G5
Northill C Beds .......... 32 G7
Northington Hants ....... 19 P12
North Kelsey Lincs ...... 52 F3
North Kessock Highld ... 107 L11
North Killingholme N Linc .. 61 K10
North Kilvington N York .. 65 Q9
North Kilworth Leics .... 41 N10
North Kyme Lincs ........ 52 G11
North Landing E R Yk ... 67 Q12
Northlands Lincs ......... 53 K11
Northleach Gloucs ....... 30 E10
North Lee Bucks ......... 20 D2
Northleigh Devon .......... 6 G4
North Leigh Oxon ........ 31 K10
North Leverton with
  Habblesthorpe Notts ... 52 B7
Northlew Devon .......... 15 J11
North Littleton Worcs .... 30 E5
North Lopham Norfk ..... 44 G12
North Luffenham Rutlnd .. 42 D9
North Marden W Susx ... 10 D6
North Marston Bucks .... 31 Q9
North Middleton Mdloth .. 86 G9
North Millbrex Abers .... 102 H6
North Milmain D & G ..... 68 E8
North Molton Devon ...... 15 M6
Northmoor Oxon .......... 31 K12

North Moreton Oxon ..... 19 P3
Northmuir Angus ......... 93 L5
North Mundham W Susx .. 10 E9
North Muskham Notts .... 52 B10
North Newbald E R Yk ... 60 F6
North Newington Oxon ... 31 K6
North Newnton Wilts .... 18 G8
North Newton Somset ... 17 J9
Northney Hants .......... 10 B8
North Nibley Gloucs ...... 29 K9
Northolt Gt Lon .......... 21 J6
Northop Flints ........... 48 E2
Northop Hall Flints ...... 48 F2
North Ormesby Middsb ... 66 D4
North Ormsby Lincs ..... 53 J5
Northorpe Kirk .......... 58 G9
Northorpe Lincs .......... 42 H3
Northorpe Lincs .......... 52 C4
North Otterington N York .. 65 P9
North Owersby Lincs ..... 52 F5
Northowram Calder ...... 58 E8
North Perrott Somset ..... 7 L2
North Petherton Somset .. 16 H9
North Petherwin Cnwll .... 4 G3
North Pickenham Norfk .. 44 E8
North Piddle Worcs ...... 30 C3
North Poorton Dorset ..... 7 M3
Northport Dorset .......... 8 D9
North Queensferry Fife ... 86 D6
North Rauceby Lincs ..... 42 E2
Northrepps Norfk ........ 45 L3
North Reston Lincs ...... 53 L6
North Rigton N York ..... 58 H4
North Rode Ches E ...... 50 B7
North Ronaldsay Ork .... 111 i1
North Ronaldsay Airport
  Ork ..................... 111 i1
North Runcton Norfk ..... 43 Q6
North Scarle Lincs ....... 52 C9
North Shian Ag & B ...... 90 C7
North Shields N Tyne .... 73 N7
North Shoebury Sthend ... 22 H6
North Shore Bpool ....... 56 F2
North Side C Pete ........ 43 J9
North Somercotes Lincs .. 53 L4
North Stainley N York ... 65 M11
North Stifford Thurr ..... 22 C7
North Stoke BaNES ...... 17 Q3
North Stoke Oxon ........ 19 Q4
North Stoke W Susx ..... 10 G7
North Street Kent ........ 23 K10
North Street W Berk ..... 19 Q6
North Sunderland
  Nthumb .................. 81 P7
North Tamerton Cnwll ... 14 F11
North Tawton Devon ..... 15 L10
North Third Stirlg ........ 85 M5
North Thoresby Lincs .... 53 J4
Northton W Isls ......... 111 b3
North Town Devon ....... 15 J9
North Town Somset ...... 17 N7
North Town W & M ...... 20 E7
North Tuddenham Norfk .. 44 G7
North Uist W Isls ....... 111 a4
Northumberland
  National Park Nthumb .. 72 F1
North Walsham Norfk .... 45 L4
North Waltham Hants .... 19 P10
North Warnborough
  Hants ................... 20 B12
North Weald Bassett
  Essex ................... 21 P3
North Wheatley Notts ... 51 Q4
Northwich Ches W ....... 49 M2
Northwick Worcs ......... 39 Q9
North Widcombe BaNES .. 17 N5
North Willingham Lincs .. 52 G6
North Wingfield Derbys ... 51 K7
North Witham Lincs ...... 42 D6
Northwold Norfk ......... 44 C10
Northwood C Stke ....... 50 B10
Northwood Gt Lon ....... 20 H5
Northwood IoW ............ 9 N8
Northwood Shrops ....... 49 J8
Northwood Green Gloucs .. 29 J5
North Wootton Dorset ... 17 P12
North Wootton Norfk .... 43 Q5
North Wootton Somset ... 17 N7
North Wraxall Wilts ..... 18 B6
North York Moors
  National Park .......... 66 G7
Norton Donc ............. 59 M10
Norton E Susx ........... 11 P9
Norton Gloucs ........... 29 M4
Norton Halton ........... 57 K11
Norton Nhants ........... 31 N2
Norton Notts ............. 51 M6
Norton Powys ............ 38 F8
Norton S on T ........... 66 C3
Norton Shrops ........... 39 N3
Norton Suffk ............. 34 F4
Norton W Susx ........... 10 E8
Norton Wilts ............. 18 C4
Norton Worcs ............ 30 D5
Norton Worcs ............ 39 Q11
Norton Bavant Wilts ..... 18 D11
Norton Bridge Staffs .... 49 Q9
Norton Canes Staffs .... 40 D6
Norton Canes Services
  Staffs ................... 40 D6
Norton Canon Herefs ... 38 H11
Norton Disney Lincs ..... 52 C10
Norton Fitzwarren
  Somset .................. 16 G10
Norton Green IoW ......... 9 K9
Norton Hawkfield BaNES .. 17 N4
Norton Heath Essex ..... 22 C3
Norton in Hales Shrops .. 49 N7
Norton in the Moors
  C Stke .................. 50 B9
Norton-Juxta-Twycross
  Leics .................... 41 J6
Norton-le-Clay N York ... 65 P12
Norton Lindsey Warwks .. 30 G2
Norton Little Green Suffk .. 34 F4
Norton Malreward BaNES .. 17 N3
Norton-on-Derwent
  N York ................... 66 H12
Norton St Philip Somset .. 17 B9
Norton Subcourse Norfk .. 45 N9
Norton sub Hamdon
  Somset .................. 17 L11
Norwell Notts ............ 51 Q8
Norwell Woodhouse
  Notts .................... 51 Q8
Norwich Norfk ............ 45 K8
Norwich Airport Norfk .... 45 K7

Norwich (St Faith)
  Crematorium Norfk .... 45 K7
Norwick Shet ............ 111 m2
Norwood Derbys ......... 85 P4
Norwood Green Gt Lon ... 21 J7
Norwood Hill Surrey ..... 11 K2
Noss Mayo Devon ......... 5 L10
Nosterfield N York ....... 65 M10
Nostie Highld ............ 97 M4
Notgrove Gloucs ......... 30 E9
Nottage Brdgnd .......... 26 H12
Nottingham C Nott ....... 51 M11
Notton Wakefd ........... 59 J10
Notton Wilts ............. 18 D6
Noutard's Green Worcs ... 39 P8
Nuffield Oxon ............ 19 Q4
Nunburnholme E R Yk ... 60 E5
Nuneaton Warwks ........ 41 J8
Nunhead Gt Lon ......... 21 M8
Nun Monkton N York .... 59 L3
Nunney Somset .......... 17 Q7
Nunnington N York ...... 66 F10
Nunsthorpe NE Lin ...... 53 J2
Nunthorpe C York ....... 59 N4
Nunthorpe Middsb ....... 66 D5
Nunthorpe Village Middsb .. 66 D5
Nunton Wilts .............. 8 H3
Nunwick N York ......... 65 N11
Nursling Hants ............ 9 L4
Nutbourne W Susx ...... 10 C8
Nutbourne W Susx ...... 10 H6
Nutfield Surrey .......... 21 L12
Nuthall Notts ............ 51 M11
Nuthampstead Herts ..... 33 L9
Nuthurst W Susx ........ 11 J5
Nutley E Susx ............ 11 N5
Nuttall Bury ............. 57 P5
Nybster Highld .......... 110 G3
Nyetimber W Susx ...... 10 E9
Nyewood W Susx ........ 10 C6
Nymans W Susx .......... 11 L4
Nymet Rowland Devon ... 15 M9
Nymet Tracey Devon .... 15 M11
Nympsfield Gloucs ....... 29 L8
Nynehead Somset ....... 16 F10
Nyton W Susx ........... 10 E8

Oadby Leics ............. 41 N7
Oad Street Kent ......... 22 G10
Oakamoor Staffs ........ 50 D11
Oakbank W Loth ......... 86 C8
Oak Cross Devon ........ 15 J11
Oakdale Caerph .......... 27 P8
Oake Somset ............. 16 F10
Oaken Staffs ............. 39 Q2
Oakenclough Lancs ...... 63 K11
Oakengates Wrekin ...... 49 M12
Oakenshaw Dur .......... 73 L12
Oakenshaw Kirk ......... 58 F8
Oakford Cerdgn .......... 36 G8
Oakford Devon .......... 16 C11
Oakham Rutlnd .......... 42 C8
Oakhanger Hants ........ 10 C3
Oakhill Somset .......... 17 P6
Oakington Cambs ....... 33 L4
Oakle Street Gloucs ..... 29 K5
Oakley Bed .............. 32 E6
Oakley Bucks ............ 31 N10
Oakley Fife .............. 86 B4
Oakley Hants ............ 19 P9
Oakley Suffk ............. 35 J2
Oakridge Lynch Gloucs .. 29 M7
Oaksey Wilts ............ 29 P9
Oakthorpe Leics ......... 40 H5
Oakwood C Derb ......... 51 J12
Oakworth C Brad ........ 58 D6
Oare Kent ............... 23 J10
Oare Somset ............. 15 N3
Oare Wilts .............. 18 H7
Oasby Lincs ............. 42 E3
Oath Somset ............. 17 K10
Oathlaw Angus .......... 93 N4
Oatlands Park Surrey .... 20 H9
Oban Ag & B ............. 90 B9
Oban Airport Ag & B .... 90 C8
Obley Shrops ............ 38 G6
Obney P & K ............. 92 F8
Oborne Dorset .......... 17 P11
Occold Suffk ............ 35 J3
Occumster Highld ...... 110 F8
Ochiltree E Ayrs ......... 76 H7
Ockbrook Derbys ........ 41 K1
Ocker Hill Sandw ........ 40 C8
Ockham Surrey .......... 20 H11
Ockle Highld ............. 89 L3
Ockley Surrey ........... 11 J3
Ocle Pychard Herefs .... 39 L11
Odcombe Somset ....... 17 M11
Odd Down BaNES ....... 17 Q4
Oddingley Worcs ........ 30 B3
Oddington Gloucs ....... 30 G8
Oddington Oxon ......... 31 M10
Odell Bed ............... 32 D5
Odiham Hants ........... 20 C12
Odsal C Brad ............ 58 F8
Odsey Cambs ............ 33 J8
Odstock Wilts ............. 8 G3
Odstone Leics ........... 41 K6
Offchurch Warwks ....... 31 J2
Offenham Worcs ......... 30 D5
Offerton Stockp ......... 50 B3
Offham E Susx ........... 11 N7
Offham Kent ............. 22 D11
Offham W Susx .......... 10 G8
Offord Cluny Cambs ..... 32 H4
Offord D'Arcy Cambs .... 32 H4
Offton Suffk ............. 34 H6
Offwell Devon ............. 6 G3
Ogbourne Maizey Wilts .. 18 H6
Ogbourne St Andrew
  Wilts .................... 18 H6
Ogbourne St George Wilts .. 18 H6
Ogle Nthumb ............ 73 K5
Oglet Lpool .............. 56 H11
Ogmore V Glam ......... 16 B2
Ogmore-by-Sea V Glam .. 16 B2
Ogmore Vale Brdgnd .... 27 K10
Okeford Fitzpaine Dorset .. 8 B5
Okehampton Devon ...... 5 M2
Oker Side Derbys ........ 50 H8
Okewood Hill Surrey .... 11 J3
Old Nhants .............. 32 B3
Old Aberdeen C Aber .... 95 Q1

Old Alresford - Perranarworthal 189


Old Alresford Hants 9 P1
Oldany Highld 108 C8
Old Auchenbrack D & G 77 M11
Old Basford C Nott 51 M11
Old Basing Hants 19 Q9
Old Beetley Norfk 44 F6
Oldberrow Warwks 30 E2
Old Bewick Nthumb 81 M9
Old Bolingbroke Lincs 53 K9
Old Bramhope Leeds 58 G5
Old Brampton Derbys 51 J6
Old Bridge of Urr D & G 70 C3
Old Buckenham Norfk 44 H10
Old Burghclere Hants 19 M8
Oldbury Sandw 40 C9
Oldbury Shrops 39 N4
Oldbury Warwks 40 H8
Oldbury-on-Severn S Glos 28 H9
Oldbury on the Hill Gloucs 18 B3
Old Byland N York 66 D9
Old Cantley Donc 51 N1
Oldcastle Mons 28 C4
Old Catton Norfk 45 K7
Old Clee NE Lin 53 J2
Old Cleeve Somset 16 E7
Old Colwyn Conwy 55 M6
Oldcotes Notts 51 N3
Old Dailly S Ayrs 76 D10
Old Dalby Leics 41 P3
Old Deer Abers 103 K6
Old Edlington Donc 51 M2
Old Ellerby E R Yk 61 K6
Old Felixstowe Suffk 35 M9
Oldfield Worcs 39 Q8
Old Fletton C Pete 42 H10
Oldford Somset 18 B10
Old Forge Herefs 28 G5
Old Grimsby IoS 2 b1
Old Hall Green Herts 33 L11
Oldham Oldham 58 B12
Oldham Crematorium Oldham 50 B1
Oldhamstocks E Loth 87 N7
Old Harlow Essex 21 P2
Old Hunstanton Norfk 44 B2
Old Hurst Cambs 33 J2
Old Hutton Cumb 63 K5
Old Inns Services N Lans 85 N7
Old Kilpatrick W Duns 84 H8
Old Knebworth Herts 32 H11
Old Lakenham Norfk 45 K8
Oldland S Glos 17 P2
Old Langho Lancs 57 M2
Old Leake Lincs 53 L12
Old Malton N York 66 H11
Oldmeldrum Abers 102 H9
Oldmill Cnwll 4 H5
Old Milverton Warwks 30 H1
Oldmixon N Som 17 J5
Old Newton Suffk 34 H4
Old Radford C Nott 51 M11
Old Radnor Powys 38 F9
Old Rayne Abers 102 E9
Old Romney Kent 13 K5
Old Shoreham W Susx 11 K8
Oldshoremore Highld 108 D4
Old Sodbury S Glos 29 K11
Old Somerby Lincs 42 D4
Oldstead N York 66 D10
Old Stratford Nhants 31 Q6
Old Struan P & K 92 C3
Old Swinford Dudley 40 B10
Old Thirsk N York 66 B10
Old Town Cumb 63 L5
Old Town E Susx 12 C9
Old Town IoS 2 c2
Old Trafford Traffd 57 P9
Oldwall Cumb 71 P4
Oldwalls Swans 26 C9
Old Warden C Beds 32 G7
Old Weston Cambs 32 F2
Old Wick Highld 110 G6
Old Windsor W & M 20 F8
Old Wives Lees Kent 23 K11
Old Woking Surrey 20 G11
Olgrinmore Highld 110 C5
Olive Green Staffs 40 E4
Oliver's Battery Hants 9 M2
Ollaberry Shet 111 K3
Ollach Highld 96 F3
Ollerton Ches E 57 P12
Ollerton Notts 51 P7
Ollerton Shrops 49 M9
Olney M Keyn 32 C6
Olrig House Highld 110 E3
Olton Solhll 40 F10
Olveston S Glos 28 H10
Ombersley Worcs 39 Q8
Ompton Notts 51 P7
Onchan IoM 56 d5
Onecote Staffs 50 D9
Onibury Shrops 39 J6
Onich Highld 90 E4
Onllwyn Neath 26 H6
Onneley Staffs 49 N6
Onslow Green Essex 33 Q12
Onslow Village Surrey 20 F12
Onston Ches W 49 L1
Opinan Highld 105 L7
Orbliston Moray 101 L4
Orbost Highld 96 B2
Orby Lincs 53 M9
Orchard Portman Somset 16 H10
Orcheston Wilts 18 F10
Orcop Herefs 28 F4
Orcop Hill Herefs 28 F4
Ord Abers 102 E4
Ordhead Abers 102 E12
Ordie Abers 94 G2
Ordiequish Moray 101 L4
Ordsall Notts 51 P5
Ore E Susx 12 G7
Orford Suffk 35 N6
Orford Warrtn 57 L10
Organford Dorset 8 D8
Orkney Islands Ork 111 h2
Orkney Neolithic Ork 111 g2
Orlestone Kent 13 J3
Orleton Herefs 39 J8
Orleton Worcs 39 M8
Orlingbury Nhants 32 C3
Ormesby R & Cl 66 D4
Ormesby St Margaret Norfk 45 P7
Ormesby St Michael Norfk 45 P7
Ormiscaig Highld 105 M4
Ormiston E Loth 86 H8
Ormsaigmore Highld 89 K4
Ormsary Ag & B 83 L8
Ormskirk Lancs 56 H7
Oronsay Ag & B 82 E5
Orphir Ork 111 h2
Orpington Gt Lon 21 P9
Orrell Sefton 56 G9
Orrell Wigan 57 K7
Orroland D & G 70 C6
Orsett Thurr 22 D7
Orslow Staffs 49 P11
Orston Notts 51 Q11
Orton Cumb 63 L1
Orton Nhants 32 B2
Orton Staffs 39 Q3
Orton Longueville C Pete 42 G10
Orton-on-the-Hill Leics 40 H6
Orton Waterville C Pete 42 G10
Orwell Cambs 33 K6
Osbaldeston Lancs 57 M3
Osbaldwick C York 59 N4
Osbaston Leics 41 K6
Osbaston Shrops 48 G10
Osborne House IoW 9 N8
Osbournby Lincs 42 F3
Oscroft Ches W 49 J3
Ose Highld 96 C2
Osgathorpe Leics 41 K4
Osgodby Lincs 52 F5
Osgodby N York 59 N7
Osgodby N York 67 M9
Oskaig Highld 96 G3
Oskamull Ag & B 89 K8
Osmaston Derbys 50 G11
Osmington Dorset 7 Q6
Osmington Mills Dorset 7 Q6
Osmondthorpe Leeds 59 J7
Osmotherley N York 66 C7
Osney Oxon 31 L11
Ospringe Kent 23 J10
Ossett Wakefd 58 H9
Ossington Notts 51 Q7
Osterley Gt Lon 21 J7
Oswaldkirk N York 66 E10
Oswaldtwistle Lancs 57 N4
Oswestry Shrops 48 F9
Otford Kent 21 Q10
Otham Kent 22 F11
Othery Somset 17 K9
Otley Leeds 58 G5
Otley Suffk 35 K5
Otterbourne Hants 9 M3
Otterburn N York 63 Q9
Otterburn Nthumb 72 F3
Otter Ferry Ag & B 83 P6
Otterham Cnwll 4 E3
Otterhampton Somset 16 H7
Otternish W Isls 111 b4
Ottershaw Surrey 20 G9
Otterswick Shet 111 k3
Otterton Devon 6 E6
Ottery St Mary Devon 6 E4
Ottinge Kent 13 M2
Ottringham E R Yk 61 M8
Oughterside Cumb 71 J7
Oughtibridge Sheff 50 H3
Oughtrington Warrtn 57 M10
Oulston N York 66 D11
Oulton Cumb 71 K5
Oulton Norfk 45 J4
Oulton Staffs 40 B1
Oulton Suffk 45 Q10
Oulton Broad Suffk 45 Q10
Oulton Street Norfk 45 J5
Oundle Nhants 42 E11
Ounsdale Staffs 39 Q4
Our Dynamic Earth C Edin 86 F7
Ousby Cumb 64 B1
Ousden Suffk 34 C5
Ousefleet E R Yk 60 E9
Ouston Dur 73 M9
Outgate Cumb 62 G3
Outhgill Cumb 64 E7
Outhill Warwks 30 E2
Outlane Kirk 58 E9
Out Rawcliffe Lancs 56 H1
Outwell Norfk 43 N8
Outwood Surrey 11 L2
Outwoods Staffs 49 P11
Ouzlewell Green Leeds 59 J8
Over Cambs 33 L3
Overbury Worcs 29 N2
Overcombe Dorset 7 Q6
Over Compton Dorset 17 N11
Overdale Crematorium Bolton 57 M7
Over Haddon Derbys 50 G7
Over Kellet Lancs 63 K8
Over Kiddington Oxon 31 K9
Overleigh Somset 17 L8
Over Norton Oxon 30 H8
Over Peover Ches E 49 P1
Overpool Ches W 56 H12
Overscaig Hotel Highld 108 H10
Overseal Derbys 40 H4
Over Silton N York 66 C8
Oversland Kent 23 K11
Overstone Nhants 32 B4
Over Stowey Somset 16 G8
Overstrand Norfk 45 L3
Over Stratton Somset 17 L11
Overthorpe Nhants 31 L6
Overton C Aber 102 H11
Overton Hants 19 N10
Overton Lancs 62 H9
Overton N York 59 M3
Overton Shrops 39 J7
Overton Swans 26 B10
Overton Wakefd 58 H10
Overton Wrexhm 48 G7
Overtown N Lans 85 N11
Over Wallop Hants 19 K11
Over Whitacre Warwks 40 G8
Over Worton Oxon 31 K8
Oving Bucks 32 A11
Oving W Susx 10 E8
Ovingdean Br & H 11 M8
Ovingham Nthumb 73 J7
Ovington Dur 65 K5
Ovington Essex 34 C8
Ovington Hants 9 P2
Ovington Norfk 44 F9
Ovington Nthumb 73 J7
Ower Hants 9 K4
Owermoigne Dorset 8 B9
Owlerton Sheff 51 J3
Owlsmoor Br For 20 D10
Owlswick Bucks 20 C3
Owmby Lincs 52 E6
Owmby Lincs 52 F3
Owslebury Hants 9 N3
Owston Donc 59 M11
Owston Leics 41 Q6
Owston Ferry N Linc 52 B4
Owstwick E R Yk 61 M7
Owthorne E R Yk 61 N8
Owthorpe Notts 41 P2
Owton Manor Hartpl 66 C2
Oxborough Norfk 44 C9
Oxcombe Lincs 53 K7
Oxenholme Cumb 63 K4
Oxenhope C Brad 58 D7
Oxen Park Cumb 62 G5
Oxenpill Somset 17 L7
Oxenton Gloucs 29 N3
Oxenwood Wilts 19 K8
Oxford Oxon 31 L11
*Oxford Airport Oxon 31 L10*
Oxford Crematorium Oxon 31 M11
Oxford Services Oxon 31 N12
Oxhey Herts 20 H4
Oxhill Warwks 30 H5
Oxley Wolves 40 B7
Oxley Green Essex 22 H1
Oxlode Cambs 43 M11
Oxnam Border 80 F9
Oxnead Norfk 45 K5
Oxshott Surrey 21 J10
Oxspring Barns 50 H1
Oxted Surrey 21 M11
Oxton Border 80 C4
Oxton N York 59 L5
Oxton Notts 51 N9
Oxwich Swans 26 C10
Oxwich Green Swans 26 C10
Oykel Bridge Hotel Highld 106 F3
Oyne Abers 102 E9
Oystermouth Swans 26 E10

## P

Pabail W Isls 111 e2
Packington Leics 41 J5
Packmoor C Stke 49 Q5
Padanaram Angus 93 M5
Padbury Bucks 31 Q7
Paddington Gt Lon 21 L7
Paddlesworth Kent 13 M3
Paddlesworth Kent 22 D10
Paddock Wood Kent 12 D2
Padiham Lancs 57 P3
Padside N York 58 F3
Padstow Cnwll 3 K1
Padworth W Berk 19 Q7
Pagham W Susx 10 E9
Paglesham Essex 22 H5
Paignton Torbay 6 B10
Pailton Warwks 41 L10
Painscastle Powys 38 D11
Painshawfield Nthumb 73 J8
Painsthorpe E R Yk 60 E3
Painswick Gloucs 29 M6
Painter's Forstal Kent 23 J10
Paisley Rens 84 H9
Paisley Woodside Crematorium Rens 84 H9
Pakefield Suffk 45 Q11
Pakenham Suffk 34 F4
Paley Street W & M 20 E7
Palfrey Wsall 40 D7
Palgrave Suffk 35 J2
Pallington Dorset 8 B8
Palmerston E Ayrs 76 H7
Palnackie D & G 70 D4
Palnure D & G 69 L6
Palterton Derbys 51 L7
Pamber End Hants 19 Q8
Pamber Green Hants 19 Q8
Pamber Heath Hants 19 Q8
Pamington Gloucs 29 N3
Pamphill Dorset 8 E7
Pampisford Cambs 33 N7
Panbride Angus 93 P8
Pancrasweek Devon 14 F10
Pandy Mons 28 D4
Pandy Tudur Conwy 55 M8
Panfield Essex 34 C10
Pangbourne W Berk 19 Q5
Pangdean W Susx 11 L7
Pannal N York 58 H4
Pannal Ash N York 58 H4
Pannanich Wells Hotel Abers 94 G3
Pant Shrops 48 F10
Pantasaph Flints 48 D1
Pant-ffrwyth Brdgnd 27 K11
Pant Glas Gwynd 46 H2
Pantglas Powys 47 M10
Panton Lincs 52 H7
Pant-y-dwr Powys 37 R6
Pant-y-mwyn Flints 48 E3
Panxworth Norfk 45 M7
*Papa Stour Airport Shet 111 j3*
*Papa Westray Airport Ork 111 h1*
Papcastle Cumb 70 H8
Papigoe Highld 110 H5
Papple E Loth 87 L7
Papplewick Notts 51 M9
Papworth Everard Cambs 33 J4
Papworth St Agnes Cambs 33 J4
Par Cnwll 3 N5
Parbold Lancs 57 J6
Parbrook Somset 17 N8
Parc Gwynd 47 P5
Parc Gwyn Crematorium Pembks 25 K6
Parc Seymour Newpt 28 E9
Pardshaw Cumb 70 H9
Parham Suffk 35 M5
Park D & G 78 E10
Park Nthumb 72 C8
Park Corner Oxon 20 B6
Park Crematorium Lancs 56 G3
Parkend Gloucs 28 H7
Parkers Green Kent 12 C1
Park Farm Kent 13 J3
Parkgate Ches W 56 F12
Parkgate D & G 78 G10
Park Gate Hants 9 N6
Park Gate Leeds 58 F6
Parkgate Surrey 11 K2
Parkgrove Crematorium Angus 93 Q6
Parkhall W Duns 84 H8
Parkham Devon 14 G7
Parkmill Swans 26 D10
Park Royal Gt Lon 21 K7
Parkside Dur 73 Q10
Parkside N Lans 85 N10
Parkstone Poole 8 F8
Park Street Herts 21 J3
Park Wood Crematorium Calder 58 E9
Parndon Essex 21 N2
Parndon Wood Crematorium Essex 21 N3
Parracombe Devon 15 L3
Parson Drove Cambs 43 L8
Parson's Heath Essex 34 G10
Partick C Glas 85 J9
Partington Traffd 57 N9
Partney Lincs 53 L9
Parton Cumb 70 F10
Partridge Green W Susx 11 J6
Parwich Derbys 50 F9
Passenham Nhants 32 A8
Paston Norfk 45 M4
Patcham Br & H 11 L8
Patching W Susx 10 H8
Patchway S Glos 28 H11
Pateley Bridge N York 58 F2
Pathhead Fife 86 F4
Pathhead Mdloth 86 H9
Path of Condie P & K 92 G12
Patna E Ayrs 76 G8
Patney Wilts 18 F8
Patrick IoM 56 b5
Patrick Brompton N York 65 L8
Patricroft Salfd 57 N8
Patrington E R Yk 61 M9
Patrington Haven E R Yk 61 M9
Patrixbourne Kent 23 M11
Patterdale Cumb 71 N11
Pattingham Staffs 39 P3
Pattishall Nhants 31 P4
Pattiswick Green Essex 34 D11
Paul Cnwll 2 C9
Paulerspury Nhants 31 Q5
Paull E R Yk 61 K8
Paul's Dene Wilts 8 G2
Paulton BaNES 17 P5
Pauperhaugh Nthumb 73 K2
Pavenham Bed 32 E5
Pawlett Somset 16 H7
Paxford Gloucs 30 F6
Paxton Border 81 K4
Payhembury Devon 6 E3
Paythorne Lancs 63 P10
Peacehaven E Susx 11 N9
*Peak District National Park 50 F3*
Peak Forest Derbys 50 E5
Peakirk C Pete 42 G8
Peasedown St John BaNES 17 Q5
Peaseland Green Norfk 44 H6
Peasemore W Berk 19 M5
Peasenhall Suffk 35 M3
Pease Pottage W Susx 11 L4
Peaslake Surrey 10 H2
Peasley Cross St Hel 57 K9
Peasmarsh E Susx 12 H5
Peathill Abers 103 J3
Peat Inn Fife 87 J1
Peatling Magna Leics 41 N8
Peatling Parva Leics 41 N9
Pebmarsh Essex 34 E9
Pebworth Worcs 30 F5
Pecket Well Calder 58 C8
Peckforton Ches E 49 K4
Peckham Gt Lon 21 M8
Peckleton Leics 41 L7
Pedlinge Kent 13 L3
Pedmore Dudley 40 B10
Pedwell Somset 17 K8
Peebles Border 79 L2
Peel IoM 56 b4
Peel Green Crematorium Salfd 57 N8
Peene Kent 13 M3
Pegsdon C Beds 32 G9
Pegswood Nthumb 73 M4
Pegwell Kent 23 Q9
Peinchorran Highld 96 G3
Peinlich Highld 104 F10
Peldon Essex 34 G12
Pelsall Wsall 40 D6
Pelton Dur 73 M9
Pelynt Cnwll 4 F8
Pemberton Carmth 26 D8
Pemberton Wigan 57 K7
Pembrey Carmth 25 P8
Pembridge Herefs 38 H9
Pembroke Pembks 24 H8
Pembroke Dock Pembks 24 G7
*Pembrokeshire Coast National Park Pembks 24 E5*
Pembury Kent 12 D2
Pen-allt Herefs 28 G3
Penallt Mons 28 F6
Penally Pembks 25 K8
Penarth V Glam 16 G2
Pen-bont Rhydybeddau Cerdgn 37 L4
Penbryn Cerdgn 36 E9
Pencader Carmth 25 Q2
Pencaitland E Loth 87 J8
Pencarnisiog IoA 54 D6
Pencarreg Carmth 37 J10
Pencelli Powys 27 M4
Penclawdd Swans 26 D9
Pencoed Brdgnd 27 K11
Pencombe Herefs 39 L10
Pencraig Herefs 28 G5
Pencraig Powys 48 B9
Pendeen Cnwll 2 B8
Penderyn Rhondd 27 K7
Pendine Carmth 25 L7
Pendlebury Salfd 57 P8
Pendleton Lancs 57 N2
Pendock Worcs 29 K3
Pendoggett Cnwll 4 C4
Pendomer Somset 7 M1
Pendoylan V Glam 16 E2
Penegoes Powys 47 M10
Pen-ffordd Pembks 25 J4
Pengam Caerph 27 N8
Pengam Cardif 27 P12
Penge Gt Lon 21 M8
Pengelly Cnwll 4 D4
Penhallow Cnwll 2 H5
Penhalvean Cnwll 2 G8
Penhill Swindn 18 H3
Penhow Newpt 28 E10
Penicuik Mdloth 86 F9
Penifiler Highld 96 F2
Peninver Ag & B 75 L7
Penistone Barns 50 G1
Penkill S Ayrs 76 D10
Penkridge Staffs 40 B5
Penley Wrexhm 48 H7
Penllyn V Glam 16 C2
Penmachno Conwy 55 L10
Penmaen Caerph 27 P8
Penmaen Swans 26 D10
Penmaenmawr Conwy 55 K6
Penmaenpool Gwynd 47 L7
Penmark V Glam 16 E3
Penmount Crematorium Cnwll 3 J6
Penmynydd IoA 54 G6
Pennal Gwynd 47 L10
Pennan Abers 102 H3
Pennant Powys 47 P10
Pennerley Shrops 38 G3
Pennines 58 C7
Pennington Cumb 62 F6
Pennorth Powys 27 M4
Penn Street Bucks 20 E4
Penny Bridge Cumb 62 F5
Pennycross Ag & B 89 L10
Pennyghael Ag & B 89 L10
Pennyglen S Ayrs 76 E8
Pennymoor Devon 15 P9
Pennywell Sundld 73 P9
Penparc Cerdgn 36 D10
Penperlleni Mons 28 C7
Penpoll Cnwll 4 E8
Penponds Cnwll 2 F7
Penpont D & G 78 D9
Pen-rhiw Pembks 36 D11
Penrhiwceiber Rhondd 27 M8
Pen Rhiwfawr Neath 26 G6
Penrhiw-llan Cerdgn 36 F11
Penrhiw-pal Cerdgn 36 F10
Penrhos Gwynd 46 F5
Penrhos Mons 28 E6
Penrhyn Bay Conwy 55 M5
Penrhyn-coch Cerdgn 37 K4
Penrhyndeudraeth Gwynd 47 K4
Penrice Swans 26 C10
Penrioch N Ayrs 75 N4
Penrith Cumb 71 Q9
Penrose Cnwll 3 K2
Penruddock Cumb 71 N9
Penryn Cnwll 2 H8
Pensarn Conwy 55 P6
Pensax Worcs 39 N8
Penselwood Somset 17 R9
Pensford BaNES 17 N4
Pensham Worcs 30 C5
Penshaw Sundld 73 N9
Penshurst Kent 11 Q2
Pensilva Cnwll 4 G6
Pensnett Dudley 40 B9
Pentewan Cnwll 3 M6
Pentir Gwynd 54 H8
Pentire Cnwll 2 H4
Pentlow Essex 34 D7
Pentney Norfk 44 C7
Pentonbridge Cumb 79 P12
Penton Mewsey Hants 19 K10
Pentraeth IoA 54 G6
Pentre Mons 28 E8
Pentre Rhondd 27 K9
Pentre Shrops 48 G11
Pentrebach Myr Td 27 M7
Pentre-bach Powys 27 J3
Pentre Berw IoA 54 F7
Pentrebychan Crematorium Wrexhm 48 F6
Pentre-celyn Denbgs 48 D5
Pentre-celyn Powys 47 P9
Pentre-chwyth Swans 26 F9
Pentre-cwrt Carmth 25 P2
Pentredwr Denbgs 48 E6
Pentrefelin Gwynd 47 J4
Pentrefoelas Conwy 55 M10
Pentregat Cerdgn 36 F9
Pentre-Gwenlais Carmth 26 E5
Pentre Hodrey Shrops 38 G6
Pentre Llanrhaeadr Denbgs 48 C3
Pentre Meyrick V Glam 16 C2
Pentre-tafarn-y-fedw Conwy 55 M8
Pentrich Derbys 51 J9
Pentridge Dorset 8 F4
Pen-twyn Mons 28 F7
Pentwynmaur Caerph 27 P9
Pentyrch Cardif 27 M11
Penwithick Cnwll 3 M5
Penybanc Carmth 26 E4
Penybont Powys 38 C8
Pen-y-bont Powys 48 E10
Pen-y-bont-fawr Powys 48 C9
Pen-y-bryn Pembks 36 C11
Penycae Wrexhm 48 F6
Pen-y-clawdd Mons 28 E7
Pen-y-coedcae Rhondd 27 M10
Penycwn Pembks 24 E4
Pen-y-felin Flints 48 D2
Penyffordd Flints 48 F4
Pen-y-Garnedd Powys 48 C10
Pen-y-graig Gwynd 46 C5
Penygraig Rhondd 27 L10
Penygroes Carmth 26 D6
Penygroes Gwynd 54 F10
Pen-y-Mynydd Carmth 26 C7
Penymynydd Flints 48 F3
Penysarn IoA 54 F4
Pen-y-stryt Denbgs 48 E5
Penywaun Rhondd 27 K7
Penzance Cnwll 2 D9
Peopleton Worcs 30 C4
Peplow Shrops 49 L9
Perceton N Ayrs 76 F4
Percyhorner Abers 103 K3
Perham Down Wilts 19 J10
Periton Somset 16 C7
Perivale Gt Lon 21 J6
Perkins Village Devon 6 D5
Perlethorpe Notts 51 N6
Perranarworthal Cnwll 2 H7

Perranporth Cnwll.....2 H5
Perranuthnoe Cnwll.....2 D9
Perranwell Cnwll.....2 H7
Perranzabuloe Cnwll.....2 H5
Perry Birm.....40 E8
Perry Barr Birm.....40 E8
Perry Barr Crematorium Birm.....40 E8
Perry Green Wilts.....18 E3
Pershall Staffs.....49 P9
Pershore Worcs.....30 C5
Pertenhall Bed.....32 F4
Perth P & K.....92 G10
Perth Crematorium P & K.....92 G10
Perthy Shrops.....48 G8
Perton Herefs.....28 H2
Perton Staffs.....39 Q3
Peterborough C Pete.....42 H9
Peterborough Crematorium C Pete.....42 G9
Peterborough Services Cambs.....42 G10
Peterchurch Herefs.....28 D2
Peterculter C Aber.....95 N2
Peterhead Abers.....103 M6
Peterlee Dur.....73 Q11
Petersfield Hants.....10 C5
Peter's Green Herts.....32 G11
Petersham Gt Lon.....21 J8
Peters Marland Devon.....14 H9
Peterstone Wentlooge Newpt.....28 B11
Peterston-super-Ely V Glam.....16 E2
Peterstow Herefs.....28 G4
Peter Tavy Devon.....5 K5
Petham Kent.....23 L12
Petherwin Gate Cnwll.....4 C3
Petrockstow Devon.....15 J9
Pett E Susx.....12 G7
Pettaugh Suffk.....35 J5
Petterden Angus.....93 M7
Pettinain S Lans.....78 F1
Pettistree Suffk.....35 L6
Petton Devon.....16 D10
Petts Wood Gt Lon.....21 N9
Pettycur Fife.....86 F5
Pettymuk Abers.....103 J9
Petworth W Susx.....10 F6
Pevensey E Susx.....12 D8
Pevensey Bay E Susx.....12 D8
Pewsey Wilts.....18 H8
Phepson Worcs.....30 C3
Philham Devon.....14 E7
Philiphaugh Border.....79 N4
Phillack Cnwll.....2 F6
Philleigh Cnwll.....3 K7
Philpstoun W Loth.....86 C6
Phoenix Green Hants.....20 C11
Phones Highld.....99 K9
Pibsbury Somset.....17 L10
Pickburn Donc.....59 L11
Pickering N York.....66 H10
Pickford Covtry.....40 H10
Pickhill N York.....65 N10
Picklescott Shrops.....38 H3
Pickmere Ches E.....57 M12
Pickney Somset.....16 G9
Pickwell Leics.....42 B7
Pickworth Lincs.....42 F4
Pickworth Rutlnd.....42 E7
Picton Ches W.....48 H2
Picton N York.....65 P6
Piddinghoe E Susx.....11 N9
Piddington Nhants.....32 B6
Piddington Oxon.....31 N10
Piddlehinton Dorset.....7 Q4
Piddletrenthide Dorset.....7 Q3
Pidley Cambs.....33 K2
Piercebridge Darltn.....65 L4
Pierowall Ork.....111 h1
Pilgrims Hatch Essex.....22 C4
Pilham Lincs.....52 C5
Pillaton Cnwll.....4 H7
Pillerton Hersey Warwks.....30 H4
Pillerton Priors Warwks.....30 H5
Pilley Barns.....51 J1
Pilley Hants.....9 K7
Pilling Lancs.....62 H11
Pilning S Glos.....28 G10
Pilsbury Derbys.....50 E7
Pilsdon Dorset.....7 K3
Pilsley Derbys.....50 G6
Pilsley Derbys.....51 K8
Pilson Green Norfk.....45 N8
Piltdown E Susx.....11 N5
Pilton Devon.....15 K5
Pilton Nhants.....42 E12
Pilton Rutlnd.....42 D9
Pilton Somset.....17 N7
Pimperne Dorset.....8 D5
Pinchbeck Lincs.....43 J5
Pin Green Herts.....33 J10
Pinhoe Devon.....6 C4
Pinley Green Warwks.....30 G2
Pinminnoch S Ayrs.....76 D11
Pinmore S Ayrs.....76 D11
Pinn Devon.....6 E5
Pinner Gt Lon.....20 H5
Pinner Green Gt Lon.....20 H5
Pinvin Worcs.....30 C4
Pinwherry S Ayrs.....68 G2
Pinxton Derbys.....51 L9
Pipe and Lyde Herefs.....39 J12
Pipe Aston Herefs.....39 J7
Pipe Gate Shrops.....49 N7
Piperhill Highld.....100 D5
Pipewell Nhants.....42 B11
Pirbright Surrey.....20 F11
Pirnie Border.....80 E8
Pirnmill N Ayrs.....75 N4
Pirton Herts.....32 G9
Pishill Oxon.....20 B5
Pistyll Gwynd.....46 E3
Pitagowan P & K.....92 C3
Pitblae Abers.....103 K3
Pitcairngreen P & K.....92 F9
Pitcalnie Highld.....107 N7
Pitcaple Abers.....102 F9
Pitchcombe Gloucs.....29 L7
Pitchcott Bucks.....31 Q9
Pitchford Shrops.....39 K2
Pitch Green Bucks.....20 C3
Pitchroy Moray.....101 J7
Pitcombe Somset.....17 P9
Pitcox E Loth.....87 M7

Pitfichie Abers.....102 E11
Pitglassie Abers.....102 F6
Pitgrudy Highld.....107 N4
Pitlessie Fife.....86 G1
Pitlochry P & K.....92 D4
Pitmachie Abers.....102 E9
Pitmain Highld.....99 L8
Pitmedden Abers.....103 J9
Pitmedden Garden Abers.....103 J9
Pitminster Somset.....16 G11
Pitmuies Angus.....93 P6
Pitmunie Abers.....102 E11
Pitney Somset.....17 L9
Pitroddie P & K.....93 J10
Pitscottie Fife.....93 M11
Pitsea Essex.....22 E6
Pitsford Nhants.....31 Q1
Pitstone Bucks.....20 F1
Pittarrow Abers.....95 M7
Pittenweem Fife.....87 K2
Pitteuchar Fife.....86 F3
Pittington Dur.....73 N11
Pittodrie House Hotel Abers.....102 F9
Pitton Wilts.....8 H2
Pittulie Abers.....103 K2
Pity Me Dur.....73 M10
Pixham Surrey.....21 J12
Plains N Lans.....85 N9
Plaish Shrops.....39 K3
Plaistow Gt Lon.....21 N6
Plaistow W Susx.....10 G4
Plaitford Hants.....9 J4
Platt Kent.....22 D11
Plawsworth Dur.....73 M10
Plaxtol Kent.....22 C11
Playden E Susx.....12 H6
Playford Suffk.....35 K7
Play Hatch Oxon.....20 B7
Playing Place Cnwll.....3 J7
Playley Green Gloucs.....29 K3
Plealey Shrops.....38 H2
Plean Stirlg.....85 P5
Pleasance Fife.....93 J12
Pleasington Bl w D.....57 M4
Pleasington Crematorium Bl w D.....57 M4
Pleasley Derbys.....51 L7
Plemstall Ches W.....49 J2
Pleshey Essex.....22 D1
Plockton Highld.....97 L3
Plowden Shrops.....38 H5
Pluckley Kent.....12 H2
Pluckley Thorne Kent.....12 H2
Plumbland Cumb.....71 J7
Plumley Ches E.....49 N1
Plumpton Cumb.....71 P7
Plumpton E Susx.....11 M7
Plumpton Nhants.....31 N5
Plumpton Green E Susx.....11 M6
Plumstead Gt Lon.....21 N7
Plumstead Norfk.....45 J3
Plumtree Notts.....41 N2
Plungar Leics.....41 Q1
Plurenden Kent.....12 H3
Plush Dorset.....7 Q3
Plwmp Cerdgn.....36 F9
Plymouth C Plym.....5 K8
Plymouth Airport C Plym.....5 K8
Plympton C Plym.....5 L8
Plymstock C Plym.....5 L9
Plymtree Devon.....6 E3
Pockley N York.....66 F9
Pocklington E R Yk.....60 D4
Podimore Somset.....17 M10
Podington Bed.....32 D4
Podmore Staffs.....49 P8
Pointon Lincs.....42 G4
Pokesdown Bmouth.....8 G8
Polbain Highld.....105 Q1
Polbathic Cnwll.....4 H8
Polbeth W Loth.....86 B9
Poldark Mine Cnwll.....2 G7
Polebrook Nhants.....42 F11
Polegate E Susx.....12 C8
Polesden Lacey Surrey.....21 J11
Polesworth Warwks.....40 H7
Polglass Highld.....105 Q2
Polgooth Cnwll.....3 M5
Polgown D & G.....77 M9
Poling W Susx.....10 G8
Poling Corner W Susx.....10 G8
Polkerris Cnwll.....4 D9
Pollington E R Yk.....59 N9
Polloch Highld.....89 Q3
Pollokshaws C Glas.....85 J10
Pollokshields C Glas.....85 J9
Polmassick Cnwll.....3 L6
Polmont Falk.....85 Q7
Polnish Highld.....97 K12
Polperro Cnwll.....4 E9
Polruan Cnwll.....4 E9
Polstead Suffk.....34 G8
Poltalloch Ag & B.....83 M4
Poltimore Devon.....6 C4
Polton Mdloth.....86 F8
Polwarth Border.....80 G4
Polyphant Cnwll.....4 G4
Polzeath Cnwll.....4 B4
Pomathorn Mdloth.....86 F9
Pondersbridge Cambs.....43 J10
Ponders End Gt Lon.....21 M4
Ponsanooth Cnwll.....2 H8
Ponsworthy Devon.....5 N5
Pont Abraham Services Carmth.....26 D7
Pontamman Carmth.....25 Q6
Pontantwn Carmth.....25 Q5
Pontardawe Neath.....26 F7
Pontarddulais Swans.....26 D7
Pont-ar-gothi Carmth.....26 C5
Pontarsais Carmth.....25 Q3
Pontblyddyn Flints.....48 F4
Pontcysyllte Aqueduct Wrexhm.....48 F7
Pontefract Wakefd.....59 L9
Pontefract Crematorium Wakefd.....59 K9
Ponteland Nthumb.....73 L6
Ponterwyd Cerdgn.....37 M4
Pontesbury Shrops.....38 H2
Pontesford Shrops.....38 H2
Pontfadog Wrexhm.....48 E7
Pontfaen Pembks.....24 H3
Pont-faen Powys.....27 L3
Pontgarreg Cerdgn.....36 F9
Ponthenry Carmth.....26 C7
Ponthir Torfn.....28 C9

Ponthirwaun Cerdgn.....36 D10
Pontllanfraith Caerph.....27 P9
Pontlliw Swans.....26 E8
Pontlottyn Caerph.....27 N7
Pontlyfni Gwynd.....54 F10
Pontneddfechan Neath.....27 J7
Pontnewydd Torfn.....28 C9
Pontrhydfendigaid Cerdgn.....37 M7
Pont-rhyd-y-fen Neath.....26 H9
Pontrhydygroes Cerdgn.....37 M6
Pontrilas Herefs.....28 D4
Pont Robert Powys.....48 C11
Pontshaen Cerdgn.....36 G10
Pontsticill Myr Td.....27 M6
Pontwelly Carmth.....36 G11
Pontyates Carmth.....26 C7
Pontyberem Carmth.....26 C6
Pontybodkin Flints.....48 F4
Pontyclun Rhondd.....27 L11
Pontycymer Brdgnd.....27 J9
Pont-y-pant Conwy.....55 L10
Pontypool Torfn.....28 C8
Pontypridd Rhondd.....27 M10
Pontywaun Caerph.....27 P9
Pool Cnwll.....2 G7
Pool Leeds.....58 G5
Poole Poole.....8 E8
Poole Crematorium Poole.....8 E8
Poole Keynes Gloucs.....18 E2
Poolewe Highld.....105 M6
Pooley Bridge Cumb.....71 P10
Poolfold Staffs.....50 B8
Poolhill Gloucs.....29 K3
Pool of Muckhart Clacks.....86 B3
Pool Street Essex.....34 C8
Poplar Gt Lon.....21 M7
Porchfield IoW.....9 M8
Poringland Norfk.....45 L9
Porkellis Cnwll.....2 G8
Porlock Somset.....15 Q3
Porlock Weir Somset.....15 P3
Portachoillan Ag & B.....83 L10
Port-an-Eorna Highld.....97 K4
Port Appin Ag & B.....90 C7
Port Askaig Ag & B.....82 F8
Port Bannatyne Ag & B.....84 B9
Portbury N Som.....17 M2
Port Carlisle Cumb.....71 K3
Port Charlotte Ag & B.....82 C10
Portchester Hants.....9 Q6
Portchester Crematorium Hants.....9 Q6
Port Driseach Ag & B.....83 Q8
Port Ellen Ag & B.....74 E4
Port Elphinstone Abers.....102 G10
Portencalzie D & G.....68 D5
Portencross N Ayrs.....76 C2
Port Erin IoM.....56 a6
Portesham Dorset.....7 N5
Portessie Moray.....101 N3
Port Eynon Swans.....26 C10
Portfield Gate Pembks.....24 G6
Portgate Devon.....5 J3
Port Gaverne Cnwll.....4 C4
Port Glasgow Inver.....84 F7
Portgordon Moray.....101 M3
Portgower Highld.....110 B11
Porth Cnwll.....3 J4
Porth Rhondd.....27 L9
Porthallow Cnwll.....2 H10
Porthallow Cnwll.....4 F9
Porthcawl Brdgnd.....26 H12
Porthcothan Cnwll.....3 K2
Porthcurno Cnwll.....2 B10
Port Henderson Highld.....105 L7
Porthgain Pembks.....24 E3
Porthgwarra Cnwll.....2 B10
Porthill Staffs.....49 Q6
Porthkerry V Glam.....16 E3
Porthleven Cnwll.....2 F9
Porthmadog Gwynd.....47 J4
Porth Navas Cnwll.....2 H9
Porthoustock Cnwll.....3 J10
Porthpean Cnwll.....3 M5
Porthtowan Cnwll.....2 G6
Porthyrhyd Carmth.....26 C5
Portincaple Ag & B.....84 D4
Portington E R Yk.....60 D7
Portinnisherrich Ag & B.....83 P2
Portinscale Cumb.....71 L10
Port Isaac Cnwll.....4 C4
Portishead N Som.....17 L2
Portknockie Moray.....101 N2
Portland Dorset.....7 P8
Portlethen Abers.....95 Q3
Portling D & G.....70 E5
Portloe Cnwll.....3 L7
Port Logan D & G.....68 E10
Portmahomack Highld.....107 Q5
Portmeirion Gwynd.....47 J4
Portmellon Cnwll.....3 M7
Port Mor Highld.....89 J1
Portnacroish Ag & B.....90 C6
Portnaguran W Isls.....111 e2
Portnahaven Ag & B.....74 B2
Portnalong Highld.....96 D2
Port nan Giuran W Isls.....111 e2
Port nan Long W Isls.....111 b4
Port Nis W Isls.....111 e1
Portobello C Edin.....86 G7
Portobello Wolves.....40 C7
Port of Menteith Stirlg.....85 J3
Port of Ness W Isls.....111 e1
Porton Wilts.....18 H12
Portpatrick D & G.....68 D8
Port Quin Cnwll.....4 B4
Port Ramsay Ag & B.....90 B7
Portreath Cnwll.....2 F6
Portreath Harbour Cnwll.....2 F6
Portree Highld.....96 F2
Port St Mary IoM.....56 b7
Portscatho Cnwll.....3 K8
Portsea C Port.....9 Q7
Portskerra Highld.....109 Q3
Portskewett Mons.....28 F10
Portslade Br & H.....11 L8
Portslade-by-Sea Br & H.....11 L8
Portslogan D & G.....68 D7
Portsmouth C Port.....9 Q7
Portsmouth Calder.....58 B8
Portsmouth Dockyard C Port.....9 Q7
Port Soderick IoM.....56 c6
Portsonachan Hotel Ag & B.....90 E11

Portsoy Abers.....102 D3
Port Sunlight Wirral.....56 G11
Portswood C Sotn.....9 M5
Port Talbot Neath.....26 G10
Portuairk Highld.....89 K3
Portway Sandw.....40 C9
Portway Worcs.....40 E11
Port Wemyss Ag & B.....74 B3
Port William D & G.....69 J9
Portwrinkle Cnwll.....4 H9
Portyerrock D & G.....69 L10
Poslingford Suffk.....34 C7
Posso Border.....79 K3
Postbridge Devon.....5 N4
Postcombe Oxon.....20 B4
Postling Kent.....13 M3
Postwick Norfk.....45 L8
Potarch Abers.....95 K3
Potten End Herts.....20 G2
Potterhanworth Lincs.....52 F9
Potterhanworth Booths Lincs.....52 F9
Potter Heigham Norfk.....45 N6
Potterne Wilts.....18 E8
Potterne Wick Wilts.....18 E8
Potters Bar Herts.....21 K3
Potters Crouch Herts.....20 H3
Potters Green Covtry.....41 J10
Potters Marston Leics.....41 L8
Potterspury Nhants.....31 Q5
Potterton Abers.....103 K11
Potto N York.....66 C6
Potton C Beds.....32 H6
Pott Shrigley Ches E.....50 C5
Poughill Cnwll.....14 D10
Poughill Devon.....15 P9
Poulner Hants.....8 H6
Poulshot Wilts.....18 E8
Poulton Gloucs.....18 G1
Poulton Wirral.....56 F10
Poulton-le-Fylde Lancs.....56 G2
Poundbury Dorset.....7 P5
Poundffald Swans.....26 D9
Pound Green E Susx.....11 P5
Pound Green Suffk.....34 C6
Pound Hill W Susx.....11 L3
Poundon Bucks.....31 N8
Poundsgate Devon.....5 N6
Poundstock Cnwll.....14 D11
Pouton D & G.....69 L9
Povey Cross Surrey.....11 L2
Powburn Nthumb.....81 M10
Powderham Devon.....6 C6
Powerstock Dorset.....7 M4
Powfoot D & G.....71 J3
Powick Worcs.....39 Q10
Powmill P & K.....86 B3
Poxwell Dorset.....7 Q6
Poyle Slough.....20 G7
Poynings W Susx.....11 L7
Poyntington Dorset.....17 P11
Poynton Ches E.....50 B4
Poynton Green Wrekin.....49 K10
Praa Sands Cnwll.....2 E9
Praze-an-Beeble Cnwll.....2 F8
Prees Shrops.....49 K8
Preesall Lancs.....62 G11
Prees Green Shrops.....49 K8
Prees Heath Shrops.....49 K7
Prees Higher Heath Shrops.....49 K8
Pren-gwyn Cerdgn.....36 G10
Prenteg Gwynd.....47 J3
Prescot Knows.....57 J9
Prescott Devon.....16 E12
Presnerb Angus.....94 C8
Prestatyn Denbgs.....56 C11
Prestbury Ches E.....50 B5
Prestbury Gloucs.....29 N4
Presteigne Powys.....38 G8
Prestleigh Somset.....17 P7
Preston Border.....87 P10
Preston Br & H.....11 L8
Preston Devon.....6 B7
Preston Dorset.....7 Q6
Preston E R Yk.....61 K7
Preston Gloucs.....18 F1
Preston Herts.....32 H10
Preston Kent.....23 K10
Preston Kent.....23 N10
Preston Lancs.....57 K3
Preston Nthumb.....81 P8
Preston Rutlnd.....42 C9
Preston Somset.....16 E8
Preston Suffk.....34 F6
Preston Torbay.....6 B9
Preston Wilts.....18 F5
Preston Bagot Warwks.....30 F2
Preston Bissett Bucks.....31 P8
Preston Bowyer Somset.....16 F10
Preston Brockhurst Shrops.....49 K9
Preston Brook Halton.....57 K11
Preston Candover Hants.....19 Q11
Preston Capes Nhants.....31 M3
Preston Crematorium Lancs.....57 L3
Preston Green Warwks.....30 F2
Preston Gubbals Shrops.....49 J10
Preston on Stour Warwks.....30 G4
Preston on the Hill Halton.....57 K11
Preston on Wye Herefs.....28 D1
Prestonpans E Loth.....86 H7
Preston Patrick Cumb.....63 K5
Preston Plucknett Somset.....17 M11
Preston-under-Scar N York.....65 J8
Preston upon the Weald Moors Wrekin.....49 M11
Preston Wynne Herefs.....39 K11
Prestwich Bury.....57 P7
Prestwick S Ayrs.....76 F6
Prestwick Airport S Ayrs.....76 F6
Prestwood Bucks.....20 E4
Prickwillow Cambs.....33 P1
Priddy Somset.....17 M6
Priest Hutton Lancs.....63 K7
Priestland E Ayrs.....77 J4
Priest Weston Shrops.....38 F3
Primrose Hill Dudley.....40 C9
Primrosehill Border.....80 H8
Primsidemill Border.....80 H8
Princes Risborough Bucks.....20 D3
Princethorpe Warwks.....41 K12
Princetown Devon.....5 M5
Priors Hardwick Warwks.....31 L3

Priorslee Wrekin.....49 N12
Priors Marston Warwks.....31 L3
Priors Norton Gloucs.....29 M4
Priory Vale Swindn.....18 G3
Priston BaNES.....17 Q4
Prittlewell Sthend.....22 G6
Privett Hants.....10 B5
Prixford Devon.....15 J5
Probus Cnwll.....3 K6
Prora E Loth.....87 K6
Prospect Cumb.....71 J7
Prospidnick Cnwll.....2 F9
Protstonhill Abers.....102 H3
Prudhoe Nthumb.....73 K8
Publow BaNES.....17 P4
Puckeridge Herts.....33 L11
Puckington Somset.....17 K11
Pucklechurch S Glos.....17 Q2
Puddinglon Ches W.....48 G2
Puddington Devon.....15 P9
Puddletown Dorset.....7 Q4
Pudsey Leeds.....58 G7
Pulborough W Susx.....10 G6
Pulford Ches W.....48 G4
Pulham Dorset.....7 Q2
Pulham Market Norfk.....45 K11
Pulham St Mary Norfk.....45 K11
Pulloxhill C Beds.....32 F9
Pumpherston W Loth.....86 C8
Pumsaint Carmth.....37 K11
Puncheston Pembks.....24 H3
Punchknowle Dorset.....7 M5
Punnett's Town E Susx.....12 C6
Purbrook Hants.....10 A8
Purfleet Thurr.....22 B7
Puriton Somset.....17 J7
Purleigh Essex.....22 G3
Purley Gt Lon.....21 L10
Purley W Berk.....19 Q5
Purse Caundle Dorset.....17 Q11
Purtington Somset.....7 K2
Purton Gloucs.....29 J7
Purton Gloucs.....29 J7
Purton Wilts.....18 G4
Purton Stoke Wilts.....18 G3
Pury End Nhants.....31 P5
Pusey Oxon.....19 L2
Putley Herefs.....28 H2
Putley Green Herefs.....28 H2
Putney Gt Lon.....21 K8
Putney Vale Crematorium Gt Lon.....21 K8
Puttenham Surrey.....10 E1
Puxley Nhants.....31 Q6
Puxton N Som.....17 K4
Pwll Carmth.....26 C8
Pwll-glâs Denbgs.....48 C5
Pwllgloyw Powys.....27 L3
Pwllheli Gwynd.....46 F4
Pwllmeyric Mons.....28 F9
Pwll Trap Carmth.....25 M5
Pwll-y-glaw Neath.....26 H9
Pye Bridge Derbys.....51 K9
Pyecombe W Susx.....11 L7
Pyle Brdgnd.....26 H11
Pyleigh Somset.....16 F9
Pylle Somset.....17 N8
Pymoor Cambs.....43 M11
Pymore Dorset.....7 L4
Pyrton Oxon.....20 B4
Pytchley Nhants.....32 C2
Pyworthy Devon.....14 F10

**Q**

Quadring Lincs.....42 H4
Quadring Eaudike Lincs.....43 J4
Quainton Bucks.....31 Q9
Quantock Hills Somset.....16 G8
Quarff Shet.....111 k4
Quarley Hants.....19 J11
Quarndon Derbys.....51 J11
Quarrier's Village Inver.....84 F9
Quarrington Lincs.....42 F2
Quarrington Hill Dur.....73 N12
Quarry Bank Dudley.....40 B9
Quarrywood Moray.....101 J3
Quarter N Ayrs.....84 D10
Quarter S Lans.....85 M11
Quatford Shrops.....39 N4
Quatt Shrops.....39 N5
Quebec Dur.....73 L11
Quedgeley Gloucs.....29 L6
Queen Adelaide Cambs.....33 P1
Queen Camel Somset.....17 N10
Queen Charlton BaNES.....17 P3
Queen Elizabeth Forest Park Stirlg.....84 H3
Queenhill Worcs.....29 M2
Queen Oak Dorset.....8 B2
Queen's Bower IoW.....9 P9
Queensbury C Brad.....58 E7
Queensferry Flints.....48 G2
Queensferry Crossing Fife.....86 D6
Queenslie C Glas.....85 L9
Queenzieburn N Lans.....85 L7
Quendon Essex.....33 N10
Queniborough Leics.....41 N5
Quenington Gloucs.....30 F12
Queslett Birm.....40 E8
Quethiock Cnwll.....4 G7
Quidenham Norfk.....44 G11
Quidhampton Wilts.....8 G2
Quinton Nhants.....31 Q4
Quintrell Downs Cnwll.....3 J4
Quixwood Border.....87 P10
Quoditch Devon.....14 H2
Quoig P & K.....92 C10
Quorn Leics.....41 M4
Quothquan S Lans.....78 G2
Quoyburray Ork.....111 h2
Quoyloo Ork.....111 g2

**R**

Raasay Highld.....96 G2
Rachan Mill Border.....79 J3
Rachub Gwynd.....55 J7
Rackenford Devon.....15 P8
Rackham W Susx.....10 G7
Rackheath Norfk.....45 L7
Racks D & G.....70 G1
Rackwick Ork.....111 g3

Radbourne Derbys....40 H1
Radcliffe Bury....57 P7
Radcliffe on Trent Notts....51 N11
Radclive Bucks....31 P7
Raddery Highld....107 L9
Radernie Fife....87 J1
Radford Covtry....41 J10
Radford Semele Warwks....31 J2
Radlett Herts....21 J4
Radley Oxon....19 N2
Radley Green Essex....22 D3
Radnage Bucks....20 C4
Radstock BaNES....17 P5
Radstone Nhants....31 N6
Radway Warwks....31 J5
Radwell Bed....32 E5
Radwell Herts....32 H9
Radwinter Essex....33 P8
Radyr Cardif....27 N11
Rafford Moray....100 G4
RAF Museum Cosford
  Shrops....39 P2
RAF Museum Hendon
  Gt Lon....21 K5
Ragdale Leics....41 P4
Raglan Mons....28 E7
Ragnall Notts....52 B8
Raigbeg Highld....99 M4
Rainbow Hill Worcs....39 Q10
Rainford St Hel....57 J8
Rainham Gt Lon....21 Q7
Rainham Medway....22 F9
Rainhill St Hel....57 J9
Rainhill Stoops St Hel....57 J10
Rainow Ches E....50 C6
Rainsbrook
  Crematorium Warwks....41 L11
Rainton N York....65 P11
Rainworth Notts....51 N8
Rait P & K....93 J9
Raithby Lincs....53 K6
Raithby Lincs....53 L9
Rake Hants....10 C5
Ralia Highld....99 K9
Ramasaig Highld....96 A2
Rame Cnwll....2 G8
Rame Cnwll....5 J9
Rampisham Dorset....7 N3
Rampside Cumb....62 E8
Rampton Cambs....33 L3
Rampton Notts....52 B7
Ramsbottom Bury....57 P5
Ramsbury Wilts....19 J6
Ramscraigs Highld....110 D9
Ramsdean Hants....10 B5
Ramsdell Hants....19 P8
Ramsden Oxon....31 J10
Ramsden Bellhouse Essex....22 E5
Ramsey Cambs....43 J11
Ramsey Essex....35 K10
Ramsey IoM....56 e3
Ramsey Forty Foot
  Cambs....43 K11
Ramsey Heights Cambs....43 J12
Ramsey Island Essex....23 J3
Ramsey Island Pembks....24 C4
Ramsey Mereside Cambs....43 J11
Ramsey St Mary's Cambs....43 J11
Ramsgate Kent....23 Q9
Ramsgill N York....65 K12
Ramshope Nthumb....80 G12
Ramshorn Staffs....50 E10
Ramsnest Common
  Surrey....10 F4
Ranby Lincs....52 H7
Ranby Notts....51 P5
Rand Lincs....52 G7
Randalls Park
  Crematorium Surrey....21 J11
Randwick Gloucs....29 L7
Ranfurly Rens....84 G9
Rangemore Staffs....40 F3
Rangeworthy S Glos....29 J10
Rankinston E Ayrs....76 H8
Rannoch Station P & K....91 L5
Ranscombe Somset....16 C7
Ranskill Notts....51 P4
Ranton Staffs....49 Q10
Ranton Green Staffs....49 Q10
Ranworth Norfk....45 M7
Raploch Stirlg....85 N4
Rapness Ork....111 h1
Rascarrel D & G....70 D6
Rashfield Ag & B....84 C6
Rashwood Worcs....30 B2
Raskelf N York....66 C12
Rastrick Calder....58 F9
Ratagan Highld....97 N6
Ratby Leics....41 L6
Ratcliffe Culey Leics....41 J7
Ratcliffe on Soar Notts....41 L2
Ratcliffe on the Wreake
  Leics....41 N5
Rathen Abers....103 K3
Rathillet Fife....93 L10
Rathmell N York....63 P9
Ratho C Edin....86 D7
Ratho Station C Edin....86 D7
Rathven Moray....101 N3
Ratley Warwks....31 J5
Ratling Kent....23 N11
Ratlinghope Shrops....38 H3
Rattar Highld....110 F2
Rattery Devon....5 P7
Rattlesden Suffk....34 F5
Ratton Village E Susx....12 C9
Rattray P & K....92 H6
Raunds Nhants....32 E3
Ravenfield Rothm....51 L2
Ravenglass Cumb....62 C3
Raveningham Norfk....45 N10
Ravenscar N York....67 L7
Ravenscraig N Lans....85 N10
Ravensden Bed....32 F6
Ravenshead Notts....51 M9
Ravensthorpe Kirk....58 G9
Ravensthorpe Nhants....41 P12
Ravenstone Leics....41 K5
Ravenstone M Keyn....32 C6
Ravenstonedale Cumb....63 N3
Ravenstruther S Lans....77 Q3
Ravensworth N York....65 K6
Rawcliffe C York....59 N4
Rawcliffe E R Yk....59 P9
Rawdon Leeds....58 G6
Rawdon Crematorium
  Leeds....58 G6

Rawling Street Kent....22 H10
Rawmarsh Rothm....51 K2
Rawreth Essex....22 F5
Rawridge Devon....6 G2
Rawtenstall Lancs....57 P4
Raydon Suffk....34 H8
Rayleigh Essex....22 F5
Rayne Essex....34 C11
Raynes Park Gt Lon....21 K9
Reach Cambs....33 P4
Read Lancs....57 P2
Reading Readg....20 B8
Reading Crematorium
  Readg....20 B8
Reading Services W Berk....20 A9
Reading Street Kent....12 H4
Reading Street Kent....23 Q9
Reagill Cumb....64 B4
Realwa Cnwll....2 F8
Rearquhar Highld....107 M4
Rearsby Leics....41 P5
Reay Highld....110 A3
Reculver Kent....23 N9
Red Ball Devon....16 E11
Redberth Pembks....25 J7
Redbourn Herts....20 H2
Redbourne N Linc....52 D4
Redbrook Gloucs....28 G6
Redbrook Wrexhm....49 K7
Redbrook Street Kent....12 H3
Redburn Highld....100 H8
Redcar R & Cl....66 E3
Redcastle D & G....70 D3
Redcastle Highld....107 J11
Redding Falk....85 Q7
Reddingmuirhead Falk....85 Q7
Reddish Stockp....50 B3
Redditch Worcs....30 D1
Redditch Crematorium
  Worcs....30 D1
Rede Suffk....34 D5
Redenhall Norfk....45 L12
Redesmouth Nthumb....72 F5
Redford Abers....95 M7
Redford Angus....93 P6
Redford W Susx....10 D5
Redfordgreen Border....79 M6
Redgorton P & K....92 G9
Redgrave Suffk....34 H2
Redhill Abers....95 M2
Red Hill Bmouth....8 G8
Redhill Herts....33 J9
Redhill N Som....17 M4
Redhill Surrey....21 L12
Redisham Suffk....45 N12
Redland Bristl....17 N2
Redland Ork....111 h2
Redlingfield Suffk....35 K3
Redlingfield Green Suffk....35 K3
Red Lodge Suffk....34 B3
Redlynch Somset....17 Q9
Redlynch Wilts....8 H3
Redmarley Worcs....39 N8
Redmarley D'Abitot
  Gloucs....29 K3
Redmarshall S on T....65 P4
Redmile Leics....42 B3
Redmire N York....65 J8
Redmyre Abers....95 M6
Rednal Shrops....48 G9
Rednal Birm....40 D10
Redpath Border....80 D7
Redpoint Highld....105 K8
Red Roses Carmth....25 L6
Red Row Nthumb....73 M2
Redruth Cnwll....2 G7
Redstone P & K....92 H8
Red Street Staffs....49 P5
Red Wharf Bay IoA....54 G5
Redwick Newpt....28 E11
Redwick S Glos....28 G10
Redworth Darltn....65 M3
Reed Herts....33 K9
Reedham Norfk....45 N9
Reedness E R Yk....60 D9
Reeds Holme Lancs....57 P4
Reepham Lincs....52 E8
Reepham Norfk....44 H5
Reeth N York....65 J7
Reeves Green Solhll....40 H11
Regil N Som....17 M4
Reiff Highld....108 A11
Reigate Surrey....21 K12
Reighton N York....67 N11
Reisque Abers....103 J10
Reiss Highld....110 G5
Relubbus Cnwll....2 E8
Relugas Moray....100 F6
Remenham Wokham....20 C6
Remenham Hill Wokham....20 C6
Rempstone Notts....41 M3
Rendcomb Gloucs....30 D1
Rendham Suffk....35 M4
Rendlesham Suffk....35 M6
Renfrew Rens....84 H9
Renhold Bed....32 F6
Renishaw Derbys....51 K5
Rennington Nthumb....81 P9
Renton W Duns....84 G7
Renwick Cumb....72 B11
Repps Norfk....45 N6
Repton Derbys....40 H3
Resaurie Highld....107 L12
Rescorla Cnwll....3 N4
Reskadinnick Cnwll....2 F7
Resolis Highld....107 K8
Resolven Neath....26 H8
Rest and be thankful
  Ag & B....84 D2
Reston Border....87 P4
Reswallie Angus....93 N5
Retford Notts....51 P5
Rettendon Essex....22 F4
Revesby Lincs....53 J10
Rewe Devon....6 C3
Rew Street IoW....9 M8
Reymerston Norfk....44 G9
Reynalton Pembks....25 J7
Reynoldston Swans....26 C10
Rezare Cnwll....4 H5
Rhandirmwyn Carmth....37 M11
Rhayader Powys....37 Q7
Rheindown Highld....106 H11
Rhes-y-cae Flints....48 E2
Rhewl Denbgs....48 C4
Rhewl Denbgs....48 D6
Rhicarn Highld....108 C10
Rhiconich Highld....108 E5

Rhicullen Highld....107 L7
Rhigos Rhondd....27 K7
Rhireavach Highld....105 Q4
Rhives Highld....107 N3
Rhiwbina Cardif....27 N11
Rhiwderyn Newpt....28 B10
Rhiwlas Gwynd....54 H8
Rhoden Green Kent....12 D2
Rhodes Minnis Kent....13 M2
Rhodiad-y-brenin Pembks....24 D4
Rhonehouse D & G....70 C4
Rhoose V Glam....16 E3
Rhos Carmth....25 P2
Rhos Neath....26 G8
Rhoscolyn IoA....54 C6
Rhoscrowther Pembks....24 F8
Rhosesmor Flints....48 E2
Rhosgoch Powys....38 G11
Rhoshill Pembks....36 C11
Rhoshirwaun Gwynd....46 C5
Rhoslefain Gwynd....47 J9
Rhosllanerchrugog
  Wrexhm....48 F6
Rhosmeirch IoA....54 F6
Rhosneigr IoA....54 D7
Rhosnesni Wrexhm....48 G5
Rhôs-on-Sea Conwy....55 M5
Rhossili Swans....25 P10
Rhostryfan Gwynd....54 G9
Rhostyllen Wrexhm....48 F6
Rhosybol IoA....54 F4
Rhos-y-gwaliau Gwynd....47 Q4
Rhosymedre Wrexhm....48 F7
Rhu Ag & B....84 E6
Rhuallt Denbgs....48 C1
Rhubodach Ag & B....83 Q8
Rhuddlan Denbgs....55 Q6
Rhunahaorine Ag & B....75 K3
Rhyd Gwynd....47 K3
Rhydargaeau Carmth....25 Q4
Rhydcymerau Carmth....26 D2
Rhyd-Ddu Gwynd....54 H10
Rhydlewis Cerdgn....36 F10
Rhydowen Cerdgn....36 G10
Rhyd-uchaf Gwynd....47 P4
Rhyd-y-clafdy Gwynd....46 E4
Rhyd-y-foel Conwy....55 N6
Rhydyfro Neath....26 F7
Rhyd-y-groes Gwynd....54 H8
Rhyd-y-pennau Cerdgn....37 K4
Rhyl Denbgs....55 Q5
Rhymney Caerph....27 N7
Rhynd P & K....92 H10
Rhynie Abers....101 P9
Rhynie Highld....107 P6
Ribbesford Worcs....39 P7
Ribbleton Lancs....57 K3
Ribchester Lancs....57 M2
Riby Lincs....52 H3
Riccall N York....59 N6
Riccarton Border....79 Q9
Riccarton E Ayrs....76 G4
Richards Castle Herefs....39 J8
Richmond Gt Lon....21 J8
Richmond N York....65 L7
Richmond Sheff....51 K4
Rickerscote Staffs....40 B4
Rickford N Som....17 L4
Rickham Devon....5 P11
Rickinghall Suffk....34 H2
Rickling Green Essex....33 N10
Rickmansworth Herts....20 G5
Riddell Border....80 C8
Riddlecombe Devon....15 K8
Riddlesden C Brad....58 E5
Ridge Dorset....8 D9
Ridge Herts....21 K4
Ridge Wilts....8 D2
Ridge Lane Warwks....40 H8
Ridgeway Derbys....51 K5
Ridgewell Essex....34 C8
Ridgewood E Susx....11 P6
Ridgmont C Beds....32 D9
Riding Mill Nthumb....72 H8
Ridlington Norfk....45 M4
Ridlington Rutlnd....42 C9
Ridsdale Nthumb....72 G4
Rievaulx N York....66 F9
Rigg D & G....71 L3
Riggend N Lans....85 M8
Righoul Highld....100 D5
Rigsby Lincs....53 L8
Rigside S Lans....78 E2
Riley Green Lancs....57 L4
Rilla Mill Cnwll....4 G5
Rillington N York....67 J11
Rimington Lancs....63 P11
Rimpton Somset....17 N10
Rimswell E R Yk....61 M8
Rinaston Pembks....24 H4
Rindleford Shrops....39 N3
Ringford D & G....69 Q7
Ringland Norfk....45 J7
Ringmer E Susx....11 N7
Ringmore Devon....5 N10
Ringmore Devon....6 C8
Ringorm Moray....101 K6
Ringsfield Suffk....45 N11
Ringsfield Corner Suffk....45 N11
Ringshall Herts....20 F1
Ringshall Suffk....34 G6
Ringshall Stocks Suffk....34 H6
Ringstead Nhants....32 E2
Ringstead Norfk....44 B3
Ringwood Hants....8 H7
Ringwould Kent....13 Q1
Ripe E Susx....11 P8
Ripley Derbys....51 K10
Ripley Hants....8 H7
Ripley N York....58 H3
Ripley Surrey....20 G11
Riplington Hants....9 Q3
Ripon N York....65 N12
Rippingale Lincs....42 F5
Ripple Kent....13 Q12
Ripple Worcs....29 M2
Ripponden Calder....58 D9
Risabus Ag & B....74 D4
Risbury Herefs....39 K10
Risby Suffk....34 D4
Risca Caerph....27 P9
Rise E R Yk....61 K6
Risegate Lincs....42 H4
Riseley Bed....32 F4
Riseley Wokham....20 B10
Rishangles Suffk....35 J3
Rishton Lancs....57 N3

Rishworth Calder....58 D9
Risley Derbys....41 L11
Risley Warrtn....57 M9
Risplith N York....58 G2
River Kent....13 P2
River W Susx....10 F5
Riverford Highld....107 J10
Riverhead Kent....21 P11
Rivington Lancs....57 L6
Rivington Services Lancs....57 L6
Roade Nhants....31 Q4
Roadmeetings S Lans....77 P2
Roadside E Ayrs....77 K7
Roadside Highld....110 D4
Roadwater Somset....16 D8
Roag Highld....96 C2
Roan of Craigoch S Ayrs....76 E9
Roath Cardif....27 P12
Roberton Border....79 N6
Roberton S Lans....78 F3
Robertsbridge E Susx....12 E5
Robertstown Kirk....58 G10
Robeston Wathen
  Pembks....25 J5
Robgill Tower D & G....71 L2
Robin Hood
  Crematorium Solhll....40 E10
Robin Hood Doncaster
  Sheffield Airport Donc....51 P2
Robin Hood's Bay N York....67 K6
Roborough Devon....5 K7
Roborough Devon....15 K8
Roby Knows....56 H10
Rocester Staffs....50 E11
Roch Pembks....24 F5
Rochdale Rochdl....58 B10
Rochdale Crematorium
  Rochdl....57 Q9
Roche Cnwll....3 L4
Rochester Medway....22 E9
Rochester Nthumb....72 E2
Rochford Essex....22 G5
Rochford Worcs....39 L8
Rock Cnwll....3 L1
Rock Nthumb....81 P9
Rock Worcs....39 N7
Rockbeare Devon....6 D4
Rockbourne Hants....8 G4
Rockcliffe Cumb....71 M4
Rockcliffe D & G....70 D5
Rockend Torbay....6 C9
Rock Ferry Wirral....56 G10
Rockfield Highld....107 Q6
Rockfield Mons....28 F6
Rockford Devon....15 N3
Rockhampton S Glos....28 H9
Rockhill Shrops....38 F6
Rockingham Nhants....42 C10
Rockland All Saints Norfk....44 G10
Rockland St Mary Norfk....45 M8
Rockland St Peter Norfk....44 G9
Rockley Notts....51 Q6
Rockville Ag & B....84 D5
Rockwell End Bucks....20 C6
Rodborough Gloucs....29 L7
Rodbourne Swindn....18 G4
Rodbourne Wilts....18 D3
Rodden Dorset....7 N6
Rode Somset....18 B9
Rode Heath Ches E....49 P4
Rodel W Isls....111 c4
Roden Wrekin....49 L11
Rodhuish Somset....16 D8
Rodington Wrekin....49 L11
Rodington Heath Wrekin....49 L11
Rodley Gloucs....29 K6
Rodmarton Gloucs....29 N8
Rodmell E Susx....11 N8
Rodmersham Kent....22 H10
Rodmersham Green Kent....22 H10
Rodney Stoke Somset....17 L6
Rodsley Derbys....50 G11
Roecliffe N York....59 J2
Roe Green Herts....21 K2
Roe Green Herts....33 K9
Roehampton Gt Lon....21 K8
Roffey W Susx....11 K4
Rogart Highld....107 M2
Rogate W Susx....10 D5
Rogerstone Newpt....28 C10
Roghadal W Isls....111 c4
Rogiet Mons....28 E10
Roke Oxon....19 Q3
Roker Sundld....73 P8
Rollesby Norfk....45 P7
Rolleston Leics....41 Q7
Rolleston Notts....51 Q9
Rolleston on Dove Staffs....40 G3
Rolston E R Yk....61 L5
Rolvenden Kent....12 G4
Rolvenden Layne Kent....12 G4
Romaldkirk Dur....64 H3
Romanby N York....65 P8
Romanno Bridge Border....86 D11
Romansleigh Devon....15 M7
Romesdal Highld....104 E10
Romford Dorset....8 F5
Romford Gt Lon....21 P5
Romiley Stockp....50 C3
Romsey Cambs....33 M5
Romsey Hants....9 L3
Romsley Shrops....39 P5
Romsley Worcs....40 C10
Rona Highld....105 J10
Ronachan Ag & B....83 L11
Rookhope Dur....72 G11
Rookley IoW....9 N9
Rooks Bridge Somset....17 K5
Rooks Nest Somset....16 E9
Rookwith N York....65 L9
Roos E R Yk....61 M7
Roothams Green Bed....32 F5
Ropley Hants....9 Q2
Ropley Dean Hants....9 Q2
Ropsley Lincs....42 D3
Rora Abers....103 L5
Rorrington Shrops....38 F3
Rosarie Moray....101 M5
Rose Cnwll....2 H5
Rose Ash Devon....15 N7
Rosebank S Lans....77 N2
Rosebush Pembks....25 J3
Rosedale Abbey N York....66 H7
Rose Green Essex....34 E10
Rose Green Suffk....34 F7
Rose Green Suffk....34 F7
Rose Green W Susx....10 E9

Rishworth Calder....58 D9
Rosehall Highld....106 H2
Rosehearty Abers....103 J2
Rose Hill Lancs....57 P3
Rose Hill Crematorium
  Donc....51 N1
Roseisle Moray....100 H2
Roselands E Susx....12 C9
Rosemarket Pembks....24 G7
Rosemarkie Highld....107 M10
Rosemary Lane Devon....16 F12
Rosemount P & K....92 H7
Rosenannon Cnwll....3 L3
Rosewell Mdloth....86 F9
Roseworth S on T....65 Q3
Rosgill Cumb....71 Q11
Roskhill Highld....96 C1
Rosley Cumb....71 M6
Roslin Mdloth....86 F9
Rosliston Derbys....40 G4
Rosneath Ag & B....84 E6
Ross D & G....69 P9
Rossett Wrexhm....48 G4
Rossett Green N York....58 H4
Rossington Donc....51 N2
Rossland Rens....84 G8
Ross-on-Wye Herefs....28 H4
Roster Highld....110 F7
Rostherne Ches E....57 N11
Rosthwaite Cumb....71 L11
Roston Derbys....50 F11
Rosyth Fife....86 D5
Rothbury Nthumb....73 J1
Rotherby Leics....41 P4
Rotherfield E Susx....12 B4
Rotherfield Greys Oxon....20 B7
Rotherfield Peppard
  Oxon....20 B7
Rotherham Rothm....51 K3
Rotherham
  Crematorium Rothm....51 L3
Rothersthorpe Nhants....31 Q3
Rotherwick Hants....20 B11
Rothes Moray....101 K5
Rothesay Ag & B....84 B9
Rothiebrisbane Abers....102 G7
Rothiemay Moray....102 D5
Rothiemurchus Lodge
  Highld....99 P7
Rothiemurchus Visitor
  Centre Highld....99 N6
Rothienorman Abers....102 F7
Rothley Leics....41 N5
Rothmaise Abers....102 F8
Rothwell Leeds....59 J8
Rothwell Lincs....52 G4
Rothwell Nhants....32 B1
Rottal Lodge Angus....94 F7
Rottingdean Br & H....11 M9
Rottington Cumb....70 F11
Roucan D & G....78 G12
Roucan Loch
  Crematorium D & G....78 G12
Rougham Norfk....44 D6
Rougham Suffk....34 E4
Rough Common Kent....23 L10
Roughpark Abers....101 L11
Roughton Lincs....53 J9
Roughton Norfk....45 K3
Roughton Shrops....39 N4
Roundbush Green Essex....22 C1
Round Green Luton....32 F11
Roundham Somset....7 K2
Roundhay Leeds....59 J6
Rounds Green Sandw....40 C9
Roundswell Devon....15 J6
Roundway Wilts....18 E7
Roundyhill Angus....93 L5
Rousay Ork....111 h1
Rousdon Devon....6 H5
Rousham Oxon....31 L8
Rous Lench Worcs....30 D4
Routenburn N Ayrs....84 D10
Routh E R Yk....61 J6
Row Cumb....63 J4
Rowanburn D & G....79 N12
Rowardennan Stirlg....84 F4
Rowarth Derbys....50 D3
Rowberrow Somset....17 L5
Rowde Wilts....18 E8
Rowen Conwy....55 L7
Rowfoot Nthumb....72 C8
Rowhedge Essex....34 G11
Rowington Warwks....40 G12
Rowland Derbys....50 G6
Rowland's Castle Hants....10 B7
Rowlands Gill Gatesd....73 L8
Rowledge Surrey....10 D2
Rowley Dur....73 J10
Rowley Regis Sandw....40 C9
Rowley Regis
  Crematorium Sandw....40 C9
Rowlstone Herefs....28 D4
Rowly Surrey....10 G2
Rowner Hants....9 P7
Rowney Green Worcs....40 D12
Rownhams Hants....9 L4
Rownhams Services Hants....9 L4
Rowrah Cumb....70 H10
Rowsham Bucks....32 C12
Rowsley Derbys....50 G7
Rowston Lincs....52 F11
Rowton Ches W....49 J3
Rowton Wrekin....49 L10
Roxburgh Border....80 F7
Roxby N Linc....60 F10
Roxton Bed....32 G6
Roxwell Essex....22 D2
Royal Leamington Spa
  Warwks....30 H2
Royal Sutton Coldfield
  Birm....40 E8
Royal Tunbridge Wells
  Kent....12 C3
Royal Wootton Bassett
  Wilts....18 F4
Royal Yacht Britannia
  C Edin....86 F6
Roy Bridge Highld....98 C11
Roydon Essex....21 N2
Roydon Norfk....34 H1
Roydon Norfk....44 B5
Roydon Hamlet Essex....21 N2
Royston Barns....59 J11
Royston Herts....33 K8
Royton Oldham....58 B11
Rozel Jersey....7 c1
Ruabon Wrexhm....48 F6

Ruaig Ag & B 88 D6
Ruan Lanihorne Cnwll 3 K7
Ruan Major Cnwll 2 G11
Ruan Minor Cnwll 2 G11
Ruardean Gloucs 28 H5
Ruardean Hill Gloucs 28 H5
Ruardean Woodside Gloucs 28 H5
Rubery Birm 40 C11
Rubha Ban W Isls 111 b6
Ruckhall Herefs 28 E2
Ruckinge Kent 13 K4
Ruckley Shrops 39 K3
Rudby N York 66 C6
Rudchester Nthumb 73 K7
Ruddington Notts 41 M2
Rudge Somset 18 C9
Rudgeway S Glos 28 H10
Rudgwick W Susx 10 H4
Rudheath Ches W 49 M2
Rudley Green Essex 22 G3
Rudloe Wilts 18 C6
Rudry Caerph 27 P10
Rudston E R Yk 61 J1
Rudyard Staffs 50 C8
Ruecastle Border 80 E9
Rufford Lancs 57 J6
Rufford Abbey Notts 51 N7
Rufforth C York 59 M4
Rugby Warwks 41 L11
Rugeley Staffs 40 D4
Ruishton Somset 16 H10
Ruislip Gt Lon 20 H6
Rùm Highld 96 D9
Rumbach Moray 101 M5
Rumbling Bridge P & K 86 B3
Rumburgh Suffk 35 M1
Rumford Cnwll 3 K2
Rumford Falk 85 Q7
Rumney Cardif 27 P11
Runcorn Halton 57 K11
Runcton W Susx 10 E9
Runcton Holme Norfk 43 P8
Runfold Surrey 10 D1
Runhall Norfk 44 H8
Runham Norfk 45 P7
Runnington Somset 16 F10
Runswick N York 66 H4
Runtaleave Angus 94 E8
Runway Visitor Park Manch 57 P11
Runwell Essex 22 F5
Ruscombe Wokham 20 C8
Rushall Herefs 28 H2
Rushall Norfk 45 K12
Rushall Wilts 18 G9
Rushall Wsall 40 D7
Rushbrooke Suffk 34 E5
Rushbury Shrops 39 K4
Rushden Herts 33 K9
Rushden Nhants 32 D4
Rushenden Kent 22 H8
Rushford Norfk 34 F1
Rush Green Essex 23 M1
Rush Green Gt Lon 21 P6
Rush Green Warrtn 57 M10
Rushlake Green E Susx 12 D6
Rushmere Suffk 45 P11
Rushmoor Surrey 10 E3
Rushock Worcs 40 B12
Rusholme Manch 57 Q9
Rushton Nhants 42 B12
Rushton Spencer Staffs 50 C8
Rushwick Worcs 39 P10
Rushyford Dur 65 M2
Ruskie Stirlg 85 K3
Ruskington Lincs 52 F12
Rusland Cross Cumb 62 G5
Rusper W Susx 11 K3
Ruspidge Gloucs 29 J6
Russell's Water Oxon 20 B5
Russ Hill Surrey 11 K3
Rusthall Kent 12 C3
Rustington W Susx 10 G9
Ruston N York 67 K10
Ruston Parva E R Yk 60 H2
Ruswarp N York 67 J5
Rutherford Border 80 E7
Rutherglen S Lans 85 K10
Ruthernbridge Cnwll 3 M3
Ruthin Denbgs 48 D4
Ruthrieston C Aber 95 Q2
Ruthven Abers 101 P6
Ruthven Angus 93 K6
Ruthven Highld 99 L8
Ruthvoes Cnwll 3 K4
Ruthwell D & G 70 H3
Ruyton-XI-Towns Shrops 48 H10
Ryal Nthumb 72 H6
Ryall Dorset 7 K4
Ryall Worcs 29 M1
Ryarsh Kent 22 D10
Rydal Cumb 62 G2
Ryde IoW 9 P8
Rye E Susx 12 H6
Rye Foreign E Susx 12 H5
Rye Street Worcs 29 M2
Ryhall Rutlnd 42 E7
Ryhill Wakefd 59 J10
Ryhope Sundld 73 P9
Ryland Lincs 52 E7
Rylands Notts 41 M1
Rylstone N York 58 C3
Ryme Intrinseca Dorset 7 N1
Ryther N York 59 M6
Ryton Gatesd 73 K7
Ryton Shrops 39 N2
Ryton-on-Dunsmore Warwks 41 J11

**S**

Sabden Lancs 57 P2
Sacombe Herts 33 K11
Sacriston Dur 73 M10
Sadberge Darltn 65 N4
Saddell Ag & B 75 L6
Saddington Leics 41 P8
Saddle Bow Norfk 43 P7
Saddlescombe W Susx 11 L8
Saffron Walden Essex 33 N8
Sageston Pembks 25 J7
Saham Hills Norfk 44 E9
Saham Toney Norfk 44 E9
Saighton Ches W 49 J3

St Abbs Border 81 J1
St Agnes Border 87 H8
St Agnes Cnwll 2 G5
St Agnes IoS 2 b3
St Agnes Mining District Cnwll 2 G6
St Albans Herts 21 J2
St Allen Cnwll 3 J5
St Andrew Guern 6 b2
St Andrews Fife 93 N11
St Andrews Botanic Garden Fife 93 N11
St Andrew's Major V Glam 16 F2
St Andrews Well Dorset 7 L4
St Anne's Lancs 56 G3
St Ann's Chapel Cnwll 5 J6
St Ann's Chapel Devon 5 N10
St Anthony Cnwll 2 H10
St Anthony's Hill E Susx 12 D9
St Arvans Mons 28 F9
St Asaph Denbgs 48 B1
St Athan V Glam 16 D3
St Aubin Jersey 7 b2
St Austell Cnwll 3 M5
St Bees Cumb 70 F12
St Blazey Cnwll 3 N5
St Boswells Border 80 D7
St Brelade Jersey 7 a2
St Brelade's Bay Jersey 7 a2
St Breock Cnwll 3 L2
St Breward Cnwll 4 D5
St Briavels Gloucs 28 G7
St Brides Major V Glam 16 B2
St Brides-super-Ely V Glam 27 M12
St Brides Wentlooge Newpt 28 C11
St Budeaux C Plym 5 K8
Saintbury Gloucs 30 E6
St Buryan Cnwll 2 C9
St Catherines Ag & B 84 C2
St Chloe Gloucs 29 L8
St Clears Carmth 25 M5
St Cleer Cnwll 4 F6
St Clement Cnwll 3 J7
St Clement Jersey 7 c2
St Clether Cnwll 4 F4
St Colmac Ag & B 83 Q9
St Columb Major Cnwll 3 K3
St Columb Minor Cnwll 3 J4
St Columb Road Cnwll 3 K4
St Combs Abers 103 L3
St Cross South Elmham Suffk 45 L12
St Cyrus Abers 95 M8
St David's P & K 92 E10
St Davids Pembks 24 D4
St Davids Cathedral Pembks 24 D4
St Day Cnwll 2 G7
St Dennis Cnwll 3 L4
St Dogmaels Pembks 36 C10
St Dominick Cnwll 5 J6
St Donats V Glam 16 C3
St Endellion Cnwll 4 C5
St Enoder Cnwll 3 K4
St Erme Cnwll 3 J6
St Erney Cnwll 4 H8
St Erth Cnwll 2 E8
St Erth Praze Cnwll 2 E8
St Ervan Cnwll 3 K2
St Eval Cnwll 3 K3
St Ewe Cnwll 3 L6
St Fagans Cardif 27 N12
St Fagans: National History Museum Cardif 27 N12
St Fergus Abers 103 M5
St Fillans P & K 91 Q10
St Florence Pembks 25 J8
St Gennys Cnwll 14 C11
St George Conwy 55 P6
St Georges N Som 17 K4
St George's V Glam 16 E2
St Germans Cnwll 4 H8
St Giles in the Wood Devon 15 J8
St Giles-on-the-Heath Devon 4 H3
St Harmon Powys 38 B7
St Helen Auckland Dur 65 L3
St Helen's E Susx 12 G7
St Helens IoW 9 Q9
St Helens St Hel 57 K9
St Helens Crematorium St Hel 57 J9
St Helier Gt Lon 21 L9
St Helier Jersey 7 b2
St Hilary Cnwll 2 E8
St Hilary V Glam 16 D2
St Ippolitts Herts 32 H10
St Ishmael's Pembks 24 E7
St Issey Cnwll 3 L2
St Ive Cnwll 4 G6
St Ives Cambs 33 K3
St Ives Cnwll 2 D7
St James's End Nhants 31 Q3
St James South Elmham Suffk 35 M1
St Jidgey Cnwll 3 L3
St John Cnwll 5 J9
St John Jersey 7 b1
St John's IoM 56 b5
St Johns Kent 21 Q11
St Johns Surrey 20 F10
St Johns Worcs 39 Q10
St John's Chapel Devon 15 J6
St John's Chapel Dur 72 F12
St John's Fen End Norfk 43 N7
St John's Kirk S Lans 78 H2
St John's Town of Dalry D & G 69 N3
St John's Wood Gt Lon 21 L6
St Just Cnwll 2 B9
St Just-in-Roseland Cnwll 3 J8
St Just Mining District Cnwll 2 B8
St Katherines Abers 102 G8
St Keverne Cnwll 2 H10
St Kew Cnwll 4 D4
St Kew Highway Cnwll 3 M1
St Keyne Cnwll 4 F7
St Lawrence Essex 23 J3
St Lawrence IoW 9 N11
St Lawrence Jersey 7 b1
St Lawrence Kent 23 Q9

St Leonards Bucks 20 E3
St Leonards Dorset 8 G6
St Leonards E Susx 12 F8
St Levan Cnwll 2 B10
St Lythans V Glam 16 F2
St Mabyn Cnwll 3 M2
St Madoes P & K 92 H10
St Margarets Herefs 28 D3
St Margarets Herts 21 M2
St Margaret's at Cliffe Kent 13 Q2
St Margaret's Hope Ork 111 h3
St Margaret South Elmham Suffk 45 M12
St Marks IoM 56 c6
St Martin Cnwll 2 H10
St Martin Cnwll 4 G8
St Martin Guern 6 b2
St Martin Jersey 7 c1
St Martin's IoS 2 c1
St Martin's P & K 92 H9
St Martin's Shrops 48 G8
St Mary Jersey 7 a1
St Mary Bourne Hants 19 M10
St Marychurch Torbay 6 C9
St Mary Church V Glam 16 D2
St Mary Cray Gt Lon 21 P9
St Mary in the Marsh Kent 13 K5
St Marylebone Crematorium Gt Lon 21 L5
St Mary's IoS 2 c2
St Mary's Ork 111 h2
St Mary's Bay Kent 13 L5
St Mary's Hoo Medway 22 F7
St Maughans Green Mons 28 F5
St Mawes Cnwll 3 J8
St Mawgan Cnwll 3 K3
St Mellion Cnwll 5 J6
St Mellons Cardif 27 P11
St Merryn Cnwll 3 K2
St Michael Caerhays Cnwll 3 L7
St Michael Church Somset 17 J9
St Michael Penkevil Cnwll 3 J7
St Michaels Kent 12 H3
St Michaels Worcs 39 L8
St Michael's Mount Cnwll 2 D9
St Michael's on Wyre Lancs 57 J1
St Minver Cnwll 3 L1
St Monans Fife 87 K2
St Neot Cnwll 4 E6
St Neots Cambs 32 H5
St Newlyn East Cnwll 3 J5
St Nicholas Pembks 24 F2
St Nicholas V Glam 16 E2
St Nicholas at Wade Kent 23 N9
St Ninians Stirlg 85 N5
St Olaves Norfk 45 P9
St Osyth Essex 23 L1
St Ouen Jersey 7 a1
St Owens Cross Herefs 28 G4
St Paul's Cray Gt Lon 21 P9
St Paul's Walden Herts 32 H11
St Peter Jersey 7 a1
St Peter Port Guern 6 c2
St Peter's Guern 6 b2
St Peter's Kent 23 Q9
St Peter's Hill Cambs 33 J3
St Pinnock Cnwll 4 F7
St Quivox S Ayrs 76 F6
St Sampson Guern 6 c1
St Saviour Guern 6 b2
St Saviour Jersey 7 b2
St Stephen Cnwll 3 L5
St Stephens Cnwll 4 H3
St Stephens Cnwll 5 J8
St Teath Cnwll 4 D4
St Tudy Cnwll 3 N1
St Twynnells Pembks 24 G8
St Veep Cnwll 4 E8
St Vigeans Angus 93 Q7
St Wenn Cnwll 3 L3
St Weonards Herefs 28 F4
Salcey Forest Nhants 32 B6
Salcombe Devon 5 P11
Salcombe Regis Devon 6 F5
Salcott-cum-Virley Essex 23 J1
Sale Traffd 57 P9
Saleby Lincs 53 M7
Sale Green Worcs 30 B3
Salehurst E Susx 12 E5
Salem Cerdgn 37 L4
Salen Ag & B 89 M7
Salen Highld 89 N4
Salford C Beds 32 D8
Salford Oxon 30 H8
Salford Salfd 57 P8
Salford Priors Warwks 30 E4
Salfords Surrey 11 L2
Salhouse Norfk 45 M7
Saline Fife 86 B4
Salisbury Wilts 8 G2
Salisbury Crematorium Wilts 8 H2
Salisbury Plain Wilts 18 F10
Salkeld Dykes Cumb 71 Q3
Salle Norfk 45 J5
Salmonby Lincs 53 K8
Salperton Gloucs 30 E9
Salt Staffs 40 C2
Saltaire C Brad 58 F6
Saltaire C Brad 58 F6
Saltash Cnwll 5 J8
Saltburn Highld 107 M8
Saltburn-by-the-Sea R & Cl 66 F4
Saltby Leics 42 C5
Saltcoats N Ayrs 76 D3
Saltdean Br & H 11 M9
Salterbeck Cumb 70 G9
Salterforth Lancs 58 B5
Salterton Wilts 18 G12
Saltfleet Lincs 53 M5
Saltfleetby All Saints Lincs 53 M5
Saltfleetby St Clement Lincs 53 M5
Saltfleetby St Peter Lincs 53 M5
Saltford BaNES 17 P3
Salthouse Norfk 44 H2
Saltley Birm 40 E9
Saltmarsh E R Yk 60 D8
Saltney Flints 48 H3
Salton N York 66 G10
Saltrens Devon 14 H7
Saltwell Crematorium Gatesd 73 M8

Saltwood Kent 13 M3
Salvington W Susx 10 H8
Salwarpe Worcs 39 Q9
Salway Ash Dorset 7 L4
Sambourne Warwks 30 D2
Sambrook Wrekin 49 N9
Sampford Arundel Somset 16 F11
Sampford Brett Somset 16 E7
Sampford Courtenay Devon 15 L11
Sampford Moor Somset 16 F11
Sampford Peverell Devon 16 D12
Sampford Spiney Devon 5 L6
Samsonlane Ork 111 i2
Samuelston E Loth 87 J7
Sanaigmore Ag & B 82 C8
Sancreed Cnwll 2 C9
Sancton E R Yk 60 F6
Sandaig Highld 97 K8
Sandal Magna Wakefd 59 J9
Sandavore Highld 96 F11
Sanday Ork 111 i1
Sanday Airport Ork 111 i1
Sandbach Ches E 49 N4
Sandbach Services Ches E 49 P4
Sandbank Ag & B 84 C6
Sandbanks Poole 8 F9
Sandend Abers 102 D3
Sanderstead Gt Lon 21 M10
Sandford Cumb 64 D4
Sandford Devon 15 P10
Sandford Dorset 8 D9
Sandford Hants 8 H7
Sandford IoW 9 N10
Sandford N Som 17 K4
Sandford S Lans 77 M3
Sandford-on-Thames Oxon 19 N1
Sandford Orcas Dorset 17 P11
Sandford St Martin Oxon 31 K8
Sandgate Kent 13 M3
Sandhaven Abers 103 K2
Sandhead D & G 68 E8
Sand Hills Leeds 59 J6
Sandhills Oxon 31 M11
Sandhills Surrey 10 F3
Sandhoe Nthumb 72 H7
Sandhole Ag & B 83 Q4
Sand Hole E R Yk 60 D6
Sandholme E R Yk 60 E7
Sandhurst Br For 20 D10
Sandhurst Gloucs 29 L4
Sandhurst Kent 12 F4
Sand Hutton N York 59 P3
Sandhutton N York 65 P10
Sandiacre Derbys 51 L12
Sandilands Lincs 53 N7
Sandleheath Hants 8 G4
Sandleigh Oxon 19 M1
Sandley Dorset 8 B3
Sandness Shet 111 j4
Sandon Essex 22 E3
Sandon Herts 33 K9
Sandon Staffs 40 C2
Sandon Bank Staffs 40 C2
Sandown IoW 9 P9
Sandplace Cnwll 4 F8
Sandridge Herts 21 J2
Sandringham Norfk 44 B4
Sandsend N York 67 J5
Sandtoft N Linc 60 D11
Sandway Kent 22 H12
Sandwell Valley Crematorium Sandw 40 D8
Sandwich Kent 23 P10
Sandwick Shet 111 k5
Sandwick W Isls 111 d2
Sandwith Cumb 70 F11
Sandy C Beds 32 G7
Sandyford D & G 79 K9
Sandygate Devon 6 B7
Sandygate IoM 56 d3
Sandyhills D & G 70 E5
Sandylands Lancs 62 H9
Sandy Lane Wilts 18 E7
Sandy Park Devon 5 P3
Sangobeg Highld 108 H3
Sangomore Highld 108 H3
Sankyn's Green Worcs 39 P8
Sanna Bay Highld 89 K3
Sanndabhaig W Isls 111 d2
Sannox N Ayrs 75 Q4
Sanquhar D & G 77 N8
Santon Bridge Cumb 62 C2
Santon Downham Suffk 44 D11
Sapcote Leics 41 L8
Sapey Common Herefs 39 M8
Sapiston Suffk 34 F2
Sapperton Gloucs 29 N7
Sapperton Lincs 42 E4
Saracen's Head Lincs 43 K5
Sarclet Highld 110 G7
Sarisbury Hants 9 N5
Sarn Gwynd 46 D5
Sarn Powys 38 E4
Sarn Powys 47 Q10
Sarnau Cerdgn 36 F9
Sarnau Powys 48 E11
Sarn Park Services Brdgnd 27 J11
Saron Carmth 26 D6
Saron Gwynd 54 G8
Sarratt Herts 20 G4
Sarre Kent 23 N9
Sarsden Oxon 30 H9
Satley Dur 73 K11
Satterleigh Devon 15 L7
Satterthwaite Cumb 62 G4
Sauchen Abers 102 F11
Saucher P & K 92 H8
Sauchieburn Abers 95 L7
Saul Gloucs 29 K7
Saundby Notts 52 B6
Saundersfoot Pembks 25 K7
Saunderton Bucks 20 C3
Saunton Devon 14 H5
Sausthorpe Lincs 53 L9
Savile Town Kirk 58 G9
Sawbridge Warwks 31 L2
Sawbridgeworth Herts 21 P1
Sawdon N York 67 K9
Sawley Derbys 51 L12
Sawley Lancs 63 P11
Sawley N York 58 G1
Sawston Cambs 33 M7
Sawtry Cambs 42 G12
Saxby Leics 42 B6

Saxby Lincs 52 E6
Saxby All Saints N Linc 60 G10
Saxelbye Leics 41 P4
Saxham Street Suffk 34 H5
Saxilby Lincs 52 C8
Saxlingham Norfk 44 G3
Saxlingham Green Norfk 45 L10
Saxlingham Nethergate Norfk 45 K10
Saxlingham Thorpe Norfk 45 K9
Saxmundham Suffk 35 N4
Saxondale Notts 51 P11
Saxon Street Cambs 34 B5
Saxtead Suffk 35 L4
Saxtead Green Suffk 35 L4
Saxtead Little Green Suffk 35 L4
Saxthorpe Norfk 45 J4
Saxton N York 59 L6
Sayers Common W Susx 11 L6
Scackleton N York 66 F11
Scafell Pike Cumb 62 E2
Scaftworth Notts 51 P3
Scagglethorpe N York 67 J11
Scalasaig Ag & B 82 E4
Scalby E R Yk 60 E8
Scalby N York 67 L9
Scaldwell Nhants 41 Q11
Scaleby Cumb 71 P3
Scalebyhill Cumb 71 P3
Scales Cumb 62 F7
Scales Cumb 71 M9
Scalford Leics 41 Q3
Scaling N York 66 G5
Scalloway Shet 111 k4
Scalpay Highld 96 H4
Scamblesby Lincs 53 J7
Scamodale Highld 90 B2
Scampston N York 67 J11
Scampton Lincs 52 D7
Scaniport Highld 99 J2
Scapegoat Hill Kirk 58 E10
Scarba Ag & B 83 K3
Scarborough N York 67 M9
Scarcewater Cnwll 3 K5
Scarcliffe Derbys 51 L7
Scarcroft Leeds 59 J6
Scarfskerry Highld 110 F2
Scarinish Ag & B 88 C7
Scarisbrick Lancs 56 H6
Scarning Norfk 44 F7
Scarrington Notts 51 Q11
Scartho NE Lin 53 J3
Scatsta Airport Shet 111 k3
Scawby N Linc 52 D7
Scawsby Donc 59 M12
Scawthorpe Donc 59 M11
Scawton N York 66 D10
Scayne's Hill W Susx 11 M5
Scethrog Powys 27 M4
Scholar Green Ches E 49 Q4
Scholemoor Crematorium C Brad 58 F7
Scholes Kirk 58 F11
Scholes Leeds 59 J6
Scholes Rothm 51 K2
Scholes Wigan 57 L7
Scissett Kirk 58 G11
Scleddau Pembks 24 G2
Scofton Notts 51 N5
Scole Norfk 35 J2
Scone P & K 92 H9
Sconser Highld 96 F4
Scoonie Fife 86 H2
Scopwick Lincs 52 F11
Scoraig Highld 105 Q3
Scorborough E R Yk 60 H5
Scorrier Cnwll 2 G7
Scorton Lancs 63 J11
Scorton N York 65 M7
Scotby Cumb 71 P5
Scotch Corner N York 65 L6
Scotforth Lancs 63 J9
Scothern Lincs 52 E7
Scotlandwell P & K 86 E2
Scotscalder Station Highld 110 C5
Scot's Gap Nthumb 73 J4
Scotsmill Abers 102 D10
Scotstoun C Glas 85 J9
Scotswood N u Ty 73 L7
Scotter Lincs 52 C4
Scotterthorpe Lincs 52 C3
Scottish Seabird Centre E Loth 87 K5
Scottish Wool Centre Stirlg 85 J3
Scotton Lincs 52 C4
Scotton N York 59 J3
Scotton N York 65 L8
Scoulton Norfk 44 G9
Scourie Highld 108 D6
Scourie More Highld 108 D7
Scousburgh Shet 111 k5
Scrabster Highld 110 C2
Scraesburgh Border 80 F9
Scrane End Lincs 43 L2
Scraptoft Leics 41 P6
Scratby Norfk 45 Q7
Scrayingham N York 60 C3
Scredington Lincs 42 F3
Scremby Lincs 53 M9
Scremerston Nthumb 81 L4
Screveton Notts 51 Q11
Scriven N York 59 J3
Scrooby Notts 51 P3
Scropton Derbys 40 G2
Scrub Hill Lincs 53 K11
Scruton N York 65 N8
Scullomie Highld 109 L4
Sculthorpe Norfk 44 E4
Scunthorpe N Linc 60 D11
Seaborough Dorset 7 K2
Seabridge Staffs 49 Q6
Seabrook Kent 13 M3
Seaburn Sundld 73 P8
Seacombe Wirral 56 G10
Seacroft Leeds 59 J7
Seafield Highld 96 F2
Seafield W Loth 86 B8
Seafield Crematorium C Edin 86 F7
Seaford E Susx 11 P9
Seaforth Sefton 56 G9
Seagrave Leics 41 N4
Seaham Dur 73 P10
Seahouses Nthumb 81 P7
Seal Kent 22 B11

Sealand - Somerford Keynes 193


**Sealand** Flints 48 G2
**Seale** Surrey 10 E1
**Seamer** N York 66 C5
**Seamer** N York 67 L10
**Seamill** N Ayrs 76 D2
**Sea Palling** Norfk 45 N5
**Searby** Lincs 52 F3
**Seasalter** Kent 23 L9
**Seascale** Cumb 62 B3
**Seathwaite** Cumb 62 E3
**Seatoller** Cumb 71 L11
**Seaton** Cnwll 4 G8
**Seaton** Cumb 70 G8
**Seaton** Devon 6 H5
**Seaton** E R Yk 61 K5
**Seaton** Kent 23 N10
**Seaton** Nthumb 73 N5
**Seaton** Rutlnd 42 C9
**Seaton Carew** Hartpl 66 D2
**Seaton Delaval** Nthumb 73 N6
**Seaton Ross** E R Yk 60 D6
**Seaton Sluice** Nthumb 73 N5
**Seatown** Dorset 7 K4
**Seave Green** N York 66 D7
**Seaview** IoW 9 Q8
**Seaville** Cumb 71 J5
**Seavington St Mary** Somset 17 K12
**Seavington St Michael** Somset 17 K12
**Sebergham** Cumb 71 M7
**Seckington** Warwks 40 H6
**Sedbergh** Cumb 63 M4
**Sedbury** Gloucs 28 G9
**Sedbusk** N York 64 F8
**Sedgeberrow** Worcs 30 D6
**Sedgebrook** Lincs 42 C3
**Sedgefield** Dur 65 P2
**Sedgeford** Norfk 44 B3
**Sedgehill** Wilts 8 C2
**Sedgemoor Crematorium** Somset 16 H7
Sedgemoor Services Somset 17 J5
**Sedgley** Dudley 40 B8
**Sedgley Park** Bury 57 P8
**Sedgwick** Cumb 63 K5
**Sedlescombe** E Susx 12 F6
**Sedrup** Bucks 20 C2
**Seend** Wilts 18 D8
**Seend Cleeve** Wilts 18 D8
**Seer Green** Bucks 20 F5
**Seething** Norfk 45 M9
**Sefton** Sefton 56 G8
**Seighford** Staffs 49 Q9
**Seion** Gwynd 54 H8
**Seisdon** Staffs 39 Q3
**Selattyn** Shrops 48 F8
**Selborne** Hants 10 C4
**Selby** N York 59 N7
**Selham** W Susx 10 E6
**Selhurst** Gt Lon 21 M9
**Selkirk** Border 79 P3
**Sellack** Herefs 28 G4
**Sellafield Station** Cumb 62 B2
**Sellafirth** Shet 111 k2
**Sellindge** Kent 13 L3
**Selling** Kent 23 K11
**Sells Green** Wilts 18 D8
**Selly Oak** Birm 40 D10
**Selmeston** E Susx 11 P8
**Selsdon** Gt Lon 21 M10
**Selsey** Gloucs 29 L7
**Selsey** W Susx 10 D10
**Selside** N York 64 E11
**Selsted** Kent 13 N2
**Selston** Notts 51 L9
**Selworthy** Somset 16 C6
**Semer** Suffk 34 G7
**Semington** Wilts 18 D8
**Semley** Wilts 8 D3
**Send** Surrey 20 G11
**Senghenydd** Caerph 27 N10
**Sennen** Cnwll 2 B10
**Sennen Cove** Cnwll 2 B9
**Sennybridge** Powys 27 K3
**Sessay** N York 66 C11
**Setchey** Norfk 43 Q7
**Seton Mains** E Loth 87 J7
**Settle** N York 63 P9
**Settrington** N York 67 J12
**Sevenhampton** Gloucs 30 D9
**Sevenhampton** Swindn 18 H3
**Seven Hills Crematorium** Suffk 35 K8
**Seven Kings** Gt Lon 21 P6
**Sevenoaks** Kent 21 Q11
**Sevenoaks Weald** Kent 21 Q12
**Seven Sisters** Neath 26 H7
**Seven Star Green** Essex 34 F10
**Severn Beach** S Glos 28 G10
**Severn Stoke** Worcs 39 Q12
Severn View Services S Glos 28 G10
**Sevington** Kent 13 K2
**Sewards End** Essex 33 P8
**Sewell** C Beds 32 E11
**Sewerby** E R Yk 61 L1
**Seworgan** Cnwll 2 G9
**Sewstern** Leics 42 C6
**Sgiogarstaigh** W Isls 111 e1
**Shabbington** Bucks 31 P11
**Shackerstone** Leics 41 J6
**Shackleford** Surrey 10 E2
**Shader** W Isls 111 d1
**Shadforth** Dur 73 N11
**Shadingfield** Suffk 45 P12
**Shadoxhurst** Kent 13 J3
**Shadwell** Norfk 44 F12
**Shaftenhoe End** Herts 33 L8
**Shaftesbury** Dorset 8 C3
**Shafton** Barns 59 K11
**Shakerley** Wigan 57 M8
**Shalbourne** Wilts 19 K7
**Shalden** Hants 10 B2
**Shaldon** Devon 6 C8
**Shalfleet** IoW 9 M9
**Shalford** Essex 34 C10
**Shalford** Surrey 10 G1
**Shalford Green** Essex 34 B10
**Shalmsford Street** Kent 23 L11
**Shalstone** Bucks 31 N6
**Shamley Green** Surrey 10 G2
**Shandford** Angus 94 H9
**Shandon** Ag & B 84 E6
**Shandwick** Highld 107 P7
**Shangton** Leics 41 Q8
**Shanklin** IoW 9 P10
**Shap** Cumb 71 Q11
**Shapinsay** Ork 111 h2
**Shapwick** Dorset 8 D7
**Shapwick** Somset 17 K8
**Shard End** Birm 40 F9
**Shardlow** Derbys 41 K2
**Shareshill** Staffs 40 C6
**Sharlston** Wakefd 59 K9
**Sharman's Cross** Solhll 40 F10
**Sharnbrook** Bed 32 E5
**Sharnford** Leics 41 L8
**Sharoe Green** Lancs 57 K3
**Sharow** N York 65 N12
**Sharpenhoe** C Beds 32 F10
**Sharperton** Nthumb 81 K12
**Sharpness** Gloucs 29 J8
**Sharrington** Norfk 44 G3
**Shatterford** Worcs 39 P6
**Shaugh Prior** Devon 5 L7
**Shavington** Ches E 49 M5
**Shaw** Oldham 58 C11
**Shaw** Swindn 18 G4
**Shaw** W Berk 19 N7
**Shaw** Wilts 18 D7
**Shawbirch** Wrekin 49 M11
**Shawbost** W Isls 111 d1
**Shawbury** Shrops 49 K10
**Shawell** Leics 41 M10
**Shawford** Hants 9 M3
**Shawhead** D & G 70 E1
**Shaw Mills** N York 58 G2
**Shawsburn** S Lans 77 N2
**Shearington** D & G 70 G3
**Shearsby** Leics 41 N8
**Shearston** Somset 16 H9
**Shebbear** Devon 14 H9
**Shebdon** Staffs 49 N9
**Shebster** Highld 110 B3
**Sheddens** E Rens 85 J10
**Shedfield** Hants 9 P5
**Sheen** Staffs 50 E8
**Sheepridge** Kirk 58 F9
**Sheepscar** Leeds 58 H7
**Sheepscombe** Gloucs 29 M6
**Sheepstor** Devon 5 L6
**Sheepwash** Devon 14 H10
**Sheepy Magna** Leics 41 J7
**Sheepy Parva** Leics 41 J7
**Sheering** Essex 21 P1
**Sheerness** Kent 22 H8
**Sheerwater** Surrey 20 G10
**Sheet** Hants 10 C5
**Sheffield** Sheff 51 J4
**Sheffield City Road Crematorium** Sheff 51 J4
Sheffield Park E Susx 11 N5
**Shefford** C Beds 32 G8
**Sheigra** Highld 108 D4
**Sheinton** Shrops 39 L2
**Shelderton** Shrops 38 H6
**Sheldon** Birm 40 F9
**Sheldon** Derbys 50 F7
**Sheldon** Devon 6 F2
**Sheldwich** Kent 23 K11
**Shelfanger** Norfk 45 J12
**Shelford** Notts 51 P11
**Shelley** Kirk 58 G11
**Shelley** Suffk 34 G8
**Shellingford** Oxon 19 K3
**Shellow Bowells** Essex 22 C2
**Shelsley Beauchamp** Worcs 39 N9
**Shelsley Walsh** Worcs 39 N9
**Shelton** Bed 32 E3
**Shelton** Norfk 45 K11
**Shelton** Notts 42 B2
**Shelton Lock** C Derb 41 J2
**Shelton Under Harley** Staffs 49 P7
**Shelve** Shrops 38 G3
**Shelwick** Herefs 39 K12
**Shenfield** Essex 22 C4
**Shenington** Oxon 31 J5
**Shenley** Herts 21 J4
**Shenley Brook End** M Keyn 32 B9
**Shenley Church End** M Keyn 32 B9
**Shenmore** Herefs 28 D2
**Shennanton** D & G 69 J6
**Shenstone** Staffs 40 E6
**Shenstone** Worcs 39 Q7
**Shenton** Leics 41 J7
**Shenval** Moray 101 J8
**Shephall** Herts 33 J11
**Shepherd's Bush** Gt Lon 21 K7
**Shepherdswell** Kent 13 N1
**Shepley** Kirk 58 G11
**Shepperton** Surrey 20 H9
**Shepreth** Cambs 33 L7
**Shepshed** Leics 41 L4
**Shepton Beauchamp** Somset 17 K11
**Shepton Mallet** Somset 17 N7
**Shepton Montague** Somset 17 P9
**Shepway** Kent 22 F11
**Sheraton** Dur 66 C1
**Sherborne** Dorset 17 P11
**Sherborne** Gloucs 30 F10
**Sherborne** Somset 17 N5
**Sherborne St John** Hants 19 Q9
**Sherbourne** Warwks 30 H2
**Sherburn** Dur 73 N11
**Sherburn** N York 67 K11
**Sherburn Hill** Dur 73 N11
**Sherburn in Elmet** N York 59 L7
**Shere** Surrey 10 H1
**Shereford** Norfk 44 E4
**Sherfield English** Hants 9 K3
**Sherfield on Loddon** Hants 20 B10
**Sherford** Devon 5 Q10
**Sheriffhales** Shrops 49 N11
**Sheriff Hutton** N York 59 P2
**Sheringham** Norfk 45 J2
**Sherington** M Keyn 32 C7
**Shernborne** Norfk 44 B4
**Sherrington** Wilts 18 E11
**Sherston** Wilts 18 C4
**Sherwood** C Nott 51 M11
**Sherwood Forest** Notts 51 N8
**Sherwood Forest Crematorium** Notts 51 P7
**Shetland Islands** Shet 111 k4
**Shettleston** C Glas 85 L9
**Shevington** Wigan 57 K7
**Sheviock** Cnwll 4 H8
**Shibden Head** C Brad 58 E8
**Shide** IoW 9 N9
**Shidlaw** Nthumb 80 H6
**Shiel Bridge** Highld 97 N6
**Shieldaig** Highld 105 M10
**Shieldhill** D & G 78 G11
**Shieldhill** Falk 85 P7
**Shieldhill House Hotel** S Lans 78 G2
**Shields** N Lans 85 N11
**Shielfoot** Highld 89 N3
**Shielhill** Angus 93 M4
**Shielhill** Inver 84 D8
**Shifnal** Shrops 39 N1
**Shilbottle** Nthumb 81 P11
**Shildon** Dur 65 M3
**Shillford** E Rens 84 H10
**Shillingford** Devon 16 D10
**Shillingford** Oxon 19 P3
**Shillingford Abbot** Devon 6 B5
**Shillingford St George** Devon 6 B5
**Shillingstone** Dorset 8 C5
**Shillington** C Beds 32 G9
**Shilton** Oxon 30 H11
**Shilton** Warwks 41 K9
**Shimpling** Norfk 45 J12
**Shimpling** Suffk 34 E6
**Shimpling Street** Suffk 34 E6
**Shincliffe** Dur 73 N11
**Shiney Row** Sundld 73 N9
**Shinfield** Wokham 20 B9
**Shinness** Highld 109 J11
**Shipbourne** Kent 22 C11
**Shipdham** Norfk 44 F8
**Shipham** Somset 17 L5
**Shiphay** Torbay 6 B9
**Shiplake** Oxon 20 C7
**Shipley** C Brad 58 F6
**Shipley** W Susx 11 J6
**Shipley Bridge** Surrey 11 L3
**Shipmeadow** Suffk 45 N11
**Shippon** Oxon 19 N2
**Shipston-on-Stour** Warwks 30 G6
**Shipton** Gloucs 30 D9
**Shipton** N York 59 M3
**Shipton** Shrops 39 K4
**Shipton Bellinger** Hants 19 J10
**Shipton Gorge** Dorset 7 M5
**Shipton Green** W Susx 10 C9
**Shipton Moyne** Gloucs 29 M10
**Shipton-on-Cherwell** Oxon 31 L10
**Shiptonthorpe** E R Yk 60 E5
**Shipton-under-Wychwood** Oxon 30 H9
**Shirburn** Oxon 20 B4
**Shirdley Hill** Lancs 56 G6
**Shirebrook** Derbys 51 M7
**Shiregreen** Sheff 51 J3
**Shirehampton** Bristl 28 G12
**Shiremoor** N Tyne 73 N6
**Shirenewton** Mons 28 F9
**Shireoaks** Notts 51 M5
**Shirland** Derbys 51 K8
**Shirley** C Sotn 9 L5
**Shirley** Derbys 50 G11
**Shirley** Gt Lon 21 M9
**Shirley** Solhll 40 E10
**Shirrell Heath** Hants 9 P5
**Shirvan** Ag & B 83 N6
**Shirwell** Devon 15 K5
**Shiskine** N Ayrs 75 N6
**Shobdon** Herefs 38 H9
**Shobrooke** Devon 15 P11
**Shoby** Leics 41 P4
**Shocklach** Ches W 48 H5
**Shoeburyness** Sthend 22 H6
**Sholden** Kent 23 Q11
**Sholing** C Sotn 9 M5
**Shop** Cnwll 14 E8
**Shoreditch** Gt Lon 21 M6
**Shoreditch** Somset 16 H10
**Shoreham** Kent 21 P10
*Shoreham Airport* W Susx 11 K8
**Shoreham-by-Sea** W Susx 11 K8
**Shorley** Hants 9 P3
**Shorne** Kent 22 E8
**Shortgate** E Susx 11 P7
**Short Heath** Birm 40 E8
**Short Heath** Wsall 40 C7
**Shortlanesend** Cnwll 3 J6
**Shortlees** E Ayrs 76 G4
**Shortstown** Bed 32 F7
**Shorwell** IoW 9 M10
**Shoscombe** BaNES 17 Q5
**Shotesham** Norfk 45 L9
**Shotgate** Essex 22 F5
**Shotley** Suffk 35 K9
**Shotley Bridge** Dur 73 J9
**Shotley Gate** Suffk 35 L9
**Shotley Street** Suffk 35 K9
**Shottenden** Kent 23 K11
**Shottery** Warwks 30 F3
**Shotteswell** Warwks 31 K5
**Shottisham** Suffk 35 M7
**Shottlegate** Derbys 50 H10
**Shotton** Dur 73 P11
**Shotton** Flints 48 F2
**Shotton Colliery** Dur 73 P11
**Shotts** N Lans 85 P10
**Shotwick** Ches W 48 G2
**Shougle** Moray 101 J4
**Shouldham** Norfk 44 B8
**Shouldham Thorpe** Norfk 43 Q8
**Shoulton** Worcs 39 P9
**Shrawardine** Shrops 48 H11
**Shrawley** Worcs 39 P8
**Shrewley** Warwks 30 G1
**Shrewsbury** Shrops 49 J11
**Shrewton** Wilts 18 F11
**Shripney** W Susx 10 F9
**Shrivenham** Oxon 19 J3
**Shropham** Norfk 44 G10
**Shucknall** Herefs 28 G1
**Shudy Camps** Cambs 33 P7
**Shuna** Ag & B 83 L2
**Shurdington** Gloucs 29 N5
**Shurlock Row** W & M 20 D8
**Shurrery** Highld 110 B4
**Shurrery Lodge** Highld 110 B4
**Shurton** Somset 16 G7
**Shustoke** Warwks 40 G8
**Shute** Devon 6 H4
**Shute** Devon 15 Q11
**Shutford** Oxon 31 J6
**Shut Heath** Staffs 49 Q10
**Shuthonger** Gloucs 29 M2
**Shutlanger** Nhants 31 Q4
**Shuttington** Warwks 40 G6
**Shuttlewood** Derbys 51 L6
**Shuttleworth** Bury 57 P5
**Siabost** W Isls 111 d1
**Siadar** W Isls 111 d1
**Sibbertoft** Nhants 41 P10
**Sibford Ferris** Oxon 31 J6
**Sibford Gower** Oxon 31 J6
**Sible Hedingham** Essex 34 C9
**Sibley's Green** Essex 33 P10
**Sibsey** Lincs 53 K12
**Sibson** Cambs 42 F10
**Sibson** Leics 41 J7
**Sibster** Highld 110 G5
**Sibthorpe** Notts 51 Q10
**Sibthorpe** Notts 51 Q6
**Sibton** Suffk 35 M3
**Sicklesmere** Suffk 34 E5
**Sicklinghall** N York 59 J5
**Sidbury** Devon 6 F4
**Sidbury** Shrops 39 M5
**Sidcot** N Som 17 K5
**Sidcup** Gt Lon 21 P8
**Siddington** Ches E 49 Q2
**Siddington** Gloucs 18 F2
**Sidestrand** Norfk 45 L3
**Sidford** Devon 6 F5
**Sidlesham** W Susx 10 D9
**Sidley** E Susx 12 E8
**Sidmouth** Devon 6 F5
**Sigglesthorne** E R Yk 61 K5
**Sigingstone** V Glam 16 C2
**Silchester** Hants 19 Q8
**Sileby** Leics 41 N5
**Silecroft** Cumb 62 D6
**Silfield** Norfk 45 J9
**Silkstone** Barns 58 H11
**Silkstone Common** Barns 58 H12
**Silk Willoughby** Lincs 42 F2
**Silloth** Cumb 70 H5
**Silpho** N York 67 L8
**Silsden** C Brad 58 D5
**Silsoe** C Beds 32 F9
**Silton** Dorset 8 B2
**Silverburn** Mdloth 86 E9
**Silverdale** Lancs 63 J7
**Silverdale** Staffs 49 P6
**Silver End** Essex 34 D11
**Silverford** Abers 102 G3
**Silverstone** Nhants 31 P5
**Silverton** Devon 6 C3
**Silvington** Shrops 39 L6
**Simonburn** Nthumb 72 F6
**Simonsbath** Somset 15 N4
**Simonstone** Lancs 57 P3
**Simprim** Border 80 H5
**Simpson** M Keyn 32 C9
**Simpson Cross** Pembks 24 F5
**Sinclair's Hill** Border 80 H4
**Sinclairston** E Ayrs 76 H7
**Sinderby** N York 65 N10
**Sinderland Green** Traffd 57 N10
**Sindlesham** Wokham 20 C9
**Sinfin** C Derb 41 J2
**Singleton** Kent 13 J2
**Singleton** Lancs 56 H2
**Singleton** W Susx 10 E7
**Singlewell** Kent 22 D8
**Sinnarhard** Abers 101 N11
**Sinnington** N York 66 G9
**Sinton** Worcs 39 P9
**Sinton** Worcs 39 Q9
**Sinton Green** Worcs 39 P9
**Sissinghurst** Kent 12 F3
**Siston** S Glos 17 P2
**Sithney** Cnwll 2 F9
**Sittingbourne** Kent 22 H10
**Six Ashes** Shrops 39 P4
**Sixhills** Lincs 52 G6
**Six Mile Bottom** Cambs 33 P5
**Sixpenny Handley** Dorset 8 E4
**Skaill** Ork 111 h2
Skara Brae Ork 111 g2
**Skares** E Ayrs 77 J7
**Skateraw** Abers 95 P4
**Skateraw** E Loth 87 N7
**Skeabost** Highld 104 F11
**Skeeby** N York 65 L7
**Skeffington** Leics 41 Q7
**Skeffling** E R Yk 61 N9
**Skegby** Notts 51 L8
**Skegby** Notts 52 B9
**Skegness** Lincs 53 P10
**Skelbo** Highld 107 N4
**Skelbo Street** Highld 107 N4
**Skelbrooke** Donc 59 L10
**Skeldyke** Lincs 43 K3
**Skellingthorpe** Lincs 52 D8
**Skellow** Donc 59 M11
**Skelmanthorpe** Kirk 58 G11
**Skelmersdale** Lancs 57 J7
**Skelmorlie** N Ayrs 84 D9
**Skelpick** Highld 109 M5
**Skelston** D & G 78 D10
**Skelton** C York 59 M3
**Skelton** Cumb 71 N8
**Skelton** E R Yk 60 D8
**Skelton** N York 59 J1
**Skelton** R & Cl 66 F4
**Skelwith Bridge** Cumb 62 G2
**Skendleby** Lincs 53 M9
**Skene House** Abers 102 G12
**Skenfrith** Mons 28 E5
**Skerne** E R Yk 60 H3
**Skerray** Highld 109 L3
**Skerricha** Highld 108 E5
*Skerries Airport* Shet 111 m3
**Skerton** Lancs 63 J9
**Sketchley** Leics 41 K8
**Sketty** Swans 26 E9
**Skewsby** N York 66 E12
**Skiall** Highld 110 B3
**Skidby** E R Yk 60 H7
**Skigersta** W Isls 111 e1
**Skilgate** Somset 16 D10
**Skillington** Lincs 42 C5
**Skinburness** Cumb 71 J4
**Skinflats** Falk 85 Q6
**Skinidin** Highld 104 C11
**Skipness** Ag & B 83 N10
**Skipper's Bridge** D & G 79 M11
**Skipsea** E R Yk 61 K3
**Skipton** N York 58 C4
**Skipton-on-Swale** N York 65 P10
**Skipwith** N York 59 P6
**Skirlaugh** E R Yk 61 K6
**Skirling** Border 78 H2
**Skirmett** Bucks 20 C5
**Skirpenbeck** E R Yk 60 D3
**Skirwith** Cumb 64 B2
**Skirza** Highld 110 H3
**Skokholm Island** Pembks 24 D7
**Skomer Island** Pembks 24 D7
**Skulamus** Highld 97 J5
**Skye Green** Essex 34 E11
**Skye of Curr** Highld 99 P4
**Slack** Calder 58 C8
**Slacks of Cairnbanno** Abers 102 H6
**Slad** Gloucs 29 M7
**Slade** Devon 15 J3
**Slade Green** Gt Lon 21 Q7
**Slade Hooton** Rothm 51 M3
**Slaggyford** Nthumb 72 C9
**Slaidburn** Lancs 63 N10
**Slaithwaite** Kirk 58 E10
**Slaley** Nthumb 72 H8
**Slamannan** Falk 85 P8
**Slapton** Bucks 32 D11
**Slapton** Devon 5 Q10
**Slapton** Nhants 31 N5
**Slaugham** W Susx 11 K5
**Slaughterford** Wilts 18 C6
**Slawston** Leics 41 R8
**Sleaford** Hants 10 C3
**Sleaford** Lincs 42 F2
**Sleagill** Cumb 64 B4
**Sleapford** Wrekin 49 L11
**Sleasdairidh** Highld 107 K3
**Sledmere** E R Yk 60 F2
**Sleetbeck** Cumb 79 P12
**Sleights** N York 67 J6
**Slickly** Highld 110 F3
**Sliddery** N Ayrs 75 P7
**Sligachan** Highld 96 F4
**Sligrachan** Ag & B 84 C5
**Slimbridge** Gloucs 29 K7
**Slindon** Staffs 49 P8
**Slindon** W Susx 10 F8
**Slinfold** W Susx 10 H4
**Slingsby** N York 66 F11
**Slip End** C Beds 32 F11
**Slip End** Herts 33 J8
**Slipton** Nhants 32 D2
**Slitting Mill** Staffs 40 D4
**Slockavullin** Ag & B 83 M4
**Sloncombe** Devon 5 P3
**Sloothby** Lincs 53 M8
**Slough** Slough 20 F7
**Slough Crematorium** Bucks 20 F7
**Slough Green** Somset 16 H11
**Slumbay** Highld 97 M2
**Slyne** Lancs 63 J8
**Smailholm** Border 80 E7
**Smallburgh** Norfk 45 M5
**Small Dole** W Susx 11 K7
**Smalley** Derbys 51 K11
**Smallfield** Surrey 11 L2
**Small Heath** Birm 40 E9
**Small Hythe** Kent 12 H4
**Smallridge** Devon 7 J3
**Smallthorne** C Stke 50 B10
**Smallworth** Norfk 34 G1
**Smannell** Hants 19 L10
**Smarden** Kent 12 G2
**Smarden Bell** Kent 12 G2
**Smart's Hill** Kent 11 Q2
**Smearisary** Highld 89 N2
**Smeatharpe** Devon 6 G1
**Smeeth** Kent 13 K3
**Smeeton Westerby** Leics 41 P8
**Smerral** Highld 110 D8
**Smestow** Staffs 39 Q4
**Smethwick** Sandw 40 D9
**Smisby** Derbys 41 J4
**Smithfield** Cumb 71 P3
**Smith's Green** Essex 33 Q8
**Smithstown** Highld 105 L6
**Smithton** Highld 107 L12
**Smoo** Highld 108 H3
**Smythe's Green** Essex 34 F11
**Snade** D & G 78 D10
**Snailbeach** Shrops 38 G2
**Snailwell** Cambs 33 Q4
**Snainton** N York 67 K10
**Snaith** E R Yk 59 N9
**Snape** N York 65 M10
**Snape** Suffk 35 N5
**Snape Street** Suffk 35 N5
**Snaresbrook** Gt Lon 21 N5
**Snarestone** Leics 41 J5
**Snarford** Lincs 52 F7
**Snargate** Kent 13 J4
**Snave** Kent 13 K4
**Sneaton** N York 67 J6
**Snelland** Lincs 52 F7
**Snelston** Derbys 50 F11
**Snetterton** Norfk 44 G11
**Snettisham** Norfk 44 B4
**Snitter** Nthumb 81 L12
**Snitterby** Lincs 52 E5
**Snitterfield** Warwks 30 G3
**Snitton** Shrops 39 K7
**Snodland** Kent 22 E10
**Snowdon** Gwynd 54 H10
*Snowdonia National Park* 47 N5
**Snow End** Herts 33 L9
**Snowshill** Gloucs 30 E7
**Soake** Hants 9 Q5
**Soay** Highld 96 E7
**Soberton** Hants 9 Q4
**Soberton Heath** Hants 9 P5
**Sockburn** Darltn 65 N6
**Soham** Cambs 33 P3
**Solas** W Isls 111 b4
**Soldridge** Hants 9 Q1
**Sole Street** Kent 22 D9
**Sole Street** Kent 23 L12
**Solihull** Solhll 40 F10
**Sollers Dilwyn** Herefs 38 H10
**Sollers Hope** Herefs 28 H3
**Solva** Pembks 24 E4
**Solwaybank** D & G 79 L12
**Somerby** Leics 41 R5
**Somerby** Lincs 52 F3
**Somercotes** Derbys 51 K9
**Somerford** Dorset 8 H8
**Somerford Keynes** Gloucs 18 E2

Somerley W Susx....10 D9
Somerleyton Suffk....45 P10
Somersal Herbert Derbys....40 F1
Somersby Lincs....53 K8
Somersham Cambs....33 K2
Somersham Suffk....34 H7
Somerton Oxon....31 L8
Somerton Somset....17 L9
Somerton Suffk....34 D6
Sompting W Susx....11 J8
Sonning Wokham....20 C8
Sonning Common Oxon....20 B7
Sopley Hants....8 H7
Sopwell Herts....21 J3
Sopworth Wilts....18 C4
Sorbie D & G....69 L9
Sordale Highld....110 D4
Sorisdale Ag & B....88 G4
Sorn E Ayrs....77 J6
Sortat Highld....110 F3
Sotby Lincs....52 H7
Sotterley Suffk....45 P12
Soughton Flints....48 E3
Soulbury Bucks....32 C10
Soulby Cumb....64 D5
Souldern Oxon....31 M7
Souldrop Bed....32 E4
Sound Ches E....49 L6
Sound Muir Moray....101 M5
Soundwell S Glos....17 P2
Sourton Devon....5 L3
Soutergate Cumb....62 E6
South Acre Norfk....44 D7
South Alkham Kent....13 N2
Southall Gt Lon....20 H7
South Allington Devon....5 Q11
South Alloa Falk....85 P5
Southam Gloucs....29 N4
Southam Warwks....31 K2
South Ambersham W Susx....10 E6
Southampton C Sotn....9 M5
Southampton Airport Hants....9 M4
Southampton Crematorium Hants....9 M4
South Anston Rothm....51 L4
South Ashford Kent....13 J2
South Baddesley Hants....9 L7
South Ballachulish Highld....90 E5
South Bank C York....59 N4
South Barrow Somset....17 N9
South Beddington Gt Lon....21 L10
South Benfleet Essex....22 F6
South Bersted W Susx....10 F9
Southborough Gt Lon....21 N9
Southborough Kent....12 C2
Southbourne Bmouth....8 G8
Southbourne W Susx....10 C8
South Bramwith Donc....59 N11
South Brent Devon....5 N8
South Brewham Somset....17 Q8
South Bristol Crematorium Bristl....17 N3
South Broomhill Nthumb....73 M2
Southburgh Norfk....44 G8
South Burlingham Norfk....45 N8
Southburn E R Yk....60 G4
South Cadbury Somset....17 P10
South Carlton Lincs....52 D8
South Carlton Notts....51 N4
South Cave E R Yk....60 F7
South Cerney Gloucs....18 F2
South Chailey E Susx....11 N6
South Charlton Nthumb....81 N9
South Cheriton Somset....17 Q10
South Church Dur....65 L2
Southchurch Sthend....22 H6
South Cliffe E R Yk....60 E7
South Clifton Notts....52 B9
South Cockerington Lincs....53 L6
South Cornelly Brdgnd....26 H11
Southcott Cnwll....4 F2
Southcott Devon....5 P4
Southcourt Bucks....20 D2
South Cove Suffk....35 P1
South Creake Norfk....44 E3
South Croxton Leics....41 P5
South Dalton E R Yk....60 G5
South Darenth Kent....22 C9
South Dell W Isls....111 d1
South Downs National Park....11 M8
South Duffield N York....59 P7
Southease E Susx....11 N8
South Elkington Lincs....53 J4
South Elmsall Wakefd....59 L11
Southend Ag & B....75 K10
Southend Airport Essex....22 G5
Southend Crematorium Sthend....22 H6
Southend-on-Sea Sthend....22 H6
Southerndown V Glam....16 B2
Southerness D & G....70 F5
South Erradale Highld....105 L7
Southerton Devon....6 E5
Southery Norfk....43 P10
South Essex Crematorium Gt Lon....22 C6
South Fambridge Essex....22 G5
South Ferriby N Linc....60 G9
South Field E R Yk....60 H8
Southfield Falk....85 P8
Southfleet Kent....22 C8
Southgate Gt Lon....21 L5
Southgate Swans....26 D10
South Gorley Hants....8 H5
South Gosforth N u Ty....73 M7
South Green Essex....22 D5
South Green Kent....22 G10
South Green Norfk....44 H7
South Gyle C Edin....86 E7
South Hanningfield Essex....22 E4
South Harting W Susx....10 C6
South Hayling Hants....10 B9
South Heath Bucks....20 E3
South Heighton E Susx....11 N9
South Hetton Dur....73 P10
South Hiendley Wakefd....59 K10
South Hill Cnwll....4 H5
South Hinksey Oxon....31 L12
South Holmwood Surrey....11 J2
South Hornchurch Gt Lon....21 P6
South Huish Devon....5 N11
South Hykeham Lincs....52 D9
South Hylton Sundld....73 P9
Southill C Beds....32 G8
Southington Hants....19 N10

South Kelsey Lincs....52 E4
South Kessock Highld....107 L11
South Killingholme N Linc....61 K10
South Kilvington N York....65 Q10
South Kilworth Leics....41 N10
South Kirkby Wakefd....59 K11
South Kyme Lincs....52 G12
South Lanarkshire Crematorium S Lans....85 L10
South Leicestershire Crematorium Leics....41 N8
Southleigh Devon....6 G4
South Leigh Oxon....31 K11
South Leverton Notts....52 A7
South Lincolnshire Crematorium Lincs....43 J4
South Littleton Worcs....30 E5
South London Crematorium Gt Lon....21 L9
South Lopham Norfk....34 G1
South Luffenham Rutlnd....42 D9
South Malling E Susx....11 N7
South Marston Swindn....18 H3
South Merstham Surrey....21 L11
South Milford N York....59 L7
South Milton Devon....5 N10
South Mimms Herts....21 K3
South Mimms Services Herts....21 K4
Southminster Essex....23 J4
South Molton Devon....15 M7
South Moor Dur....73 L9
Southmoor Oxon....19 L2
South Moreton Oxon....19 P3
Southmuir Angus....93 L5
South Mundham W Susx....10 E9
South Newbald E R Yk....60 F7
South Newington Oxon....31 K7
South Newton Wilts....8 G1
South Normanton Derbys....51 K9
South Norwood Gt Lon....21 M9
South Ockendon Thurr....22 C6
Southoe Cambs....32 H4
Southolt Suffk....35 K3
South Ormsby Lincs....53 L8
Southorpe C Pete....42 F9
South Otterington N York....65 N9
Southover Dorset....7 N4
South Owersby Lincs....52 F5
Southowram Calder....58 E9
South Oxfordshire Crematorium Oxon....19 M2
South Park Surrey....11 K1
South Perrott Dorset....7 L2
South Petherton Somset....17 L11
South Petherwin Cnwll....4 G4
South Pickenham Norfk....44 E8
South Pill Cnwll....5 J8
South Pool Devon....5 Q11
South Poorton Dorset....7 M4
Southport Sefton....56 G5
Southport Crematorium Lancs....56 G6
South Queensferry C Edin....86 D6
South Rauceby Lincs....42 E2
South Raynham Norfk....44 E5
South Reddish Stockp....50 B3
Southrepps Norfk....45 L3
South Reston Lincs....53 L6
Southrey Lincs....52 G9
South Ronaldsay Ork....111 h3
Southrop Gloucs....30 G12
Southrope Hants....19 Q10
South Runcton Norfk....43 Q8
South Scarle Notts....52 B10
Southsea C Port....9 Q7
South Shian Ag & B....90 C7
South Shields S Tyne....73 P7
South Shields Crematorium S Tyne....73 N8
South Shore Bpool....56 F3
Southside Dur....65 K3
South Stainley N York....58 H2
South Stoke BaNES....17 Q4
South Stoke Oxon....19 P4
South Stoke W Susx....10 G7
South Street Kent....23 K10
South Street Kent....23 L9
South Tarbrax S Lans....86 B10
South Tawton Devon....5 N2
South Tehidy Cnwll....2 F7
South Thoresby Lincs....53 L7
Southtown Norfk....45 Q8
South Uist W Isls....111 b6
Southwaite Cumb....71 P6
Southwaite Services Cumb....71 P6
South Walsham Norfk....45 M7
Southwark Gt Lon....21 L7
South Warnborough Hants....10 B1
Southwater W Susx....11 J5
South Weald Essex....22 C5
Southwell Notts....51 P9
South West Middlesex Crematorium Gt Lon....20 H8
South Weston Oxon....20 B4
South Wheatley Notts....51 Q4
Southwick Hants....9 Q6
Southwick Nhants....42 E10
Southwick Sundld....73 P8
Southwick W Susx....11 K8
Southwick Wilts....18 C7
South Widcombe BaNES....17 N5
South Wigston Leics....41 N7
South Willesborough Kent....13 K2
South Willingham Lincs....52 H6
South Wingfield Derbys....51 J9
South Witham Lincs....42 D6
Southwold Suffk....35 Q2
South Woodham Ferrers Essex....22 F4
South Wootton Norfk....43 Q5
South Wraxall Wilts....18 C7
South Zeal Devon....5 N2
Sovereign Harbour E Susx....12 D9
Sowerby Calder....58 D9
Sowerby N York....66 B10
Sowerby Bridge Calder....58 D9
Sowood Calder....58 D9
Sowton Devon....5 K7
Sowton Devon....6 D4
Soyland Town Calder....58 D9
Spain's End Essex....33 Q8
Spalding Lincs....43 J5
Spaldington E R Yk....60 D7

Spaldwick Cambs....32 G3
Spalford Notts....52 B9
Spanby Lincs....42 F3
Sparham Norfk....44 H6
Spark Bridge Cumb....62 F5
Sparkford Somset....17 N10
Sparkhill Birm....40 E10
Sparkwell Devon....5 M8
Sparrowpit Derbys....50 E5
Sparrows Green E Susx....12 D4
Sparsholt Hants....9 M2
Sparsholt Oxon....19 L4
Spaunton N York....66 G9
Spaxton Somset....16 G8
Spean Bridge Highld....98 C11
Spearywell Hants....9 K2
Speen Bucks....20 D4
Speen W Berk....19 M7
Speeton N York....67 N11
Speke Lpool....56 H11
Speldhurst Kent....12 B2
Spellbrook Herts....33 M12
Spencers Wood Wokham....20 B9
Spen Green Ches E....49 P4
Spennithorne N York....65 K9
Spennymoor Dur....65 M2
Spetchley Worcs....30 B4
Spetisbury Dorset....8 D7
Spexhall Suffk....35 N2
Spey Bay Moray....101 L3
Speybridge Highld....100 G9
Speyview Moray....101 K6
Spilsby Lincs....53 L9
Spinkhill Derbys....51 L5
Spinningdale Highld....107 L4
Spital Hill Donc....51 N3
Spital E Loth....87 J6
Spittal Highld....110 D5
Spittal Nthumb....81 L4
Spittal Pembks....24 G4
Spittalfield P & K....92 G7
Spittal of Glenmuick Abers....94 E5
Spittal of Glenshee P & K....94 B7
Spittal-on-Rule Border....80 D9
Spixworth Norfk....45 L7
Splatt Devon....15 K10
Splayne's Green E Susx....11 N5
Splottlands Cardif....27 P12
Spofforth N York....59 J4
Spondon C Derb....41 K1
Spooner Row Norfk....44 H10
Sporle Norfk....44 E7
Spott E Loth....87 M7
Spottiswoode Border....80 E4
Spratton Nhants....41 Q12
Spreakley Surrey....10 D2
Spreyton Devon....15 M11
Spriddlestone Devon....5 L9
Spridlington Lincs....52 E6
Springburn C Glas....85 K8
Springfield D & G....71 M2
Springfield Essex....22 E2
Springfield Fife....93 L12
Springholm D & G....70 D2
Springside N Ayrs....76 F4
Springthorpe Lincs....52 C5
Springwell Sundld....73 M8
Springwood Crematorium Lpool....56 H10
Sproatley E R Yk....61 K7
Sproston Green Ches W....49 N3
Sprotbrough Donc....51 M1
Sproughton Suffk....35 J7
Sprouston Border....80 G7
Sprowston Norfk....45 L7
Sproxton Leics....42 C5
Sproxton N York....66 E10
Spurstow Ches E....49 K4
Spyway Dorset....7 M4
Stableford Shrops....39 N3
Stacey Bank Sheff....50 H3
Stackhouse N York....63 P8
Stackpole Pembks....24 H9
Staddiscombe C Plym....5 K9
Stadhampton Oxon....19 Q2
Stadhlaigearraidh W Isls....111 a5
Staffield Cumb....71 Q7
Staffin Highld....104 G8
Stafford Staffs....40 B3
Stafford Crematorium Staffs....40 C3
Stafford Services (Northbound) Staffs....40 B2
Stafford Services (Southbound) Staffs....40 B2
Stagsden Bed....32 E7
Stainburn Cumb....70 G9
Stainby Lincs....42 C5
Staincross Barns....59 J11
Staindrop Dur....65 K4
Staines-upon-Thames Surrey....20 G8
Stainforth Donc....59 N10
Stainforth N York....63 P8
Staining Lancs....56 G2
Stainland Calder....58 E9
Stainsacre N York....67 K6
Stainton Cumb....63 K5
Stainton Cumb....71 P9
Stainton Donc....51 M3
Stainton Dur....65 J4
Stainton Middsb....66 C5
Stainton by Langworth Lincs....52 F7
Staintondale N York....67 L7
Stainton le Vale Lincs....52 H5
Stainton with Adgarley Cumb....62 F7
Stair E Ayrs....76 G6
Stairhaven D & G....68 G7
Staithes N York....66 H4
Stakes Hants....10 B8
Stalbridge Dorset....17 Q11
Stalbridge Weston Dorset....17 Q11
Stalham Norfk....45 N5
Stalisfield Green Kent....23 J11
Stallen Dorset....17 N11
Stallingborough NE Lin....61 K11
Stalmine Lancs....62 G12
Stalybridge Tamesd....50 C2
Stambourne Essex....34 C8
Stambourne Green Essex....34 B8
Stamford Lincs....42 E8
Stamford Nthumb....81 P9
Stamford Bridge Ches W....49 J3
Stamford Bridge E R Yk....60 C3
Stamfordham Nthumb....73 J6

Stamford Hill Gt Lon....21 M6
Stanbridge C Beds....32 D11
Stanbury C Brad....58 D6
Stand N Lans....85 M8
Standburn Falk....85 Q7
Standeford Staffs....40 B6
Standen Kent....12 G3
Standerwick Somset....18 B10
Standford Hants....10 D3
Standingstone Cumb....70 H8
Standish Wigan....57 K6
Standlake Oxon....31 K12
Standon Hants....9 M3
Standon Herts....33 L11
Standon Staffs....49 P8
Stane N Lans....85 P10
Stanfield Norfk....44 F6
Stanford C Beds....32 G8
Stanford Kent....13 L3
Stanford Bishop Herefs....39 M11
Stanford Bridge Worcs....39 N8
Stanford Dingley W Berk....19 P6
Stanford in the Vale Oxon....19 L3
Stanford le Hope Thurr....22 D7
Stanford on Avon Nhants....41 N10
Stanford on Soar Notts....41 M3
Stanford on Teme Worcs....39 N8
Stanfree Derbys....51 L6
Stanghow R & Cl....66 F4
Stanground C Pete....42 H10
Stanhoe Norfk....44 D3
Stanhope Border....79 J3
Stanhope Dur....72 H11
Stanion Nhants....42 D11
Stanley Derbys....51 K11
Stanley Dur....73 L9
Stanley P & K....92 G8
Stanley Staffs....50 B9
Stanley Crook Dur....73 L12
Stanley Pontlarge Gloucs....30 D7
Stanmer Br & H....11 M7
Stanmore Gt Lon....21 J5
Stanmore Hants....9 M2
Stannersburn Nthumb....72 D4
Stanningfield Suffk....34 D5
Stannington Nthumb....73 L5
Stannington Sheff....50 H4
Stannington Station Nthumb....73 L5
Stansbatch Herefs....38 G9
Stansfield Suffk....34 D6
Stanstead Suffk....34 D7
Stanstead Abbotts Herts....21 M2
Stansted Kent....22 C10
Stansted Airport Essex....33 N11
Stansted Mountfitchet Essex....33 N10
Stanton Gloucs....30 E7
Stanton Nthumb....73 K3
Stanton Staffs....50 E10
Stanton Suffk....34 F3
Stanton by Bridge Derbys....41 J3
Stanton by Dale Derbys....51 L12
Stanton Drew BaNES....17 N4
Stanton Fitzwarren Swindn....18 H3
Stanton Harcourt Oxon....31 K11
Stanton in Peak Derbys....50 G7
Stanton Lacy Shrops....39 J6
Stanton Lees Derbys....50 G8
Stanton Long Shrops....39 L4
Stanton on the Wolds Notts....41 N2
Stanton Prior BaNES....17 P4
Stanton St Bernard Wilts....18 G8
Stanton St John Oxon....31 M11
Stanton St Quintin Wilts....18 D5
Stanton Street Suffk....34 F4
Stanton under Bardon Leics....41 L5
Stanton upon Hine Heath Shrops....49 K10
Stanton Wick BaNES....17 N4
Stanway Essex....34 F11
Stanway Gloucs....30 D7
Stanwell Surrey....20 G8
Stanwick Nhants....32 E3
Stanwix Cumb....71 N4
Staoinebrig W Isls....111 a5
Stape N York....66 H8
Stapeley Ches E....49 M5
Stapenhill Staffs....40 G3
Staple Kent....23 P11
Staple Cross Devon....16 D11
Staplecross E Susx....12 F5
Staplefield W Susx....11 L5
Staple Fitzpaine Somset....16 H11
Stapleford Cambs....33 M6
Stapleford Herts....33 K12
Stapleford Leics....42 B6
Stapleford Lincs....52 C11
Stapleford Notts....51 L12
Stapleford Wilts....18 F12
Stapleford Abbotts Essex....21 P5
Staplegrove Somset....16 G10
Staplehay Somset....16 G10
Staplehurst Kent....12 F2
Staplestreet Kent....23 K10
Stapleton Herefs....38 G8
Stapleton Leics....41 K7
Stapleton N York....65 M5
Stapleton Shrops....39 J2
Stapleton Somset....17 L11
Stapley Somset....16 G12
Staploe Bed....32 G5
Staplow Herefs....29 J1
Star Fife....86 G2
Star Pembks....25 M2
Star Somset....17 L4
Starbeck N York....59 J3
Starbotton N York....64 G11
Starcross Devon....6 C6
Stareton Warwks....41 J12
Starlings Green Essex....33 M9
Starston Norfk....45 K12
Startforth Dur....65 J4
Startley Wilts....18 D4
Statenborough Kent....23 P11
Statham Warrtn....57 M10
Stathe Somset....17 K9
Stathern Leics....41 Q4
Staughton Green Cambs....32 G4
Staunton Gloucs....28 G4
Staunton Gloucs....29 K3
Staunton on Arrow Herefs....38 G9
Staunton on Wye Herefs....38 G12

Staveley Cumb....62 H5
Staveley Cumb....63 J3
Staveley Derbys....51 K6
Staveley N York....59 J2
Staverton Devon....5 Q7
Staverton Gloucs....29 M4
Staverton Nhants....31 M2
Staverton Wilts....18 C8
Stawell Somset....17 K8
Stawley Somset....16 E10
Staxigoe Highld....110 H5
Staxton N York....67 L10
Staynall Lancs....62 G12
Stean N York....65 J11
Stearsby N York....66 E12
Steart Somset....16 H7
Stebbing Essex....33 Q11
Stechford Birm....40 F9
Stedham W Susx....10 D5
Steelend Fife....86 B4
Steele Road Border....79 Q9
Steen's Bridge Herefs....39 K10
Steep Hants....10 C5
Steep Lane Calder....58 D9
Steeple Essex....22 H3
Steeple Ashton Wilts....18 D9
Steeple Aston Oxon....31 L8
Steeple Bumpstead Essex....34 B8
Steeple Claydon Bucks....31 P8
Steeple Gidding Cambs....32 G1
Steeple Langford Wilts....18 F12
Steeple Morden Cambs....33 J8
Steeton C Brad....58 D5
Stein Highld....104 C10
Stelling Minnis Kent....13 M1
Stembridge Somset....17 K11
Stenalees Cnwll....3 M4
Stenhouse D & G....77 N11
Stenhousemuir Falk....85 P6
Stenscholl Highld....104 F8
Stenson Fields Derbys....41 J2
Stenton E Loth....87 M7
Steornabhagh W Isls....111 d2
Stepaside Pembks....25 K7
Stepford D & G....78 E11
Stepney Gt Lon....21 M7
Steppingley C Beds....32 E9
Stepps N Lans....85 L8
Sternfield Suffk....35 N5
Stert Wilts....18 F8
Stetchworth Cambs....33 Q5
Stevenage Herts....32 H10
Stevenston N Ayrs....76 E3
Steventon Hants....19 P10
Steventon Oxon....19 M3
Steventon End Essex....33 P8
Stevington Bed....32 E6
Stewartby Bed....32 E8
Stewartfield S Lans....85 K11
Stewarton E Ayrs....76 G3
Stewkley Bucks....32 C10
Stewley Somset....17 J11
Steyning W Susx....11 J7
Steynton Pembks....24 G7
Stibb Cnwll....14 D9
Stibbard Norfk....44 G4
Stibb Cross Devon....14 H8
Stibb Green Wilts....19 J8
Stibbington Cambs....42 F9
Stichill Border....80 F6
Sticker Cnwll....3 L6
Stickford Lincs....53 K10
Sticklepath Devon....5 M2
Stickney Lincs....53 K11
Stiffkey Norfk....44 F2
Stilligarry W Isls....111 a5
Stillingfleet N York....59 N6
Stillington N York....59 N1
Stillington S on T....65 P3
Stilton Cambs....42 G11
Stinchcombe Gloucs....29 K8
Stinsford Dorset....7 Q5
Stiperstones Shrops....38 G3
Stirchley Wrekin....39 M1
Stirling Abers....103 M6
Stirling Stirlg....85 N4
Stirling Castle Stirlg....85 N4
Stirling Services Stirlg....85 N5
Stirtloe Cambs....32 H4
Stirton N York....58 C4
Stisted Essex....34 D10
Stithians Cnwll....2 G8
Stivichall Covtry....41 J11
Stixwould Lincs....52 H9
Stoak Ches W....48 H2
Stobo Border....79 K2
Stoborough Dorset....8 D9
Stobs Castle Border....80 C11
Stobswood Nthumb....73 L2
Stock Essex....22 E4
Stock N Som....17 L4
Stockbridge Hants....9 L1
Stockbriggs S Lans....77 N4
Stockbury Kent....22 G10
Stockcross W Berk....19 M7
Stockerston Leics....42 B9
Stock Green Worcs....30 C3
Stocking Herefs....28 H3
Stockingford Warwks....41 J8
Stocking Pelham Herts....33 M10
Stockland Devon....6 H2
Stockland Bristol Somset....16 H7
Stockleigh English Devon....15 P10
Stockleigh Pomeroy Devon....15 P10
Stockley Wilts....18 E7
Stocklinch Somset....17 K11
Stockport Stockp....50 B3
Stockport Crematorium Stockp....50 B3
Stocksbridge Sheff....50 H2
Stocksfield Nthumb....73 J8
Stockton Herefs....39 K9
Stockton Norfk....45 N10
Stockton Shrops....39 N3
Stockton Warwks....31 K2
Stockton Wilts....18 E12
Stockton Wrekin....49 P11
Stockton Brook Staffs....50 B9
Stockton Heath Warrtn....57 L10
Stockton-on-Tees S on T....66 C4
Stockton on Teme Worcs....39 N8
Stockton on the Forest C York....59 P3
Stockwell End Wolves....40 B7
Stockwood Bristl....17 P3

Stockwood Dorset ...... 7 N2
Stock Wood Worcs ...... 30 D3
Stodmarsh Kent ...... 23 N10
Stody Norfk ...... 44 H3
Stoer Highld ...... 108 B9
Stoford Somset ...... 17 N12
Stoford Wilts ...... 8 F1
Stogumber Somset ...... 16 E8
Stogursey Somset ...... 16 G7
Stoke Covtry ...... 41 J10
Stoke Devon ...... 14 E7
Stoke Hants ...... 10 B9
Stoke Hants ...... 19 L9
Stoke Medway ...... 22 G8
Stoke Abbott Dorset ...... 7 L3
Stoke Albany Nhants ...... 42 B11
Stoke Ash Suffk ...... 35 J3
Stoke Bardolph Notts ...... 51 N11
Stoke Bliss Worcs ...... 39 M9
Stoke Bruerne Nhants ...... 31 Q4
Stoke-by-Clare Suffk ...... 34 C7
Stoke-by-Nayland Suffk ...... 34 G8
Stoke Canon Devon ...... 6 C3
Stoke Charity Hants ...... 19 N11
Stoke Climsland Cnwll ...... 4 H5
Stoke Cross Herefs ...... 39 L11
Stoke D'Abernon Surrey ...... 20 H10
Stoke Doyle Nhants ...... 42 E11
Stoke Dry Rutlnd ...... 42 C10
Stoke Edith Herefs ...... 28 H1
Stoke Farthing Wilts ...... 8 F3
Stoke Ferry Norfk ...... 44 B9
Stoke Fleming Devon ...... 6 B11
Stokeford Dorset ...... 8 C9
Stoke Gabriel Devon ...... 6 B10
Stoke Gifford S Glos ...... 28 H11
Stoke Golding Leics ...... 41 K7
Stoke Goldington M Keyn ...... 32 B7
Stokeham Notts ...... 52 A7
Stoke Hammond Bucks ...... 32 C10
Stoke Holy Cross Norfk ...... 45 K9
Stokeinteignhead Devon ...... 6 C8
Stoke Lacy Herefs ...... 39 L11
Stoke Lyne Oxon ...... 31 M8
Stoke Mandeville Bucks ...... 20 D2
Stokenchurch Bucks ...... 20 C4
Stoke Newington Gt Lon ...... 21 M6
Stokenham Devon ...... 5 Q10
Stoke-on-Trent C Stke ...... 50 B10
Stoke Orchard Gloucs ...... 29 M3
Stoke Poges Bucks ...... 20 F6
Stoke Prior Herefs ...... 39 K10
Stoke Prior Worcs ...... 30 C1
Stoke Rivers Devon ...... 15 L5
Stoke Rochford Lincs ...... 42 D5
Stoke Row Oxon ...... 20 B6
Stoke St Gregory Somset ...... 17 J10
Stoke St Mary Somset ...... 16 H10
Stoke St Michael Somset ...... 17 P6
Stoke St Milborough
    Shrops ...... 39 K5
Stokesby Norfk ...... 45 N7
Stokesley N York ...... 66 D6
Stoke sub Hamdon
    Somset ...... 17 L11
Stoke Talmage Oxon ...... 20 B4
Stoke Trister Somset ...... 17 Q9
Stoke upon Tern Shrops ...... 49 M9
Stolford Somset ...... 16 G7
Stondon Massey Essex ...... 22 C4
Stone Bucks ...... 20 C2
Stone Gloucs ...... 29 J9
Stone Rothm ...... 51 M3
Stone Staffs ...... 40 B1
Stone Worcs ...... 39 Q7
Stone Allerton Somset ...... 17 K6
Stonebridge N Som ...... 17 K4
Stonebridge Warwks ...... 40 G10
Stonebroom Derbys ...... 51 K8
Stone Cross Kent ...... 23 P11
Stonecrouch Kent ...... 12 E4
Stoneferry C KuH ...... 61 J7
Stonefield Castle Hotel
    Ag & B ...... 83 N8
Stonegate E Susx ...... 12 D4
Stonegrave N York ...... 66 F11
Stonehaven Abers ...... 95 P5
Stonehenge Wilts ...... 18 G11
Stonehouse C Plym ...... 5 K9
Stonehouse Gloucs ...... 29 L7
Stonehouse S Lans ...... 77 M3
Stone in Oxney Kent ...... 12 H5
Stoneleigh Warwks ...... 41 J11
Stonesby Leics ...... 42 B5
Stonesfield Oxon ...... 31 K10
Stones Green Essex ...... 35 J10
Stone Street Kent ...... 22 C11
Stone Street Suffk ...... 35 N1
Stonewells Moray ...... 101 K3
Stoneybridge W Isls ...... 111 a5
Stoneyburn W Loth ...... 86 B9
Stoneygate C Leic ...... 41 N7
Stoneykirk D & G ...... 68 E8
Stoney Middleton Derbys ...... 50 G6
Stoney Stanton Leics ...... 41 L8
Stoney Stoke Somset ...... 17 Q9
Stoney Stratton Somset ...... 17 P8
Stoneywood C Aber ...... 103 J11
Stoneywood Falk ...... 85 N6
Stonham Aspal Suffk ...... 35 J5
Stonnall Staffs ...... 40 E6
Stonor Oxon ...... 20 B5
Stonton Wyville Leics ...... 41 Q8
Stony Houghton Derbys ...... 51 L7
Stony Stratford M Keyn ...... 32 B8
Stoodleigh Devon ...... 15 L6
Stoodleigh Devon ...... 16 C11
Stop 24 Services Kent ...... 13 L3
Stopham W Susx ...... 10 G6
Stopsley Luton ...... 32 F11
Stornoway W Isls ...... 111 d2
Stornoway Airport W Isls ...... 111 d2
Storrington W Susx ...... 10 H7
Storth Cumb ...... 63 J6
Storwood E R Yk ...... 60 C5
Stotfield Moray ...... 101 J2
Stotfold C Beds ...... 32 H9
Stottesdon Shrops ...... 39 M5
Stoughton Leics ...... 41 N7
Stoughton Surrey ...... 20 F12
Stoughton W Susx ...... 10 C7
Stoulton Worcs ...... 30 B4
Stourbridge Dudley ...... 40 B10
Stourbridge
    Crematorium Dudley ...... 40 B10
Stourhead Wilts ...... 8 B1

Stourpaine Dorset ...... 8 C5
Stourport-on-Severn
    Worcs ...... 39 P7
Stour Provost Dorset ...... 8 B3
Stour Row Dorset ...... 8 B3
Stourton Staffs ...... 39 Q5
Stourton Warwks ...... 30 H6
Stourton Wilts ...... 8 B1
Stourton Caundle Dorset ...... 17 Q12
Stove Shet ...... 111 k5
Stoven Suffk ...... 35 P1
Stow Border ...... 87 J12
Stow Lincs ...... 52 C7
Stow Bardolph Norfk ...... 43 P8
Stow Bedon Norfk ...... 44 F10
Stowbridge Norfk ...... 43 P8
Stow-cum-Quy Cambs ...... 33 N5
Stowe Shrops ...... 38 F7
Stowe by Chartley Staffs ...... 40 D3
Stowell Somset ...... 17 P10
Stowey BaNES ...... 17 N4
Stowford Devon ...... 5 J3
Stowlangtoft Suffk ...... 34 F3
Stow Longa Cambs ...... 32 G3
Stow Maries Essex ...... 22 H4
Stowmarket Suffk ...... 34 H5
Stow-on-the-Wold Gloucs ...... 30 F8
Stowting Kent ...... 13 L2
Stowting Common Kent ...... 13 L2
Stowupland Suffk ...... 34 H5
Straanruie Highld ...... 99 P6
Strachan Abers ...... 95 L4
Strachur Ag & B ...... 84 B3
Stradbroke Suffk ...... 35 K3
Stradishall Suffk ...... 34 C6
Stradsett Norfk ...... 43 Q8
Stragglethorpe Lincs ...... 52 C11
Straiton Mdloth ...... 86 F8
Straiton S Ayrs ...... 76 G9
Straloch Abers ...... 102 H10
Straloch P & K ...... 92 F3
Stramshall Staffs ...... 40 E1
Strang IoM ...... 56 c5
Strangeways Salfd ...... 57 P8
Strangford Herefs ...... 28 G4
Stranraer D & G ...... 68 E7
Stratfield Mortimer
    W Berk ...... 19 Q7
Stratfield Saye Hants ...... 20 B10
Stratfield Turgis Hants ...... 20 B10
Stratford Gt Lon ...... 21 M6
Stratford St Andrew Suffk ...... 35 M5
Stratford St Mary Suffk ...... 34 H9
Stratford sub Castle Wilts ...... 8 G12
Stratford Tony Wilts ...... 8 G3
Stratford-upon-Avon
    Warwks ...... 30 G3
Strath Highld ...... 105 L6
Strathan Highld ...... 108 C10
Strathan Highld ...... 109 K3
Strathaven S Lans ...... 77 L3
Strathblane Stirlg ...... 85 J7
Strathcanaird Highld ...... 106 C3
Strathcarron Highld ...... 97 N2
Strathcoil Ag & B ...... 89 N9
Strathdon Abers ...... 101 L11
Strathkinness Fife ...... 93 M11
Strathloanhead W Loth ...... 85 Q8
Strathmashie House
    Highld ...... 98 H10
Strathmiglo Fife ...... 86 E1
Strathpeffer Highld ...... 106 H10
Strathtay P & K ...... 92 D5
Strathwhillan N Ayrs ...... 75 Q5
Strathy Highld ...... 109 P3
Strathy Inn Highld ...... 109 P3
Strathyre Stirlg ...... 91 N11
Stratton Cnwll ...... 14 E10
Stratton Dorset ...... 7 P4
Stratton Gloucs ...... 30 D12
Stratton Audley Oxon ...... 31 N8
Stratton-on-the-Fosse
    Somset ...... 17 P6
Stratton St Margaret
    Swindn ...... 18 H4
Stratton St Michael Norfk ...... 45 K10
Stratton Strawless Norfk ...... 45 K6
Streat E Susx ...... 11 M7
Streatham Gt Lon ...... 21 L8
Streatley C Beds ...... 32 F10
Streatley W Berk ...... 19 P5
Street Devon ...... 6 G5
Street Somset ...... 17 L8
Street Ashton Warwks ...... 41 L10
Street Dinas Shrops ...... 48 G7
Street End Kent ...... 23 M11
Street End W Susx ...... 10 D9
Streethay Staffs ...... 40 F5
Streetlam N York ...... 65 N7
Streetly Crematorium
    Wsall ...... 40 E7
Streetly End Cambs ...... 33 P7
Street on the Fosse
    Somset ...... 17 N8
Strelitz P & K ...... 92 H8
Strelley Notts ...... 51 L11
Strensall C York ...... 59 N3
Strensham Services
    (northbound) Worcs ...... 29 M1
Strensham Services
    (southbound) Worcs ...... 29 M2
Stretcholt Somset ...... 16 H7
Strete Devon ...... 5 R10
Stretford Traffd ...... 57 P9
Strethall Essex ...... 33 M8
Stretham Cambs ...... 33 N2
Strettington W Susx ...... 10 E8
Stretton Derbys ...... 51 K8
Stretton Rutlnd ...... 42 D7
Stretton Staffs ...... 40 B5
Stretton Staffs ...... 40 G3
Stretton Warrtn ...... 57 L11
Stretton Grandison
    Herefs ...... 39 L12
Stretton-on-Dunsmore
    Warwks ...... 41 K11
Stretton on Fosse Warwks ...... 30 G6
Stretton Sugwas Herefs ...... 28 E1
Stretton under Fosse
    Warwks ...... 41 L10
Stretton Westwood
    Shrops ...... 39 L3

Stromeferry Highld ...... 97 M3
Stromness Ork ...... 111 g2
Stronachlachar Stirlg ...... 84 G2
Stronafian Ag & B ...... 83 Q6
Stronchrubie Highld ...... 108 E11
Strone Ag & B ...... 84 D6
Strone Highld ...... 98 A11
Strone Highld ...... 98 G4
Stronenaba Highld ...... 98 B11
Stronmilchan Ag & B ...... 90 F10
Stronsay Ork ...... 111 i2
Stronsay Airport Ork ...... 111 i2
Strontian Highld ...... 89 Q4
Strood Medway ...... 22 E9
Strood Gloucs ...... 29 L7
Stroud Hants ...... 10 B5
Stroud Green Gloucs ...... 29 L7
Stroxton Lincs ...... 42 C4
Struan Highld ...... 96 D3
Struan P & K ...... 92 B3
Strumpshaw Norfk ...... 45 M8
Strutherhill S Lans ...... 77 M2
Struthers Fife ...... 86 H1
Struy Highld ...... 98 E2
Stuartfield Abers ...... 103 K6
Stubbers Green Wsall ...... 40 D7
Stubbington Hants ...... 9 P6
Stubbins Lancs ...... 57 P5
Stubton Lincs ...... 42 C11
Stuckton Hants ...... 8 H5
Studham C Beds ...... 32 E12
Studland Dorset ...... 8 F10
Studley Warwks ...... 30 E2
Studley Wilts ...... 18 E6
Studley Roger N York ...... 65 N12
Studley Royal N York ...... 65 M12
Studley Royal Park &
    Fountains Abbey
    N York ...... 58 H1
Stuntney Cambs ...... 33 N2
Sturmer Essex ...... 34 B7
Sturminster Common
    Dorset ...... 8 B5
Sturminster Marshall
    Dorset ...... 8 D7
Sturminster Newton
    Dorset ...... 8 B5
Sturry Kent ...... 23 M10
Sturton N Linc ...... 52 D3
Sturton by Stow Lincs ...... 52 C7
Sturton le Steeple Notts ...... 52 B6
Stuston Suffk ...... 35 J2
Stutton N York ...... 59 L6
Stutton Suffk ...... 35 J9
Styal Ches E ...... 57 Q11
Stynie Moray ...... 101 L3
Styrrup Notts ...... 51 N3
Succoth Ag & B ...... 84 E2
Suckley Worcs ...... 39 N10
Sudborough Nhants ...... 32 D1
Sudbourne Suffk ...... 35 N6
Sudbrook Lincs ...... 42 D2
Sudbrook Mons ...... 28 F10
Sudbrooke Lincs ...... 52 E8
Sudbury Derbys ...... 40 F2
Sudbury Gt Lon ...... 21 J6
Sudbury Suffk ...... 34 E8
Suffield N York ...... 67 L8
Suffield Norfk ...... 45 K4
Sugnall Staffs ...... 49 P8
Sugwas Pool Herefs ...... 28 E1
Suisnish Highld ...... 96 H6
Sulby IoM ...... 56 d3
Sulgrave Nhants ...... 31 M5
Sulham W Berk ...... 19 Q6
Sulhamstead W Berk ...... 19 Q7
Sullom Shet ...... 111 k3
Sullom Voe Shet ...... 111 k3
Sully V Glam ...... 16 F3
Sumburgh Airport Shet ...... 111 k5
Summerbridge N York ...... 58 G2
Summercourt Cnwll ...... 3 K5
Summerfield Norfk ...... 44 C3
Summerhill Pembks ...... 25 K7
Summerhouse Darltn ...... 65 L4
Summersdale W Susx ...... 10 D8
Summerseat Bury ...... 57 P6
Summertown Oxon ...... 31 L11
Sunbury-on-Thames
    Surrey ...... 20 H9
Sundaywell D & G ...... 78 D11
Sunderland Ag & B ...... 82 C9
Sunderland Cumb ...... 71 J8
Sunderland Lancs ...... 62 H10
Sunderland Sundld ...... 73 P9
Sunderland Bridge Dur ...... 73 M12
Sunderland
    Crematorium Sundld ...... 73 P9
Sundhope Border ...... 79 M4
Sundon Park Luton ...... 32 F10
Sundridge Kent ...... 21 P11
Sunningdale W & M ...... 20 F9
Sunninghill W & M ...... 20 F9
Sunningwell Oxon ...... 19 N1
Sunniside Dur ...... 73 K12
Sunniside Gatesd ...... 73 L8
Sunnyhill C Derb ...... 41 J2
Sunnyhurst Bl w D ...... 57 N4
Sunnylaw Stirlg ...... 85 N4
Sunnymead Oxon ...... 31 L11
Surbiton Gt Lon ...... 21 J9
Surfleet Lincs ...... 43 J5
Surlingham Norfk ...... 45 M8
Surrex Essex ...... 34 E11
Surrey & Sussex
    Crematorium W Susx ...... 11 L3
Sustead Norfk ...... 45 K3
Susworth Lincs ...... 52 B3
Sutcombe Devon ...... 14 F9
Sutcombemill Devon ...... 14 F9
Sutterby Lincs ...... 53 L8
Sutterton Lincs ...... 43 J3
Sutton C Beds ...... 32 H7
Sutton C Pete ...... 42 F9
Sutton Cambs ...... 33 M2
Sutton Devon ...... 5 N10
Sutton E Susx ...... 11 P9
Sutton Gt Lon ...... 21 K9
Sutton Kent ...... 23 P12
Sutton N York ...... 59 L8
Sutton Norfk ...... 45 N5
Sutton Notts ...... 51 Q12
Sutton Oxon ...... 31 K11
Sutton Shrops ...... 39 N5
Sutton Staffs ...... 49 N10
Sutton Suffk ...... 35 M7
Sutton W Susx ...... 10 F7

Sutton-at-Hone Kent ...... 22 B9
Sutton Bassett Nhants ...... 41 Q9
Sutton Benger Wilts ...... 18 D5
Sutton Bonington Notts ...... 41 L3
Sutton Bridge Lincs ...... 43 M6
Sutton Cheney Leics ...... 41 K7
Sutton Coldfield Birm ...... 40 E8
Sutton Coldfield
    Crematorium Birm ...... 40 F7
Sutton Courtenay Oxon ...... 19 N2
Sutton cum Lound Notts ...... 51 P4
Sutton Green Surrey ...... 20 G11
Sutton Howgrave N York ...... 65 N10
Sutton-in-Ashfield Notts ...... 51 L8
Sutton-in-Craven N York ...... 58 D5
Sutton Maddock Shrops ...... 39 N2
Sutton Mallet Somset ...... 17 K8
Sutton Mandeville Wilts ...... 8 E2
Sutton Montis Somset ...... 17 P10
Sutton-on-Hull C KuH ...... 61 J7
Sutton on Sea Lincs ...... 53 N7
Sutton-on-the-Forest
    N York ...... 59 M2
Sutton on the Hill Derbys ...... 40 G2
Sutton on Trent Notts ...... 52 B9
Sutton St Edmund Lincs ...... 43 L7
Sutton St James Lincs ...... 43 L6
Sutton St Nicholas Herefs ...... 39 K11
Sutton Scotney Hants ...... 19 M11
Sutton-under-Brailes
    Warwks ...... 30 H6
Sutton-under-
    Whitestonecliffe
    N York ...... 66 C10
Sutton upon Derwent
    E R Yk ...... 60 C5
Sutton Valence Kent ...... 12 F1
Sutton Veny Wilts ...... 18 D11
Sutton Waldron Dorset ...... 8 C4
Sutton Weaver Ches W ...... 57 K11
Sutton Wick BaNES ...... 17 N4
Sutton Wick Oxon ...... 19 N2
Swaby Lincs ...... 53 L7
Swadlincote Derbys ...... 40 H4
Swaffham Norfk ...... 44 D8
Swaffham Bulbeck Cambs ...... 33 N4
Swaffham Prior Cambs ...... 33 N4
Swafield Norfk ...... 45 L4
Swainby N York ...... 66 C7
Swainsthorpe Norfk ...... 45 K9
Swainswick BaNES ...... 18 B7
Swalcliffe Oxon ...... 31 J6
Swalecliffe Kent ...... 23 L9
Swallow Lincs ...... 52 H3
Swallow Beck Lincs ...... 52 D9
Swallowcliffe Wilts ...... 8 E3
Swallowfield Wokham ...... 20 B9
Swallownest Rothm ...... 51 K4
Swanage Dorset ...... 8 F10
Swanbourne Bucks ...... 32 B10
Swan Green Ches W ...... 49 N2
Swanland E R Yk ...... 60 G8
Swanley Kent ...... 21 P9
Swanley Village Kent ...... 21 Q9
Swanmore Hants ...... 9 P4
Swannington Leics ...... 41 K4
Swannington Norfk ...... 45 J6
Swanpool Lincs ...... 52 D9
Swanscombe Kent ...... 22 C8
Swansea Swans ...... 26 E9
Swansea Airport Swans ...... 26 D9
Swansea Crematorium
    Swans ...... 26 E8
Swansea West Services
    Swans ...... 26 E8
Swanton Abbot Norfk ...... 45 L5
Swanton Morley Norfk ...... 44 G6
Swanton Novers Norfk ...... 44 G4
Swan Village Sandw ...... 40 C8
Swanwick Derbys ...... 51 K9
Swanwick Hants ...... 9 N5
Swarby Lincs ...... 42 F3
Swardeston Norfk ...... 45 K9
Swarkestone Derbys ...... 41 J2
Swarland Nthumb ...... 81 N12
Swarraton Hants ...... 19 P12
Swarthmoor Cumb ...... 62 F6
Swaton Lincs ...... 42 G3
Swavesey Cambs ...... 33 K3
Sway Hants ...... 9 J7
Swayfield Lincs ...... 42 E5
Swaythling C Sotn ...... 9 M4
Sweetham Devon ...... 15 Q11
Sweethaws E Susx ...... 11 P4
Sweets Cnwll ...... 4 E2
Sweetshouse Cnwll ...... 3 N4
Swefling Suffk ...... 35 M4
Swepstone Leics ...... 41 J5
Swerford Oxon ...... 31 J7
Swettenham Ches E ...... 49 P3
Swilland Suffk ...... 35 K6
Swillington Leeds ...... 59 J7
Swimbridge Devon ...... 15 L6
Swimbridge Newland
    Devon ...... 15 K6
Swinbrook Oxon ...... 30 H10
Swincliffe N York ...... 58 G3
Swinderby Lincs ...... 52 C10
Swindon Gloucs ...... 29 N4
Swindon Staffs ...... 39 Q4
Swindon Swindn ...... 18 G4
Swine E R Yk ...... 61 K7
Swinefleet E R Yk ...... 60 D9
Swineshead Bed ...... 32 F4
Swineshead Lincs ...... 43 J3
Swiney Highld ...... 110 E8
Swinford Leics ...... 41 M10
Swingfield Minnis Kent ...... 13 M2
Swingfield Street Kent ...... 13 N2
Swingleton Green Suffk ...... 34 F7
Swinhoe Nthumb ...... 81 P8
Swinithwaite N York ...... 65 J9
Swinside Cumb ...... 71 K10
Swinstead Lincs ...... 42 E5
Swinton Border ...... 80 H5
Swinton N York ...... 65 L10
Swinton N York ...... 66 G11
Swinton Rothm ...... 51 K2
Swinton Salfd ...... 57 P8
Swithland Leics ...... 41 M5
Swordale Highld ...... 107 J3
Swordland Highld ...... 97 L10
Swordly Highld ...... 109 M4
Swynnerton Staffs ...... 49 Q8
Swyre Dorset ...... 7 M5
Sychtyn Powys ...... 38 B1
Syde Gloucs ...... 29 N6
Sydenham Gt Lon ...... 21 M8

Sydenham Oxon ...... 20 B3
Sydenham Damerel
    Devon ...... 5 J5
Syderstone Norfk ...... 44 D4
Sydling St Nicholas Dorset ...... 7 P3
Sydmonton Hants ...... 19 N8
Syerston Notts ...... 51 Q10
Sykehouse Donc ...... 59 N10
Symbister Shet ...... 111 k3
Symington S Ayrs ...... 76 G5
Symington S Lans ...... 78 G2
Symondsbury Dorset ...... 7 L4
Symonds Yat (West)
    Herefs ...... 28 G5
Syre Highld ...... 109 M7
Syreford Gloucs ...... 30 D9
Syresham Nhants ...... 31 N6
Syston Leics ...... 41 N5
Syston Lincs ...... 42 D2
Sytchampton Worcs ...... 39 Q8
Sywell Nhants ...... 32 B4

## T

Tackley Oxon ...... 31 L9
Tacolneston Norfk ...... 45 J10
Tadcaster N York ...... 59 L5
Taddington Derbys ...... 50 F6
Tadley Hants ...... 19 P8
Tadlow Cambs ...... 33 J7
Tadmarton Oxon ...... 31 K6
Tadworth Surrey ...... 21 K11
Taff's Well Rhondd ...... 27 N11
Taibach Neath ...... 26 G10
Tain Highld ...... 107 M6
Tain Highld ...... 110 E3
Tairbeart W Isls ...... 111 c3
Takeley Essex ...... 33 P11
Takeley Street Essex ...... 33 N11
Talaton Devon ...... 6 E3
Talbenny Pembks ...... 24 E6
Taleford Devon ...... 6 E4
Talerddig Powys ...... 47 Q10
Talgarreg Cerdgn ...... 36 G9
Talgarth Powys ...... 27 N3
Talisker Highld ...... 96 D4
Talke Staffs ...... 49 P5
Talke Pits Staffs ...... 49 P5
Talkin Cumb ...... 71 Q4
Talladale Highld ...... 105 N8
Talla Linnfoots Border ...... 79 J5
Tallaminnock S Ayrs ...... 76 G10
Tallarn Green Wrexhm ...... 49 J6
Tallentire Cumb ...... 70 H8
Talley Carmth ...... 26 E3
Tallington Lincs ...... 42 F8
Talmine Highld ...... 109 K3
Talog Carmth ...... 25 N4
Talsarn Cerdgn ...... 37 J9
Talsarnau Gwynd ...... 47 K4
Talskiddy Cnwll ...... 3 K3
Talwrn IoA ...... 54 G6
Tal-y-Bont Cerdgn ...... 37 K3
Tal-y-Bont Conwy ...... 55 L7
Tal-y-bont Gwynd ...... 47 J7
Tal-y-bont Gwynd ...... 54 H7
Talybont-on-Usk Powys ...... 27 N4
Tal-y-Cafn Conwy ...... 55 L7
Tal-y-coed Mons ...... 28 E6
Talysarn Gwynd ...... 54 G10
Tamar Valley Mining
    District Devon ...... 5 J7
Tamerton Foliot C Plym ...... 5 K7
Tamworth Staffs ...... 40 G6
Tamworth Services
    Warwks ...... 40 G7
Tandridge Surrey ...... 21 M12
Tanfield Dur ...... 73 L9
Tanfield Lea Dur ...... 73 L9
Tangley Hants ...... 19 K9
Tangmere W Susx ...... 10 E8
Tangusdale W Isls ...... 111 a7
Tankerness Ork ...... 111 h2
Tankersley Barns ...... 51 J2
Tankerton Kent ...... 23 L9
Tannach Highld ...... 110 G6
Tannachie Abers ...... 95 N5
Tannadice Angus ...... 93 M5
Tanner's Green Worcs ...... 40 E11
Tannington Suffk ...... 35 L4
Tannochside N Lans ...... 85 L10
Tansley Derbys ...... 51 J8
Tansor Nhants ...... 42 F11
Tantobie Dur ...... 73 L9
Tanworth in Arden
    Warwks ...... 40 E12
Tan-y-groes Cerdgn ...... 36 E10
Taobh Tuath W Isls ...... 111 b3
Taplow Bucks ...... 20 E7
Tarbert Ag & B ...... 75 J3
Tarbert Ag & B ...... 83 N8
Tarbert W Isls ...... 111 c3
Tarbet Ag & B ...... 84 F3
Tarbet Highld ...... 97 L10
Tarbet Highld ...... 108 D6
Tarbolton S Ayrs ...... 76 G6
Tarbrax S Lans ...... 86 B10
Tardebigge Worcs ...... 30 D1
Tarfside Angus ...... 94 H6
Tarland Abers ...... 94 H2
Tarleton Lancs ...... 57 J5
Tarlton Gloucs ...... 29 N8
Tarnock Somset ...... 17 K5
Tarporley Ches W ...... 49 K3
Tarrant Crawford Dorset ...... 8 D6
Tarrant Gunville Dorset ...... 8 D5
Tarrant Hinton Dorset ...... 8 D5
Tarrant Keyneston Dorset ...... 8 D6
Tarrant Launceston
    Dorset ...... 8 D5
Tarrant Monkton Dorset ...... 8 D5
Tarrant Rawston Dorset ...... 8 D6
Tarrant Rushton Dorset ...... 8 D6
Tarring Neville E Susx ...... 11 N9
Tarrington Herefs ...... 28 H1
Tarskavaig Highld ...... 96 H7
Tarves Abers ...... 102 H8
Tarvin Ches W ...... 49 J3
Tasburgh Norfk ...... 45 K10
Tatenhill Staffs ...... 40 G3
Tathwell Lincs ...... 53 K6
Tatsfield Surrey ...... 21 N11
Tattenhall Ches W ...... 49 J4
Tatterford Norfk ...... 44 E5
Tattersett Norfk ...... 44 E4

Tattershall Lincs 52 H11
Tattershall Thorpe Lincs 52 H10
Tattingstone Suffk 35 J8
Tattingstone White
  Horse Suffk 35 J8
Tatton Park Ches E 57 N11
Tatworth Somset 7 J2
Tauchers Moray 101 M5
Taunton Somset 16 G10
Taunton Deane
  Crematorium Somset 16 G10
Taunton Deane Services
  Somset 16 G11
Taverham Norfk 45 J7
Tavernspite Pembks 25 L6
Tavistock Devon 5 K5
Tavistock Devon 5 K5
Taw Green Devon 15 L11
Tawstock Devon 15 K6
Taxal Derbys 50 D5
Tay Bridge C Dund 93 M9
Taychreggan Hotel Ag & B 90 E11
Tay Forest Park P & K 92 B4
Tayinloan Ag & B 75 K4
Taynton Gloucs 29 J4
Taynton Oxon 30 G10
Taynuilt Ag & B 90 D9
Tayport Fife 93 M9
Tayvallich Ag & B 83 L5
Tealby Lincs 52 G5
Tealing Angus 93 M7
Team Valley Gatesd 73 M8
Teangue Highld 97 J7
Teanord Highld 107 K9
Tebay Cumb 63 L2
Tebay Services Cumb 63 L2
Tebworth C Beds 32 E10
Tedburn St Mary Devon 5 L2
Teddington Gloucs 29 N3
Teddington Gt Lon 21 J8
Tedstone Delamere
  Herefs 39 M9
Tedstone Wafer Herefs 39 M9
Teesside Crematorium
  Middsb 66 C4
Teeton Nhants 41 P12
Teffont Evias Wilts 8 E2
Teffont Magna Wilts 8 E2
Tegryn Pembks 25 L3
Teigh Rutlnd 42 C7
Teigngrace Devon 6 B7
Teignmouth Devon 6 C8
Teindside Border 79 P7
Telford Wrekin 39 M1
Telford Crematorium
  Wrekin 49 N12
Telford Services Shrops 39 N1
Tellisford Somset 18 B9
Telscombe E Susx 11 N8
Tempar P & K 91 Q5
Templand D & G 78 H10
Temple Cnwll 4 E5
Temple Mdloth 86 G9
Temple Bar Cerdgn 37 J9
Temple Cloud BaNES 17 P5
Templecombe Somset 17 Q10
Temple Grafton Warwks 30 E3
Temple Guiting Gloucs 30 E8
Temple Hirst N York 59 N8
Temple Normanton
  Derbys 51 K7
Temple of Fiddes Abers 95 N6
Temple Sowerby Cumb 64 B3
Templeton Devon 15 Q9
Templeton Pembks 25 K6
Templetown Dur 73 K10
Tempsford C Beds 32 G6
Tenbury Wells Worcs 39 L8
Tenby Pembks 25 K8
Tendring Essex 35 J11
Tendring Green Essex 35 J10
Tendring Heath Essex 35 J10
Ten Mile Bank Norfk 43 P10
Tenterden Kent 12 H4
Terling Essex 22 F1
Ternhill Shrops 49 L8
Terregles D & G 78 F12
Terrington N York 66 F12
Terrington St Clement
  Norfk 43 N6
Terrington St John Norfk 43 N7
Teston Kent 22 E11
Testwood Hants 9 L5
Tetbury Gloucs 29 M9
Tetchill Shrops 48 H8
Tetcott Devon 14 F11
Tetford Lincs 53 K8
Tetney Lincs 53 K4
Tetsworth Oxon 20 B3
Tettenhall Wolves 40 B7
Tettenhall Wood Wolves 39 Q3
Teversal Notts 51 L8
Teversham Cambs 33 M5
Teviothead Border 79 N7
Tewin Herts 21 L1
Tewkesbury Gloucs 29 M3
Teynham Kent 23 J10
Thackley C Brad 58 F6
Thainstone Abers 102 G10
Thakeham W Susx 10 H6
Thame Oxon 20 B3
Thames Ditton Surrey 21 J9
Thamesmead Gt Lon 21 P7
Thamesport Medway 22 G8
Thanet Crematorium
  Kent 23 Q9
Thanington Kent 23 L11
Thankerton S Lans 78 F2
Tharston Norfk 45 K10
Thatcham W Berk 19 N7
Thaxted Essex 33 P9
Theakston N York 65 N10
Thealby N Linc 60 F9
Theale Somset 17 L7
Theale W Berk 19 Q6
Thearne E R Yk 61 J6
The Beeches Gloucs 18 F1
Theberton Suffk 35 P4
The Braes Highld 96 G3
The Brunt E Loth 87 M7
The Bungalow IoM 56 d4
The Burf Worcs 39 P8
The Butts Gloucs 29 M5
The City Bucks 20 C4
The Common Wilts 9 J2
The Counties
  Crematorium Nhants 31 Q3

Theddingworth Leics 41 P9
Theddlethorpe All
  Saints Lincs 53 M6
Theddlethorpe St Helen
  Lincs 53 M6
The Den N Ayrs 76 F2
The Forstal Kent 13 K3
The Garden of England
  Crematorium Kent 22 H9
The Green Cumb 62 D5
The Green Essex 34 C11
The Green N York 66 H6
The Green Wilts 8 C2
The Headland Hartpl 66 D1
The Hill Cumb 62 D5
The Lee Bucks 20 E3
The Lhen IoM 56 d2
Thelnetham Suffk 34 G2
The Lochs Moray 101 L3
Thelveton Norfk 35 J1
Thelwall Warrtn 57 M10
Themelthorpe Norfk 44 H5
The Middles Dur 73 L9
The Moor Kent 12 F4
The Mumbles Swans 26 E10
The Murray S Lans 85 K11
The Neuk Abers 95 M3
Thenford Nhants 31 M6
The Park Crematorium
  Hants 10 E1
The Reddings Gloucs 29 M5
Therfield Herts 33 K8
The Ross P & K 92 B10
The Stocks Kent 12 H5
The Strand Wilts 18 D8
Thetford Norfk 44 E12
Thetford Forest Park 44 D11
The Vale Crematorium
  Luton 32 G10
Theydon Bois Essex 21 N4
Thickwood Wilts 18 C6
Thimbleby Lincs 53 J9
Thimbleby N York 66 C8
Thingwall Wirral 56 F11
Thirkleby N York 66 C10
Thirlby N York 66 C10
Thirlestane Border 80 D5
Thirn N York 65 L9
Thirsk N York 65 Q10
Thistleton Lancs 56 H2
Thistleton Rutlnd 42 D6
Thistley Green Suffk 33 Q2
Thixendale N York 60 E3
Thockrington Nthumb 72 G5
Tholomas Drove Cambs 43 L8
Tholthorpe N York 59 L2
Thomastown Abers 102 D7
Thompson Norfk 44 F10
Thongsbridge Kirk 58 F11
Thoralby N York 64 H9
Thoresway Lincs 52 G4
Thorganby Lincs 52 H4
Thorganby N York 59 P6
Thorgill N York 66 G7
Thorington Suffk 35 N2
Thorington Street Suffk 34 G9
Thorlby N York 58 C4
Thorley Herts 33 M11
Thorley Street IoW 9 L9
Thornaby-on-Tees
  S on T 66 C4
Thornage Norfk 44 H3
Thornborough Bucks 31 Q7
Thornborough N York 65 N10
Thornbury C Brad 58 G7
Thornbury Devon 14 G9
Thornbury Herefs 39 L9
Thornbury S Glos 28 H10
Thornby Nhants 41 P11
Thorncliff Staffs 50 D8
Thorncliffe
  Crematorium Cumb 62 G7
Thorncombe Dorset 7 K3
Thorndon Suffk 35 J3
Thorndon Cross Devon 5 L2
Thorne Donc 59 P10
Thorner Leeds 59 J6
Thorne St Margaret
  Somset 16 E11
Thorney C Pete 43 J8
Thorney Notts 52 C8
Thorney Somset 17 K10
Thorney Hill Hants 8 H7
Thorney Island W Susx 10 C9
Thornfalcon Somset 16 H10
Thornford Dorset 17 N12
Thorngrafton Nthumb 72 E7
Thorngumbald E R Yk 61 L8
Thornham Norfk 44 C2
Thornham Magna Suffk 34 H3
Thornham Parva Suffk 35 J3
Thornhaugh C Pete 42 F9
Thornhill C Sotn 9 M5
Thornhill Cumb 62 B1
Thornhill D & G 78 E9
Thornhill Derbys 50 G4
Thornhill Kirk 58 G9
Thornhill Stirlg 85 L3
Thornholme E R Yk 61 J2
Thornicombe Dorset 8 C6
Thornington Nthumb 81 J7
Thornley Dur 73 K12
Thornley Dur 73 P11
Thornliebank E Rens 85 J11
Thorns Suffk 34 C6
Thornsett Derbys 50 D4
Thornthwaite Cumb 71 K9
Thornthwaite N York 58 H3
Thornton Angus 93 M6
Thornton Bucks 31 Q7
Thornton C Brad 58 E7
Thornton E R Yk 60 D5
Thornton Fife 86 F3
Thornton Lancs 56 G1
Thornton Leics 41 L6
Thornton Middsb 66 C5
Thornton Nthumb 81 K5
Thornton Curtis N Linc 61 J9
Thornton Garden of
  Rest Crematorium
  Sefton 56 G8
Thorntonhall S Lans 85 K11
Thornton Heath Gt Lon 21 L9
Thornton Hough Wirral 56 F11
Thornton-in-Craven
  N York 58 B5

Thornton in Lonsdale
  N York 63 M7
Thornton-le-Beans N York 65 P9
Thornton-le-Clay N York 59 P2
Thornton-le-Dale N York 67 J10
Thornton le Moor Lincs 52 F4
Thornton-le-Moor N York 65 P9
Thornton-le-Moors
  Ches W 48 H1
Thornton-le-Street N York 65 P9
Thorntonloch E Loth 87 N7
Thornton Rust N York 64 G9
Thornton Steward N York 65 L9
Thornton Watlass N York 65 M9
Thornydykes Border 80 E5
Thornythwaite Cumb 71 N10
Thoroton Notts 51 Q11
Thorp Arch Leeds 59 K5
Thorpe Derbys 50 F10
Thorpe E R Yk 60 G5
Thorpe N York 58 D2
Thorpe Notts 51 Q10
Thorpe Surrey 20 G9
Thorpe Abbotts Norfk 35 K2
Thorpe Arnold Leics 41 Q4
Thorpe Audlin Wakefd 59 L10
Thorpe Bassett N York 67 J11
Thorpe Bay Sthend 22 H6
Thorpe by Water Rutlnd 42 C10
Thorpe Constantine Staffs 40 H6
Thorpe End Norfk 45 L7
Thorpe Green Essex 35 J11
Thorpe Green Suffk 34 F6
Thorpe Hesley Rothm 51 J2
Thorpe in Balne Donc 59 N11
Thorpe Langton Leics 41 Q8
Thorpe Lea Surrey 20 G8
Thorpe-le-Soken Essex 35 K11
Thorpe le Street E R Yk 60 E5
Thorpe Malsor Nhants 32 B2
Thorpe Mandeville Nhants 31 M5
Thorpe Market Norfk 45 L3
Thorpe Marriot Norfk 45 K7
Thorpe Morieux Suffk 34 F6
Thorpeness Suffk 35 P5
Thorpe on the Hill Lincs 52 C9
Thorpe Park Surrey 20 G9
Thorpe St Andrew Norfk 45 L8
Thorpe St Peter Lincs 53 M10
Thorpe Salvin Rothm 51 M5
Thorpe Satchville Leics 41 Q5
Thorpe Thewles S on T 65 P3
Thorpe Tilney Lincs 52 G11
Thorpe Underwood
  N York 59 L3
Thorpe Waterville Nhants 32 E1
Thorpe Willoughby N York 59 M7
Thorrington Essex 34 H11
Thorverton Devon 6 C3
Thrandeston Suffk 35 J2
Thrapston Nhants 32 E2
Threapwood Ches W 48 H6
Threapwood Staffs 50 D11
Threave S Ayrs 76 F9
Three Bridges W Susx 11 L3
Three Chimneys Kent 12 G3
Three Cocks Powys 27 N2
Three Counties
  Crematorium Essex 34 D10
Three Crosses Swans 26 D9
Three Cups Corner E Susx 12 D6
Threekingham Lincs 42 F3
Three Leg Cross E Susx 12 D4
Three Legged Cross
  Dorset 8 F6
Three Mile Cross Wokham 20 B9
Threemilestone Cnwll 2 H6
Three Miletown W Loth 86 C7
Three Oaks E Susx 12 G7
Threlkeld Cumb 71 M9
Threshers Bush Essex 21 P2
Threshfield N York 58 C2
Thrigby Norfk 45 P7
Thringstone Leics 41 K4
Thrintoft N York 65 N8
Thriplow Cambs 33 M7
Throcking Herts 33 K10
Throckley N u Ty 73 K7
Throckmorton Worcs 30 C4
Throop Bmouth 8 G8
Thropton Nthumb 72 H1
Throsk Stirlg 85 P5
Throughgate D & G 78 E11
Throwleigh Devon 5 N3
Throwley Forstal Kent 23 J11
Thrumpton Notts 41 L2
Thrumster Highld 110 G6
Thrunscoe NE Lin 53 K2
Thrupp Gloucs 29 M7
Thrussington Leics 41 P4
Thruxton Hants 19 K10
Thruxton Herefs 28 E2
Thrybergh Rothm 51 L2
Thulston Derbys 41 K2
Thundersley Essex 22 F6
Thurcaston Leics 41 M5
Thurcroft Rothm 51 L3
Thurgarton Norfk 45 K3
Thurgarton Notts 51 P10
Thurgoland Barns 50 H1
Thurlaston Leics 41 L7
Thurlaston Warwks 41 L12
Thurlbear Somset 16 H11
Thurlby Lincs 42 F6
Thurlby Lincs 52 C10
Thurlby Lincs 53 M8
Thurleigh Bed 32 F5
Thurlestone Devon 5 N10
Thurloxton Somset 16 H9
Thurlstone Barns 58 G12
Thurlton Norfk 45 N9
Thurmaston Leics 41 N5
Thurnby Leics 41 N6
Thurne Norfk 45 N7
Thurnham Kent 22 F11
Thurning Nhants 42 F12
Thurning Norfk 44 H4
Thurnscoe Barns 59 L11
Thursby Cumb 71 M5
Thursford Norfk 44 G4
Thursley Surrey 10 E3
Thurso Highld 110 D3
Thurstaston Wirral 56 F11
Thurston Suffk 34 F4
Thurstonfield Cumb 71 M4
Thurstonland Kirk 58 F11
Thurton Norfk 45 M9

Thurvaston Derbys 50 G12
Thuxton Norfk 44 G8
Thwaite N York 64 F7
Thwaite Suffk 35 J3
Thwaite Head Cumb 62 G4
Thwaite St Mary Norfk 45 M10
Thwing E R Yk 67 M12
Tibbermore P & K 92 F10
Tibbers D & G 78 E9
Tibberton Gloucs 29 K4
Tibberton Worcs 30 B3
Tibberton Wrekin 49 M10
Tibenham Norfk 45 J11
Tibshelf Derbys 51 K8
Tibshelf Services Derbys 51 K8
Tibthorpe E R Yk 60 G3
Ticehurst E Susx 12 E4
Tichborne Hants 9 P2
Tickencote Rutlnd 42 E8
Tickenham N Som 17 L2
Tickhill Donc 51 N3
Ticklerton Shrops 39 J4
Ticknall Derbys 41 J3
Tickton E R Yk 60 H6
Tidcombe Wilts 19 K8
Tiddington Oxon 31 P12
Tiddington Warwks 30 G3
Tidebrook E Susx 12 C4
Tideford Cnwll 4 H8
Tidenham Gloucs 28 G9
Tideswell Derbys 50 F6
Tidmarsh W Berk 19 Q6
Tidmington Warwks 30 H6
Tidworth Wilts 19 J10
Tiers Cross Pembks 24 F6
Tiffield Nhants 31 P4
Tigerton Angus 95 J8
Tigh a Ghearraidh W Isls 111 a4
Tigharry W Isls 111 a4
Tighnabruaich Ag & B 83 P8
Tigley Devon 5 P7
Tilbrook Cambs 32 F3
Tilbury Thurr 22 D8
Tile Cross Birm 40 F9
Tile Hill Covtry 40 H11
Tilehurst Readg 19 Q6
Tilford Surrey 10 E2
Tilgate W Susx 11 L3
Tilham Street Somset 17 M8
Tillicoultry Clacks 85 Q4
Tillietudlem S Lans 77 N3
Tillingham Essex 23 J3
Tillington Herefs 39 J12
Tillington W Susx 10 F6
Tillington Common Herefs 39 J11
Tillybirloch Abers 95 L1
Tillyfourie Abers 102 E11
Tillygreig Abers 103 J10
Tillyrie P & K 86 D2
Tilmanstone Kent 23 P12
Tilney All Saints Norfk 43 P6
Tilney High End Norfk 43 N6
Tilney St Lawrence Norfk 43 N7
Tilshead Wilts 18 F10
Tilstock Shrops 49 K7
Tilston Ches W 49 J5
Tilstone Fearnall Ches W 49 K4
Tilsworth C Beds 32 E11
Tilton on the Hill Leics 41 Q6
Tiltups End Gloucs 29 L8
Timberland Lincs 52 G10
Timbersbrook Ches E 50 B8
Timberscombe Somset 16 C7
Timble N York 58 F4
Timpanheck D & G 71 M1
Timperley Traffd 57 P10
Timsbury BaNES 17 P4
Timsbury Hants 9 L3
Timsgarry W Isls 111 c2
Timsgearraidh W Isls 111 c2
Timworth Suffk 34 E3
Timworth Green Suffk 34 E3
Tincleton Dorset 8 B8
Tindale Cumb 72 B8
Tingewick Bucks 31 P7
Tingrith C Beds 32 E9
Tingwall Ork 111 h2
Tinhay Devon 5 J3
Tinsley Sheff 51 K3
Tinsley Green W Susx 11 L3
Tintagel Cnwll 4 C3
Tintern Parva Mons 28 F8
Tintinhull Somset 17 M11
Tintwistle Derbys 50 D2
Tinwald D & G 78 G11
Tinwell Rutlnd 42 E8
Tipton Sandw 40 C8
Tipton Green Sandw 40 C8
Tipton St John Devon 6 E5
Tiptree Essex 34 E12
Tiptree Heath Essex 22 G1
Tirabad Powys 37 P11
Tiree Ag & B 88 C7
Tiree Airport Ag & B 88 C7
Tiretigan Ag & B 83 K9
Tirley Gloucs 29 L3
Tiroran Ag & B 89 K10
Tirphil Caerph 27 N7
Tirril Cumb 71 P9
Tisbury Wilts 8 D2
Tissington Derbys 50 F9
Titchberry Devon 14 E6
Titchfield Hants 9 P6
Titchmarsh Nhants 32 F2
Titchwell Norfk 44 C2
Tithby Notts 51 P12
Titley Herefs 38 G9
Titsey Surrey 21 N11
Titson Cnwll 14 E10
Tittensor Staffs 49 Q7
Tittleshall Norfk 44 E6
Titton Worcs 39 P7
Tiverton Ches W 49 K4
Tiverton Devon 6 C1
Tivetshall St Margaret
  Norfk 45 K11
Tivetshall St Mary Norfk 45 J11
Tixall Staffs 40 C3
Tixover Rutlnd 42 D9
Toab Shet 111 k5
Tobermory Ag & B 89 L5
Toberonochy Ag & B 83 L2
Tobha Mor W Isls 111 a5
Tocher Abers 102 F8
Tochieneal Moray 101 P3

Tockenham Wilts 18 F5
Tockholes Bl w D 57 M4
Tockington S Glos 28 H10
Tockwith N York 59 L4
Todber Dorset 8 B4
Toddington C Beds 32 E10
Toddington Gloucs 30 D7
Toddington Services
  C Beds 32 E10
Todenham Gloucs 30 G7
Todhills Abers 93 M7
Todhills Services Cumb 71 N3
Todmorden Calder 58 C8
Todwick Rothm 51 L4
Toft Cambs 33 K5
Toft Lincs 42 F6
Toft Shet 111 k3
Toft Hill Dur 65 K2
Toft Monks Norfk 45 N10
Toft next Newton Lincs 52 E6
Toftrees Norfk 44 F5
Togston Nthumb 73 M1
Tokavaig Highld 96 H7
Tokers Green Oxon 20 B7
Tolastadh W Isls 111 e1
Toll W Isls 111 d2
Tolland Somset 16 E9
Tollard Royal Wilts 8 D4
Toll Bar Donc 59 M11
Toller Fratrum Dorset 7 N4
Toller Porcorum Dorset 7 N3
Tollerton N York 59 L2
Tollerton Notts 41 N1
Tollesbury Essex 23 J2
Tolleshunt D'Arcy Essex 22 H2
Tolleshunt Knights Essex 22 H1
Tolleshunt Major Essex 22 H1
Tolpuddle Dorset 8 B8
Tolsta W Isls 111 e1
Tolworth Gt Lon 21 J9
Tomatin Highld 99 M4
Tomchrasky Highld 98 C6
Tomdoun Highld 98 B8
Tomich Highld 98 D4
Tomich Highld 107 J11
Tomich Highld 107 K2
Tomich Highld 107 L8
Tomintoul Moray 101 J10
Tomnacross Highld 98 G2
Tomnavoulin Moray 101 J9
Tonbridge Kent 12 C2
Tondu Brdgnd 27 J11
Tonedale Somset 16 F11
Tong C Brad 58 G7
Tong Kent 23 J11
Tong Shrops 39 P1
Tonga W Isls 111 d2
Tonge Leics 41 K3
Tongham Surrey 10 E1
Tongland D & G 69 Q8
Tong Norton Shrops 39 P1
Tongue Highld 109 K4
Tongwynlais Cardif 27 N11
Tonmawr Neath 26 G8
Tonna Neath 26 G8
Tonwell Herts 33 K12
Tonypandy Rhondd 27 L9
Tonyrefail Rhondd 27 L10
Toot Baldon Oxon 19 P1
Toot Hill Essex 21 P3
Toothill Swindn 18 G4
Tooting Gt Lon 21 L8
Tooting Bec Gt Lon 21 L8
Topcliffe N York 65 P11
Topcroft Norfk 45 L10
Topcroft Street Norfk 45 L10
Toppesfield Essex 34 C8
Toprow Norfk 45 J9
Topsham Devon 6 C5
Torbeg N Ayrs 75 N6
Torboll Highld 107 M3
Torbreck Highld 99 J2
Torbryan Devon 5 Q6
Torcastle Highld 90 F1
Torcross Devon 5 Q10
Tore Highld 107 K10
Torinturk Ag & B 83 M9
Torksey Lincs 52 B7
Tormarton S Glos 18 B5
Tormore N Ayrs 75 N6
Tornagrain Highld 107 M11
Tornaveen Abers 95 K2
Torness Highld 98 H4
Toronto Dur 65 L2
Torpenhow Cumb 71 K7
Torphichen W Loth 86 A7
Torphins Abers 95 K2
Torpoint Cnwll 5 J8
Torquay Torbay 6 C9
Torquay Crematorium
  Torbay 6 B9
Torquhan Border 87 J11
Torran Highld 104 H11
Torrance E Duns 85 K8
Torranyard N Ayrs 76 F3
Torridon Highld 105 N10
Torridon House Highld 105 M10
Torrin Highld 96 G5
Torrisdale Ag & B 75 M5
Torrisdale Highld 109 M4
Torrish Highld 110 A11
Torrisholme Lancs 63 J9
Torroble Highld 107 K2
Torry C Aber 95 Q2
Torryburn Fife 86 B5
Torteval Guern 6 a2
Torthorwald D & G 78 G12
Tortington W Susx 10 G8
Torton Worcs 39 Q7
Tortworth S Glos 29 J9
Torvaig Highld 96 F2
Torver Cumb 62 F4
Torwood Falk 85 P6
Torwoodlee Border 79 P2
Torworth Notts 51 P4
Toscaig Highld 97 J3
Toseland Cambs 33 J4
Tosside Lancs 63 P10
Tostock Suffk 34 F4
Totaig Highld 104 B11
Tote Highld 104 F11
Tote Highld 104 G9
Totland IoW 9 K9
Totley Sheff 50 H5
Totnes Devon 5 Q7
Toton Notts 41 L1
Totronald Ag & B 88 E5

| Place | County | Page | Grid |
|---|---|---|---|
| Totscore | Highld | 104 | E8 |
| Tottenham | Gt Lon | 21 | M5 |
| Tottenhill | Norfk | 43 | Q7 |
| Totteridge | Gt Lon | 21 | K5 |
| Totternhoe | C Beds | 32 | E11 |
| Tottington | Bury | 57 | P6 |
| Totton | Hants | 9 | L5 |
| Toulton | Somset | 16 | G9 |
| Toulvaddie | Highld | 107 | P6 |
| Tovil | Kent | 22 | F11 |
| Toward | Ag & B | 84 | C8 |
| Toward Quay | Ag & B | 84 | B9 |
| Towcester | Nhants | 31 | P4 |
| Towednack | Cnwll | 2 | D7 |
| Tower of London | Gt Lon | 21 | M7 |
| Towersey | Oxon | 20 | B3 |
| Towie | Abers | 101 | N11 |
| Tow Law | Dur | 73 | K11 |
| Town End | Cambs | 43 | L10 |
| Townend | W Duns | 84 | G7 |
| Townhead | Barns | 50 | F1 |
| Townhead | D & G | 78 | G10 |
| Townhead of Greenlaw | D & G | 70 | C3 |
| Townhill | Fife | 86 | D4 |
| Town Littleworth | E Susx | 11 | N6 |
| Towns End | Hants | 19 | P8 |
| Townshend | Cnwll | 2 | E8 |
| Town Street | Suffk | 44 | C11 |
| Town Yetholm | Border | 80 | H8 |
| Towthorpe | C York | 59 | N3 |
| Towton | N York | 59 | L6 |
| Towyn | Conwy | 55 | P6 |
| Toxteth | Lpool | 56 | G10 |
| Toynton All Saints | Lincs | 53 | L10 |
| Toy's Hill | Kent | 21 | P12 |
| Trabboch | E Ayrs | 76 | G7 |
| Trabbochburn | E Ayrs | 76 | H7 |
| Tradespark | Highld | 100 | D4 |
| Trafford Park | Traffd | 57 | P9 |
| Trallong | Powys | 27 | K3 |
| Tranent | E Loth | 86 | H1 |
| Tranmere | Wirral | 56 | G10 |
| Trantelbeg | Highld | 109 | Q5 |
| Trantlemore | Highld | 109 | Q5 |
| Trapp | Carmth | 26 | E5 |
| Traprain | E Loth | 87 | L1 |
| Traquair | Border | 79 | M3 |
| Trawden | Lancs | 58 | B6 |
| Trawsfynydd | Gwynd | 47 | L4 |
| Trealaw | Rhondd | 27 | L9 |
| Treales | Lancs | 56 | H3 |
| Trearddur Bay | IoA | 54 | C6 |
| Treaslane | Highld | 104 | E10 |
| Trebetherick | Cnwll | 4 | B5 |
| Treborough | Somset | 16 | D8 |
| Trebullett | Cnwll | 4 | H5 |
| Treburley | Cnwll | 4 | H5 |
| Trecastle | Powys | 27 | J3 |
| Trecwn | Pembks | 24 | G3 |
| Trecynon | Rhondd | 27 | L7 |
| Tredegar | Blae G | 27 | N7 |
| Tredington | Gloucs | 29 | M3 |
| Tredington | Warwks | 30 | H5 |
| Tredunnock | Mons | 28 | D9 |
| Treen | Cnwll | 2 | B10 |
| Treeton | Rothm | 51 | K4 |
| Trefasser | Pembks | 24 | F2 |
| Trefecca | Powys | 27 | N3 |
| Trefeglwys | Powys | 37 | Q3 |
| Treffgarne | Pembks | 24 | G4 |
| Treffgarne Owen | Pembks | 24 | F4 |
| Trefforest | Rhondd | 27 | M10 |
| Trefilan | Cerdgn | 37 | J8 |
| Trefin | Pembks | 24 | E3 |
| Trefnant | Denbgs | 48 | B2 |
| Trefonen | Shrops | 48 | F9 |
| Trefor | Gwynd | 46 | F3 |
| Trefriw | Conwy | 55 | L8 |
| Tregadillett | Cnwll | 4 | G4 |
| Tregare | Mons | 28 | E6 |
| Tregaron | Cerdgn | 37 | L8 |
| Tregarth | Gwynd | 54 | H7 |
| Tregeare | Cnwll | 4 | F3 |
| Tregeiriog | Wrexhm | 48 | D8 |
| Tregele | IoA | 54 | E4 |
| Treglemais | Pembks | 24 | F4 |
| Tregonetha | Cnwll | 3 | L3 |
| Tregonning & Gwinear Mining District | Cnwll | 2 | E9 |
| Tregony | Cnwll | 3 | K6 |
| Tregorrick | Cnwll | 3 | M5 |
| Tregoyd | Powys | 27 | P2 |
| Tre-groes | Cerdgn | 36 | G10 |
| Tregynon | Powys | 38 | C3 |
| Tre-gynwr | Carmth | 25 | P5 |
| Trehafod | Rhondd | 27 | L10 |
| Trehan | Cnwll | 5 | J8 |
| Treharris | Myr Td | 27 | M9 |
| Treherbert | Rhondd | 27 | K8 |
| Trekenner | Cnwll | 4 | H5 |
| Treknow | Cnwll | 4 | E4 |
| Trelawnyd | Flints | 56 | C11 |
| Trelech | Carmth | 25 | M3 |
| Treleddyd-fawr | Pembks | 24 | D3 |
| Trelewis | Myr Td | 27 | M9 |
| Trelights | Cnwll | 4 | B4 |
| Trelill | Cnwll | 4 | C5 |
| Trellech | Mons | 28 | F7 |
| Trelogan | Flints | 56 | D11 |
| Tremadog | Gwynd | 47 | J4 |
| Tremail | Cnwll | 4 | F4 |
| Tremain | Cerdgn | 36 | D10 |
| Tremaine | Cnwll | 4 | G3 |
| Tremar | Cnwll | 4 | G6 |
| Trematon | Cnwll | 5 | J9 |
| Tremeirchion | Denbgs | 48 | C2 |
| Trenance | Cnwll | 3 | J3 |
| Trenance | Cnwll | 3 | L2 |
| Trench | Wrekin | 49 | M11 |
| Trenear | Cnwll | 2 | G9 |
| Treneglos | Cnwll | 4 | F3 |
| Trent | Dorset | 17 | N11 |
| Trentham | C Stke | 49 | Q7 |
| Trentishoe | Devon | 15 | L3 |
| Trent Vale | C Stke | 49 | Q7 |
| Treoes | V Glam | 27 | K12 |
| Treorchy | Rhondd | 27 | K8 |
| Trequite | Cnwll | 3 | M1 |
| Trerhyngyll | V Glam | 27 | L11 |
| Trerulefoot | Cnwll | 4 | H8 |
| Tresaith | Cerdgn | 36 | E9 |
| Tresco | IoS | 2 | b2 |
| Trescowe | Cnwll | 2 | E9 |
| Tresean | Cnwll | 3 | J5 |
| Tresham | Gloucs | 29 | L9 |
| Treshnish Isles | Ag & B | 88 | G7 |
| Tresillian | Cnwll | 3 | K6 |
| Treskinnick Cross | Cnwll | 14 | D11 |
| Tresmeer | Cnwll | 4 | F3 |
| Tresparrett | Cnwll | 4 | F2 |
| Tressait | P & K | 92 | C4 |
| Tresta | Shet | 111 | k4 |
| Tresta | Shet | 111 | m2 |
| Treswell | Notts | 52 | A7 |
| Treswithian Downs Crematorium | Cnwll | 2 | F7 |
| Tre Taliesin | Cerdgn | 37 | L3 |
| Trethevey | Cnwll | 4 | D3 |
| Trethewey | Cnwll | 2 | B10 |
| Trethurgy | Cnwll | 3 | M5 |
| Tretire | Herefs | 28 | F4 |
| Tretower | Powys | 27 | P5 |
| Treuddyn | Flints | 48 | F4 |
| Trevalga | Cnwll | 4 | D3 |
| Trevalyn | Wrexhm | 48 | H4 |
| Trevarrian | Cnwll | 3 | J2 |
| Trevarren | Cnwll | 3 | J3 |
| Treveal | Cnwll | 2 | H4 |
| Treveighan | Cnwll | 4 | C4 |
| Trevellas Downs | Cnwll | 2 | H5 |
| Trevelmond | Cnwll | 4 | G7 |
| Treverva | Cnwll | 2 | H9 |
| Trevescan | Cnwll | 2 | B10 |
| Treviscoe | Cnwll | 3 | L5 |
| Trevone | Cnwll | 3 | K1 |
| Trevor | Wrexhm | 48 | F7 |
| Trewalder | Cnwll | 4 | D4 |
| Trewarmett | Cnwll | 4 | D3 |
| Trewavas Mining District | Cnwll | 2 | E9 |
| Trewen | Cnwll | 4 | F4 |
| Trewint | Cnwll | 4 | F4 |
| Trewithian | Cnwll | 3 | K8 |
| Trewoon | Cnwll | 3 | L5 |
| Treyford | W Susx | 10 | D6 |
| Trimdon | Dur | 65 | P1 |
| Trimdon Colliery | Dur | 65 | P1 |
| Trimdon Grange | Dur | 65 | P1 |
| Trimingham | Norfk | 45 | L3 |
| Trimley St Martin | Suffk | 35 | L8 |
| Trimley St Mary | Suffk | 35 | L9 |
| Trimsaran | Carmth | 26 | B7 |
| Trimstone | Devon | 15 | J4 |
| Trinafour | P & K | 91 | Q4 |
| Tring | Herts | 20 | E2 |
| Trinity | Angus | 95 | K9 |
| Trinity | Jersey | 7 | b1 |
| Trinity Gask | P & K | 92 | E11 |
| Triscombe | Somset | 16 | F8 |
| Trislaig | Highld | 90 | E2 |
| Trispen | Cnwll | 3 | J6 |
| Tritlington | Nthumb | 73 | L3 |
| Trochry | P & K | 92 | E7 |
| Troedyraur | Cerdgn | 36 | E10 |
| Troedyrhiw | Myr Td | 27 | M8 |
| Troon | Cnwll | 2 | F8 |
| Troon | S Ayrs | 76 | F5 |
| Tropical World Roundhay Park | Leeds | 59 | J6 |
| Trossachs | Stirlg | 84 | H2 |
| Trossachs Pier | Stirlg | 84 | H2 |
| Troston | Suffk | 34 | E3 |
| Trotshill | Worcs | 30 | B3 |
| Trottiscliffe | Kent | 22 | D10 |
| Trotton | W Susx | 10 | D5 |
| Troutbeck | Cumb | 62 | H2 |
| Troutbeck Bridge | Cumb | 62 | H3 |
| Troway | Derbys | 51 | K5 |
| Trowbridge | Wilts | 18 | C8 |
| Trowell | Notts | 51 | L11 |
| Trowell Services | Notts | 51 | L11 |
| Trowse Newton | Norfk | 45 | L8 |
| Trudoxhill | Somset | 17 | Q7 |
| Trull | Somset | 16 | G10 |
| Trumpan | Highld | 104 | C9 |
| Trumpet | Herefs | 28 | H2 |
| Trumpington | Cambs | 33 | M6 |
| Trunch | Norfk | 45 | L3 |
| Truro | Cnwll | 3 | J6 |
| Trusham | Devon | 6 | B6 |
| Trusley | Derbys | 40 | G1 |
| Trusthorpe | Lincs | 53 | N6 |
| Trysull | Staffs | 39 | Q4 |
| Tubney | Oxon | 19 | M2 |
| Tuckenhay | Devon | 5 | Q8 |
| Tuckhill | Shrops | 39 | P5 |
| Tuckingmill | Cnwll | 2 | F7 |
| Tuckingmill | Wilts | 8 | D2 |
| Tuckton | Bmouth | 8 | G8 |
| Tuddenham | Suffk | 34 | C3 |
| Tuddenham | Suffk | 35 | K7 |
| Tudeley | Kent | 12 | C2 |
| Tudhoe | Dur | 65 | M1 |
| Tudweiliog | Gwynd | 46 | D4 |
| Tuffley | Gloucs | 29 | L6 |
| Tufton | Hants | 19 | M10 |
| Tufton | Pembks | 24 | H3 |
| Tugby | Leics | 41 | Q7 |
| Tugford | Shrops | 39 | K5 |
| Tughall | Nthumb | 81 | P8 |
| Tullibody | Clacks | 85 | P4 |
| Tullich | Highld | 99 | J4 |
| Tullich | Highld | 107 | P7 |
| Tulliemet | P & K | 92 | E5 |
| Tulloch | Abers | 102 | G8 |
| Tullochgorm | Ag & B | 83 | P4 |
| Tulloch Station | Highld | 98 | H12 |
| Tullymurdoch | P & K | 92 | H5 |
| Tullynessle | Abers | 102 | D10 |
| Tulse Hill | Gt Lon | 21 | L8 |
| Tumble | Carmth | 26 | D6 |
| Tumby | Lincs | 53 | J10 |
| Tumby Woodside | Lincs | 53 | J11 |
| Tunbridge Wells | Kent | 12 | C3 |
| Tundergarth | D & G | 79 | J11 |
| Tunley | BaNES | 17 | Q4 |
| Tunstall | E R Yk | 61 | M7 |
| Tunstall | Kent | 22 | H10 |
| Tunstall | Lancs | 63 | L7 |
| Tunstall | N York | 65 | L8 |
| Tunstall | Norfk | 45 | N8 |
| Tunstall | Staffs | 49 | Q5 |
| Tunstall | Suffk | 35 | M6 |
| Tunstall | Sundld | 73 | P9 |
| Tunstead | Derbys | 50 | E6 |
| Tunstead | Norfk | 45 | L6 |
| Tunstead Milton | Derbys | 50 | D5 |
| Turgis Green | Hants | 20 | B10 |
| Turkdean | Gloucs | 30 | E9 |
| Tur Langton | Leics | 41 | Q8 |
| Turleigh | Wilts | 18 | B8 |
| Turnastone | Herefs | 28 | D2 |
| Turnberry | S Ayrs | 76 | D9 |
| Turnditch | Derbys | 50 | H10 |
| Turner's Hill | W Susx | 11 | M3 |
| Turnhouse | C Edin | 86 | D7 |
| Turnworth | Dorset | 8 | B6 |
| Turriff | Abers | 102 | F5 |
| Turton Bottoms | Bl w D | 57 | N6 |
| Turves | Cambs | 43 | K10 |
| Turvey | Beds | 32 | D6 |
| Turville | Bucks | 20 | C5 |
| Turweston | Bucks | 31 | N6 |
| Tushielaw Inn | Border | 79 | L5 |
| Tutbury | Staffs | 40 | G2 |
| Tutshill | Gloucs | 28 | G9 |
| Tuttington | Norfk | 45 | K5 |
| Tuxford | Notts | 51 | Q6 |
| Twatt | Ork | 111 | g2 |
| Twatt | Shet | 111 | k4 |
| Twechar | E Duns | 85 | L7 |
| Tweedbank | Border | 80 | C7 |
| Tweedmouth | Nthumb | 81 | L4 |
| Tweedsmuir | Border | 78 | H4 |
| Twelveheads | Cnwll | 2 | H7 |
| Twemlow Green | Ches E | 49 | P2 |
| Twenty | Lincs | 42 | G6 |
| Twerton | BaNES | 17 | Q4 |
| Twickenham | Gt Lon | 21 | J8 |
| Twigworth | Gloucs | 29 | L4 |
| Twineham | W Susx | 11 | K6 |
| Twinstead | Essex | 34 | E9 |
| Twitchen | Devon | 15 | N6 |
| Two Dales | Derbys | 50 | H8 |
| Two Gates | Staffs | 40 | G7 |
| Twycross | Leics | 41 | J6 |
| Twycross Zoo | Leics | 40 | H6 |
| Twyford | Bucks | 31 | P8 |
| Twyford | Hants | 9 | N3 |
| Twyford | Leics | 41 | Q5 |
| Twyford | Norfk | 44 | G5 |
| Twyford | Wokham | 20 | C8 |
| Twynholm | D & G | 69 | P8 |
| Twyning Green | Gloucs | 29 | M2 |
| Twynllanan | Carmth | 26 | G4 |
| Twywell | Nhants | 32 | D2 |
| Tyberton | Herefs | 28 | D2 |
| Tyburn | Birm | 40 | F8 |
| Tycroes | Carmth | 26 | E6 |
| Tycrwyn | Powys | 48 | C12 |
| Tydd Gote | Lincs | 43 | M6 |
| Tydd St Giles | Cambs | 43 | L6 |
| Tydd St Mary | Lincs | 43 | M6 |
| Tye Green | Essex | 33 | P9 |
| Tyldesley | Wigan | 57 | M8 |
| Tyler Hill | Kent | 23 | L10 |
| Tylorstown | Rhondd | 27 | L9 |
| Ty-nant | Conwy | 48 | B6 |
| Tyndrum | Stirlg | 91 | J9 |
| Ty'n-dwr | Denbgs | 48 | E7 |
| Tynemouth | N Tyne | 73 | P7 |
| Tynemouth Crematorium | N Tyne | 73 | N7 |
| Tyne Tunnel | S Tyne | 73 | N7 |
| Tyninghame | E Loth | 87 | L6 |
| Tynron | D & G | 77 | N11 |
| Tynygraig | Cerdgn | 37 | L6 |
| Ty'n-y-Groes | Conwy | 55 | L7 |
| Tyn-y-nant | Rhondd | 27 | M10 |
| Tyringham | M Keyn | 32 | C7 |
| Tyseley | Birm | 40 | E9 |
| Tythegston | Brdgnd | 27 | J11 |
| Tytherington | Ches E | 50 | B6 |
| Tytherington | S Glos | 29 | J10 |
| Tytherington | Wilts | 18 | D11 |
| Tytherleigh | Devon | 7 | J3 |
| Tytherton Lucas | Wilts | 18 | D6 |
| Tywardreath | Cnwll | 3 | N5 |
| Tywyn | Gwynd | 47 | J10 |

## U

| Place | County | Page | Grid |
|---|---|---|---|
| Ubbeston Green | Suffk | 35 | M3 |
| Ubley | BaNES | 17 | M5 |
| Uckfield | E Susx | 11 | P6 |
| Uckinghall | Worcs | 29 | M2 |
| Uckington | Gloucs | 29 | M4 |
| Uddingston | S Lans | 85 | L10 |
| Uddington | S Lans | 78 | E3 |
| Udimore | E Susx | 12 | G6 |
| Udny Green | Abers | 103 | J9 |
| Udny Station | Abers | 103 | J9 |
| Uffculme | Devon | 16 | E12 |
| Uffington | Lincs | 42 | F8 |
| Uffington | Oxon | 19 | K3 |
| Uffington | Shrops | 49 | K11 |
| Ufford | C Pete | 42 | F8 |
| Ufford | Suffk | 35 | L6 |
| Ufton | Warwks | 31 | J2 |
| Ufton Nervet | W Berk | 19 | Q7 |
| Ugadale | Ag & B | 75 | L6 |
| Ugborough | Devon | 5 | N8 |
| Uggeshall | Suffk | 35 | P2 |
| Ugglebarnby | N York | 67 | J6 |
| Ughill | Sheff | 50 | G3 |
| Ugley | Essex | 33 | N10 |
| Ugley Green | Essex | 33 | N10 |
| Ugthorpe | N York | 66 | H5 |
| Uibhist A Deas | W Isls | 111 | b6 |
| Uibhist A Tuath | W Isls | 111 | a4 |
| Uig | Ag & B | 88 | E5 |
| Uig | Highld | 104 | B10 |
| Uig | Highld | 104 | E9 |
| Uig | W Isls | 111 | c2 |
| Uigshader | Highld | 104 | F12 |
| Uisken | Ag & B | 89 | J11 |
| Ulbster | Highld | 110 | G7 |
| Ulcat Row | Cumb | 71 | N9 |
| Ulceby | Lincs | 53 | L9 |
| Ulceby | N Linc | 61 | J10 |
| Ulceby Skitter | N Linc | 61 | J10 |
| Ulcombe | Kent | 12 | G1 |
| Uldale | Cumb | 71 | L7 |
| Uley | Gloucs | 29 | K8 |
| Ulgham | Nthumb | 73 | M3 |
| Ullapool | Highld | 106 | B4 |
| Ullenhall | Warwks | 30 | E1 |
| Ulleskelf | N York | 59 | M6 |
| Ullesthorpe | Leics | 41 | L9 |
| Ulley | Rothm | 51 | L4 |
| Ullingswick | Herefs | 39 | L11 |
| Ullinish Lodge Hotel | Highld | 96 | C3 |
| Ullock | Cumb | 70 | H10 |
| Ullswater | Cumb | 71 | N10 |
| Ullswater Steamers | Cumb | 71 | N11 |
| Ulpha | Cumb | 62 | E4 |
| Ulrome | E R Yk | 61 | K3 |
| Ulsta | Shet | 111 | k3 |
| Ulva | Ag & B | 89 | J8 |
| Ulverley Green | Solhll | 40 | F10 |
| Ulverston | Cumb | 62 | F6 |
| Ulwell | Dorset | 8 | F10 |
| Ulzieside | D & G | 77 | N9 |
| Umberleigh | Devon | 15 | M7 |
| Unapool | Highld | 108 | E8 |
| Underbarrow | Cumb | 63 | J4 |
| Under Burnmouth | Border | 79 | P11 |
| Undercliffe | C Brad | 58 | F7 |
| Underdale | Shrops | 49 | J11 |
| Under River | Kent | 22 | B11 |
| Underwood | Notts | 51 | L10 |
| Undy | Mons | 28 | E10 |
| Union Mills | IoM | 56 | C5 |
| Unst | Shet | 111 | m2 |
| Unstone | Derbys | 51 | J5 |
| Upavon | Wilts | 18 | G9 |
| Upchurch | Kent | 22 | G9 |
| Upcott | Devon | 15 | N10 |
| Up Exe | Devon | 6 | C3 |
| Upgate | Norfk | 45 | J6 |
| Uphall | Dorset | 7 | M3 |
| Uphall | W Loth | 86 | C7 |
| Upham | Devon | 15 | Q9 |
| Upham | Hants | 9 | N4 |
| Uphampton | Herefs | 38 | H9 |
| Uphampton | Worcs | 39 | Q8 |
| Uphill | N Som | 17 | J5 |
| Up Holland | Lancs | 57 | K7 |
| Uplawmoor | E Rens | 84 | G11 |
| Upleadon | Gloucs | 29 | K4 |
| Upleatham | R & Cl | 66 | E4 |
| Uploders | Dorset | 7 | M4 |
| Uplowman | Devon | 16 | D11 |
| Uplyme | Devon | 7 | J4 |
| Up Marden | W Susx | 10 | C7 |
| Upminster | Gt Lon | 22 | C6 |
| Up Mudford | Somset | 17 | N11 |
| Up Nately | Hants | 20 | B11 |
| Upottery | Devon | 6 | G2 |
| Upper Affcot | Shrops | 39 | J5 |
| Upper Ardchronie | Highld | 107 | K5 |
| Upper Arley | Worcs | 39 | N6 |
| Upper Basildon | W Berk | 19 | P5 |
| Upper Beeding | W Susx | 11 | K7 |
| Upper Benefield | Nhants | 42 | E11 |
| Upper Bentley | Worcs | 30 | C2 |
| Upper Bighouse | Highld | 109 | Q4 |
| Upper Boddington | Nhants | 31 | M4 |
| Upper Brailes | Warwks | 30 | H6 |
| Upper Breakish | Highld | 97 | J3 |
| Upper Broadheath | Worcs | 39 | P10 |
| Upper Broughton | Notts | 41 | P3 |
| Upper Bucklebury | W Berk | 19 | P7 |
| Upper Burgate | Hants | 8 | H4 |
| Upperby | Cumb | 71 | N5 |
| Upper Caldecote | C Beds | 32 | G7 |
| Upper Chapel | Powys | 27 | L1 |
| Upper Chicksgrove | Wilts | 8 | E2 |
| Upper Chute | Wilts | 19 | K9 |
| Upper Clapton | Gt Lon | 21 | M6 |
| Upper Clatford | Hants | 19 | L11 |
| Upper Cound | Shrops | 39 | K2 |
| Upper Cumberworth | Kirk | 58 | G11 |
| Upper Dallachy | Moray | 101 | M3 |
| Upper Deal | Kent | 23 | Q11 |
| Upper Dean | Bed | 32 | F4 |
| Upper Denby | Kirk | 58 | G11 |
| Upper Dicker | E Susx | 12 | B7 |
| Upper Dounreay | Highld | 110 | B3 |
| Upper Dovercourt | Essex | 35 | K9 |
| Upper Drumbane | Stirlg | 85 | L2 |
| Upper Dunsforth | N York | 59 | K2 |
| Upper Eashing | Surrey | 10 | F2 |
| Upper Eathie | Highld | 107 | M9 |
| Upper Egleton | Herefs | 39 | M12 |
| Upper Elkstone | Staffs | 50 | D8 |
| Upper Ellastone | Staffs | 50 | E11 |
| Upper Farringdon | Hants | 10 | B3 |
| Upper Framilode | Gloucs | 29 | K6 |
| Upper Froyle | Hants | 10 | C2 |
| Upperglen | Highld | 104 | D11 |
| Upper Godney | Somset | 17 | L7 |
| Upper Gravenhurst | C Beds | 32 | G9 |
| Upper Green | W Berk | 19 | L7 |
| Upper Grove Common | Herefs | 28 | G4 |
| Upper Hale | Surrey | 10 | D1 |
| Upper Halliford | Surrey | 20 | H9 |
| Upper Hambleton | Rutlnd | 42 | C8 |
| Upper Harbledown | Kent | 23 | L10 |
| Upper Hartfield | E Susx | 11 | P3 |
| Upper Hatherley | Gloucs | 29 | M5 |
| Upper Heaton | Kirk | 58 | F9 |
| Upper Helmsley | N York | 59 | P3 |
| Upper Hergest | Herefs | 38 | F10 |
| Upper Heyford | Nhants | 31 | P3 |
| Upper Heyford | Oxon | 31 | L8 |
| Upper Hill | Herefs | 39 | J10 |
| Upper Hopton | Kirk | 58 | G9 |
| Upper Hulme | Staffs | 50 | D8 |
| Upper Inglesham | Swindn | 18 | H2 |
| Upper Killay | Swans | 26 | D9 |
| Upper Kinchrackine | Ag & B | 90 | G10 |
| Upper Lambourn | W Berk | 19 | K5 |
| Upper Landywood | Staffs | 40 | C6 |
| Upper Langford | N Som | 17 | L4 |
| Upper Langwith | Derbys | 51 | L6 |
| Upper Largo | Fife | 87 | J2 |
| Upper Leigh | Staffs | 50 | D12 |
| Upper Lochton | Abers | 95 | L3 |
| Upper Longdon | Staffs | 40 | D5 |
| Upper & Lower Stondon | C Beds | 32 | G9 |
| Upper Lybster | Highld | 110 | F8 |
| Upper Lydbrook | Gloucs | 28 | H6 |
| Upper Lye | Herefs | 38 | H8 |
| Uppermill | Oldham | 58 | C11 |
| Upper Milton | Worcs | 39 | P7 |
| Upper Minety | Wilts | 18 | E3 |
| Upper Mulben | Moray | 101 | L5 |
| Upper Netchwood | Shrops | 39 | L4 |
| Upper Nobut | Staffs | 40 | D1 |
| Upper Norwood | W Susx | 10 | F6 |
| Upper Poppleton | C York | 59 | M4 |
| Upper Ratley | Hants | 9 | K3 |
| Upper Rissington | Gloucs | 30 | G9 |
| Upper Rochford | Worcs | 39 | L8 |
| Upper Ruscoe | D & G | 69 | N6 |
| Upper Sapey | Herefs | 39 | M8 |
| Upper Seagry | Wilts | 18 | D5 |
| Upper Shelton | C Beds | 32 | E7 |
| Upper Sheringham | Norfk | 45 | J2 |
| Upper Skelmorlie | N Ayrs | 84 | D9 |
| Upper Slaughter | Gloucs | 30 | F9 |
| Upper Soudley | Gloucs | 28 | H6 |
| Upper Standen | Kent | 13 | N3 |
| Upper Stoke | Norfk | 45 | L9 |
| Upper Stowe | Nhants | 31 | N3 |
| Upper Street | Hants | 8 | H4 |
| Upper Street | Norfk | 45 | M6 |
| Upper Street | Norfk | 45 | M6 |
| Upper Street | Suffk | 34 | C6 |
| Upper Street | Suffk | 34 | H6 |
| Upper Sundon | C Beds | 32 | F10 |
| Upper Swell | Gloucs | 30 | F8 |
| Upper Tasburgh | Norfk | 45 | K10 |
| Upper Tean | Staffs | 50 | D11 |
| Upperthong | Kirk | 58 | F11 |
| Upperton | W Susx | 10 | F5 |
| Upper Town | Herefs | 39 | L11 |
| Upper Town | N Som | 17 | M3 |
| Upper Town | Suffk | 34 | F4 |
| Upper Tumble | Carmth | 26 | D6 |
| Upper Tysoe | Warwks | 31 | J5 |
| Upper Victoria | Angus | 93 | P8 |
| Upper Wardington | Oxon | 31 | L5 |
| Upper Welland | Worcs | 29 | K1 |
| Upper Wellingham | E Susx | 11 | N7 |
| Upper Weybread | Suffk | 35 | K2 |
| Upper Wield | Hants | 19 | Q11 |
| Upper Winchendon | Bucks | 31 | Q10 |
| Upper Woodford | Wilts | 18 | G12 |
| Upper Wraxall | Wilts | 18 | B6 |
| Uppingham | Rutlnd | 42 | C9 |
| Uppington | Shrops | 49 | L12 |
| Upsall | N York | 66 | C9 |
| Upsettlington | Border | 81 | J5 |
| Upshire | Essex | 21 | N4 |
| Up Somborne | Hants | 9 | L2 |
| Upstreet | Kent | 23 | N10 |
| Upton | Bucks | 31 | Q10 |
| Upton | C Pete | 42 | G9 |
| Upton | Cambs | 32 | H2 |
| Upton | Ches W | 48 | H2 |
| Upton | Cnwll | 4 | G6 |
| Upton | Cnwll | 5 | N10 |
| Upton | Devon | 6 | E3 |
| Upton | Dorset | 7 | Q6 |
| Upton | Dorset | 8 | E8 |
| Upton | Halton | 57 | J10 |
| Upton | Hants | 9 | L4 |
| Upton | Hants | 19 | L9 |
| Upton | Leics | 41 | J7 |
| Upton | Lincs | 52 | C6 |
| Upton | Norfk | 45 | N7 |
| Upton | Notts | 51 | Q5 |
| Upton | Notts | 51 | Q9 |
| Upton | Oxon | 19 | N4 |
| Upton | Slough | 20 | F7 |
| Upton | Somset | 16 | D9 |
| Upton | Somset | 17 | L10 |
| Upton | Wakefd | 59 | L10 |
| Upton | Wirral | 56 | F10 |
| Upton Bishop | Herefs | 28 | H4 |
| Upton Cheyney | S Glos | 17 | Q3 |
| Upton Cressett | Shrops | 39 | M4 |
| Upton Grey | Hants | 10 | B1 |
| Upton Hellions | Devon | 15 | P10 |
| Upton Lovell | Wilts | 18 | D11 |
| Upton Magna | Shrops | 49 | K11 |
| Upton Noble | Somset | 17 | Q8 |
| Upton Pyne | Devon | 6 | C3 |
| Upton St Leonards | Gloucs | 29 | M6 |
| Upton Scudamore | Wilts | 18 | C10 |
| Upton Snodsbury | Worcs | 30 | C4 |
| Upton-upon-Severn | Worcs | 29 | L1 |
| Upton Warren | Worcs | 30 | B1 |
| Upwaltham | W Susx | 10 | F7 |
| Upwell | Norfk | 43 | N9 |
| Upwood | Cambs | 43 | J12 |
| Urchfont | Wilts | 18 | F8 |
| Urmston | Traffd | 57 | P9 |
| Urquhart | Moray | 101 | K3 |
| Urquhart Castle | Highld | 98 | G4 |
| Urra | N York | 66 | D7 |
| Urray | Highld | 106 | H10 |
| Usan | Angus | 95 | N9 |
| Ushaw Moor | Dur | 73 | M11 |
| Usk | Mons | 28 | D8 |
| Usselby | Lincs | 52 | F5 |
| Usworth | Sundld | 73 | N8 |
| Utkinton | Ches W | 49 | K3 |
| Utley | C Brad | 58 | D5 |
| Uton | Devon | 15 | P11 |
| Utterby | Lincs | 53 | K5 |
| Uttoxeter | Staffs | 40 | E2 |
| Uxbridge | Gt Lon | 20 | G6 |
| Uyeasound | Shet | 111 | m2 |
| Uzmaston | Pembks | 24 | G6 |

## V

| Place | County | Page | Grid |
|---|---|---|---|
| Vale | Guern | 6 | c1 |
| Vale of Glamorgan Crematorium | V Glam | 16 | F3 |
| Valley | IoA | 54 | D6 |
| Valtos | Highld | 104 | G9 |
| Valtos | W Isls | 111 | c2 |
| Vange | Essex | 22 | E6 |
| Vatsetter | Shet | 111 | k2 |
| Vatten | Highld | 96 | C2 |
| Vaynor | Myr Td | 27 | L6 |
| Veensgarth | Shet | 111 | k4 |
| Velindre | Powys | 27 | P2 |
| Venngreen | Devon | 14 | G9 |
| Venn Ottery | Devon | 6 | E5 |
| Ventnor | IoW | 9 | P11 |
| Venton | Devon | 5 | M8 |
| Vernham Dean | Hants | 19 | K9 |
| Vernham Street | Hants | 19 | L8 |
| Verwood | Dorset | 8 | G5 |
| Veryan | Cnwll | 3 | K7 |
| Vickerstown | Cumb | 62 | E8 |
| Victoria | Cnwll | 3 | L4 |
| Vidlin | Shet | 111 | k3 |
| Viewfield | Moray | 101 | K3 |
| Viewpark | N Lans | 85 | M10 |
| Vigo | Kent | 22 | D10 |
| Village de Putron | Guern | 6 | c2 |
| Vines Cross | E Susx | 12 | C6 |
| Vinters Park Crematorium | Kent | 22 | F11 |

198 Virginia Water - Westlington


Virginia Water Surrey 20 G9
Virginstow Devon 4 H2
Vobster Somset 17 Q6
Voe Shet 111 k3
Vowchurch Herefs 28 D2

## W

Waberthwaite Cumb 62 C4
Wackerfield Dur 65 K3
Wacton Norfk 45 K10
Wadborough Worcs 30 B5
Waddesdon Bucks 31 Q10
Waddesdon Manor Bucks 31 Q10
Waddeton Devon 6 B10
Waddingham Lincs 52 E4
Waddington Lancs 63 N12
Waddington Lincs 52 D9
Wadebridge Cnwll 3 L2
Wadeford Somset 7 J1
Wadenhoe Nhants 42 E12
Wadesmill Herts 33 K12
Wadhurst E Susx 12 D4
Wadshelf Derbys 50 H6
Wadworth Donc 51 M2
Wainfleet All Saints Lincs 53 N10
Wainfleet St Mary Lincs 53 M10
Wainhouse Corner Cnwll 4 E2
Wainscott Medway 22 E8
Wainstalls Calder 58 D8
Waitby Cumb 64 D6
Waithe Lincs 53 J4
Wakefield Wakefd 59 J9
Wakefield Crematorium Wakefd 58 H10
Wake Green Birm 40 E10
Wakehurst Place W Susx 11 M4
Wakerley Nhants 42 D9
Wakes Colne Essex 34 E10
Walberswick Suffk 35 P2
Walberton W Susx 10 F8
Walbutt D & G 70 C2
Walcombe Somset 17 M6
Walcot Lincs 42 F3
Walcot Shrops 49 L11
Walcot Swindn 18 H4
Walcote Leics 41 M10
Walcot Green Norfk 35 J1
Walcott Lincs 52 G11
Walcott Norfk 45 M4
Walden Stubbs N York 59 M10
Walderslade Medway 22 F10
Walderton W Susx 10 C7
Walditch Dorset 7 L4
Waldridge Dur 73 M10
Waldringfield Suffk 35 L7
Waldron E Susx 12 B6
Wales Rothm 51 L4
Wales Somset 17 N10
Walesby Lincs 52 G5
Walesby Notts 51 P6
Wales Millennium Centre Cardif 16 G2
Walford Herefs 28 G5
Walford Herefs 38 H7
Walford Heath Shrops 49 J10
Walgherton Ches E 49 M6
Walgrave Nhants 32 B3
Walkden Salfd 57 N8
Walker N u Ty 73 M7
Walkerburn Border 79 M2
Walkeringham Notts 51 Q3
Walkerith Lincs 52 B5
Walkern Herts 33 J10
Walker's Heath Birm 40 D10
Walkerton Fife 86 F3
Walkford Dorset 8 H8
Walkhampton Devon 5 L6
Walkington E R Yk 60 G6
Walkley Sheff 51 J3
Walk Mill Lancs 57 Q3
Walkwood Worcs 30 D2
Wall Nthumb 72 G7
Wall Staffs 40 E6
Wallacetown S Ayrs 76 E10
Wallacetown S Ayrs 76 F6
Wallands Park E Susx 11 N7
Wallasey Wirral 56 F9
Wall Heath Dudley 40 B9
Wallingford Oxon 19 P3
Wallington Gt Lon 21 L9
Wallington Hants 9 P6
Wallington Herts 33 J9
Wallisdown Poole 8 F8
Walls Shet 111 j4
Wallsend N Tyne 73 N7
Wallyford E Loth 86 H7
Walmer Kent 23 Q12
Walmer Bridge Lancs 57 J4
Walmley Birm 40 F8
Walmley Ash Birm 40 F8
Walpole Suffk 35 M2
Walpole Cross Keys Norfk 43 N6
Walpole Highway Norfk 43 N7
Walpole St Andrew Norfk 43 N6
Walpole St Peter Norfk 43 N6
Walsall Wsall 40 D7
Walsden Calder 58 C9
Walsgrave on Sowe Covtry 41 J10
Walsham le Willows Suffk 34 G3
Walshford N York 59 K4
Walsoken Norfk 43 M7
Walston S Lans 86 C12
Walsworth Herts 32 H10
Walter's Ash Bucks 20 D4
Waltham Kent 13 L1
Waltham NE Lin 53 J3
Waltham Abbey Essex 21 M4
Waltham Chase Hants 9 P4
Waltham Cross Herts 21 M4
Waltham on the Wolds Leics 42 B5
Waltham St Lawrence W & M 20 D7
Walthamstow Gt Lon 21 M5
Walton Cumb 71 Q3
Walton Derbys 51 J7
Walton Leeds 59 K5
Walton Leics 41 N9
Walton M Keyn 32 C9
Walton Powys 38 F9
Walton Somset 17 L8
Walton Suffk 35 L9
Walton W Susx 10 D8
Walton Wakefd 59 J10
Walton Wrekin 49 L10
Walton Cardiff Gloucs 29 M3
Walton East Pembks 24 H4
Walton-in-Gordano N Som 17 K2
Walton Lea Crematorium Warrtn 57 L10
Walton-le-Dale Lancs 57 K4
Walton-on-Thames Surrey 20 H9
Walton-on-the-Hill Staffs 40 C4
Walton on the Hill Surrey 21 K11
Walton-on-the-Naze Essex 35 L11
Walton on the Wolds Leics 41 N4
Walton-on-Trent Derbys 40 G4
Walton Park N Som 17 K2
Walton West Pembks 24 F6
Waltonwrays Crematorium N York 58 C4
Walworth Darltn 65 M4
Walworth Gt Lon 21 M7
Walwyn's Castle Pembks 24 F6
Wambrook Somset 6 H2
Wanborough Surrey 10 E1
Wanborough Swindn 18 H4
Wandsworth Gt Lon 21 K8
Wangford Suffk 35 P2
Wanlip Leics 41 N5
Wanlockhead D & G 78 E6
Wannock E Susx 12 C8
Wansford C Pete 42 F9
Wansford E R Yk 60 H3
Wanshurst Green Kent 12 F2
Wanstead Gt Lon 21 N6
Wanstrow Somset 17 Q7
Wanswell Gloucs 29 J8
Wantage Oxon 19 L3
Wappenbury Warwks 41 J12
Wappenham Nhants 31 N5
Warbleton E Susx 12 C6
Warborough Oxon 19 P3
Warboys Cambs 33 K2
Warbreck Bpool 56 G2
Warbstow Cnwll 4 F3
Warburton Traffd 57 M10
Warcop Cumb 64 D5
Warden Nthumb 72 G7
Ward End Birm 40 E9
Wardington Oxon 31 L5
Wardle Ches E 49 L4
Wardle Rochdl 58 B10
Wardley Gatesd 73 N8
Wardley Rutlnd 42 B9
Wardlow Derbys 50 F6
Wardy Hill Cambs 33 M1
Ware Herts 21 M1
Wareham Dorset 8 D9
Warehorne Kent 13 J4
Warenford Nthumb 81 N8
Wareside Herts 21 N1
Waresley Cambs 33 J6
Warfield Br For 20 E8
Warfleet Devon 6 B11
Wargrave Wokham 20 C7
Warham All Saints Norfk 44 F2
Warham St Mary Norfk 44 F2
Wark Nthumb 72 F5
Wark Nthumb 80 H6
Warkleigh Devon 15 L7
Warkton Nhants 32 C2
Warkworth Nhants 31 L6
Warkworth Nthumb 81 P11
Warlaby N York 65 N8
Warleggan Cnwll 4 E6
Warley Town Calder 58 D8
Warlingham Surrey 21 M10
Warmfield Wakefd 59 J9
Warmingham Ches E 49 N4
Warmington Nhants 42 F11
Warmington Warwks 31 K5
Warminster Wilts 18 C10
Warmley S Glos 17 P2
Warmsworth Donc 51 M1
Warmwell Dorset 7 Q5
Warner Bros Studio Tour Herts 20 H4
Warnford Hants 9 Q3
Warnham W Susx 11 J4
Warningcamp W Susx 10 G8
Warninglid W Susx 11 K5
Warren Ches E 50 B6
Warren Pembks 24 G8
Warrenhill S Lans 78 F2
Warren Row W & M 20 D7
Warren Street Kent 22 H11
Warrington M Keyn 32 C6
Warrington Warrtn 57 L10
Warriston C Edin 86 F7
Warriston Crematorium C Edin 86 F7
Warsash Hants 9 N6
Warslow Staffs 50 E8
Warter E R Yk 60 E4
Warthermaske N York 65 L10
Warthill N York 59 P3
Wartling E Susx 12 D8
Wartnaby Leics 41 P3
Warton Lancs 56 H3
Warton Lancs 63 J7
Warton Warwks 40 H6
Warwick Warwks 30 H2
Warwick Bridge Cumb 71 P4
Warwick Castle Warwks 30 H2
Warwick Services Warwks 31 J3
Wasbister Ork 111 h1
Wasdale Head Cumb 62 E1
Washaway Cnwll 3 M2
Washbourne Devon 5 Q8
Washbrook Suffk 35 J8
Washfield Devon 16 C11
Washford Somset 16 E7
Washford Pyne Devon 15 N9
Washingborough Lincs 52 E8
Washington Sundld 73 N9
Washington W Susx 10 H7
Washington Services Gatesd 73 M9
Washwood Heath Birm 40 E9
Wasperton Warwks 30 H3
Wass N York 66 D10
Wast Water Cumb 62 D2
Watchet Somset 16 E7
Watchfield Oxon 19 J3
Watchgate Cumb 63 K3
Water Devon 5 P4
Waterbeach Cambs 33 M4
Waterbeach W Susx 10 E8
Waterbeck D & G 79 L12
Water End E R Yk 60 D6
Waterfall Staffs 50 E9
Waterfoot E Rens 85 J11
Waterford Herts 21 L1
Waterheads Border 86 F11
Waterhouses Staffs 50 E10
Wateringbury Kent 22 E11
Waterloo Highld 97 J5
Waterloo N Lans 85 N11
Waterloo P & K 92 F8
Waterloo Pembks 24 G7
Waterloo Sefton 56 G8
Waterlooville Hants 10 B7
Watermillock Cumb 71 P10
Water Newton Cambs 42 G10
Water Orton Warwks 40 F8
Waterperry Oxon 31 N11
Waterrow Somset 16 E10
Watersfield W Susx 10 G6
Waterside Bl w D 57 N4
Waterside E Ayrs 76 G9
Waterside E Ayrs 76 H3
Waterside E Duns 85 L8
Waterstein Highld 104 A11
Waterstock Oxon 31 N11
Waterston Pembks 24 G7
Water Stratford Bucks 31 P7
Waters Upton Wrekin 49 L10
Watford Herts 20 H4
Watford Nhants 31 N1
Watford Gap Services Nhants 31 N1
Wath N York 58 F1
Wath N York 65 N11
Wath upon Dearne Rothm 51 K1
Watlington Norfk 43 P7
Watlington Oxon 20 B5
Watten Highld 110 F5
Wattisfield Suffk 34 G2
Wattisham Suffk 34 G6
Watton Dorset 7 L4
Watton E R Yk 60 H4
Watton Norfk 44 F9
Watton-at-Stone Herts 33 K11
Wattston N Lans 85 N8
Wattsville Caerph 27 P9
Waulkmill Abers 95 K4
Waunarlwydd Swans 26 E9
Waunfawr Cerdgn 37 K4
Waunfawr Gwynd 54 G9
Wavendon M Keyn 32 C8
Waveney Crematorium Suffk 45 P11
Waverbridge Cumb 71 K6
Waverton Ches W 49 J3
Waverton Cumb 71 K6
Wawne E R Yk 61 J6
Waxham Norfk 45 P5
Wayford Somset 7 K2
Waytown Dorset 7 L4
Way Village Devon 15 Q9
Weacombe Somset 16 F7
Weald Oxon 19 K1
Wealdstone Gt Lon 21 J5
Weardley Leeds 58 H5
Weare Somset 17 K5
Weare Giffard Devon 14 H7
Wearhead Dur 72 F11
Wearne Somset 17 K9
Wear Valley Crematorium Dur 65 M2
Weasenham All Saints Norfk 44 E6
Weasenham St Peter Norfk 44 E5
Weaste Salfd 57 P8
Weaverham Ches W 49 L1
Weaverthorpe N York 67 L12
Webheath Worcs 30 D2
Wedderlairs Abers 102 H8
Weddington Warwks 41 J8
Wedhampton Wilts 18 F8
Wedmore Somset 17 L6
Wednesbury Sandw 40 C8
Wednesfield Wolves 40 C7
Weedon Bucks 32 B12
Weedon Nhants 31 N3
Weedon Lois Nhants 31 N5
Weeford Staffs 40 F6
Weeke Hants 9 M2
Weekley Nhants 32 C1
Week St Mary Cnwll 14 E11
Weel E R Yk 60 H6
Weeley Essex 35 J11
Weeley Crematorium Essex 35 J11
Weeley Heath Essex 35 J11
Weem P & K 92 C6
Weethley Warwks 30 D3
Weeting Norfk 44 C11
Weeton E R Yk 61 N9
Weeton Lancs 56 H2
Weeton N York 58 H5
Weetwood Leeds 58 H6
Weir Lancs 57 Q4
Weir Quay Devon 5 J7
Weisdale Shet 111 k4
Welborne Norfk 44 H7
Welbourn Lincs 52 D11
Welburn N York 60 C1
Welbury N York 65 P7
Welby Lincs 42 D3
Welcombe Devon 14 E8
Weldon Nhants 42 D11
Welford Nhants 41 N10
Welford W Berk 19 L6
Welford-on-Avon Warwks 30 F4
Welham Leics 41 Q8
Welham Notts 51 Q5
Welham Green Herts 21 K3
Well Hants 10 C2
Well Lincs 53 M8
Well N York 65 M10
Welland Worcs 29 L2
Wellbank Angus 93 N8
Wellesbourne Warwks 30 H3
Well Head Herts 32 H10
Welling Gt Lon 21 P8
Wellingborough Nhants 32 C3
Wellingham Norfk 44 E6
Wellingore Lincs 52 E11
Wellington Cumb 62 C2
Wellington Herefs 39 J11
Wellington Somset 16 F11
Wellington Wrekin 49 M12
Wellington Heath Herefs 29 J1
Wellow BaNES 17 Q5
Wellow IoW 9 L9
Wellow Notts 51 P7
Wells Somset 17 M7
Wells-next-the-Sea Norfk 44 F2
Wellstye Green Essex 33 Q11
Welltree P & K 92 E10
Wellwood Fife 86 C5
Welney Norfk 43 N10
Welshampton Shrops 48 H8
Welsh Frankton Shrops 48 G8
Welsh Newton Herefs 28 F5
Welshpool Powys 38 E1
Welsh St Donats V Glam 16 D2
Welton Cumb 71 M6
Welton E R Yk 60 G8
Welton Lincs 52 E7
Welton Nhants 31 N2
Welton le Marsh Lincs 53 M9
Welton le Wold Lincs 53 J6
Welwick E R Yk 61 N9
Welwyn Herts 32 H12
Welwyn Garden City Herts 21 K2
Wem Shrops 49 K9
Wembdon Somset 16 H8
Wembley Gt Lon 21 J6
Wembury Devon 5 L9
Wembworthy Devon 15 L9
Wemyss Bay Inver 84 D8
Wendens Ambo Essex 33 N9
Wendlebury Oxon 31 M9
Wendling Norfk 44 F7
Wendover Bucks 20 D2
Wendron Cnwll 2 G9
Wendron Mining District Cnwll 2 G8
Wendy Cambs 33 K7
Wenhaston Suffk 35 N2
Wennington Cambs 33 J2
Wennington Gt Lon 22 B7
Wennington Lancs 63 L8
Wensley Derbys 50 H8
Wensley N York 65 J9
Wentbridge Wakefd 59 L10
Wentnor Shrops 38 H4
Wentworth Cambs 33 M2
Wentworth Rothm 51 J2
Wenvoe V Glam 16 F2
Weobley Herefs 38 H10
Wepham W Susx 10 G8
Wereham Norfk 44 B9
Werrington C Pete 42 G9
Werrington Cnwll 4 H3
Wervin Ches W 48 H2
Wesham Lancs 56 H3
Wessex Vale Crematorium Hants 9 N4
Wessington Derbys 51 J8
West Acre Norfk 44 C7
West Alvington Devon 5 P10
West Anstey Devon 15 P6
West Ashby Lincs 53 J8
West Ashling W Susx 10 D8
West Ashton Wilts 18 C9
West Auckland Dur 65 L3
West Ayton N York 67 L9
West Bagborough Somset 16 G9
West Bank Halton 57 K11
West Barkwith Lincs 52 G7
West Barnby N York 66 H5
West Barns E Loth 87 M6
West Barsham Norfk 44 E4
West Bay Dorset 7 L5
West Beckham Norfk 45 J3
West Bedfont Surrey 20 H8
Westbere Kent 23 M10
West Bergholt Essex 34 F10
West Berkshire Crematorium W Berk 19 P7
West Bexington Dorset 7 M5
West Bilney Norfk 44 B7
West Blatchington Br & H 11 L8
West Boldon S Tyne 73 P8
Westborough Lincs 42 C2
Westbourne Bmouth 8 F8
Westbourne W Susx 10 C8
West Bowling C Brad 58 F7
West Bradenham Norfk 44 F8
West Bradford Lancs 63 N12
West Bradley Somset 17 M8
West Bretton Wakefd 58 H10
West Bridgford Notts 51 N12
West Bromwich Sandw 40 D8
Westbrook Kent 23 Q8
Westbrook W Berk 19 M6
West Buckland Devon 15 L6
West Buckland Somset 16 G11
West Burrafirth Shet 111 j4
West Burton N York 64 H9
Westbury Bucks 31 N7
Westbury Shrops 38 G1
Westbury Wilts 18 C9
Westbury Leigh Wilts 18 C10
Westbury on Severn Gloucs 29 J6
Westbury-on-Trym Bristl 28 G12
Westbury-sub-Mendip Somset 17 M6
West Butterwick N Linc 52 B3
Westby Lancs 56 H3
West Byfleet Surrey 20 G10
West Cairngaan D & G 68 F11
West Caister Norfk 45 Q7
West Calder W Loth 86 B9
West Camel Somset 17 N10
West Chaldon Dorset 8 B10
West Challow Oxon 19 L3
West Charleton Devon 5 P10
West Chiltington W Susx 10 H6
West Chinnock Somset 17 L12
West Clandon Surrey 20 G11
West Cliffe Kent 13 Q2
Westcliff-on-Sea Sthend 22 G6
West Coker Somset 17 M12
Westcombe Somset 17 P8
West Compton Somset 17 N7
West Compton Abbas Dorset 7 N4
Westcote Gloucs 30 G9
Westcote Barton Oxon 31 K8
Westcott Bucks 31 Q10
Westcott Devon 6 D2
Westcott Surrey 11 J1
West Cottingwith N York 59 P6
Westcourt Wilts 19 J8
West Cowick E R Yk 59 P9
West Cross Swans 26 E10
West Curthwaite Cumb 71 M6
Westdean E Susx 11 Q9
West Dean W Susx 10 D7
West Dean Wilts 9 J3
West Deeping Lincs 42 G8
West Derby Lpool 56 H9
West Dereham Norfk 43 Q9
West Down Devon 15 J4
Westdowns Cnwll 4 C4
West Drayton Gt Lon 20 G7
West Drayton Notts 51 P6
West Dunnet Highld 110 E2
West Ella E R Yk 60 H8
West End Bed 32 E6
West End Hants 9 M5
West End N Som 17 L3
West End Norfk 45 Q7
West End Surrey 20 F10
West End Wilts 8 E3
West End Green Hants 19 Q8
Wester Aberchalder Highld 98 H5
Westerdale Highld 110 D5
Westerdale N York 66 F6
Westerfield Suffk 35 K7
Westergate W Susx 10 F8
Westerham Kent 21 N11
Westerhope N u Ty 73 L7
Westerland Devon 6 B9
Westerleigh S Glos 29 J11
Westerleigh Crematorium S Glos 29 J12
Western Isles W Isls 111 c3
Wester Ochiltree W Loth 86 B7
Wester Pitkierie Fife 87 K2
Wester Ross Highld 105 P6
Westerton of Rossie Angus 93 R5
Westerwick Shet 111 j4
West Farleigh Kent 22 E11
West Farndon Nhants 31 M4
West Felton Shrops 48 G9
Westfield BaNES 17 P5
Westfield Cumb 70 G9
Westfield E Susx 12 F7
Westfield Highld 110 C3
Westfield N Lans 85 M8
Westfield Norfk 44 G8
Westfield W Loth 85 Q8
Westfields of Rattray P & K 92 H6
Westgate Dur 72 G12
Westgate N Linc 60 D11
Westgate on Sea Kent 23 P8
West Grafton Wilts 19 J8
West Green Hants 20 C11
West Grimstead Wilts 8 H3
West Grinstead W Susx 11 J5
West Haddlesey N York 59 M8
West Haddon Nhants 41 N12
West Hagbourne Oxon 19 N3
West Hagley Worcs 40 B10
Westhall Suffk 35 N1
West Hallam Derbys 51 K11
West Halton N Linc 60 F9
Westham Dorset 7 P7
Westham E Susx 12 D8
West Ham Gt Lon 21 N6
Westham Somset 17 K6
Westhampnett W Susx 10 E8
West Handley Derbys 51 K5
West Hanney Oxon 19 L3
West Hanningfield Essex 22 E4
West Harnham Wilts 8 G2
West Harptree BaNES 17 M5
West Harting W Susx 10 C6
West Hatch Somset 16 H11
West Hatch Wilts 8 D2
West Haven Angus 93 P8
Westhay Somset 17 L7
West Heath Birm 40 D11
West Helmsdale Highld 110 B11
West Hendred Oxon 19 M3
West Hertfordshire Crematorium Herts 20 H3
West Heslerton N York 67 K11
West Hewish N Som 17 K4
Westhide Herefs 39 L12
Westhill Abers 95 N1
West Hill Devon 6 E4
West Hoathly W Susx 11 M4
West Holme Dorset 8 C9
Westhope Herefs 39 J11
Westhope Shrops 39 J5
West Horndon Essex 22 D6
Westhorpe Lincs 42 H4
Westhorpe Suffk 34 H3
West Horrington Somset 17 N6
West Horsley Surrey 20 H11
West Hougham Kent 13 N3
Westhoughton Bolton 57 M7
Westhouse N York 63 M7
Westhouses Derbys 51 K8
West Howe Bmouth 8 F8
Westhumble Surrey 21 J11
West Huntingtower P & K 92 G10
West Huntspill Somset 17 J7
West Hythe Kent 13 L3
West Ilsley W Berk 19 M4
West Itchenor W Susx 10 C9
West Kennett Wilts 18 G7
West Kilbride N Ayrs 76 D2
West Kingsdown Kent 22 C10
West Kington Wilts 18 B5
West Kirby Wirral 56 E10
West Knapton N York 67 J11
West Knighton Dorset 7 Q5
West Knoyle Wilts 8 C2
Westlake Devon 5 M9
West Lambrook Somset 17 K11
West Langdon Kent 13 P1
West Lavington W Susx 10 E6
West Lavington Wilts 18 E9
West Layton N York 65 K5
West Leake Notts 41 M3
Westleigh Devon 14 H6
Westleigh Devon 16 E11
West Leigh Somset 16 F9
Westleton Suffk 35 P3
West Lexham Norfk 44 D6
Westley Suffk 34 D4
Westley Waterless Cambs 33 P5
West Lilling N York 59 P2
Westlington Bucks 31 Q11

West Linton - Winmarleigh 199


West Linton Border 86 D10
Westlinton Cumb 71 N3
West Littleton S Glos 18 B5
West Lockinge Oxon 19 M4
West London Crematorium Gt Lon 21 K7
West Lothian Crematorium W Loth 86 B8
West Lulworth Dorset 8 B10
West Lutton N York 60 F1
West Lydford Somset 17 N9
West Lyng Somset 17 J9
West Lynn Norfk 43 P6
West Malling Kent 22 D10
West Malvern Worcs 39 N11
West Marden W Susx 10 C7
West Markham Notts 51 Q6
Westmarsh Kent 23 P10
West Marsh NE Lin 61 L11
West Marton N York 58 B4
West Melbury Dorset 8 C4
West Meon Hants 9 Q3
West Mersea Essex 23 J2
Westmeston E Susx 11 M7
West Midland Safari Park Worcs 39 P7
Westmill Herts 33 K10
West Milton Dorset 7 M4
Westminster Gt Lon 21 L7
West Minster Kent 22 H8
Westminster Abbey & Palace Gt Lon 21 L7
West Molesey Surrey 21 J9
West Monkton Somset 16 H9
West Moors Dorset 8 F6
West Morden Dorset 8 D8
West Morriston Border 80 E6
West Mudford Somset 17 N11
Westmuir Angus 93 L5
West Ness N York 66 F10
Westnewton Cumb 71 J6
West Newton E R Yk 61 L6
West Newton Norfk 44 B5
West Newton Somset 16 H9
West Norwood Gt Lon 21 L8
West Norwood Crematorium Gt Lon 21 L8
Westoe S Tyne 73 P7
West Ogwell Devon 5 Q6
Weston BaNES 17 Q3
Weston Ches E 49 N5
Weston Devon 6 F3
Weston Devon 6 F5
Weston Hants 10 B6
Weston Herts 33 J10
Weston Lincs 43 J5
Weston N York 58 F5
Weston Nhants 31 N5
Weston Notts 51 Q7
Weston Shrops 39 L4
Weston Shrops 48 F9
Weston Staffs 40 C3
Weston W Berk 19 L6
Weston Beggard Herefs 28 G1
Westonbirt Gloucs 18 C3
Weston by Welland Nhants 41 Q8
Weston Colville Cambs 33 P6
Weston Corbett Hants 10 B1
Weston Coyney C Stke 50 C11
Weston Favell Nhants 32 B4
Weston Green Cambs 33 P6
Weston Heath Shrops 49 P11
Westoning C Beds 32 E9
Weston-in-Gordano N Som 17 L2
Weston Jones Staffs 49 N10
Weston Longville Norfk 45 J7
Weston Lullingfields Shrops 48 H9
Weston Mill Crematorium C Plym 5 K8
Weston-on-the-Green Oxon 31 M9
Weston Park Staffs 49 P12
Weston Patrick Hants 10 B1
Weston Rhyn Shrops 48 F8
Weston-sub-Edge Gloucs 30 E6
Weston-super-Mare N Som 17 J4
Weston-super-Mare Crematorium N Som 17 J4
Weston Turville Bucks 20 D2
Weston-under-Lizard Staffs 49 P12
Weston under Penyard Herefs 28 H4
Weston-under-Redcastle Shrops 49 K9
Weston under Wetherley Warwks 41 J12
Weston Underwood Derbys 50 H11
Weston Underwood M Keyn 32 C6
Weston-upon-Trent Derbys 41 K2
Westonzoyland Somset 17 J8
West Orchard Dorset 8 B4
West Overton Wilts 18 G7
Westow N York 60 D2
West Park Abers 95 N3
West Parley Dorset 8 G7
West Peckham Kent 22 D11
West Pelton Dur 73 M9
West Pennard Somset 17 M8
West Pentire Cnwll 2 H4
West Perry Cambs 32 G4
West Porlock Somset 15 P3
Westport Somset 17 K11
West Putford Devon 14 G8
West Quantoxhead Somset 16 F7
Westquarter Falk 85 Q7
West Rainton Dur 73 N10
West Rasen Lincs 52 F5
Westray Ork 111 h1
Westray Airport Ork 111 h1
West Raynham Norfk 44 E5
Westrigg W Loth 85 Q9
West Road Crematorium N u Ty 73 L7
Westrop Swindn 18 H3
West Rounton N York 65 P6
West Row Suffk 34 B2
West Rudham Norfk 44 D5
West Runton Norfk 45 K2
Westruther Border 80 E4
Westry Cambs 43 L9
West Saltoun E Loth 87 J8
West Sandford Devon 15 N10
West Sandwick Shet 111 k3
West Scrafton N York 65 J10
West Stafford Dorset 7 Q5
West Stockwith Notts 52 B5
West Stoke W Susx 10 D8
West Stour Dorset 8 B3
West Stourmouth Kent 23 N10
West Stow Suffk 34 D3
West Stowell Wilts 18 G8
West Street Suffk 34 G3
West Suffolk Crematorium Suffk 34 D4
West Tanfield N York 65 M10
West Taphouse Cnwll 4 E7
West Tarbert Ag & B 83 M9
West Tarring W Susx 10 H8
West Thirston Nthumb 73 L2
West Thorney W Susx 10 C9
West Thorpe Notts 41 N3
West Thurrock Thurr 22 C7
West Tilbury Thurr 22 D7
West Tisted Hants 9 Q2
West Torrington Lincs 52 G7
West Town Hants 10 B9
West Town N Som 17 L3
West Tytherley Hants 9 J2
West Walton Norfk 43 M7
West Walton Highway Norfk 43 M7
Westward Cumb 71 L6
Westward Ho! Devon 14 H6
Westwell Kent 13 J1
Westwell Oxon 30 G11
Westwell Leacon Kent 13 J1
West Wellow Hants 9 K4
West Wembury Devon 5 L9
West Wemyss Fife 86 G4
Westwick Cambs 33 L4
West Wickham Cambs 33 P6
West Wickham Gt Lon 21 M9
West Williamston Pembks 24 H7
West Wiltshire Crematorium Wilts 18 D8
West Winch Norfk 43 Q6
West Winterslow Wilts 9 J2
West Wittering W Susx 10 C9
West Witton N York 65 J9
Westwood Devon 6 D3
Westwood Kent 23 Q9
Westwood Wilts 18 B8
West Woodburn Nthumb 72 F4
West Woodhay W Berk 19 L8
Westwoodside N Linc 51 Q2
West Worldham Hants 10 C3
West Worthing W Susx 11 J9
West Wratting Cambs 33 P6
Wetheral Cumb 71 P5
Wetherby Leeds 59 K5
Wetherby Services N York 59 K4
Wetherden Suffk 34 G4
Wetheringsett Suffk 35 J4
Wethersfield Essex 34 B9
Wetherup Street Suffk 35 J4
Wetley Rocks Staffs 50 C10
Wettenhall Ches E 49 L4
Wetton Staffs 50 E9
Wetwang E R Yk 60 F3
Wetwood Staffs 49 P8
Wexcombe Wilts 19 J8
Weybourne Norfk 45 J2
Weybourne Surrey 10 D1
Weybread Suffk 35 L1
Weybread Street Suffk 35 L2
Weybridge Surrey 20 H9
Weycroft Devon 7 J3
Weydale Highld 110 D3
Weyhill Hants 19 K10
Weymouth Dorset 7 P7
Weymouth Crematorium Dorset 7 P7
Whaddon Bucks 32 B9
Whaddon Cambs 33 K7
Whaddon Gloucs 29 L6
Whaddon Gt Lon 21 L9
Whaddon Wilts 8 H3
Whaddon Wilts 18 C8
Whaley Derbys 51 L6
Whaley Bridge Derbys 50 D5
Whaley Thorns Derbys 51 M6
Whaligoe Highld 110 G7
Whalley Lancs 57 N2
Whalsay Shet 111 m3
Whalton Nthumb 73 K5
Whaplode Lincs 43 K5
Whaplode Drove Lincs 43 K7
Wharf Warwks 31 K4
Wharfe N York 63 P8
Wharles Lancs 57 J2
Wharley End C Beds 32 D7
Wharncliffe Side Sheff 50 H2
Wharram-le-Street N York 60 E2
Wharton Herefs 39 J10
Whashton N York 65 K6
Whasset Cumb 63 K6
Whatcote Warwks 30 H5
Whateley Warwks 40 G7
Whatfield Suffk 34 G7
Whatley Somset 7 J2
Whatley Somset 17 Q6
Whatlington E Susx 12 F6
Whatton Notts 51 Q11
Whauphill D & G 69 K8
Wheal Peevor Cnwll 2 G6
Wheatacre Norfk 45 P10
Wheathampstead Herts 21 J1
Wheatley Hants 10 C3
Wheatley Oxon 31 N11
Wheatley Hill Dur 73 P11
Wheatley Hills Donc 59 N12
Wheaton Aston Staffs 49 Q11
Wheddon Cross Somset 16 C8
Wheelock Ches E 49 N4
Wheelton Lancs 57 L5
Wheldrake C York 59 P5
Whelford Gloucs 18 H2
Whelpley Hill Bucks 20 F3
Whempstead Herts 33 K11
Whenby N York 66 E12
Whepstead Suffk 34 D5
Wherstead Suffk 35 J8
Wherwell Hants 19 L11
Wheston Derbys 50 F5
Whetsted Kent 12 D2
Whetstone Leics 41 M7
Whicham Cumb 62 D6
Whichford Warwks 30 H7
Whickham Gatesd 73 L8
Whiddon Down Devon 5 N2
Whigstreet Angus 93 N6
Whilton Nhants 31 N2
Whimple Devon 6 E4
Whimpwell Green Norfk 45 N4
Whinburgh Norfk 44 G8
Whinnie Liggate D & G 70 B5
Whinnyfold Abers 103 M8
Whippingham IoW 9 N8
Whipsnade C Beds 32 E12
Whipsnade Zoo ZSL C Beds 32 E12
Whipton Devon 6 C4
Whisby Lincs 52 C9
Whissendine Rutlnd 42 B7
Whissonsett Norfk 44 F5
Whistlefield Ag & B 84 D4
Whistlefield Inn Ag & B 84 C4
Whistley Green Wokham 20 C8
Whiston Knows 57 J9
Whiston Nhants 32 C5
Whiston Rothm 51 K3
Whiston Staffs 40 B5
Whiston Staffs 50 D10
Whitbeck Cumb 62 D5
Whitbourne Herefs 39 N10
Whitburn S Tyne 73 P8
Whitburn W Loth 85 Q9
Whitby N York 67 J5
Whitchester Border 87 N9
Whitchurch BaNES 17 N3
Whitchurch Bucks 32 B11
Whitchurch Cardif 27 N11
Whitchurch Devon 5 K5
Whitchurch Hants 19 M10
Whitchurch Herefs 28 G5
Whitchurch Oxon 19 Q5
Whitchurch Pembks 24 E4
Whitchurch Shrops 49 K7
Whitchurch Canonicorum Dorset 7 K4
Whitchurch Hill Oxon 19 Q5
Whitcombe Dorset 7 Q5
Whitcot Shrops 38 H4
Whitcott Keysett Shrops 38 F5
Whiteacre Heath Warwks 40 G8
White Ball Somset 16 E11
Whitebridge Highld 98 G6
Whitebrook Mons 28 G7
Whitecairns Abers 103 J10
Whitechapel Gt Lon 21 M7
White Chapel Lancs 57 K1
Whitecliffe Gloucs 28 G6
White Colne Essex 34 E10
Whitecraig E Loth 86 G8
Whitecrook D & G 68 F7
White Cross Cnwll 2 G10
Whitecross Falk 85 R7
Whiteface Highld 107 L5
Whitefarland N Ayrs 75 N4
Whitefaulds S Ayrs 76 E8
Whitefield Bury 57 P7
Whitefield Somset 16 E9
Whiteford Abers 102 F9
Whitegate Ches W 49 L2
Whitehall Ork 111 i2
Whitehaven Cumb 70 F11
Whitehill and Bordon Hants 10 C4
Whitehills Abers 102 E3
Whitehouse Abers 102 E11
Whitehouse Ag & B 83 M10
Whitehouse Common Birm 40 F7
Whitekirk E Loth 87 L6
White Lackington Dorset 7 Q3
Whitelackington Somset 17 K11
White Ladies Aston Worcs 30 B4
Whiteleaf Bucks 20 D3
Whiteley Hants 9 N5
Whiteley Bank IoW 9 P10
Whitemire Moray 100 F5
Whitemoor C Nott 51 M11
Whitemoor Cnwll 3 L4
Whiteness Shet 111 k4
White Notley Essex 34 D11
Whiteparish Wilts 9 J3
White Pit Lincs 53 L7
Whiterashes Abers 102 H9
White Roding Essex 22 C1
Whiterow Highld 110 G6
Whiterow Moray 100 F4
Whiteshill Gloucs 29 L7
Whitesmith E Susx 11 Q7
Whitestaunton Somset 6 H1
Whitestone Cross Devon 6 B4
White Waltham W & M 20 D7
Whitewell Lancs 63 M11
Whitfield C Dund 93 M8
Whitfield Kent 13 P2
Whitfield Nhants 31 N6
Whitfield Nthumb 72 E8
Whitfield S Glos 29 J9
Whitford Devon 6 H4
Whitford Flints 56 D12
Whitgift E R Yk 60 E9
Whitgreave Staffs 40 B2
Whithorn D & G 69 L10
Whiting Bay N Ayrs 75 Q7
Whitkirk Leeds 59 J7
Whitland Carmth 25 L5
Whitlaw Border 80 C10
Whitletts S Ayrs 76 F6
Whitley N York 59 M9
Whitley Readg 20 B8
Whitley Sheff 51 J2
Whitley Wilts 18 C7
Whitley Bay N Tyne 73 N6
Whitley Bay Crematorium N Tyne 73 N6
Whitley Chapel Nthumb 72 G8
Whitley Lower Kirk 58 G10
Whitminster Gloucs 29 K7
Whitmore Staffs 49 P7
Whitnage Devon 16 D11
Whitnash Warwks 31 J2
Whitney-on-Wye Herefs 38 F11
Whitsbury Hants 8 G4
Whitsome Border 81 J4
Whitson Newpt 28 D11
Whitstable Kent 23 L9
Whitstone Cnwll 14 E11
Whittingham Nthumb 81 M10
Whittingslow Shrops 38 H4
Whittington Derbys 51 J6
Whittington Gloucs 30 D9
Whittington Lancs 63 L7
Whittington Norfk 44 B9
Whittington Shrops 48 G8
Whittington Staffs 39 Q5
Whittington Staffs 40 F6
Whittington Warwks 40 H7
Whittington Worcs 39 Q10
Whittlebury Nhants 31 P5
Whittle-le-Woods Lancs 57 L5
Whittlesey Cambs 43 J10
Whittlesford Cambs 33 M7
Whitton N Linc 60 F8
Whitton Nthumb 73 J1
Whitton Powys 38 F8
Whitton S on T 65 P3
Whitton Shrops 39 L7
Whittonstall Nthumb 73 J9
Whitway Hants 19 M8
Whitwell Derbys 51 M5
Whitwell Herts 32 H11
Whitwell IoW 9 N10
Whitwell N York 65 M7
Whitwell Rutlnd 42 D8
Whitwell-on-the-Hill N York 60 C2
Whitwell Street Norfk 44 H6
Whitwick Leics 41 K4
Whitworth Lancs 58 B9
Whixall Shrops 49 K8
Whixley N York 59 K3
Whorlton Dur 65 K5
Whyle Herefs 39 K9
Whyteleafe Surrey 21 M10
Wibsey C Brad 58 F7
Wibtoft Warwks 41 L9
Wichenford Worcs 39 P9
Wichling Kent 22 H11
Wick Bmouth 8 H8
Wick Highld 110 G5
Wick S Glos 17 Q2
Wick V Glam 16 C2
Wick W Susx 10 G8
Wick Worcs 30 C5
Wicken Cambs 33 P3
Wicken Nhants 31 Q6
Wicken Bonhunt Essex 33 N9
Wickenby Lincs 52 F7
Wicken Green Village Norfk 44 D4
Wickersley Rothm 51 L3
Wicker Street Green Suffk 34 F8
Wickford Essex 22 E5
Wickham Hants 9 P5
Wickham W Berk 19 L6
Wickham Bishops Essex 22 G2
Wickhambreaux Kent 23 N10
Wickhambrook Suffk 34 C6
Wickhamford Worcs 30 E6
Wickham Green Suffk 34 H3
Wickham Market Suffk 35 M5
Wickhampton Norfk 45 N8
Wickham St Paul Essex 34 D9
Wickham Skeith Suffk 34 H3
Wickham Street Suffk 34 H3
Wick John o' Groats Airport Highld 110 G5
Wicklewood Norfk 44 H9
Wickmere Norfk 45 J4
Wick St Lawrence N Som 17 K3
Wicksteed Park Nhants 32 C2
Wickwar S Glos 29 J10
Widdington Essex 33 N9
Widdrington Nthumb 73 M2
Widdrington Station Nthumb 73 M3
Widecombe in the Moor Devon 5 P5
Widegates Cnwll 4 G8
Widemouth Bay Cnwll 14 D10
Wide Open N Tyne 73 M6
Widford Essex 22 E3
Widford Herts 33 L12
Widmer End Bucks 20 E4
Widmerpool Notts 41 N2
Widmore Gt Lon 21 N9
Widnes Halton 57 K11
Widnes Crematorium Halton 57 K10
Widworthy Devon 6 G3
Wigan Wigan 57 L7
Wigan Crematorium Wigan 57 L7
Wigborough Somset 17 L12
Wiggaton Devon 6 E4
Wiggenhall St Germans Norfk 43 P7
Wiggenhall St Mary Magdalen Norfk 43 P7
Wiggenhall St Mary the Virgin Norfk 43 P7
Wigginton C York 59 N3
Wigginton Herts 20 F2
Wigginton Oxon 31 K7
Wigginton Staffs 40 G6
Wigglesworth N York 63 P10
Wiggonby Cumb 71 L5
Wighill N York 59 L5
Wighton Norfk 44 F3
Wightwick Wolves 39 Q3
Wigley Hants 9 K4
Wigmore Herefs 38 H8
Wigmore Medway 22 F9
Wigsley Notts 52 C9
Wigsthorpe Nhants 32 F1
Wigston Leics 41 N7
Wigston Parva Leics 41 L9
Wigthorpe Notts 51 N4
Wigtoft Lincs 43 J3
Wigton Cumb 71 L6
Wigtown D & G 69 L7
Wike Leeds 59 J5
Wilbarston Nhants 42 B11
Wilberfoss E R Yk 60 C4
Wilburton Cambs 33 M2
Wilby Nhants 32 C4
Wilby Norfk 44 G11
Wilby Suffk 35 L3
Wilcot Wilts 18 G8
Wilcott Shrops 48 H10
Wildboarclough Ches E 50 C7
Wilden Bed 32 F6
Wilden Worcs 39 P7
Wildmanbridge S Lans 85 N11
Wildmoor Worcs 40 C11
Wildsworth Lincs 52 B4
Wilford C Nott 51 M12
Wilford Hill Crematorium Notts 41 M1
Wilkesley Ches E 49 L7
Wilkhaven Highld 107 Q5
Wilkieston W Loth 86 D8
Willand Devon 6 D1
Willaston Ches E 49 M5
Willaston Ches W 56 G12
Willen M Keyn 32 C8
Willenhall Covtry 41 J11
Willenhall Wsall 40 C7
Willerby E R Yk 60 H7
Willerby N York 67 L10
Willersey Gloucs 30 E6
Willersley Herefs 38 G11
Willesborough Kent 13 K2
Willesborough Lees Kent 13 K2
Willesden Gt Lon 21 K6
Willesley Wilts 18 C3
Willett Somset 16 F9
Willey Shrops 39 M3
Willey Warwks 41 L9
Willey Green Surrey 20 F12
Williamscot Oxon 31 L5
Willian Herts 32 H9
Willingale Essex 22 C2
Willingdon E Susx 12 C9
Willingham Cambs 33 L3
Willingham by Stow Lincs 52 C6
Willington Bed 32 G6
Willington Derbys 40 H2
Willington Dur 65 L1
Willington Kent 22 F11
Willington N Tyne 73 N7
Willington Warwks 30 H6
Willitoft E R Yk 60 C7
Williton Somset 16 E7
Willoughby Lincs 53 M8
Willoughby Warwks 31 M1
Willoughby-on-the-Wolds Notts 41 N3
Willoughby Waterleys Leics 41 M8
Willoughton Lincs 52 D5
Willows Green Essex 34 C11
Willtown Somset 17 K10
Wilmcote Warwks 30 F3
Wilmington Devon 6 G3
Wilmington E Susx 12 B8
Wilmington Kent 21 Q8
Wilmslow Ches E 57 Q11
Wilpshire Lancs 57 M3
Wilsden C Brad 58 E6
Wilsford Lincs 42 E2
Wilsford Wilts 18 G11
Wilsford Wilts 18 G8
Wilshaw Kirk 58 E11
Wilsill N York 58 F2
Wilson Leics 41 K3
Wilsontown S Lans 85 Q11
Wilstead Bed 32 F7
Wilsthorpe Lincs 42 F7
Wilstone Herts 20 E1
Wilton Herefs 28 G4
Wilton N York 67 J10
Wilton R & Cl 66 E4
Wilton Wilts 8 G2
Wilton Wilts 19 J8
Wilton Dean Border 80 C10
Wimbish Green Essex 33 P9
Wimbledon Gt Lon 21 K8
Wimblington Cambs 43 L10
Wimboldsley Ches W 49 M3
Wimborne Minster Dorset 8 E7
Wimborne St Giles Dorset 8 F5
Wimbotsham Norfk 43 P8
Wimpole Cambs 33 K6
Wimpstone Warwks 30 G4
Wincanton Somset 17 Q9
Winchburgh W Loth 86 C7
Winchcombe Gloucs 30 D8
Winchelsea E Susx 12 H6
Winchester Hants 9 N2
Winchester Services Hants 9 N1
Winchet Hill Kent 12 E2
Winchfield Hants 20 C11
Winchmore Hill Bucks 20 E4
Winchmore Hill Gt Lon 21 L5
Wincle Ches E 50 C7
Wincobank Sheff 51 J3
Windermere Cumb 62 H3
Windermere Steamboats & Museum Cumb 62 H3
Winderton Warwks 31 J6
Windhill Highld 107 J11
Windlesham Surrey 20 E9
Windmill Cnwll 3 K2
Windmill Hill E Susx 12 D7
Windmill Hill Somset 17 J11
Windrush Gloucs 30 F10
Windsole Abers 102 D4
Windsor W & M 20 F7
Windsor Castle W & M 20 F7
Windsoredge Gloucs 29 L8
Windsor Green Suffk 34 E6
Windy Arbour Warwks 40 H12
Windygates Fife 86 G3
Wineham W Susx 11 K6
Winestead E R Yk 61 M8
Winfarthing Norfk 45 J11
Winford IoW 9 P9
Winford N Som 17 M3
Winforton Herefs 38 F11
Winfrith Newburgh Dorset 8 B9
Wing Bucks 32 C11
Wing Rutlnd 42 C9
Wingate Dur 73 P12
Wingerworth Derbys 51 J7
Wingfield C Beds 32 E10
Wingfield Suffk 35 K2
Wingfield Wilts 18 B9
Wingham Kent 23 N11
Wingrave Bucks 32 C11
Winkburn Notts 51 P8
Winkfield Br For 20 E8
Winkfield Row Br For 20 E8
Winkhill Staffs 50 D9
Winkleigh Devon 15 L9
Winksley N York 65 M12
Winlaton Gatesd 73 L8
Winless Highld 110 G5
Winmarleigh Lancs 63 J11

Winnall Hants .......... 9 N2
Winnersh Wokham .......... 20 C8
Winnington Ches W .......... 49 M1
Winscombe N Som .......... 17 K5
Winsford Ches W .......... 49 M3
Winsford Somset .......... 16 B8
Winsham Somset .......... 7 K2
Winshill Staffs .......... 40 H3
Winshwen Swans .......... 26 F9
Winskill Cumb .......... 64 B1
Winsley Wilts .......... 18 B8
Winslow Bucks .......... 31 Q8
Winson Gloucs .......... 30 E11
Winsor Hants .......... 9 K5
Winster Cumb .......... 62 H4
Winster Derbys .......... 50 G8
Winston Dur .......... 65 K4
Winston Suffk .......... 35 K5
Winstone Gloucs .......... 29 N6
Winswell Devon .......... 15 J9
Winterborne Came Dorset .......... 7 Q5
Winterborne Clenston
   Dorset .......... 8 C6
Winterborne Houghton
   Dorset .......... 8 B6
Winterborne Kingston
   Dorset .......... 8 C7
Winterborne Monkton
   Dorset .......... 7 P5
Winterborne Stickland
   Dorset .......... 8 C6
Winterborne
   Whitechurch Dorset .......... 8 C7
Winterborne Zelston
   Dorset .......... 8 D7
Winterbourne S Glos .......... 28 H11
Winterbourne W Berk .......... 19 M6
Winterbourne Abbas
   Dorset .......... 7 N5
Winterbourne Bassett
   Wilts .......... 18 G6
Winterbourne
   Dauntsey Wilts .......... 8 H1
Winterbourne Earls Wilts .......... 8 H1
Winterbourne Gunner
   Wilts .......... 8 H1
Winterbourne Monkton
   Wilts .......... 18 G6
Winterbourne
   Steepleton Dorset .......... 7 P5
Winterbourne Stoke Wilts .......... 18 F11
Winterburn N York .......... 58 C3
Winteringham N Linc .......... 60 F9
Winterley Ches E .......... 49 N4
Winterslow Wilts .......... 9 J2
Winterton N Linc .......... 60 F9
Winterton-on-Sea Norfk .......... 45 P6
Winthorpe Notts .......... 52 B11
Winton Bmouth .......... 8 G8
Winton Cumb .......... 64 E5
Wintringham N York .......... 67 J11
Winwick Cambs .......... 32 F1
Winwick Nhants .......... 41 N11
Winwick Warrtn .......... 57 L9
Wirksworth Derbys .......... 50 H9
Wirral Ches E .......... 56 F10
Wirswall Ches E .......... 49 K6
Wisbech Cambs .......... 43 M8
Wisbech St Mary Cambs .......... 43 L8
Wisborough Green
   W Susx .......... 10 G5
Wiseman's Bridge
   Pembks .......... 25 K7
Wiseton Notts .......... 51 Q3
Wishaw N Lans .......... 85 N11
Wishaw Warwks .......... 40 F8
Wisley Garden RHS Surrey .......... 20 G10
Wispington Lincs .......... 52 H8
Wissett Suffk .......... 35 M2
Wissington Suffk .......... 34 F9
Wistanstow Shrops .......... 38 H5
Wistanswick Shrops .......... 49 M9
Wistaston Ches E .......... 49 M5
Wiston Pembks .......... 24 H5
Wiston S Lans .......... 78 F3
Wiston W Susx .......... 11 J7
Wistow Cambs .......... 33 J1
Wistow N York .......... 59 N7
Wiswell Lancs .......... 57 N2
Witcham Cambs .......... 33 M2
Witchampton Dorset .......... 8 E6
Witchford Cambs .......... 33 N2
Witcombe Somset .......... 17 L10
Witham Essex .......... 22 G1
Witham Friary Somset .......... 17 Q7
Witham on the Hill Lincs .......... 42 F6
Withcall Lincs .......... 53 J6
Withdean Br & H .......... 11 L8
Witherenden Hill E Susx .......... 12 D5
Witheridge Devon .......... 15 N8
Witherley Leics .......... 41 J7
Withern Lincs .......... 53 L7
Withernsea E R Yk .......... 61 N4
Withernwick E R Yk .......... 61 K6
Withersdale Street Suffk .......... 35 L1
Withersfield Suffk .......... 33 Q7
Witherslack Cumb .......... 62 H5
Withiel Cnwll .......... 3 M3
Withiel Florey Somset .......... 16 D9
Withington Gloucs .......... 30 D10
Withington Herefs .......... 39 K12
Withington Manch .......... 57 Q9
Withington Shrops .......... 49 L11
Withington Staffs .......... 40 D1
Withleigh Devon .......... 6 B1
Withnell Lancs .......... 57 L4
Withybed Green Worcs .......... 40 D11
Withybrook Warwks .......... 41 K10
Withycombe Somset .......... 16 D7
Withyham E Susx .......... 11 P3
Withypool Somset .......... 15 P5
Withywood Bristl .......... 17 N3
Witley Surrey .......... 10 F3
Witnesham Suffk .......... 35 K6
Witney Oxon .......... 31 J11
Wittering C Pete .......... 42 F9
Wittersham Kent .......... 12 H5
Witton Birm .......... 40 E8
Witton Norfk .......... 45 M4
Witton Norfk .......... 45 M4
Witton Gilbert Dur .......... 73 M10
Witton le Wear Dur .......... 65 K2
Witton Park Dur .......... 65 L2
Wiveliscombe Somset .......... 16 E9
Wivelrod Hants .......... 19 R12
Wivelsfield E Susx .......... 11 M6
Wivelsfield Green E Susx .......... 11 M6


Wivenhoe Essex .......... 34 G11
Wiveton Norfk .......... 44 G2
Wix Essex .......... 35 J10
Wixford Warwks .......... 30 E3
Wixoe Suffk .......... 34 C8
Woburn C Beds .......... 32 D9
Woburn Safari Park
   C Beds .......... 32 D9
Woburn Sands M Keyn .......... 32 D9
Woking Surrey .......... 20 G10
Woking Crematorium
   Surrey .......... 20 F11
Wokingham Wokham .......... 20 D9
Woldingham Surrey .......... 21 M11
Wold Newton E R Yk .......... 67 M11
Wold Newton NE Lin .......... 53 J4
Wolfclyde S Lans .......... 78 G2
Wolferton Norfk .......... 43 Q4
Wolfhill P & K .......... 92 H8
Wolf's Castle Pembks .......... 24 G4
Wolfsdale Pembks .......... 24 G5
Wollaston Dudley .......... 40 B9
Wollaston Nhants .......... 32 C4
Wollaston Shrops .......... 48 G11
Wollaton C Nott .......... 51 M11
Wollaton Hall & Park
   C Nott .......... 51 M11
Wollerton Shrops .......... 49 L9
Wollescote Dudley .......... 40 B10
Wolseley Bridge Staffs .......... 40 D4
Wolsingham Dur .......... 73 J12
Wolstanton Staffs .......... 49 Q6
Wolston Warwks .......... 41 K11
Wolvercote Oxon .......... 31 L11
Wolverhampton Wolves .......... 40 B7
Wolverhampton
   Halfpenny Green
   Airport Staffs .......... 39 P4
Wolverley Worcs .......... 39 P6
Wolverton Hants .......... 19 P8
Wolverton M Keyn .......... 32 B8
Wolverton Warwks .......... 30 G2
Wolverton Wilts .......... 8 B2
Wolvesnewton Mons .......... 28 E8
Wolvey Warwks .......... 41 K9
Wolvey Heath Warwks .......... 41 K9
Wolviston S on T .......... 66 C3
Wombleton N York .......... 66 F10
Wombourne Staffs .......... 39 Q4
Wombwell Barns .......... 51 K1
Womenswold Kent .......... 23 N12
Womersley N York .......... 59 M9
Wonersh Surrey .......... 10 G2
Wonford Devon .......... 6 C4
Wonston Dorset .......... 7 Q2
Wonston Hants .......... 19 M11
Wooburn Bucks .......... 20 E6
Wooburn Green Bucks .......... 20 E6
Woodacott Devon .......... 14 G9
Woodall Rothm .......... 51 L5
Woodall Services Rothm .......... 51 L5
Woodbastwick Norfk .......... 45 M7
Wood Bevington Warwks .......... 30 D4
Woodborough Notts .......... 51 N10
Woodborough Wilts .......... 18 G8
Woodbridge Suffk .......... 35 L7
Woodbury Devon .......... 6 D5
Woodbury Salterton
   Devon .......... 6 D5
Woodchester Gloucs .......... 29 L8
Woodchurch Kent .......... 12 H3
Woodcombe Somset .......... 16 C6
Woodcote Gt Lon .......... 21 L10
Woodcote Oxon .......... 19 Q4
Woodcote Wrekin .......... 49 P11
Woodcroft Gloucs .......... 28 G9
Wood Dalling Norfk .......... 44 H5
Woodditton Cambs .......... 33 Q5
Woodeaton Oxon .......... 31 M10
Wood End Gt Lon .......... 20 H7
Wood End Herts .......... 33 K10
Woodend Highld .......... 89 Q4
Woodend Nhants .......... 31 N4
Woodend W Loth .......... 85 Q8
Woodend W Susx .......... 10 D8
Wood End Warwks .......... 40 E11
Wood End Wolves .......... 40 C7
Wood Enderby Lincs .......... 53 J10
Woodfalls Wilts .......... 8 H4
Woodford Cnwll .......... 14 D9
Woodford Gloucs .......... 29 J9
Woodford Gt Lon .......... 21 N5
Woodford Nhants .......... 32 D2
Woodford Stockp .......... 50 B4
Woodford Bridge Gt Lon .......... 21 N5
Woodford Halse Nhants .......... 31 M4
Woodford Wells Gt Lon .......... 21 N5
Woodgate Birm .......... 40 D10
Woodgate Devon .......... 16 E12
Woodgate W Susx .......... 10 F8
Woodgate Worcs .......... 30 C2
Wood Green Gt Lon .......... 21 L5
Woodgreen Hants .......... 8 H4
Woodhall N York .......... 64 H9
Woodhall Spa Lincs .......... 52 H10
Woodham Bucks .......... 31 P9
Woodham Surrey .......... 20 G10
Woodham Ferrers Essex .......... 22 F4
Woodham Mortimer
   Essex .......... 22 F3
Woodham Walter Essex .......... 22 F3
Wood Hayes Wolves .......... 40 C7
Woodhead Abers .......... 102 G7
Woodhill Shrops .......... 39 N5
Woodhill Somset .......... 17 J10
Woodhorn Nthumb .......... 73 N3
Woodhouse Leeds .......... 58 H7
Woodhouse Leics .......... 41 M5
Woodhouse Sheff .......... 51 K4
Woodhouse Wakefd .......... 59 J9
Woodhouse Eaves Leics .......... 41 M5
Woodhouselee Mdloth .......... 86 F8
Woodhouselees D & G .......... 71 N1
Woodhouses Oldham .......... 50 B1
Woodhouses Staffs .......... 40 F4
Woodhurst Cambs .......... 33 K2
Woodingdean Br & H .......... 11 M8
Woodkirk Leeds .......... 58 H8
Woodland Abers .......... 103 J9
Woodland Devon .......... 5 M8
Woodland Devon .......... 5 Q6
Woodland Dur .......... 65 J3
Woodlands S Ayrs .......... 76 D1
Woodlands Abers .......... 95 N3
Woodlands Donc .......... 59 M11
Woodlands Dorset .......... 8 F5
Woodlands Hants .......... 9 K5


Woodlands N York .......... 59 J3
Woodlands (Coleshill)
   Crematorium Warwks .......... 40 F9
Woodlands Park W & M .......... 20 D7
Woodlands
   (Scarborough)
   Crematorium N York .......... 67 L9
Woodlands
   (Scunthorpe)
   Crematorium N Linc .......... 60 F11
Woodleigh Devon .......... 5 P9
Woodley Wokham .......... 20 C8
Woodmancote Gloucs .......... 29 K8
Woodmancote Gloucs .......... 29 N4
Woodmancote N Som .......... 30 D11
Woodmancote W Susx .......... 10 C8
Woodmancote W Susx .......... 11 K7
Woodmancott Hants .......... 19 P11
Woodmansey E R Yk .......... 60 H6
Woodmansgreen W Susx .......... 10 D5
Woodmansterne Surrey .......... 21 L10
Woodmanton Devon .......... 6 D5
Woodnesborough Kent .......... 23 P11
Woodnewton Nhants .......... 42 E10
Wood Norton Norfk .......... 44 G5
Woodplumpton Lancs .......... 57 J2
Woodrising Norfk .......... 44 G9
Wood's Corner E Susx .......... 12 D6
Woodseaves Staffs .......... 49 P9
Woodsetts Rothm .......... 51 M4
Woodsford Dorset .......... 8 A8
Wood's Green E Susx .......... 12 D4
Woodside Br For .......... 20 E8
Woodside Fife .......... 86 H1
Woodside Gt Lon .......... 21 M9
Woodside P & K .......... 93 J7
Woodside Crematorium
   Inver .......... 84 E7
Woodstock Oxon .......... 31 K10
Woodston C Pete .......... 42 H10
Wood Street Norfk .......... 45 N6
Wood Street Village
   Surrey .......... 20 F12
Woodton Norfk .......... 45 L10
Woodtown Devon .......... 14 G7
Woodvale Crematorium
   Br & H .......... 11 L8
Wood Walton Cambs .......... 32 H1
Woofferton Shrops .......... 39 K8
Wookey Somset .......... 17 M7
Wookey Hole Somset .......... 17 M6
Wool Dorset .......... 8 C9
Woolacombe Devon .......... 14 H4
Woolage Green Kent .......... 23 N12
Woolaston Gloucs .......... 28 G8
Woolaston Common
   Gloucs .......... 28 G8
Woolavington Somset .......... 17 J7
Woolbeding W Susx .......... 10 E5
Woolbrook Devon .......... 6 F5
Wooler Nthumb .......... 81 L8
Woolfardisworthy Devon .......... 14 F7
Woolfardisworthy Devon .......... 15 P9
Woolfords S Lans .......... 86 B10
Woolhampton W Berk .......... 19 P7
Woolhope Herefs .......... 28 H2
Woolland Dorset .......... 8 B6
Woolley BaNES .......... 17 Q3
Woolley Cambs .......... 32 G2
Woolley Wakefd .......... 58 H10
Woolley Edge Services
   Wakefd .......... 58 H10
Woolmere Green Worcs .......... 30 C2
Woolmer Green Herts .......... 33 J11
Woolminstone Somset .......... 7 K2
Woolpit Suffk .......... 34 F4
Woolstaston Shrops .......... 39 J3
Woolsthorpe Lincs .......... 42 B4
Woolsthorpe-by-
   Colsterworth Lincs .......... 42 D5
Woolston C Sotn .......... 9 M5
Woolston Shrops .......... 48 G9
Woolston Somset .......... 16 E8
Woolston Somset .......... 17 P9
Woolston Warrtn .......... 57 M10
Woolstone Gloucs .......... 29 N3
Woolstone M Keyn .......... 32 C8
Woolstone Oxon .......... 19 K4
Woolston Green Devon .......... 5 Q7
Woolton Lpool .......... 56 H10
Woolton Hill Hants .......... 19 M8
Woolverstone Suffk .......... 35 K8
Woolverton Somset .......... 18 B9
Woolwich Gt Lon .......... 21 N7
Woonton Herefs .......... 38 G10
Woore Shrops .......... 49 N7
Wootten Green Suffk .......... 35 K3
Wootton Bed .......... 32 E7
Wootton Kent .......... 23 N2
Wootton N Linc .......... 61 J10
Wootton Nhants .......... 31 Q3
Wootton Oxon .......... 19 N1
Wootton Oxon .......... 31 K9
Wootton Staffs .......... 50 E10
Wootton Bassett Wilts .......... 18 F4
Wootton Bridge IoW .......... 9 P8
Wootton Courtenay
   Somset .......... 16 C7
Wootton Fitzpaine Dorset .......... 7 K4
Wootton Rivers Wilts .......... 18 H8
Wootton St Lawrence
   Hants .......... 19 P9
Wootton Wawen Warwks .......... 30 F2
Worcester Worcs .......... 39 Q10
Worcester
   Crematorium Worcs .......... 39 Q10
Worcester Park Gt Lon .......... 21 K9
Wordsley Dudley .......... 40 B9
Worfield Shrops .......... 39 N3
Workington Cumb .......... 70 G9
Worksop Notts .......... 51 N5
Worlaby N Linc .......... 60 H10
Worlds End Hants .......... 9 Q5
Worlds End W Susx .......... 11 L6
Worle N Som .......... 17 J4
Worleston Ches E .......... 49 M4
Worlingham Suffk .......... 45 P11
Worlington Devon .......... 15 N9
Worlington Suffk .......... 34 B3
Worlingworth Suffk .......... 35 K3
Wormbridge Herefs .......... 28 E3
Wormegay Norfk .......... 43 Q7
Wormelow Tump Herefs .......... 28 F3
Wormhill Derbys .......... 50 E6
Worminghall Bucks .......... 31 N11
Wormington Gloucs .......... 30 D6


Wormit Fife .......... 93 M9
Wormleighton Warwks .......... 31 K4
Wormley Herts .......... 21 M3
Wormley Surrey .......... 10 F3
Wormshill Kent .......... 22 G11
Wormsley Herefs .......... 38 H11
Worplesdon Surrey .......... 20 F11
Worrall Sheff .......... 50 H3
Worsbrough Barns .......... 51 J1
Worsbrough Bridge Barns .......... 59 J12
Worsbrough Dale Barns .......... 59 J12
Worsley Salfd .......... 57 N8
Worstead Norfk .......... 45 M5
Worsthorne Lancs .......... 57 Q3
Worston Devon .......... 5 M9
Worston Lancs .......... 57 P1
Worth Kent .......... 23 P11
Wortham Suffk .......... 34 H2
Worthen Shrops .......... 38 G2
Worthenbury Wrexhm .......... 48 H6
Worthing Norfk .......... 44 G6
Worthing W Susx .......... 11 J9
Worthing Crematorium
   W Susx .......... 10 H8
Worthington Leics .......... 41 K4
Worth Matravers Dorset .......... 8 E11
Wortley Barns .......... 50 H2
Wortley Leeds .......... 58 H7
Worton N York .......... 64 G9
Worton Wilts .......... 18 E8
Wortwell Norfk .......... 45 L12
Wotton-under-Edge
   Gloucs .......... 29 K9
Wotton Underwood
   Bucks .......... 31 P10
Woughton on the
   Green M Keyn .......... 32 C8
Wouldham Kent .......... 22 E9
Wrabness Essex .......... 35 K9
Wrafton Devon .......... 15 J5
Wragby Lincs .......... 52 G7
Wragby Wakefd .......... 59 K10
Wramplingham Norfk .......... 45 J8
Wrangaton Devon .......... 5 N8
Wrangle Lincs .......... 53 L12
Wrangway Somset .......... 16 F11
Wrantage Somset .......... 17 J10
Wrawby N Linc .......... 52 E2
Wraxall N Som .......... 17 L2
Wraxall Somset .......... 17 N8
Wray Lancs .......... 63 L8
Wraysbury W & M .......... 20 G8
Wrayton Lancs .......... 63 L7
Wrea Green Lancs .......... 56 H3
Wreay Cumb .......... 71 N6
Wrecclesham Surrey .......... 10 D2
Wrekenton Gatesd .......... 73 M8
Wrelton N York .......... 66 G9
Wrenbury Ches E .......... 49 L6
Wreningham Norfk .......... 45 J9
Wrentham Suffk .......... 35 Q1
Wrentnall Shrops .......... 38 H2
Wressle E R Yk .......... 60 C7
Wressle N Linc .......... 52 D2
Wrestlingworth C Beds .......... 33 J7
Wretton Norfk .......... 44 B9
Wrexham Wrexhm .......... 48 G5
Wrexham Industrial
   Estate Wrexhm .......... 48 H5
Wribbenhall Worcs .......... 39 P7
Wrinehill Staffs .......... 49 N6
Wrington N Som .......... 17 L4
Writhlington BaNES .......... 17 Q5
Writtle Essex .......... 22 D3
Wrockwardine Wrekin .......... 49 L11
Wroot N Linc .......... 60 C12
Wrose C Brad .......... 58 F6
Wrotham Kent .......... 22 C10
Wroughton Swindn .......... 18 G5
Wroxall IoW .......... 9 P10
Wroxall Warwks .......... 40 G12
Wroxeter Shrops .......... 39 K1
Wroxham Norfk .......... 45 L6
Wroxham Barns Norfk .......... 45 M6
Wroxton Oxon .......... 31 K6
Wyaston Derbys .......... 50 F11
Wyberton East Lincs .......... 43 K3
Wyboston Bed .......... 32 G5
Wybunbury Ches E .......... 49 M5
Wychbold Worcs .......... 30 B2
Wychnor Staffs .......... 40 F4
Wyck Rissington Gloucs .......... 30 F9
Wycliffe Dur .......... 65 K5
Wycoller Lancs .......... 58 C6
Wycomb Leics .......... 41 Q3
Wycombe Marsh Bucks .......... 20 E5
Wyddial Herts .......... 33 L9
Wye Kent .......... 13 K1
Wyke C Brad .......... 58 F8
Wyke Dorset .......... 8 B3
Wyke Champflower
   Somset .......... 17 P8
Wykeham N York .......... 67 L10
Wyken Covtry .......... 41 J10
Wyken Shrops .......... 39 N3
Wyke Regis Dorset .......... 7 P7
Wykey Shrops .......... 48 H9
Wylam Nthumb .......... 73 K7
Wylde Green Birm .......... 40 E8
Wylye Wilts .......... 18 E12
Wymeswold Leics .......... 41 N3
Wymington Bed .......... 32 D4
Wymondham Leics .......... 42 C6
Wymondham Norfk .......... 45 J9
Wynford Eagle Dorset .......... 7 N4
Wyre Forest
   Crematorium Worcs .......... 39 P7
Wyre Piddle Worcs .......... 30 C5
Wysall Notts .......... 41 N3
Wythall Worcs .......... 40 E11
Wytham Oxon .......... 31 L11
Wythenshawe Manch .......... 57 P10
Wyton Cambs .......... 33 J3
Wyton E R Yk .......... 61 K7
Wyverstone Suffk .......... 34 G3
Wyverstone Street Suffk .......... 34 G4


Yapton W Susx .......... 10 F9
Yarborough N Som .......... 17 K5
Yarburgh Lincs .......... 53 K5
Yarcombe Devon .......... 6 H2
Yard Devon .......... 15 N7
Yardley Birm .......... 40 F9
Yardley Crematorium
   Birm .......... 40 F9
Yardley Gobion Nhants .......... 31 Q5
Yardley Hastings Nhants .......... 32 C5
Yardley Wood Birm .......... 40 E10
Yarkhill Herefs .......... 28 H1
Yarley Somset .......... 17 M7
Yarlington Somset .......... 17 P9
Yarm S on T .......... 65 P5
Yarmouth IoW .......... 9 L9
Yarnbrook Wilts .......... 18 C9
Yarnfield Staffs .......... 49 Q8
Yarnscombe Devon .......... 15 K7
Yarnton Oxon .......... 31 L10
Yarpole Herefs .......... 39 J8
Yarrow Border .......... 79 M4
Yarrow Feus Border .......... 79 M4
Yarrowford Border .......... 79 N3
Yarwell Nhants .......... 42 F9
Yate S Glos .......... 29 J11
Yateley Hants .......... 20 D10
Yatesbury Wilts .......... 18 F6
Yattendon W Berk .......... 19 P6
Yatton Herefs .......... 38 H8
Yatton N Som .......... 17 L3
Yatton Keynell Wilts .......... 18 C5
Yaverland IoW .......... 9 Q9
Yaxham Norfk .......... 44 G7
Yaxley Cambs .......... 42 H10
Yaxley Suffk .......... 35 J2
Yazor Herefs .......... 38 H11
Yeading Gt Lon .......... 20 H7
Yeadon Leeds .......... 58 H6
Yealand Conyers Lancs .......... 63 J7
Yealand Redmayne Lancs .......... 63 J7
Yealmpton Devon .......... 5 M9
Yearsley N York .......... 66 E11
Yeaton Shrops .......... 48 H10
Yeaveley Derbys .......... 50 F11
Yeavering Nthumb .......... 81 K7
Yedingham N York .......... 67 J10
Yelford Oxon .......... 31 J12
Yell Shet .......... 111 k3
Yelling Cambs .......... 33 J4
Yelvertoft Nhants .......... 41 N11
Yelverton Devon .......... 5 L6
Yelverton Norfk .......... 45 L9
Yenston Somset .......... 17 Q11
Yeoford Devon .......... 15 N11
Yeolmbridge Cnwll .......... 4 G3
Yeovil Somset .......... 17 M11
Yeovil Crematorium
   Somset .......... 17 M11
Yeovil Marsh Somset .......... 17 M11
Yeovilton Somset .......... 17 M10
Yesnaby Ork .......... 111 g2
Yetminster Dorset .......... 7 N1
Yettington Devon .......... 6 E5
Yetts o'Muckhart Clacks .......... 86 B2
Yew Tree Sandw .......... 40 D8
Y Felinheli Gwynd .......... 54 G7
Y Ferwig Cerdgn .......... 36 C10
Y Ffor Gwynd .......... 46 G4
Y Gyffylliog Denbgs .......... 48 C4
Yielden Bed .......... 32 E4
Yieldshields S Lans .......... 77 P2
Yiewsley Gt Lon .......... 20 G7
Y Maerdy Conwy .......... 48 B6
Ynysboeth Rhondd .......... 27 M9
Ynysddu Caerph .......... 27 P9
Ynyshir Rhondd .......... 27 L9
Ynystawe Swans .......... 26 F8
Ynysybwl Rhondd .......... 27 M9
Yockleton Shrops .......... 48 H12
Yokefleet E R Yk .......... 60 E8
Yoker C Glas .......... 84 H8
York C York .......... 59 N4
York City Crematorium
   C York .......... 59 N5
Yorkletts Kent .......... 23 L10
Yorkley Gloucs .......... 28 H7
York Minster C York .......... 59 N4
Yorkshire Dales National
   Park .......... 64 F11
York Town Surrey .......... 20 D10
Youlgreave Derbys .......... 50 G7
Youlthorpe E R Yk .......... 60 D3
Youlton N York .......... 59 L2
Yoxall Staffs .......... 40 F4
Yoxford Suffk .......... 35 N3
Y Rhiw Gwynd .......... 46 D6
Ysbyty Ifan Conwy .......... 55 M10
Ysbyty Ystwyth Cerdgn .......... 37 M6
Ysceifiog Flints .......... 48 D2
Ystalyfera Neath .......... 26 G7
Ystrad Rhondd .......... 27 L9
Ystrad Aeron Cerdgn .......... 36 H9
Ystradfellte Powys .......... 27 K6
Ystradgynlais Powys .......... 26 H6
Ystrad Meurig Cerdgn .......... 37 L7
Ystrad Mynach Caerph .......... 27 N9
Ystradowen V Glam .......... 27 L12
Ythanbank Abers .......... 103 J8
Ythanwells Abers .......... 102 E7
Ythsie Abers .......... 103 J8

Zeal Monachorum Devon .......... 15 M10
Zeals Wilts .......... 8 B2
Zelah Cnwll .......... 3 J5
Zennor Cnwll .......... 2 C7
Zouch Notts .......... 41 L3
ZSL London Zoo Gt Lon .......... 21 L6
ZSL Whipsnade Zoo
   C Beds .......... 32 E12

Yaddlethorpe N Linc .......... 52 C3
Yafforth N York .......... 65 N8
Yalberton Torbay .......... 6 B10
Yalding Kent .......... 22 E12
Yanwath Cumb .......... 71 Q9
Yanworth Gloucs .......... 30 E10
Yapham E R Yk .......... 60 D4